LOVE IS IN THE EARTH-

A KALEIDOSCOPE OF CRYSTALS

UPDATE

Copyright © 1995 by
EARTH-LOVE PUBLISHING HOUSE
3440 Youngfield Street, Suite 353
Wheat Ridge, Colorado 80033 USA

Published by
EARTH-LOVE PUBLISHING HOUSE
3440 Youngfield Street, Suite 353
Wheat Ridge, Colorado 80033 USA

First Printing 1995	Ninth Printing 1999
Second Printing 1995	Tenth Printing 1999
Third Printing 1995	Eleventh Printing 2000
Fourth Printing 1996	Twelfth Printing 2001
Fifth Printing 1996	Thirteenth Printing 2001
Sixth Printing 1997	Fourteenth Printing 2002
Seventh Printing 1998	Fifteenth Printing 2002
Eighth Printing 1998	Sixteenth Printing 2003
Seventeenth Printing 2004	Eighteenth Printing 2004

This book is a reference work based upon research by the author and by those who are mentioned in the acknowledgements. The opinions expressed herein are not necessarily those of, or endorsed by, the Publisher. The information as stated in this book is in no way to be considered as a substitute for consultation with a duly licensed holistic physician.

Library of Congress Catalogue Card Number: 94-061710

ISBN: 0-9628190-3-4

Printed in the United States of America

LOVE IS IN THE EARTH-

A KALEIDOSCOPE OF CRYSTALS

UPDATE

THE REFERENCE BOOK

DESCRIBING

THE METAPHYSICAL PROPERTIES OF THE MINERAL KINGDOM

BY: '♪, **MELODY** ♪, ♪

illustrator: julianne guilbault

EARTH-LOVE PUBLISHING HOUSE

3440 Youngfield Street, Suite 353
Wheat Ridge, CO. 80033

Illustrations created by Julianne Guilbault - I would like to thank Julianne Guilbault for creating the illustrations shown within this Updated **Love Is In The Earth - A Kaleidoscope Of Crystals**. Julianne and I have been friends through many lifetimes and have worked together toward the furtherance of the "brotherhood" of "All That Is". She has been active in crystal awareness for years and is truly the personification of creativity, both living and being the essence of originality and ingenuity. She has been involved in graphics design and illustrating for over twenty years, utilizing the mediums of watercolour, pastels, charcoal, pen and ink, and acrylic. She has sculpted fantasy art deco crystal/crystal ball holders; previous sculptures, including flower faeries and crystal holders, are in private collections throughout the world. She is also continuing work in completing her first fiction/fantasy novel. I thank her also for her encouragement and support in both the preparation of this Update and in the compilation and illustration of my workshop materials. Julianne may be contacted c/o Earth-Love Publishing House LTD.

Cover Art created by Charley Berryhill - I would like to thank Charlie Berryhill for his aesthetic creation of the cover art, entitled "Crystals Of Life", which he created for this Updated **"Love Is In the Earth - A Kaleidoscope Of Crystals"**. Charley and I have been friends for many lifetimes - he is a Native American who truly understands the peace of the universal "brotherhood" and has actualized the creative talents of his inherent precision. His art is in collections throughout the world and is available through his studio, "The Wildlife Art Studio" in Cheney, Washington, USA. With his sensitivity to, and practical application of, the many mediums available, Charley conceives, creates, and originates the captivating and enchanting. Charlie may also be contacted c/o Earth-Love Publishing House LTD.

Back cover Photography created by Rich Szempruch - I would like to thank Rich Szempruch for the photography of the author which is shown on the back cover of **LOVE IS IN THE EARTH - A KALEIDOSCOPE OF CRYSTALS UPDATE**. Rich and I have been friends for over ten years. He has been active in all aspects of photography for twenty years and his photography always exhibits the extra expertise which is required to convey the inner depth of his subject. The talent for photography which Rich demonstrates is highly regarded and many of his creations are in private collections throughout the country. I would like to thank him for his patience and perseverence in photographing just the "right" moment in time. Rich may be contacted c/o Earth-Love Publishing House LTD.

I am especially grateful and give my warmest thanks to Lynn Fielding, our attorney, through whom this book and the the prior books in the "Love Is In The Earth..." series have become a reality. Lynn and I are very good friends and I sincerely appreciate his help, his guidance, his love, and his encouragement in pursuing my path. His expertise and his expediency has enabled us to continue to make this book available to you, my friends.

Colour Separations by Peter Hoyt, Pacific Scanning.

Original artwork photography by Colorado Camera.

The author may be contacted c/o Earth-Love Publishing House LTD.

♪   ♫

DEDICATION

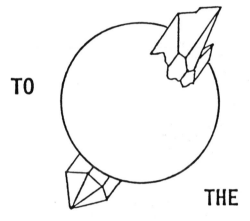

TO

THE

EARTH

ACKNOWLEDGEMENTS

I would like to thank the following people for their assistance in helping to make this book a reality.

Jose Orizon, Maria Inez, Ricardo, and Daniel de Almeida - for their lovely gifts of, and for my first introduction, to the Faden Quartz from Brasil, to the zoned smokey/clear and smokey/citrine quartz configurations, for their true hospitality during the times we have shared, and for their love.

Charley Berryhill - for his love and encouragement and for taking time to teach me more about the Native American ways.

Bob Beck - for his being and for my first introduction to the record-keeper Quartz crystal, to singing crystals, and to chevron amethyst.

Carlos do Prado Barbosa - for his being and for my first introduction to Phenacite.

Mike Brown - for his love and encouragement in all areas of my life, for his sensitivity to the sanctity of the Native American ways, and for his awareness and practice within crystal-consciousness.

Debi & Guvan Cankur - for their lovely gifts of Diaspor and for providing mineralogical information about Diaspor available and for providing insight to some of the researched qualities of same.

Pai Carumbe - for his being and for our connection of understanding and love between Brasil and America.

Edward Salisbury Dana - for teaching me, via his textbooks of mineralogy, about the multitude of crystalline structures which exist today.

Howard Dolph - for his love and for his being and for my first introduction to Biggs-formation picture Jasper, to the Nephrite/Quartz structures, and to electric-blue sheen obsidian.

Lynn Fielding - for his assistance in making the "Love Is In The Earth" series a reality and for his continuing friendship and expertise applied to my life.

Si Frazier - for my first introduction to Growth Interference Crystals.

Monika Friedrich - for her love and encouragement, and for her lovely gifts of stones from Madagascar.

Jose Roberto Bortoluzzi - and his family, for their love and their hospitality, and for making the lovely minerals of Brasil available to all.

Arthur Goldstein - for my first introduction to Charoite from Russia.

Karen Gillespie - for my first introductin to, and for her gift of, the lovely rainbow Boji Stones.

Betty & Wayne Green - for their lovely gift of, and my first introduction to, the naturally carved quartz crystal configuration, and for their lovely smiles and love.

Julio and Solange Gros - for my first introduction to the Asbestos-Included Quartz and for their continued love and encouragement.

Lucy and Joe Gross [Mama & Papa] - for their being, their love, encouragement, reassurance, motivation, patience, and support in all that I attempt and all that I am, for stimulating my interest in all of the kingdoms of the Earth, and for further helping me to both recognize and understand my heritage.

Gypsy Blue Eyes - for his being and for his emanation of the ideal that minerals are truly alive.

Robert Haag - for my first introduction to Moldavite from Czechoslovakia.

Wendy Hafferkamp - for her love and encouragement in all areas of my life.

W. R. Horning - for his love and encouragement, for stimulating my interest in the mineral kingdom, and for his lovely gifts of, and my first introductions to, Hanksite, to Indicolite, to the Faden Quartz Crystals, and to the pyrite/quartz mineralogical formation.

Barbara Hontalas - for providing information for several of the minerals listed herein and for her continued love and encouragement.

Robert Jackson - for his love and encouragement in my life, for his patience, for his assistance in editing this book, for his quotable words shown herein, for making available [via Pleasant Company Ltd. & Earth-Love Minerals, 3440 Youngfield Street, Suite 353, Wheat Ridge, CO 80033 USA, and via Earth-Love Gallery, 3266 Youngfield Street, Wheat Ridge, CO 80033 USA] the wonderful minerals of the world, for his creations as a silver/goldsmith, for my first introduction to many minerals, and for sharing in the adventure that is my life and my road.

Judy & Ray (Sedona, AZ) - for my first introduction to, and for their lovely gift of, Rhonite.

Herbert Kiesler - for providing information about several minerals listed herein, for his continuing progression toward the understanding of the unknown, and for his blessings.

Gunnard and Betty Kuoppala - for their being, and for my first introduction to the Elestial crystal and to Covellite.

Paul Lawrenz - for his gift of, and for my first introduction to, Arizona Lizard Stone Jasper.

Jose Maria - for his being, for his love of the beautiful minerals of Brasil, and for his hospitality.

Marguerite Martin - in memory and for stimulating my interest in the greater realm of minerals and for her love and encouragement toward continuing interest in the mineral kingdom.

Antony Malakou - for his love and encouragement, for my first introduction to the Ajoite crystal, and for creating the innovative title for this book.

Ed Maslovicz and Sue Neil - for their gifts of, and for my first introduction to, strombolite and ussingite.

Mano - for his love, for his appreciation of the mineral kingdom, and for his hospitality.

Barbara & Bruce McDougall - for their lovely gift of Boulder Matrix Fire Opal, for my first introduction to Boulder Opal and Parti Sapphire, and for providing information for Opal and Zeolite listed herein, and for their love and encouragement.

Max Gros Moyano - for teaching me about the alaranjado tourmaline and the ametista rutilado, and for his true hospitality during the time we shared.

Monty Montague - for his gift of, and my first introduction to, the Ruby record-keeper crystal from Africa.

Scott Nelson - for his encouragement and for his assistance in working with and describing portions of the properties of several of the minerals discussed herein.

Elenita, Natalino, Rackel, Gustavo, and Mariana Oliveira - for my first introduction to the prime specimens of rutilated quartz and asterated quartz, for their true hospitality during the times we have shared, for their gifts of lovely mineral specimens, and for their love.

Chris Pittario - for her love and encouragement and for her assistance in working with and describing portions of the properties of several of the minerals discussed herein.

Antar Pushkara - for his love and encouragement in my life, for his poetry shown herein, for being my kinsman, and for sharing his radiance and manifestation of inner calm, peace, and understanding with all who touch his life.

Jean Schroeder - for her continued love and encouragement.

Ms Sigari - for her lovely gifts of, and for my first introduction to, Skan, Phosphorite, the Biotite Lens, Serefina, Diaspor, the Kyanite/Ruby combination, and the Maqui-Marbel, and for her continued inspiration.

Bob Simmons and Kathy Warner - for their lovely gift of, and for my first introduction to Azeztulite, and for their continuing love and encouragement.

Gregory Sluszka - for his love and encouragement, for my first introduction to Kyanite, and for his assistance in working with/describing portions of the properties of over 75 minerals discussed herein.

Milt Szulinski - in his memory, for his being, for his love, and for his encouragement.

Michael Sherer - for my first introduction to the Ruby crystal from India.

Rob Smith - for his love and encouragement, for my first introduction to the Ajoite crystal and to Sphaerocobaltite, and for making available the wonderful minerals from the African continent.

Don Toth - for his love and encouragement and for providing his recipe for the Angovar Elixir which is shown in this book.

Gil Nelson - for his lovely smile, and his lovely gifts of, and my first introduction to, Purple Sage Agate.

Layton Talbott - for my first introduction to drusy Chrysocolla, a most beautiful and powerful mineral formation.

Angel Torrecillas - for my first introduction to, and for his loving gifts of, Peacock Rock, the Oaxacca Herkimer, the Amethyst Herkimers from Mexico, Ruby Silver, and for his lovely smile.

Clara Utter - for her assistance in working with/describing portions of the properties of several of the minerals discussed herein and for her continued blessings.

Josef Vajdak - for his love and encouragement and for making the fine specimens of the world available to all.

Liza Van De Linde - for her love and encouragement, for her openness and care, and for her friendship.

Antonio Viana - for his being, for his love of the beautiful minerals of Brasil, and for his hospitality.

John Wittman - for his love and encouragement in all areas of my life.

I also thank Jose Eduardo, Salim, Villani, and Jose Estrada, for their assistance and their kindnesses. In addition, I want to thank those people who have provided poetry shown herein. I truly am thankful to all of those people who have touched my life and have, thereby, assisted in the furtherance of my being. Thanks to Osho for initiating consciousness and thanks to my many friends on this wonderful Earth.

To The Reader

The information contained in the subsequent <u>updated</u> alphabetical listing for the members of the mineralogical kingdom has been derived from "hands-on" experience, geological research, folklore, experimentation, and channeled information; the channeled information and the experiences have both been validated via further experimentation and in a controlled environment.

Certain minerals [e.g., uranium, gallium, mercury, etc.] were not included due to their highly radioactive state and/or highly toxic or poisonous nature. Zinc was not included because it does not occur in the native state. Tortoise shell and "new" ivory were not included due to the potential increase in demand for the exploitation of the animals from which these materials are derived. If there is a question concerning the toxic nature of a mineral, one needs to research the chemical composition prior to utilization of that mineral - always listen to the guidance from the inner self.

The colours and structures listed in the description of the minerals are those which occur naturally. It should be noted that there are some gemstones "on the market" which have been colour-enhanced, either via artificial radiation or heat; these processes have not affected the energies of the minerals which have been tested by the author. It should also be noted that some gemstones which are available still emit radiation - it is the policy in the USA that artificially irradiated stones are not permitted to be resold until after dissipation of the radiation. Many other countries do not have the same policy, and not every stone which enters the United States is tested for radioactivity; consequently, there are those who are in unknowing possession of radioactive minerals and gemstones.

The astrological signs assigned to the minerals are indicative of the attributes of the minerals. Where the term "elemental" is used, the attributes which are intrinsic to all forms of the mineral are reflected by that sign.

Now continues the journey into the multi-faceted energies of the mineral kingdom. May you harvest the benefits of the stones, be receptive to the wisdom from within, and enjoy your life in this physical form while maintaining respect for the Earth which sustains you.

I wish you peace within yourself, love to guide you, and the understanding leading to bliss. May you heal yourself in all ways.

TABLE OF CONTENTS

INTRODUCTION

INTRODUCTION

This updated book is meant to take the reader on an intimate journey into the subtle realms of crystal energy, providing for an adventure into the avantgarde and assisting one in developing a loving affinity with crystals.

Crystals are the blossoms of the mineralogical portion of the Earth; the recognition of the beauty and loving energies of these forms can greatly enhance ones personal development. They are the myriad fireworks of both creativity and individual universal energies.

The crystal is defined as any portion of a mineralogical body exhibiting characteristic internal structure and enclosed by symmetrically arranged plane surfaces, intersecting at definite and characteristic angles. It is the "regular" form which a substance tends to assume, during the process of solidification, through the inherent power of cohesive attraction.

Crystals have been used and/or revered since the dawning of civilization. The Christian Bible refers to crystals over 200 times. Recall, the spiritually crystalline city whose walls were made of crystals, whose gates were of pearl, whose streets have no dust but gold dust, whose crystalline light falls upon the crystal sea and crystal river, and where souls that are clear as crystal are jewels forever in the crown of the redeemer. Precious stones of crystalline formation were used in the foundation of New Jerusalem [Revelations]. They were also used in the breastplate of Aaron, the Hebrew high priest [Exodus]; note that there are several translations regarding the stones used in the breastplate - hence, each stone, which has been previously defined as having been used in the breastplate [a total of 27 from the various translations] is referenced within the text describing the stone. Crystalline structures have been found in the ruins of Babylonia and in the ancient tombs of Egyptian and Chinese rulers.

Crystals exhibit the properties of both piezoelectricity [pronounced pie-ee-zo electricity] and pyroelectricity. Piezoelectricity is the quality whereby electricity, and sometimes light, is produced via compression. Many of the early civilizations of the Earth [e.g., Mayan, Aztec, American Indian, African Native, Celtic] often used quartz crystals in ceremonies and struck the crystals in order to produce a flash of visible light. Compression produces the release of electrons. Release of compression allows expansion [albeit minute] of the crystal and concurrent re-absorption of electrons; hence, producing mechanical energy [vibration]. A high energy source applied to a crystal may cause it to fracture. [There are numerous examples of personal crystals fracturing during use.] Pyroelectricity is the quality of an electrified state, or polarity, which is produced by, and changes with, variation in temperature. The pyroelectric state activates expansion of the inherent energy when the crystal is heated; subsequently, when cooled, the energy contracts and remains within the structure. It has been known for centuries in India and Ceylon, that tourmaline, when heated in the embers of a fire, first attracted ashes and then repelled ashes. Other crystals [e.g., topaz] will either attract or repel bits of paper, thread, or ashes. This phenomenon is due to electrical charges which accumulate on the surface of the crystal [i.e., heat producing an evident electrical energy]. The topaz will continue to hold the electrical excitation for several hours.

The energies of the mineral kingdom are "universal energies". Hence, when one contacts and is willing to receive this energy, and begins to exercise personal creativity via exercise of the Higher Will, one can contact and synthesize the energies from which the entire universe is comprised. This is the reason that crystals and other minerals are so very powerful and also why their powers must only be used through the highest consciousness of the individual. The individual universal energies contained within each mineralogical structure is activated and directed by interaction and/or contact with same. Right intention during use of the mineral further stimulates the melding of ones personal energy with that of the mineral kingdom, furthering the propagation of the light, the love, and "the good of all".

Although each of us has the infinite power of the universe within the self, we tend to find it easier and are predisposed to accept support from that which is from outside of ourselves. Each crystalline structure/form has its own individual energy and its own "personality". Mineralogical structures which contain more than one mineral possess a melding of the energies of the minerals contained. Each can be used in unique ways to assist one in understanding the multi-faceted nature of existence on the Earth plane.

The consciousness of the planet is leading humanity to the re-discovery of an ancient and forgotten healing art in which the utilization of crystals is prominent. Dis-ease and disorder in ones life usually entails lessons which will allow one to release the burdens of unconsciousness. Although one must ultimately heal oneself, the healing process may be facilitated by the catalytic presence of many things. To experience dis-ease is to experience a total or partial disconnection from wholeness, a loss of awareness of the innate and universal source of perfection. The members of the mineralogical kingdom have been used for centuries to act as catalysts and to assist one in becoming re-united with that source.

CONFIGURATIONS

CONFIGURATIONS

The shapes and structures of the members of the mineralogical kingdom vary with natural occurrence and with enhancement by humanity. Both unpolished/natural and polished crystalline forms of any given crystal configuration embrace and provide the same energies. Some shapes which are fabricated provide for properties identical to those shapes found within the Earth; fabrication of other shapes will not produce identical properties. Other fabricated shapes provide unique properties of both direction and use to the contained energy.

The following list provides both examples of varying configurations and descriptions of the configurations of specialty crystals; these configurations occur in the structures of quartz crystals, as well as in the structures of other crystals.

Additional information, relative to the qualities of these specialty crystals, is presented in the QUARTZ section of this book and, in some cases, in the applicable section describing the variation of the crystalline form which exhibits the attributes [e.g., information relevant to ruby record keeper crystals would be found in the "record keeper" subsection of the QUARTZ section of this book and in the RUBY section of this book].

Where reference to the configuration is not addressed in the section addressing the specific mineral, the additional properties listed in the QUARTZ section are also applicable.

The ankh is a symbol which has been found in many ancient civilizations [e.g., Egypt]. It represents the "key of life" and the approach to the infinite realm of wisdom. The configuration has been used for dowsing, to enhance creativity, to enhance fertility in both mind and body, and to bring long life. The fabricated and natural shapes exhibit identical properties.

The asterated [star] crystalline structure exhibits the rays of a star within the structure, when held in direct light. The asterism usually occurs as a four-ray or six-ray star. The energy available brings forth the light of the universe, integrating it with the light of the inner self, such that one may speak, act, and perform the will of the Divine. The associated attributes are not exhibited by fabrication of this form.

The barnacle crystal is recognized as a crystal covered or partially covered with smaller crystals. The associated attributes will not be exhibited by fabrication of this form.

The bridge crystal is recognized by a small crystal partially in and partially out of a larger crystal. The associated attributes will not be exhibited by fabrication of this form.

The cartouche is a symbol from ancient Egypt; it is used as an amulet/talisman, and was one of the pieces of jewelry found in the tomb of Tutankhamen. It contains hieroglyphics which represent "that which encircles the Earth". It was used for protection and is said to have provided a link between those of the Earth and those of other planes. The shape is fabricated from gold, silver, platinum, and other non-metallic minerals.

Carved crystals occur both naturally and are create by man. The naturally carved crystal is recognized by the existence of a carved triangular face - the carving outlines the face and is etched such that the location of the engraved portion is normally a dull shade of the colour of the crystal in appearance. These crystals tend to provide for a peeling effect to uncover that which is hidden. Those carved crystals that are created by man bring the energy of the carving to the user and act to assist one in connections with the subject.

Crystal balls [i.e., spheres] which have been contoured in the spherical configuration send energy in all directions and are the most unified of all shapes. These spheres facilitate smoother communication in group gatherings by rounding-off rough edges. They are often used as "windows" to faraway places - the past and the future. They have been used in the activity of "gazing", as if from afar, in order to assist one in the evaluation of a present situation or circumstance. Crystal balls have been used to purify and to fill the gaps in the entire auric field when worn or held. Small spheres are also used as charms and worn or carried, to prevent and/or to ameliorate degenerative diseases. The fabricated and naturally occurring shapes exhibit identical properties.

Clusters of crystals bring the "group" energy of the associated crystal to the surrounding environment. They enhance harmony and peace in groups, in the family, and in other social and/or business environments. Both the fabricated and the naturally occurring cluster configurations exhibit identical properties.

Crystal bowls, usually fabricated, have been used for gazing and for energizing and awakening other crystals. The energy of the crystalline structure of which the bowl is comprised tends to supplement the energy, providing for a furtherance of the intrinsic energies of the crystals placed within the bowl. Bowls of quartz have been used in rain-making ceremonies; they have also been used to activate the resonance of the "OM" vibration, enhancing the meditative and centering states. The fabricated and natural shapes exhibit identical properties.

The crystal cross is recognized by the cruciform shape, and occasionally, by the Celtic cross configuration. It is a tool of the light worker, assisting in the removal of unwanted other-worldly implants. It represents the idea of multiplicity while stabilizing the center of the self, promoting a further uninterrupted connection with the ethereal perfection. The fabricated configuration also exhibits identical properties.

Crystal earrings, when worn on both sides of the head, assist in balancing the left and the right sides of the brain with respect to the energy of the crystalline form which is contained within the jewelry.

The curved crystal is produced during the developmental stages of growth and is rather a rare occurrence. The associated attributes will not be exhibited by fabrication of this form.

The dendritic crystal is recognized by a branching figure or marking resembling a tree, fern, or moss-like form. The associated attributes will not be exhibited by fabrication of this form.

Double-Terminated crystals are recognized as those which exhibit terminations on both ends of the crystals. The associated attributes are also exhibited by the fabrication of this form.

The egg shape, usually fabricated, is extremely versatile. Held sideways between the thumb and fingers, it can be easily used to scan the auric field of the body. Pointing the small end forward, it can be used for reflexology, zone-therapy, acupressure, and shiatsu. The curve of the egg allows it to fit perfectly in the curve of the hand; hence, allowing ease of use during meditation. In addition, the egg shape has been used in reading the aura of another: by holding the egg shaped crystalline structure in the hand of preference and scanning the body from head to foot, one may check for blockages and "muddy" areas; where cold and/or vacuousness is felt, there is generally a resistance - where heat and/or tingling is felt, the area is usually clear. After the areas are defined, a crystal can be used in a counter-clockwise motion [northern hemisphere] to relieve the blockage and/or to dispel the "muddiness". The fabricated and natural shapes exhibit identical properties.

Elestiated Crystals is recognized by natural terminations and/or over-growth of crystals over the body and face of an etched and/or layered crystal. The associated attributes will not be exhibited by fabrication of this form.

Etched Crystals can be recognized by the existence of abrasions located upon the outer areas of the crystal. The abrasions appear to be a type of hieroglyphics. The associated attributes will not be exhibited by fabrication of this form.

Faceted Stones can determine the direction in which the energy flows from a crystal. The angles and shape of the facets will give direction to the energy. This is also true for the faces of natural crystals. It should be noted that when a stone is faceted, the energy is somewhat smoother and the magnitude tends to increase. However, as long as one is working in the realm of light and love, the faceted form of any mineral will not be over-intense or over-powering; ones capacity tends to adapt with the amount of energy available.

The gateway crystal is recognized by the existence of a portal going from the face or side of the crystal to the interior. Fluorite, amethyst, calcite, etc., occasionally exhibit this structure. The gateway crystal can be used to gain access to other worlds and other lives. It has been used to assist one in gaining admittance to akashic records and has assisted one in the attainment of the state of ascension required in order to view both past and future lives. This crystal can also provide for stability of the chakras and the aura, initiating cleansing and purification as necessary. The associated attributes will not be exhibited by fabrication of this form.

The generator crystal is recognized by a configuration of crystal faces all joining at the top of each crystal face, in the same location, in order to form the terminated apex. The fabricated configuration can also be used to exhibit the identical properties.

Headbands have been configured with one major crystal located at the third-eye, with crystals placed at locations around the circumference, and with crystals inside a hollow copper tubing. These configurations are fabricated to bring the energies of the specified stones to the areas of the third-eye and the crown chakra for a variety of effects.

The inner cross is recognized by the shape of a cross or an "X" lying within the mineral; fluorite and quartz, for example, occasionally exhibit this anomaly (in the quartz, it is sometimes caused by fractures and/or by phantom inclusions). The cross is usually off-centered, with the smaller portion being at the top. The inner cross is the symbol of ones quest for enlightenment; it assists one in opening the crown chakra and in stimulating the movement of the Kundalini. It also allows one to "skim the cream" from experiences, learning - doing - being that which is most beneficial to ones development. The associated attributes will not be exhibited by fabrication of this form.

The key crystal is recognized, in the quartz crystal, by a six-sided [varying-sided in other crystals] indented shape which is located on a face of, or on a side of, the crystal. The indent usually becomes narrower as it goes within the crystal, ending within the crystal [in an apex termination in the quartz crystal; in a variety of termination configurations in other crystals]. The associated attributes will not be exhibited by fabrication of this form.

Large crystals can be used to stimulate areas of the environment with the energies contained within the structure. They are conducive to providing increased quantities of energy to the user and/or to a subject of healing. They have been used to assure security of living quarters and as protection from negativity external to ones environment. The fabricated and natural shapes exhibit identical properties.

The manifestation crystal is recognized as a crystal in which a smaller crystal is totally enclosed. The associated attributes will not be exhibited by fabrication of this form.

The obelisk is a tapering four-sided shaft of stone, having a pyramidal apex. It stimulates the marking of time and has been used to promote connection with the ancient cultures of Egypt. This form is of the fabricated variety.

Crystals formed as octahedrons can be used to discourage chaotic growth and to assist the body, mind, and emotions to recognize that "as above" in the universal perfection of "All That Is", "so below" on the Earth plane, in the physical form. This shape has also been used to stabilize the throat chakra and to provide for exactitude in communication and analytical pursuits. The fabricated shape also exhibits identical properties.

Pendants have been used for eons to bring the energies of the mineral to the wearer. In the Victorian days, minerals were used in pendants to spell names and/or to spell words for protection, charms, and enchantments; the first letter of the name of the mineral was equal to the first letter of the name or word that was spelled - for example, to wear "Daniel", the first mineral would be one beginning with a "D" (e.g., Dioptase), the next would be one beginning with an "A" (e.g., Amethyst), and then, for example, Nephrite, Iolite, Emerald, and Labradorite. This is a very unique way to bring the numerical vibrations to ones being and to enhance ones energy field.

The phantom crystal is recognized by a "phantom" crystal within the crystal. The phantom, an image of the structure of another crystalline mineral, is comprised of a white or colored mineral and may be partial or complete. The associated attributes will not be exhibited by fabrication of this form.

Crystals formed as pyramids focus and amplify through the pyramidal shape and molecular structure of the crystal. The pyramid focuses energy in a tight beam through the apex and has been used to both charge and preserve objects. The fabricated shape also exhibits identical properties.

The rainbow crystal is recognized by fractures, producing rainbows within the crystal. The associated attributes will not be exhibited by fabrication of this form.

The record keeper crystal is recognized by a raised [or several raised] perfect triangle[s] located on one or more of the crystal faces. The associated attributes will not be exhibited by fabrication of this form.

The "rutilated crystal" is recognized by the inclusion of rutile, goethite, or sagenite, rarely curved, within the crystal. Fabrication of this form is not possible.

The scarab is an ancient symbol of protection, originally used as a protective amulet during the time of the Middle Kingdom [2133 - 1633 B.C.]. It also represents the qualities of long endurance and stamina. It is said to bring abundance to the holder. The shape is fabricated from malachite, quartz, amethyst, onyx, etc.

The self-healed crystal is recognized by small crystalline structures at the location where the crystal was removed from its matrix or home. Another type of self-healed crystal is one which has been broken [exhibiting the break in the horizontal plane or close to the horizontal strata], with the break being healed and the crystal structure being again complete. The associated attributes will not be exhibited by fabrication of this form.

The sheet or lens crystal occurs in the formation of flat layers. The fabricated configuration also exhibits identical properties.

The tabular crystal is recognized as a flat crystal with "notches" on one or both of the flat sides. The associated attributes will not be exhibited by fabrication of this form.

The tourmalinated crystal" is recognized by the inclusion of tourmaline, rarely curved, within the crystal. Fabrication of this form is not possible.

The transformation crystal can be found in any and all configurations. It is usually not recognized until the beginning of the transformation [i.e., changes in shape, quality, and/or colour]. Fabrication of this form is not possible.

The tumbled crystal is one that has been tumble-polished to smooth the configuration. It has been used as a massage tool, to stimulate the meridians of the body, to promote invention with ingenuity and skill, and to promote a free state of mind; the fabricated shape also exhibits identical properties.

The twin crystal is recognized as a growing-together of two or more individual crystals such that certain portions of each crystal are in parallel alignment and other portions of each crystal are in reverse positions with respect to each other. The associated attributes will not be exhibited by fabrication of this form.

The <u>window crystals</u> is recognized by the presence of a large diamond-shaped "window" located in the center front of the crystal, such that the top point of the diamond connects with the line leading directly to the termination, the side points connect with angles forming the opposing faces, and the bottom point connects with a line leading to the base of the crystal. The associated attributes have been exhibited by fabrication of this form.

NUMERICAL VIBRATIONS

Judi Lynn Cross
1 349 3755 39611
8   2   2

(3)

missing #'s 2 & 8

NUMERICAL VIBRATIONS

Numerologists maintain that every name vibrates and is dynam
Numbers are associated with each letter of the alphabet and each i
a particular frequency.

When representing ones name in numbers, it is said that the numbers which are
excluded indicate those experiences which are needed during this lifetime to assist the
spirit, and the physical manifestation of the spirit, in the experiences necessary to
facilitate the completion of the cycle of successive re-birth.

It is also said that those numbers which are included in ones name represent the
minerals which will support the actualization of that which is required during this
lifetime.

Since particular vibrations/frequencies attract, enhance, and assist in the actualization
of certain experiences, the utilization of members of the mineral kingdom, which
vibrate to specialized frequencies, may help one to complete and to understand the
experiences which are necessary to further ones development.

The following listing provides a method to examine ones name in order to detect the
missing numbers.

<u>1</u>	<u>2</u>	<u>3</u>	<u>4</u>	<u>5</u>	<u>6</u>	<u>7</u>	<u>8</u>	<u>9</u>
A	B	C	D	E	F	G	H	I
J	K	L	M	N	O	P	Q	R
S	T	U	V	W	X	Y	Z	

The numerical vibration, for each mineralogical form discussed herein, is listed within
the alphabetical cataloging of the text of this book.

♪45♫

MASTER NUMBERS

MASTER NUMBERS

Supplementary to the doubling of the effects of the qualities attributable to the numbers from one to nine, the "Master Numbers" also possess distinct properties. The following information is given to provide the user with additional details relevant to "Master Numbers".

Master Number 11: The connection between "brotherhood" and "sisterhood" is combined to reflect the androgynous and spiritual connection between all which exists, which has ever existed, and which will ever exist. The concept that "*I am also a you*" is reflected in the "eleven" vibration.

Master Number 22: Actualization of the God within the self, recognition that God is in the totality of existence, and understanding of the God outside of the self, produce a combined vibration in "realization" of the self, of others, and of the whole. The concept of the parallel dimensions with respect to the four cardinal directions is reflected in the "twenty-two" vibration.

Master Number 33: Power over the total physical realm is revealed and the application of same is facilitated. Understanding of the "right time" is expedited and the act of non-action is furthered; patience is a keyword. The concept of ease in actualization and the understanding of the abstraction of manifestation is reflected in the "thirty-three" vibration.

Master Number 44: Metamorphosis and continued change throughout all times is concentrated with determination of both the acceleration and the ease of reformation of the self. The concepts of impetus and catalytic motion are reflected in the "forty-four" vibration.

Master Number 55: The extension of occurrences to facilitate knowledge with ease is advanced such that approach to each event/condition/experience is with absolute precision and beneficial construction. The concept of approach via strategic techniques is reflected in the "fifty-five" vibration.

Master Number 66: Arrangement of the divine order of personal life, the sacred order upon, and within, the Earth, and the celestial order of the universe, is facilitated. The concepts of organization and systematic resolutions, and the implementation of same, are reflected in the "sixty-six" vibration.

Master Number 77: Transcendence of the creation of advancement combines the energies of non-restriction with the application of a devoted stamina. The synthesis of the vibratory messages of "twenty-two" and our Mother Earth and Father Sky brings the correspondence to consummation of all within each dimension. The concept of wholeness in entirety is reflected in the "seventy-seven" vibration.

Master Number 88: The elevation of the personal and the infinite consciousness is facilitated to encompass the actuality of "knowing" <u>and</u> the receipt of meaningful, revealing, and significant revelations [and implementation of same] with respect to ones unlimited and unrestricted capabilities. The concepts of sensitivity and compassion, with the experiencing of each moment, is reflected in the "eighty-eight" vibration.

Master Number 99: Revolution and evolution on all levels are expedited and a comprehension of the appropriate paths to completion is imparted. Flexibility in consciousness and in the unification of past, present, and future actions gains appreciation. The concept of supple adaption to facilitate the integration of all which has transpired, is transpiring, and will transpire, is reflected in the ninety-nine" vibration.

PREPARATORY METHODOLOGY

PREPARATORY METHODOLOGY

The following information is provided as guidance for those who wish to accelerate personal progress upon the spiritual path. The methods shown contain examples of techniques which have achieved the desired results; the reader is encouraged to discover additional methods which relate in the application to personal energy. The subsequent material takes one from the acquisition of the crystal [or mineral] through the preliminary phases which are conducive to preparing one for the utilization, on this plane, of the mineralogical energies.

Acquiring Crystals

"Finding" crystals or being open to crystals "finding" you are the techniques for obtaining crystals. One may acquire crystals by actually unearthing them, by buying them, and/or by receiving them as gifts.

One may find them in mines, in quarries, in the forests and mountains, in a shop, or disguised as a gift. It seems that since our lives are so busy, many of us have only the time to "find" crystals in shops. This is certainly a great way to exchange the energy, which you have given in acquiring your money, for the energy that the crystal has accumulated in making its way to you. The crystals you "find" in shops have been exposed to, and in some cases have acquired, the positive energies of the miner, the buyer, the importer, and the various forms of transportation which were utilized in order to reach the seller.

Using the "first impression" method to "find" your crystal in a shop is excellent:

o   Stand in front of a group of crystals.

o   Close your eyes and relax.

o   Open your eyes quickly and pick-up the first crystal you see.

At other times, one may be drawn to a particular crystal without knowing the reason. This crystal has "found" you and wants to be with you [at least for the present]. Meditation may provide the answer with respect to its purpose in sharing your life. The crystal could, however, be for someone else [even someone you have not yet met], and you can facilitate that person having the crystal by buying it and by remaining as its Earth-keeper until the "right" time occurs and it may be presented to the "right person".

If one is choosing crystals for a specific purpose [e.g, healing, mediation, etc.], that purpose can be held in the mind and/or projected to the crystals; subsequent openness, to which crystal[s] responds, is necessary. Some people will actually sense an energy response from a certain crystal. The energy response can take the form of, for example, a flash of light, a vibration, a resonance, a tingling sensation, a euphoric awareness or even the sense of the crystal jumping up and down and saying "take me! take me! with you".

Choosing a crystal for someone else is also quite easy. One method involves visualizing the person for whom the crystal is being chosen, projecting that visualization to the crystals, and selecting the crystal which responds [or the crystal to which you respond while visualizing the other person]. Another method is to close the eyes, visualize the person for whom the crystal is being chosen, and, upon opening the eyes, be aware of which crystal[s] responds.

"Attraction" is the key word; when personal attraction is over, personal need is over. When you are "finished" with a certain crystal in your life, the Universal consciousness will facilitate the presence of the new Earth-keeper and will draw that person to you.

Dedication

Upon receiving a "new" crystal, a dedication is always recommended. This may be accomplished by holding the crystal while consciously "willing" that the crystal be used only in love, in light, and for the good of all.

Cleansing Crystals

There are a multitude of methods which have been utilized for crystal cleansing. The following provides several examples of workable techniques.

o Take the crystal to the sea, cleanse in sea water [via allowing the water to "wash" over it], and energize in the sun.

o Smudge the crystal [e.g., with sweetgrass, cedar, sage, incense, etc.]. This method of cleansing has been used for centuries by Native American and Native African tribal cultures.

o Soak the crystal in sea salt for 7-24 hours, rinse with pure water, and energize in the sun. Caution: With some of the softer crystalline forms, salt or abrasive substances may mar the surface; this will not, however, affect the properties of the crystal.

o Place the crystal on a large crystal cluster or on another mineral [which is a specific energizer] for 12-24 hours.

o Soak the crystal in saltwater for a duration of from one to seven days; this method uses approximately three tablespoons of salt to a cup of water [water must cover the stones] in a glass container with the water and crystals in a location which will receive sunlight.

o Beam white light from the area of the third-eye and surround the crystal, sweeping any negativity to a black hole which is filled with a white light; the white light in the black hole transforms the negativity to a positive light energy such that the negativity is released from existence. Concentration and intention must be maintained.

o Surround the crystal with a visualized white or golden light, intending any present negativity to be transformed to positive light energy. Concentration and intention must be maintained.

o Move a tape de-magnetizer up and down the length of the crystal, removing and dissipating the negative vibratory essences.

o Cleanse the crystal in flowing spring, river, lake, or tap water and energize in the sun. [Water is the universal cleanser and is effective in cleansing undesirable energies from all physical forms.]

o Soak the crystal in flowers [e.g., rose petals, orange blossoms, honeysuckle, etc.] for twenty-four hours; the essence strips away negativity and cleanses the stone while the purity and energy of the flower is transmitted to the stone.

o Soak the crystal in brown rice for twenty-four hours; the rice balances and centers the energy, removing the negativity, while dissipating and transforming the negative to the positive. Upon completion of the "soak" the rice is purified and energized and is quite wonderful to eat.

Awakening Crystals

During the times of ancient civilization, tribal ceremonies involved the activation of crystals. Once a year, North American Indians and Native Africans ran, with the head shaman of their respective tribes, to the ocean to awaken the crystals held by the tribe. Upon arriving at the ocean, the shaman or tribal medicine man hit a large rock with the base of the crystal. It was said that if the crystal broke, the world would end. Although this appears to be a drastic consequence, in actuality, only the world of the shaman would possibly end - due to the large amount of energy which would be released from the crystal.

Crystals have also been awakened via;

- o impacting the crystal upon the energized sand of the ocean beaches and/or sand dunes;

- o sounding a meditative gong in proximity to the crystal [this method stimulates the activation of the resonance of the crystal]; and

- o gently sounding Tibetan prayer bells [or other bells] in proximity to the crystal [this method aligns the energy of the crystal structure such that it can be efficiently directed].

Charging Crystals

- o Place the crystal on a large crystal cluster.

- o Place the crystal in the center of a circle, where the circle is comprised of other crystals whose terminations are pointing toward the center.

- o Place the crystal in sunlight and/or in the light of the moon; the days related to the summer and winter solstices, the vernal equinox, the autumnal equinox, the full moon, and the new moon are more heavily charged.

Pre-Programming Crystals

Prior to any specialized crystal programming, the following pre-programming is recommended:

- o Program the crystal to receive Divine will such that the results will reflect actualization for the good of all.

- o Program the crystal for protection in the light.

Programming

Programming is the process of instructing the energies of the crystal in the method in which to use its qualities of transformation, stability, and attunement. Precise directions are required, or the response will be less than that which is intended. [This precision in intent is beneficial training for those utilizing crystals - with the use of crystals, one may also become "crystal clear" in the use of personal energies.]

The act of holding a crystal and intending to use it for a specific purpose is the simplest form of programming [e.g., for healing or meditation crystals].

Another method, primarily relevant to the programming of thoughts, and universal energies which are inherent to the mineralogic formation, involves the following:

o Formulate a precise phrase which accurately describes the nature of the programming [i.e., angelic/other-worldly communication, harmony, balance, love, special healing or protection for someone, etc.].

o Hold the crystal in the left hand [if left-handed, hold the crystal in the right hand], relax for several minutes, initiate circular breathing, and center the consciousness. Consciously align the personal conscious awareness with the higher-self and/or other [pre-defined] appropriate other-worldly beings.

o Ask for guidance, protection, and assistance in the programming process. Open the center of consciousness and allow receptivity to flow through to the inner being.

o Repeat the formulated phrase 20-30 times in succession while visualizing and/or feeling the desired effect of the program. [Be open to higher assistance during this process.]

As the phrase is repeated, an energy field will build and culminate in the energy pattern necessary to represent the desired program.

o While maintaining full awareness of the energy field, bring total awareness and consciousness to the area of the third-eye or the heart chakra. Place the crystal in front of the area of the third-eye or the heart chakra and allow the self to feel the connection with it.

o Direct the energy field into the crystal for 30-60 seconds and allow the program to be transferred to within the crystal. Intuitive recognition will signal when the transmittal is complete.

o Detach consciousness from the crystal and allow the universal energies to act.

PRACTICAL APPLICATIONS

PRACTICAL APPLICATIONS

The following information is included to assist the reader in the application of various methods which may be utilized to access and implement the energies available from the mineral kingdom.

Meditation with Crystals

Crystals [and many of the other mineralogical formations reported in this book] can assist one in contacting the perfection of the Divine and can allow one to reach the higher spiritual levels during meditation. Attainment of these levels provides for discovery of the Divine being inherent to the self. The crystal magnifies ones personal energy by merely focusing and connecting it with the universal powers.

Contacting the higher intelligence of the mineralogical kingdom via meditation may provide substantive information about the mineral kingdom and the various ways the minerals may help humanity.

The techniques of allowing minerals to assist in mediation involve holding a pre-selected stone in the hand [or hands] or placing the stone on the floor or on a table and allowing the self to focus on it during entry to the meditative state.

In group meditations, sitting in a circle, with a mineral[s] in the center, is quite effective. Assure, prior to meditation, that all participants hold the precise intention of the group. [The energy of intention is directed into the mineral and is focused as clearly and precisely as possible.]

Holding a crystal during meditation with music will often allow the user to "see" the music in terms of color and shape. When harmonious music is played in the presence of a crystal, much of the intention of the composer is impressed in the crystal structure, and if one "listens" to the crystal at a later time during a meditative state, one will often be able to "hear" and understand the etheric message of the music.

Manifestation

In manifestation there is a thin line between "helping the universe provide that which is necessary" and "attempting to force the universe to provide that which is desired". One must strive to remember that unfulfilled "want" is one of the true sources of unhappiness; if one "wants" something desperately enough and is unable to obtain it in this lifetime, one may keep drawing the self into additional lifetimes until the "want" is fulfilled. "Need", however, will always be fulfilled - as long as it is not blocked by "want". Those things which are truly needed are those which fulfill the personal specific plan for ones present incarnation. One may, however, need to work for the manifestation of that which is "needed".

When the energies of desire, need, and intention are directed concurrently through the crystal in order to bring that which is necessary to fulfill ones life plan, one can propagate an energy appropriate to facilitation of the fulfillment of the "need".

Protection

Protective energies have been gained from the mineralogical kingdom for eons. Minerals have been worn as amulets and talismen and have been programmed for protection in the light and love of the universal forces.

One method which has been used during programming for protection [e.g., against psychic attack] entails visualization of a protective shield or a bubble of white light emanating from the crystal. The protection of ones possessions or of the home can also be facilitated via this method; another technique involves gridding the home or ones possessions and/or using the laser wand to enclose same.

Elixirs/Energizing Liquids

An elixir is a preparation of "mineral water" which contains the essence of the energies of the crystalline form with which it is fortified. In order to prepare the energies of a crystal for the assimilation into an elixir, conscious programming is recommended to facilitate enhanced transfer of the special energies desired.

Without conscious programming, all of the energies are transmitted, and no specific direction for these energies is delineated; this method is conducive to activation of "spring tonics" and for general daily use. The minerals listed within the book, except for those specifically designated, can be used in the preparation of elixirs. The minerals which indicate that preparation of an elixir should not be via the normal method can be used in the preparation of an elixir via the alternative method.

The **normal method** for the manufacture of a mineral elixir requires a mineral, distilled water [or other non-polluted liquid], a glass jar or bowl, and patience. The mineral is placed within the liquid within the glass jar; no metal should contact the liquid. The container is then placed in the sun/moon for at least 24 hours, after which the resultant elixir may be consumed.

A general enhancement of any type of water is an obvious benefit of the 24 hour elixir. A simple test, conducted throughout many parts of the world [including Africa, India, Kathmandu, and the USA], has evidenced that the energized water tends to taste "sweeter" and less "flat" than water which has been "standing" for the same time period. The members of the mineral kingdom have also been used to energize and enhance wine.

An **enhanced normal method** of elixir preparation involves placing the container, containing the mineral and <u>distilled water,</u> in the sun on the day of the full [or new] moon, allowing for the energy transfer to progress during the following seven days. The container is then placed in a dark location for seven days with the placement of seven, of the same minerals of which the elixir is being prepared, surrounding and pointing toward the center of the elixir; if the seven like-minerals are not available, quartz crystals may be substituted. After the fourteen days, one ounce of brandy [or other food-grade alcohol] is mixed with the liquid in order to stabilize and maintain the frequencies of the contained energies; this preparation is known as the "mother" elixir. The mother elixir should be stored in glass and in a dark location. It may be consumed via placing 2-3 drops under the tongue and/or via drinking a reconstituted liquor [reconstitution is accomplished by placing 2-3 drops in one gallon of distilled water].

An **alternative method** for preparation of unusual elixirs is to place the mineral within a glass container and to place this container within the distilled water; the remainder of the procedure is the same as described above. This method alleviates the potential of contamination of the elixir by toxic chemicals contained within or upon the mineral and prevents the dissipation of minerals which are soluble in water and/or are very soft.

Example of United Elixirs

The Angovar Elixir is an example of an elixir created with more than one mineral; this specific elixir has been used to transmit energy to others and to the world, during healing circles and medicine wheels; in addition, it can be used to activate the third-eye. The procedure which has been used to create this elixir is in recipe form as follows (please note that the time period includes creation and activation during three new moons):

During first new moon, a gem elixir is prepared with Amethyst, Citrine, Rose Quartz - (about 1/2 gallon); during the second new moon, natural Iron or Copper is added to the elixir; during the third new moon, take one cup of the gem elixir and add 1/2 tsp. sage, 1/2 tsp. cedar, and 9 rose hips - then boil to make a "tea", strain the tea and, after cooling, add to the gem elixir. Add 1 ounce of food grade alcohol for each 1 ounce of elixir. The elixir may be taken as 2-3 drops under the tongue during a 24 hour period or can be used to annoint the third-eye (approximately the same amount is used for the third-eye).

Treating Food

A mineral may be programmed to help neutralize harmful chemicals and harmful energies contained within processed food. In this case, the mineral facilitates the de-programming and release of the molecular links which bind the essence of the harmful substances/energies together. During the programming, it is very important to include direction for the transmutation of the harmful substances/energies into helpful substances/energies.

Minerals have also been placed in aquariums and in the water dishes of pets -larger specimens, eliminating the possibility of ingestion, are recommended for pet dishes.

Treating Plants

Plants have been treated with mineral-sweetened water. A small portion of sand [high in quartz crystal content] mixed with potting soil has also tended to increase the health of plants.

For outside plants, minerals have been programmed, for the highest good of all beings, and then placed in a grid formation around the garden, around shrubs, and/or around the base of trees. This technique can be augmented by placing another mineral at the base of any plant which needs encouragement -this mineral should be programmed to act for the highest good of all beings within the energy field and to balance and strengthen the plant individually.

Within the text of the multitude of crystals listed in the subsequent sections of this book, the reader will find reference to specific stones which have been used in the treatment of plants.

Treating the Aura

The aura, an energy field surrounding the body, can be charged by wearing and/or carrying minerals and by placing minerals within ones environment. The frequency and duration with which a mineral is worn/carried/handled determines the level of attunement which is attainable with that mineral. Attuning to a mineral facilitates the energizing of ones aura with the energies contained within the mineral.

The aura may be scanned with a mineral in order to determine energy blockages and/or the existence of auric "holes" which allow the drain of energy from the physical body. Minerals have also been successfully used to cleanse and stabilize the aura - directing the mineral toward the auric field while performing a "sweeping" motion from the top to the bottom or from the bottom to the top of the auric body; both a pre-determined direction and an intended receiving source for any negativity are recommended. In addition to the quartz crystal, one will be guided by the subsequent alphabetized text and the intuitive self to the additional minerals which are quite useful for balancing, cleansing, stabilizing, and scanning and correcting any problematic areas in the aura.

Treating the Automobile

Gasoline mileage has been enhanced by placing a quartz crystal on the carburetor and/or on the fuel line. Increases of up to 50% have been reported.

Mechanical portions of the automobile have also been "treated" by placing a crystal on, or pointing the crystal toward, the equipment.

There have been many reports of minerals which have been placed in automobiles to encourage both the protection of the driver/passengers and to enhance and/or maintain the abilities of the components.

ADDITIONAL DEFINITIONS

ADDITIONAL DEFINITIONS

The following definitions are included to provide clarification of many terms which are used within the text of this book.

Akashic Records

The akashic records are ethereal records of all actions and thoughts which have or which will occur.

Aura

The aura is a subtle, but luminous, emanation which surrounds a structure [e.g., the physical body, plants, minerals, etc.], providing a protective field. The magnitude, density, and colours of the auric field are relative to the spiritual development of that which it surrounds.

Chakras

Chakras [translated from Sanskrit as "wheels" of rotating energy and pronounced "shock-ras"], as defined by the Eastern Masters, are intersections of vital energy flows present in the ethereal body and in related locations of the physical body.

There are hundreds of these intersections, each related to an acupressure/acupuncture point. Of these hundreds of points, there are seven [or eight] major chakras associated with the physical body; these major chakras are the areas where the major energy flows intersect. The health of an area of the physical body and the condition of its associated chakra are considered interdependent [e.g., when a chakra is clear and vital, the associated portions of the body should also be in the optimum state]. As chakras are cleared, vitalized, and expanded in clarity and development, one may experience the actualization of qualities which have not previously been manifest.

Base Chakra - The base chakra [first chakra] is located in the area of the base of the spine in the area of the lumbar. It is the center of vitality, physical energy, and self-preservation. It activates and strengthens the will [e.g., the will to live, to survive, to manifest, etc.], assists one in living on the physical plane, and stimulates the life-sustaining energies. It is the location of the resting Kundalini. It is the center which vitalizes the kidneys, the suprarenal glands, and the spinal column in the physical body. The colours associated with the base chakra include red [representing the essential, idealistic, and confident passion for life] and black [representing stability and grounding to the source of security].

Sacral Chakra - The sacral chakra [second chakra] is located in the area 1" to 2" below the navel. It is the center of desire, emotion, creativity, sexuality, and intuition. It stimulates the creative life force, forces required for existence on the physical plane, and the bases of life, itself. It is the center which vitalizes the digestive system, reproductive organs, sexual activity, and the gonads where sex hormones are produced. The second chakra has been known as the pathway to health; it is attuned to emotions and thoughts concerning well-ness and is, usually, the center which allows the condition of dis-ease to manifest in order to cleanse the body, mind, and/or emotions.

The second chakra has also been said to be located under the area of the rib cage, at the location of the spleen. It has been called the splenic chakra and is considered, by some, to be a major chakra. In addition to the attributes of the sacral chakra, it is the center which allows for vitalization of the entire physical form. It also acts as an open door to both the receipt and the assimilation of the life-giving energies of the universe.

The colours associated with the second chakra include orange [representing wisdom, equity, creativity, and benevolence to all] and blue/green [representing the synthesis of Divine guidance in the areas of healing.

Solar Plexus Chakra - The solar plexus chakra [third chakra] is located at the solar plexus area, below the breastbone and behind the stomach. It is sometimes considered to be located at the navel. Looking at the solar plexus chakra from the back of the body, the location is just below the shoulder blades. It is the center of personal power, ambition, intellect, astral force, desire and emotions based on intellect, and touch.

The third chakra contains a protective energy, protecting against any negativity which is contained within any of the other chakras. It is the center which vitalizes the stomach, liver, gall bladder, sympathetic nervous system [activating involuntary muscles which enhance the mobilization of the physical body], pancreas, and adrenal glands. The colour associated with the third chakra is yellow [representing meditative analytical thought and intellectual activity].

Heart Chakra - The heart chakra [fourth chakra] is located in the center of the chest, at the level of the heart. It is the center of compassion, love, group consciousness, and spirituality associated with a "oneness" with "All That Is". The fourth chakra provides for a desegregation between the loving energy of the heart and the analytical energy of the intellect; it provides for a "sprinkling" of love and compassion to all of the chakras. It is the center which vitalizes the heart, thymus, circulatory system, blood, cellular structure, and the involuntary muscles which assist in the restoration of both physical and loving energy. The colours associated with the fourth chakra include pink [representing softness in strength, compassion, empathy, and unconditional love to all that exists] and green [representing soothing, smoothing healing, ecstasy and exhilaration, and a joyful and fulfilling anticipation].

Throat Chakra - The throat chakra [fifth chakra] is located at the neck, the center being recognized as the area of the throat located above the collar bone. It is the center of communication, sound, and expression of creativity via thought, speech, and writing. The fifth chakra has been called the communication center, acting to provide the energy for, and the understanding of, both verbal and mental communications. It is the center which vitalizes the thyroid gland, throat and jaw areas, alimentary canal, lungs, vocal cords, and the breath. The colour associated with the fifth chakra is blue [representing the knowledge of <u>and</u> oneness with Divine guidance].

Third-Eye Chakra - The third-eye chakra [sixth chakra], also known as the brow chakra, is located between and about one finger-breadth above the eyebrows. On the back of the body, the corresponding location is at the base of the skull in the area of the medulla oblongata. It is the center of psychic power, higher intuition, the energies of the spirit, magnetic forces, and light. It enables focusing of the higher intuitive information and stimulates the wisdom for "right" intent. The sixth chakra, when activated and clear, is the center for outside guidance and the intuitive "aha". It also assists in the purification of negative tendencies and in the elimination of selfish attitudes. It is the center which vitalizes the cerebellum, nose, central nervous system, the pituitary gland, and the left eye. The combined interaction of the pineal and pituitary glands activates this center. The colour associated with the sixth chakra is indigo [representing the attainment, the search, and those who search for the spiritual purpose of life].

Crown Chakra - The crown chakra [seventh chakra] is located at the crown of the head. It is the center of spirituality, enlightenment, dynamic thought, and energy. It allows for the inward flow of wisdom from the ethers and brings the gift of cosmic consciousness. When stimulated and clear, it enables one to see the truth concerning illusory ideals, materialistic pursuits, self-limiting concepts, pride, and vanity; it further allows one to experience continuous self-awareness and conscious detachment from personal emotions. It is the center which vitalizes the cerebrum, the right eye, and the pineal gland. The colours associated with the seventh chakra are violet [representing royalty in enlightenment and the search and attainment of the true meanings of spirituality, life, and existence] and a shimmering golden-white [representing the state of perfection in body, mind, emotions, and spirituality].

The areas where few energy flows intersect are called minor chakras. These minor chakras include, for example, centers at the palm of the each hand, at the sole of each foot, behind each eye, in front of each ear where the jawbone is connected, above each breast, and at the back of each knee.

Chakras can be opened by a variety of methods. One method is via the use of a laser wand or another wand-type crystal, rotated in a counter-clockwise direction or in a clockwise direction. Research throughout the world has found that the opening of the chakras can be different for each person - in some cases the chakras can be opened by rotating the laser wand in the counter-clockwise direction and in other cases the chakra can be opened by rotating the laser wand in a clockwise direction. In addition, the chakras may change directions for opening and/or closing. The practitioner will need to "feel" the rotation each time, such that the proper directional opening is facilitated; the practitioner will sense an increase of heat, of vibration, or of energy when the chakra is open.

The assignment of a type of crystal to a specific chakra is not given within the text of this book; it is recommended that the crystal which contains the colour associated with the chakra is used when one is beginning to practice chakra stimulation and balancing, auric healing, and the "laying-on-of-stones" in the art of crystal lay-outs.

In addition to the qualities listed within the text relative to each stone, the organs located in the area of the chakra and the properties inherent to each chakra can be treated with minerals exhibiting the colour associated with said chakra. As one becomes more attuned to the crystals and to the self, intuition will guide the practitioner to the most beneficial crystals and the most beneficial locations for placement. When one utilizes these arts with a loving and open heart, there can be no errors and there can be no detrimental or adverse effects.

Cloud-busting/weather control

Cloud-busting is a method of weather control which uses a type of divining rod. The equipment required includes a 10-foot length of 2" diameter galvanized pipe, steel wool, duct tape, and a 5 to 6-foot length of 1" diameter conduit steel [e.g., BX cable from the plumbing section of any hardware store]. The steel wool is wrapped around the end of the conduit steel and this assembly is pressed into the galvanized pipe. Contact between the conduit steel and the galvanized pipe is created and maintained via wrapping the conduit steel and the galvanized pipe with duct tape at the area of connection.

Pointing the assembly [outdoors] in a north-westerly direction has initiated rain; the rod can be aimed at any cloud, subsequently producing an ethereal hole in the cloud, and often bringing rain or, at least, helping the cloud to move. Pointing the assembly in an easterly direction has helped in moving weather through an area. Pointing the assembly at a 55 gallon drum which is full of water and mounted at an angle, such that the water trickles slowly from the drum, has been used to help the movement and intensity of weather to return to its natural state or course.

Positioning the rod on the shoulder, while aiming it in the direction where an observer can recognize the colour of blue and/or purple emanating from it, has facilitated increased activity in the natural processes required to clear an area of pollution and/or radioactivity. It can further be used to help to clear pollution from streams.

One can also point the rod at the self in order to both clean and restore the chakras.

The rod, pointed toward the heavens, while the thought process focuses on the eternal bonding with those on other planets, has also been used to attract ships from other worlds. The rod, again pointed toward the heavens, while the thought process focuses on the spiritual connection with those in the spiritual worlds, has been used to facilitate contact with those from the "other side".

The utilization of crystalline forms [e.g., attached via natural fiber wrapping to the sides of the rod] have increased the powers, the stamina, and the intensity of the divining rod.

Dowsing

Dowsing is defined as the act of searching for something and/or facilitating a specific condition via the utilization of a divining rod.

Etheric Body

The etheric body is an energy field, perfect in composition, which is connected to, and assists in maintaining, the physical form. It acts as a buffer for energy forces which are relayed to the physical form from higher dimensions; it transmits these forces via the central nervous system and the endocrine and circulatory systems.

It provides for the vitalization of the physical cells and, when in alignment with the physical body, stimulates the quest toward the attainment of the perfection of health and form.

It further assists in promoting the stimulation of the higher intuition and in the transmission and receipt of telepathic messages.

Grand Formation

The "Grand Formation" is defined as one which is comprised of several minerals bringing in the properties of same and the synthesis of the minerals to produce further properties; it is one through which we may access knowledge of other civilizations and other worlds and gain knowledge of activities and actions of those times/places;

it has come to us at this time to assist in many activities associated with the furtherance of the "brotherhood" and the actualization of our innate perfection.

Gridding

The localities within the Earth and in which minerals reside are connected by an inter-dimensional grid. This grid allows, for example, for the transmittal of energies from one mineral to another. Those minerals which are removed from within the Earth tend to retain an ethereal connection to those remaining within the grid. In order to activate and to enhance the connection between the minerals which are on the Earth plane and those which are a part of the interdimensional grid, a graphic design is accessed via the alignment of the energies of the specific tangible selected minerals and those minerals which remain within the Earth.

When gridding a specific location, the tangible minerals are placed on ley lines within the location of concern. This placement facilitates enhanced energy transfer and subsequent results due to the increase in the focusing ability of the minerals between the points of the grid.

Hand-of-Preference

The right hand is the hand-of-preference for those who are "right-handed"; the left hand is the hand-of-preference for those who are "left-handed".

Karma

Karma is the doctrine of inevitable consequence. It is defined, by the religions of Hinduism and Buddhism, to be the cosmic operation of retribution which acts to determine the status and experiences of a person based upon the actions of that person during a previous incarnation [or a previous era of this lifetime]. The philosophy of karma allows for the realization that ones actions in this life may also affect future lives and that ones experiences in this life are based upon ones actions during a previous life. To phrase the doctrine succinctly,"one receives that which one gives".

Laying-on-of-stones

"Love Is In The Earth - Laying-On-Of-Stones" provides information with respect to laying-on-of-stones; this activity involves placing the members of the mineral kingdom upon the body of another. Those from ancient civilizations have used this art to facilitate healing of another on all levels; first affecting an aligned connection between the perfection of the etheric body and the physical form and, subsequently, promoting the energy transfer from the minerals to the physical form.

The laying-on-of-stones can be used to initiate healing, astral travel, travel to the center of ones being, etc.

There are no set procedures and no rules; the intuition is the teacher; one will make no mistakes because there are no mistakes. It is, however, recommended that appropriate minerals be used at the areas of the hand and feet chakras in order to produce grounding to the physical plane; this grounding assists one in the acceptance of the transfer of the mineralogical healing energies during healing activities.

Ley Lines

Ley lines are geometrically straight lines of energy which are arranged in a web-like pattern over the Earth. When two or more ley lines intersect, a power point emanates the concentration of the natural energy forces.

Utilization of a crystal in the area of a power point enhances both the energy of the crystal and the ability of the user; power points are excellent areas for psychic endeavors and for the actualization of that which is necessary in ones life.

The location of power points can be determined most conveniently via dowsing; using two dowsing rods, a power point lies where the rods cross. In addition to various other methods, the pendulum can also be used to determine the location of power points.

Stone Of The Seventh Mansion

"A stone of the seventh mansion" is one of spiritual development and subsequent enlightenment - it is spiritually attuned to the ethereal realm and to ones progression, advancement, and cultivation.

Transcending The Third Dimension

We live in a "third dimensional" world - transcending the third dimension means that we can go beyond the limitations of same and experience the unfathomable ideas, ideals, events, conditions, etc., which exist in other dimensions, on other planes. Transcending our self-imposed limitations is quite important for our perfect manifestation - one may exemplify this on the physical plane via manifesting an accelerated spiritual and psychological growth, etc.

Vortex

A vortex is the intersection of multiple ley lines, creating an intensely powerful area with respect to the concentration of natural energy forces. The area of the vortex tends to enhance all psychic abilities and to facilitate experiences which bring healing energies to unusual manifestations.

The areas upon the Earth where these forces are abundant include locations in the proximity of Table Mountain, Cape Town, RSA; Sedona, Arizona, USA; Topo Do Mundo, close to Belo Horizonte, Brasil; Kathmandu, Nepal; Pune, India; South Of England, UK; Browns Mountain, close to Spokane Washington, USA; and many areas in the mountains of Peru.

Wands

Silver, gold, copper, or platinum used on a crystalline form or as a wand [with a natural crystal, faceted gem, or polished mineral located at one or both ends] facilitates amplification of the energies of the crystalline form, promoting maximum utilization of the potential energy. The wand, itself, provides for the directional focus required to provide the maximum penetration of the energy. The energies associated with the mineral comprising the wand also supplement those of the contained minerals.

The "whirling wand", designed by R.R. Jackson of Colorado, USA, produces an amplification and directed-ness of the mineralogical components. The structure provides the energy of the spiral, bringing synthesis to the energies of the physical plane and the spiritual worlds. The energies of the attached minerals are enhanced by the design, allowing for intensification and sensitivity with respect to the direction of energy transmission.

The action of a wand comprised of a combination of copper, brass, and iron provides for a balancing of the energies of the bodies and assists in maintaining an overall well-being within the chemistry of the physical, emotional, and intellectual bodies.

Yin-Yang

As defined by the I Ching [pronounced "yee-jing"], the yin aspect is feminine, one of change; the yang aspect is masculine, one of harmony.

YOU ARE THE BRIGHT SHINING STAR OF LOVE

ACANTHITE   [Astrological Sign of Scorpio]

Acanthite crystallizes in the form of iron-black orthorhombic configurations.

In ancient times this mineral was revered by the Saxons as a protective force. Many warriors carried Acanthite in a small carved bottle to dispel evil and to provide safety and preservation of the self. It was also revered as a stone bringing wisdom and foresight.

It can be used to bring strength in times of need, to assist on in the removal of obstacles (via dissolution on the ethereal plane), and to induce a state of well-being in the physical, mental, and emotional bodies.

It can be used as a mirror to internal dis-ease, stimulating the sight of the self from outside of the body. This sight is without judgmental attitudes and can provide for a stepping-stone to the furtherance of holistic well-ness. It provides one with patience and perseverance in the healing of the body and allows one to understand the underlying reasons for the problem and the amelioration process. It assists in increasing perception and helps to regulate the emotional and the intuitive energies.

Acanthite has been used in the treatment of bacterial and viral infections and to ameliorate the symptoms of colds and flus. It has also been used to eliminate toxins at the cellular level. It can be used to increase the assimilation of Vitamins A and E, and to ameliorate disorders associated with deficiency in the immune system.

This mineral's softness precludes its use in the normal method of preparation of an elixir.

Vibrates to the number 9.

ACTINOLITE   [Astrological Sign of Scorpio]

Actinolite crystals are long-bladed and are usually found in fibrous or columnar aggregates. The typical colours are green or black. A compact green variety [nephrite, a form of jade] has properties similar to jade albeit somewhat smoother [i.e., mellow]. Further information with respect to nephrite is found in the NEPHRITE section of this book. The black variety helps to produce a wearing-away of that which is unwanted.

Actinolite is an immensely important tool. It is a phenomenal shielding device and expands the energy bodies [especially when used in conjunction with sheen obsidian].

The expansion of the energy bodies provides for a connection to "All That Is" and facilitates the "brotherhood" of all.

This mineral also provides for a familiarity with all of those who one encounters, withholding all aspects of that which causes the familiar smile, action, or being, to appear objectionable.

By focusing the mineral on an unwanted condition, lessening is both facilitated and enhanced. All colours can be used to help one with strengthening basic conditions and/or decreasing unwanted conditions.

Vibrates to the number 9.

ADAMITE   [Astrological Sign of Cancer]

Adamite occurs in crystalline form as a bright yellowish-green tabular crystal or as a druse [an overgrowth of small, usually interlocked crystals] on other minerals. It characteristically has a vitreous luster and sometimes fluoresces under ultra-violet light.

Adamite can be used to facilitate the synthesis of the intellect [third chakra] with the heart [fourth chakra] in order to help produce the stability of the heart [e.g., emotional, loving, caring] as guided by the intellect.

It also provides for inner strength when dealing with emotional issues, and helps one to vocalize personal sentiments.

It instills one with courage to pioneer into the unknown and stimulates the prosperous conduct of business and attainment of the material aspects of this reality. It also provides stimulus for one to attempt new "things" and to inspire avantgarde thinking.

It can be used in the treatment of disorders of the heart, lungs, and ductless glands. It also has been used to treat discordant conditions related to the throat.

Vibrates to the number 8.

ADULARIA   [Astrological Sign of Cancer]

Adularia is a form of orthoclase [also a feldspar] which is usually found in the form of crystals configured with eight sides, four which are trapezoidal and four which are triangular. The colour range includes white, colourless, pale yellow, peach, pink, grey, and, occasionally green.

In addition to the properties listed in the ORTHOCLASE and FELDSPAR sections of this book, adularia can also be used to enhance devotion to a cause, purpose, or person. The energies of the mineral increase ones ability to see the positive attributes in all.

It can be used to stimulate the opening of the heart and crown chakras and to provide for clarity of the mental processes and an openness to love.

It also encourages the practical side of ones nature and is conducive to facilitation of increased performance in situations of ones "life work". It has been used to advance one in employment and to assist one in gaining employment in ones chosen field.

It can also be used in the treatment of the parasympathetic nervous system to stabilize and calm, for example, the heart and mind. It has been used to treat snow-blindness.

Vibrates to the number 4.

AEGIRINE   [Astrological Sign of Pisces]

Aegirine is a mineral which can assist one in following personal convictions and morality and to do that which is required - it actually provides the strength for one to be true to oneself. It further dispenses with the effects of group pressure, bringing acceptance of the self without conformance.

Utilization of this mineral for energy generation is excellent. It acts to concentrate the positive energy in an area and to interact with all who are present, providing revitalizing, mental stimulation, concentration of healing energy for other minerals, and unifying the group effort.

It has been used to remove emotional blockages, to allow one to reflect personal attitudes, opinions, and conceptions, and to accept the state of sufficiency. It further strengthens personal integrity and conviction.

Aegirine has been used in the treatment of deficiencies of the immune system, to protect one from negative energy and psychic attack, and to increase the amount of energy applied by other minerals when used in <u>any</u> healing situation.

Vibrates to the number 5.

Agate is a variegated class of chalcedony, usually exhibiting coloured bands or other markings. Some agate is not patterned.

In addition to the properties listed in the CHALCEDONY section of this book, agate also provides for balancing of yin-yang energy and for balancing of the physical, emotional, and intellectual bodies with the etheric energies. It stabilizes the aura, providing for a cleansing effect which acts to smooth dysfunctional energies and to both transform and eliminate negativity. It further assists one in the development of precision in examination of oneself and of circumstances relevant to ones well-being.

Agate is said to have been one of the stones used in the breastplate of the high priest.

In historic times, it was placed in water for use in cooking and/or for drinking in order to dispel sickness.

Agate can be used to stimulate analytical capabilities and precision. It provides for perceptiveness to situations and awakens ones inherent talents and adroitness. It is also used to produce inspiration from and connected-ness with the entities residing in the spiritual worlds.

It has been reported to strengthen the sight, to diminish thirst, and to promote marital fidelity.

Vibrates to the number 7.

In addition to the above properties common to the agate family, specific types of agates possess further qualities.

Angel Wing Agate   [Astrological Signs of Taurus & Aries]

Angel wing agate exhibits tubes within the structure, sometimes hollow and sometimes solid; in the cases where a tube is solid, there is usually a hollow space surrounding it.

It can be used to diminish distractions and to further the abilities of concentration. It allows one to realize alternatives to situations and to weigh the varied actions which are viewed as possibilities. It helps one to imagine a life with no cares, no worries, and no anxieties - one which is perfectly calm and continually serene; it further helps to stimulate the insight require to attain this state.

Angel wing agate has been used at the crown chakra to encourage the initiation of movement of the Kundalini, providing an opening and clearing of the major chakras and a short-circuiting of dysfunctional energies.

It can also be used to facilitate the opening of the pathway for communication with those other-worldly beings, both of the spiritual world and the other planetary worlds. It activates clairaudient capabilities and provides additional energy to amplify thought transfer and to facilitate telepathic endeavors.

It has been used to produce a communication between the physical cellular structure and the perfect ethereal body, such that the physical body can more readily repair itself.

It can also be used in the treatment of disorders of the ears, lungs, stomach, and intestines.

Vibrates to the number 9.

<u>Blue Lace Agate</u>   [Astrological Sign of Pisces]

Blue lace agate displays a blue and white lace pattern. It can help one to reach extremely high spiritual spaces. It contains the qualities of flight, air, movement, and grace. It is a highly inspirational influence when used for inner attunement.

The energy of this mineral is most useful at the locations of the throat chakra, the heart chakra, the third-eye, and crown chakra. Activating these chakras, it helps one to enter into high-frequency states of awareness.

Blue lace agate is especially suited to those gentle people with shades of pale blue in their aura.

It can be used in the treatment of arthritic conditions and in cases of "hereditary" bone deformity; it can also be used to strengthen the skeletal structure. It is quite helpful when used to enhance the mending of breaks and fractures, and for the regulation of the developmental processes of the fingernails and toenails. Blue lace agate can help to remove blockages from the nervous system and from the capillaries of the body. It can be used in the treatment of disorders of the pancreas and of those glands inherently associated with digestion. It is of assistance in eliminating outwardly manifested growths.

This mineral can also be used for fluid balance around the brain; the hydrocephalic may find relief from the condition by using a liquid elixir of this stone. It also is used for the attunement within the fleshy cellular structure, promoting cohesiveness in thought and maintenance of the state of health. It has also been used as an elixir to soothe the eyes and to diminish dilation of the blood vessels of the iris.

Vibrates to the number 5.

Botryoidal Black Agate   [Astrological Signs of Sagittarius & Scorpio]

Botryoidal black agate displays a nodular configuration which presents, when polished, both tubular/orbicular configurations and plumes.

This mineral can be used to enhance communication on the physical plane and to strengthen the connection with other worlds and with beings in those worlds.

It can also be used to alleviate distractions and to provide for intensified concentration. It can enable one to predict future events and can be used to enhance the abilities of a divining rod. It can facilitate clairaudient experiences and may be used to grid an area to enhance the energy to welcome spaceship landings.

It is a "stone for peace and healing", allowing one to go to the center of the Earth, to the center of ones being, and/or to the center of any stress or conflict in order to initiate the self-healing properties of the energy of perfection.

It provides for grounding and centering, promoting an energy which facilitates entry to both the "heart space" and the meditative state. It assists one in maintaining the connection with the ethereal meridians and further helps to both relieve and remove energy blockages within the emotional and physical bodies.

It is a stone which can be used for the healing of the Earth, helping with the dissipation of negativity and with the instilling of the "positive" within the hearts of humanity.

It can also be used in the treatment of disorders of the intestines, alimentary canal, veins, ears, nose, and throat. It has been used to dissipate pain on all levels.

Vibrates to the number 4.

Botswana Agate   [Astrological Sign of Scorpio]

Botswana agate is a purplish-grey fortification agate exhibiting white patterns of, usually, circles or ovoids. It is generally found in the form of nodules.

It can be used to stimulate the exploration of the unknown and to further ones quest toward the enlightened state. It enhances creativity and helps one to release the emotional nuances which have been repressed. It also allows one to look toward the solution, rather than dwell on the problem.

It stimulates the crown chakra and energizes the auric body, encouraging eternal love and allowing for the recognition that eternal love is a constant in the ever changing universe. It also encourages conscientiousness and vigilance in tasks and helps one to maintain an ever-present watchfulness during the activities requiring circumspection, deliberation, and/or vigilance.

It helps one to maintain a forthright character and to sustain an attentiveness to detail which further facilitates the sensitivity to, and the recognition and the understanding of, the complete picture [regardless of distortion].

Botswana Agate can be used in the treatment of disorders of the nervous system and to help to rid the body of toxins. It is said to counteract poisoning on the physical, emotional, and intellectual planes. It can also be used to ameliorate depression amd stress.

Vibrates to the number 3.

Brasilian Agate   [Astrological Sign of Aries]

Brasilian Agate is a translucent to transparent fortification agate exhibiting patterns of ovoids or circles in a variety of colours. Many Brasilian Agates have been dyed, but many are natural in colour.

This mineral can be used to activate success in dowsing and in divining. Fastened with twine or leather upon the end of a willow, it has led the user to lost items.

Brasilian Agate can be used to facilitate immense strength, to assist one in diversification in fields of endeavor, and to promote, during meditative states and astral projection, a wandering in unregimented directions [producing a variety of scenes, situations, and messages for consideration to the user]. It provides for a protective structure over the field of astral travel so that one can relax in the protective barrier.

It has been used to expedite the whirling state of the dervishes and is honoured by the shamen of South America as a pathway leading both to and from the other worlds.

The mineral can also bring relief to bruises, strains, and sprains. It can help to bring temporary relief to painful conditions. It has also been used in the treatment of various kinds of elimination problems, to strengthen the walls of the intestines, and to promote the production of the proper range of gastric fluids to enhance digestion. It has been used to balance the energies of the heart, to stabilize the heart and pulse rate, and to increase circulation. An elixir (of non-dyed Brasilian Agate) is also quite effective in treatment of these disorders.

Vibrates to the number 2.

Carnelian   [See Carnelian]

Damsonite   [See Damsonite]

Dendritic Agate   [Astrological Sign of Gemini]

Dendritic agate is a transparent to translucent form of agate containing dendrites [branching forms], often comprised of manganese minerals.

It enhances gentleness and encourages one to walk lightly through the gardens of life, taking time to enjoy each moment.

It helps one to remain as a directed energy during situations of discordant and/or dis-orienting confusion. It further assists one in maintaining the centering of the self in all situations.

The message which dendritic agate conveys is that in ones awakening, one must only recognize and accept the inception of ones origin.

It is used to assist one in connecting to the natural states of the universe and to enhance communication between ones intellectual world and the plant kingdom.

It is a stone to help in healing the Earth, stabilizing the center and energy vortices, and stimulating a peacefulness within the structure of the inner environment.

It both opens and activates the chakras, maintaining the opening to accept and integrate the energy of the higher consciousness.

It is a "stone of plenitude", providing abundance and fullness in ones life. It was used in ancient Greece to produce plentiful crops, and is conducive to generous yields in both business and agricultural pursuits.

It can also be used to treat disorders of the skeletal system and to provide alignment of the bone structure supporting ones physical reality.

It can be used in the treatment of disorders of the nervous system and to ameliorate degraded conditions of the small capillaries which are located in the structure of the blood veins. It can also be used to relieve pain.

When the inner structure of the dendritic agate includes the manganese minerals, the properties from the MANGANESE section of this book also apply.

Vibrates to the number 3.

Dry-Head Agate   [Astrological Sign of Capricorn]

Dry-head agate is a fortification agate which displays shades of brown, white, and orange.

The energy of dry-head agate is conducive to deep meditative states. It furthers the understanding of the idea of universal "brotherhood", and helps one to maintain peace within the inner being.

It affords one patience and encourages the acceptance of responsibility - the responsibility being for ones actions and for ones personally created reality.

It allows one to understand that the universal will recognizes only complete peace and joy; it also promotes the realization that refusal to acknowledge this aspect is that which brings converse and/or unpleasant experiences.

It has further been used to facilitate the state of meditation, producing a calming and soothing effect upon the mind and facilitating a release of tension from the physical body.

It is used in the treatment of colds and allergies, and for further strengthening of the immune system. It can also be used to stabilize psychological disorders. When used as an elixir and applied topically, it can both soothe and smooth the hair and skin.

Vibrates to the number 9.

Ellensburg Blue Agate   [Astrological Sign of Leo]

Ellensburg blue agate is a blue agate found in the vicinity of Ellensburg, Washington, USA.

It can be used to enhance ones stature, to eliminate suppression, and to bring happiness through understanding. It provides the energy to allow one to fully appreciate ones abilities, characteristics, and situations.

It is useful for opening and activating the throat chakra. It provides assistance in communication and in speech.

Ellensburg blue agate has been used in the treatment of disorders of the throat and to improve the eyes.

Vibrates to the number 9.

Fire Agate   [Astrological Sign of Aries]

Fire agate occurs due to the inclusion of very thin layers of iridescent limonite.

It represents the spiritual flame of absolute perfection. It is said to dispel fear from the very depths of the inner being and to provide a protective shield which reflects all threat of harm back to the source such that the source may personally understand the act.

It also helps to dispel undesirable desires, "undesirable" being defined as those which would not further one in the pursuit and acceptance of the enlightened state, and those which produce an inner understanding of aversion.

It is also a stone to encourage one to be the "best" possible. Its energy provides an impetus to actions and stimulates both progression and advancement.

It further provides the energy for initiating introspection and inspiration.

It has been used on the triple-burner acupressure/acupuncture meridians to dissolve blockages and to assist in the treatment of circulatory disorders and disorders of the central nervous system. It can also be used in the treatment of disorders of the eyes, to bring clarity to the sight, and to enhance night-vision.

Vibrates to the number 9.

Flame Agate   [Astrological Sign of Sagittarius]

Flame agate is known as Mexican Flame Agate, Graveyard Plume Agate and Carey Plume Agate.

When the agate is sliced, there is an appearance of flames which seem to spring from the base of the slice.

The Mexican Flame Agate and Carey Plume flames are usually comprised of a red jasper intrusion. The Graveyard Plume flames are white.

This mineral is a "prodder", providing stimulus for one to seek the light and the hope of the eternal. It renews the passion and enhances physical vitality.

It also stimulates attentiveness and diligence.

The flame agates containing the red jasper also exhibit the properties listed in the JASPER section of this book.

The Graveyard Plume, in addition, stimulates the crown chakra and both strengthens and initiates the movement of the Kundalini. It further helps, during states of transition, to enhance understanding.

Flame agate can be used in the treatment of burns, to eliminate the pain and to initiate the healing and renewal processes. It has also been used successfully in the treatment of disorders of the eyes.

Flame Agate, in general, vibrates to the number 8.

Mexican Flame Agate vibrates to the number 5, Carey Plume Agate vibrates to the number 9, and Graveyard Plume Agate vibrates to the number 4.

Holly Blue Agate   [Astrological Sign of Virgo]

Holly blue agate is an agate from the vicinity of Holly, Oregon, USA. It is similar in appearance to the Ellensburg blue agate, except that the blue colouring includes a tinge of violet. The combination of these colours produces a lovely violet-blue agate.

It is a "stone of spirituality and psychic actualization" and can be used to facilitate communication in this world, and between this world and the spiritual world. It works to eliminate mental and emotional conditions which produce distortion in judgment.

It also helps to refine ones communication skills and provides encouragement to verbalize ones feelings.

It activates and stimulates both the throat and the crown chakras, allowing for verbalization of the inner states of meditation with concomitant understanding via intellectual response. It also enhances mental acuity and clarity.

Holly blue agate helps one to realize that all that one teaches, one learns; hence, to teach love, is to learn that love is within and that one is indeed the pure representation of the essence of love. It also expedites the eradication of heartaches.

It can be used in the therapy for debilitating conditions, to protect from typhoid fever, and to improve jaundiced conditions of the body. It has also been used in the treatment of disorders of the heart and throat, and to stabilize imbalances in the brain.

Vibrates to the number 2.

Iris Agate   [Astrological Sign of Sagittarius]

Iris agate is a translucent to transparent fortification agate with fine close bands, producing a pattern of diffraction from which is emitted an iridescence.

It helps to awaken the inner self and makes one receptive to truth. It promotes happiness, longevity, good health, and the friendship of others.

The rainbow effect, produced when this agate is sliced very thin, brings the serenity and peacefulness of "rainbows" into ones life. It has also been used to increase the abilities required for psychic "seeing", producing an activation of the intuition and the inner knowing which is attained with wisdom. In addition, it has been used for gazing during shamanistic rituals and during soul-journeying to the interior of the body and/or mind.

It can be used in the treatment of disorders of the eyes, skin, hair, and nails. It has also been used to eliminate dehydration.

Vibrates to the master number 44.

Laguna Agate   [Astrological Sign of Taurus]

Laguna agate is a type of banded agate which exhibits patterns of irregular circular-square design.

It can be used to increase flexibility in ones life and in ones body and mind. In addition, it assists in decreasing the shallowness of ones character.

It enhances precision and provides stimulus to intellectual pursuits. It is an excellent stone for mathematical endeavors.

Laguna agate has been used to help one return from the depths of depression to a state of openness and acceptance of that which "is". It further encourages one to continue in the dreams of life while remaining aware of the purposes of the worldly visit.

It assists in the assimilation of zinc, and Vitamins A and D. It can also be used in the treatment of disorders of the lower digestive tract and colon, and to enhance the elasticity of the intestinal walls.

Vibrates to the number 9.

Lake Superior Agate   [Astrological Signs of Scorpio & Leo]

Lake Superior Agate is a banded-agate which is found in the area around Lake Superior [of course]. It is rather uncommon at times [depending upon the movement of the tides within and around the lake].

This agate elevates ones personal worth, and facilitates contact with the higher-self. It furthers ones self-confidence in exploration of the mythical and mystical realms, bringing the unknown into conscious recognition, and enhancing the understanding of the rites and rituals involved to maintain access to these hidden worlds.

It also facilitates contact with information sources beyond the physical plane of this planet. It allows one to recognize that it is quite natural to communicate with the other planes of existence - the other planes are there, so.... why not?

It can be used to stimulate the medulla oblongata and to correct defective reasoning patterns.

Vibrates to the number 4.

Mexican Lace Agate   [Astrological Sign of Aries]

Mexican lace agate [sometimes called Mexican Crazy Lace Agate] displays the colours of red and white lace configurations or paisley patterns, sometimes exhibiting greys and yellows.

It can be used to help one to reach extremely high physical levels. It is also quite helpful during physical bio-rhythmic "lows", to bring the physical energies into a balanced and steady state. It also helps one to understand the plan of the "perfect human" - providing insight to the many paths which are available to take one to the heights of awareness. It allows one to laugh, heartily, and to comprehend the games of this world.

It has been used in the treatment of the heart and to provide vitality to the vital organs. It is excellent as an elixir to soothe, smooth, and treat disorders of the skin.

Vibrates to the number 7.

Montana Agate   [Astrological Sign of Scorpio]

Montana agate is a transparent to translucent agate which contains inclusions; some inclusions within the structures of Montana agate tend to resemble the configurations of ferns and dendrites, while others resemble a variety of patterns.

It can be used to stimulate the crown chakra, while providing grounding to the Earth plane.

It has also been used to clear and to energize all of the chakras and to cleanse and activate other minerals.

When Montana agate contains a mossy structure, the qualities listed in the MOSS AGATE section of this book also apply; when it contains dendrites, the qualities listed in the DENDRITIC AGATE section of this book also apply.

Vibrates to the number 4.

Moss Agate   [Astrological Sign of Virgo]

Moss agate is a transparent to translucent agate containing inclusions of minerals resembling moss or foliage. It is usually found in massive form and, occasionally, within the configuration of a thunderegg. The colour range includes red, green, yellow, brown, and brown-black.

Moss agate leads one toward the characteristics of agreeability, persuasiveness, strength in all endeavors, and efficacy in all pursuits. It helps to improve ego and self-esteem, providing for emotional balancing and strengthening of the positive personality traits. It allows one to see the beauty within all that ones eyes touch.

It can be used to provide for communication with and between the plant and mineral kingdoms; the information is often relative to methods for enhancing the stability of the planet. It has also been used in agricultural pursuits and has been successful in promoting the growth of new crops.

In early times, it was used by the Native American Indians as a power stone. It has successfully been used in the art of "cloud-busting" and in helping the weather patterns to reach ultimate equilibration.

It is said to help one in the acquisition of riches. It is also said to bring one the powers of speed.

It can be used in the treatment of dehydration and disorders of the eyes, to ameliorate fungal infections, to stimulate digestion and the elimination of toxins from the body, and to relieve the symptoms of colds, internal infections, and flu. When used as an elixir, it is quite effective in an elixir for the topical treatment of skin disorders and infections.

Vibrates to the number 1.

Ocean Spray Agate   [Astrological Sign of Aquarius]

Ocean Spray Agate is a lustrous agate with transparency to translucency. The colour ranges through the spectrum of greens.

This mineral can be used to enhance ones mental and emotional flexibility, to engender precise and decisive decision-making, and to quicken resolution and settlements of disputes and conflicts.

Ocean Spray Agate is a catalyst for bringing that which is desired and for assisting in the release of that which is no longer essential. It also helps one to determine that which is desired and to recognize and to release that which is not necessary and/or enjoyable.

It has been used to stimulate movement of body fluids, and to treat sinusitis, congestion, fluid retention, mucoid formation, and dehydration.

Vibrates to the number 7.

Orbicular Agate   [Astrological Sign of Libra]

Orbicular agate is a fortification agate which exhibits, usually upon cutting, a pattern of ring-like designs.

It can be used to attune oneself with the other planets of this solar system and to recognize the most amenable times to do so; the influence of the full moon will increase and provide stimulation to these endeavors.

It stimulates the quality of grace in physical movements and actions.

It provides a force to balance the energy fields of the chakras, and to stimulate an awareness and the fulfillment of well-being.

It can be used in the treatment of disorders of the reproductive system and to increase fertility [conscious attunement is required]. It can also be used to treat growths, and to stimulate regenerative properties.

Vibrates to the number 7.

Plasma Agate   [Astrological Sign of Taurus]

Plasma Agate is transparent to translucent in shades of green and red, with a veinular structure in beige to yellow to brown.

This mineral can assist on in the attainment of direction, both in the determination of the direction required for the improvement of the self and in the stability and resolution required to maintain progress on that chosen path.

Plasma Agate has been worn by runners to facilitate speed and stamina.

It can also be used in gridding the Earth to provide protection from disasters and turmoil. It has been used successfully in areas of violence to alleviate the disturbance.

This mineral has been used in the treatment of disorders of the blood, veins, circulation, and heart. It has been used in the opening of arterial passageways (as an elixir), in the amelioration of cuts and bruises, and in the therapeutic removal of skin growths.

Vibrates to the number 5.

Polka-Dot Agate   [Astrological Sign of Gemini]

Polka-Dot Agate is an agate which displays polka-dots. The colour of the agate and of the colour and the size of the polka-dots is variable.

This mineral has been used to assist one in releasing painful experiences, facilitating the integration of the experience into "life's records" such that one may look at those events as history of the past.

It has also been used to bring a happy state to ones environment, encouraging cheerfulness and a synthesis of energies.

Polka-Dot Agate has been used in the amelioration of measles, chicken-pox, skin eruptions, and eye disorders. It can also be used in the treatment of liver dis-ease and to provide a stable increase in energy for whole-body wellness.

Vibrates to the number 2.

<u>Plume Agate</u>   [Astrological Signs of All]

Throughout this section, there are several varieties of Plume Agate discussed. The general properties of all Plume Agate are as follows.

Plume Agate can facilitate the re-birthing process and can help one to deal with both the information and the events of the past which have instilled blockages within the meridians and energy centers of the body. It provides for a gentle release of those conditions which have been inhibiting ones growth.

It has been used to provide for a deep state of meditation, allowing the mind to be entirely uninhibited and clear. Prior to this utilization of the stone, one can consciously decide whether to use the meditative state as a vehicle of emptiness, or as a vehicle to further the psychic process and to provide visions with respect to pre-defined questions.

This mineral has been used in the treatment of flows; energy flows, blood flows, etc.; it can provide assistance in balancing the white blood cell count with the red blood cell count and can facilitate the normalization of that ratio. It can also be used in the treatment of dermatitis.

Vibrates to the number 2.

<u>Priday Plume Agate</u>   [Astrological Sign of Scorpio]

Priday plume agate occurs within the thundereggs which are found in the areas outlying Madras, Oregon, USA. The plume appears in a variety of colours and is configured similar to a beautiful flowering desert plant.

It can be used to open and activate the heart chakra and to assist one in recognizing the beauty in all of life.

It brings insight to allow one to remember that all things, events, encounters, circumstances, and situations lead to ones growth, and are truly helpful in ones development.

It inspires creativity and helps one to delve into the unknown. It brings peace to the birthing and re-birthing processes and promotes tranquility through all phases of transitions.

Priday plume agate provides one with a fresh outlook and encourages one to enjoy the moment. It stimulates and inspires the endeavors of life and helps one to relate in a loving manner.

It also inspires creativity, allowing one to see the flower within each person and the budding growth which is waiting to bloom into perfection. It promotes imagination with personal freedom, allowing one to accept changes with alacrity.

It can be used to eliminate negativity from ones environment, by simply being a part of that environment. Worn, carried, or used as an elixir, it removes the opposing forces of positive energy from ones energy field and provides a barrier against further entry of same.

It can be used in the treatment of disorders associated with the sense of smell, to encourage the even flow of blood and nerve impulses, and to lower the blood pressure. It has also been used in the treatment of the eyes and to initiate further mending capabilities of the skeletal structure.

When the interior of a thunдеregg contains Priday plume agate, the additional properties listed in the THUNDEREGG section of this book also apply.

Vibrates to the number 3.

Purple Sage Agate   [Astrological Signs of Virgo and Scorpio]
                                     [Also Known As Lurelite]

Purple Sage Agate is an agate which has been recently found in Arizona, USA, and which resembles, in colour and in formation, the Holly Blue Agate. It is similar in appearance to the Ellensburg blue agate, except that the blue colouring includes a tinge of violet. The combination of these colours produces a lovely violet-blue agate which occurs in seams, masses, and druses.

This mineral has been found to activate the occurrence of change by assisting one to love oneself. It helps one to question that which is of value and to release confrontation with the values of others. Heightening ones sensitivity, it acts to reduce vulnerability and brings profound insight. The natural attention-gathering ability increases and delivers an energy to bring the "new" into ones realm of activity and being.

It can assist in the activation of the throat chakra and the crown chakra such that one may speak that which will be beneficial for advancement toward enlightenment.

Purple Sage Agate is a "stone of completion", assisting one to complete that which has been initiated, to achieve that which one desires, and to perfect that which one attains. It further brings the energy to allow one to relax in the ease with which things, events, and people come to ones life, providing an opening to opportunity for the release of manipulation.

It further stimulate empathy - not sympathy - such that one may truly understand the conditions and situations of others. Also helping one to follow ones own inner convictions, it produces a strength for one to be "true" to the self.

This mineral has been used in the treatment of emphysema, the reproductive system, and depression. It has also been successful in use in the therapy for debilitating conditions, and in the treatment of disorders of the throat and the brain.

Vibrates to the numbers 1 and 3.

Regency Rose Agate   [Astrological Sign of Virgo]

Regency Rose Agate is a translucent to transparent silicated agate occurring in a lovely rose colour.

This mineral can be used to bring to one the state of dignity in all matters, lessening any and all embarrassment about any and all things. It allows one to recognize that we can laugh about ourselves, be comfortable with ourselves, and love ourselves.

In the days of the "Old West", the miners who carried a piece of "Regency Rose" believed it would bring them happiness, luck, and wealth.

Regency Rose Agate has been used in the treatment of depression, despondency, and despair. It assists one in recognizing that hopelessness need not exist and that resignation to less than perfection is inappropriate.

It has also been used in the treatment of hair loss (as an elixir), PMS, chronic fatigue syndrome, and heart dis-ease.

Vibrates to the number 6.

Rose-Eye Agate   [Astrological Sign of Gemini]

Rose-Eye Agate is a translucent to transparent white to yellow agate with a rose-colour in the center.

This mineral has been used to stimulate the balancing of the masculine and feminine energies, to bring lustre to ones life, and to assist in balancing the reactive state with the active state, furthering the calmness of action and diminishing the distress of reaction.

It has been used to stimulate the third-eye, to induce channeling and visioning, and to enhance clairvoyance.

The alleviation of tension, and the calming of the outer bodies and the physical body, which is produced by this mineral, also helps to align the energy structure of the user.

Rose-Eye Agate has been used in the treatment of cataracts, retina damage, healing after surgery, and dis-ease/discomfort of the tear ducts. It can also be used in the cleansing of the liver and the pancreas. It has been effective in the elimination of blood clots.

Vibrates to the number 9.

Snakeskin Agate   [Astrological Sign of Scorpio]

Snakeskin agate is similar to the skin of a snake in appearance.

It provides for strength during times of activity and promotes a pleasant personality via both inner peace and the recognition of the joy of living. It also brings cheerfulness to the inner emotional systems, facilitating the outward manifestation of the love of life and self.

It has been used to assist one in eliminating mundane worries, promoting self-esteem and self-awareness.

It can be used to help one to become lost in a crowd, and to fade into the background, when consciously directed. It is quite useful in detective work, and can also help one to find lost "things". In addition, it can bring the energy of reclamation and orientation to the user.

It has been used to initiate the rise of the Kundalini.

It is used in the treatment of hearing problems and stomach disorders. It has also been used successfully to diminish wrinkles and to soothe the skin.

Vibrates to the number 2.

Stinking Water Plume Agate   [Astrological Sign of Sagittarius]

Stinking Water Plume Agate is a lustrous blue to yellow agate with plumes.

It can bring the synthesis and melding of the intellect with the throat chakra such that one may speak astutely and wisely. It has facilitated poise, confidence, and composure during speech-making, oral examinations, dissertations, and when representing oneself for the benefit of the self.

It emits a calming, cooling energy which can work on all of the chakras to gently remove negativity and to reinstate the loving, gentle forces of self-love. It provides the message that there is no need for haste in any situation, bringing calmness and clarity to the emotions and restoring the mind to harmony after chaotic or crisis situations.

It can be used [as an elixir] to clear the skin and is said to reduce wrinkles and to provide the wearer/carrier with a soft complexion. It has also been used in the treatment of disorders of the intestines, the colon, and the prostate.

Vibrates to the number 1.

Turritella Agate   [Astrological Signs of Cancer & Aquarius]

Turritella agate can be recognized by the sea creature and fossil snail patterns within the stone.

It can be used to dispel pomposity within an individual, diminishing actions emanating due to a superiority complex.

It is a protective stone which also allows one to recognize that the idea of safety is actually the relinquishment of the idea of attack.

It also provides for an opening of the communication channels between the plant and mineral world, allowing one access to information which would be beneficial to the healing of the Earth. It is a stone to help one through transition and to apply to the amelioration of discordant thought forms during trials and tribulations. It gives one the insight to know that regardless of the outcome, one will be the winner. It further provides impetus toward surviving, and in some cases, winning with ease.

It can be used as a general medicinal and to ameliorate conditions of fatigue. It is soothing to the stomach, and can stimulate proper peristaltic action in the alimentary canal. It can also be beneficial in the assimilation of nutrients and in the absorption of zinc, calcium, magnesium, and Vitamin A. The turritella agate has been used to treat swellings and "normal" distentions of the abdomen [one must consume the proper foods to facilitate this remedial action].

Vibrates to the number 8.

<u>Woodward Ranch Plume Agate</u>   [Astrological Sign of Sagittarius]

Woodward ranch plume agate is found in Texas, USA, in the form of nodules. The plume within the nodule is, generally, red or black, and in the configuration of a bush.

It can be used to stimulate the base chakra and to concurrently provide for grounding. It enhances physical vitality, encourages creativity, and inspires maturity. It is a "bestower" of that which is considered "good".

It provides for progress through variety and stimulates peace through understanding. It activates the process of giving of oneself and can provide the strength to release the gift of oneself. It dispels rigidity in action and mind.

It can also be used in the treatment of disorders of the spine, reproductive system, and elimination processes.

Vibrates to the number 5.

AJOITE   [Astrological Sign of Virgo]

Ajoite, mainly in the form of phantoms within crystals, was discovered in Messina, Republic of South Africa. It is quite an unusual occurrence. These phantom crystals are powerful tools for the new age. Ajoite is, rarely, also found as a drusy crystalline structure and as an inclusion in calcite. Although ajoite is the name of the primary mineral contained within these crystals, other minerals which may also be present within include hematite, limonite, and papagoite.

Ajoite produces a melding between the heart chakra and the throat chakra and facilitates speaking that which is in ones heart. This quality provides for a peacefulness within ones emotional system and a joyful acceptance of ones surroundings, circumstances, and environment.

The energy of ajoite also brings peace within the self, regardless of ones actual physical or mental location; it stimulates understanding and total acceptance.

The Earth-keeper of the ajoite phantom crystal will find clarity of spirit through communication via the heart, bringing to fruition the perfection of love and facilitating communion with all of the integral parts of the Earth, Sky, and life.

It can also be used to eliminate hostility - it is quite difficult for one to remain hostile toward oneself; in addition, and following the same logic, it can also be used to eliminate anger, abrasiveness, jealousy, prejudice, ..., and all of the negative attributes one could imagine. What an exciting thought!

It allows for recognition of the native state and provides a bonding and synthesis between ones energy and the pure and inviolate energy of "All That Is".

It enhances creativity and is an adjuvant to communication.

Ajoite is also said to energize and to activate the peace "chakra" (an energy field between the throat and heart chakras).

It symbolizes the awareness of the "All" and represents the purity of both the Earth and the infinite potential available for ones access.

It has been carried by those of similar spirituality to facilitate the "brotherhood" connection and to promote recognition between strangers and friends. It stimulates a bonding between souls who are on the Earth plane and have agreed to meet again during this lifetime; it also stimulates the connection between the kindred spirits of both the spirit world and the other worlds, providing for transfer of information.

It has been used successfully to remove extra-terrestrial, Lemurian, Atlantean, and current implants. This has been facilitated by the property of the ajoite energy which acts to extract dysfunctional energy from within a body [or substance], and concurrently fills the empty space with pure loving energy.

Ajoite can be used for preservation and rejuvenation on all levels and can facilitate the polarization of the bodies and the alignment with the optimum self to stimulate total well-being.

It also provides the proper reception frequency for the cellular structure of the body, allowing for transmission of the message of perfection from the ethereal body. It is both a master healer and a medium for access to the higher worlds.

The ajoite phantom crystal is one of the most beautiful, loving, and joyous crystals which has come from our Earth.

Vibrates to the number 6.

ALABASTER   [Astrological Sign of Sagittarius]

Alabaster is a fine-grain variety of gypsum, coloured white or somewhat delicately shaded.

This mineral can help to unlock the "secrets of the pyramids"; when used in meditation, it helps to take one to the days when the pyramids were being constructed.

It can also be used to energize other minerals; this can be accomplished by placement of the other mineral[s] on the alabaster.

Carved alabaster, in geometrical forms can be useful as stimulus for meditation, to promote the centering of the self, and to further ones mental acuity.

Alabaster can show one how to be forgiving; it provides succinct messages to the user with respect to living on this plane.

It also enhances the skills employed for providing service to "man", providing for maturity and bestowing composure during times of stress. It alleviates the tension associated with seeking, allowing for the recognition that one will ultimately acquire the heavenly state.

It is also helpful in the treatment of disorders of the heart. It assists in diminishing the internal anger which is directly proportional to the severity of a dis-ease.

Vibrates to the number 7.

ALBITE [Astrological Sign of Aquarius]

Albite is a form of feldspar which crystallizes in the pattern of masses, tabular crystals, and plate-like crystals. The colour range includes blue, brown, red, white, and colourless.

In addition to the properties listed in the FELDSPAR section of this book, this mineral encourages one to flow with relationships, situations, and the activities of interactions. It enhances the qualities of tact and cooperation.

It eliminates fear of the unknown and supports personal freedom through change. It encourages one to action, providing insight to certainty of purpose while sustaining ones confidence and resolution.

It also stimulates clarity in thought and enhances the stabilization of the frequency of brain wave transmissions. It can provide for a connection to the psychic self, awakening the energy of the third-eye and expediting the verbalization of the experience.

It has been used to clarify and to treat disorders of the eyes, restrictions of the blood flow, and ambulatory disorders. It is a purifier for the disturbed portions of the physical body.

Vibrates to the master number 22.

ALTAITE [Astrological Sign of Pisces]

Altaite is a lead telluride ranging in colour from tin-white to yellow to bronze. It occurs in masses and, rarely, forms in octahedral or cubic crystals.

This mineral is a "stone of harmony", stimulating interaction on all levels, and assisting in the decrease of self-limiting ideas. This mineral provides for access to ones spiritual guides when questions related to course of action are pending.

It acts to incite the intellect and to ground and to provide expansiveness concurrently. It assists in the elimination of sedentary aspects and encourages being "on the move", adding strength to the physical and mental bodies.

It can be used to locate energy blockages within the body; placing the Altaite upon the different areas of the body, one can usually feel a slight resonance at the location of the obstruction.

It is said to reduce inflammations and to heal skin eruptions on the body, and to be beneficial to the blood and olfactory system. It can be used to increase the assimilation of selenium and zinc, to stimulate circulation, and to treat disorders of the veins.

This lead base of this mineral precludes its use in the normal method of preparation of an elixir.

Vibrates to the number 5.

ALEXANDRITE   [Astrological Sign of Scorpio]

Alexandrite is a variety of chrysoberyl which is usually found with the pleochroic [exhibiting different colours in different directions when viewed via transmitted light] property. The mineral exhibits the colour green by sunlight and red-violet by artificial light. The attributes of chrysoberyl apply to alexandrite; the following properties are in addition to those listed in the CHRYSOBERYL section of this book.

Recently, rare alexandrite crystals, configured as twins and triplets, have been found in Africa. These crystals have been used to provide for the synthesis between the third-eye chakra, heart chakra, and base chakra, and have produced excellent results in astral travel via the spectrum of colour. Use of these crystals can help one to return to the origin of time and to connect with the beginning of ones development; this facilitates the understanding of, and the sensitivity to, that which remains to be learned and provides for insight into the effortless way to attain higher realization.

Alexandrite is a rare gemstone regarded as having regenerative power. It enhances the rebirth of both the inner and the outer self, providing impetus to expedite the changing of ones world while producing the qualities of expansiveness, creativity, and awareness in the realm of manifestation. The energy of the crystalline form is especially conducive to the art of manifestation.

This mineral can assist one in centering the self, reinforcing self-esteem, and augmenting ones ability to experience joy and to both acknowledge and appreciate the interconnected-ness of all of nature.

It can also be used to facilitate the alignment of the mental, emotional, and etheric bodies, creating a more balanced emotional state.

In the Orient, it is regarded as a magical gemstone bringing good fortune to its owner.

It has been used in the treatment of disorders of the spleen, testicles, and pancreas, and in the regeneration of neurological tissue on the cellular level. It has helped to improve dis-eases of the nervous system, to treat disorders which are associated with leukemia, and to enhance the assimilation of protein.

Vibrates to the number 5.

ALMANDINE   [Astrological Signs of Scorpio & Virgo]

Almandine, a variety of garnet, crystallizes forming dodecahedra or trapezohedra forms. Compact or granular masses are also found. The colour is deep red, violet-red, or brownish-black, displaying a resinous lustre. In addition to the qualities listed in the GARNET section of this book, the following attributes are noted.

This mineral inspires during times of contemplation, engendering peace, and balancing the time allotted for solitude.

It represents profound love, stimulates physical vitality, and provides for energizing and opening of the path between the base and crown chakras.

It allows one to both access and integrate truth, providing the affinity to the higher-self and the universal will; the resultant knowledge and subsequent "knowing", bringing forth the understanding that the end of ones world is not destruction, but, indeed, the inculcation of perfect order.

It initiates charitable actions, and provides for connection with the higher intellect. It is also useful to those exploring the fields of astronomy, astrology, and mathematics.

It has been used in the treatment of heart disorders, to stimulate the inner cellular structure of the eyes, and to treat the liver and pancreas. It can strengthen the proper functioning of the body to the depths of the cells, and can help to promote action toward regeneration.

Vibrates to the number 1.

ALURGITE   [Astrological Sign of Leo]

Alurgite is a type of mica, crystallizing in the form of compacted to loosely compacted plates. The colour is copperish-red.

This mineral provides one with the view of oneself from an superficial perspective and can produce perspicacity with respect to the methods available for painlessly correcting the attributes which are unwanted; this is occasionally in opposition to the way one consciously appraises the self. It helps one to make these corrections in an uncomplicated manner, and provides for periodic reminders of any uncorrected and unwanted personal qualities.

It also shows one how one may appear dull to others and encourages one to "shine".

It further awakens and illumines the senses and the intellect, bringing tranquility to ones expressiveness and dispelling both the use of impulsive words and the actions of impatience.

It has been used in the treatment of the elimination system, for cleansing the intestines, for relief of tension and stress related disorders, and to increase the assimilation of manganese and potassium.

This softness and fragility of this mineral precludes its use in the normal method of preparation of an elixir.

Vibrates to the number 3.

AMAZONITE   [Astrological Sign of Virgo]

Amazonite is a type of feldspar which crystallizes in the form of short prismatic crystals, tabular crystals, or masses. It usually occurs in the turquoise colour and is sometimes found with yellow, white, or grey portions.

In addition to the properties listed in the FELDSPAR section of this book, this mineral provides for pacification and eliminates aggravation. It soothes the emotional processes, providing for subjugation of worries and fears. It is soothing to the nerves and dispels both irritating and negative energy.

It soothes all chakras and is particularly rejuvenating to the heart center and throat chakra; it enhances communications concerning love.

It is said to have been one of the stones used in the breastplate of the high priest.

It aligns the physical body with the etheric and astral bodies producing a balancing and preventive energy; this attribute makes it a lovely stone to carry, wear, or use for general health maintenance. It is excellent when used as an elixir.

It can balance the male/female energies, bringing forth the qualities of clarity, clear spirit, and balancing of the many aspects of ones personality.

This mineral also helps one to simultaneously attune to both the spiritual dimension and the province of chaos in order to facilitate the complete traversing of all boundaries; this aspect of the energy of amazonite helps one to access the harmonious center within the kingdom of perfection and to integrate and synthesize the duality. It helps one to both manifest and retain the pure energy of universal love.

It can be used in the treatment of disorders of the nervous system and to dissipate energy blockages which could propagate the improper flow of neural impulses. It has been used to facilitate balancing of the metabolic processes related to calcium assimilation; an elixir of amazonite taken three times a day can be used to rectify a calcium deficiency. It is also useful for resisting tooth decay and osteoporosis, and for diminishing calcium deposits within the body. It is an excellent remedy for dispelling spasms of the muscle tissue.

Vibrates to the number 5.

AMBER   [Astrological Signs of Leo & Aquarius]

Amber is a fossilized resin and is usually golden to yellow-brown in colour. Some amber has been found to contain red, blue, or green hues.

Amber allows the body to heal itself by absorbing and transmuting negative energy into positive energy. It emits a sunny and bright soothing energy which helps to calm nerves and to enliven the disposition.

The different colours of amber may be used on the appropriate chakras to facilitate opening and cleansing.

It is a stone dedicated to the connection of the conscious self to universal perfection. It helps one in the art of manifestation to bring that which is desired to the state of reality. It stimulates the intellect and opens the crown chakra. It also transmutes the energy of physical vitality toward the activation of unconditional love.

Amber provides an energy to kindle the realization and subsequent response of choice, helping one to choose and to be chosen.

It has been used as a symbol for renewal of marriage vows and to assure promises. It has been said to bring good luck to warriors.

It is a sacred stone to both the Native American and Eastern Indians. It has also been used in the fire ceremonies of ancient tribal healers. It was burned, beginning in the medieval days, as a fumigant and as an incense to clear the environment of negativity.

It is said to have been one of the stones used in the breastplate of the high priest.

It aligns the ethereal energies to the physical, mental, and emotional bodies, providing for an even flow of perfect order to the requirements of the Earth plane while balancing the electro-magnetics of the physical body.

It cleanses the environment in which it rests and is an excellent mineral for use in purifying birthing and re-birthing rooms. It also acts to purify ones body, mind, and spirit when worn, carried, or used as an elixir.

It has been used in the treatment of goiter and other dis-eases of the throat. It has also been successful in the treatment of disorders of the kidneys and bladder. In ancient times it was used as a penicillin-type remedy, ground and ingested or soaked [as in an elixir] and subsequently drunk.

Vibrates to the number 3.

AMBLYGONITE   [Astrological Sign of Taurus]

The mineral amblygonite crystallizes as prismatic crystals or as masses demonstrating perfect cleavage. It has a vitreous luster and occurs, usually, in a very light pink, light lilac, or a very light yellow colour. Occasionally, the lightness of the mineral causes lack of definition of the colour, causing the appearance to be white or colourless.

Amblygonite can be used to calm and soothe. It can be used to grid classrooms, shopping malls, or other areas which may be conducive to energy equilibration and stabilization.

It is considered a "food" of the gods, imparting the sense of divinity and immortality.

The energy of amblygonite is helpful to those in the pursuit of music, poetry, and the arts.

It helps one to both recognize and identify the co-existence of opposite and conflicting feelings, providing insight into the resolution of duality. It can help to ease the unpleasantness and to enhance understanding when one is forced to end a relationship.

It can be used in the treatment of ambulatory disorders, to increase the clarity of the vision, and to relieve genetic defects.

Vibrates to the number 6.

AMETHYST
[Astrological Signs of Pisces, Virgo, Aquarius, & Capricorn]

Amethyst is a variety of quartz which occurs [throughout the world] either in crystalline or massive form. The associated colour ranges from deep purple to pale lavender. The presence of manganese in clear quartz produces amethyst, while additional amounts of iron content vary the purple colouration. The deepest amethyst colours occur in those crystals from Uruguay, Siberia, Africa, and Colorado. The most common occurrence is a medium purple colour which is found in Brazil. Double terminated crystals from Vera Cruz occur in the light amethyst colour - this type is said to provide an immediate Beta state; in addition, it provides for stimulation of the throat chakra, then providing a calming effect - stimulating the heart chakra, then providing a calming effect; stroking it brings energy emission; placement on the arm also provides for tranquility. Double terminated crystals from the locality of Brandenberg in The Republic of South Africa occur in a very deep amethyst colour [sometimes with phantoms]. The very pale lavender variety of amethyst has been found in Oregon; the configuration is quite noticeable due to the three large and three small sides. Amethyst elestials, sometimes combined with smokey quartz, have been found in Montana and Brasil; they exhibit the properties of the elestial [see the QUARTZ section of this book] and those of amethyst and/or smokey quartz. Plates of flowers consisting of amethyst and quartz have also been found in Brasil - this configuration includes some clear quartz and brings a lightness and loving-ness to ones environment.

Amethyst is a "stone of spirituality and contentment". It facilitates transmutation of lower energies into the higher frequencies of both the spiritual and ethereal levels. It is representative of the principles of complete metamorphosis.

It balances the energies of the intellectual, emotional, and physical bodies and provides a clear connection between the Earth plane and the other worlds. It clears the aura and stabilizes and transmutes any dysfunctional energy located within ones body. Amethyst also bestows stability, strength, invigoration, and peace; the peace being the perfect peace which was present prior to birth.

♪ 109 ♫

It is also a "stone of meditation", being excellent in conducting the energy of calm and peacefulness to help one to both enter and maintain the state. It opens and activates the crown chakra.

It is said to have been one of the stones used in the breastplate of the high priest.

Amethyst can be used to protect against psychic attacks; the energy of the attack being transmitted to the universe after its transformation into positive, loving energy.

It is "warm and cuddly" as well as a regal and ruling. It brings one the energies of serenity and composure while inciting fairness in decisions and enhancement in the ability to manage any and all responsibilities.

It enhances cooperation and co-efficiency between ones mental, physical, and emotional bodies, between the physical and spiritual worlds, and during activities of this world.

It provides the "sense" of common sense and encourages flexibility in decisions. It controls temperament by imparting a soothing, calming, and tranquilizing influence, while clearing-away unproductive and unkind vibrations. It is also said to help business affairs to prosper.

It assists in the assimilation of new ideas; by carrying, wearing, or using amethyst, one can remember and apply the myriad of ways which can be used to overcome any crystallized/stationary areas within ones physical form, intellectual activities, emotional attitudes, and state of consciousness.

By directing love to the structure of the amethyst, the energy is increased by orders of magnitude and returned to the region in which the amethyst is located.

Consciously holding the amethyst allows one to activate the energy to produce re-alignment of the energy bodies, while providing for stimulus to rectify dis-association between the aspects of cause and effect.

It further allows for the integration of cause and effect, providing insight into which portion of the actualized self requires remodeling in order to facilitate change toward the ultimate state of perfection.

It has, since historic times, been used to encourage and support sobriety. It is an excellent stone for one who is attempting to find freedom from addictive personalities [oneself, or another].

It is also useful in the situation of debating, affording advantage to the holder of the amethyst; the advantage being attained via spiritual insight coupled with intellectual reasoning.

Amethyst has been used in conjunction with chlorite to expedite the removal of unwanted energy implants from ones physical and auric bodies. The combination, when placed in the energy field of the physical body, provides a connection with universal mind which, in turn, confers the information with respect to the location of the implant.

It can be used in the treatment of hearing disorders, to both strengthen the skeletal system and reinforce ones posture, and to stimulate both the sympathetic nervous system and the endocrine glands to proper and precise performance. It is quite useful in the treatment of disorders of the nervous system, digestive tract, heart, stomach, skin, and teeth. It can help cellular disorders to re-adjust and re-align in order to eliminate distressful conditions.

It has been used in the treatment of insomnia and to ameliorate pain from headaches and other disorders; the pain being dissipated completely. It is also useful in stabilizing mental disorders. It has been used, with excellent results, as an elixir in the treatment of arthritis.

An elixir of amethyst can be used in all of the areas mentioned.

"Rutilated" amethyst is a rare form of amethyst which does not contain rutile, but contains goethite. This formation combines the qualities of the amethyst with the qualities of goethite [see GOETHITE section in this book]. It should be noted that goethite inclusions in amethyst are infrequent; but, however unique, the beauty of this configuration is tantamount, bringing the beauty to the field of the user.

In addition, amethyst is also found in combination with Cacoxenite, to provide a very powerful energy, and combining the qualities of both minerals.

Vibrates to the number 3.

CHEVRON AMETHYST   [Astrological Sign of All]

The Chevron Amethyst is of the variety exhibiting one of the deepest colours of the purple hue. There are two primary structures of the chevron - one structure exhibits a chevron of two or more colours [purple and rusty/rose-red/orange/yellow], with additional hues; and, one structure features a chevron containing several hues of purple. It is found in Siberia and in India. Since several of the arrays within this guidebook have recommended the utilization of the Chevron Amethyst, a brief description of the attributes are given below.

In addition to the properties of amethyst which have been previously discussed, this mineralogical formation possesses the energies which allow it to be represented as one of the finest third-eye stones, stimulating vision into unknown realms both within the self and into the exterior worlds.

It can also be used to facilitate both the perception and the interpretation of the aura, assisting in diagnostic techniques and in the furtherance of auric cleansing. It emanates a concentrated energy, allowing for direction such that a larger area than is usual [with terminated crystals] is impacted. The forceful, yet subtle, rays provide for clearing of the aura and for the release and dissipation of negativity. The enhancement of the aura has been shown by Kirlian photography. After the utilization of this stone to cleanse ones aura, one can, literally, become absorbed in the light of its radiance. It further stimulates the "brighter" aspect of the individual, as well as encouraging the emanating warmth and the purity of love within ones being.

Placement of the Chevron Amethyst on a chakra serves to release the tensions of that chakra and to further energize the areas which have heretofore been static.

It is an excellent stone for journeying and for inner-self evaluation and evolution. It brings one the strength and the loving essence to continue in any and all pursuits. It is an energy for psychic research, assisting one to transport and to retrieve [on both the tangible and intangible levels] patterns of force, movement, and space-time relationships. It also allows one to re-trace any negative energies which attempt to penetrate ones protective shield, providing information with respect to the reasons for, and the origin of, the negativity.

It stimulates the understanding of a positive answer to any imaginable problem, assisting one in the selection of the resolution, which would best be suited to ones purpose, and to the doctrine of universal love. It also assists in the implementation of same, bringing forth a perceptible manifestation. It has been called the "breath of life", assisting one to actualize that which is required for personal and universal development.

The Chevron Amethyst allows one to gain knowledge in the arts of spiritual healing; it furthers ones acceptance of the unseen forces which are available to complete the actions to facilitate the perfect state. Carried upon ones person, it can act to repel negativity.

It assists one in the application of the central unity of all religions, all men/women - all of existence. It helps one to understand the abstract forms of ones being and to develop the "resistance to resistance" via the total release of resistance.

With this larger forcefield, the Chevron Amethyst can affect a greater area and can stimulate the emergence of a synthesis between the various organs in the body. It assists the members of the body to act in a cooperative manner, bringing balance to the structure and autonomic and sympathetic nervous systems and the generative systems. It has been used successfully to eliminate headaches, pain, symptoms of viral and infectious dis-ease. It can be used in the treatment of disorders of the lungs, the intestines, the pancreas, and the liver. It further acts to stimulate the thymus and the immune system. It has also been used [via placement upon the closed eyes] to increase the proper functioning of the eyes.

Vibrates to the number 7.

AMETRINE   [Astrological Sign of Libra}

Ametrine is a mixing of citrine and amethyst. It occurs in both crystalline and massive form. In addition to the properties listed in the AMETHYST and CITRINE sections of this book, the following properties relate to the combined force of these two powerful crystalline structures.

It is a stone to enhance universal equilibrium and provides a clear connection between the physical form and the ultimate state of perfection. It provides for balancing of the male/female qualities and for an intellectual synthesis of spirituality.

It stimulates the intellect to reach beyond the worldly aspects toward the development of the consciousness.

In meditation and attunement, ametrine can help one to reach higher states more quickly; the expanded clearing effect bringing in the higher mental openings, leading to peace, tranquility, and cooperation.

It disperses negativity from the aura and fills the voids with energizing and stabilizing qualities of pure light energy.

It penetrates and facilitates the release of blockages in the physical, mental, emotional, and auric bodies, allowing for the release of the associated tension and for the initiation of proper functioning of that which was affected.

Negative emotional programming can be released via the energy of ametrine, facilitating the transformation of those feelings to both a beneficial and constructive level. In clearing emotional blockage, it provides one with insight regarding the necessity of cooperation and interaction.

It allows one access to the knowledge concerning the connected-ness of all, and helps one to recognize the need for and to be comfortable with the actions to eliminate prejudice.

It enhances all aspects of compatibility, allowing one to recognize that each "other" is both likened and bonded to oneself. It also combines the qualities of the intellect with spirituality, in such a way as to promulgate intellectual awareness, both on the physical and spiritual planes.

It is useful at the astral level to raise the consciousness and to allow one to attune to the gift of flight; it helps one to enter the state of astral travel, providing protection and awareness of the differences between the physical realm and the astral world.

Ametrine works quickly in all areas; the amethyst raising the clearing quality of citrine to a higher level of vibration while expanding the extent of the energy.

It can be used to stabilize and/or correct the RNA/DNA structuring within the body. It is useful for stimulating oxygenation of the body - providing the effect at the locations necessary without conscious knowledge of the locations by the user. It can also be used to help one to both consciously recognize and accept changes to the body [e.g., during periods of growth from childhood through physical maturation, and when one is provided with artificial organs, implants, etc.].

Vibrates to the number 4.

AMMONITE   [Astrological Sign of Aquarius]

Ammonite is a fossilized animal which was present on the Earth in eons past; it is similar in its structure to the snail. Pyritized ammonite is a rarer form and combines the properties of ammonite with the properties of pyrite.

The properties of ammonite include stimulus to architects and those in the fields of construction.

It provides for insight to the basis from which to start and allows one to retain the "whole picture" from conception to use.

Ammonite is a protective stone, giving stability and structure to ones life. It can eliminate the caustic attributes and can transform negativity into a smooth, flowing energy. It also tends to encourage and to supplement ones survival instincts. It is a stone to assist one in the promulgation of the requirements, and the actions necessary, for world survival.

It can alleviate the burdens of the birthing process and can provide for ease of relaxation, with a constant reminding of the patterns and rewards of circular breathing. It can also help to alleviate the depression sometimes associated with the re-birthing process.

It can be used in the treatment of disorders of the lungs and limbs. It can be quite helpful in the rectification of degenerative disorders.

Vibrates to the number 9.

ANALCIME   [Astrological Sign of Cancer]

Analcime crystallizes in the form of trapezohedral crystals, modified cubic crystals, and masses. The colour range includes white, grey, yellow, pink, green, white, and colourless.

This mineral helps one toward mental clarity and stimulates and clears the heart chakra.

It also allows one to maintain individuality and creativity, especially when subjected to the constraints of others.

It provides assistance to the mental, emotional, and physical states when one is entering into the realm of change and transformation.

It is a stone which enhances all aspects of teamwork and brings harmony to group activities.

It is interesting to note that analcime occasionally occurs within the rubies which are found in Thailand. The combination of analcime and ruby [the location from which the ruby emerged is unimportant] is quite important for physical vitality, communication skills, and strength in all endeavors.

It dispels weakness in all bodies and produces an energy conducive to stabilization rather than activation.

It can be used in the treatment of water retention, diabetes, and pancreatic secretory functions, and can provide strength to atrophied muscular structures.

Vibrates to the number 4.

ANATASE
[Astrological Sign of Scorpio]
[Also Known as Octahedrite]

Anatase crystallizes in the form of prismatic, bi-pyramidal, and tabular crystals. The colour range includes black, brown, blue, yellow, and green-yellow.

It can be used to teach that the alteration of oneself and ones circumstances can be attained painlessly. The mineral aids in amelioration of side-effects from changes and helps one to overcome resistance to change. It also contains the energy to help one in collecting, retaining, and assimilating information.

It is an excellent stone for teaching technical ideas, as well as for enlightening others in the aspects of peace and unity.

It helps one to look within, without, through, back, and forward - culminating in decisiveness in all aspects of ones life.

It also produces insightful-ness and stimulates insight during activities of "gazing".

Anatase can be used in the treatment of allergic reactions, sensitivity to medications, and disorders of the eyes. It can stimulate the assimilation of Vitamin A, calcium, magnesium, and iodine. It has also been used to stabilize and to balance the metabolic processes.

Vibrates to the numbers 7 and 1.

ANDALUSITE
[Astrological Sign of Virgo]

Andalusite crystallizes forming prismatic crystals or is formed in massive and columnar configurations.

The mineral usually occurs in the colours of white, red, violet, grey, pink, red/brown, or green; in some forms it is pleochroic [i.e., exhibiting different colours in three different directions when viewed via transmitted light]. When exhibiting pleochroism, the colour range includes yellow and green.

Andalusite can be used to promote viewing the different facets of ones character and ones emotional, physical, and intellectual being while allowing one to remain grounded and unbiased about the results.

It encourages one to look at issues rationally by helping one to see the various sides to a problem or situation. It also helps one to realize that self-sacrifice is "okay", but never required. It provides a message that in order to gain access and awareness in the kingdom of spirituality, one must only focus full attention upon the intent.

It is a stimulant to memory and recollection, promoting expertise in allegorical interpretation and providing for clarification of material from ancient texts. It awakens the inner knowledge allowing one to connect to the ancestral awareness and to access knowledge from the spiritual plane via channeling. It assists in facilitating clarity in the messages received and in enhancing the understanding and appreciation of same.

It promotes the chivalrous aspects of ones character and encourages moderation in all things [including moderation].

It further helps one to recover when "thrown" out of balance by circumstances or individuals, facilitating advance in re-alignment to the centering and to the balancing of the self.

It can be used in the treatment of disorders related to deficient oxygenation and orderly chromosome development. It has also been used in the treatment of cellular disorders of the hands and eyes.

Vibrates to the number 7.

ANDESINE   [Astrological Sign of Leo]

Andesine is a type of Oligoclase/Feldspar and crystallizes in granular and volcanic rocks of medium silica content. The colour ranges from white to yellow.

This mineral is an excellent choice for use in activities related to thought transference; one may transfer information, ideas, and loving emotional messages to another and receive, in return, the touching interpersonal experiences of the energy of the universe.

This mineral produces an energy which is predisposed to discourage chaotic, disruptive, and disorganized growth. It emits an energy which can be used to stabilize and to produce order within the mental, physical, emotional, and spiritual systems. It can be used to bring order to chaos.

It helps to impart impartial and objective, detached reasoning in situations where it would be beneficial to both view and act upon information objectively.

Andesine has been used in the treatment of high cholesterol and can act as a carrier for the energies of other minerals. It also provides for the transmission of energy to the location of disorder and serves to bring the relinquishment of the dis-ease.

Vibrates to the number 8.

ANDRADITE   [Astrological Sign of Aries]

Andradite, a variety of garnet, crystallizes in the form of grains, masses, plate-like layers, and crystals configured as dodecahedron, trapezohedron, and combinations of the dodecahedral/trapezohedral structures. The colour range includes wine, green-yellow, orange-yellow, lime green to emerald green, brown-red, grey-green, dark green, brown, grey-black, and black.

There is also a "new" rainbow Andradite which displays the complete colour range, or a portion of same. The following properties are in addition to those listed in the GARNET section of this book.

This mineral works mainly to stabilize and enhance the male qualities; hence, providing strength, stamina, courage, etc.

One type of andradite is known as demantoid garnet. Demantoid is a green colour; within this garnet is a twist of green fire, a "coal" fire which generates energy at an atomically high-powered rate of oscillation.

It is an excellent conductor and can be used to assist in the alignment of the magnetic fields of the body.

Andradite also enhances the attractive aspects in relationships, attracting to one not that which is necessarily wanted, but bringing into ones life that which is essential for ones development.

The rainbow Andradite also assists in clearing the aura, to expand the vision etherically, and to further encounters with others such that sharing and giving are accentuated. It further dispels isolation and dis-connectedness and abates unwarranted fears. It also has been used to activate mysticism, bringing total experiences of the body, mind, and spirit and allows one to dissolve with the known and the unknown.

It can be used to facilitate calcium, magnesium, and iron assimilation within the body and to treat associated disorders of the body.

Vibrates to the number 4.

ANGELITE   [Astrological Sign of Aquarius]

Angelite crystallizes in the form of blue and white masses, nodules, and crystals; it occasionally, contains a splash of red hematite. It was discovered in Peru, South America, during the time of the harmonic convergence and is a symbol of the verbalization and communication of love and light to the world.

It is an excellent balancing agent, polarizing and aligning the physical body with the ethereal network.

It provides a protective field around the environment in which it is placed; use of an elixir tends to install a shield of protection around the physical body, while an elixir applied to areas of agriculture has been used to suppress infestations of insects.

Angelite is both a sender and receiver; telepathic communication is enhanced, contact with other worldly beings is initiated, and communication with ones spirit totem is either introduced or the intensification of information is facilitated.

It helps one in spiritual journeys and in astral travel, allowing for the experience of flight to be second-nature.

It is an excellent stone for promotion of both astrological and mathematical understanding and comprehension.

It represents peace to the world and the "brotherhood" both within and without of the galactic configurations.

It is a "stone for raising the state of conscious awareness" and for promoting clear and orderly communication.

It dispels anger, renews ones connected-ness with universal knowledge, and initiates a parting-of-the-impediments during innovative pursuits.

It can be used to induce the re-birthing process, to provide impetus and guidance in psychic healing, and to open the pathway for channeling.

In the energy transfer to facilitate psychic healing, angelite provides for the linking of the network between the psychic and the infrastructure of the ethereal energy field.

It has been used in the treatment of infectious dis-eases, to correct deficiencies of the hemoglobin, and to renew and repair that which has degraded. It can also be used in the treatment of inflammations and afflictions of the throat, to correct any "atrophication" of the thymus, and to alleviate symptoms relative to proper functioning of the heart. It can help to renew the blood vessels and to provide rectification with respect to loss of sensory perceptiveness.

Vibrates to the number 1.

ANGLESITE   [Astrological Sign of Pisces]

Anglesite crystallizes as tabular crystals or as masses. The colour range includes white, colourless, pale green, yellow, and blue.

Anglesite has been reported to facilitate contact with entities "on the other side" and has been used extensively in channeling. It allows one to stay grounded during communication with entities in those worlds other than the Earth plane.

The mineral is quite loving and allows for open communication with others with respect to spiritual issues; it helps to bring forth dreams into this reality.

It can be used in the treatment of nervous disorders, to stimulate neural transmitters, and to promote the circulation of blood.

Vibrates to the number 2.

ANHYDRITE   [Astrological Signs of Cancer, Pisces, & Scorpio]

Anhydrite crystallizes as tabular crystals or as granular masses. It occurs as a colourless mineral or in the colours ranging from blue to grey.

This mineral facilitates strength on the physical plane and allows one to understand that the physical body is, in fact, transient. It acts to guide one toward acceptance of that which may come tomorrow. It has been used to help one to develop stamina and to provide for loving communication with those of a different mind. It enhances understanding via supporting the authorization for clearing the distractions from the mind.

It also provides the energy for "glad acceptance" of all of the changes and situations which one has the opportunity to experience; allowing one to recognize that the past is gone, except for the memories of beauty, and that nothing remains except the grace through which one can accept the benefit of each episode.

It has been used in the treatment of disorders of the throat and to ameliorate water retention and swelling.

Vibrates to the number 5.

ANNABERGITE   [Astrological Sign of Capricorn]

Annabergite crystallizes in capillary crystals and masses. The colour is a fine apple-green.

This mineral instills the knowledge that there is perfect harmony within the self, where nothing is unbelievable, unimaginable, or impossible; the inner self, which one may access at will, is where the perfection and the excellence of "All That Is" resides.

It facilitates intuition, imagination, and visualization, and helps one to both understand and to use the qualities and the attribures of the mystic; it can bring one into communication with the past spiritual masters of this world and can expedite transfer of knowledge.

Annabergite can also assist in the alignment of the subtle bodies and in strengthening and arranging the meridians of the physical body.

It increases the bio-magnetic forces in the body, aligns the body with the magnetic fields of the Earth, and has been used extensively in magnetic healing and to provide receptivity to radionic treatment.

Annabergite can be used in the treatment of cancer, cellular disorders, and dehydration. It is said to be the stone to "eliminate all infections".

Vibrates to the number 6.

ANTHROPHYLLITE   [Astrological Sign of Capricorn]

Anthrophyllite crystallizes in massive, fibrous, lamellar [e.g., layers of thin plates], and crystalline form. The mineral occurs in the colours of green and brown.

It has been used to teach one that the bonds, restrictions, and constraints placed upon a person are self-imposed and easily discarded. It helps one to decide, with the heart, that which is really important, and to plan for, and to initiate, the release of any binding ideas.

It has been used in the treatment of disorders of the lower digestive tract, the colon, and the duodenum, and to facilitate assimilation of nutrients throughout the body.

Vibrates to the number 3.

ANTIGORITE   [Astrological Sign of Capricorn]

Antigorite is a lamellar variety of Serpentine ranging in colour from green to black, white to grey, and yellow-brown to red-brown.

In addition to the properties of Serpentine, this mineral can be used to activate alignment of the chakras, to increase mental fortitude, and to stimulate the structure of ones life.

It has also been used to release negativity from the emotional body, to assist in retrieval of information from the memory, and to activate intuition. Ranging through the chakras, it can assist in activation of same and in the removal of the etheric cords of attachment from the self to another and from another to the self.

It also facilitates knowledge with ease and advances ones awareness such that approach to each event/condition/experience is with absolute precision and beneficial construction.

Antigorite is a mineral for bringing changes and for activating separations which are beneficial - allowing for the release of separation with ease and with a loving attitude. It acts to bring the energy of love to all actions.

This mineral has been used in the treatment of spinal aligmnent, to provide interference and corrective action to cellular disorder, and to assist in the release of toxins from the body.

♪ 122 ♫

This softness and lamellar structure of this mineral precludes its use in the normal method of preparation of an elixir.

Vibrates to the master number 55.

ANTIMONY   [Astrological Sign of Aquarius]

Antimony is light gray with a metallic luster and occurs in both massive and granular forms.

It is said to have been one of the stones used in the breastplate of the high priest.

It stimulates advancement in all areas of pursuit and gives one the tenacity to pursue all situations of interest. It has been said that this mineral encourages one to progress with the speed required to allow others to "just watch the dust". It dispels opposition, as long as ones pursuit is not detrimental to another, and encourages and stimulates access to an instinctive knowledge of the most efficient plan of action.

Antimony has been used successfully to reduce fever and to generally cool the physical body. It has also been used to reduce swelling and to ameliorate water retention.

Holding the mineral in the hand of preference and/or placing it on the affected part of the body, while continuing and persisting in a calm, meditative state has produced these results.

It has also been used as an anti-toxin, helping with the elimination of same. It can also check inflammation and tends to work as a shield against the "normal" dis-eases [e.g., colds, flu, measles, etc.]. It has been used for disorders of the throat and the thymus.

Vibrates to the number 3.

ANTLERITE   [Astrological Sign of Gemini]

Antlerite crystallizes as tabular crystals or as fibrous aggregates. The colour is emerald green to dark green.

It can be used to open the heart chakra and to provide a working connection between the heart [emotions/love] and the mind. This connection helps to promote an unbiased evaluation of ones feelings and to provide for a loving evaluation of ones thoughts. Antlerite can also be used to stimulate the thought processes, to enhance mental clarity, and to produce a melding of the heart and the mind.

It can be used in the treatment of mental disorders and epilepsy. It provides stimulus to the heart to transmit love to the brain, hence, ameliorating dysfunctional behavior.

Vibrates to the number 5.

ANYOLITE   [Astrological Sign of Aries]

Anyolite crystallizes in the form of masses composed of ruby crystals embedded in green zoisite. This mineral possesses the properties listed in the ZOISITE and RUBY sections of this book in addition to the qualities listed below.

Anyolite increases the awareness of ones individuality while allowing one to maintain connected-ness with humanity. It enhances contact with the etheric bodies and stimulates the crown chakra toward spirituality.

It can create altered states of consciousness and can serve as a vehicle for both reaching and utilizing the talents and abilities of the mind. All of the psychic abilities can be stimulated and amplified via the use of these consolidated energies.

In addition, it provides for amplification of the entire energy field of the body. It has also been used by healers in the Asian countries for both diagnostic healing and communicating with the spirits.

It acts to improve disorders of the heart and to help one to recover from those disorders associated with diminished physical vitality.

Vibrates to the number 2.

APACHE TEAR   [See Obsidian]

APACHE GOLD   [Astrological Sign of Leo]

Apache Gold is a combination of Steatite and Pyrite, occurring in the colours of gold and black.

In addition to the merging of the properties of Steatite and Pyrite, this mineral can be used to produce a state of mind which is free from impressions. It allows one to see the duality of ones nature, rectifying the negative and building the positive.

It can produce deep silence interspersed with visions of the luminous terrain emitted from the crown chakra.

It is an excellent stone for grounding during meditation, bringing clarity to the "no-mind" meditation while providing for a protective environment.

Apache Gold also provides one with awareness, on the emotional and physical levels, of those who do and/or do not have ones well-being in their heart. It provides for an electrical stimulus, facilitated through the subtle bodies, which produces a dielectric charge due to the alignment and/or the affiliation of the "other" with opposing electrical energy.

It is quite interesting to use this stone as a check against ones intuition and to check ones awareness level with respect to the stimulation which is actually received. It further encourages one to act on the impulses which are instinctual.

It can assist in the alignment of the subtle bodies and in strengthening and arranging the meridians of the physical body. It increases the bio-magnetic forces in the body, aligns the body with the magnetic fields of the Earth, and has been used extensively in magnetic healing and to provide receptivity to radionic treatment. Wearing or carrying the stone is recommended to facilitate remedial actions and to stabilize alignment.

The Mexican Indians have used Apache Gold in ceremonial magic and during shamanic journeying.

It can be used to increase the ability to assimilate vitamins and minerals. It can also assist in the treatment of disorders of the teeth and to enhance the integrity of the bones and alimentary canal. It has been used in the treatment of hearing disorders which are related to the integrity of the organ itself.

Vibrates to the number 9.

APATITE   [Astrological Sign of Gemini]

Apatite crystallizes as prismatic crystals or as compact masses. The mineral occurs in the range of colour which includes yellow, white, olive green, deep blue, purple, brown, red/brown, or colourless; the usual occurrence, however, produces yellow to yellow/green crystals.

This mineral can be used to stimulate the intellect and to promote realization that ones strength occurs through both spiritual avenues and via love; hence, dissolving aloofness and negativity.

Use of apatite while working with other crystals will facilitate results with greater ease since the apatite enhances the "coming-to-results".

Apatite is related to service and to the development of the humanitarian pursuits - it is attuned to healing, storing information, communicating, balancing energy, and teaching. It enables one to both recognize and experience information which can be used individually and collectively. One can use apatite as an interface point, between the consciousness and matter, in order to practically apply ones insight and powers of manifestation. It is extremely useful in the expansion of knowledge and in the disclosure of the "truth to freedom".

It can help to integrate, co-ordinate, and balance the emotional, intellectual, physical, and etheric bodies. It can also help to eliminate over-activity, under-activity, blockage, or congestion from any of the chakras.

It can be used to stimulate the development of clairvoyance, clairaudience, clairsentience, and the awareness of the devic worlds. It can further the connection with UFOs and can provide access to past-life insights and telepathy.

When applied with spiritual discipline, apatite can be used to assist one in the development of deeper states of meditation and reflection, yin-yang balancing, raising of Kundalini energy, self-insight, inner clarity, peace, and oneness with the higher-self.

Apatite enhances creativity. It is a stone of the future and will bring knowledge to those attuned to it by clearing mental confusion. It truly awakens the finer, inner self.

Wearing/carrying apatite has successfully produced hunger suppression; an elixir made of the mineral has also produced the same results. It can be used at the physical level to focus healing energy on the systems, glands, meridians, and organs of the body.

Vibrates to the number 9.

APHRIZITE   [See Black Tourmaline]

APOPHYLLITE   [Astrological Signs of Libra & Gemini]

Apophyllite crystallizes as pseudo-cubic crystals, granular masses, natural pyramidal structures, and as druse upon another mineral. The select grades of apophyllite have been found to occur in Pune, India, primarily, in green, white, and clear/colourless forms.

Apophyllite has been used to create a conscious connection between the physical form and the spiritual realm. It facilitates attunement to ones body as well as to the higher dimensional life forms.

It allows one to both recognize and act upon the truth in all situations. It enhances mindful analysis, tinged with universal love, and helps one to realize that the state of perfection is the natural state of being.

It has been used to facilitate astral travel and to provide a clear and definite connection to the physical body during the travel. It allows one to send information, which has been gleaned during the travel, back to the conscious self - this is one of the stones which helps one to remain totally conscious while experiencing the activities of astral travel [e.g., access to akashic records, exchange of communication with those of the spirit world, and past-life experiences].

The mineral also produces a reflective aspect to allow for the recognition of ones behavior/attitudes and to encourage one to seek, to recognize, and to correct deficiencies, while providing for an energy gain during these times. It allows one to see into the future - this is facilitated when one looks sideways into the crystal; it is similar in action to the art of "gazing".

The natural apophyllite pyramids [usually, white/greyish white, clear, and rarely, green] have been used successfully for enhanced energy stimulation and as an elixir to bring "light" and energy to ones being and love to ones heart. They can also be used to charge objects and to preserve.

They can be used to enhance and stimulate ones intuitive vision; the augmentation of these capabilities has been produced by application of the base of the pyramid to the third-eye. The natural pyramids have been used to induce access to the spiritual world in order to facilitate the channeling state. One can look through the bottom of the pyramidal structure and traverse time and space, arriving at the "star gate".

Green apophyllite has also been used to activate the heart chakra and to provide energy and forthright-ness in decisions of the heart. It allows one to absorb the energies one needs from the universal supply of perfect energy. It stimulates a joyful glee.

It has also been used in fire-walking, to help one to hold the meditative state and, after the "walk", it has been used to provide a cool clear energy surrounding the feet; in this case, there has been no burning sensation and no physical burn to the feet. This green crystal has been used to facilitated removal of unwanted historical and present day energy/control implants.

Apophyllite can be used to maintain the energy necessary to assist in the actions required for preservation and rejuvenation. It can further clear and refresh the eyes via the utilization of two apophyllite pyramids, placed with the base section of each upon each eyelid.

Vibrates to the number 4.

AQUAMARINE   [Astrological Signs of Gemini, Pisces, & Aries]

Aquamarine is a variety of beryl which crystallizes prismatically, sometimes vertically striated and, occasionally, terminated with small pyramidal faces. The colour ranges from light blue to green.

It is a "stone of courage". It enhances ones ability for rapid intellectual response and helps one to remain impeccable through assimilation of knowledge concerning ones beginning and the reality which one has actualized. It accelerates the intellectual reasoning processes and makes one unconquerable through learning -not only about the physical world, but about oneself. It provides a shielding property for the aura and the subtle bodies.

It encourages the innate ability to "always be prepared". One way of protecting oneself, temporarily, from pollutants is to imagine the essence of aquamarine in the air on all sides - the difference in the air quality is usually recognizable. It has also been used to guard against injury during battle.

There is a flowing quality to the energy of aquamarine; at the same time, the energy is also structured so that balance and order are maintained. It provides for alignment of the chakras and balancing of the network of structures connecting the physical and ethereal bodies.

It helps one to attune to more spiritual levels of awareness; for those who are involved in spiritual development, it provides emotional and intellectual stability and enhances the connection with the higher-self. It enables one to travel deep within the self and to understand the complexities, to simplify the resultant information, and to concurrently remain centered.

It emits a gentle and compassionate energy, exhibiting moderation; it helps judgmental people to be more tolerant, and can help one who is "swamped" by responsibility to bring order to the process. It also helps one to take responsibility for ones actions and encountered situations.

Aquamarine stimulates, activates, and cleanses the throat chakra, facilitating communication of a higher quality than the mundane.

This crystalline structure provides stimulus to the ideal of service to the world, and to the development of a humanity which is both attuned to healing and to furthering the subsequent eradication of dis-ease.

It provides for access to stored information concerning the perfection of the body and enhances ones insight into the art and practice of actualizing the perfection; it provides for inspiration and for an inculcation of the truths of the universe and the universal perfection.

It has been used in the treatment of swollen glands. It can also be used to balance and fortify the glands, is excellent for the eyes and for improving vision, and assists in the maintenance of the teeth and with the formative bone structure.

Please note that the Aquamarine Phantom Crystal combines the qualities of Aquamarine with the qualities of a phantom crystal. This crystal has been used extensively in the activation of memory of past-life experiences.

In addition, the configuration of Cat's Eye Aquamarine, brings the qualities of the Cat's Eye mineral to the energies of Aquamarine. This configuration has also been used to stimulate the clairvoyant state during discussions with others.

Vibrates to the number 1.

ARAGONITE   [Astrological Sign of Capricorn]

Aragonite crystallizes forming acicular [needle-shaped] crystals which are elongated along the c-axis. The mineral formation can also be fibrous, columnar, and stalactitic. Quite frequently the crystals will be twinned and/or inter-penetrating. The predominant colours include white, yellow/yellow-gold, green/green-brown, and blue.

It provides for ease of centering oneself and is especially helpful during periods of stress and anger, or during the preparation for the state of meditation.

It can also provide for insight into the basis of the problems which one confronts on the physical plane and can stimulate communication on the higher planes.

It enhances ones patience and helps one to "maintain" comfortably during conditions requiring the acceptance of an abundance of responsibilities.

It can, when consciously directed, help one to maintain strict discipline within ones activities. It also enhances reliability and practicality.

Aragonite can be useful to combat chills and to bring warmth to extremities. For chills, an elixir can be utilized; for warmth to the extremities, one would place the mineral upon the affected location. An aragonite elixir can also be used as a "spring-tonic" and for the amelioration of general aches and pains. It is also helpful when applied locally to problem areas of the skin. It has been used successfully to combat deficiencies in Vitamins A and D.

The varieties from Tsumeb, Namibia, have purported values against hair loss and in the amelioration of wrinkled and coarse skin.

Vibrates to the number 9.

ARGENTITE   [Astrological Signs of Sagittarius and Scorpio]

Argentite crystallizes as octahedral and cubic crystals (which are often distorted and frequently grouped in reticulated or arborescent formation), and in masses and druse.

This mineral is one of alteration, bringing altered states readily, altered conditions when one desires such, and altered requirements to ones being.

In addition to the properties of Silver, Argentite also stimulates the augmentation of beneficial change to ones life, bringing the energy of action without reaction and a clear purpose for advancement.

It helps to show one that which is internal to the self and to others with respect to emotional, physical, and intellectual circumstances. It can draw forth negativity from these centers while transferring the positive forces of another mineral to same; hence, performing as a balancing agent.

Argentite has been used in the treatment of cellular disorders, tumors, and bone structure, and to increase the T-Cell count. It has also been used to increase the stability of the body and the organs of the body, to cleanse the body of toxins, and to assist in the equilibration of the pulse and heart rates.

It has also been used as an activation stone in the preparation of elixirs.

This softness of this mineral precludes its use in the normal method of preparation of an elixir.

Vibrates to the number 9.

ARTHURITE   [Astrological Sign of Leo]

Arthurite crystallizes as prismatic crystals or as globular aggregates. The colour ranges from apple green to emerald green.

This mineral helps one in areas and situations which require both perseverance and tenacity. It can be used to enhance ones position in any area of life; it can be especially helpful to those involved in romantic pursuits.

It also helps one to understand that the only deficiency which is real is the situation of the actualization of ones separation from the perfection of "All That Is".

It is useful in the treatment of infectious disorders and to enhance fertility. It has also been used in the treatment of vertigo, acrophobia, and ambulatory dysfunctions.

Vibrates to the number 3.

ARTINITE   [Astrological Sign of Libra]

Artinite crystallizes in the form of acicular [needle-like] crystals or fibrous aggregates. The colour is white and the mineral is vitreous, silky, and/or transparent.

This mineral has been used to combat abrasiveness and to bring ease to the user with respect to "smoothing-over" disagreements and jealousies.

It appears to aid in bringing ones consciousness to bear in situations requiring crucial decisions and to help one to stay alert to ones surroundings and environment.

It enhances creativity and artistic pursuits. It also instills diplomacy and cooperation in group activities.

Artinite can be used in the treatment of disorders of the parathyroid gland, kidneys, and throat.

Vibrates to the number 6.

ASH [Volcanic]   [Astrological Signs of Taurus & Leo]

Volcanic ash can be used to soothe the emotions and to help one to both recognize and give sufficient attention to details. Using the ash itself or the ash contained as an ingredient in pottery or glass items will provide the same results.

It also stimulates initiative and independence, furthering ones quest for self-assurance and self-reliance. It can be used in the treatment of disorders associated with fever, and to help in the alleviation of digestive disruptions, intestinal disorders, and stomach ulcers. It has been used in the treatment of acidosis.

The normal preparation of an elixir of the volcanic ash is only recommended if adequate filtering equipment is available.

Vibrates to the number 1.

ASTROPHYLLITE   [Astrological Sign of Scorpio]

Astrophyllite crystallizes as bladed crystals in star-shaped groups. The crystals range in colour from a golden-yellow to a bronze-yellow and have somewhat of a metallic lustre.

The crystalline structure exhibits the properties of facilitating astral travel, of providing a method for one to view oneself from the outside, and of producing the recognition of ones inherent self-esteem. It allows for the recognition that one has no limitations and that "we are, in fact, all stars".

It can help to bring to life hidden forces and to show one that as one door closes, another door opens. It also assists in absolving one from responsibility and in purging from ones life that which should be eliminated such that one can continue to both develop and to progress.

Astrophyllite can be used in the elimination of fatty deposits, to increase the sensitivities of touch, and to aid in remedial action for seizures. It can also be used in the treatment of disorders of the reproductive system and in regeneration at the cellular level.

Vibrates to the number 9.

ATELESTITE   [Astrological Sign of Virgo]

Atelestite crystallizes as tabular crystals and as spherical crystalline aggregates. The colour ranges from yellow to green.

This crystal can be used to facilitate speaking and, especially, speaking automatically about those memories which one has consciously forgotten. Retrieval of this information often results in the integration of solutions to problems which have been persistently causing disruption in ones physical, emotional, and/or intellectual bodies.

It is also a "stone for business and possessions", helping to supplement ones energy and assisting one in directing ones thoughts and energy toward successful ventures.

It can be used in the treatment of disorders of the throat, eyes, and ears. It is said to enhance the assimilation of protein, to stabilize the mind [especially when there are schizophrenic tendencies], and to promote the balancing of the metabolic processes.

Vibrates to the number 8.

AUGELITE   [Astrological Sign of Cancer]

Augelite crystallizes as tabular crystals, masses, or triangular plates. The colours of occurrence include colourless, white, yellow, blue, or pink.

This mineral can be useful to dispel and/or to isolate contrariness and discordant temperaments.

Sleeping with a piece of augelite close to the head can produce a restful sleep and can help to dispel intractability.

It can also help to provide for "smooth sailing" in relationships, assisting one in releasing animosity, resentment, and hostility which have culminated from reasons born of the past.

Augelite can be used in the treatment of obesity and circulatory disorders, and to enhance the digestive/elimination processes.

Vibrates to the number 8.

AUGITE   [Astrological Sign of Capricorn]

Augite is found as short vitreous [glassy] prismatic crystals or as compact masses or grains. It may occur in the colour range of purple, brown, or black with a grey-green streak.

Augite can be used to enhance the understanding of metamorphosis in ones life. As one is in the state of constantly experiencing change of form, structure, and substance, augite can be used to ameliorate the more trying transformations.

The purple augite can be useful for providing guidance during spiritual growth; the brown augite can be useful for help in clearing the self of "muddy" emotional, physical, or spiritual issues; the streaked black augite has been used for healing the painful transformations while allowing one to remain grounded and centered in this reality.

All colours of the augite can be used to ameliorate problems associated with calcium deficiencies; an augite elixir can also be helpful in deficiency cases.

Vibrates to the number 9.

AURICHALCITE   [Astrological Sign of Aquarius]

Aurichalcite crystallizes in the form of needle-like crystals, tufted aggregates, encrustations, and granular, columnar, and laminated configurations. The colour ranges from pale green to blue-green to green-blue.

This mineral encourages stability and fearlessness. It enables one to recognize that "the only thing to fear is fear itself". It can produce a protective shield around the user and within the environments in which it is placed.

Aurichalcite acts to enhance tact during social situations and tends to activate harmony within the self; when there is harmony and accord within the inner being, there is peace and serenity in the outer manifestation of ones life.

It enhances ones personal freedom, allowing one to release the old, non-productive practices and to reach for and attain the new, hopefully constructive, situations.

It also clears the aura, smoothing the energy field, and provides for opening to the perfection of the energy of originality.

It can be used in the treatment of the pineal gland, the thalamus, and the circulatory system.

Vibrates to the number 2.

AUTUNITE   [Astrological Sign of Aries]

Autunite crystallizes as tabular crystals, crusts, or aggregates. The colour range includes bright yellow, with hues ranging from pale to deep green.

This mineral allows one to reap the highest rewards from changes; to actually seek the changes which would bring increased development and to continue in action until completion. It helps one to gain increased stability in ones environment and to understand the relationship of the environment to both ones life and ones emotional structure.

Do not use this mineral in the preparation of an elixir via the normal method. It is recommended that the use of autunite be confined to an established location in ones environment, from which the powers would emanate.

The energy emanating from autunite has been used to soothe the temper and to ameliorate heart disorders. It also has been used to encourage the dissipation of malfunctioning cells and to renew and regenerate at the cellular level.

Vibrates to the number 5.

AVENTURINE   [Astrological Sign of Aries]

Aventurine is a variety of mineral [usually quartz or feldspar] which is spangled with bright particles of mica, hematite, etc. The properties listed in the MICA section of this book also apply. In conditions where the reader can recognize the inclusion of another mineral in an aventurine specimen, the qualities of the included mineral also apply. [It should be noted that all crystals and minerals which grow together are quite compatible.]

The most common colour of aventurine is green; it is used primarily at the heart chakra to both activate and clear. It is also an excellent protector of the heart chakra, providing for a shield to block the entry from those who wish to "tap-in" and use the energy of another.

Aventurine provides for balancing of the male/female energies, enhancing ones creativity, supplementing motivation in activities, and augmenting the "pioneering" spirit.

It also reinforces ones decisiveness, amplifies ones leadership qualities, and is a willing participant in instinctive action.

It facilitates balancing and alignment of the intellectual, emotional, physical, and auric bodies.

It has been used in rituals of the medicine wheel, to show to the spirit guides the connection with the healing light of the heart. In these ceremonies it is held at the heart of each participant around the medicine wheel; it has been reported that, during contact with the spirit guides, the participants have felt a "wash of love" fall around them.

It has been used in the treatment of disorders of the lungs, heart, adrenal glands, and the muscular and urogenital systems.

Vibrates to the number 3.

AVOGADRITE   [Astrological Signs of Virgo & Sagittarius]

Avogadrite crystallizes in granular masses or as eight-sided tabular crystals. The colour is pure white.

This mineral facilitates direct communication with the sub-conscious self and, hence, enhances intuition. It promotes the purification of ones bodies and selves and provides for an avenue for one to always see that small patch of blue sky on cloudy days.

It stimulates the analytical capabilities, and provides for rapidity in perception, mental acuity, and insight. It gives impetus to the expression of assumptions and to the presentation of theories, providing for a freedom from repression. It is a stone for frankness, openness, eagerness, and validation.

It inspires one toward occupations and hobbies which will aid in ones development. It is a useful stone for the pursuit of mathematics, physics, and chemistry.

It also is a protective stone, assisting one to come through peril [actual or potential] without suffering serious consequences. It also helps one to remove oneself from that which is harmful or undesirable.

It has been used in the treatment of wounds, disorders of the liver and pituitary, and discomforts associated with the lungs and brain. It can also assist in the assimilation of lipo-proteins, Vitamin A, and the proper combinations of amino acids.

Vibrates to the number 3.

AXINITE   [Astrological Sign of Aries]

Axinite takes the form of tabular crystals which resemble the shape of a wedge. It may also occur in lamellar masses [e.g., very thin layers of plate]. The colours of the mineral include a range of violet/brown and colourless-to-yellow.

This crystal has been useful in helping one to submit gratefully to changes; it acts to stimulate insight into the "that" which could be replaced and the "what" which could successfully provide a positive replacement.

It provides for grounding in all endeavors. It is also a polarizing stone, aligning the energies of the physical with the energies of the Earth.

It inspires friendship, exhibiting an energy which is conducive to stabilizing relationships.

It provides for impetus to an intelligent direction with respect to pursuits, guiding one to the areas behind the scenes and facilitating focus on the actual mechanics of a situation. It allows one to understand that the solution to any problem is one which will not cause injury to another.

It can be used in the treatment of disorders of the adrenal glands, muscular system, and ambulatory functions. It has also been used in the alignment of the vertebrae of the spine, to assist in maintaining the alignment, and to help in the process of mending breaks and fractures.

Vibrates to the number 1.

AZEZTULITE   [Astrological Sign of All]

The composition of Azeztulite has not yet been defined. It was found in a Beryllium mine and does contain silica.

When using it in meditation, it facilitates a cleaner and easier entry and assists one in attaining the state of "no mind".

When holding the mineral, it tends to provide for an encircling spiral; in meditation, the spiral is predisposed to become the Kundalini -rising, and surrounding ones essence at the same time it is within ones body.

During some third-eye placement of Azeztulite there is stimulation of quite vivid "motion" pictures which can assist in self-directing; i.e., bringing "pictures" and scenes from the future, both personal and universal. Following the guidance that one, with ease, sees, one has the ability to make major decisions and to reach-out to others on this and other planes so very easily.

When holding the mineral, the message is clear "...AND WHAT A LOVELY LIGHT". This light is inextinguishable and will shine for the user through all events and conditions.

The energy of the stone shows no negativity or even neutrality - it is a positive stone, and, one of four stones, recognized to-date, of the mineral kingdom which never needs cleansing or energizing (it appears to have a connective cord to the infinite supply of energy from a very loving spot).

In healing, Azeztulite brings a clear energy similar to the quartz crystal and can be applied to further the transference of other energies to the affectation.

In addition, it has been used it can be used in the treatment of cellular disorders, cancer, and inflammation of tissue. It has been used with the infirm to provide insight to purpose and to assist in the restoration of the will.

Vibrates to the number 1.

AZULICITE   [Astrological Signs of Sagittarius & Leo]

The azulicite feldspar crystal is a light grey-blue to grey-green iridescent mineral which is coated [prior to cleaning] with chlorite and limonite. After cleaning, the azulicite is a light sunshine colour with blue/gray adularescence. In addition to the properties listed in the FELDSPAR section of this book, the following qualities are applicable.

The energies of azulicite are related to the synthesis of qualities from the third chakra [intellect] and fifth chakra [throat]. The synthesis can produce the speech of the intellect, and has proven quite useful for those who experience difficulty in intellectual communication and/or in understanding avantgarde topics of conversation.

It has been used to advance communication with entities from other worlds, providing for exchange, especially, of technical information. It maintains the encounter in the purity of the universal white light and provides for strength of endurance in maintaining the altered state required.

It is also a stone for astral travel, helping one to access the information desired, more than facilitating the state. It assists in precision, especially during memory recall of the information. It also balances the male/female qualities, exhibiting a delicate energy filled with vitality.

Allowing the chlorite coating to remain partially upon the azulicite also has produced excellent results in healing, where the stimulation of the intellect produces answers to questions concerning health and well-being.

It can be used in the treatment of disorders of the optical nerves, the digestive system, and the liver. It has also been used in stabilizing incontinent brain waves and in controlling dizziness.

Vibrates to the number 7.

AZURITE   [Astrological Sign of Sagittarius]

Azurite crystallizes forming masses, nodular concretions [nodules], films, stains, and, more rarely, tabular and/or short prismatic crystals. The colour ranges from light to deep blue and the mineral, occasionally, produces a vitreous lustre.

It is known as a "stone of heaven". It stimulates the pursuit of the heavenly self, providing for guidance via the third-eye and allowing for precise verbalization of psychic experiences. It awakens the development of the psychic self and provides for insight into all areas of ones life. It also promotes the recognition of intuitive information which is relevant to the loving ways to further the talents. It is the "great benefactor", controlling the flow of energy and emitting precisely the amount of energy required in any situation.

It enhances creative ability and helps to eliminate indecision and worries which are quietly agitating in the "back of ones mind". One simply holds the azurite and asks to have the troublesome thoughts evaporate.

The form of the azurite nodule is excellent for stimulation of the third-eye and the intuitive and psychic selves. It can also be used to enable the focusing of the intuitive self, via the third-eye, at the etheric level, to induce to memory the portions of ones life or character which require attention; it brings forth the idea that "the truth will-out".

It can work very well with the sacral chakra and the heart chakra, allowing for the recognition and manifestation of the "bestower of good" within each person.

It enhances creativity, mellows the intellect with love, helps one to maintain communication from the "heart space", and stimulates ones compassionate and empathetic nature. It also enhances self-confidence, allowing for invincibility when required.

In the Native American Indian history, azurite has been used as a sacred stone. The nodule and crystal forms have been used to facilitate contact with ones spiritual Indian guide; to allow one to both feel the presence and to understand the message. In many other ancient civilizations, it has been a symbol of status.

The Mayans used the stone to stimulate and inspire the actualization of the psychic and mystical self and to facilitate the transfer of information, knowledge, and wisdom via thought.

It aligns the chakras and attunes the structure of the physical body to the ethereal nervous system, providing for an unimpaired flow of energy. It works quite well in the dissolution of energy blockages.

The energy of azurite is also conducive to the dissolution of impediments and restraints in ones progress; focusing on the mineral, with directed thought to the actualization of the release all barriers in ones path, initiates and expedites the process.

It can help to give one direction and to bring forth required information which will help one to both understand and to release the vitiated energy from within the self; this energy being the antecedent to, and catalyst for, the continuation of dis-ease.

During radionic analysis [where one holds a sample specimen and places a sample on the witness], or when used as a pendulum, the energy of the stone permeates the energy of the user and points to the problem[s] involved and/or to the answers required.

In meditation, it provides for relaxation and for the easy entry to the void of the state of "no-mind". It allows one to travel deep within the inner being and to maintain the depth, while integrating the myriad of visual images which are made available.

When in the non-meditative state, it further combines the abilities of relaxation with the stimulus toward awareness, precision, and global thought.

It has been used in the treatment of disorders of spinal alignment, and to ameliorate the arrangement of the vertebrae, rib cage, and small bones, in particular, which are malformed. It can also be used in the treatment of circulatory disorders, to disseminate and disperse growths, to clear toxins from the body, and to stimulate the functioning of the synapses. It emits an energy conducive to enhancing the flow of motion and can be helpful in allaying spasms and "tics".

Vibrates to the number 1.

AZURITE - MALACHITE   [Astrological Signs of Sagittarius
                                                      & Capricorn]

The synthesis of azurite and malachite produces a mineral which exhibits the properties of each individual mineral as listed in the AZURITE and MALACHITE sections of this book.

In addition, the energy of the combination helps one to meditate by going deep within in order to be reborn into the light - the change being profound or minor, as necessary. It generally allows one to reach into the inner depths without fear, so that one is sustained, absolved, and is aware of the genesis of all time.

It bestows upon one the cleansing of the immutable forces and freshens ones outlook to be as the "wind in the willow". It produces a flow to actions and a willingness toward flexibility.

It assists in dissolving egocentric characteristics, dispelling conceit, arrogance, and vanity, while instilling individuality based upon the connection to the "All". The action of the stone in this regard does not need conscious direction; it will work without consciousness of purpose.

It could be considered one of the requisite minerals for ones collection because of its proclivity for reconstruction during the transformation process.

It gives comfort by calming anxiety associated with "dis-ease", and allows the thought process to follow its course; this enable one to render emotionally charged thoughts ineffective, while facilitating the stability of the intellect to produce rationality.

It can be used to enhance flexibility in motion and to treat disorders associated with the skin, bones, teeth, and circulatory system. It assists in the balancing of the secretory organs, including the gall bladder, liver, etc. It can also be used in the prevention and treatment of ulcers, asthma, and other problems arising from stress.

Vibrates to the number 1.

AZURITE - MALACHITE - CHRYSOCOLLA   [Astrological Signs of Sagittarius, Capricorn, Scorpio, Gemini, Virgo, Taurus]

Azurite-Malachite-Chrysocolla is a combination of these three minerals and is often silicated, containing quartz.

In addition to the combination of properties listed for each of the individual minerals, this combination can help one to extend oneself to others, in the spirit of "brotherhood" and love. It provides for a demonstration of compassion and intelligence, promoting both philanthropic tendencies and attachment to "right-mindedness". On the other hand, it provides stamina against weariness from adulation.

This combination has been used in the treatment of proper healing for breaks and fractures. It has also been used to correct imbalances in RNA/DNA and in the metabolic rate.

Vibrates to the number 6.

ONLY IN THIS BEING DO I FIND LIFE

[r.r.jackson,1990]

BABINGTONITE   [Astrological Sign of Gemini]

Babingtonite crystallizes forming short prismatic or plate-like crystals which range in colour from green to black-brown.

Babingtonite has been used to facilitate ascension, providing for a viewing of ones life on this plane ["this time around"]. It can be used during "re-birthing" sessions to enhance ones understanding of both the blockages which are removed and the reasons for which they existed.

The mineral can be used to overcome shyness in speech and to rectify a negative outlook with respect to possessions and the worldly aspects of ones character.

It provides for grounding to communicative skills and activates and energizes the heart chakra, culminating in the actualization of ones ability to verbalize with subtlety and alacrity.

It can be used in the treatment of disorders of the thyroid, to eliminate restrictions within the structures of the veins, and to ameliorate distressed conditions related to the throat and heart. It also enhances the sense of taste.

Vibrates to the master number 55.

BACULITES   [Astrological Sign of Scorpio]

Baculites are known in the fossil state and are a genus of many-chambered cephalopods.

In addition to the qualities listed in the FOSSIL section, the following information applies.

This mineral has been used to awaken one to the actuality of ones life, bringing consciousness to eliminate the elements of guilt, self-deception, and role-playing which contribute to destructive behavior. It assists one in recognizing the type of negative thinking one is experiencing, and to be able to initiate cognitive thinking to reverse the effects.

Baculites can be used in the treatment of disorders of capillaries, blood vessels, the intestines, atrophy, circulation, and dexterity.

Vibrates to the number 2.

Barite crystallizes as tabular crystals, aggregates, plate-like masses, fibrous masses, and, occasionally, stalactites. The mineral occurs in a range of colours including colourless, blue, white, grey, yellow, brown, and a brownish-rose.

The desert rose is a barite concretion symbolizing the realization that all things are possible; it occurs in the brownish-rose colour. It is an excellent stone for use in the healing of the Earth.

In the Native American religion, it is said that Indian warriors, who had shifted from the physical world to the spiritual world, returned at night and carved the barite roses. The scattering of the roses over a vast area was affected so that those on the physical plane would not know where the warriors had congregated. The energy of the roses can be used to enhance love, to facilitate clandestine meetings, and to stimulate teamwork. The message which the energy of this rose conveys is that the most sacred areas of ones life are those in which ancient hatred has been transformed to present love.

All forms of barite produce an incentive to "go for" ones dreams without restraint. Barite continues to bring the energy toward ending the processes of finite thought while facilitating the expansion of all aspects of ones world.

This mineral enhances friendship, harmony, and love, and can provide insight into the "relationship connection". It also initiates independence and motivation; assisting one in attaining personal freedom from the "requirements" of others, as well as from oneself.

It can be a cathartic to the emotional self, allowing for release of trapped emotions and feelings; bringing calm and self-assurance to the inner state after removal of the pain.

It can also be used to both stimulate and cleanse the throat chakra, to assist in renewal of the intuitive energies, and to provide for communication of new ideas and thoughts [with shyness diminished]. It provides a strong, yet delicate, connection to the spiritual world, assisting one on the path toward the journey and the goal.

Barite can be used in the removal of toxins from the body, to stimulate vision, and to assist in the recovery from addictions. It also helps to soothe and smooth the nervous system.

Vibrates to the number 1.

BASALT   [Astrological Signs of Taurus & Cancer]

Basalt is an igneous volcanic rock [produced under conditions of intense heat] and solidified from molten lava. The colour ranges from grey to black.

It can provide one with the strength to continue through difficult times and can produce solidarity in ones life. It can be quite useful in dissipating anger and can provide understanding and guidance in situations which require one to "bounce back".

It is a mineral to help one through changes and to provide stability to ones life. It also assists in diminishing the negative aspects of ones character, promoting positive modifications of ones behavior.

It is best activated and energized during full and new moon cycles.

It can be used in the treatment of the reproductive system, to enhance fertility, and to help one in the development of muscle structures.

Vibrates to the number 1.

BASINITE   [Astrological Sign of Sagittarius]

Basinite is a very fine-grained Basalt. The colour is black.

In addition to the properties listed in the BASALT section, this mineral can be used to smooth and to soothe the emotional and the intellectual bodies while applying a grounding effect. It assists one in reaching the summit of self-realization and facilitates the psychological experience of focusing inward such that the realm of the unconscious opens; this further enhances the innate integration of the total range of thoughts and actions.

It is also used in shamanic ceremonies to support the removal of the dis-ease from the body; one travels with the Basinite to the affected area of the body and visually brings the affectation to the surface, surrounding and transmuting it into white light.

It is a lovely stone for inducing creativity in all endeavors and for providing grounding.

Basinite has been used in the treatment of disorders associated with assimilation and the intestines. It can also be used in the amelioration of muscular spasms and tenseness, and is an excellent elixir to be applied during massage. It has been used to support the detoxification of the liver and the lymphatic system and to support digestion.

Vibrates to the number 7.

BAVENITE   [Astrological Sign of Libra]

Bavenite crystallizes in the form of fibrous-radial groupings of prismatic crystals. The colour is white.

This mineral can be used to enhance ones self-image and to provide incentive to grow spiritually, emotionally, and intellectually. It brings a softness to ones spirit, yet encourages a righteousness with respect to ones privilege to grow in the highest direction.

It promotes "flowering" of the self during the right season. The message of the energy of bavenite instills the knowledge that one must never accept deficiencies within oneself; if one accepted less than perfection, one would be grasping the belief that "lack" is universal will.

It allows one to delay judgment until all relevant information is available. It also provides for proficiency in intellectual endeavors.

It continues to encourage one to open to creativity, providing for a vast expanse of information with respect to the nature of creation.

Bavenite can be used in the treatment of disorders of speech, hearing, sight, smell, and touch. It can stimulate the "wellness" attribute within the inner being, allowing for mental and structural alignment and physical well-being.

Vibrates to the master number 33.

BEAVERITE   [Astrological Sign of Libra]

Beaverite crystallizes as crumbly masses of hexagonal plates. The colour is yellow.

This mineral can provide protection by providing insight with respect to "what to say" when one encounters difficult communication situations which require response; hence, aiding the intellect in determining the best course of action, while allowing for the understanding of the many facets of the difficulty.

It can also be used to enhance diversification of activities and to produce a well-balanced character.

It is conducive to the development of a wide range of intellectual powers and can be used to stimulate and to enhance ones abilities of discretion and judgment.

It can be used in the treatment of disorders associated with the presence of fatty deposits, to rectify states of mental imbalance, and, as an elixir, for the skin and hair.

Since the mineral is rather crumbly, carrying it in a pouch is recommended.

Preparation of an elixir via the normal method is not recommended.

Vibrates to the number 6.

BENITOITE   [Astrological Sign of Virgo]

Benitoite crystallizes forming slightly flattened pyramid-shaped or tabular crystals. The colour ranges from colourless to blue, pink, purple, and white; some of the crystals are partially colourless and partially coloured. It has been found exclusively in California, USA.

This mineral can be used to enhance contact with extra-terrestrial beings, once contact has been established [see, for example, the MOLDAVITE section of this book for energies available in establishing contact].

It can also aid in allowing transmission of thoughts between two people [i.e., without verbalization]. The stone has been used successfully in the "laying-on-of-stones" to raise the experience of astral travel to a higher degree.

Benitoite brings lightness and joy with depth of beauty and thought to the wearer, enhancing movement and activity.

It is a great benefactor to the well-being of ones physical, emotional, and intellectual selves; the energy brings the message and helps one to realize that ones passage through time and space is not arbitrary and indiscriminate and that one is, indeed, at all times, "in the right place, at the right time".

It is an excellent healing stone, useful for expediting the healing process and for integrating and releasing the basic cause of dis-ease.

It has been used in the treatment of disorders of the blood, to ameliorate conditions of excessive bleeding, and to strengthen the walls of the veins.

Vibrates to the number 9.

BERLINITE   [Astrological Sign of Aquarius]

Berlinite crystallizes as granular masses and occurs as a grey to pink colour.

This mineral provides help in removing oneself from entangling situations, allowing one to "bide ones time" until the time is right. It enhances the power of ones will to endure. It provides a message that when any situation has been dedicated totally to the aspect of truth, tranquility is inevitable.

In addition, Berlinite can be used to stimulate independence and autonomy, allowing for the recognition of self-assurance and self-sufficiency.

It has been used in the treatment of disorders of peripheral nerves, pain associated with paralysis of the extremities, swelling of the body, and emaciation of the fleshy tissues. It aids in the assimilation of the B-complex vitamins.

Vibrates to the number 4.

BERTHIERITE   [Astrological Sign of Aries]

Berthierite crystallizes as prismatic crystals or as masses. The usual grey colour generally tarnishes to a deep brown.

This mineral can produce insight with respect to "everyday" concerns and can facilitate decision-making on those levels. The decisions made, although not always in accord with the opinions of others, will best suit the life and needs of the decision-maker. This mineral will also provide support to the decision-maker with respect to the resolution of a problem.

Berthierite can be used to help one to overcome undue modesty, to become more assertive in living through choice, and to encourage one to overcome introversion. It further stimulates the qualities of tact and cooperation.

It can be used in the elimination of skin disorders and external growths. It provides for stabilization during the process of birth and can ease pain and alleviate stress due to anxiety. It can also enhance the security of the newly born. It has been used in the treatment of conditions associated with infertility.

Vibrates to the number 2.

BERTRANDITE   [Astrological Sign of Aquarius]

Bertrandite crystallizes forming prismatic or thin tabular crystals. The crystals are transparent and range from colourless to pale yellow.

This mineral can help one to go through "changes" and can help to provide for a smooth transition.

It can assist one in conservatism in judgment, in generosity with respect to favour, and in stimulating the growth of appreciation. It provides for energy direction with respect to both discernment in ideals and improvement in articulation. It also assists one in the verbalization of those ideas and/or feelings which have been hidden.

It can also help one in the conduct of business and in the promotion of same.

Bertrandite can be used in the treatment of obesity, psychopathic tendencies, hair disorders, and stomach upsets. It has also been used to strengthen the muscles of the legs.

Vibrates to the number 8.

BERYL   [Astrological Signs Are Relative to the Type of Beryl]

Beryl crystallizes as prismatic crystals which are sometimes striated and sometimes terminated by small pyramid-like faces.

The forms of beryl include aquamarine, bixbite, emerald, goshenite, heliodor, morganite, and golden [or yellow] beryl. Golden beryl is addressed below; the remaining beryl crystals are addressed individually in specific sections of this book.

The astrological sign related to golden beryl is Leo.

Golden beryl represents purity in all aspects of all planes of being. It provides for initiative and independence in thought and action. It also supports the potential of the individual, instilling guidance from the source of all life.

It opens and activates both the crown and solar plexus chakras, providing for synthesis between the intellect and spirituality, and inducing a "wise" intellect. It stimulates activity, adaptability, and vitality.

It is said to have been one of the stones used in the breastplate of the high priest.

It can also be used to provide insight into the rites of ceremonial magic. It promotes the will to succeed, even when ones courage fails, and contributes to the process of finalization.

The message of golden beryl is that there is no obstacle in any circumstance that confidence and conviction cannot resolve; there is only the need to assure that one remains open to, and has not withdrawn from, the solution.

It has been used in the treatment of disorders of the heart and spine. It can also be useful in the treatment of concussions and damage to the cranial portion of the head.

Golden beryl vibrates to the number 1.

BERYLLONITE   [Astrological Sign of Aries]

Beryllonite crystallizes as tabular prismatic colourless, white, or yellow crystals.

This mineral can encourage a pleasant disposition and can combat fatigue. It has been used to relieve anxiety concerning personal expression. It helps one to understand that one cannot interpret the actions or the qualities of another; it further helps one in looking beneath the layers of the world and in allowing the light of love to display the likeness of another to oneself.

It can be used to assist in the healing of dis-ease and discomfort in the reproductive system. It can also be used as a prognostic, promoting ones ability to use the insight given in order to determine the cause, course, and subsequent termination of a dis-ease.

Vibrates to the number 2.

BERZELIITE   [Astrological Sign of Gemini]

Berzeliite crystallizes in the isometric form of grains, masses, or, less commonly, as trapezohedra. The colour is orange-yellow to red-yellow.

This mineral enhances personal power when one is dealing with issues of intuition, creativity, sexuality, and emotions. It provides for a strong base on which to stand when one is confronted in any situation, further helping one to "stand-up" for oneself.

It opens and activates the navel and solar plexus chakras, providing for clarity in intuition coupled with intellect - this is a powerful combination. It can also be used to stabilize the emotions, helping one to channel desire toward the "proper" goals, and aiding one to adjust and to be comfortable in all situations.

It provides for a smooth transition from the beta state to the alpha level, where extra-sensory perception is stimulated.

Berzeliite can be used in the treatment of disorders associated with the stomach, to balance the intake of Vitamin A and Vitamin E, and to assist in establishing continuity in areas of incontinence. It can also be used to initiate cellular renewal.

Vibrates to the number 3.

BETA QUARTZ   [Astrological Sign of Virgo]

Beta Quartz is a variety of quartz which occurs in the configurations of hexagonals and trapezohedral-hemihedrals. The colour ranges from beige to bronze-brown.

In addition to the qualities listed in the QUARTZ section, this mineral has been used for both dowsing and divining, providing clear directional information and responding to all questions. There is a response and resolution to each question, no matter where, when, or what kind of question is posed and answer is solicited.

It has been used for de-coding/encoding of patterns from dreams and visions, assisting in clear channels of communication from both the higher-self and the inner self; hence, the information flows freely and contributes information which assists one in determining the appropriate and foremost actions which will enhance and strengthen ones continuation on the selected path.

It tends to bring the energies of responsibility to the qualities of systematic intuition. It represents the height of mental achievement, facilitating a limitless range of avenues for exploration.

Beta Quartz is known as a DNA crystal for re-tuning the DNA. It has been used extensively in the treatment of violent and/or highly infective dis-ease, as well as by others who are working with those affected in order to provide protection from the affectation. It has been used in the treatment of tumors - at the beginning stages of their growth.

It can be used in the treatment of both the structure of the bone and the composition and formation of the cells. It has been used to assist in the prevention of RNA/DNA damage and can be used in repair of same.

Vibrates to the number 5.

BETAFITE   [Astrological Sign of Scorpio]

Betafite crystallizes in the configurations of octahedrons and dodecahedrons. The colour ranges from green to rust to black.

This mineral has been used, placed above ones body, for diagnostic operations. One can feel a directional energy which focuses upon the area which needs attention.

Used to grid the body, via wearing and/or carrying, Betafite provides a protective shield to psychic attack, emotional pollution, and general uneasiness.

It has been used to prompt a definite and distinct connection between the astral body and the physical body during astral travel. This connection tends to lessen the fear of astral travel and fosters the competence in leaving the body.

Betafite has been used in the treatment of varicose veins, the circulatory system, hormonal balance, and thyroid and metabolic balancing.

Vibrates to the number 5.

BEUDANTITE   [Astrological Sign of Taurus]

Beudantite crystallizes as rhombohedral [i.e., six rhombic sides] crystals exhibiting the colour range of dark green to black.

This mineral can help one to eliminate disparaging thoughts and can provide one with impetus to continue onward toward the light. It has been used in cases of depression and to help one to understand that the times perceived as less than wonderful were, in fact, quite necessary to provide the learning experience one was seeking [consciously, or not]. The message provided from beudantite is "that which one believes about the self determines ones talents". When one is convinced that the human structure is comprised of love, one can give and receive only love; when one is convinced that perfection is inherent, then one can but manifest that perfection.

Beudantite can be used to dispel odor from the body, to treat disorders of the stomach and heart, and has been said to be efficacious against poison. It can help to remove toxins from the body and to provide relief from "aches and pains".

Do not prepare an elixir of this mineral via the normal method.

Vibrates to the number 2.

BIEBERITE   [Astrological Sign of Pisces]

Bieberite crystallizes in the form of red stalactites and crusts.

This mineral helps one to stay in tune with the physical body and to recognize changes within the body when they occur.

It can also enhance ones spirituality during the initial stages of growth. It provides a mirror of the self and the inner workings of the body, allowing one to see into the emotional, mental, and physical structures.

It helps one to refrain from delusion and to recognize and extinguish the self-limiting ideas which have been instilled.

It can be used in the treatment of disorders of the teeth, the skeletal structure, and the muscular composition. It has also been quite useful in stabilizing the nerves, calming during stressful situations, and increasing ones energy and stamina.

Vibrates to the number 3.

BIOTITE   [Astrological Sign of Scorpio]

Biotite is a form of mica which crystallizes forming massive scaly aggregates or sheet-like disseminates. The colour ranges from red-brown to brown to green and displays a metallic lustre. It is a member of the mica group; in addition to the qualities listed below, those discussed in the MICA section of this book also apply.

This mineral, as does mica, allows one to look rationally at both ones environment and the issues affecting ones environment. It also promotes "seeing" farther than the issue and assists one in looking at the issue intelligently, but with input from the loving side. While allowing one to discard insignificant and irrelevant details, it provides for a clear picture of each issue.

It has been called a "stone of life" and has been used in diagnosing disorders associated with disorganized cellular patterns. It can also be used in the treatment of the eyes, to release and wilt growths, and to regulate the secretion of bile.

Biotite Lens

The Biotite Lens is configured as a brown, dark brown, reddish-brown lens shape. In addition to the properties listed above, it has been used to assist in the maintenance and order of information - both within the mind and in the structure of organizations. Used in an office situation, the tendency toward orderliness and systematic and methodical approach is increased.

It also increases the vision of the third-eye, bringing information concerning structures in ones life and structures from past times and civilizations. The pathway to channeling information from other realms is unobstructed with the application of this mineral.

It is a stone of the crown chakra, bringing connected-ness with the higher-self and enhancing ones true consciousness. It assists one in changing ones ideas, preconceived notions, and beliefs, such that progression toward the realization of the spiritual self is enhanced.

It has also been used in the treatment of motor abilities and the eyes. Use during acupuncture, such that the subject of treatment holds the lens, tends to increase the flow of energy to the directed locations.

Biotite vibrates to the number 8 and the Biotite Lens also vibrates to the number 4.

BISMUTH   [Astrological Sign of Aquarius]

Bismuth crystallizes in the form of masses and, occasionally, hexagonal crystals. It is a silver-white colour which transforms to red.

It can be used to help one to transit from the physical plane to the astral state and/or to the spiritual realms. In this case, it provides for the opening for, and the continuity of travel with respect to, a pre-established travel plan.

It relieves conditions of emotional and spiritual isolation, allowing one to feel the connected-ness with "All That Is". It allows one to abide within serenity, regardless of ones physical location, enhancing the state of the moment with the illumination of wisdom.

Bismuth has been used as a stone of transformation; it directs the change to orderliness and calms the state of change, providing a supplemental physical vitality to the user. It transforms the energy of the crown chakra to energize the base chakra [in contrast with most stones] and actualizes the power of wisdom.

It stimulates cohesiveness in groups and relationships, allowing for independence in progression toward a common goal. It also helps one to enjoy the journey.

Bismuth can be used to assist in diminishing fevers and in lessening catatonic states. It can also stimulate the energy and can be used to clear the biological field.

Vibrates to the number 2.

BITYITE   [Astrological Sign of Libra]

Bityite crystallizes as thin tabular crystals, rosettes, and aggregates of tiny platelets. The colour ranges from white to yellow.

This mineral can be used as a calming agent and to reduce the crystallization of any aspect of ones life. It is excellent when used as an elixir.

It can be used to support gridding exercises associated with the promotion and the enhancement of the condition of stability; in this case, a piece of the mineral would be placed beneath each piece of the other minerals chosen for the gridding.

Bityite provides for the awareness that certain signs and actions precede certain events; the energy emitted allows one to recognize "the signs" and to formulate readiness.

It instills the property of symmetry to ones thoughts and actions, allowing for forethought prior to action and for recognition that reactive emotional states are unproductive.

It can be used to help one to understand, to accept, and to actively pursue the "moral norm"; this is facilitated when conscious direction of the energy of bityite is focused to eliminate that which is considered to be "abnormal".

It can also be used in the treatment of skin abrasions, to help one to stabilize after operative restructuring, and to stimulate the release of toxins from the lungs.

Vibrates to the number 9.

BIXBITE   [Astrological Signs of Taurus & Aries]

Bixbite is a variety of red beryl which crystallizes prismatically, sometimes vertically striated and, occasionally, terminated with small pyramidal faces. This variety of beryl has sometimes been designated as "red emerald" due to the brilliance, quality, and the aspect of rare occurrence. Bixbite is a relatively newly discovered mineral [early 1980's, Colorado, USA].

It can be used to establish ones natural progression toward wisdom and the enlightened state. It can enhance physical energy and power, bringing in the clear state of universal love. It opens and energizes the base chakra, providing stimulus to the initiation of the Kundalini movement. It can also be used to raise the energy of the base chakra to the level of devotion.

It activates the heart chakra with a powerful and distinct energy of sacredness, stimulating to action the innate qualities of unconditional love and respect for all of life. It is a stone of love for the new age and is useful in relationships to provide cooperation, compatibility, and harmony. It deals with issues of co-dependence and brings the energy of the stars to the reality of the Earth plane.

It helps one to concentrate on inner growth and allows for the release of negativity. It shows one that the worldly aspects of ones life will remedy themselves. The energy of bixbite provides insight with respect to "the right time" to change ones mind, to change ones direction, or to "do" something.

It inspires one to complete old projects and to contemplate the new.

It is also a powerful and stable influence upon business and possessions.

It stimulates ones awareness and promotes the recognition of those beings who are from other planetary worlds. It allows for clarity in judgment and provides the message to "accept, accept, accept" all events and conditions, and to know that, being in the perfect state, one has no concerns and must adhere to no requirements - except to impart love. It also provides for a protective energy which clearly disallows becoming "caught-up" in fear; it allows one to remember that, indeed, there is nothing to fear.

Its healing power lies in the absence of ignorance and negativity, which is indicative of the perfect balance of creative force. It can be used in the treatment of disorders of the heart, lungs, spleen, liver, kidneys, pancreas, thyroid, parathyroid, and stomach. It also provides for a cleansing action which can affect both the respiratory tract and the digestive system.

Vibrates to the number 8.

BIXBYITE   [Astrological Sign of Pisces]

Bixbyite crystallizes in the form of black metallic cubic/octahedral crystals.

It is a mineral for intuition, sensitivity, imagination, adaptability, and spirituality. It enhances each aspect of these qualities and provides for teaching, with integrity, via insight.

This mineral can be used to dispel headaches and painful conditions of the body. It can provide strength while one is being subjected to pain and can condition one to "let go" of same. While providing for a grounding and centering of the self, it often provides insight into the connection between pain and karma.

Vibrates to the number 6.

BLENDE   [See Sphalerite]

BLOEDITE   [Astrological Sign of Cancer]

Bloedite crystallizes in the form of compact masses and as prismatic crystals. The colour ranges from colourless to grey to blue-green.

This mineral can produce an effect of preservation on the physical and mental bodies and can provide for guidance and understanding [when used during meditation] with respect to the methods which can be used to maintain this preservation.

It provides for insight into ones basic impulses and responses, and stimulates receptiveness and intuition. It allows for the recognition and understanding that ones belief systems are responsible for ones present position in life and it promotes insight into the techniques available for elimination of the belief patterns which do not serve in a positive manner.

It can be used in the treatment of painful swellings in the muscles, to renew the membranes and muscular walls of the organs, and to eliminate parasitic invasions. It can also be used to ameliorate water retention, chills, and fevers.

Vibrates to the number 9.

BLOODSTONE   [Astrological Signs of Aries, Pisces, & Libra]
                                           [Also Known as Heliotrope]

Bloodstone is a variety of quartz which occurs in massive formations. The colour is green with flecks of red; in smaller pieces of the mineral, the red does not appear.

In addition to the properties listed in the CHALCEDONY section of this book, the following attributes apply.

This mineral is a intense healing stone and a "stone of courage". It can be used to awaken and to introduce uniformity within the vibrations of energy in the base, navel, sacral, and heart chakras. It helps one to accept the change in energy fields, and to recognize the beneficial aspects of turmoil prior to perfection.

It also provides one with the centering and grounding energy of the heart, and is conducive to balancing the total body in order to help one to overcome any distress and anxiety which is associated with the re-alignment of the energies.

The message which lies within bloodstone is to "be here now". It grants one the mastery of renewal - for renewal of the physical, mental, and emotional. It also provides for the revitalization of love, relationships, and friendships.

There is an inherent strength to the energy of the stone, allowing for transmittal of practical and dispassionate guidance; it also provides introductory information with respect to the application of the advice and counsel. It further instills the wisdom and sensitivity to facilitate the application and provides for unification of the energy bodies to advance the attributes of harmony, adaptability, and strength.

It helps one to demonstrate unselfishness and idealism, to improve ones talents and abilities, to enhance creative efforts, and to support the decision-making processes. It has been used in accessing the principles of mysticism, providing for insight into the immediate spiritual intuition of truths which transcend ordinary understanding.

It also helps one toward the direct union with the Divine through contemplation, meditation, and love.

Bloodstone has also been used to facilitate admittance to the spiritual realms of the ancestors, providing for an open avenue of communication with same. The information received is, usually, via the intuitive state.

It can be used to dispel states of bewilderment and obscure thought.

It has been used in the treatment of the spleen, and to purify the blood, kidneys, bladder, intestines, and liver. It can neutralize the toxins within the body and can provide for elimination of same. It has been used in the treatment of leukemia, and to stabilize, balance, and increase or decrease, as necessary, the flow of blood. It has also been used to aid in the rectification of failing eyesight, lung congestion, and rashes.

Vibrates to the numbers 4 and 6.

BOJI STONE   [Astrological Signs of Aquarius, Scorpio, Leo, & Taurus]
[Boji is pronounced "boh-ji"]

The boji stone [a registered trademark] was brought to the light by a trance-channeler in Colorado, USA. It is a blackish-brownish concretion with, usually, a flattened spherical shape. Occasionally, the stone appears in other forms [e.g., figure-eight shape, thin oval shape, etc.]. Each stone is distinguished by the characteristic of a small, smooth pattern of crystallization or a larger uneven pattern of crystallization; the smoother stone being defined as the female, and the more heavily crystallized stone [sometimes with platelets protruding] being defined as the male. Some are said to be androgenous.

In addition, the boji stone has been found with rainbows upon the surface; the rainbows truly make a lovely expansion of the energies of the mineral.

The crystallization mineral within the boji stone is, primarily, pyrite. Analysis of the composition of the stone has also indicated the presence of palladium, an excellent healing mineral. Further studies have shown a variety of other minerals, but written test results have not yet been available to the author.

In addition to the properties listed below, the information listed in the PYRITE, PALLADIUM and CONCRETION sections of this book also apply.

The boji stone aligns all of the subtle bodies and both balances and aligns the chakras. It is useful for removal of energy blockages.

It is an excellent energy source, exhibiting an electro-magnetic energy field, and providing for the transfer of energy from the etheric body to the physical. It also cleans, charges, and fills the voids in the aura.

It combines the qualities of initiative and independence with the furthering of the "brotherhood" of all, producing a circular energy which penetrates from the crown to the base chakra.

An effective "everyday" use of the boji is facilitated by allowing it to remain in ones energy field; this will provide for continuous balancing of ones energy. It is not necessary that one be aware of the presence of the boji in order for the balancing and alignment to occur.

It is quite effectual to use a pair of boji stones [female and male consisting of the "team"] to balance ones body and energy fields. Using the male on one side of the body and the female on the other side of the body [the reader will determine which side for which stone], the stones can be used to balance the acupressure or acupuncture meridians and to remove energy blockages.

Blockages are often not removed in one session, but the decrease is usually quite apparent. It should be noted that when one begins work with the boji, an accepted method is to hold the stones in the fingers [one stone in the fingers of one hand and the other stone in the fingers of the other hand], moving the stones toward and then away from each other; then turn one over and go through the procedure again; then turn the other one over and go through the procedure again - whichever position the bojis maintained when the strongest sensation [push or pull or tingling, etc.] occurred is the position of greatest power for the stones.

In addition, it is an excellent grounding stone.

It has been reported that boji stones also facilitate growth of plants, as well as telepathic communication between the self and plants and/or animals. The stones, however, if placed in ones fields or garden, may disintegrate after discharging their energy to enhance the well-being and stability of the environment in which they were placed. If you have an abundant supply of these stones and want to use them to help your plants and garden, beware that they may disappear, becoming a part of the Earth again.

The boji stone has been used in general healing and in tissue regeneration.

Exhibiting a similar property to the quartz crystal when placed on a painful area of the body, it has been used to relieve the discomfort. The presence of palladium, a very strong healing mineral, provides impetus to the boji energy during activities ordered toward the restoration of the healthy state.

Vibrates to the numbers 1 and 9.

BOLEITE   [Astrological Sign of Taurus]

Boleite crystallizes in an indigo-blue colour with the form closely resembling cubes.

This mineral can provide one with stability during work with the sixth chakra [third-eye]. It can be very helpful during the pursuit of opening and actuating the third-eye; in this case it promotes, as well, an understanding that one cannot become lost in the process.

It provides for courage in the face of actual danger or rejection, producing daring, unhesitating action while supporting the maintenance of the protective forces of the universal light.

It emits a penetrating energy which is conducive to halting or encouraging an action, dependent upon the conscious direction of the power.

It can be used in the treatment of suppurating inflammations and microbic infections. It has been used in the treatment of disorders of the upper chest and dis-eases of the throat. It can also be used to smooth the skin and to stabilize the thyroid.

Vibrates to the number 5.

BOLIVARITE   [Astrological Sign of Leo]

Bolivarite is not formed into any distinct shape, but occurs as crusts and botryoidal [consisting of a group of round prominences] masses. The botryoidal form is easiest to use since the crusts are somewhat fragile. The colour is a bright yellow-green.

This mineral can stimulate the intellect to facilitate the procurement of "this-world" items. It provides for insight into the attainment of that which is required in order to procure and promotes insight into the most logical and readily accessible methods which are available.

It also enhances ones self-esteem and leadership qualities, and stimulates revolutionary ideas.

It can be carried/worn to facilitate both financial improvement and successful business ventures.

It expedites the transfer of energy - between one and the ethereal body, between crystals and minerals, between people, etc. - eliminating the resistive forces which are present in the environment.

It can be used in the treatment of circulatory disorders, dis-eases of the nervous system, and minor complaints accompanying the development of the physical body.

Vibrates to the number 5.

BOOTHITE   [Astrological Sign of Aries]

Boothite crystallizes as light blue masses.

This mineral can be used to help one to determine which direction one should take when confronted by many choices. It provides for a stable influence and a "guiding light" in matters occurring when one approaches a crossroads in decision-making. It also allows one to remain calm when discussion of the matter occurs.

Boothite provides for a strength coupled with a small protective cover for immediate circumstances. It promotes swift motion in the realms of physical and intellectual action.

It can be used in the treatment of genital disorders, irritations of the mucus membranes, and to enhance the functioning of the thymus.

Vibrates to the number 4.

BORNITE   [Astrological Sign of Cancer]
                                             [Also Known as Peacock Rock]

Bornite crystallizes in the form of masses and, occasionally, in the form of cubic and rhombdodecahedral [twelve faces, each the shape of a rhombus] crystals. The colour is a red-brown and is enhanced by an iridescent tarnish produced in a variety of colours [e.g., purple, yellow, blue, turquoise, rose, etc.].

This mineral can facilitate the synthesis of the chakras and can be useful in the individual activation of the chakras.

This mineral can bring freshness and newness to ones life. It stimulates the inner spirit to seek further heights and substantiates ones ability to enjoy happiness in the moment.

It is an excellent stone for use during activities of re-birthing, helping one to integrate and to unite the existing separation of the emotions with the intellect. It helps one to release that which is no longer useful. It also promotes insight into the aspects of grief and relief - allowing one to both recognize and accept the differences.

It is a "stone of happiness", providing a message that life is truly joyful to experience.

It also assists one in recognizing that there need be no deficiency in any aspect of ones life, for one is the image of the creation, now and for all times.

It protects one from negative energy bombardment and assists one in the recognition of the source of negativity. It also provides for insight to the obstacles which may block ones progression toward a specific goal, furthering awareness of the avenues available for use in the circumvention of same.

It produces an energy similar to the energy of alignment. It also emits a circular energy which returns to itself; upon the return, it transforms any negative forces, which have been gathered, into pure beneficial energy. When the energy of bornite is applied to a part of the body, it affects the remaining portions, as well.

Bornite is an excellent healing stone. It can be used to assist in the building of the structures of the physical body and to renew perfection to the growth of the cellular composition and arrangement.

It performs a major role in the amelioration of the origin, nature, and course of disease; it is quite useful in the treatment of imbalances in cellular metabolism and in alterations of tissue formation within the body.

It can bring harmony to the cellular structure of the body, allowing for total cooperation at the level of the cellular heart.

When used in the healing situation, in or on the area of the body above the waist, it can help to regulate the flow of adrenaline, to increase alkalinity when there is an over-acid state, to increase the assimilation of potassium, and to decrease excess levels of calcium [especially in conditions of undesirable deposited calcium]. It can also be useful in the elimination of fevers and swelling, and to decrease protein assimilation, when required, in order to facilitate the state of orderliness within the body [e.g., for conditions of gout, etc.].

When used in the healing situation, in or on the areas of the body below the waist, it can help to provide for increased circulation of the blood, to increase acidity when there is an over-alkaline state, to stabilize the assimilation and retention of sodium, and to stimulate the flow of adrenaline. It can also be useful in the treatment of convulsive and spasmatic conditions, in the elimination of fevers, and to ameliorate dehydration.

It can be used as an elixir to assist in the elimination of disruptive forces in the body, balancing the upper body with the lower body in the situations and in the conditions listed above.

Vibrates to the numbers 2 and 4.

BOTRYOGEN   [Astrological Sign of Taurus]

Botryogen crystallizes in the form of prismatic crystals and botryoidal masses. The colour is a lustrous orange.

This mineral can be useful for activation and stimulation of the second [emotional] chakra. It can enhance both creativity and intuition and can provide insight to the thoughts and issues related to desires and sexuality.

Botryogen is quite helpful when one is dealing with relationships and creative endeavors. The energy available from this stone is both tranquilizing and soothing. It also facilitates growth in extra-sensory perception.

It can be used in the treatment of the fleshy organs of the body. It can help to stimulate circulation and to relieve mental instability. It is also helpful for elimination of undesirable residue from the area of the intestines. It has been used during pregnancy to ease the expansion of the skin and to facilitate ease in the birthing process. Botryogen, when placed on the stomach, has produced both calming for the unborn child and rectification of digestive disorders.

Vibrates to the number 4.

BOULANGERITE   [Astrological Sign of Aries]

Boulangerite crystallizes in the form of prismatic and tabular crystals and masses. The colour is a lustrous metallic blue-grey.

This mineral has been used to assist one in finding that which has been lost; it expedites and facilitates the knowledge to either return the lost item or to allow it to remain astray. It encourages sedentary habits and inspires one to proceed and to advance.

It assists in the conduction of energy to the non-flexible portions of the body and the mind, serving to bring patience, perseverance, composure, and stamina.

It actually tends to awaken ones innate sense of well-being and to bring elevated energy toward the furtherance of goals.

Boulangerite has been used in the treatment of the immune system, to increase the number of T-cells, to assist in the assimilation of vitamins and minerals, and to stimulate cleansing activity within the body.

Preparation of an elixir via the normal method is not recommended.

Vibrates to the number 3.

BRANDTITE   [Astrological Sign of Sagittarius]

Brandtite crystallizes in the form of prismatic crystals, reniform [kidney-shaped] masses, and radial groupings. The colour ranges from colourless to white.

It can be used to stimulate the receipt of information, via meditation, which is relevant to the reasons for being in the physical body.

It grants support to emotional issues and allows one to recognize the supreme connection to the primal source, and to regain clarity of the ultimate goal of all being.

It is conducive to sudden inspiration and can provide for insight, allowing one to recognize the approaching end of a situation.

It has been used to contact a "council of experts" from other planes in order to gain information concerning a specific question, dilemma, or situation; the council members being automatically selected and notified when the question is posed.

This mineral treats the body as a unit and can be quite useful in decreasing general malaise. It can both stimulate and soothe the kidneys, and can aid in the removal of skin growths and discolourations.

It can also be used to balance the neuron response within the brain, to steady the brain waves, and to treat inflammations of the brain and spinal column.

Vibrates to the number 3.

BRAUNITE   [Astrological Sign of Leo]

Braunite crystallizes in the form of masses or pyramid-like striated crystals. The colour ranges from metallic black to brown.

This mineral, used in meditation, can provide information concerning both past and future "weathering" one has/will endure. Note that "endure" is a key word; braunite, actually, provides insight to methods, useful and relatively painless, which can increase ones "staying power". The energy of the mineral is both strengthening and invigorating.

It can be used in the treatment of respiratory dysfunctions, for amelioration of disorders of the mammary glands, and to decrease hunger.

Vibrates to the number 9.

BRAVOITE   [Astrological Sign of Leo]

Bravoite crystallizes in the form of fragmented shapes, grains, and, occasionally, in cubic configuration. The colour is pale yellow and the mineral is often covered with a red tarnish.

This mineral can be useful to both stimulate physical activity and intellectual activity; it can help one to understand the importance of both types of activity and can provide insight into the uses of these activities to assist one in advancement in spirituality.

It is conducive to amplification of courageous endurance and provides for confidence in the face of difficulty.

It helps to produce a noble valour, reflecting from an innate quality of mind and spirit that which assists one to both confront and endure difficulties without fear and without excitement.

It is helpful to stimulate creativity in the musician, both in the field of performance and in the area of creation.

It can be used in the treatment of wounds, cuts, bruises, and other outward manifestations of physical discomforts. It can also be used in the removal of blockages in the veins and to rectify impairments in speech.

Vibrates to the number 2.

BRAZILIANITE   [Astrological Sign of Capricorn]

Brazilianite crystallizes in the form of globules or short striated prismatic crystals. The colour ranges from colourless to pale yellow to a yellow-green.

This mineral works quite well in the synthesis of the third [intellect] and fourth [heart] chakras. It promotes understanding of difficult situations and allows for decisions to be made via the utilization of a "team" of personal qualities such that the loving-intellect produces the end result.

It further encourages close examination of situations and relationships, helping one to attain the insight necessary for attainment of that which is desired. It also assists one in releasing that which is not desired.

It provides for stimulation to the acupressure/acupuncture meridians, decreasing the areas of obstruction and providing for the flow of the etheric energy throughout the body.

It is useful as an elixir for application, topically, to sensitive skin areas. It has been used to diminish fevers and to stabilize the body temperature.

Brazilianite can also be used to alleviate the conditions of both heatstroke and sunstroke.

Vibrates to the number 9.

BROCHANTITE   [Astrological Sign of Capricorn]

Brochantite crystallizes in the form of acicular crystals, drusy crusts, and masses. The colour ranges from a lustrous emerald-green to blackish green.

In addition to the qualities listed in the COPPER section, it can be used to both strengthen and to align all chakras, meridians, and subtle bodies. It actually elevates all chakras and can facilitate attunement between the physical level and the higher planes of existence. It can bring any and all energies to a higher level. It does, however, primarily stimulate the heart and base chakras, bringing survival skills to emotional issues while allowing for the application of surety and protection in all issues.

It is excellent for spiritual attunement, for healing and cleansing of both the energy centers and the physical body, and for providing protection.

It has been said that Brochantite looses its lustre to warn of impending danger and/or to indicate duplicity and disloyalty in thought or action. It can be used to protect against environmental contaminates as well.

It has also been used for water-retention and to rid food of free-radical oxides. It also tends to work well in disorders associated with the exterior of the body. It has been used in the treatment of the pancreas, the prostate, and the spleen.

Vibrates to the number 7.

BRONZITE   [Astrological Sign of Leo]

Bronzite crystallizes in the form of masses, fibrous or lamellar, and (rarely) crystals. The colour is bronze.

This mineral has been used to assist one in achieving the state of certainty without willful-ness, such that one may continue to be adaptable with respect to the methodology of attainment. It can help one in all facets relative to service, bringing the value of assistance to the forefront.

It is a "stone of courtesy", promoting loving equitability and unprejudiced discernment within the user. It also provides the stimulus for decisiveness of that which has not been resolved in ones life.

It provides one with the courage to "do" during the action of "being".

In healing, it can be useful to bring an alkaline body state to the acid condition. It can also be used to assist the body in normal transforming cycles. It can quicken the assimilation of iron and can provide for increased duration of iron within the physical body.

Vibrates to the number 1.

BROOKITE   [Astrological Sign of Cancer]

Brookite crystallizes in the form of tabular and plate-like crystals. The colour ranges from red-brown to black and the finish ranges from metallic to a diamond-like lustre.

This mineral helps one to withstand intolerable situations, and to flow with the moment. It also helps one to understand that the "systems of belief" have brought one to the position one has today; it further assists one in correcting those beliefs which do not benefit progression.

Brookite attracts and retains energy. It is excellent for use in energizing ones chakras, energy fields, environment, etc., and for supplementing the energy forces of other crystals and minerals. It can be used to dispel lethargy and apathy, prompting ones hidden energy toward imaginative endeavors and responsiveness.

It can also be useful in the treatment of debilitating conditions, circulation problems, and under-activity with respect to fertility [when consciously directed].

Vibrates to the number 5.

BUNSENITE   [Astrological Sign of Sagittarius]

Bunsenite crystallizes in the form of vitreous [i.e., resembling glass] green octahedra.

This mineral can be used to stimulate the heart chakra and to provide centering during meditation. It provides for protection from subtle annoyances and for tenacity in affairs of the heart. It also initiates and encourages the movement of the Kundalini.

It is an excellent healing stone, bringing a type of coziness to the environment of those suffering from disorders. It is also useful for the treatment of chills, cold extremities, swellings, contusions, and disorderly growth.

Vibrates to the number 1.

BUSTAMITE   [Astrological Sign of Libra]
                                       [A Powerful Stone For Energy Work]

Bustamite crystallizes in the form of masses and tabular crystals with rounded edges. The colour ranges from pink to raspberry to brownish-red and the specimens sometimes contain black manganese. Bustamite has been recently found in Brasil in combination with Rhodonite.

This is truly a stone for the new age. Although it was discovered years ago and was available from the state of New Jersey, in the United States, it was not until the bustamite from The Republic of South Africa became available that the mineral was brought to the attention of those working with crystals and minerals. This is truly a stone for powerful energy work -- thanks, South Africa!

Bustamite is also a powerful stone for initiation, movement, and stabilization of energy. It has been used successfully in the removal of energy blockages and in re-aligning the energy channels to their proper locations. It can be used to both activate and clear the heart chakra, and to provide calming action during stressful activities.

Used in meditation, it provides one with both a safe and sacred place where the soul is honored and where the inner being can feel the perfection of health, harmony, and the congruity of the universe.

It is conducive to the dream state and stimulates the state of awareness during dream time; hence, cultivating the dream state as a vehicle for meditation. It also provides for access to angelic beings in the purity of the light.

The energy of bustamite can allow one to remove oneself from a situation while remaining physically present; it provides a "stand-in" capability which allows for intellectual or emotional discussions while the user connects and enjoys the meditative state. It can also provide for the fortitude necessary for one to remove from an unpleasant or non-productive physical situation.

The gemmy Rhodonite with Bustamite which has become available from Brasil, combines the properties of Rhodonite with Bustamite, for a dynamic, active, and powerful energy.

It can be taken as an elixir, and can be worn, carried, or used during the "laying-on-of-stones" for body work. It is helpful to circulation and can be used in the treatment of calcium deficiencies and to increase muscular structure. It can be used in the treatment of heart disorders, to provide strength to the heart muscles. It has been used to clear the lungs, to both stabilize and balance the actions of the pancreas and liver, and to clear and smooth the skin. It can be used to dispel pain, to eliminate the cause and the symptoms of migraine headaches, and to help the user to eliminate personal emotional pain.

Vibrates to the number 2.

BUTLERITE

Butlerite crystallizes in the form of octahedra and as tabular crystals. The colour is a vitreous orange.

This mineral can be used to help one to accept responsibility and to enable one to excel at the performance of tasks or management of same; it provides one with access to information concerning the methods of installing a "buffer zone" between oneself and the outside.

It can provide insight to allow one to recognize and to accept the dualities of ones nature, inciting one toward self-appraisal, self-discovery, self-awareness, and self-correction.

It can also be used to both stimulate and clear the second chakra, facilitating creativity, emotional stability, and adaptability.

It is a stone for those in the fields of service to others. It stimulates social abilities and versatility.

It is also a "stone of travel", bringing forth the avenues through which one can learn.

Butlerite can be used in the treatment of cellular disorders, dysfunctions of the muscular structure, to enhance the skeletal structure and improve the posture, and to provide for additional strength and integrity to the enamel and the inner portions of the teeth.

Vibrates to the number 9.

CELEBRATE YOUR EXISTENCE!

ARE YOU UP TO YOUR DESTINY?

CACOXENITE [Astrological Sign of Sagittarius]

Cacoxenite crystallizes in radiated tufts of yellow to brown colour. One of the most exquisite formations occurs within amethyst.

The formation with amethyst is said to instill the concept that there are truly "new" things and ideas to be brought forth; the energy of this combination provide a mode of creativity that foster the occurrence of thoughts that have never "been thought before". Hence, the mineral assists one in bringing new ideas to our humanity.

This mineral is a "stone of ascension", being used by many during the myriad of planetary alignments, world meditations, and during the full and new moons, in order to increase spiritual awareness on all levels, to transfer healing energy to the Earth, and to provide a loving and ethereal connection between all of the universe.

It has been used with Moldavite extensively by the ancient tribes of Czechoslovakia during spiritual ceremonial activities, to bring in the higher macrocosmic energies.

It is a mineral to bring rainbows to ones life, allowing one to see the positive, beneficial, and constructive forces of all events and conditions. It serves to activate discretion based upon wisdom and discernment.

Using Cacoxenite during meditation stimulates awareness of the abounding nature of ones existence. It can also awaken memories of the nature of ones prior existences.

It has been used in holistic treatment, to allow one to recognize all of the relationships between each integral part of the body, mind, and emotions. The energy of this mineral can act to carry information both within and between the cellular structure and can be used in the treatment of cellular disorders, hormonal responses, and to relieve stress. It appears to have a cytophylactic effect upon the body and has been used to increase the renewal of cells and to promote healing.

Vibrates to the number 9.

CAFARSITE [Astrological Sign of Gemini]

Cafarsite crystallizes as well-formed crystals in the cubic system. The colour ranges from yellow-brown to deep brown.

This mineral can be used to facilitate the cohesiveness of groups of people working together. It helps to decrease the judgmental and prejudicial "qualities" of people and assists one in both recognizing and understanding these characteristics within oneself; hence, allowing one to rectify negativity within ones life.

It helps to purify the emotions, providing for an effective discharge of negativity. It not only provides symptomatic relief, but assists in the clearing of the underlying pathology.

It also helps one to break "free" from intellectual and emotional confinement.

It can be used in ceremonies of the medicine wheel to bring a stronger connection between the four directions; it further binds those around the wheel.

It can be used to ameliorate mental instability and has been used in the treatment of disorders associated with nervousness. It is also useful to aid in the metabolizing of nutrients within the body.

Vibrates to the number 1.

CALAVERITE   [Astrological Sign of Leo]

Calaverite crystallizes forming masses and thin prisms which are striated in the same direction as their length. It is an ore of gold, containing a little silver and tellurium. The colour is white with, often, enhancement by varying shades of yellow.

In addition to the properties listed in the TELLURIUM, GOLD, and SILVER sections of this book, the following information is applicable.

This mineral is a "stone to eliminate compulsiveness" and to promote thought before action.

It can also be used to stimulate the intellect toward the rectification of monetary concerns, prompting one to take the most beneficial action in the most beneficial manner.

It is preferable to carry this mineral in a pouch or to allow it to remain stationary in ones environment. It brings a positive and lasting influence to the environment in which it resides; a clarity and simplicity, a crisp wholesomeness, and a natural easiness. Do not use this mineral as an elixir.

Vibrates to the number 6.

The various crystallized forms of calcite include masses, grains, stalactites, scalenohedrons [twelve-faced crystals, each face exhibiting three unequal sides], and rhombohedrons [six-faced crystals, each face the shape of a rhombus]. It is, however, characterized by the rhombohedron crystallization. Calcite is colourless or white and can become green, pink, peach, golden, orange, yellow, red, blue, grey, or black when other compounds blend with it during formation.

This mineral releases electrical impulses when placed under pressure, and is an energy amplifier. It is said to help the mind and body to remember - the mind, to remember information brought to bear during astral travel and channeling experiences; the body, to remember the state of perfection during dis-ease in order to return to the natural state of flawless-ness.

It is useful in multi-directional energy distribution; it appears that the energy, which is directed inward toward the central forces of the mineral, separates and returns at double the intensity. It brings forth a polarizing prismatic energy, which engenders a spectrum of energy to clear and to activate all of the chakras.

Calcite is a world teacher for all of humanity, facilitating macrocosmic awareness and appreciation of the creative forces of nature. It is an excellent stone when studying the arts and sciences.

Placement of the various colours of calcite upon the body has induced amplification of ones energy field. Placing calcite, of the appropriate chakra colour, upon the chakra, has not only cleared and activated that chakra, but has provided a "sweeping" action which cleared the remaining centers. The clear calcite and golden calcite are excellent energy sources for use at the crown chakra; the clear calcite has also been used at all chakras to provide for the amplification of the energy available.

Note that there are Calcite Enhydros which also combine the qualities of the Enhydro with the qualities of Calcite.

Calcite can be used to ameliorate dis-ease associated with the improper functioning of the kidneys, pancreas, and spleen. It can be used to promote the de-calcification of bone growths; in addition, it is a balancing agent for the assimilation of calcium within the body.

Calcite Phantoms have recently been discovered; each phantom is composed of minute Pyrite crystals. This combination of Calcite and Pyrite merges the properties of Calcite with those listed in the PYRITE section of this book. In addition, the properties of the phantom crystal are integrated, providing a dynamic stone for advancement.

Green calcite has also been used to rid the body of infections and to provide a barrier to diminish the effect of dis-ease producing micro-organisms; in addition, it has been used with Lepidolite and quartz to eliminate candida.

Optical quality calcite - Iceland Spar - has the additional property of double refraction. This stone can also be used to remind one of the double meaning of words and to, hence, assist one in communication during difficult conversations. It is an excellent mineral for use when cleansing and clearing the outer bodies.

Vibrates to the number 8.

CALEDONITE   [Astrological Sign of Pisces]

Caledonite crystallizes forming masses, coatings, and small elongated prismatic crystals. The colour ranges from a transparent dark blue to blue-green.

This mineral can be used to stimulate the navel chakra, throat chakra, and the third-eye chakra. It can initiate the actualization of psychic power and can facilitate intuition on the physical, etheric, and spiritual levels; it also assists in providing for coherency in communication of same.

It helps one in the realm of public speaking and induces calm action in speaking that which is foremost in ones mind.

It has been used to assist one in obtaining the state of astral projection, and provides for an opening of the pathways, during altered states, toward the expansion of knowledge.

It can be used in the alleviation of chills, to bring warmth to cold extremities, and to enhance the healing of wounds and disturbances of the epithelial tissues.

Vibrates to the number 7.

CALOMEL   [Astrological Sign of Aquarius]

Calomel crystallizes in the form of coatings, tabular crystals, and pyramid-like crystals. The colour ranges from white to yellow to brown.

The mineral can be used to produce a stabilizing influence while one is experiencing significant changes. It can also act as a catalyst to help one to initiate changes which would be beneficial.

It is enhances one vitality and provides for stimulation to the intellect. It helps to bring maturity to the intellect, assisting in emotional well-being.

It can be used to provide a leveling effect on the blood flow of the body, helping to calm the heart rate and to steady the blood pressure. It has also been used as a purgative.

Vibrates to the number 7.

CANCRINITE   [Astrological Sign of Aries]

Cancrinite crystallizes as masses and as prismatic crystals. The colour range includes pink, blue, white, orange, and yellow.

This mineral can be use to stimulate the heart chakra [pink], throat chakra [blue], solar plexus chakra [yellow], navel chakra [orange], and the crown chakra [white].

It enhances ones worldly abilities and powers and also assists one in courageous endeavors, facilitating approval from others, when required.

It also helps to produce strong will with respect to succumbing to undesirable temptations.

It can be used in the treatment of congestive disorders and infections, and to facilitate order within the elimination system. It has also been used in the treatment of disorders of the neck and throat.

Vibrates to the number 6.

CAPPELENITE   [Astrological Signs of Aquarius, Gemini, & Cancer]

Cappelenite crystallizes as green-brown prismatic crystals.

This mineral can assist one to overcome any negative attributes assigned to the astrological signs listed above.

It also provides an energy to stimulate awareness of any negative attribute and to provide insight to the action required to overcome.

It can be useful in grounding ones heart energy and in facilitating meditative states.

It provides for left brain/right brain balancing, as well as for balancing of the male/female energies.

It can be used to treat Vitamin A, Vitamin D, and calcium deficiencies. It has been used in the treatment of disorders of the teeth, bone structure, and eyes. It has also been successful when applied to enhance circulation.

Vibrates to the number 7.

CARNALLITE   [Astrological Sign of Aries]

Carnallite crystallizes in the form of granular masses and as crystals which hold a resemblance to hexagons. The colour ranges from white to yellow or from white to red.

This mineral can help to purify ones body and ones surroundings. It can be worn, carried, used as an elixir, or stationed in ones environment.

It acts as a calming, yet purifying agent. The energy is mainly concerned with the physical world, but also provides for a connective "thread" between the intellect and spirituality and between physical vitality and meditation.

It enhances passionate and procreative energies and directs one toward eloquence. It stimulates motive for activity and helps to facilitate the opportunity required to bring the activity to fruition.

It has been used during gaming to "give one the edge"; conscious direction of the energy is required.

It has also been used to assist in dispelling trauma associated with abuse.

It can be used to ameliorate potassium deficiencies and to relieve water retention. It can also be used in the treatment of degenerative conditions of the body.

Vibrates to the number 5.

CARNELIAN

Carnelian is a form of chalcedony and usually occurs in the uniform colour of red, orange, or red-brown. In addition to the properties listed in the AGATE and CHALCEDONY sections of this book, the following attributes are applicable.

This mineral stimulates analytical capabilities and precision. It provides for perceptiveness to situations and awakens ones inherent talents and adroitness. It is also used to produce inspiration from, and connected-ness with, the spiritual worlds.

It protects against envy, fear, and rage, and helps to banish sorrow from the emotional structure.

It further assists in providing for awareness of the association between the emotional state and the inner condition of the self.

It provides an energy conducive to the stabilization of energy in the home. It provides, also, a strong, yet tender energy when used in the mode of retreat. The message of carnelian is that since one is love, there is nothing to do but to offer the love - each offering of love bringing an exponential increase in the quantity of love returned. Pink carnelian, especially, can encourage love between parents and children, and between parents and parents.

Carnelian stimulates inquisitiveness and subsequent initiative.

It can be used to dispel apathy, indolence, and passivity.

The energy of carnelian is favorable with respect to cleansing negativity from other stones. When directed, it provides for a clearing action while directing any negative energy, which is within the area, toward the light of transmutation.

Carnelian is said to have been one of the stones used in the breastplate of the high priest.

It can assist one in drama and in pursuits related to theatrical presentations.

It is useful in work on the first, second, third, and fourth chakras, and can help to increase physical energy, personal power, creativity, and compassion.

In addition the utilization of Carnelian and Kammererite together, has been used to facilitate connection between the physical self and the higher-self.

The employment of Carnelian with Chlorite and Ruby Crystals has been used to eliminate psychic attack and to assist earth-bound spirits to leave an area. Gridding of these three minerals can protect one and ones environment from the return of negative energies.

It can be used in the treatment of neuralgia, gall stones, kidney stones, pollen allergies, and colds. It can also be useful to aid in the amelioration of disorders of the spine, spleen, and pancreas. It has been used as an elixir to help heal cuts and abrasions.

Vibrates to the numbers 5 and 6.

CARNIGORM   [See Smokey Quartz]

CARNOTITE   [Astrological Sign of Cancer]

Carnotite crystallizes as a yellow druse and in the form of yellow powder.

This mineral has been used to activate and to stimulate the nurturing aspects of ones nature, to promote and to advance a fostering and nurturing care and consideration, without activating the clinging nature and with the utilization of instinctive behavior and habit patterns.

It assists one in the establishment of belonging-ness, to create security of ones environment, and to be capable of honestly expressing need.

Carnotite instills the ability of direct response and instinctual behavior, and promotes the integration of all parts of the personality, contributing to the understanding of the habits and reactions in any given environment with respect to ones instinctive behavior.

It has been used in the treatment of the digestive system, the stomach, breasts, sympathetic nervous system, regulation of body fluids, assimilation of the necessary nutrients, and in childbirth.

Preparation of an elixir via the normal method is <u>not</u> recommended.

Vibrates to the number 6.

CARROLLITE [Astrological Sign of Pisces]

Carrollite crystallizes as granular masses and as octahedral crystals. The colour is a silvery grey; the silvery-grey being partially covered by the colour range of peach to red to violet.

This mineral can be useful for providing grounding of each chakra; it can also facilitate the closure of the chakras, allowing for protection of the self against psychic attack.

The message of carrollite is that love transcends fear; since one establishes everything that transpires within ones personal realm [i.e., one creates ones own reality], each response to each perception is personal - the mind determining the perception, and the emotions determining the fear.

It can be used to enhance the voice and to stimulate clarity with respect to the verbalization of communication between one and other-worldly beings.

Carrollite can add swiftness to recovery. It can also be used in the treatment of ambulatory complaints and to aid in tissue regeneration. An elixir applied to burns can provide soothing and can diminish the manifestation of the burn.

Vibrates to the number 9.

CASSITERITE [Astrological Sign of Sagittarius]
[Also Known As Tinstone]

Cassiterite is a form of tin which crystallizes in masses, grains, and pyramid-type or short prismatic crystals. The colour range includes yellow, black, and red-brown.

This crystal is quite lustrous and can be used for grounding [black], energy stimulation [red], and intellect actuation [yellow]. It can provide for a syncronicity within the self and can provide for protection from physical dangers.

It helps to eliminate feelings of separateness and prejudice. It can be used to ameliorate rejection, to dispel energy related to disapproval, and to encourage optimism.

It is useful in the fields of mathematics, astrology, and astronomy to provide precise insight into problems which are encountered.

It can be used in the treatment of obesity and hormonal imbalance, and to balance the functions of the secretory organs.

Vibrates to the numbers 2 and 8.

CATLINITE
[Astrological Sign of Sagittarius]
[Also Known as Pipestone]

Catlinite is a solidified clay-like mineral which is of a red-pink colour.

This mineral has been used for hundreds of years by the Native American Indian; sacred pipes and renditions of totems [i.e., fetishes] have been carved from catlinite and used in sacred ceremonies, as protective devices, and to enhance skills.

The American culture is, today, drawn to many of the "old ways" and is becoming more aware of the power of ceremony to enhance a pursuit. Many of us have looked to our lineage to try to discover even a small connection to the Native American Indian heritage, assuming that the connection would give us the privilege of using the same ceremonies.

May I suggest that if you truly want to participate in the aspects of historical Native American Indian ceremonial ways, please read as much literature as possible and communicate with and request help from the Native Americans.

If you wish to use pipestone in an intuitive way, I encourage you and suggest that you ask for guidance from the spirit world to provide you with the "correctness" which is both necessary and required.

Would that one could walk in the shoes of another, but only at the times that one would choose.

Vibrates to the numbers 2 and 3.

CAT'S EYE
[Astrological Signs of Capricorn, Taurus, & Aries]

Cat's eye, usually a variety of quartz or chrysoberyl, exhibits a chatoyancy which allows the stone to resemble a cat's eye. This chatoyancy is usually caused from the inclusion of straight fibers of asbestos. The colour range is endless due to the numerous stones in which it may occur. The properties of the mineral which hosts the cat's eye configuration are also applicable.

The structure of this mineral represents happiness and serenity. It can also amplify ones "luck".

It can act to stimulate intuition and to enhance awareness.

It is effective in dispelling unwanted energy from ones etheric fields. It also provides a protective energy to the user.

This mineral can be used in the treatment of eye disorders, to increase vision responses during night-driving, and to relieve facial and sciatic affectations. It has also been used to relieve headaches and pains associated with the nervous system.

Vibrates to the number 6.

CAVANSITE   [Astrological Sign of Aquarius]

Cavansite crystallizes in the orthorhombic system with the colour ranging from green-blue to ink blue.

This mineral has been used to stimulate the intuition, to instill second-sight, and to activate channeling abilities. It is an excellent stone for psychic healing and to provide protection during same such that the dis-ease will not have the ability to return.

It can also be used to enable the focusing of the intuitive self, via the third-eye, at the etheric level, to induce to memory the portions of ones life or character which require attention.

It has been used to bring thoughtfulness to ones environment and to stimulate the pensive action which precedes unwarranted reaction. It prompts reflection, inspires conception of new ideas, and assists in the removal of faulty thoughts and beliefs.

Cavansite has been used in gridding activities to further the instinct and to modify deleterious behavior patterns.

This mineral has been used in the treatment of disorders of the eye, the teeth (bone loss associations), and the blood. It can be used to assist in the release of endorphins, to promote healing at the cellular level, and to stabelize the pulse rate.

Vibrates to the number 5.

CELESTITE   [Astrological Sign of Gemini]
                                            [Also Known as Celestine]

Celestite crystallizes as nodules, granular masses, and as tabular orthorhombic crystals. The colour range includes blue [the most beautiful being from Madagascar], white, yellow, orange [usually massive and on matrix], red, and red-brown.

It is quite good for mental activities - one can use this stone for help in analysis of complex ideas or physical realities by synchronizing ones conscious with the mineralogical structure; this integration of consciousness and instinct allows one to recognize the method of approach. It renders, in outline form, the range of actions most easily accomplished, such that one may both recognize and comprehend all facets of a problem, situation, or idea. It actually attunes one to heightened powers of rationality.

It works well with the comprehensive state, allowing one to recall and to acknowledge both ones spirituality and the gifts of the Divine.

It is a stone for balance, acting as an equilibrant to outside forces, and stabilizing the yin-yang values within ones energy field. It assists in the alignment of the n-dimensional energy centers with those of the ethereal domain, and promotes continence in clearing and perfecting the chakras.

It can also promote a pleasant disposition and can provide for fluency in communication. Celestite has "stories to tell". It can provide for access to, and transfer of, information from the purity of the angelic realms. It assists in clairaudient endeavors, affording lucid, distinct, and articulate verbalization of the messages received. It also contains an innate wisdom which is accessible to the user; the data, from within the stone, is useful with respect to ones advancement in the spiritual kingdom, and to the aspects of perfection and the patterns involved in the attainment of that which is desired. In this manner, it can help one to achieve that which would be helpful as the end-product of manifestation, and to recognize the difference between worldly manifestation and a manifestation which would further ones development.

It is also a stone for astral travel, providing for the freedom to access pre-determined sites and assisting one to surrender to the inner peace required. It is an excellent assistant for dream recall.

It is a "bright hope" in days of despair, bringing calmness and harmony to ones life, and providing for increase in ones avocation. It sometimes appears that the stone is inhabited by the "fairy of good fortune"; the dismissal of worries, the freedom of movement, and the energetic pursuit of intangibility being fostered -with clarity of, and approval by, the intellect.

It is an excellent stone for use in the pursuit of music, in the production of delicate arts [e.g., watercolour, scrimshaw, jewelry fabrication and design, etc.], and, especially, in the quest of bliss.

Celestite is an exquisite stone to give - in the spirit of love and with the blessing of respect.

It is an excellent healing stone. The blue celestite seems to cleanse the area of affectation, transmuting pain and chaos into light and love.

It has been used in the treatment of disorders of the eyes, to increase the range of hearing, and to balance mental dysfunctions. It advances the order of the cellular state, balancing the structure and facilitating elimination of the toxins of negativity and destruction. It has been used to ameliorate digestive disorders, and in the treatment of a dysfunctional intestinal system.

Vibrates to the numbers 8 and 2.

CERULEITE   [Astrological Sign of Taurus]

Ceruleite crystallizes as masses, sometimes comprised of tiny rhombic octahedral crystals. The colour is a beautiful cerulean or azure blue.

This mineral is useful for work on the throat chakra; providing both relief from throat ailments and a promoting a clear, precise, and explicitly accurate channel for communication. It has also been used to promote distinction during the transfer of knowledge from the channeling state.

It relates to ones lifework, providing support and insight toward that pre-defined goal. It is helpful when searching for employment or when arriving at a decision concerning a future avocation; in the quest for employment, the energy of ceruleite stimulates the actualization of both intuition and good fortune - helping one to determine which avenue to pursue, and, upon establishment of the path, enables one to secure the position which will bring the most advancement and the most evolution toward development.

It can be used to decrease problems associated with dehydration. It has also been used in the treatment of the fear of water, the fear of drowning, and the fear of success. It can be used to stabilize the muscular structure, to provide ease to the movement of the limbs, and to provide strength to weak areas of the body.

Vibrates to the master number 44.

CERUSSITE   [Astrological Sign of Virgo]

Cerussite crystallizes in the form of masses, grains, stalactites, crystal clusters, and single crystals. It occasionally occurs in the form of six-rayed twinned crystals, comprised of three individual crystals in a configuration of a star-like formation. It also, occasionally, occurs in a structure similar to that resembling branching trees with icicles. The colour range includes transparent white, grey, grey-black, clear with a tinge of blue, clear with a tinge of green, and pale yellow.

This mineral is a wonderful grounding stone and allows one to feel "comfortable" and "at-home" in all environments. It is a useful stone for business-travelers, as well as pleasure-travelers. It allows one to easily adapt to situations and to change as is required; it enables one to realize that these changes are transient and, hence, helps one to be accommodating.

It helps one to understand responsibility and to increase the capabilities required to sustain ones composure. It provides for the strength to manage the conditions of ones reality, relieving tension and anxiety, and allowing one to recognize that which one can and must change - and that which one must release from ones being.

Cerussite encourages growth in all areas of ones life. It assists by providing the strength of wisdom to all areas of relationships. It can be utilized to help one with decision-making and to initiate diversity in ones life.

It is excellent in both stimulating and enhancing communication; it is quite conducive to all aspects of correspondence. It also assists one in the art of complete listening. It has been used to balance the left brain and right brain, encouraging creativity in the intellect as well as encouraging intelligently directed ingenuity.

It helps to align the network of the nervous system and to provide for free flow of energy. It is also a powerful grounding stone, providing for a clear connection to the powerful basis of love.

It can be used to alleviate introversion, to provide tact to situations, and to instill the art and beauty of cooperation.

It is excellent to use in the ceremonial aspect, promoting a bond between participants while sustaining grounding of the energy centers. It also provides for guidance and assured-ness to activities.

It is useful in helping one to recognize those who have been a part of ones past-lives. The star-like configuration can also facilitate access to a connection with other-planetary beings, allowing for the remembering of other worlds and other times.

As an elixir it is an excellent energizer and protector of house plants; it can also be used in the garden or field situation to help to relieve infestations. It has been used in the home environment to protect against pests.

It can be used in the treatment of insomnia, in disorders affecting the coordination of voluntary movements, and to ameliorate mental discontinuity. It can provide strength and renewal to the inner organs and skeletal system. It is an excellent stone for increasing the vitality of those experiencing dis-ease.

Vibrates to the number 2.

CHABAZITE   [Astrological Sign of Virgo]

Chabazite crystallizes in the form of crystals exhibiting the configurations of rhombohedrons [similar to a cube], hexagons, and tabular hexagonal prisms. The colour range includes colourless, red, yellow, pink to red, and green.

This mineral may be used to help in structuring ones life, allowing for the focus of the energy to be directed to the area which would be most beneficial at the time. It allows one to be "alone in the midst of a crowd", providing for centering and contemplation in all surroundings.

It is conducive to gaining and maintaining the meditative state and assists one in the attainment of the depths of the central light of universal peace.

The message of the energy of chabazite is that although reality relates only to the spirit, the intellect which benefits the spirit is invulnerable. It consequently produces a stillness of the mind which allows the intellect to adjust to the higher realms, bringing forth those thoughts and realizations which are conducive to, and actually stimulate, higher learning.

It has been used to lessen the degrees of addiction and to both comfort and stabilize the addictive personality. It allows the adjacent energies to transform to positive forces, and brings the focus of the user toward recovery, toward rejuvenation, and toward reclamation of the true self.

When focused properly, this mineral initiates a chain-reaction of energies within the body, allowing one to sustain oneself for long periods. Endurance, perseverance, and tenacity are enhanced.

The initiative to take control of ones life is instilled with the utilization of this mineral.

Chabazite can be useful as an elixir, taken as a "spring tonic" or applied locally to sore muscles. It can also be helpful to lessen conditions of obesity, to increase hormonal balance, and to treat disorders of the thyroid; topical application of the stone or internal use of an elixir can be beneficial to these afflictions.

Vibrates to the number 3.

CHALCANTHITE   [Astrological Sign of Aquarius]

Chalcanthite crystallizes in the form of flattened crystals, masses, stalactites, and reniform and fibrous structures. The colour ranges through the various shades of blue and may occasionally have a green tinge. Since the mineral is readily soluble in water, it may "disappear" if not stored in a humidity-free environment.

This mineral can be used to eliminate the feeling of abandonment and restraint, and to assist one in continuing toward ones goals without confinement.

It is an excellent mineral for activation of the throat chakra, bringing a smooth flow of communication and elocution in all situations.

It has also been used to assist one in the selection of choice - the energy of Chalcanthite tends to reflect the choice of preference which will further ones objectives and desires.

This mineral has been used in the treatment of arthritis, to reduce the presence of free-radical oxides, to cleanse the arteries, to alleviate water retention, and to treat disorders of the reproductive system.

Do not prepare an elixir of this mineral via the normal method.

Vibrates to the number 5.

CHALCEDONY   [Elemental Astrological Signs of Cancer
                                                              & Sagittarius]

Chalcedony is considered as a member of the quartz family. It is either transparent, translucent, or opaque. It occurs as stalactites, in botryoidal form, and in the lining of cavities of rocks. It occasionally contains a small amount of opal.

Some of the many types of chalcedony which are discussed in the appropriate sections of this book include agate, bloodstone, chrysoprase, carnelian, chert, flint, jasper, onyx, sardonyx, touchstone, and petrified wood; the following properties apply to these stones as well as to the remaining forms of chalcedony.

It was used as a sacred stone by the Native American Indians, promoting stability within the ceremonial activities of the tribes. It has successfully been used to provide a pathway for receiving thought transmissions.

Chalcedony is useful for balancing the energy of the body, mind, emotions, and spirit.

It is a stone to encourage "brotherhood" among all. It symbolizes benevolence and good will, the benevolence stemming from the nurturing energy within the stone. It alleviates hostilities, irritability, and melancholy.   It enhances generosity, responsiveness, and receptivity.

It can be used to improve the assimilation of minerals and to help combat build-up of materials in the veins. It is said to cure varying forms of dementia, to rectify senility, and to increase mental stability.

Vibrates to the number 9.

CHALCOPYRITE   [Astrological Sign of Capricorn]

Chalcopyrite crystallizes in the form of tetrahedrals with sphenoidal faces, in octahedrals, and compact botryoidal or reniform masses. The colour range includes brass-yellow which may tarnish to green or iridescent. It often occurs with copper and/or zinc.

This mineral has been used to assist one in finding "lost" objects; it also often "disappears" to accumulate information which will be beneficial to the user.

It can be used to enhance ones abilities of perception and to strengthen ones contact with the ancient cultures of the universe. It acts as a connective force between one and the other cultures such that one may readily receive information. It is a "stone of the mystic", bringing information for the self and for others relative to the ethereal energies surrounding. It possesses an energy which can remove energy blockages and can totally open the crown chakra, cleansing and activating at the same time. It is excellent for use in meditation [no-mind] and assists one in attaining and in maintaining the state.

Chalcopyrite can inspire the infinite energies of the universe to activate the maintaining energies of the body, assisting one in the achievement of the paramount state of physical perfection. It allows one to recognize the uniformity of the universe and to understand that each portion of the universe preserves an intrinsic perfection in order to allow the unfolding of irreproachability.

It has been used to assist in acupressure/acupuncture treatments to incite the movement of the Chi, to treat disorders of the brain, to relieve the pressure of tumors and growths and to constrict same, and to assist in the natural composition and formation of the cells. It has been used to assist in the prevention of RNA/DNA damage and can be used in repair of same. It can be used in the treatment of bronchitis and disorders of the lungs. It has been used in the treatment of violent and/or highly infective dis-ease, as well as by others who are working with those affected, in order to provide protection from the affectation. It has also been used to lessen fevers, to reduce inflammation, and to promote hair growth.

Vibrates to the number 9.

CHALCOSIDERITE   [Astrological Sign of Scorpio]

Chalcosiderite crystallizes as crusts and prismatic crystals. The colour range is from tree-green to dark green.

This mineral can be used to soften the effects of stimulation to the third-eye; this is especially useful in healing when one uses the "laying-on-of-stones" - it softens that which is brought to the surface from the depths of ones inner being.

It promotes concentration and persistence in endeavors and assists in the activities of astrology and future-telling, stimulating the understanding of all information intuitively presented with respect to the unknown.

It is a "stone of enchantment", allowing for the direction of "crystal clear" energy toward another, for purposes which are "for the good of all".

It is said to have been used in mystical rites and ceremonies by the ancient ones of Babylonia.

Chalcosiderite has been used, with conscious direction, to facilitate one blending with the environment such that ones presence is not recognized.

It can be used in the treatment of arthritis and neuralgia. It can also help to relieve the symptoms of colds and infections.

Vibrates to the number 5.

CHAROITE   DEC 2022   [Astrological Signs of Sagittarius & Scorpio]

Charoite crystallizes in the form of masses and as tiny druse upon a host mineral. The major discovery location is Russia, and the colour range includes purple and pink to purple, sometimes with inclusions of quartz and manganese.

Charoite is a stone for this age. It provides for a synthesis between the heart and crown chakras and combines the higher spiritual dimensions with unconditional love from the physical plane. It allows one to recognize, to integrate, and to understand those attributes exhibited on the physical plane which are thought to emit a negative vibration; hence, facilitating the acceptance of others, regardless of the development and/or actualization level in which they appear.

This mineral provides for transmutation of negativity and for grounding to the spiritual self. It can be useful in cleansing the auric body, filling the chakras with a loving spiritual emotion of purity, and in assisting one in comprehension of self-inflicted "lessons". It enhances ones "giving" nature, opening the heart to allow one to "see" with love, and to recognize the connection between "All".

It awakens analytical abilities and precision, providing for scrutiny in the investigation of the unknown.

It instills a "brotherhood of light" between the individual, the dualities, and the total environment of the planet; hence, promulgating the idea of relationships and stimulating flexibility with respect to "letting go".

It sustains ones attention span, allows for discrimination between validity and fiction, and helps one to realize that "as one door closes, another opens". It is a "stone for transformation", within this world, and from this world to another.

It also can assist one in realizing that one is, in fact, where one should be during this very moment.

It is a "bestower" of "good", bringing forth the ultimate benefits in situations encountered.

It assists in the actualization of "second-sight" and visioning.

It aligns the meridians in the upper portion of the body, activating the mechanism which expedites the approval of the self while further providing for an active pursuit of forward motion; the forward motion rapidly occurring when the total integration between the heart and spirit produce complete alignment of the physical body with the perfect self.

Charoite tends to transmute the symptoms of illness and dis-ease to well-ness. It can be used to treat disorders of the eyes and heart, to provide improvement in autistic pursuits, to allay headaches and general aches and pains, to improve degraded conditions of the liver [e.g., due to excess alcohol], to improve degraded conditions of the pancreas [e.g., due to excess refined sugars], and to stimulate and regulate the blood pressure and the pulse rate.

It can be an excellent cleanser of the body when taken as an elixir.

Vibrates to the number 7.

CHERT   [Astrological Sign of Leo]
                                                   [Also Known as Hornstone]

Chert is a form of chalcedony which resembles flint, but is more brittle. The colour range is from grey to black.

In addition to the properties listed in the CHALCEDONY section of this book, the following attributes apply.

This mineral can be used to provide stability and to assist one in remembering, both during the daily routine and during specific times when one decides to either "look-back" at this life or to view previous lives. It can also be used to help one to find lost items.

Chert was important in the ceremonies of the Algonquin Indians. It is said to have been used as an implement with which to request the presence of the spirit guides.

It can be used in the treatment of chemical imbalances, to soothe allergic reactions, and to aid in the decrease of fatty deposits.

Vibrates to the numbers 2 and 9.

CHIASTOLITE   [Astrological Sign of Libra]
                                                [Also Known as Cross-Stone]

Chiastolite is a variety of andalusite which occurs in the form of stout crystals, exhibiting the axis and angles in a different colour from the rest and producing a coloured cross. The properties discussed in the ANDALUSITE section of this book are in addition to those listed below.

The "cross-stone" was, in yesteryear, associated with deflection of the "evil eye". It is now used as a sign of devotion, especially, devotion toward awareness, which can, in itself, dispel negativity. The energy of chiastolite opposes and thwarts contrary action by transmuting dissension to the state harmony.

It signifies both death and re-birth, bringing one to the state of realization with respect to understanding immortality.

It is a bridge for "crossing-over" - providing the means of transportation as well as the unobstructed avenue.

It can be quite helpful during the state of change, assisting one to traverse disquieting situations and to gain a foothold in the new. It can also be instrumental in both astral and mind travel, again providing the "password" for entry.

It can also be used for problem-solving and to provide insight to answers to mysterious occurrences.

It assists in both creativity and practicality, balancing ones perspective in all matters.

It is helpful to the maintenance of spirituality during illness - being readily available to provide insight into those ideas and ideals which stimulate protective forces and perfection.

It can be used to lessen fevers, to balance the flow of blood, to increase the secretion of milk in nursing mothers, and to repair chromosome damage.

Vibrates to the numbers 3 and 4.

CHILDRENITE   [Astrological Sign of Leo]

Childrenite crystallizes in the form brown or yellow plates and tabular crystals.

This mineral can be used to control temper and to promote receptiveness to new ideas. It is useful for facilitating growth on the emotional, intellectual, and physical planes. It may also be used to encourage endurance in relationships.

It is an excellent stone for the enhancement of business pursuits and resources, assisting in both procurement and beneficial results.

It can be used in the treatment of fevers, flu, measles, chicken pox, mumps, etc., especially via providing a protective barrier against the transmittal of "communicable" dis-ease.

Vibrates to the number 8.

CHINESE WRITING ROCK   [Astrological Sign of Pisces]

Chinese writing rock is a porphyry with lath-like crystals of, usually, feldspar, grouped into patterns resembling the Chinese script.

This mineral helps one to access information from both the ancient sacred texts and the akashic records, providing for clarity in translation with respect to the writing and furthering the interpretation of that which is written.

It is an excellent stone for dreaming, assisting one into the dream state and directing ones dreams toward the subject that one has pre-determined.

It is a stone for re-affirmation, re-alignment, and re-commitment; it validates and then helps one to execute plans and strategies. It also helps one to adjust to change, to accept responsibility for newly found personal freedom, and to stimulate originality in living.

It can be used in the treatment of disorders of the eyes, spine, and legs. It can also be used to increase the assimilation of protein, to treat malaria and yellow fever, and to soothe the muscular structures of the hands. It is excellent as an elixir in all aspects of energy utilization.

Vibrates to the number 3.

Chlorite is the designation for a group of minerals. The minerals of the chlorite collection which are addressed in the appropriate sections of this book include CLINOCHLORE, DIABANTITE, DAPHNITE, KAMMERERITE, and PENNINITE.

These minerals, in addition to the other chlorite minerals, also possess the following qualities.

Chlorite is one of the most favorable healing stones. Worn, carried, placed within ones environment, or used as an elixir, the properties of chlorite are overwhelmingly positive.

It brings the energy to enhance cooperation and stimulates ones personal affinity with "All". It is a purifier and is quite useful for cleansing the aura, the chakras, and the energy meridians.

It attacks anger, hostility, and exasperation, and dissipates the dissenting energy.

Forms of chlorite have been used with amethyst to remove unwanted energy implants; the presence of chlorite and amethyst within ones energy field has also successfully protected against both energy implants and psychic attack.

Please note that a type of Chlorite which is now available from Russia is named "Serefina" and derivatives of same. It has been used to enhance circulation, both of energy and of the blood. Used as an elixir it has relieved "chills" and has also assisted in weight loss (seems to be a "melting away" of fat). In addition, it has been used as an antihistamine. During the meditative state, it has produced celestial contact with the highest order of angels, with information imparted which was extremely relevant and of vast importance to the users. Used at the crown chakra, it has aligned the chakras and has bestowed a centering effect. At the heart chakra, it seems to clean the area and to promote protection and love concurrently. It assists one in seeing and in understanding the stages of ones life and acts to provide insight to changes required to promote peace and happiness within ones life.

The employment of Chlorite with Carnelian and Ruby Crystals has been used to eliminate psychic attack and to assist earth-bound spirits to leave an area. Gridding of these three minerals can protect one and ones environment from the return of negative energies.

Chlorite can be used to increase the assimilation of Vitamins A and E, calcium, iron, and magnesium. It has also been used to eliminate toxins from the body, to stimulate the production of beneficial bacteria within the body, and to act as an anesthetic during times of pain. It can also be used to remove growths from the outer layers of the skin and to diminish the appearance of "liver spots".

Chlorite vibrates to the number 9. Serefina vibrates to the number 5.

CHLOROCALCITE   [Astrological Sign of Aquarius]
                                           [Also Known as Hydrophilite]

Chlorocalcite crystallizes in the form of encrustations and as crystals configured similar to cubes. The colour is white.

It combines the properties listed in the CHLORITE and CALCITE sections of this book and also exhibits the following attributes. It is a dynamite stone for furthering analytical capabilities, study habits, and exactness.

It can be used in meditation to aid in viewing previous civilizations and in understanding the transitions [i.e., why? how? when? where? what? etc.] which occurred.

It is also a calming agent and can be used to produce an inner reflection concerning that which can potentially cause stress in ones life.

This mineral can be used to ameliorate calcium deficiencies, either via an elixir or by placement upon the body.

Vibrates to the number 7 and the master number 77.

"CHOCOLATE MARBLES"   [Astrological Sign of Scorpio]

Chocolate marbles are similar in appearance to round chocolate spheres. They are actually petrified mud balls from volcanic action [found, for example, in Arizona, USA].

They are joyful stones and, when held, tend to eliminate worries and to enhance ones state of well-being. They help with transitions, with variations in ones life, and to relieve states of anger.

This mineral is mainly for the young and old; the young, because they have not yet lost the wisdom which they brought to Earth during this lifetime; the old, because they have regained and supplemented the wisdom which they brought to the Earth during this lifetime.

They also provide a grounding force, allowing for an increase in mental faculties, while stimulating amiability toward others.

They can be used in the treatment of potassium deficiency, disorders of the throat, and in the dissipation of growths.

Vibrates to the number 8.

CHROMITE   [Astrological Sign of Gemini]

Chromite crystallizes in the form of masses and octahedral crystals. The colour range includes brown, black, and, occasionally, a blend of yellow-red which usually occurs in the formation of thin mineralogical sections.

This mineral can provide a state of non-reaction to unpleasant situations. It leads one to awareness and incites suspicion, when necessary, to protect ones physical, emotional, and intellectual beings.

It further provides for cleverness and perceptiveness coupled with initiative and independence. It also stimulates intrepidity.

It can be used to stimulate the energy of the throat and provides an excellent energy to supplement the process of "toning".

It is a good stone for use during for healing work on a cellular level. It can also be used to stimulate the absorption of Vitamins A and D, to aid in the treatment of disorders of the eyes, and to provide strength to those inflicted with inveterate disorders.

Vibrates to the number 1.

CHRYSANTHEMUM STONE   [Astrological Signs of Taurus
                                                        & Aquarius]

Chrysanthemum stone is comprised of dolomite, gypsum-bearing clay, limestone, or porphyry with lath-like crystals of andalusite, celestite, feldspar, or calcite which are grouped into a pattern resembling blooming autumnal chrysanthemum flowers. This stone has been found in Japan, China, Canada, and in the Lake Superior region of the USA.

In addition to the attributes listed below, the attributes of the minerals comprising the stone also apply.

This stone allows one to take the time to drift slowly through the blossoms of life instead of trampling the flowers of experience. It is a "stone of harmony and change", encouraging one to understand the correlation between the two. It enhances compatibility, is excellent for renewal of relationships, and helps one to progress toward unity.

It is a parody of the "Peter Pan" principle which has been taken to its logical extremes - one need not loose the radiance of youth nor "grow-up"; one needs only to progress toward spiritual growth while remaining in a state of fresh, fun-loving, innocence. It also helps one to understand that the flower is always within the self; both prior to and after, as well as, during ones physical experience on this plane.

It brings the message to enjoy each moment, allowing one to both recognize and to understand that time, so often, does not become precious and cherished until it is already past. It helps one to "bloom" and to progress on the path toward the perfect self.

The chrysanthemum stone inspires, enlivens, and enkindles. It is quite useful in providing the impetus to begin, or to continue, that which is important in the path of development. It dispels superficiality and mental distractions which can often weaken the mind.

It dispels ignorance, bigotry, and self-righteous attitudes, showing one that a prime reason for being in the physical body is to bring love to all and to, thus, further the amplification of the positive-ness of this world. It also helps to eliminate jealousy, animosity, and resentment from ones character.

It assists in the removal of obstructions from ones path, provides calm confidence, and increases ones inherent strength of character. It yields insight to the equality of "man" and helps one to understand the idea of respect.

It also brings one the joy of achievement, helping to support endeavors to fruition.

The ability to "see the big picture" is facilitated and narrow-minded attitudes are dissipated.

It is helpful for time travel, assisting one to, via inner sight, progress or ascend to the specific time periods desired.

It can be used to lessen the traumas associated with physical maturity, to aid in transitions, and to stimulate radiance. It can be used in the treatment of disorders of the eyes, skin, and skeletal system. It is also useful in combating growths and in eliminating toxins.

It can be used as an elixir, worn, carried, or placed in ones environment.

Vibrates to the number 3.

CHRYSOBERYL   [Astrological Sign of Leo]

Chrysoberyl crystallizes in the form of hexagonal-type and tabular crystals. It occasionally occurs in the form of a six-ray star configuration comprised of three individual crystals. The colour range includes various shades of green, yellow, honey, and red.

Alexandrite and cymophane are both varieties of chrysoberyl. The properties listed below apply to the yellow and honey chrysoberyl and are also supplementary properties to the qualities, which are listed in this book, for ALEXANDRITE and CYMOPHANE.

This mineral provides for increase in personal power and spirituality. It synthesizes the energy of the third chakra with the energy of the seventh chakra, providing for utilization of the intellect in ones endeavors.

It helps to both open and activate the crown chakra and brings the energy of astuteness to the furtherance of spirituality.

It is a "stone of immortality", assisting one to both overcome and to progress toward excellence. It elevates ones sense of self-worth and helps one to understand and to actualize the intrinsic state of perfection which is available.

Chrysoberyl increases generosity and "charitability". It allows one to forgive family members or friends who may have performed an injustice. It brings peace of mind to the user and promotes understanding of interactive relationships.

It also promotes the feeling of peace within the physical and intellectual bodies and helps one to be charitable to the self.

It allows one to see the good in ones surroundings and to understand opposing views.

The energy of the stone is strong, yet mellifluous. It promotes continuity of those aspects of ones life which would lend themselves toward developmental continuity. It also helps one to release and to discontinue unproductive energy patterns.

It helps to facilitate permanence in physical healing by helping one to both understand and integrate the reasons behind the disorder. Using chrysoberyl concurrently with other stones, which emit the requisite healing energy for specific disorders, actually tends to enhance the energy transmittal from the other stones.

It has been used in the treatment of disorders of incontinuity, to regulate the secretion of adrenalin and cortin, to moderate the cholesterol levels, and to ameliorate disorders of the liver, pancreas, and kidneys. The action of the energy of chrysoberyl also tends to stimulate "un-infection" to infected parts of the body.

Vibrates to the number 6.

CHRYSOCOLLA   [Astrological Signs of Gemini, Virgo, & Taurus]

Chrysocolla crystallizes in the form of crusts, layers, masses, botryoidal configurations, and microscopic needle-like crystals. There is also a form called drusy chrysocolla which exhibits small crystals covering one or more of the faces of a specimen. Colours range from blue to green and are sometimes brown to black.

Chrysocolla in its gemmy state is known as gem silica.

This mineral revitalizes and calms the base, navel, and solar plexus chakras. At the heart chakra, it can help to ease emotional heartache and to give renewed strength and balance; it further increases ones capacity to love. At the throat chakra, it can give strength and balance in expression and communication; it also helps one to refrain from verbalization when silence would be beneficial to all concerned. It provides for grounding while transmitting and furthering these stabilizing and balancing energies.

It can help one to become attuned to the Earth and can provide direction to assist one in increasing the ionization of the atmosphere.

It can also assist one in communication with the spiritual forces of the Earth and can help one to understand that which is required in order that the Earth may heal itself.

It can produce great inner strength, helping to sustain one during stressful and/or long-enduring situations. It promotes and enhances physical vitality, stimulating the initiative qualities of ones character.

It promotes harmony by helping one to release the distress culminating from negative emotions; e.g., animosity, indignation, remorse, etc. It also furthers ones understanding of others, while helping one to recognize that there is, indeed, more to life than that which is evidenced in materiality.

Chrysocolla purifies the home and the environment, and can work to eliminate negativity from within a person. It imparts an energy conducive to stabilizing the home and re-building relationships.

The drusy chrysocolla, occasionally appearing with quartz crystals, combines the energies of the mineral with the clarity of force, enabling acceleration in the process for which it is used.

Gemmy chrysocolla also enhances the rapidity of the energy amelioration. In addition, it stimulates the crown chakra and provides for alignment of the physical structure to the ethereal network; this further stimulates the action toward perfection of the physical state. It also initiates powerful visionary experiences when used at the third-eye.

In healing, chrysocolla helps one to attune to the perfection of the universe, providing for insight into that which is necessary to the physical body, intellect, and emotions in order to facilitate re-alignment toward the perfect state of health.

It can help to regenerate the pancreas, to assist in the regulation of insulin, and to balance the blood sugar. It can strengthen the muscular structure of the legs, arms, back, and abdomen. It has been used in the treatment of blood disorders [e.g., leukemia, etc.] and cellular inadequacies. It has also been used to ameliorate disorderly conditions of the lungs [e.g., tuberculosis, asthma, emphysema, etc.] and has produced excellent results in re-oxygenation of the cellular structure - in fact, it seems to furnish greater lung capacity and to instill increased breathing capabilities. It has also been used in the treatment of muscle cramps and spasms.

Vibrates to the number 5.

CHRYSOLITE   [See Peridot]

CHRYSOPRASE   [Astrological Sign of Libra]

Chrysoprase crystallizes in the same form as chalcedony and is actually an apple-green type of chalcedony. In addition to the attributes listed in the CHALCEDONY section of this book, the following properties are applicable.

This mineral is useful for balancing the yin-yang energy and for aligning the chakras with the ethereal plane. It activates, opens, and energizes the heart chakra, bringing the energy necessary to the physical body, through the loving energy of the heart.

It instills a state of grace within the user, facilitating deep meditative states, compassion, and clemency. It provides for non-judgmental attitudes, acceptance of others, acceptance of self, and savoir-faire.

Chrysoprase helps one to recognize the trinity within oneself; assisting one in extricating oneself from states of imperfection. It encourages the maximum beneficial outcome to situations and facilitates adaptability. It can also help to heal a "broken heart", enabling one to understand the patterns of growth.

It can reduce superiority or inferiority complexes and can confer fluency of speech with presence of mind.

It has also been used to encourage fidelity in business and personal affairs.

It has been used in the treatment of disorders of the heart, to increase the assimilation of Vitamin C, to increase ones dexterity, and to ameliorate frailty and infirmity. It can also be used to treat the reproductive organs and to stimulate an increase in fertility [when consciously directed].

Vibrates to the number 3.

CHRYSOTILE   [Astrological Sign of Taurus]
                                        [Also Known As Chrysotite]

Chrysotile crystallizes in the form of flexible and easily separating delicate fibers. The colour range includes green-white, olive-green, green, green-black, yellow, and brown, brown-yellow, brown-red, and white.

This mineral can be used to bring a bonding action between one and the object of ones desires, such that one may easily release the object whenever the need has been fulfilled.

It brings an energy of resourcefulness and integrity and serves to instill honesty and sincerity.

In addition, the energy of Chrysotile assists one in "finding" the "true" self by clearing the "baggage" of the past and by recognizing ones individual controlling modes. It assists one in the release of control over others, but assists one in maintaining control with respect to ones life.

It has been used in telepathic endeavors to both send and to receive messages, assisting one in assuring delivery and acceptance of the information.

It assists one in recognizing the extension of occurrences to facilitate knowledge with ease and advances that approach to each event/condition/experience such that each encounter is with absolute precision and beneficial construction.

Chrysotile has been used in the treatment of disorders of the veins and arteries, the pores of the skin (i.e., inflammations and abrasions), lung disorders (including emphysema and irritations precipitating coughs), multiple sclerosis, tissue regeneration, and chronic fatigue.

Due to the asbestos content, do not prepare an elixir of this mineral via the normal method.

Vibrates to the number 8 and the master number 55.

CHUDOBAITE   [Astrological Sign of Taurus]

Chudobaite crystallizes as small crystals, pink in colour.

This mineral can help one to overcome obstacles in the physical, mental, and emotional realms.

It can also be used to stimulate and to activate the heart chakra and to bring love into ones life, the love being a self-love; please note that, often, when one has finally attained an egoless self-love, love from "without" manifests in the physical reality.

Chudobaite allows one to "flow within the river of humanity" and to commune with the natural forces of the universe. It helps one to approach problems in a timely manner, and enhances ones position relative to each specific problem. It furthers attempts toward the elimination of procrastination and encourages patience.

It provides for sincerity, clarity of thought, and inducement to accept the invitations of life. It heightens ones instincts and ones innate loyalty to the fostering of humanity.

It has been used in the treatment of disorders of the teeth, bones, and skeletal system. It can help one in the assimilation of calcium, magnesium, and zinc.

Vibrates to the number 7.

CHURCHITE   [Astrological Sign of Virgo]

Churchite crystallizes in the form of minute tabular crystals. The colour is a pale smoke-grey tinged with red.

This mineral can be used to activate the first chakra while providing grounding and centering; this energy brings forth conscious knowledge of anger, encounters of all types, and primordial reactions - prior to their occurrence, such that conscious action can be accomplished without unconscious reaction.

It tends to initiate the evolution of awareness of intuitiveness and assists in dream interpretation. It further acts to assist one in recognizing the guidance from the inner self that flows through out daydreaming moments, and acts to replace negative thoughts with positive conceptions.

It has also been used to open and to active the crown chakra, enhancing ones knowledge of spirituality and bringing forth an interactive balance between the physical and the spiritual realms.

Churchite has been used in the treatment of disorders of the spleen, the intestinal tract, and the colon.

Vibrates to the number 5.

CINNABAR   [Astrological Sign of Leo]

Cinnabar crystallizes in the form of compact granular masses and rhombohedral, thick tabular, or needle-like crystals. The colour ranges from a beautiful vermillion [red] to brown-red, and grey. It is interesting to note that the name "cinnabar" is said to have been derived from the Eastern Indian word for "dragons' blood".

This mineral bestows both an aesthetically appealing and elegant demeanor. It stimulates dignity, vitality and power; it is quite beneficial in the world of business and finance, assisting one in the recognition of historical trends and enabling one toward invincibility, while serving to remove obstructions.

It is been reported that cinnabar is one of the stones to be called the "merchant's stone"; placing a cluster or a crystal of cinnabar in ones cash box has produced an increase in income for the merchant. It not only assists the merchant in acquiring wealth, but helps one to maintain the state of wealth.

It also brings one the qualities of fluency, persuasiveness, and effectiveness in ones aspirations. It furthers ones assertiveness while eliminating aggression. It is helpful in community work and in the organization structure, assisting one in remembering the "giving" qualities of the Divine.

It connects one with the source of all being, promoting the acceptance that "everything is, indeed, okay". It is excellent in extracting energy blockages, yielding ease in alignment of the energy centers.

It can be used in the treatment of disorders of the blood, to bring strength to the physical body, to provide flexibility in ones movement, and to help in the treatment of weight disorders. It has also been helpful in correcting fertility deficiencies.

Vibrates to the number 8.

CITRINE   [Astrological Signs of Gemini, Aries, Libra, & Leo]

Citrine is a variety of quartz, the colour being in the range from yellow to golden brown to burnt amber.

It is one of the two minerals on the planet which does not hold and accumulate negative energy, but dissipates and transmutes it, working-out problems on both the physical and subtle levels. It, hence, never needs clearing or cleansing.

It has also been reported that citrine is one of the stones to be called the "merchant's stone"; placing a cluster or a crystal of citrine in ones cash box has produced more income for the merchant. It not only assists the merchant in acquiring wealth, but helps to maintain the state of wealth.

This mineral is useful for balancing the yin-yang energy and for aligning the chakras with the ethereal plane.

It activates, opens, and energizes the navel and solar plexus chakras, directing, via personal power, creativity, and intelligent decisiveness, the energy necessary to enhance the physical body. It stimulates both mental focus and endurance.

It emits an elevated energy which provides one with supplemental initiative coupled with emotional balance. It stimulates the intuitive self and promotes contact with the higher forces of intelligence.

It also illuminates the energy of the root chakra, delivering both comfort and optimism. It can help one to dispense with the fundamental level of fear. It further promotes a radiance from within the self, culminating in a constant happy disposition. It brightens even the darkest corner of ones perceived reality, and helps one to "laugh without restraint".

It is quite efficient in conveying, when necessary, information relative to the appropriate aspects of survival.

It also allows for clarification of problems related to the realms of the intellect and emotions.

It influences, in a positive manner, the areas of education, business pursuits, and interpersonal relationships. It is an excellent stone for smoothing family or group problems and, subsequently, producing cohesiveness within the associative members. It acts similarly to the cutting edge of a sword, penetrating problems and expediting solutions.

Citrine, especially in the faceted form, stimulates the crown chakra, allowing for synthesis between the intellect and total perfection; it is, therefore, quite helpful in problem solving, for facilitating recognition of resolutions to mental conundrums, and for promoting mental awareness on a moment-to-moment basis. It is said to stimulate openness and to accelerate the wakening of the mind.

It is an excellent stone for clearing the aura and for aligning the auric body with the physical structure, diminishing the "muddy" areas in both the aura and the physical body. It can act to stabilize the emotions, to dispel anger, and to encourage one to "look toward the sunrise", the freshness of beginnings, and the reality of excellence.

It is said to have been one of the stones used in the breastplate of the high priest.

In addition, there is a formation of Citrine/Smokey Quartz (sometimes with "clear quartz") with clean definition between the colours, which has been found in Brasil. This alliance of forces merges the energy of all three minerals and for a dynamic healing stone. The citrine acts to cleanse the energies of the smokey and "clear" quartz, while the smokey quartz provides grounding for all endeavors. The faceted form provides a distinct and bright energy for application to all aspects, combining the singular energies of the three minerals to provide an energy greater than the sum.

It can aid in digestion, can assist in the treatment of digestive disorders, and can promote the circulation of the blood. It has been used in the treatment of degenerative disorders and to facilitate the diminishment of growths.

It has also been used to increase visual abilities, to balance the thyroid, and to activate the thymus.

Vibrates to the number 6.

CLEVELANDITE   [Astrological Sign of Libra]

Clevelandite crystallizes in the formation of lamellar masses. The colour is usually white.

This energy of this mineral spans the life forces of the physical, astral, and ethereal realms, bringing one knowledge of personal conditions as they are currently and of personal conditions as the perfect state. It is a mineral to substantiate ones plans and ones goals.

It brings the energy for conception of plans and for outlining and perfecting transactions. It also stimulates the initiation of journeys and provides for a safe passage.

This mineral furthers relationships and assists one in all undertakings. It assists one in understanding the many facets of others and in appreciating the qualities which are dissimilar and distinct from ones personal attributes.

Clevelandite has been used to strengthen new cell membranes, to ameliorate the deficiencies which tend to underlie bronchial asthma, allergies, skin diseases, ulcerative colitis, and heart disease.

It also tends to block the oxidation of tissue and has been used to treat chronic illnesses such as arteriosclerosis, cerebrovascular disorders, degenerative joint disease, and strokes.

Vibrates to the number 4.

CLINOCHLORE

Clinochlore crystallizes in the form of foliated and granular masses and as tabular crystals. The colour range includes colourless, white, yellow, and green. This mineral is the most common of all of the chlorite minerals and also exhibits the properties listed in the CHLORITE section of this book.

It can be used to enhance cohesiveness in relationships and to heal on all levels. The chlorite faction in the mineral is one of the best healing minerals for the physical, emotional, and mental bodies.

It helps one to achieve complete independence, yet allows one to still exhibit "companion-ability" and diplomacy.

It helps one to appreciate that which is growing spiritually, teaching one the refinements of tenderness and care. It also provides one with a sense of order - order of ones life, order of the universe, and, even, order of chaos - allowing one to understand that one is neither helpless nor hopeless in the realm of the creation or correction of personal reality.

It is especially helpful during confinement to provide a comforting energy and to assist in stabilizing ones condition. It assists in cellular restructuring and integration of the healthy state.

Vibrates to the number 6.

CLINOZOISITE

Clinozoisite crystallizes in the form of prismatic formations, fibers, grains, and masses. The colour range includes colourless, light yellow, green, and pink.

This mineral can provide for disintegration of dissention and for transformation of the opposing energies to constructive force-fields; the constructive fields, enclosing more aggregate energy than the entirety of the energy contained in the negativity.

It grants a focused attachment, via the cognitive processes, to the celestial latitudes [especially during the astrological cycle of Cancer]; this can promote progress in all realms of ones life. In addition, Clinozoisite furthers the completion of projects to successful conclusions; it is a favorable energy for those in search of anything and has been used to stimulate healing of discord and to bring friendship.

The occurrence with quartz combines the energies of Clinozoisite and Quartz to produce a powerful mineral for healing and for progression.

It has been used in the treatment of disorders associated with the heart, spleen, pancreas, and lungs.

Vibrates to the number 3.

COBALTITE   [Astrological Sign of Leo]

Cobaltite crystallizes in the form of granular masses and as cubes and related shapes. The colour range includes silver-white [sometimes with a red inclination], steel-grey [with a violet hue], or greyish-black.

This mineral can be helpful in developing and furthering creative endeavors, bringing the forces of creativity to the zenith. It is said to be quite uplifting to ones emotional experiences.

The message of cobaltite is that there exists a place within one which contains perfect harmony and where nothing is inconceivable, unimaginable, or impossible; this place, which one may access at will, is where the perfection of "All That Is" resides and where the all-knowing may be accessed.

Cobaltite can be used in the treatment of cancer, cellular disorders, and dehydration. It is said to be the stone to "heal all infections".

Vibrates to the master number 33.

COLEMANITE   [Astrological Sign of Aries]

Colemanite crystallizes in the form of masses, grains, and short prismatic crystals. The colour range includes milk-white, white with a shade of yellow, and grey.

This mineral can be useful to teach one about survival; not only physical survival, but spiritual survival.

It further provides light to the darkness of ones soul.

It can provide stimulus for the attainment of education in the arts, and for study in the fields of herbal and holistic healing.

It also assists one in maintaining patience and tolerance, and in moderating indulgence.

It can be used in the treatment of disorders of the reproductive system and to enhance fertility [when consciously directed]. It stimulates the triple-burner acupressure and acupuncture meridians and can be used to enhance the circulatory functions. It can also be used as a de-toxifying agent.

Vibrates to the number 7.

COLUMBITE   [Astrological Sign of Aquarius]

Columbite crystallizes in the form of short prismatic prisms, rectangular prisms, thin tabular crystals, pyramids, and masses. The colour range includes iron-black, grey, brown, brown-black, and red-brown.

This mineral can be used to activate all chakras and to provide for equilibrium between the physical and the spiritual selves. It has been used to provide protection in ones environment and of ones personal property.

It has acted to bring flashes of insights with respect to problems concerning one now and with respect to future problems which have not yet manifested - hence, eliminating the need for anxiety when the imminent obstacles emerge.

The energy of the mineral has served to assist one in decision-making and in the release of pensive action.

It has also been used to dispel indolent and lethargic behavior, and is an excellent grounding stone.

Columbite has been used to assist in the assimilation of iron and manganese, to ameliorate deficiencies in eyesight, and to assist in the relief of skin disorders (including psoriasis).

Vibrates to the number 1.

CONCRETION   [Astrological Sign of Taurus]

The concretion is a mass of mineral, found, generally, within a rock of a dissimilar composition. It is created by deposition of the mineral, via aqueous solution [within the dissimilar rock]. Succinctly, the concretion is a coalescence of separate particles of matter into one body, sometimes exhibiting an arrangement of concentricity. Many concretions, when opened, display a fossil tracery.

The bezoar concretions are found chiefly in the alimentary organs of ruminants, and have been said to possess magical properties.

The partially hollow concretions, containing particles of sand or gravel, have been known as "Indian Rattle Boxes", and have been used in Native American Indian and Native African ceremonial activities. They are said to have the power to ward-off venomous snakes, to increase strength and vigor, and to elevate ones state of consciousness to the visionary condition. Non-rattling concretions have also been used in Native American Indian healing ceremonies.

Some concretions are fossilized marine invertebrates which have been covered by minerals, such as, sulphides. The boji stone, discussed within this book, is an example of the fossilized marine invertebrates which have experienced metamorphosis. The Mochi Balls and the Maqui Marbels discussed in this book are also concretions.

In addition, there are some light shades of pink, peach, and violet concretions found in Indiana that have a true healing spirit.

The ancient and revered Churinga Stones have been said to be concretions; these stones are esteemed for their magical powers by the Australian aborigines, and can be used in activities of enchantment and in the performance of white magic rituals. They are, usually, used in pairs [as are the boji stones]; one stone representing the force of the creative nurturing and sustaining of the "Great Mother", and one stone representing the force of the strength, intensity, fervor, and effectiveness of the "Great Father".

The concretion is a symbol of life after life. It shows one that the beginning of death is, in fact, the beginning of another facet of ones life.

This stone can be used to attune one to the electromagnetic waves of transmitted communication from within and without of the universe. It stimulates thought transference and helps one in the comprehension of the messages. It can produce a spontaneous coming-together, a coalescence of loving intellectual energies converging and fusing to become one.

It can also both take one back through the many lives of existence and can progress ones thought processes forward to eternity.

The concretion is a protective stone, providing both grounding and shielding of the physical, mental, and emotional bodies.

It is a "stone for regulation" [toward perfection] of spiritual, mental, and physical prowess.

It promotes both calming and understanding on the emotional level.

It enhances ones feeling and condition of well-being and provides for a merging with ones inherent energies - in this case, the sum of the energy of the concretion and the energy of the user, being greater than the whole.

It is also quite useful when one is in need of information concerning the direction in which to progress.

The concretion loves to be held, emanating a loving, kind, and sincere energy pattern; allowing one to know that there is always comfort available from the purity of that which transforms.

In addition, it exhibits a fostering energy, being conducive to both business pursuits and material acquisitions.

With the concretion, one can connect with the depths of ones being, to gain information concerning the purpose of ones physical condition; the knowledge gleaned, producing incentive to modify portions of ones character or outlook, in order to rectify the problem.

The minty, peach/apricot, and violet pastel concretions are said to provide healing energy to the spirit.

It is an excellent stone for pain relief; one takes the concretion, visually, to within the pain, and allows the gentle action of the energy to facilitate transformation and a gentle release of same. This technique also assists in the elimination of other internal physical disorders.

It is also a "stone of preservation", acting to enhance the conservation of resources within the body. It can be used to regenerate the cellular structure. It has also been successful in the treatment of gout and in the balancing of protein and uric acid within the body.

Vibrates to the number 8.

CONICHALCITE   [Astrological Sign of Pisces]

Conichalcite crystallizes in the form of crusts, kidney-shaped masses, and prismatic crystals. The colour range includes yellow and green.

This mineral is another which brings the heart and the intellect together to enhance communication and personal power in a loving manner.

Giving strength to sway with changes, it also provides stability.

It is also helpful in beginning meditation; it produces a barricade to ones concerns of the physical world. It stimulates intuition, imagination, and adaptability. It helps one to realize the boundless-ness of ones abilities.

It can be used in the treatment of disorders of the kidneys and bladder, and in the elimination of toxins. It is conducive to improvement in disorders of the mucoid system.

Vibrates to the number 3.

COOKEITE   [Astrological Sign of Sagittarius]

Cookeite crystallizes in the form of plates and round aggregates. It also occurs as an outer coating on crystals of pink tourmaline. The colour range includes white, yellow, green, pink, and brown.

This mineral can be used for gridding and produces a calming effect.

It can also be useful for taming inflexibility [both physical and mental] and for furthering adaptability.

It assists one in problem-solving via facilitating objective examination and study of all relevant data, disallowing, via insightful guidance, the judgment prior to completion.

It also stimulates cooperation and tact and is quite useful in communal activities.

Cookeite can be use to treat allergies and muscle spasms, and to combat insomnia. It has also been used to enhance the assimilation of nutrients.

Vibrates to the number 2.

COPAL   [Astrological Sign of Gemini]

Copal is a fossil resin of vegetable origin and is similar to Amber. The colour ranges from yellow to red to brown.

This mineral has been used to activate the crown chakra and, concurrently, to maintain physical consciousness. It assists one in remaining aware during meditation, and in maintaining the knowledge of emptiness within the spiritual centers of ones being.

Copal can be used in the removal of energy blockages and to strengthen the meridians of the physical body, such that one becomes aligned with the perfection of the ethereal body.

It serves to increase the awareness of ones individuality while allowing one to maintain association with humanity.

It enhances contact with the etheric bodies and stimulates the crown chakra toward spirituality. It can also create altered states of consciousness and can serve as a vehicle for both reaching and utilizing the talents and abilities of the mind. All of the psychic abilities can be stimulated and amplified via the use of these consolidated energies. In addition, it provides for amplification of the entire energy field of the body.

It has also been used by healers in the European countries for both diagnostic healing and communicating with the spirits. It acts to improve disorders of the heart and to help one to recover from those disorders associated with diminished physical vitality.

Copal has been used in the treatment of disorders of the kidneys and bladder. In ancient times it was used as a penicillin-type remedy, ground and ingested or soaked [as in an elixir] and subsequently drunk. It has also been used to provide rejuvenating energy to those recovering from hospitalization, and to stimulate cellular renewal.

Vibrates to the number 2.

COPPER   [Astrological Signs of Taurus & Sagittarius]

Copper crystallizes in the form of dendrites, free-forms, plates, and rhombic dodecahedral crystals. The colour is copper-red.

This mineral can combat lethargy, passivity, restlessness, excitability, and non-acceptance of oneself. It can stimulate initiative, optimism, diplomacy, and independence. It conveys the messages that there is no need to seek love or to constantly search for life, and that there definitely is a need to seek and release all of the restrictions which one has installed within the self. It emits a philosophic energy, free of orthodoxy and bias. It is excellent for use in policy-making and policing, providing insight into the avenues for right-attainment in all areas.

Copper provides a harmonic connection between the physical and astral bodies and aligns the subtle bodies. It has been used successfully to amplify and to transmit thought. It is said to be a "bestower" of "good", bringing benefit to the user. It is also reported to bring "luck" to persons, especially in the recovery of property.

Copper activates and opens the base and sacral chakras, advancing and stabilizing the energies of intuition, sexuality, desire, and vitality - directing these energies toward the pursuit of ones path of evolution. It allows one to recognize the barriers which are in the path of ones development.

It can conduct electrical impulses and can magnify the energy transfer, from the healer or from minerals, to the subject of the healing. Used with brass and iron, it can balance the energies of the body and can maintain stability and wellness within the chemistry of the blood and cellular structures.

Copper can be used to stabilize and to balance the flow of blood within the body; helping to increase circulatory functions when necessary. It can be used to cleanse wounds and to fight bacterial infection. It has also been used in the treatment of arthritis, bursitis, and rheumatism, and to stimulate the metabolic processes.

Vibrates to the number 1.

CORAL   [Astrological Sign of Pisces - Elemental]

Coral comes from the sea and is the vacated housing of a marine animal. The colour range includes black, pink, red, white, and blue. In addition to the properties listed in the SHELL section of this book, the following attributes apply.

It represents diplomacy and concurrence. It is also said to quiet the emotions and to bring peace to within the self.

It facilitates intuition, imagination, and visualization, and helps one to both understand and to use the qualities of the mystic; it can bring one into communication with the past spiritual masters of this world and can expedite and accelerate the transfer of knowledge.

It can be used to strengthen both the circulatory system and the bones of the body. It can be used to stimulate tissue regeneration and has been used to nourish the blood cells. It can also be used in the treatment of disorders of the spinal canal, the alimentary canal, the nervous system, and the thalamus.

Vibrates to the master number 22.

In addition to the above qualities, the following categories list further qualities for specific colours.

<u>Black Coral</u>   [Astrological Signs of Capricorn & Scorpio]

Black coral is reported to both absorb and transform negativity when worn, carried, taken as an elixir, or placed in ones environment.

It elevates the aspects of the significant creative forces and imparts tranquility to action.

It can dispel fear of darkness and can bring hidden matters to the forefront, allowing one to utilize original thinking and the meditative state to actualize the elimination of problems.

It is a "stone of regeneration and purification" and can be used in the treatment of disorders related to the internal organs, to the skin and the pores, and to the elimination of toxins.

Vibrates to the master number 33.

<u>Blue Coral</u>   [Astrological Signs of Sagittarius & Aquarius]

Blue coral can activate and energize the throat chakra and can act as a clearing agent for the navel chakra.

It has also been used to illuminate the third-eye, enhancing the psychic awareness and capabilities of the user.

It has been used to facilitate improvement and permanence in pursuits of commerce and in the maintenance and accrual of the tangible.

It can also improve ones communicative abilities and can help one to understand the process of relating to others.

It can be used in the treatment of throat ailments and for cleaning and purging the mucoid system.

It has also been used to ameliorate disorders and to enhance remediation of the liver, the pituitary gland, the pineal gland, and the circulatory system.

Vibrates to the number 8.

Horn Coral   [Astrological Sign of Aquarius]
                                         [Also Known As Dragon Tooth Coral]

Horn Coral occurs in the shape of a horn and/or a large tooth.

It can be used to increase ones knowledge of ancient civilizations and of the animal kingdom. It has also been used to assist one in finding and in maintaining contact with ones totem animal.

It is reported to act to bring information concerning ones safety and security in all situations.

In addition, it has been used in the treatment of hearing disorders, degeneration of the bone structure, muscular disorders, and carpel tunnel syndrome.

Vibrates to the numbers 5 and 6.

Pink Coral   [Astrological Sign of Cancer]

Pink coral represents continuity, activity, and structure. It is a building block of human physiology. It helps to stimulate sensitivity with respect to ones emotions and ones physical condition.

It stimulates and activates the heart chakra and enhances the intuitive aspects of love.

It also helps one to act in the "caring" manner supported by the knowledge that everyone and everything is connected by the bonds of love.

In addition, it assists one to maintain both awareness and continuity during the normal ebb and flow of ones life.

It can be used in the treatment of disorders of the heart, breasts, stomach, and reproductive organs.

Vibrates to the number 9.

Red Coral   [Astrological Sign of Libra]

Red coral helps one to become in harmony with the natural forces of the universe and with the wilderness within ones own being.

It provides for practicality with respect to ones avocation, balancing the material with the spiritual, and further aligning one with the source of all wisdom.

It both opens and activates the base chakra, stimulating the energetic pursuit of pre-determined goals.

It is also said to protect one from depression and despondency.

It has been used in the treatment of hiccups, colic, and heartburn. It is also used to stimulate the metabolic processes and to provide for release of impurities from the muscular system. It can be used in the treatment of disorders of the cellular structure of the kidneys, bladder, and parathyroid.

Vibrates to the number 4.

White Coral   [Astrological Sign of Pisces]

White coral can be used to open and clear the crown chakra and to align the major chakras of the body with the energies of the ethereal plane.

It provides for a distinct connection with the ethereal plane, stimulating energy flow and helping to both dissipate energy blockages in the physical body and to fill any voids in ones aura.

It can also stimulate clairaudient abilities, bringing forth information which is beneficial to assist humanity.

It has been used to facilitate renewal of the cellular structure of the brain and olfactory structure.

Vibrates to the number 6.

CORDIERITE   [See Iolite]

CORNETITE   [Astrological Sign of Aries]

Cornetite crystallizes as crusts and as prismatic crystals. The colour ranges from blue to green.

This mineral can be used to enable one to both focus upon and to understand the nature of personal duality. It helps one to go forward, to progress.

The message of the energy helps one to understand that the quality of grace rests in forgiveness and love.

It also helps one to "bear the load", with patience and fortitude, acknowledging problems and advancing toward solutions.

It opens and activates the heart and throat chakras, bringing charity and clarity to communication, while instilling an affinity for the truth of self-expression.

It is a "stone for exploration into the unknown", providing one with both enterprise and direction.

It helps one to maintain freedom and assists one in the process of adequate deliberation prior to decisions.

Using cornetite on the area of the head can increase awareness, can lessen headaches, and can stimulate mental acuity.

It can be used in the treatment of disorders of the feet and legs, the nervous system, and the blood vessels.

Vibrates to the number 1.

CORUNDUM   [Astrological Sign of Sagittarius - Elemental]

Corundum, the second hardest of all minerals, crystallizes in the form of grains, masses, and tabular prisms with rhombohedra and bi-pyramidal structures. The colour range includes red [ruby], blue, orange, yellow, grey-to-brown, black, bronze with a pearly luster, pink [when yellow is transmuted by heat], green, and purple. The designation of "sapphire" is often applied to indicate the corundum gems of any colour except red. Additional properties of the corundum family are listed in the sections of this book addressing RUBY and SAPPHIRE.

Occasionally, the outer surface of the mineral alters to margarite [a form of mica]; when this structure is exhibited, the properties listed in the MARGARITE section of this book are also inherent. In addition, the mica/corundum mixture provides for a stone which can be used to enhance change, helping one toward the proper direction for growth.

Corundum promotes insight to the unknown. It provides for a "parting of the way" for all endeavors and acts to enhance ones intuitive awareness. It stimulates ambition and confidence. It also dispels harsh and irritating attitudes, subdues the emotions, and helps one to release anger in a positive manner.

It is said to have been one of the stones used in the breastplate of the high priest.

It can be used in the treatment of disorders of the eyes, to soothe and smooth the skin, and to bring peace to the body.

Vibrates to the number 1.

COVELLITE   [Astrological Sign of Sagittarius]

Covellite crystallizes forming plates, foliates, masses, and rarely, in the form of a crystalline structure. The colour is a deep indigo blue with, sometimes, a purple-rose iridescence. It is also known as covelline. The most beautiful covellite I have seen has been found in the Butte, Montana, USA, copper mine.

This mineral has been used successfully to stimulate the third-eye and to initiate psychic power.

It enhances ones communication skills and stimulates a positive outlook; it encourages verbalization of that which is positive.

It can assist in transforming conscious "dreams" into realities, allowing one to maintain humility of spirit and to recognize that energy, properly directed and understood, can bring "miracles" to ones life.

Covellite also helps one to be reflective and acts as a mirror, showing one the defective reasoning which leads to problems.

It can be used to relieve despondency, instilling a constructive approach toward the solution of problems.

It assists one in accepting gratification and in eliminating the aspects of vanity which are attached to ones being; hence, helping one to understand and to appreciate the perfection of "All".

It also helps to heal the wounds of vanity, when necessary.

It assists in matters of birth and re-birth. The message of covellite is that to be born again is to release the past and to be able to see the present without anxiety and disapproval.

This mineral has been used in the treatment of cancer, to stimulate disordered cells to re-order themselves and to purge any toxins from within the body.

Placing a polished piece of the covellite on or near the navel chakra tends to stimulate the process; placement on the affected area has also been conducive to relief. As the mineral recognizes the destructive condition, a temperature increase can, usually, be detected in the stone; this is an indication that work on the problem is being accomplished.

Covellite is also associated with the healing of disorders of the ears, eyes, nose, and mouth/throat. It can, in addition, provide for an ordering of the mental processes.

An elixir should be made only from the polished mineral.

Vibrates to the numbers 4 and 7.

COWRIE   [Astrological Sign of Pisces]

Cowrie is a shell from the sea and is recognized as an ancient symbol for creation, birth, and re-birth. In addition to the properties listed in the SHELL section of this book, the following attributes apply.

It is said to inspire the creativity of excellence, to provide for both intuitive and intellectual control, and to promote achievement in aesthetic and artistic endeavors. It has been reported to be useful in stimulating ones learning and retention capabilities, to provide initiative to the user to advance in scholarship, and to assist in the recognition of the self as a vehicle for understanding.

The cowrie shell has been used in the art of manifestation and has been said to bring both good fortune and affluence to the user. It was used, in ancient times, by the Native American Coastal Indians to indicate wealth.

It can be used to enhance fertility, to treat disorders of the reproductive system, and to aid in the assimilation of iodine, Vitamins A and D, calcium, and magnesium.

Vibrates to the number 1.

CREEDITE   [Astrological Sign of Virgo]

Creedite crystallizes in the form of colourless to white [and, occasionally, purple] needle-like or prismatic crystals.

This mineral helps to align the throat and crown chakras and provides for clarity in expression in the spiritual realm. It enhances spirituality and is a tool to be used in channeling meditation to provide clarity in the verbalization of the message which is transmitted.

It also helps one to gain access to the sacred texts, and to understand the subtle messages within the structure of knowledge. It further assists one by providing for a driving force toward an objective, promoting insight into the obstruction and initiating the wisdom to circumvent or the ability to penetrate the obstacle.

This mineral can be used to assist in mending broken bones and torn muscles. It can be used to aid in the assimilation of Vitamins A, E, and B, and can help to cleanse the liver and to regulate the heartbeat.

Vibrates to the number 6.

CRISTOBALITE   [Astrological Sign of Capricorn]

Cristobalite normally crystallizes in the form of white octahedral crystals. It is, occasionally, found as a patterned red crystal formation in moon rock.

It has been used at the crown chakra to stimulate movement of the Kundalini. It can also be used to stimulate the third-eye, and it facilitates advanced sight in the psychic realm. Cristobalite helps to bring one to the state of recognition of other worldly beings, merging the intuitive self with the willingness to acknowledge "the signs". It is a "stone for journeys", both within and without.

This mineral can be used to lessen fevers and to help one withstand the heat of summer, assisting in the dissipation of heat from the body.

It can also be used in the treatment of problems associated with the lower intestines, the elimination and digestive systems, and the male reproductive system. It has been used successfully to treat failing vision.

Vibrates to the number 7.

CROCOITE   [Astrological Sign of Aries]

Crocoite crystallizes in the form of masses, aggregates, and prismatic crystals. The colour ranges from a hyacinth-red to a lovely saffron.

This mineral relates to the navel chakra and can stimulate and enhance intuition, creativity, and sexuality.

It is a transition stone, assisting one in the progression from this life to another, from this life to the next, from one state of change to another situation, in a non-complex and very self-possessed method.

It stimulates recovery from physical, mental, or emotional distress. It can be used in the treatment of disorders of the emotions and of the reproductive system.

Do not prepare an elixir of this mineral via the normal method.

Vibrates to the number 7.

CRYOLITE   [Astrological Sign of Gemini]

Cryolite crystallizes as masses, and, occasionally, as cube-like crystals. The colour range includes colourless, snow-white, red, brown, brown to black, and black.

It assists one in public speaking and has been effective and constructive in the amelioration of speech disorders which have culminated due to emotional and/or psychological needs.

It can also be used to stimulate the connection between the base and crown chakras, providing for continuity in the flow of energy throughout the body.

It further increases ones stability, especially during stress-related situations, and can promote increased awareness to both ones self and ones environment.

This mineral can be used to treat eye infections, to reduce chills, and to combat the effects of cold weather on the physical body.

Vibrates to the master number 44.

CUBANITE   [Astrological Sign of Aquarius]

Cubanite crystallizes in the form of vertically striated, elongated prisms. The colour ranges from brass to bronze. This mineral is strongly magnetic.

It can assist in the alignment of the subtle bodies and in strengthening and arranging the meridians of the physical body.

It increases the bio-magnetic forces in the body, aligns the body with the magnetic fields of the Earth, and has been used extensively in magnetic healing and to provide receptivity to radionic treatment. Wearing or carrying the stone is recommended to facilitate remedial actions and to stabilize alignment.

Cubanite can provide one with a magnetic attraction; would that one could attract only those or that which is desired.

Placing the stone on an affected area of the body can stimulate rejuvenation of the organs within that area.

Vibrates to the number 3.

CUMBERLANDITE   [Astrological Sign of Virgo]

The Cumberlandite formation known to the author is massive, with the colour ranging from grey to black.

This mineral enhances the intellect, activating both the left and right sides of the brain concurrently.

It provides increased mental perception, increases capabilities for both mental and physical communication, and encourages the exchange of information. The reasoning process is truly enhanced.

It is a very useful "merchant's stone", quickening the exchange of merchandise and/or commodities, and expediting an increase in both services and monetary gain.

It helps to reinforce and to augment the ability of communication of ideas to others and especially helpful to those in the teaching profession. It also acts to increase receptivity, the inquisitive mind, and the desire to learn on the part of students and has been used for gridding classroom environments.

It has been used in debate situations to instill excellence and attention to detail.

Cumberlandite has been used to impart a sense of purpose to ones activities and ones life path.

It has been used in the treatment of disorders related to movement, mental acuity and strain, and uncontrolled nervous energy. It can assist in the treatment of disorders of the brain, the sympathetic nervous system and the thyroid and parathyroid glands.

Vibrates to the number 8.

CUPRITE   [Astrological Signs of Virgo, Capricorn & Taurus]

Cuprite crystallizes in the form of masses and octahedral, dodecahedral, and cubic crystals. The colour is a very deep red, leaning toward a black-red.

This mineral stimulates the base chakra while providing a grounding effect on the total body. It can increase physical vitality and energy. It is a survival tool, attracting that which can satisfy ones physical needs. It has also been used to alleviate worries, especially worries concerning situations over which one has no control.

It can be used in the treatment of water retention, dysfunctional elimination, and bladder and kidney disorders. It can also be helpful in the treatment of vertigo, altitude sickness, and reproductive disorders.

Vibrates to the number 2.

CUPROADAMITE   [Astrological Sign of Capricorn]

Cuproadamite crystallizes in the form of small orthorhombic crystals, orthorhombic crystal clusters, druses, and granular aggregations. The colour is green.

In addition to the combination of the qualities listed in the Copper and Adamite sections, this mineral can be used to amplify the capabilities to construct, to organize, to express willful-ness, and to accept responsibility.

It acts to encourage one toward self-discipline, toward defining oneself in terms of understanding, and to realize that any limitations and restrictions which are personally perceived are self-imposed.

It functions well to manifest distinct goals in the architecture of advancement. It tells the story that we can always realize the technique and accomplish patient persistence in well-doing.

It is also a supportive and beneficial transition stone, assisting one to recognize the benefits of the inevitable and representing the methods to release self-crystallization.

Cuproadamite assists one in powerful adjustments of personal affairs, to re-order ones life, and to understand structure.

It is also a "stone of patience", bringing calmness, composure, and tranquility to ones life. It assists one in learning from ones mistakes and in understanding and completing the changes in life direction and or level.

The energy tends to reduce inhibition and intolerance, affecting reliability, trustworthiness, responsibility, and endurance.

It has been used in the treatment of the skin, teeth, bones and acid formations in joints, gall bladder, spleen, vagus nerve, and depression. It can also be used in the treatment of colds, poor circulation, and in the conditions generally associated with increase in age.

Vibrates to the number 7.

CUSPIDINE   [Astrological Sign of Cancer]

Cuspidine crystallizes in the form of masses and tiny, spear-shaped crystals. The colour range includes pale rose-red, green, green-grey, grey, and white.

This mineral can be used to soften problems associated with love by allowing one to both feel contentment within the self and to be willing to give, without any thought of receiving.

It is an excellent help to one caught in the realm of decision-making. It helps one to verbalize personal feelings and inner thoughts without apprehension.

Cuspidine can be used to treat problems of the teeth. It can enhance the tooth structure and form. It is not, however, used for problems associated with loose teeth. It is also useful in the treatment of stomach problems related to digestive complaints and to the secretion of digestive enzymes.

Vibrates to the number 1.

CYANOTRICHITE   [Astrological Sign of Aries]

Cyanotrichite crystallizes in velvet-like druses and in spherical forms. The colour ranges from blue to colourless.

This mineral tends to stimulate initiative, to arouse the energy to pursue personal desires and to act (without reacting) upon ones own motivation, and to seek and to attain new beginnings.

It assists one to be direct in approach, to be a strong leader in crises situations, and to genuinely and guilelessly respond in a positive, confident, and lively manner to all situations.

It has also been used to stimulate the communication of information received during sessions involving clairaudience activities. It helps one to speak clearly and concisely and to recall the details of the information given.

Cyanotrichite can be used to amplify planning abilities and to decrease the application of quarrelsome and hasty speech.

It has been used in the treatment of muscular disorders, dis-ease associated with the adrenal glands, the urogenital system, the gonads, the red blood corpuscles, and the kidneys. An elixir applied to cuts and burns has shown efficacy in healing. It has also been used in the regulation and for the ease of handling of dietary constraints, for the regulation of the blood and cholesterol levels, and as the silent supervisor of same.

Preparation of an elixir via the normal method is not recommended.

Vibrates to the number 6.

CYLINDRITE   [Astrological Sign of Capricorn]

Cylindrite crystallizes in the form of cylinders which, under pressure, break apart into forms of shells and folia. The colour is a metallic grey-black.

This mineral can provide intuitive awareness and enhanced communication with the plant and animal kingdoms, assisting one in understanding the lessons of the Earth Mother. It enhances both growth toward the light and orderliness, with spontaneity, of both ones presence and character.

Cylindrite can also be used to enhance ones dancing, aerobic, and exercising abilities.

It can be used to increase the ability to assimilate vitamins and minerals. It can also assist in the treatment of disorders of the blood vessels and to enhance the integrity of the intestines and alimentary canal. It has been used in the treatment of hearing disorders which are related to the integrity of the organ itself.

Vibrates to the number 2.

CYMOPHANE   [Astrological Sign of Gemini]

Cymophane is a type of cat's eye which crystallizes in the form of masses and hexagonal-type and tabular crystals. The colour is green with a chatoyant property. Cymophane is a form of chrysoberyl; the properties listed in the CHRYSOBERYL and CAT'S EYE sections of this book are also applicable to cymophane. In addition, the following should be noted.

This mineral has been used to stimulate the intellect, providing a stabilizing influence, thereby, strengthening ones approach to, and rectification of, problems and situations. It can help one to see clearly all aspects of a situation prior to action.

It also assists in helping one to look at love in the physical world and to recognize the need for unconditional love; cymophane further supports the strength required for giving unconditional love. It can also help one to be both fluid in movement and flexible in mind.

It has been used to treat intestinal disorders, heart irregularities, and night-blindness, and to provide relief from feminine discomforts.

Vibrates to the number 1.

CRYSTAL IN THE SUN
LAUGHS IN RAINBOW HUES
REFLECTING RED, ELECTRIC BLUES
IN THE COZY DARKNESS

OF A WINTERS NIGHT
CRYSTAL WILL CAPTURE EVERY HEART
AND DANCE A DANCE OF PURE DELIGHT
OF RAINBOW HUES IN DARKEST NIGHT

[rodney spurlock, 1990]

DAMSONITE

Damsonite is a type of jasper which occurs in massive form. It is a lovely violet colour, often with "flowers of yellow" and other colours showing when designed into the style of a cabochon.

In addition to the qualities listed in the JASPER section of this book, the following attributes apply.

This mineral stimulates the feminine aspects of a person, allowing for freer expression of emotions. It stimulates both love and a happiness with the life one has chosen.

It also enhances meditation and spiritual development and provides a clear channel between the intellect and the spiritual self; this produces an understanding of the reasons one is on this life plane and allows one to recognize that which must be accomplished before one is permitted to "go on".

It also stimulates mental acuity and proficiency in the aspects of ones choice.

It can be used to stimulate and to calm the heart, to enhance fertility [when consciously directed], and to administer to disorders of the kidneys, bladder, and spleen.

Vibrates to the number 1.

DANALITE

Danalite crystallizes in the form of masses and octahedral and dodecahedral crystals. The colour range includes red, yellow, brown, and grey.

Danalite is a comforting stone and will encourage one to "pour-out all troubles" to the stone; hence, removing the burden from the inner self and the mind.

It is said to bring honour upon the holder and to heighten ones standing with oneself, ones peers, and ones environment.

It has been used to remove the "muddy" areas from ones aura and to stimulate the clarity of connection between the aura and the physical, emotional, and ethereal bodies.

Danalite can be used to clarify the eyes and to treat disorders of the cellular structure of the body.

Vibrates to the number 3.

DANBURITE   [Astrological Sign of Leo]

Danburite crystallizes in the form of prismatic crystals resembling topaz in configuration. The colour range includes colourless, yellow-white, yellow-brown, pale wine-yellow, pink, and dark wine-yellow.

This mineral encourages one to "let your light shine", and helps people to get-along with others. It is a powerful intellectual activator, bringing both stimulus and responsiveness to the user. It is also helpful in the rectification of recalcitrant attitudes, allowing one to maintain personal identity while flowing with the structure of the world.

The pink colour has been used to activate the heart chakra and to bring self-love to the user.

It can be used to facilitate motor capabilities and to provide catalytic action to the muscular structure.

In addition, occasionally Danburite exhibits a "Buddha Crystal" configuration, bringing the aspects of enlightenment and love toward realization. It intensifies all of the attributes of Danburite and assists one in actualization of that which will promote ease of traveling ones path.

It can be used in the treatment of ailments of the gall bladder and the liver. If consciously directed, it will help one to add weight to the body. It further assists in the removal of toxins from the body.

Vibrates to the number 4.

DAPHNITE   [Astrological Sign of Libra]

Daphnite crystallizes in the form of deep green spherical and botryoidal aggregates.

In addition to the qualities listed in the CHLORITE section of this book, this mineral facilitates communication with the plant world and is an enhancement to gardens and plants. It is especially useful for those involved in agricultural pursuits and for those cultivating herbs, flowers, and any vegetation.

It is a "stone for transformation and transmutation". It can help one to smoothly flow through the many changes necessary in the physical world. It is also a stone for balancing the physical, emotional, and intellectual bodies, as well as the male/female qualities [both within themselves and between each other]. Daphnite also provides for an open channel to the spiritual world, facilitating communication with those on that plane and providing for access to the akashic records.

It can be used in the treatment of hearing disorders and physical and mental instabilities, and to combat nightmares.

Vibrates to the number 5.

DATOLITE   [Astrological Sign of Aries]

Datolite crystallizes in the form of masses, grains, globular and botryoidal columnar structures, and prismatic and tabular crystals. The colour range includes white, red, yellow, green, grey, and violet.

This mineral is used to increase ones stature and respect. It can help one with problem-solving and with remembering significant details. It can help to bring one closer to those one loves.

It can also instill an understanding of transience to those experiencing changes; allowing one to know that all situations will eventually fade into the aspect of memory.

Datolite can be used in the treatment of diabetes and hypoglycemia. It has also been used to enhance the memory.

Vibrates to the number 5.

DAVYNE   [Astrological Sign of Pisces]

Davyne crystallizes in both white and colourless masses and hexagonal crystals.

This mineral creates a balance for those under stress and would be a stone conducive to traveling with those in service. It helps one to be "okay" with not being in control of the situation; however, it also provides one with a strength to take control and to make the "correct" decisions whenever necessary and/or possible.

It helps one to see beyond the moment when that moment is uncomfortable and/or embarrassing, and enables one to see beyond the exterior facade of another in order to attain understanding, appreciation, and acceptance of the other. In addition it assists one in recognizing the appreciation of others for oneself.

It can be used in the treatment of disorders of the hands and the personality.

Vibrates to the number 8.

DECHENITE   [See Dicinite]

DESCLOIZITE   [Astrological Sign of Taurus]

Descloizite crystallizes in the configuration of orthorhombic crystals, druses, masses, and radiated fibers. The colour range includes black, cherry to brownish red, and light to dark brown.

This mineral promotes the advancement of the extension of occurrences to facilitate knowledge with ease, such that approach to each event/condition/experience is with absolute precision and beneficial construction; the concept of approach via strategic techniques is reflected.

It has been used to strengthen ones inventiveness, to intensify ones movement toward future visions, to assist one in releasing old social patterns and out-dated conditions while finding innovative and new directions, and to advance altruistic and humanitarian pursuits.

It is a stone of unconditional love, assisting one to consider the highest good in all.

It has been used to assist in the assimilation of information related to science and aeronautics, and to encourage creativity and originality. It has also been used by those associated with radio and television to enhance personal image and to provide for effective presentation.

Descloizite can be used to stimulate independence, versatility, and the release of restriction by the self and by others. It brings forth, when consciously directed, a dynamic change with no concomitant suffering or distress.

It has been used in the treatment of the circulatory system, paralysis, cramping of muscular structures, and nervous breakdown. It can assist in transition of physical changes, allowing those who are experiencing the changes to understand, graciously accept, and be thankful for lessons learned.

Vibrates to the master number 55.

DIABANTITE [Astrological Sign of Pisces]

Diabantite is a type of chlorite which crystallizes as compact fibrous masses, usually filling seams of cavities in igneous rocks. The colour is a deep green.

The attributes listed in the CHLORITE section of this book are in addition to those listed below.

This mineral can be useful to provide incentive in ending relationships and other situations which one feels are harmful to oneself or another.

It can also facilitate psychic development and ritualistic order, and is conducive to the furtherance of white magic.

It is helpful in diagnostic situations, can be used in the treatment of disorders of the pancreas and spleen, and is excellent in general healing of the physical and emotional bodies.

Vibrates to the number 4.

DIASPOR [Astrological Sign of Leo, Libra, and Pisces]

Diaspor crystallizes in the formation of thin flattened and, sometimes, acicular crystals, foliated masses, thin scales, and stalactites. The colour range includes whit, greyish white, greenish grey, brown, yellowish, and colourless. At times, the mineral exhibits pleochroism; in this case, the X-axis displays a dark violet or red-brown colour and the Z-axis displays a faint yellow colour.

Carrying Diaspor has assisted in the increase of "reading" people and in understanding exactly what is being communicated, more on a spiritual plane; subsequently, the application to the mental and material plane is enhanced. In our society there are so many ways to misunderstand intent - the intent is quite clear when this mineral is used.

Sleeping with Diaspor can facilitate the vividness of dreams and enhancement of the recall of same - the actual detail becomes "crystal" clear in the mind that it is similar to recalling a scene that one has just experienced; having sufficient time to record dreams would no longer be a problem with the use of this stone. In addition, past-life dreams are prevalent. During meditation with this mineral, one may ask questions and expect to receive clear, concise, and accurate answers.

Diaspor is said to be part of an ancient symbol worn in civilizations throughout Eurasia. Entering meditation with this mineral, one may visit a desert, where there is a community of healers - the time pre-dates the continental shifts and the community is a lovely peaceful area. The visuals involve the scene of robed people, wearing pendants that were created for use (the pendants were configured and constructed with gold/silver/bronze/brass octagonal shapes with the Diaspor hanging within (either in rough or in polished freeform octagonal shape or faceted octagonal shape; there were eight other stones at the corners of the octagon - one of each of the rainbow colours and one white/clear stone). There was also a sacred inscription mounted around the octagon on all sides - it was information about each stone, but in a language that appears to be the old symbols. The inscription around the octagon differs from person to person due to the difference in the stones used. One can visit this location during the meditative state and learn many lessons from the wise population.

Diaspor has also been used to bring the freshness of spring to ones environment, assisting one in maintaining openness and calm in all situations. It tends to facilitate the building of ones life upon a strong foundation, a foundation which is maintained and protected by the energies of universal strength.

It has been used to enhance the production of documents and other texts of the written word, allowing for concentration and self-centering which intensifies and heightens the quality of the result.

It provides activation of the crown chakra while initiating grounding; this action tends to produce increased perception and comprehension of that which occurs in trance states, while affording the perpetuation of security and safety within the self.

The utilization of Diaspor with the elestial formation promotes a strengthening of stability and protection when one is initiating and fulfilling changes and metamorphosis.

In addition, with the Diaspor, the one tends to feel less vulnerable, more dispassionate, and calm, when evaluating the need and the actual path for the change.

This mineral also can be used to align the outer bodies, to provide grounding, and to create a pathway to the higher-self energy seems to go straight up, when consciously directed.

It is interesting to note that the Diaspor cave in Turkey is a vortex.

For the twin configuration, there is a "V" between the two crystals, the energy is similar to a mini-vortex; when one places two of these crystals in the pattern of an "X" over the body, the energy permeates the heart chakra to cleanse and to assist one in understanding matters of the heart.

Diaspor assists the body in maintaining the proper acid/alkaline balance, enhancing the solubility of alkaline deposits within the body. It has assisted in the removal of free-radical oxides from the body, providing for stability within ones own temple. It has also been used to eliminate water retention, and to promote weight loss, and to reduce fevers. It is currently being used in the treatment of Parkinson's dis-ease. It has also been used in the amelioration of the rash associated with Agent Orange and to diminish the presence of this toxin. In addition, it is said to provide for an increased T-cell count in AIDS patients.

Vibrates to the number 1.

DICINITE   [Astrological Sign of Pisces]
                                                 [Also Known As Dechenite]

Dicinite crystallizes in the formation of botryoidal and nodular masses. The colour range includes a silvery red, brown, and/or yellow.

This mineral can be used to facilitate instilling trust in others and to initiate the experience of trust in oneself. It acts to eliminate the need for deception, treachery, and betrayal between the self and the self, between the self and others, and between others and the self, allowing one to merge in honesty with others with a faith born of conviction.

It can promote a compassion with decisiveness and practicality, and the elimination of anxiety associated with the issues of trust. It assists in dispelling confusion in the metaphysical realm, expediting advancement in intuition, in the creation of altered states, in the demonstration of spiritual values, and, in mystic pursuits.

Dicinite is a "stone of divinity", bringing contact, when the energy is consciously directed, with spiritual beings and allowing for celestial communication to be initiated and enhanced. This communication transcends the "normal" channeling ideals; it actually brings the information with ease in a conversational form, and with comfort and guardianship from the unknown.

It has been successfully used in "cloud-busting" and in assisting the weather patterns to increase rainfall.

Dicinite can be used to assist in businesses associated with navigation, prisons, hospitals, artistic endeavors, religious ministries, dancing, and poetry. It has also been used to eliminate erratic and careless behavior.

It has been used in the treatment of dryness of skin, psoriasis, bloating, disorders of the thalamus, and dis-ease of the spinal canal. It can also be used to stabilize both mental and nervous processes, to lessen addictions to drugs, and to reduce the after-effects of poisons and anesthetics.

Do not prepare an elixir via the normal method.

Vibrates to the number 1.

DICKITE   [Astrological Sign of Pisces and Virgo]

Dickite crystallizes in the formation of tabular crystals. The colour ranges from white to transparent.

This mineral can be used to enhance travel and the prospects of travel, and to protect one during travel. It can assist one in intuitively knowing the acceptable customs and lore of the location visited and can guide one to areas which will be of immense importance to the furtherance of oneself.

In addition, it instills dignity and good taste.

When consciously directed, the energy of Dickite can facilitate the finding of travel companions - ones who will rejoice in the sharing of the newly found locations and information.

It also assists one in communication with those of other languages and in meeting people under pleasant circumstances.

It is an excellent mineral to further higher education, to assist in studying and in comprehension of information, to augment knowledge associated with philosophy, teaching, and religion, to enhance mental exploration and cognitive understanding, and to further the study of languages.

It is another mineral for dreaming, bringing flashes of insight through dreams which concern travel and study.

In combination with Pumpellyite, this mineral portrays a truly phenomenal and magnificent energy.

Vibrates to the number 5.

DIAMOND   [Astrological Signs of Aries, Leo & Taurus]

Diamond crystallizes in the form of octahedral, dodecahedral, and trapezohedral crystals. The colour range includes colourless, white, black, and various shades [usually pale] of pink, yellow, red, orange, green, blue, and brown.

This mineral is known as "the king of the crystals", symbolizing the central "sun" of the solar system, a force which maintains itself as the perfect state, never requiring re-charging. The ability of the diamond to dissipate light into flashing prisms conveys the force to enhance the powers of other minerals, bringing strength and endurance to the action of the energies.

It was used during ancient times as a talisman against cowardice and was recognized as a "stone to enhance invulnerability". It rallies strength with age and maintains the energy to stimulate unity and love of oneself and of others.

Traditionally, the power of the diamond worked only when the diamond was freely given; in ancient times it was given to insure love and harmony and to dispel anger. It is a reminder of ones goals towards spiritual awareness; as the evolution and growth required becomes manifest within the heart, one can transfer the feeling and the being to others, via the diamond.

It is also known as a "stone of innocence", bringing forth purity, constancy, and the loving and open nature with which one came into the physical realm.

It is said to have been one of the stones used in the breastplate of the high priest.

It can instill the aspect of trust to relationships and situations, bringing confidence to ones emotional and intellectual characteristics, and bringing fidelity to interpersonal associations.

It has been used to the remove voids from ones aura and to fill the emptiness with a loving energy of purity. It inspires creativity, imagination, ingenuity, inventiveness, and brilliance in the world of the "new".

It can activate the crown chakra and can produce a connected force between the intellect and higher knowledge. It assists in removal of the "fog" from ones mind such that one can recognize the obstructions to be avoided on the path towards enlightenment.

The diamond can also inspire the forces of accumulation; helping one to manifest abundance in all areas of ones life.

It has been used in the treatment to counteract poisoning, to clarify and stimulate the sight, and as a metabolic balancing agent.

Vibrates to the master number 33.

DINOSAUR BONE   [Astrological Sign of Aries]

Dinosaur bone is a portion of a fossilized dinosaur. In addition to the properties listed below, further attributes are listed in the FOSSIL section of this book.

Use of the dinosaur bone can help to diminish the barriers separating the ancient ones and their inherent knowledge from the modern representatives of the human kingdom.

It can open avenues of communication and insight, assisting one in understanding the Earth changes, the role of evolution, and the issues of dominance and endurance in all situations.

It stimulates the adventuresome nature, helping one to proceed from one point to another with both the faith and the strength to understand and to attain the ultimate value of a situation.

The dinosaur bone has been used to facilitate mind travel, providing for a stabilizing force to ground the user while allowing the mind to wander toward a pre-set goal.

It can also be used to help alter ones "recognizability" with respect to verbal response, assisting one toward spontaneity and instinctive undeliberate reply.

It can be used to assist in the assimilation of phosphorus within the body, to stimulate orderly growth of tissues, to control the temperature and the release of fevers from the body, and to re-build and to re-structure confused and disarranged skeletal structures.

Vibrates to the number 2.

DIOPSIDE [Astrological Sign of Virgo]

Diopside crystallizes in the form of masses, thin plates, grains, and slender prismatic crystals. The colour range includes white, colourless, yellow, grey, green, red-brown, and black.

This mineral can be used to stimulate the intellect and can provide assistance in mathematical and analytical pursuits. It enhances academic learning and couples the practical side of ones nature to both the sciences and arts.

It helps one to wield pride objectively, providing both humility and respect for the superior exhibition of intelligence. It allows one to recognize that the strength of the opposition is less than that which is within oneself.

It also allows one to understand the duality within the self, and further stimulates retrieval of the feminine side of nature, being a good stone for healing those who will not allow themselves to cry.

It can be used in the treatment of physical weakness and psychological disorders. It is an excellent stone for runners, helping to eliminate the muscular spasms and "stitches" during the run.

It has also been used to calm pets.

Vibrates to the number 9.

DIOPTASE [Astrological Signs of Sagittarius & Scorpio]

Dioptase crystallizes forming emerald-green masses, prismatic crystals, and crystalline aggregates. It is a relatively rare mineral and is found in only a few localities. The most beautiful dioptase I have seen comes from Tsumeb, Namibia. It is one of the best healing stones of the age.

This mineral can be used to both clear and stimulate all chakras to the higher level of awareness and action, bringing an invigoration and a refreshing energy to the physical, emotional, and intellectual bodies. It further instills a clarity of connection between the physical body and the perfection of the ethereal body.

Dioptase brings forth and helps one to understand the message that "yesterday is but a memory, tomorrow is but a vision, and TODAY is REAL"; <u>living in the moment</u> is the energy of this mineral.

It is an excellent stone for furthering spiritual attunement; use of dioptase over the third-eye can help one to see to the root of a problem and can help one to gain the wisdom to correct the neglect.

It stimulates the memory of past-lives and assists one in obtaining attunement to both conscious awareness of these lives and to the inner reality which has been the bases for these lives. It also "brings to light" hidden forces which one can utilize in attaining that which is required.

It assists in the enrichment of ones life, ones environment, and ones planet. One can hear the silence of the resonance of the Earth and can help to heal the Earth with the energies of dioptase.

Dioptase can be very beneficial in eliminating "lack". It helps one to eliminate oppressive feelings and situations, to realize the richness and surplus of ones personal resources, and to utilize, to the fullest, ones capabilities.

It also helps to raise the consciousness such that one may employ the universal energies of awakening while stimulating the actualization of well-being.

This mineral is useful for balancing the yin-yang energy and for aligning the chakras with the ethereal plane. It activates, opens, and energizes the heart chakra, bringing the energy necessary to the physical body, through the loving energy of the heart.

Dioptase can promote inner cellular awareness such that each cell affected by a disorder can singularly, and collectively, recognize the reason for the malfunction and then release the anomaly, facilitating both alignment with the perfect self and the healing state.

It can also produce a natural calming energy which desensitizes both the body and the mind, when required. It can help to relieve pain; an elixir would be excellent for headaches, migraines, pain from surgery, or "things" that hurt generally. It can be used to ease high blood pressure and to release stress and tension. It can be helpful in correcting problems associated with inadequacies in nourishment, disturbed equilibrium, disorders of the heart and lungs, and in general, all cells and structures.

It has also been used in the treatment of Meniere's symptoms, to alleviate the dizziness and to remove the cause. It has also been used in the amelioration of the rash associated with Agent Orange and to diminish the presence of this toxin. In addition, it is said to provide for an increased T-cell count in AIDS patients.

Vibrates to the number 8.

DOLOMITE   [Astrological Sign of Aries]

Dolomite crystallizes in the form of masses, grains, rhombohedral and prismatic crystals, and crystal aggregates. The colour range includes white, grey, green-white, red, rose-red, green, pink, brown, and black. The rhombohedral crystals which are quite characteristic of dolomite are in the tri-rhombohedral class with phenacite.

Dolomite encourages charitable actions and relieves sorrow in such a way as to assist one to recognize that there are actually no reasons to be sorrowful [i.e., "everything happens for a reason"]. It encourages energetic and impulsive original thinking and manifestation. It also assists in producing stamina when one is dealing with hyper-active individuals.

It can be worn, carried, and used as an elixir [stable crystallized forms are recommended]. When used to enhance a room, the massive, granular forms may also be used. The tri-rhombohedral crystalline structure is useful for energy alignment, balancing, and blockage removal. It can also be used to arrest leakages of energy from the chakras.

This mineral can be used to build the body; including muscular structure, blood cells, bones, teeth, nails, and skin. It can be used to provide oxygenation to the lungs and cellular structures, to relieve chills, and to treat disorders associated with the adrenal glands and urogenital system.

Vibrates to the number 3.

DOMEYKITE   [Astrological Sign of Scorpio]

Domeykite crystallizes as reniform and botryoidal formations and as masses. The colour ranges from tin-white to steel-grey.

This mineral can be used to both sustain and "maintain" one during changes, helping to fortify and to strengthen one for transformation, and allowing for the gentle comprehension of the hidden layers of "cause" which support the states of distress and dis-ease. It further assists one in detaching one from the cause; hence, reducing or abating the effect. It helps one to understand that any control is personal control and that in order to actualize ones full potential, the state of personal action is required. It brings the unconscious guiding thoughts to the surface.

In addition, it serves to rejuvenate, to restore, and to renew, while actually triggering powerful cycles of change, and assisting one to direct the beginnings and endings of all phases of ones life. It provides an energy to bring the capability for one to make a "fresh-start" in unfavourable circumstances. It allows one to recognize that metamorphosis and continued change throughout all times is concentrated with determination of both the acceleration and the ease of reformation of the self.

Domeykite has been used to grid areas subject to volcanic action and earthquakes, to stabilize and to balance the energies associated with same.

It has been used to heighten "big business", promoting an aptitude for commerce and promoting financial security.

Ones analytical capabilities are reinforced and power over ones creation is magnified. Honesty is elevated and criminal tendencies are lessened.

This mineral has been used to augment the creative and regenerative forces of the body. It has also been used in the treatment of skin eruptions, skin growths, and the gonads.

Vibrates to the master number 44.

DOUGLASITE   [Astrological Sign of Leo]

Douglasite crystallizes as green granular masses which alter to red when exposed to air.

This mineral can be used to combat prejudicial judgmental ideas and to provide incentive to higher aspirations.

It provides for a connection between the heart chakra and the base chakra, allowing for the transformation of love to personal power.

It allows one to see into the past aspects of ones lives and to recognize the connection between the self and the universal/galactic spirit.

It can be used to grid ones garden or to stimulate the strength and growth of plants; use of an elixir or placing the mineral at four corners of the garden/in the planter have both achieved results.

It can be used in the treatment of disorderly spinal alignment, dysfunctional physical vitality, and disorders related to conditions of atrophy.

Vibrates to the number 5.

DRAVIDE   [See Brown Tourmaline]

DUFTITE   [Astrological Sign of Scorpio]

Duftite crystallizes in the form of crusts and tiny crystals coloured from apple-green to deep green.

This mineral helps to rid one of inferiority complexes, to increase ones attention span, and to provide for assistance in artistic activities and pursuits.

It can be used to both activate and open the heart chakra, facilitating openness in communication with others and with oneself.

It can also be used in the treatment for obesity, to help one withdraw less painfully from smoking, and in circumstances where it is necessary for the body to accept a replacement for some portion or item of which it has grown accustomed.

Vibrates to the number 4.

DUMONTITE   [Astrological Sign of Libra]

Dumontite crystallizes in the form of tiny elongated crystals. When viewed from one axis [X], the colour is pale yellow; when viewed from another axis [Y], the colour is golden yellow.

This mineral induces one to participate actively in affairs, increases ones imaginative capabilities, enhances genuineness, stimulates the intellect, enhances speech, and eliminates severity in ones manner. It stimulates and activates both the crown chakra and the solar plexus chakra, bringing intelligence to the pursuit of spirituality. It provides for the reinstatement of the aptitude which one was born.

It is an excellent stone for communal bonding, stimulating practicality in lifework and life-pursuits; the practicality allowing for one to remain centered and functional within the world while progressing on the path toward total attunement with "All That Is".

It can also be used in the treatment of elevated cholesterol, and infections of the bladder and the urinary tract.

Do not prepare an elixir of this mineral via the normal method.

Vibrates to the number 4.

DUMORTIERITE   [Astrological Sign of Leo]

Dumortierite crystallizes in granular or fibrous masses in the colours of blue-to-violet and pink-to-brown.

This mineral can be used to reduce excitability and to eliminate stubbornness while facilitating the continuance of "standing-up" for oneself; it can also assist in providing the stamina to retain the self when one is subjected to harsh environments.

It is an excellent stone for patience, allowing for the recognition of the potential of any or all with whom one is involved. It can actually provide an element of accommodation to bazaar reality, helping one to both realize and understand that reality is illusion, and illusion is real.

It can stimulate verbalization of spiritual ideas [blue-violet colour] and can provide grounding in love matches while clearing-away unsettled areas in relationships [pink-brown colour].

It can be used to diminish wasting disorders, to provide strength in dealing with conditions of dis-ease, and to provide insight into the basis of a condition in order to help one to understand and correct the cause.

Vibrates to the number 4.

DUNDASITE   [Astrological Sign of Sagittarius]

Dundasite crystallizes in the form of white crusts and small round aggregates of radiating needle-like crystals.

This mineral can be used to increase ones analytical capabilities and can stimulate precision, where required, in ones life.

It can also be used to facilitate expertise in design, dance, and poetry.

It is a "stone for accomplishment", rather than planning; helping one to the goal and encouraging the carefree attitude that "life is perfect" and all goals can be easily attained.

Dundasite also increases ones talents for cleverness, imagination, inventiveness, and humour, assisting ones alertness and vigilance, when consciously directed, and facilitating the release of tendencies associated with and proclivities for lethargy and idleness.

It can be used in the treatment of conditions associated with disorderly ambulation and dexterity. It has also been used to calm extreme states of confusion and anxiety.

Vibrates to the number 7.

DYSCRASITE   [Astrological Sign of Aquarius]

Dyscrasite crystallizes in massive formation and, occasionally, in the form of hexagonal-type crystals. It is a metallic silver colour.

This mineral can be used to bring "luck". It can also stimulate mental acuity, such that one can "make" ones "luck".

It has been used to align the meridians of the physical body with the ethereal body in order to assure proper flow to, and sufficiency of energy within, the physical body. It also assists in providing balance to the male/female qualities within one, to stabilize the emotions, and to counteract negativity.

It can be used to supplement other healing stones in order to eliminate the potential difficulties encountered in the healing process.

It can also be used in the treatment of disorders of the intestines, digestive tract, muscles, and bladder. It can help during pregnancy to provide health and warmth to the unborn.

Vibrates to the number 6.

**WHEREVER YOU ARE, WHATEVER YOU DO,
A PART OF YOU IS EXPERIENCING UNIVERSAL LOVE**

ECKERMANNITE   [Astrological Sign of Virgo]

Eckermannite crystallizes in the form of aggregates and long prismatic crystals in the colour range of dark blue to green.

This mineral can be used to access insight into the mystic realm, transcending ordinary human knowledge. One can facilitate trance channeling with this mineral and can receive a direct union of the spirit with all of divinity through contemplation and love.

It is an excellent stone to assist one in initiating and completing changes; it helps one to bring variety to ones life and to continue progress in the areas defined.

It also provides a lightening effect on the body and is conducive to out-of-body experiences.

It produces an intuitive connection to others and is excellent for use in the field of teaching and instructive situations, facilitating an understanding with respect to the comprehension of others.

In addition, this mineral can be used in the treatment of disorders of the eyes, to aid in the amelioration of unbalanced cholesterol levels, and to assist in the assimilation of the amino acids required to maintain the physical body.

Vibrates to the master number 55.

EGLESTONITE   [Astrological Sign of Libra]

Eglestonite crystallizes in the formation of isometric minute crystals of dodecahedral habit. The colour range includes brown to yellow, darkening to black upon exposure to air.

This mineral can assist one in the establishment of values and in the expression of ones personal values. It assists one in minimizing vanity and egotism with respect to ones abilities and/or possessions.

It assists one in magnetically attracting that which one desires and to enhance practicality and carelessness. It further acts to reduce parasitic behavior.

Eglestonite serves to reinforce the creation of harmony, unison, and beauty. It symbolizes feminine energies, bringing love and the power to love, coalition, honesty to ones feelings, and intimate union. It assists one to act in a gentle, kind, and free manner, bringing romance, thoughtfulness, adaptability, appreciation, and refinement to ones life.

It facilitates the energies to stimulate one in the adeptness of love and the social arts. It has been used in socio-emotional situations to stimulate harmonious partnerships.

It is a mineral to advance possessions, money, and beauty; in addition, it has been used to advance employment in the arts, social life, fabrication of adornment, and creation of fashion.

Eglestonite has been used in the treatment of emotional disorders, to ameliorate disorders associated with the feminine organs, the circulatory system, and the hands. It has also been used to in the correction of dis-ease associated with the lumbar, the throat, the kidneys, and the parathyroid glands. It can be used in the elimination of free-radicals from the body.

Preparation of an elixir via the normal method is not recommended.

Vibrates to the number 5.

EILAT STONE   [Astrological Sign of Sagittarius]

The eilat stone is a massive form containing copper, turquoise, chrysocolla, and a few other minerals which are required to stabilize the structure. It occurs in veins of blues and greens. It can usually be purchased, when available, in the polished form.

This stone combines the properties of CHRYSOCOLLA, TURQUOISE, and COPPER [see appropriate sections of this book].

In addition, it helps one in the attainment of growth toward wisdom. This stone is known as "the sage", sage being a wise man; it provides for insight to the most beneficial course of action, and stimulates creative problem-solving.

It also can be used to cleanse negativity from the environment in which it resides.

Vibrates to the number 3.

ELBAITE   [See Pink Tourmaline]

EMBOLITE   [Astrological Sign of Scorpio]

Embolite crystallizes in the form of masses and cubes. The colour range includes yellow, yellow-green, and grey-green.

This mineral helps to purify the auric field as well as the physical body. It can be used to remove toxins from the physical form and to remove darkness from the auric field. It assists in purification of the emotional system, relieving characteristics of selfishness from ones aspects.

The major healing action of the stone provides for purification of the body; it can also be also useful for dyspepsia. In addition, it can be used to stimulate the methodical and systematic growth of the skeletal and cellular systems of the body.

Vibrates to the number 9.

EMERALD   [Astrological Signs of Taurus, Gemini, & Aries]

Emerald is a form of beryl and crystallizes in the structure of prismatic crystals, sometimes vertically striated and terminated by small pyramid-like faces. The colour is emerald green. Please note that there is a stone on the market which is, sometimes, designated "red emerald" - it is actually a red beryl, identified as bixbite; information relative to this "red emerald" is listed in the BIXBITE section of this book.

In addition to the properties listed in the BERYL section, emerald is known as a "stone of successful love". It is said to provide for domestic bliss and to instill both sensitivity and loyalty within the self and within others.

It can be used to enhance the memory and to stimulate the use of greater mental capacity. The emerald helps to combine intelligence with discernment, allowing for the choice of "right" action to be the only choice available.

It can be used to open, to activate, and to stimulate the heart chakra, while helping to quiet the emotions. It is a stone to bring harmony to all areas of ones life.

It can also assist in inciting one to activity and to facilitate intensity and focus in ones actions. It can be used to eliminate negativity from ones life and to bring forth the positive actions required to assist one in remaining centered in the practicality of ones lifework.

It can help to bring awareness of the unknown to conscious recognition, helping one to access the laws of order within the universe and to eliminate from ones life that which impedes progress.

It can help one to maintain the rhythmic breathing conducive to entering and to attaining depth in the meditative state. After the meditative state, it helps one to maintain the cool brilliance of the deliberate reflection and to emit the radiance of the light.

It is said to have been one of the stones used in the breastplate of the high priest.

It is also said to bring beneficial consequences to matters involving the legal affairs.

It can be used in the treatment of disorders of the spine, lungs, heart, and muscular system. It has also been used to soothe the eyes.

Vibrates to the number 4.

EMMONSITE   [Astrological Sign of Aquarius]

Emmonsite crystallizes as yellow-green compact masses and scalular formations.

This mineral can be used to help one to remember how small, yet significant, one is in the overall scheme of the world.

It helps to teach one to reach toward others and to understand the personal state of contribution while maintaining both personal freedom and progression in ones life. It can also be used to sustain both intellectual and emotional pursuits.

It can be used to help correct eye deficiencies and to provide for increased assimilation of iron. It has been used to soften and relax body tissues and to provide support for menopausal discomforts.

Vibrates to the number 5.

ENARGITE   [Astrological Sign of Pisces]

Enargite crystallizes in massive, granular, and columnar form, as well as in small crystals with vertical striations, and star-shaped trillings [six-rayed crystal structure consisting of three individual crystals]. The colour is grey to black.

This mineral combines the aspects of intuition with analysis, bringing forth evaluation via inspiration.

Holding the stone provides a grounding effect with concurrent stimulus to "get-with-it". To stimulate the power of the stone, it may be carried or worn.

Enargite can be used for problems with the joints of the body as well as the back. It can also be used to increase physical vitality.

Do not prepare an elixir via the normal method.

Vibrates to the number 7.

ENDLICHITE   [Astrological Sign of Cancer]

Endlichite crystallizes in the formation of prismatic crystals, cavernous crystals, globules, and druses. The colour range includes yellow, red, and brown.

This mineral can be used to promote a blending and supporting between two or more people through the achievement of outside resources.

It acts to bring a request for assistance to the appropriate location and facilitates the endowment of support. It serves to bring support from friends and to foster growth and expression.

It has been used to bring a state of balance which furthers ones sharpening of consciousness and heightening of awareness, such that one cannot remain passive.

The energy represents and enhances activity directed toward building that which is relatively easy; it attracts opportunity and assists one in completion.

It further stimulates the intellect and provides for an intellectual grounding during times of study.

Endlichite has been used in the treatment of disorders of the stomach, the ears, the mouth, excessive mucoid formation, and the cortex.

Do not prepare an elixir via the normal method.

Vibrates to the number 8.

ENHYDRO   [Astrological Signs of Cancer, Pisces, & Scorpio]

The enhydro is a mineral which contains fluid; the fluid being that from which chalcedony, agate, or quartz was deposited. The fluid can be eons in age and is most likely quite pure. In addition to the qualities of the host mineral, the following attributes apply.

This mineral can be used to help one to "put oneself in the shoes of another", and to both recognize and understand the true feelings of that person. Not being a stone to stimulate sympathy, it supports the empathetic state.

It provides for the coupling of imagination and practicality, inducing sensibility in employment, relationships, and in the acceptance of responsibilities. It brings honour to ones associated circumstances.

It also contains a life-sustaining energy, initiating adaptability in situations which could, otherwise, become stressful.

The enhydro assists in metamorphosis and continued change throughout all times; it provides for concentrated determination of both the acceleration and the ease of reformation of the self. The concepts of impetus and catalytic motion are enhances.

In healing, it is useful to have an enhydro available; it assists in bringing the body to the state or specified condition that one is attempting to attain. It is rather a strength to help other minerals perform in the requisite manner. The enhydro can help to treat conditions related to the degraded integrity of tissue and/or organs.

Vibrates to the master number 44.

ENSTATITE   [Astrological Sign of Aries]

Enstatite crystallizes in the form of masses, plate-like shapes, fibers, and distinct prismatic rare crystals. The colour range includes colourless, yellow, green, brown, and grey. It is found in association with diamonds in the Republic of South Africa and is contained in meteorite formations.

This mineral can be quite helpful in situations where one wishes to "best" an opponent; the enstatite found in meteorites seems to provide an instant connection to an intelligent force in these cases, while the enstatite found in the diamond mines seems to produce more of a conquering, yet modest, unassuming, and assured attitude to the user.

It also assists one in achieving the state of determination without willful-ness, such that one may continue to be flexible with respect to the methodology of attainment. It can help one in all facets relative to service, activating the value of assistance.

Enstatite is a "stone of chivalry", promoting loving fairness and unbiased judgment within the user. It also provides the stimulus for decisiveness.

In healing, it can be useful to bring an alkaline body state to the acid condition. It can also be used to assist the body in normal changing cycles. It can stimulate the assimilation of iron and can provide for increased duration of iron within the physical body.

Vibrates to the number 5.

EOSPHORITE   [Astrological Sign of Leo]

Eosphorite crystallizes as radial aggregates, masses, and prismatic crystals. The colour range includes pink, colourless, yellow, red, blue, and black. The pink colour is often exhibited in a beautiful "gemmy" structure.

This mineral can provide for a shield of protection along the path to ones past-lives and to early periods of civilization on the planet. It also helps to produce and/or to stimulate the acceptance of oneself, and can assist one in conquering inherent long-enduring hostilities and feelings of inferiority.

The gemmy pink eosphorite is truly wonderful for clearing and subsequently activating the heart chakra.

When consciously attuned, this mineral provides a "GOD SPEED" to ones endeavors.

Eosphorite can be used to help with stabilizing and/or correcting the RNA/DNA structure within the body, and with the assimilation of the minerals necessary for body functioning.

Vibrates to the number 4.

EPIDIDYMITE   [Astrological Sign of Aquarius]

Epididymite crystallizes in the form of spherical aggregates and tabular crystals. The colour range includes white, colourless, grey, blue, yellow, and violet. Eudidymite is quite similar in structure and colour and exhibits properties similar to those of Epididymite.

This mineral is quite useful to provide support in "new beginnings" and to help to provide for a visualization of the path required.

It promotes enhanced auric and physical protection and protects against psychic attacks.

It also provides for a stable comforting "blanket" upon which the further unconstrained connections to the etheric body are both stimulated and facilitated.

It aligns the chakras with the universal nervous system, bringing both tact and cooperation to the forces of stability.

It can help to protect one from contagious dis-eases and is used in the treatment of disorders of the male reproductive system, the skin, the fleshy tissue, and the central nervous system.

Vibrates to the number 2.

EPIDOTE   [Astrological Sign of Gemini]

Epidote crystallizes in the form of plates, needle-like and prismatic crystals [the prismatic crystals being sometimes longitudinally striated and terminated on one end], granular masses, fibers, and deeply striated masses. The colour range includes yellow, yellow-green, pistachio green, brown-green, green-black, grey, and black; it also occurs in transparent reds and yellows.

This mineral can provide for increase in that to which one attunes it. This short but clear statement shows that epidote is truly a stone to experience in all aspects of one life.

It dispels critical-ness, enhances keen perception, stimulates participation and interaction, and supplements personal power.

It is also useful to combat dehydration and can be used as an elixir for softening and smoothing skin. It can be used in the treatment of disorders associated with the nervous system, brain, and thyroid.

Vibrates to the number 2.

EPISTILBITE   [Astrological Sign of Sagittarius]

Epistilbite crystallizes in the form of granular masses, radial spherical aggregates, and prismatic crystals. The colour range includes white and pink; the crystals occur in a beautiful red.

This mineral can be used to investigate the origin, nature, methods, and lack of limitations with respect to human "knowing". It should be noted that this "knowing" is based on a mechanism which extends far beyond the intellect. One can access this information and then understand and utilize the fact that man has no limitations.

Epistilbite also assists one in writing personal thoughts clearly. It is also helpful in verbal communication and in enhancing ones listening abilities. It can provide for stimulus to allow one to connect with other worlds via automatic writing. It can be used to calm the emotions, to stimulate the aspect of unconditional love, and to help one to flow through stressful situations.

It can be used in the treatment of incontinence and uncontrolled kidney/bladder functions, and to support the stability of the structure of the teeth and gums.

Vibrates to the number 9.

ERIONITE   [Astrological Signs of Taurus, Cancer, Pisces, & Scorpio]

Erionite forms in white fibrous masses resembling wool, and occurs in opal deposits.

This mineral can help to dissipate controversy and is quite useful during disputes. Placement of another mineral on this "stone" will remove discordant vibrations from the other mineral; allowing a piece of erionite to be a member of ones environment will produce the removal of discordant vibrations from that environment. Having Erionite in ones surroundings is similar to "smudging" with sage, other herbs, or incense, with respect to the removal of negativity.

It can provide one with insight into the methodology which may be utilized to stimulate the intuitive nature.

It helps one in matters of personality modifications and stimulates the recognition of the multiplicity of patterns which are existing within ones life.

It can also be useful in the rectification of concerns of ownership and lawsuits.

Erionite can be used to reinforce ones strength, to treat disorders associated with the stomach and digestive system, and to assist in regeneration.

Vibrates to the number 5.

ERYTHRITE   [Astrological Signs of Virgo, Capricorn, & Taurus]

Erythrite crystallizes in the form of bladed aggregates, globular and reniform structures [formed with a small crystalline structure covering or as a part of the outer surface] stellate shapes, and vertically striated prismatic crystals. The colour range includes the hues from pale pink to deep purple, crimson, peach-red, and grey. The structure sometimes occurs exhibiting a pleochroic quality [i.e., where a pale pink colour is displayed through the X-axis, pale violet is displayed through the Y-axis, and red is displayed through the Z-axis].

This mineral can be used to provide for a strong and flowing connection between all of the chakras, bringing the use of a loving personal power to the realm of spirituality.

It can bring harmony to communications and can impart responsiveness to the user.

Erythrite can help one to "see in many directions" and to assimilate the knowledge coming from each; for example, looking within oneself, into ones environment, and into the auric field can produce answers concerning health and development issues. The other possibilities are endless and are left to the reader.

This mineral can be worn, carried, or allowed to rest in ones environment. Do not use as an elixir.

It can be used in the treatment of skin disorders, inflammations, and dis-eases related to bone marrow, red blood cells, and infectious conditions [primarily of the throat].

Vibrates to the number 2.

ERYTHROSIDERITE   [Astrological Signs of Aries, Aquarius,
                                                        Gemini, & Libra]

Erythrosiderite crystallizes in the form of red tabular crystals and crystals configured similar to octahedrons.

This mineral can bring universal orderliness in the midst of chaos. It can expedite organization within ones life, and provides for both a balancing in relationships and an elimination of reproach. It also assists in the eradication of symptoms of irritability.

It can provide a personal magnetism to the user, bringing those desired closer to the heart.

Erythrosiderite is also quite helpful in providing continuity of stamina when activity is intense and over-extended.

This mineral can be helpful in the treatment of disorders of the veins and the muscle structures of the body. It can also be used to help during weight-loss struggles, and has been effective in the reduction of growths. It can be carried by runners and athletes to assist in the elimination of sprains and spasms.

Vibrates to the number 9.

ETTRINGITE   [Astrological Sign of Gemini]

Ettringite crystallizes in the form of colourless fibers, hexagonal double pyramids, and tiny needle-like crystals.

This mineral activates more of the yin qualities, but also provides for emotional and physical balancing and provides strength and vitality to the physical body.

It can be used to allow one to be able to distinguish between sincerity and insincerity, truthfulness and untruthfulness, loving attitudes and unloving attitudes, etc. It actually provides for a mechanism to clarify situations of duality.

It helps one to experience the diversions in life with openness, to be receptive and understanding of fluctuating emotional states, and to augment ones knowledge with the pieces of each anomaly.

A message of ettringite is that if one looses faith in another, one will find faith in oneself.

It can be used in the treatment of disorders of the tendons and the throat, and to support the cycles of toxin elimination.

Vibrates to the master number 55.

EUCHROITE   [Astrological Sign of Libra]

Euchroite crystallizes in the form of lovely emerald green or garden green prismatic crystals resembling dioptase.

This mineral enhances beauty and splendor, both superficially and from within the self.

It provides for a strength to ones character and a satisfaction with oneself so that one is never lonely, and can stand alone in any situation. It helps one to understand that "one is always alone, yet one is never alone".

It helps one to be "quick-witted" and to become "more alive". It can also provide for a steadiness in decisions and actions.

Euchroite can be used in healing to facilitate wholeness; i.e., it can be useful in re-knitting activities associated with the skin, bones, muscular structure, and internal organs.

Vibrates to the number 5.

EUCLASE   [Astrological Signs of Virgo & Sagittarius]

Euclase crystallizes as long prismatic crystals. The colour range includes blue, green, and colourless.

This mineral has been called the "stone of happiness". It can stimulate happiness in ones life through activity, not only governed by reason, but governed by the heart, intuition, and serendipity.

It inspires pride in accomplishment, a loving pride which gently restrains one from repeating "old lessons".

Euclase helps one to reach for, and to attain, the "ultimate" in all areas. It teaches one to "watch the stars" and to not allow the gaze to be diverted by lesser illuminants.

It is an excellent stone for enhancing communication skills, stimulating the crown chakra, the throat chakra, and the heart chakra, to combine energies and to facilitate beneficial clarity. It awakens the creative force from within the perfect self.

It can also be used to provide assistance in the mathematical fields, primarily geometry.

It can be used in the treatment of dis-aligned energy fields and assists in providing flowing lines of energy conductivity through the body.

It can also be used to provide for relief from aches, pains of arthritis, muscle tension, minor cuts and scratches, bruises, muscular cramps, inflammation, swelling, constriction of the blood vessels, and spasmatic conditions. It can also be used as an anti-bacterial and antiseptic.

Vibrates to the number 3.

EULITE   [See Hypersthene]

EVANSITE   [Astrological Sign of Virgo]

Evansite crystallizes in the form of massive stalactitic, reniform, and botryoidal shapes. The colour range included colourless, white, yellow-green, and blue.

This mineral allows one to see the truth, when the truth appears to be elusive. It provides insight into personal experience and acts to incite reconciliations, such that the hostilities involved which initiated a separation are vanquished.

It is helpful to teachers and lecturers, providing for an increase in the capabilities required to elicit understanding and the capacity to maintain audiences in a state of calm, balanced rationality.

The mineral can be used in the treatment of dis-eases of the "wearing-away" variety. It can also be used to ease the states of dizziness and disorientation and to ameliorate the symptoms of vertigo.

Vibrates to the number 5.

EVEITE   [Astrological Sign of Virgo]

Eveite crystallizes in the form of apple green tabular crystals. The ones I have seen are beautiful and come from Sweden.

This mineral assists one to attain, and to remain in, the "always-be-prepared" state and has been called the "stone of living".

It helps one to be precise in expression, to remain calm, impartial, and uniform in action, and to maintain a "level-headed" demeanor. It is a mineral for living on the Earth plane.

It helps to alleviate temptation which would be non-productive to ones advancement, and to enhance purity in ideals.

It can also be used in ameliorating discomforts associated with nervousness, mental dis-continuity, and stress.

Vibrates to the number 3.

FOLLOW YOUR BLISS

FAUJASITE   [Astrological Signs of Gemini & Aries]

Faujasite crystallizes in the form of octahedral crystals. The colour range includes colourless and white, but the mineral is sometimes stained with other minerals to produce other colours.

This mineral can be used to enhance perception and to guide one in the adventures to the unknown.

Faujasite, when sliced into thin sections, exhibits the quality of transparency and can be used to induce the psychic state. It assists one in maintaining and in going quite deeply into the state.

It can also be used to assist one to look within the inner being of the self or another and to evaluate the matters which are affecting ones actualization [without exhibiting judgmental feelings].

The mineral also acts to keep one true to ones feelings and to help one to maintain propriety when counseling others. It discourages unproductive speaking and assists one in attaining the direct, yet loving, approach in conversations.

It can be used in the treatment for loss of smell and for decreasing an overabundance of mucus in ones system. It is also helpful for stabilizing ones growth patterns and for treating disorders associated with disruptive physical states.

Vibrates to the number 2.

FAUSTITE   [Astrological Sign of Virgo]

Faustite crystallizes in the form of compact masses. The colour is apple-green.

This mineral can be used by those who are actively engaged in outdoor activities related to forests and meadows. It provides one with an even keener sense of appreciation of the life surrounding ones reality and allows for deeper communication with the plant and animal life in those locations.

Communication with the plant life can produce information concerning herbal remedies, while communication and an ethereal connection with the animal life can provide one with information concerning the freedom of spirit and the understanding which is required to suspend and eliminate exploitation. The communication aspects are endless and the reader is encouraged to venture into the realm of discovery.

Communication with the plant and animal kingdoms can actually, heal ones spirit and ones life.

Faustite stimulates innovation and exploration with respect to the nature of the universe and the nature of the moment. It allows for release of emotional inhibitions, bringing forth verbalization of feelings in a loving and "allowing" manner.

It assists in dispelling the negative, being as a "sweet rose nodding in the sunshine" and obliterating that which is not desired. It also helps one to remove physically from situations which would not be both beneficial and constructive to ones life.

It can be used in the treatment of fungus disorders, rickets, scurvy, muscular rigidity, and to increase the assimilation of Vitamins D and E, calcium, and protein.

Vibrates to the number 2.

FELDSPAR   [Astrological Sign of Aquarius - Elemental]

Feldspar is the name of a family of silicates which are related in crystalline structures and chemical compositions. The feldspars addressed in this book include ALBITE, ADULARIA, AMAZONITE, AZULICITE, LABRADORITE, MOONSTONE, OLIGOCLASE, ORTHOCLASE, PARACELSIAN, and SUNSTONE. The general properties of the feldspar group are listed below.

This mineral assists one in detaching from the old, encouraging unconventional and exciting methods to attains ones goals. It provides for support in issues of self-awareness and self-love, for with realization of love one can become united with all aspects of the world.

It has been found as a constituent of moon rock and provides for a connection with inter-galactic intelligence. Feldspar also enables one to access the communicative forces of this intelligence.

It assists one in locating that which has been mis-placed and in discovering and understanding previously unidentified messages from both within and without of the self.

It can be used in the treatment of disorders associated with the skin and muscular structure.

Vibrates to the number 9.

FERGUSONITE   [Astrological Signs of Aquarius & Virgo]

Fergusonite crystallizes in the form of grains, scales, pyramid-type crystals, and prismatic crystals. The colour ranges from brown to black. The occurrence of this mineral in massive quartz is lovely.

Fergusonite can be used to enhance ones self-esteem, to stimulate mathematical abilities, and to increase ones sensibility.

It enhances leadership qualities and self-assuredness and control of ones life, while allowing one to recognize and to act upon the pragmatic issues which are encountered.

It is an assistant for initiation of the rise of the Kundalini and helps to produce impetus for the continuance of ones inner "journey toward the light".

It can be used in the treatment of blood disorders, to increase circulation in the veins of the neck and head, to relieve sciatic pain, and to ameliorate burns.

Vibrates to the number 4.

FERRIERITE   [Astrological Sign of Aries]

Ferrierite crystallizes in the form of thin tabular crystals, often in radial-shaped groups. The colour ranges from colourless to white.

This mineral can help to keep one suspended in meditation [after one has attained the meditative state].

It emanates a joyful reality and acts to transmit the joy to the user. It provides energy to assist one in transforming ones life.

It also helps one to cleanse the mind of unfortunate and stress-producing memories, allowing for release, with integration of same.

It is useful in matters concerning transportation over long distances [i.e., distances of the length or physical composure that one would not want to walk]. In this case, the mineral can help one to have "smooth sailing" during the travel involved. Please note that this travel is relative to the physical, mental, and astral wanderings which one may experience.

Ferrierite can be used in the treatment of chills, dizziness, and motion sickness. It has also been used to accelerate the healing process.

Vibrates to the number 5.

FERSMANNITE   [Astrological Sign of Cancer]

Fersmannite crystallizes in light to dark brown tetragonal-type forms.

It can be used to stimulate the mind, bringing superb independent thought and contentment to the user; it is quite helpful in the development of rational and systematic thought.

It can assist one in gaining prominence, providing for conditions of opportunity for encounters both desired and necessary. It also enables one to realize that, indeed, "the time has arrived"; allowing one to recognize that deferral, in most cases, is non-productive, and assisting one in the release of all delay.

This mineral can remove "muddy" spots from the chakras and from the auric field and can draw-out pain from within the body. It is supportive when used with other minerals, tending to instill a calming and tranquil energy.

It has also been used in the treatment of disorders of the arms, feet, and hands.

Vibrates to the number 7.

FIEDLERITE   [Astrological Sign of Taurus]

Fiedlerite crystallizes in the form of white tabular crystals.

This mineral is a loving companion, emanating energy to encourage one to express ideas and opinions, and to act with grace.

It also helps one to be comfortable with idleness and to "use the idleness" in a constructive way.

Fiedlerite can also be helpful when one is in search of a home; it can direct one toward the "perfect place" and can help one to recognize, to acknowledge, and to secure same.

It also helps one to recognize the body as the "temple of spirit", and to subsequently remember the methods to gratify the physical without detriment.

It can be used in the treatment for shock.

Vibrates to the number 3.

FILLOWITE   [Astrological Sign of Leo]

Fillowite crystallizes in the form of granular masses and rhombohedral-type crystals. The colour range includes yellow, yellow to red-brown, and colourless.

This mineral can be used to help eliminate procrastination [unless one procrastinates in the use of fillowite], and to bring abundance into ones life.

It enables one to flow with all situations, imparting the energy to stimulate less rigidity in ones "belief" structures.

It can be used in the treatment of disorders associated with cholesterol, cellulite, and other substance build-ups within ones system. It can also help to relieve tension associated with the shoulder and neck areas.

Vibrates to the number 3.

FLINT   [Astrological Sign of Scorpio]

Flint is a variety of chalcedony, occurring in grey, smoky-brown, and brown-black colours. In addition to the qualities listed in the CHALCEDONY section of this book, the following information applies.

This mineral is an excellent choice for use in activities related to thought transference; one may transfer information, ideas, and loving emotional messages to another and receive, in return, the touching interpersonal experiences of the energy of the universe.

It can help to relieve shyness and to promote both intimate and personal experiences.

It also assists one in severing the emotional ties through which one is attached to problems and distressful situations.

It has been revered by the ancient tribes of this planet to produce protective energy and to dispel negativity from "haunted" localities.

It assists one in viewing the unknown, providing for insight into the methods by which to oppose contrary forces; it can further enhance ones abilities toward meticulous judgment concerning the manifested character of others. It can also be helpful in money management.

It has been used as a talisman to bring intellectual, psychological, rational, and physical strength during confrontations, arguments, and disputes.

Flint has been used in the treatment for kidney stones, liver disorders, calcium deposits, lung disorders, skin lesions, and digestion, and to prevent nightmares. It can be used as an elixir to enhance the integrity of the skin and to help in the diminishment of superficial growths.

It has also been used as a tool for psychic surgery.

Vibrates to the number 7.

FLORENCITE   [Astrological Sign of Taurus]

Florencite crystallizes in the form of rhombohedral pink or pale yellow crystals.

This mineral can be used to stimulate and to further energize flower essences. It can also stimulate right-brain/left-brain synthesis in action and can provide for creativity with intellectual support.

It is excellent for clearing and gently balancing the heart chakra. It can be used to kindle romantic love, bringing to ones emotions the freshness of the breezes and the tranquility of tropical seas. It has been used to bring harmony to business relationships and to help to assure the safe-keeping and appropriate use of ones resources.

It is good to use around areas of the head and is quite supportive to astral travel by facilitating the remembering processes.

It can be used in the treatment of mental disorders and in those dysfunctions associated with heart regulation and tension.

Vibrates to the number 8.

FLUOR SPAR   [See Fluorite]

FLUORITE   [Astrological Signs of Pisces & Capricorn]
                                                [Also Known As Fluor Spar]

Fluorite crystallizes in the form of masses, grains, columns, cubes, octahedra, and rhombdodecahedra crystals. The colour range includes pink, blue, green, yellow, purple, magenta, red, black, and colourless, and shades of all.

This mineral produces an energy which is predisposed to discourage chaotic, disruptive, and disorganized growth. It emits an energy which can be used to stabilize and to produce order within the mental, physical, emotional, and spiritual systems. It can be used to bring order to chaos.

It helps to impart impartiality and unbiased, detached reasoning in situations where it would be beneficial to both view and to act upon information objectively.

It has been known as a "stone of discernment and aptitude", bringing the energies of responsibility to the qualities of systematic intuition. It represents the height of mental achievement, facilitating a limitless range of avenues for exploration.

It increases the ability to concentrate, balancing the positive and negative relationships of the mind. It helps one to see both reality and truth behind illusion.

It is excellent in helping one to understand the balances intrinsic to relationships. It provides for a stabilizing energy, helping relationships, groups, and individuals to flourish in the realm of that which is beneficial to all.

The energy of fluorite can inspire the universal energies to activate the nourishing energies of the body, assisting one in the attainment of the ultimate state of physical perfection. It allows one to recognize the purity of the universe and to understand that each portion of the universe maintains an inherent perfection in order to allow the unfolding of the perfect universe.

It also encourages and sustains the flawless ideal of health, intellect, and emotional well-being. It provides for purification, cleansing, and elimination of that which is in disorder. It can be used to dispel disorders at the commencement of the symptoms. It is useful to dissipate the states associated with colds, flu, staph and strep infections, infectious cankers, herpes, ulcers, and similar infections. It has been used in the treatment of violent and/or highly infective dis-ease, as well as by others who are working with those affected in order to provide protection from the affectation. It has been used in the treatment of tumors - at the beginning stages of their growth.

It can be used in the treatment of both the structure of the bone and the composition and formation of the cells. It has been used to assist in the prevention of RNA/DNA damage and can be used in repair of same.

Fluorite vibrates to the number 7 and Fluor Spar vibrates to the number 9.

The following list provides additional properties for several colours of fluorite. The manifestation of these colours within the fluorite can promote the manifestation of the additional qualities.

Blue Fluorite helps one to develop orderly, sequential thoughts. It is also quite good for promoting orderly record-keeping.

It produces a calm energy, which is non-directive; this enables one to both easily and competently direct the energies toward the appropriate medium. It is an excellent energy for stimulating clear, concise communicative skills, both within the physical reality and between this plane and the other worlds.

It can be used in the treatment of eye problems, blocked tear ducts, inflammation, and disorders of the inner nasal passages, inner ear, throat, and speech.

Vibrates to the number 2.

Chinese Fluorite combines the properties of the appropriate colour of the fluorite with the qualities listed in the PYRITE section of this book.

It is an excellent stone for both protecting against, and for amelioration of, dis-ease.

Vibrates to the number 7.

Colourless Fluorite has been used to stimulate the crown chakra and to clear and energize the aura. It brings accordance between the intellect and the spiritual, assisting one in recognizing that which is not conducive to furthering the spiritual nature.

It has been used to align the chakras, to open the pathways between the universal energy and the physical body, and to facilitate transmittal of energy from other minerals during the healing state.

It has been used to clear the eyes, to eliminate obstructions from the area of the iris and pupil, and to stimulate improvement in sight.

Vibrates to the number 2.

Green Fluorite can bring a cleansing, tidying, mint-like freshness of spring time and renewal to the chakras. It can be used to help diminish mild trauma in the emotional body and to eliminate negativity within a room, the negative vibratory states being transmuted toward the light and love of the universe.

It can be used extensively in the treatment of disorders of the stomach; it acts to circulate a soothing energy throughout the intestinal tract. It also helps to ease discomforts of colitis, heartburn, sore throat, and similar maladies.

Vibrates to the number 2.

Purple Fluorite is a third-eye stone bringing rationality to the intuitive qualities and assisting one in precise communication of that which is psychically presented.

It also brings an orderly connection and conscious association to both psychic and spiritual growth.

It assists quite well in disorders associated with the bone and bone marrow, expediting suitable balancing within the body, bone, and cellular structures. It is excellent in helping to prepare the physical, emotional, intellectual, and/or spiritual realms of ones being for healing.

Vibrates to the master number 77.

Yellow Fluorite can be used to enhance creativity and to provide support with intellectual pursuits.

It is also beneficial in stabilizing group energy, promoting a cooperative connection between the members. It enables one to recognize the connective structure of love among and between all that exists.

It has been used in the treatment of unbalanced cholesterol, disorders of the liver, and mental discontinuity, and to assist in the release of toxins from the fatty deposits within the body.

Vibrates to the number 9.

Yttrian-Fluorite occurs in massive and granular form and is usually found in violet, grey, red-brown, green, yellow, and brown.

This mineral does not have the perfect cleavage that produces the octahedral formation; it does not, therefore, emit the energies to correct disorganization. It does, however, possess the remaining qualities listed above.

In addition, yttrian-fluorite is quite lustrous and provides the qualities of promoting increase in wealth and mental acuity. It helps one to initiate the state of self-fulfillment, bringing to fruition the self-actualizing characteristics and the properties of manifestation. It is an excellent stone for assisting in service-oriented activities.

Vibrates to the number 6.

FLUOROAPATITE   [Astrological Signs of Gemini, Pisces, and Capricorn]

Fluorapatite crystallizes in the form of masses, grains, columns, cubes, octahedra, prismatic, and rhombdodecahedra crystals. The colour range includes translucent green, blue, pink, etc.

In addition to combining the properties of Fluorite and Apatite, this mineral can stimulate a fine-tuning between the self and another, through the activation of delicate adjustments; aggravations, irritability, and annoyances are ameliorated and each person is encouraged to express his/her latent abilities.

It further provides a for a gentle challenging motivation through dynamic confrontation such that conflicts are resolved, frustrations are abolished, and growth toward change is both clarified and simplified. The energy is a catalyst for ease of change.

Fluorapatite also supports a blending and enhancing of one with another through the combination of talents; it acts to bring the proficiencies of groups together to produce new forms which are created without the loss of personal identities.

It furthers an interconnected-new of talents, bringing resolution, equilibrium, and a creative flow with universal energies.

It has also been used in the treatment of cancer, disorders of the eyes, the lungs, and the extremities, and in amelioration of olfactory degradation.

Vibrates to the number 9.

FORSTERITE   [Astrological Sign of Leo]

Forsterite crystallizes in the form of masses, vertically-striated thick tabular crystals exhibiting wedge-shape terminations, and equal-dimensional crystals. The colour range includes green, pale yellow, and white.

This mineral helps one to not deny feelings, hence, enhancing ones self-image and intuitive capabilities concurrently. It helps to provide for contact with ones spirit guides and facilitates the understanding of the messages received. I remind again that when one calls-in spirit guides, it is very important to ask, prior to beginning the session, for protection in the light and that the information given be for the good of all.

It can also increase ones awareness and ones conscious recognition of that which is in the "now". It further calms the intellect and the emotions while providing for a centering effect on the total energy field. It enhances the caring nature and helps one to become attuned to the energies of the earth and mountains.

It assists in helping one to maintain a consistent and steady course, providing support to eliminate obstructions and to enhance clarity in order that one may recognize the advantageous side-trips which would heighten the journey.

It can be used in the treatment of disorders associated with motor capabilities, and fungus and yeast infections, and to provide strength to overcome dis-ease.

Vibrates to the number 9.

FOSSIL   [Astrological Sign of Virgo]

The fossil is a preserved remnant of the past. Most fossils are organic matter which has transformed to stone; in many cases, a mineral [e.g., quartz, calcite, opal, pyrite, agate, jasper, etc.] merely infiltrates the empty cellular spaces in wood or bone, so that much of the original organic matter remains and retains its cellular structure. The range of fossils includes bone, shell, insects, animals, fish, and impressions left by plants, animals, and even natural resources.

In addition to the qualities listed for the mineral which assists in the fossilization process, the following properties apply.

In ancient times, fossils were believed to have been stony casts of that which was once alive and which were grown in the Earth from seeds descendant from the realms of the stars. This gift from the stars has been used to enhance telepathic communication between this present reality and the prior worlds, as well as the current other worlds.

It can be used to both heighten and supplement ones accomplishments in the business realm and to instill quality and excellence within ones environment.

It helps one to dispense with old "programming" and schedules, and to be open and receptive to, and perceptive of, the fresh innovative forces which are available.

It can be used in the stimulation of the thymus, and in the treatment of disorders associated with atrophication, the skeletal system, and the hands and feet.

Vibrates to the number 8.

FOURMARIERITE   [Astrological Sign of Capricorn]

Fourmarierite crystallizes in the form of red tabular crystals. Zaire is the recognized source for these lovely crystals.

This mineral can be used during ceremonies of the medicine wheel to represent the synthesis of the four directions. It has been used successfully, via placement in the middle of the wheel, to facilitate the binding-together of those around the medicine wheel during the ceremony.

Fourmarierite can help with the pursuits of the mathematician and analyst, bringing forth the heights of precision, meticulousness, and accuracy.

It can help to bring patience, tolerance, and strength to all pursuits, allowing one to recognize and to accept personal responsibility, and to relinquish those responsibilities [e.g., for others] which are not appropriate.

It can also enhance constancy in a given situation and can assist in bringing one those elements which are both necessary to, and suitable for expanding ones interests.

It can be used in the treatment of apoplexy, to promote circulation, and to stabilize the conditions relative to dis-ease. It has also been used in the treatment of wounds, breaks, and fractures. Use of an elixir, both internally and as a topical application, has tended to increase the mending qualities of the cellular structure.

Vibrates to the master number 77.

FRANCKEITE   [Astrological Sign of Leo]

Franckeite crystallizes in the formation of tabular crystals and masses. The colour range includes blackish-grey to black.

This mineral brings challenges and re-direction through the presentation of viable alternatives. It assists in showing one the path and methods which are compatible with reaching a defined goal. It eliminates the potential of surprises at the culmination of ones path and facilitates an intervening energy to preclude crises. It further assists one in advancing ones path with knowledge of potential detours and promotes adjustment to conditions which could otherwise become overwhelming.

It encourages the act of compromise, prompting one to recall all circumstances relevant to a problem. It serves to bring balance and a perspective to consider alternatives prior to decision-making.

It is a mineral which activates knowledge of the processes which are commencing and/or originating both within and outside of one. It assists in "setting-the-stage" for examining and resolving issues related to expanded experiences and worldly concerns.

It promotes genial interactions with others, allows for recognition of shared interests, and assists one to consider "other-oriented" systems. It further assists in relationships and social interaction, where mental exchanges occur and where experiences involving communication and inter-relatedness are supported.

It sustains one in both the recognition of and the stability of ones identity. It furthers interaction between business and emotional partners, cooperative efforts, and clients, and strengthens ones position during negotiations. It may also be employed to expedite ones finding a marriage partner.

Franckeite has been used in the treatment of disorders of the throat, the legs, and pain sensitivity. It can be used in the treatment of bruises and to ameliorate weakness in ones muscular structure - acting to release toxins. It is an excellent mineral for stimulating the growth of hair.

Vibrates to the number 2.

FRANKLINITE   [Astrological Sign of Gemini]

Franklinite crystallizes in the formation of black masses, granules, and octahedral crystals.

This mineral is quite useful in preservation, in the physical or emotional realm, of the self or another.

It is an excellent grounding stone, allowing for centering of the self in any situation.

It can be used to stimulate inventiveness and self-expression, to provide perceptiveness, and to enhance the characteristic of diplomacy.

It can also be useful to stimulate hair growth and can be used in the treatment of disorders of the male reproductive system. It is conducive to clearing the eyes.

Vibrates to the number 2.

FREIBERGITE   [Astrological Sign of Sagittarius]

Freibergite crystallizes in isometric-tetrahedral configurations, masses, and grains. The colour ranges from light steel-grey to iron-black.

In addition to combining the qualities of both Silver and Copper, this mineral also acts to ease developmental tension and developmental energy, through which progress and growth are accomplished.

With this mineral, "things happen".

It facilitates the commencement and origination of processes in ones private life, setting the stage for understanding and resolving issues and potential problems which are related to ones basic foundations, ones creation, and ones personal concerns and daily routine.

It assists one in explorations of the self, to define personal interests, and to comprehend self-orientation.

Freibergite promotes enthusiastic behavior to support experiences associated with expressiveness and inspiration.

The energy brings forth definite identity, adding impetus to the care of ones persona, outside behavior, appearance, and role.

It assists one in personality development, positive disposition, equitable temperament, and knowledge of how, where, when, etc., to claim ones personal roles.

It is an excellent stone to promote general vitality and to insure positive "first impressions".

The utilization of this mineral in combination with Owyheeite produces a dynamic effect for both healing and for self-actualization.

Do not prepare an elixir via the normal method.

Vibrates to the number 5.

FUCHSITE   [Astrological Signs of Aquarius]

Fuchsite is a form of Mica which crystallizes in the form of plate-like layers, scales, masses, and tabular crystals. The colour is green due to the presence of Chromium.

In addition to the properties listed in the MICA section, this mineral assists in the understanding of process that are both adapting and dispersing. It promotes the examination of issues related to basic foundations and personal concerns, including problems and solutions directly related to interactions with others and the material world, shared interests, vocational objectives, physical being and well-ness, and productivity.

In the context of meditation with Fuchsite, one may access information concerning the maintenance of physical health, daily routine, schedules and scheduling, stress, pets, mainstream environments, co-workers, and career.

It also assists one in eliminating any type of servitude issues, bringing the light of knowledge of innate perfection being within each person. It further helps one to "bounce-back" after tense situations in the physical and/or emotional realm.

It has been used to enhance knowledge and right action in the field of law enforcement and holistic medicine.

When used in channeling activities, Fuchsite can bring information concerning herbal remedies and holistic remediation. It is one of the stones which also facilitates the transfer of energy from other minerals; hence, using this mineral in conjunction with other minerals during healing sessions promotes an increase in energy transfer.

It has also been used in the balancing of red and white blood cell count, in the treatment of carpel tunnel syndrome, to assist the stabilization of the alignment of the spinal column, and to increase flexibility of muscles.

Due to the flakiness of this mineral, it is recommended that an elixir is not prepared by the normal method.

Vibrates to the number 9.

FULGURITE   [See Glass - Natural]

**THE OPEN MIND RECOGNIZES
THAT WHICH CANNOT BE MEASURED AS REAL**

GALENA   [Astrological Sign of Capricorn]

Galena crystallizes in the form of cubes, octahedron, skeletal shapes, net-like shapes, masses, and fibers. The colour is grey.

This mineral can be used to provide grounding and to enhance the centering of ones energies. It helps to open the pathway between the physical and ethereal bodies in order to allow for the alignment of energies and the stimulation of the nervous system.

It is a "stone of harmony", stimulating interaction on all levels, and assisting in the decrease of self-limiting ideas.

It is quite helpful for those studying the field of medicine and can promote holistic, homeopathic, and herbal medicine studies, providing insights and, when required, the skepticism to induce further testing.

Internal consumption of an elixir of this mineral is <u>not</u> recommended.

It is said to reduce inflammations and to heal skin eruptions on the body, and to be beneficial to the blood and olfactory system. It can be used to increase the assimilation of selenium and zinc, to stimulate circulation, and to treat disorders of the veins. It can also assist in the stimulation of hair growth and in bringing the healthy state to the hair.

Vibrates to the master number 22.

GANOPHYLLITE   [Astrological Sign of Sagittarius]

Ganophyllite crystallizes in the form of foliated masses, rosettes, and short prismatic and tabular crystals. The colour range includes brown and brown-yellow.

This mineral can be used for physical protection, and to facilitate contact with ones power animal. Ganophyllite can be used to contact the spirit-animal world and to allow one to "fly-off on the wings of an eagle" during meditation; this flight may bring one to the akashic records, past-life scenes, and/or present-life scenes. The reader is encouraged to enjoy this travel and to determine further avenues which are opened by this stone.

It brings expansion and maturity to the user, allowing for a broad-minded optimistic attitude concomitant with generosity. It emits an energy which can bring the advantage to one in a given situation, and, concurrently assists one in understanding the loving relationship between the self and others. It also calms the intellect, affording the user with clarity of perception and astuteness of insight.

This mineral can also help to relieve dizziness and to provide balance. It can be used in the treatment of circulation disorders and Vitamin A deficiencies. It has been used in the treatment of disorders of the throat.

Vibrates to the number 9.

GARNET
[Elemental Astrological Signs of Leo, Virgo, Capricorn, & Aquarius]

Garnet crystallizes in the form of dodecahedral and trapezohedral crystals, combinations of dodecahedral/trapezohedral crystals, masses, granules, and plate-like layers. The colour range includes all of those colours listed under the various types of garnets in this book; these types of garnets are almandine, andradite, grossular/grossularite, pyrope/rhodolite, uvarovite, and spessartine/spessartite.

Specific properties of each of these types of garnets will be found in their respective sections. The general properties of all forms of the garnet are given below.

Garnet is a "stone of health", extracting negative energy from the chakras, and transmuting the energy to the beneficial state.

It is said to have been one of the stones used in the breastplate of the high priest.

It has been used as a sacred stone by the Native American Indians, the South American Indians, the Aztecs, the African tribal elders, and the Mayans. It acts with speed due to the flash of lightening contained within, helping one to change ones world by producing both expansiveness in awareness and manifestation. It enhances ones internal fire, bringing the creative powers to the stage of implementation. It allows one to recognize inherent responsibility with respect to personal freedom and patience, inciting personal magnetism and cooperation in instances of change.

It has also been known as a "stone of commitment" - to purpose, to others, and to oneself. The loving powers of garnet tend to reflect the attributes of devotion, bringing the love of others to expressions of warmth and understanding. It is quite helpful in moods of abandonment, allowing one to realize that surrender to discontinuity brings freshness to ones life.

The garnet balances and stimulates the development and movement of the Kundalini. It stimulates from both the base and crown chakras to provide for free flow of movement, via the spinal column and the inner pathway of light, helping to distribute the appropriate amount of energy to each portion of the body. It provides for a stable connection between the physical and ethereal nervous systems, energizing the total system to vitality. It etherically controls and dispenses the amount of energy that is best for the system. It also allows one to flow with the energies available.

It both monitors and adjusts the flow of energy, providing for a balanced energy field around the physical body and aligning the emotional and intellectual bodies with the perfection of "All That Is".

The energies of the garnet help to amplify the functions of emotional and intellectual regeneration <u>and</u> the processes therein; in order to achieve the integration of experiences and the acceptance of emotions, with subsequent renewal of the aspects of self-discovery, one must re-affirm the direction of inherent thoughts and feelings.

The individual effort to alter ones state of mind and emotions, through the self-adjustment of personal dissonance, in order to regain integration and/or balance, can be promoted via working with, and identifying through, the garnet. The garnet provides a protective influence and a calming stable vitality during use.

Rutilated garnet combines the properties of garnet with the properties listed in the RUTILE section of this book.

Star garnet additionally promotes connection to the other worlds, helps one to remember dreams, and helps one toward success. It is also a "stone of majesty", allowing for rightness in will and providing support in action. It can produce flashes of insight to assist in guiding one to "right" and honourable endeavors. It also brings counsel to assist one in "hitting the target", expediting the state of victory to ones endeavors.

This mineral produces an energy which is predisposed to discourage chaotic, disruptive, and disorganized growth. It emits an energy which can be used to stabilize and to produce order within the mental, physical, emotional, and spiritual systems. It can be used to bring order to chaos.

It provides for purification, cleansing, and elimination of that which is in disorder. It can be used to dispel disorders at the commencement of the symptoms.

It is also an excellent stone for treating disorders of the spine and spinal fluid, bone, cellular structure and composition, heart, lungs, and blood. It has been used in the treatment to equilibrate sexual energies and to enhance the assimilation of iodine, calcium, magnesium, and Vitamins A, D, and E. It can help to both repair and prevent damage to RNA/DNA structures. It can be helpful in all conditions requiring regenerative forces.

Vibrates to the number 2.

GAUDEFROYITE   [Astrological Sign of Sagittarius]

Gaudefroyite crystallizes in the form of black prismatic crystals exhibiting a glassy luster. This mineral is caused by the replacement of quartz, in the crystal form, by black hematite; hence, a black hematite [quartz] crystal. This mineral combines the properties of hematite with the properties of quartz, creating a "dynamite" healing stone.

In addition, gaudefroyite stimulates vividness in dreams, and assists in ones memory capabilities. It encourages one to take the initiative and furthers independence in thought and action.

It can also assist one in stabilizing and crystallizing ones goals such that one can appreciate and aspire toward the philosophical realm of "all knowing". It enables a directed approach, diminishing vacillation and indecisiveness.

Gaudefroyite helps one to eliminate pretentious and ostentatious mannerisms, bringing the state of grace to actualization.

It activates clairaudience while providing grounding; this enables one to contact the other worlds while remaining totally conscious of the self.

It can also be used in the treatment of hearing disorders, to stimulate circulatory functions, and to assist one in regaining flexibility of muscular structures.

Vibrates to the number 1.

GEHLENITE   [Astrological Sign of Sagittarius]

Gehlenite crystallizes in the form of masses, grains, rolled pebbles, and short prismatic crystals. The colour range includes, grey, green-to-brown, yellow, and colourless.

This mineral enhances second-sight, intuition, and visualization propagating manifestation.

In addition, it awakens the practical side of ones nature, allowing for the application of spiritual awareness to aspects of employment and lifework.

It also intensifies ones optimism and furthers the display of a "happy disposition".

Gehlenite can provide for an inner warmth and can stimulate circulation as well as well-being. This attribute applies to both the emotional and physical bodies - the outer world or relationships and the inner world of physical structure.

This mineral can be used in the treatment of osteoporosis, bruxism, disorders of the liver, disorders of the eyes, and to lessen leg cramps. It can also be used to improve conditions causing extreme cases of suffering and/or distress.

Vibrates to the number 4.

GENTHELVITE   [Astrological Sign of Sagittarius]

Genthelvite crystallizes in the form of rounded aggregates and tetrahedral crystals. The colour range includes white, yellow, emerald green, purple, pink, and brown-to-black.

This mineral can be used to combine the loving aspects of the heart with intelligence applied toward spiritual awareness.

It incites change toward the progressive and reformative state, assisting in the transformation and transmutation of negativity and inspiring reformative, liberal, and tolerant attitudes.

It enhances anti-prejudicial attitudes, and amplifies deliberate and voluntary kindness and forbearance; it brings honour and respect to the user. It encourages gentleness in all actions and situations, initiates "proper" rapport, and encourages an affinity for composure.

This mineral can be used in the treatment of depression, confusion, vertigo, swelling of the lymphatics, frontal headache, colic, and general restlessness and prostration.

Vibrates to the master number 55.

GEODE   [Astrological Sign of Virgo]

The geode is recognized, usually, by a spherical configuration which contains a cavity lined with a crystalline structure growing toward the center. It is configured in the form of a closed shell, usually containing quartz, amethyst, citrine, or calcite, and partially filled with crystals projecting into the hollow interior; it is separated from the usual limestone or "mud" matrix by a film of clay. Some of the crystals described in this book are found in geodes.

The geode structure itself exhibits several properties in addition to the properties of the contained minerals. These properties include facilitation of astral travel, and assistance in the pursuits of mathematics.

The geode also allows one to both recognize and analyze the total picture prior to decision-making. It allows one the freedom to mold and to shape ones own future, and assists one in attaining highly effective communication skills. It furthers ones connection to the higher forces and the higher planes, stimulating the bridge of association with those of like pursuits.

It can also be used in the treatment of disorders associated with the hands, lungs, and nervous system. The "brain geode" which is found with a conglomerate on the exterior of the geode, has also been used in the treatment of brain tumors and mental imbalances.

Vibrates to the number 9.

GIBBSITE   [Astrological Sign of Aries]
                                            [Also Known as Hydrargillite]

Gibbsite crystallizes in the form of stalactites, spherical concretions, and tabular-hexagonal crystals. The colour range includes white, greyish-white, reddish-white, and greenish-white.

This mineral can be used to provide independence in employment and initiative toward accomplishment. It allows one to release inhibitions, bringing power in decisions and spontaneity to actions.

It can help one to see the "big picture" in situations, enabling one to withhold judgment until the bases become obvious, and augmenting the qualities of articulation in matters of import. Gibbsite can be useful for one in the pursuit of knowledge in physics, astronomy, astrology, and writing. It stimulates the receiving nature, allowing for recognition of information from other realms. It also promotes freedom of movement and freedom from constraint.

This mineral can be used in the treatment of disorders of the neck, the upper back and arms, and for reduction in swelling.

Vibrates to the numbers 1 and 4.

GIRASOL   [See Blue Opal]

GISMONDINE   [Astrological Sign of Pisces]

Gismondine crystallizes in the form of tetragonal-type double pyramids. The colour range includes white, colourless, grey, and red.

This mineral supports the essential part of ones being and helps one to "maintain" and to influence the circumstances, of which one is a part, to be beneficial to the inner essence.

It facilitates the "granting of permission" by the spirit-guides so that one may access the "unknown". [Many times, without permission, one struggles to become one with the metaphysical aspects of ideas or things - with this stone, the struggle is lessened.]

Gismondine helps to produce "boundlessness" in intuition and adaptability. It heightens ones perception of change, brings diversity to ones life, and augments ones mystical proclivities.

It can be used in the treatment of disorders of the liver, gall bladder, thalamus, and thymus.

Vibrates to the master number 55.

GLASS - [NATURAL]   [Astrological Signs of Virgo & Gemini]
                                [Also Known as Lechatelierite]

Lechatelierite is the name given to naturally occurring glass which is, actually, fused quartz. This mineral occurs as fulgurites, as inclusions in volcanic rocks, and, occasionally, in meteorite craters. Libyan Desert Glass (Libya) and Darwin Glass (Tasmania) are two types of the fusion glass available.

Please note that the Libyan Desert Glass, specifically, has been used to increase profits in sales.

It is helpful in assisting one in fulfilling ones "duties" and in completing tasks; it provides for a basis of "knowing" from which one can progress toward higher learning and spirituality.

This mineral can also provide for the actualization of leadership qualities, stability, and sudden progress. It provides an excellent energy for encouraging the practical side of group work and for imparting a shared knowledge and understanding throughout the group.

Natural glass can be used to align the energy centers of the physical body and to balance the nervous systems of both the physical and ethereal bodies.

It can be used in the treatment of tumors and other growths. It has been used to enhance the assimilation of nutrients and to provide for strengthening of the muscles and tissues of the body. It has also been used to activate the thymus and to improve the immune system.

Fulgurite, a natural glass tube formed in sand or rock by the action of lightning, also enhances communication on the physical plane and strengthens the connection with other worlds and beings in those worlds. It can be used to alleviate distractions and to provide for intensified concentration. The tube can also enable one to predict future events and can be used to enhance the abilities of a divining rod for divining and/or "cloud-busting" [e.g., rain-making]. It can also facilitate clairaudient experiences. In addition, fulgurite may be used to grid an area to enhance the energy for welcoming spaceship landings. Fulgurite can also be used in the treatment of disorders of the ear, nose, throat, intestinal walls, colon, alimentary canal, and esophagus.

Vibrates to the numbers 4 and 6.

GMELINITE   [Astrological Sign of Pisces]

Gmelinite crystallizes in the form of pyramid-type hexagonal crystals and rhombohedrons which are, usually, striated. The colour range includes green, white, colourless, yellow, red, and pink.

This mineral promotes "second sight" and helps to produce a well-balanced philosophy such that one can "see" around the corners of life. It assists in realistic pursuits, allowing one to recognize that reality is that which is tangible with respect to personal perception.

It also enhances ones self-esteem, providing for progress with humility, and growth through modesty.

This mineral can be used to facilitate either weight gain or weight reduction - the user must consciously focus on gain or loss. It can also be used to treat glaucoma, disorders of the gums, and deficiencies in the assimilation of Vitamin C.

Vibrates to the number 4.

GOETHITE   [Astrological Sign of Aries]

Goethite crystallizes in the form of scales, fibrous masses, prismatic crystals which are vertically striated, needle-like structures, granular masses, stalactites with a radial central structure, and in forms similar to small pipe organs [quite lovely in the exhibition of the various colours]. The colour range includes yellow, orange, red, and black-brown.

This mineral can teach one to enjoy the journey in life while enhancing progression toward the goal. It inspires pragmatism with imagination, bringing energy to pursuits of discovery.

Goethite helps one to attune to the ethereal realms, and enhances communication with "the angels". It also facilitates clairaudience and, sometimes, allows one to hear the music of the ethers. It enhances communication on the physical plane and strengthens the connection with other worlds and beings in those worlds. It can be used to alleviate distractions and to provide for intensified concentration.

It can enable one to predict future events and can be used to enhance the abilities of a divining rod. It can also facilitate clairaudient experiences. In addition, goethite may be used to grid an area to enhance and strengthen the energy for welcoming spaceship landings.

This mineral can be used in the treatment of anemia, menorrhagia, convulsions, and to facilitate body-building activities. It can also be used in the treatment of disorders associated with the ears, nose, throat, intestines, alimentary canal, veins, and esophagus.

Vibrates to the master number 44.

GOLD

Gold crystallizes in massive forms, grains, flakes, dendritic forms, plates, nuggets, and, rarely, in octahedral, cubic, and rhombdodecahedral crystals. The occurrence of gold within a quartz crystal is not only beautiful, but rare. The colour range includes shades of golden yellow, silver-white, and orange-red.

If one is fortunate enough to become an Earth-keeper for a quartz crystal containing gold, the uses are extensive. The properties of gold and the properties of the quartz crystal are combined and produce "dynamite" results.

Gold symbolizes the purity of the spiritual aspect of "All That Is". It is symbolic of spirituality and development in the realm of complete understanding, allowing one to both attain and maintain communion with the source of all being.

It emits an energy to prompt one to allow beauty to come forth from the inner being as one travels in, and through, the world of experiences.

It helps one to improve ones character via learning, lessening the trauma associated with the situations experienced during the gain of knowledge. It assists one to activate, to mobilize, and to actualize the intrinsic potential of the self.

The energy of gold can be used to balance the energy fields and to assist one in the elimination of ego conflicts and feelings of futility.

It can also help to assuage the overburden of responsibility, to combat feelings of depression and inferiority, to allow one to both understand and to dispense with self-reproach, and to calm excitation and states of anger.

Gold has been used in the development, purification, and balancing of the heart chakra and for the amplification of thought-forms. The purity of gold is said to help one to preserve higher thought forms for later retrieval.

Gold has also been used to open and to activate the third-eye and crown chakras.

It has been said to attract honors, wealth, and happiness, to provide composure, to stabilize the emotional system, to alleviate tension and stress, and to amplify positive feelings. It also assists one in attuning to nature and its healing forces.

Gold has been called "the master healer". It is an excellent mineral for purification of the physical body.

It can clear negativity from the chakras and the energy fields of the physical, emotional, intellectual, and spiritual bodies, while transferring the vitality of any companion mineral to the affected area.

It produces an energy which is both cooperative and receptive, allowing for extensive use with other gem stones; gold is capable of attracting and maintaining those qualities which are inherent within the additional stone.

Gold, when in proximity to another mineral, provides a stabilizing influence to the energies of that mineral.

It has been used to enhance mental faculties, to rebuild the nervous system [e.g., in the treatment of multiple sclerosis], to improve digestion, circulation, and breathing, and to increase warmth. It can be used for the treatment of arthritis, skin cancer, blood disorders, pneumonia, vascular diseases, heart disease, eye problems, paralysis, rheumatism, skin disorders, tuberculosis, nightmares, and spinal problems.

It has been used to assist in the rejuvenation of the endocrine system, in the absorption of vitamins and minerals, and in the regeneration of tissue and the skeletal structure. It can be used to balance the right brain/left brain and to treat conditions associated with autism, dyslexia, epilepsy, and physical coordination.

Vibrates to the number 2.

GOSHENITE   [Astrological Sign of Libra]

Goshenite is a type of colourless beryl which crystallizes in the form of prismatic crystals, sometimes vertically striated, and sometimes terminated by small pyramid-like faces.

This mineral encourages truth in ones word. It brings one toward a state of plentitude and comfort.

Proper use of goshenite helps one to maintain composure and self-control through the "surprises" of life and to direct the energy of each revelation toward the higher aspects of ones being. It can facilitate creativity, originality, and aesthetically rewarding pursuits. It is also an excellent stone for stabilizing relationships.

It has been used to open and to activate the crown chakra, bringing a loving and companionable energy to the user.

It can be used in the treatment of afflictions which indicate that one is being influenced by outside forces. It has also been used in the treatment of disorders related to the muscular structures of the legs.

Vibrates to the number 3.

GOYAZITE   [Astrological Sign of Cancer]

Goyazite crystallizes in the form of pebbles, and rhombohedral and cubic-type crystals. The colour range includes pink, yellow, and colourless.

This mineral can provide one with incentive to follow the basic impulses and to furnish sensitive and intuitive responses. It assists one in attaining the state of receptivity and allows one to feel the unification of the energies of the "All".

It provides one with strength during trials of endurance, balances the male/female aspects of ones character, and opens and gently activates the navel, heart, and crown chakras. The energy is delicate, enabling one to easily direct and control the movement of the force to the location desired.

Goyazite can provide support in endeavors of artistic painting and etching.

It can help in the assimilation of iodine [in the correct quantities] for body stability. It can also be used in the treatment of disorders associated with the eyes and the speech.

Vibrates to the number 9.

GRANDIDIERITE   [Astrological Sign of Leo]

Grandidierite crystallizes in the form of masses and elongated crystals. The colour range includes green-blue, colourless, and dark green.

This mineral helps one to be precise and correct in judgments in cases requiring evaluation of evidence prior to decision-making.

It also provides one with a strength and stability in social situations which may be beyond the ordinary [i.e., beyond the ordinary social situations in which one is comfortable and/or beyond a social situation which is quite out of the ordinary].

Grandidierite also provides a cohesiveness with respect to family ties and closeness within a group. Improvement and refinement in communication is reported; both for inter/intra family structures, work environments, social environments, and other worlds. It can assist one in exhibiting an openness from the heart space, to display real feelings of love and generosity, and to maintain dignity.

It is also quite effective for amplifying nutrients which are required in vegetarian diets. It can be used in the treatment of disorders associated with the lungs, throat, spleen, and heart.

Vibrates to the number 6.

GRANITE   [Astrological Sign of Libra]

Granite is primarily composed of quartz and orthoclase [feldspar]. The colour range includes grey, white, pink, black, and yellow-brown. In addition to the properties listed in the QUARTZ, ORTHOCLASE, and FELDSPAR sections of this book, the following qualities are applicable.

Granite can be used to enable one to "see the big picture" instead of being in the mind-set to "see the puddle, when there is an ocean awaiting". It helps to banish the negative traits of skepticism and to train the user in the difference between beliefs and "knowing".

It helps one to maintain balance in relationships and cooperative efforts, facilitating diplomacy and discretion in all matters of import. It also enables one to "nip" disagreeable situations at the onset, defeating negativity with ease.

It has been revered, in ancient times by the Mayan nation, and more recently by the aboriginal tribes, to be a sacred, magical stone; affording protection and increase to the user.

It has been reported that granite also brings one an increase in money; the mineral inducing recognition of, and generous overtures to, the user, while allowing for continuity in modesty by the user.

Granite can be used in the treatment of disorders associated with the hair, face, and head.

Vibrates to the number 2.

GRAPHITE   [Astrological Sign of Aquarius]

Graphite crystallizes in the form of masses, flakes, columnar and radial configurations, and flat, six-sided crystals. The colour ranges from iron-black to a deep steel-grey.

This mineral is one of the best electrical conductors and can be used during healing activities to enhance the energy transfer from a healer, or from other minerals, to the subject of the healing. It is an excellent component in wands.

It also can be used to align the chakras and to order the connection between the ethereal and physical nervous systems.

Graphite is a "stone of personal freedom", providing impetus for one to "take charge" of ones life and to enter into the activities and associated realms which are "calling".

It improves ones writing abilities and mathematical astuteness, and stimulates thought. It helps one to access the sphere of automatic writing, providing access to information concerning the history of "mankind". It also assists in improvement of conversational skills, discouraging hostility, and relieving anger.

It has been used in the treatment of spinal dis-alignment, cataracts, hearing loss, and disorders of the elimination system.

Do not prepare an elixir via the normal method.

Vibrates to the number 3.

GREENOCKITE   [Astrological Sign of Leo]

Greenockite crystallizes in the form of coatings, short hexagonal crystals, and rare hemimorphic pyramid-like crystals. The colour ranges from honey-orange to orange-yellow.

This mineral can be used in the field of radionics to enable the user to more easily recognize the response. It facilitates the attunement of the radionics operator with the subject.

It improves ones intuitive responses and response time and allows for the intellect to be an approving part of those responses. This enables one to feel the response and to then understand why that response occurred. It also encourages functional relationships. It stimulates emotional stability and advances the art of imaging. It allows for the realization that, that which one can imagine in fantasy can, in fact, produce the biological responses to expedite the reality.

It can be an assistant in the field of drama and can help one to maintain a role, whenever necessary.

Greenockite can be used in the treatment of skin disorders and to improve potassium assimilation within the body. It can smooth the emotional system and can assist in the enhancement of the immune system.

Vibrates to the number 4.

GROSSULAR GARNET   [Astrological Sign of Cancer]

Grossular garnet [also known as Grossularite] is a type of garnet which crystallizes in the form of masses, grains, and crystals in the configuration of dodecahedral, trapezohedral, and combinations of the varying shapes of dodecahedral/trapezohedral formations. The colour range includes wine-yellow, brown, emerald green, pale green, yellow, red-brown, red, orange, colourless-to-white, grey, and black.

In addition to the information listed in the GARNET section of this book, the following qualities are applicable.

This mineral strengthens stability in lawsuits and challenges. It transforms the lower forms of response and reaction to loving forms of reply.

It also inspires the ideal of service, providing for cooperative effort and ingenuity in maintaining the effort.

Grossular garnet enhances fertility when the consciousness is specifically directed toward that goal during meditation with this mineral. It also assists in the assimilation of Vitamin A.

Vibrates to the numbers 2 and 6.

GUERINITE   [Astrological Sign of Cancer]

Guerinite crystallizes in the monoclinic system in a vitreous pearly colourless to white configuration.

This mineral facilitates activation on all levels, for all bodies, and automatically. It stimulates the loving nature of ones essence, bringing nurturing and cultivation of ones innate talents.

It can be used to cleanse the chakras, to clear the aura, and to purify ones mind by eliminating thought-patterns which are not conducive to growth.

Guerinite is conducive to bringing expanded experiences in worldly concerns; it channels energy in the direction of that which is consciously desired and assists in bringing that conscious desire to actualization.

This mineral has been used in the treatment of leukemia, CFS, bone loss, menopausal complaints, and the intestines.

Due to the softness of this mineral, do <u>not</u> prepare an elixir via the normal method.

Vibrates to the number 9.

GYPSUM   [Astrological Sign of Aries]

Gypsum crystallizes in the form of granular masses, fibrous shapes, and prismatic, needle-like, and tabular crystals. The colour range includes white, colourless, greenish, yellow-to-brown, grey, pink, honey-yellow, yellow, blue, red, red-brown, brown, and black.

Gypsum, in the form of crystals, is known as selenite and is discussed in the SELENITE section of this book.

Gypsum, in the form of masses, is known as alabaster and is discussed in the ALABASTER section of this book.

Gypsum, in the fibrous form, is "really" gypsum, and is discussed here.

This mineral can be used to mold ones character toward both the ideals of growth and improvement. Stagnation is eliminated and progression is strengthened.

It also helps one to sustain the self when events of life are "happening too quickly".

It is a lovely stone to place in the middle of the medicine wheel; it can bring together the four directions of the medicine wheel and can induce the synthesis of these directions with Mother Earth and Father Sky.

It can also bring the members of the wheel into the conditions of "right" thought and action, while maintaining a connection between the members via the heart chakras.

Gypsum is considered the "Lucky Stone". It provides a strong influence for bringing good fortune to the fortunate Earth-keeper.

It has been used in ceremonies of rain-making by the aboriginal tribes; these ceremonies required that gypsum be "thrown into the air" such that upon the return and dispersement of the fibers, the god of rain would know where to allow the rain to fall.

Fibrous gypsum also helps to produce strong bones and can renew and enhance the elasticity in ones skin and tissue. An elixir applied to the skin and/or taken internally could produce lasting results. It has also been used by the ancient tribes to stimulate fertility.

Vibrates to the number 2.

GYROLITE   [Astrological Sign of Scorpio]

Gyrolite is a member of the Zeolite Division and crystallizes in rhombohedral-tetartohedral patterns of lamellar-radiate concretions. The colour ranges from white to green.

This mineral has been used to stimulate the healing properties of other minerals, to cleanse and to activate other minerals, and to disperse universal energy to the meridians of the body. It is excellent for use in connecting the auric bodies to the physical body and to assist one in the attainment of the perfect state of well-being on all levels.

Used in meditation, it has stimulated the "all knowing" wisdom of the ancient civilizations. It has been used by the masters of India to instill discernment and insight, to energize the will, and to promote stability. It is said to be one of the stones accessed by Buddha, bringing knowledge and erudition.

Gyrolite has been used to assist in the alignment of the spinal column, to support the maintenance of cellular and bone structure, and to stimulate the assimilation of calcium. It can also be used in acupuncture/acupressure treatments to assist in the flow of energy through the nervous system.

Vibrates to the number 3.

THE HITCH-HIKER

HIS PRESENCE ALONG THE ROAD BROUGHT ME JOY
SOMEONE NEW, SOMETHING NEW
DEEPLY, I LISTENED -
THE WORDS CAME ON AND ON.
WORDS WITH QUITE THE SOUND
WORDS WITHOUT A THREAD
THERE SEEMS TO BE A WEALTH OF KNOWLEDGE,
THE WORDS KEEP COMING ON
FANTASY
WISDOM, NOT KNOWLEDGE
TRUTH, NOT WORDS.
I GO.

[antar pushkara, 21st century]

Halite crystallizes in the form of masses, columnar structures, and cubic crystals [some with concave faces]. The range of colour includes colourless and shades of yellow, red, and blue.

This mineral enhances good will, elevates ones moods, ameliorates mood swings, and diminishes negativity. It is excellent in rectifying the "mood of abandonment", inciting initiative and independent thought.

It can also provide insight to allow greater freedom with respect to meeting contingencies.

It stimulates the acupressure/acupuncture meridians and can be used for the preservation of same.

It also allows one to go deep within the self in order to find the ancient solutions to present-day problems.

Due to the solubility of Halite, do <u>not</u> prepare an elixir of this mineral via the normal method.

It can be used in the treatment of disorders of the colon and lower intestinal tract, for amelioration of water retention, and to augment strength during physical activities. A word of caution: it is recommended that halite is not placed on the abdominal area during pregnancy; it can, however, be placed upon other portions of the body.

Halite occurs in special hues which require mentioning. The pink, deep pink, and cranberry colours occur in a deposit in California, USA. These colours occur in the halite which is based by a pink-to-cranberry shaded Burkeite; the colouring is caused by a seaweed-type plant growth within the mineral. This formation of halite has additional attributes, including clearing of the heart chakra, assisting in regenerative growth, dispelling oppression, and for use as a diuretic. It is not suitable for wearing; for carrying, it should be provided protection due to fragility. Having a small cluster in ones environment can facilitate feelings of love and well-being.

Another rare hue of halite manifests in the colour of indigo blue, where the indigo blue is as an inclusion within the crystallized halite. The astrological sign of Pisces represents this mineralogical formation. Indigo halite has been found in Germany and has additional attributes, including the stimulation of psychic power, mysticism, and intuition. It is also said to encouraging adaptability. It aids in the assimilation of the proper amount of iodine, and can be used in the treatment of disorders of the thalamus, thymus, and thyroid. One can use small amounts of this mineral as an elixir and as a mineral additive in cooking [small amounts being one to four drops].

Vibrates to the number 1.

HAMBERGITE [Astrological Sign of Taurus]

Hambergite crystallizes in the form of prismatic crystals. The colour is greyish-white.

This mineral can be used as a "pick-me-up", and, in states of trance, provides for a feeling of euphoria; the euphoria stemming from the nearness of the outer bodies. When this condition is nigh, it is recommended that the metaphysician access information.

Hambergite can be used in the treatment of dysfunctional disorders of the iris, for conditions when the heart is producing an excess pulse rate, and in the diminishment of chills. It can also be helpful in the stabilization of weight.

Vibrates to the number 7.

HANKSITE [Astrological Sign of Taurus]

Hanksite crystallizes in the form of tabular and prismatic crystals. The range of colour includes grey-green, yellow, yellow-green, white, yellow, and almost black.

This mineral helps one to understand the experience of leaving ones body for the final time during this life [some call this experience death], and to understand and to flow with the "unwanted" changes which occur during this life. It also helps to combat restlessness and unwarranted "wants", while providing for insight into the difference between "wants" and "needs".

Hanksite provides insight to information to help combat trickery and illusion, inciting the qualities of perception and adeptness, while allowing for awareness with respect to ones environment.

It enhances the solar plexus chakra and helps one to become totally open to another, facilitating both a "melding" into another and a recognition of the subsequent connection between the self and the "non-self".

It is also a wonderful stone to use during meditation and during advancement toward spirituality.

It has been called "the juggler's stone". It dispels introversion, allows one to utilize the inherent creative forces and the creative forces of the universe, and increases ones flexibility in the mental, emotional, and physical bodies. In addition, it can be used to provide a stabilizing effect on ambulatory activities, and has been used to stimulate hair growth and health, and to ameliorate "head colds".

Vibrates to the master number 33.

HARKERITE   [Astrological Sign of Virgo]

Harkerite crystallizes in the form of colourless octahedral crystals.

This mineral can be used to improve ones attention span and to promote the expansion and progression of ones clairaudient abilities.

Harkerite stimulates the throat chakra and the crown chakra; it helps one to connect to the spiritual world and inspires highly-effective communication. It is truly a gift from the angelic kingdom, allowing one to "reach the pavement of gold" along the pathway of enlightenment.

It can help one to eliminate somnambulistic "consciousness", to be attentive to the moment, and to connect in the conscious state to the glorious present.

It assists one in dealing with negative situations and provides for a barrier of unassailable strength when one confronts danger. It also helps one to grow emotionally, with change.

Harkerite can promote inner cellular awareness such that each cell affected by a disorder can singularly, and collectively, recognize the reason for the malfunction and then release the anomaly, facilitating both alignment with the perfect self and the healing state.

It can be useful for treatment of throat disorders, can support the improvement of hearing disorders, can help to correct improper cellular growth, and can assist in the amelioration of RNA/DNA disorders. It is also useful as an elixir for topical application to bruises and sores.

Vibrates to the number 5.

HARMOTOME   [Astrological Signs of Gemini & Capricorn]

Harmotome crystallizes in the form of radial aggregates, and square prismatic crystals with a pyramid-like structure on the diagonal. The colour range includes white, colourless, grey, pink, red, yellow, and brown.

This mineral can help one to "stay-on-schedule", allowing routine work to be more enjoyable [one is able to understand the importance of the routine work in the overall scheme of life or one may recognize the methods to eliminate that facet of ones life].

It can help one to reach out to others, in the spirit of "brotherhood" and love. It is expressive of warmth and intelligence, promoting both altruistic tendencies and devotion to "right-mindedness". On the other hand, it provides stamina against weariness from adulation.

It improves congruency and consistency in groups and is quite useful to have in the vicinity when a group is in the formative stages.

It assists one in learning and assimilating the unusual.

It is also useful to one who is actively engaged in musical pursuits.

This mineral can be used in the prevention of periodontal disorders which result in cavities, to relieve muscle spasms, to increase blood flow, and to improve conditions resulting from external injuries.

Vibrates to the number 9.

HAUSMANNITE   [Astrological Sign of Virgo]

Hausmannite crystallizes in the form of tetragonal octahedrons, twins, and granular masses. The colour is a brownish black.

This mineral represents metamorphosis and continued change throughout all times. The energy is centered with the perseverance of both expedition and the ease of reorganizing and improving the self. The concepts of impetus and catalytic motion are reflected so that one may be grounded and stimulated concurrently.

It can be used to temporarily align the chakras, the subtle bodies, and the meridians of the physical and etheric bodies. It has been used to dispel anguish, anxiety, exasperation, and attachment. It enhances the desire for, and facilitates the attainment of, those ideals which assist in the evolution of ones spirituality. It also provides the energy conducive to both ease of entry to, and maintenance of, the deep meditative state. One can feel the connection to the universal energy during meditation with Hausmannite.

It is a "stone of security" and can be used to attract love. It has been quite instrumental in activities of manifestation, assuring stability both during and after the item is attained. It also assists in balancing the emotions with reason, in encouraging the trust of ones intuition, and in producing mental lucidity with respect to the determination of the additional minerals which would be beneficial in ones life.

It can be used in the treatment of disorders of the bone structure, hair, skin, blood vessels, and the flesh. It has also been used in the treatment of nose bleed. It can help one to "attract" the healing energies necessary for recovery from disorders.

Vibrates to the master number 44.

HAZELWOODITE   [Astrological Sign of Aries]

Hazelwoodite is found in the configuration of masses, often with Serpentine and/or Zaratite. The colour ranges from a metallic grey to black.

This mineral is a stone to encourage longevity and to balance both the physical and etheric bodies.

It has been used to increase awareness and to assist in the release of negative-memory trauma while reinforcing positive retention.

It acts to create a feeling of higher spiritual awareness and is an excellent mineral for activating the meditative state.

Hazelwoodite has also been used to stimulate right-brain energy and to strengthen the connection between the higher-self, the inner self, and the conscious self. It further stimulates wise decision-making and can serve to place one in the "right place at the right time".

It has been used in the treatment of the male hormonal system, to alleviate sciatica and spinal dis-alignment, and to stabilize pulse rate and cholesterol level.

Vibrates to the number 8.

HEDENBERGITE   [Astrological Sign of Virgo]

Hedenbergite crystallizes in the form of prismatic crystals, twins, and lamellar masses. The colour range includes light to dark green to black. Recently in the Amazon, Hedenbergite has been found within quartz crystals with amethyst.

This mineral is one of transition, assisting in the progression from one state to another and from one circumstance to another. It melds the extremes in ones life to bring a synthesis of opposing forces to expedite ease of development.

It brings forth an arrangement of the divine order of personal life, the sacred order upon, and within, the Earth, and the celestial order of the universe. It further facilitates the concepts of organization and systematic resolutions, and reflects the implementation of same.

It is an energy of success and patience, bringing forth the correct actions to accelerate the achievement of goals and promoting new friendships.

This mineral, when occurring with quartz and amethyst brings together the qualities of these minerals to produce a dynamic stone for meditation, healing, and for telepathic endeavors.

Hedenbergite has been used to assist in the assimilation of manganese, calcium, and iron. It has also been used in the treatment of bone loss, peridontal disorders, and for the healing of chronic illness of the immune system.

Vibrates to the master number 66.

HEINRICHITE   [Astrological Signs of Virgo & Libra]

Heinrichite crystallizes in the form of yellow-green tabular crystals.

This mineral facilitates the blending together of lives between two or more people. It is useful in relationships of all types which are in need of blending; it tends to further understanding between those involved.

It can provide access to guidance to both substantiate agreements between oneself and another and to improve leadership qualities.

It also assists one in exhibiting affection and in dispelling condemnation. It allows one to assess the general view of the "whole", or of the principal parts of a subject.

Heinrichite brings impetus to the user, allowing for the recognition of innate power and for direction of that power toward that which is ultimately beneficial to all. It is said to bring wealth to ones life.

It helps one to remain an impartial observer, at a comfortable distance, when dealing with ones problems, the problems of another, or when channeling.

It can be useful in eliminating the symptoms of acrophobia, to improve hearing with respect to pitch dominance, and to provide for increase in endurance.

Vibrates to the number 9.

HELIODOR   [Astrological Sign of Leo]

Heliodor is a type of beryl which crystallizes in the form of prismatic crystals which are sometimes vertically striated and terminated by small pyramid-like faces. The colour is golden yellow. In addition to the properties listed in the BERYL section of this book, the following qualities are applicable.

Heliodor can be used to activate the third chakra, the location of personal power and intellect. It enables one to communicate on a higher level and improves communication, via thought waves, between one and those at a distance.

This mineral also activates the seventh chakra [crown] and influences the mental plane, bringing balance between the intuitive and conscious levels of oneself. It assists in the elimination of duality within ones character, leading one to the entrance toward higher knowledge.

It also serves to enable one to both expertly and sympathetically contend with delicate issues. It assists one in exhibiting both sympathetic and compassionate understanding.

When one is in the protective mode, heliodor can prove quite valuable by facilitating the beaming of white/golden light around persons/objects, and by beaming purification around objects which may be "contaminated" by others during the "cold-and-flu" seasons.

It can also be used in the treatment of disorders associated with the liver, spleen, and pancreas.

Vibrates to the number 5.

HELIOTROPE   [See Bloodstone]

HEMATITE   [Astrological Signs of Aries & Aquarius]

Hematite crystallizes in the form of tabular and rhombohedral crystals, masses, columnar and granular shapes, plate-like layers, rosettes, and botryoidal [uncommon] configurations. The colour range includes grey-to-black, brown-red, and red - all with a metallic lustre.

Hematite can be called a "stone for the mind". It helps one to "sort-out" things in ones mind, and can be used for mental attunement, memory enhancement, original thinking, and technical knowledge. It assists one in mathematical pursuits and in the development of both mental and manual dexterity.

Although this stone enhances mental capability, it provides for a calming atmosphere concurrently, and, in addition, encourages one to "reach for the sun". It helps one to realize that the only limitations which exist are those self-limiting concepts within the mind.

It is also capable of helping the body to remain cool, or of dispelling heat at the physical level; one could use it on the forehead to draw-out the heat from a fever, or one could take it as an elixir internally.

It facilitates balancing of the yin-yang energies, utilizing, in addition, the magnetic qualities of the energy to balance the meridians within the body and to provide a stable equilibrium between the ethereal nervous system and the physical nervous system.

It assists in the focusing of energy and emotions for balance between the body, mind, and spirit.

It also assists in the dissolution of negativity, transforming the negativity, in the dissolved state, to the purity of the universal light of love.

It can be used to stimulate the desire for, and to facilitate the attainment of, peace, self-control, and inner happiness. It is also conducive to enabling one to enter into a loving relationship. It has been said to attract "kind" love.

It helps one to attain a "soft" meditative state, providing for smooth grounding and bringing tranquility and emotion clarity.

It can be used in the treatment of leg cramps, blood disorders [such as anemia], nervous disorders, and insomnia. It can also be used to assist in spinal alignment and in the proper healing of breaks and fractures; placing a piece of hematite on the base of the spine, on the area of mis-alignment, and on the top of the spine, has provided adjustment to the vertebrae.

Vibrates to the number 9.

HEMIMORPHITE   [Astrological Sign of Libra]

Hemimorphite crystallizes in the form of fan-shaped aggregates, masses, stalactites, thin tabular striated crystals, and botryoidal configurations. The colour range includes colourless, white, blue, green, and grey.

This mineral can be used to decrease "self-centeredness" and to encourage the state of egoless-ness while facilitating the staying power of the self.

It allows one to take responsibility for happiness or unhappiness, for creating ones personal reality, and for recognizing and utilizing the powers of self-concept.

It can further enhance ones self-esteem when one maintains the honesty of ones relationship to reality. It is an excellent stone to assist one in growing toward an egoless self-confidence and self-respect.

It provides for the manifestation of practicality and sensibility, relieving feelings of hostility and anger. It assists in smoothing emotional irritations and reinforces ones understanding of the origin of these provocations or aggravations such that one may easily deter future exposure to like-situations.

It is said to bring one "luck", a discerning mind, and a charming manner; allowing one to actualize the beneficial character traits.

Hemimorphite provides a symmetry between the physical plane and the other planes of existence [including emotional, intellectual, astral, etc.], allowing one to grow simultaneously on all planes.

It assists one in self-transformation, personal evolution, and maintaining and/or regaining health.

It helps one to recognize methods which will enable one to fully "know thyself" and to, subsequently, reach ones highest human potential; it also emits an energy to encourage one to develop inner strengths and resources, to live a joyous and creative life, and to contribute to the well-being of the social structure of all of humanity.

Hemimorphite can help one to understand and to utilize the powerful ancient techniques of healing. It was used in ancient times to ward-off poisoning and malice.

It can be used in the treatment of disorders of the blood and cellular composition, to soothe ulcers, to reduce pain, and to act as an emetic. It has been used to treat genital dis-eases, including herpes. It can also be used to provide support for dieting, body maintenance and shaping, and agility.

Vibrates to the number 4.

HERDERITE   [Astrological Sign of Aries]

Herderite crystallizes in the form of fibrous aggregates, and prismatic and tabular crystals. The colour range includes pale yellow and green.

This mineral can be used for treatment of imbalance in behavior patterns, and to stimulate psychic abilities. It encourages the exploration in all areas of ones life.

It stimulates directness and passion, allowing one to recognize both the needs of the moment and the impact of the potential future consequences.

It can be used to promote leadership qualities and is an excellent stone for facilitating tact and cooperation within groups, bringing an interactive harmony to the collective relationships.

Herderite can also be useful in the treatment of disorders of the pancreas, spleen, and gall bladder.

Vibrates to the number 2.

HERKIMER DIAMOND   [Astrological Sign of Sagittarius]

The herkimer diamond is a unique form of quartz which crystallizes in the configuration of double-terminated short, stout, clear or included prismatic crystals. This mineral was given the name due to the discovery of this pseudo-diamond in Herkimer, NY, USA.

There are now herkimer diamonds which are also available from Oaxacca, Mexico and from Spain; the ones from Oaxacca often contain rutile or goethite.

Amethyst Herkimer Diamonds are available from Tanzania and Mexico. They integrate the properties of the Amethyst with the properties of Herkimer Diamonds and a truly powerful stones.

This mineral provides an energy of delicate harmony, enhancing distinct awareness and unbridled spontaneity. It helps one to "be", providing for an alliance of surrender and a strength allowing for the further recognition of the essential being within the self; recognition of this aspect also provides for the acknowledgment and appreciation of the essential being, which is not the self, but is within each of us.

The energy of the herkimer diamond helps one to begin again in this lifetime, while allowing one to recognize ones inner space and to remember that there is "nothing to become" - that one _is_ that which one has been seeking and only needs to allow the actualization. It also assists one in clearing the body-mind system of unconscious fears and repressions, allowing for total relaxation and expansion of the life energy.

The herkimer diamond is known as an "attunement stone". It can be used to attune oneself with another person, environment, or activity.

It is quite important to use a herkimer diamond prior to the "laying-on-of-stones", or in other healing situations when the practitioner and the subject are not well acquainted; in these cases, a suggested method is for the practitioner and the subject to hold the herkimer diamond, as one, for several minutes prior to the session. [It is a lovely practice to give the subject the herkimer diamond after the session.]

Placement of a portion of a cluster in one location, while carrying another segment of that cluster on ones person, can provide for attunement to the activities or the energy of that environment.

For a continual attunement between two people, two herkimers can be held simultaneously by these people and each person can subsequently carry one of the herkimers. This approach can also be applied to groups.

In addition, the herkimer diamond stimulates clairvoyant and clairaudient abilities and can assist one in prescience and in telepathic communication.

It can accept and retain information which can be retrieved at a later time; information can also be stored within the herkimer prior to giving the mineral to another [the reason for the gift ranging from healing facilitation to the transfer of

♪ 319 ♬

thoughts of love]. After implanting thought-forms of love, it has been used in gridding environments to facilitate healing and well-being for others and for the Earth.

Some people who work in proximity to radioactive materials either wear or carry this stone as a form of protection and to facilitate the dissipation of any harmful rays.

The herkimer diamonds containing rutile combine the qualities of the herkimer with the properties of rutile listed in the RUTILE section of this book. The herkimer diamonds containing goethite combine the qualities of the herkimer with the properties of goethite listed in the GOETHITE section of this book.

The herkimer diamond is quite useful for dispersal of toxins which have accumulated in the body and for re-building the cellular structure. It has been used to correct imbalances in RNA/DNA and in the metabolic rate.

The alleviation of tension, and the calming of the outer bodies and the physical body, which is produced by this mineral, helps to align the energy structure of the user.

It is also quite helpful in releasing the tensions and rigidities of body tissues, further assisting in the recovery of memory by these areas, in order to facilitate healing.

Vibrates to the number 3.

HESSONITE   [Astrological Sign of Aries]

Hessonite crystallizes in the form of a grossularite and is, in fact, another form of the grossular garnet. Hessonite occurs in the colours of cinnamon, and yellow; it has been called the "cinnamon stone".

In addition to the properties listed in the GARNET and GROSSULAR GARNET sections of this book, hessonite also exhibits the following qualities.

It helps to eliminate feelings of inferiority, encourages one to seek new challenges via unexplored areas on the Earth plane, and provides courage for one to continue in personal endeavors.

Hessonite also carries one to the locations of the etheric realm where one wishes to travel, advancing the meditative state and bringing one to the circumstances and to the situations desired.

It further helps those dedicated to service, activating the intellectual qualities which are necessary and sufficient for the maintenance of both directness and good will.

It can be used as a carminative, to ameliorate disorders of the olfactory system, to cleanse the blood, and to clear ones environment of the negative influences which are often detrimental to the healthy state.

Vibrates to the number 6.

HETEROSITE   [Astrological Sign of Scorpio]

Heterosite crystallizes in the configuration of masses. The colour ranges from rose to red-purple, to black.

This mineral provides strong dissipation capabilities, assisting one to remove oneself from conditions requiring old patterns and conditions.

It allows one the insight to that which would occur if one would withdraw along the pathway leading to security in the successes already achieved; it also facilitates insight into that which one could accomplish if the choice would be to travel far into the unknown.

It stimulates the crown chakra, while providing for a grounding effect, and increases ones spiritual aspirations.

It also provides one with a freedom from the material world and rids one of undue modesty. Heterosite provides for access to expedient materialization of that which is chosen. It produces a purity within ones being that both stimulates higher conceptions and facilitates both conceptual design and performance to help one to continue on ones selected path.

It assists one in expressing oneself with both assurance and autonomy, providing for protection from interfering energies during the verbalization of ideals and concepts.

It can be used in the treatment of hemorrhages, bruises, and superficial wounds. It can assist in providing proper transport of the blood from the heart to the lungs. It can be used to control the level of uric acid and to stabilize the pulse rate. It can also assist in the purification of the blood.

Vibrates to the number 7.

HEULANDITE   [Astrological Sign of Sagittarius]

Heulandite crystallizes in the form of granular masses, globular shapes, and trapezoidal crystals. The colour range includes white, colourless, grey, yellow, pink, red, and brown.

This mineral may be used to "take one back" to the ancient civilizations of Atlantis/Lemuria where transfer of ancient information concerning traditions, techniques, and standards would be facilitated.

It also assists one in exploring, and in the discovery of both the "old" and the "new", bringing a synthesis of times together for the actualization of the "best". It helps one to diminish those ideas and conditions which are distressing, allowing one to release the bonds of custom, privilege, condescension, conceit, and jealousy.

The energy also furthers the replacement of these constraints with openness and willingness to maintain the centered-ness relative to the loving aspects of the perfect state.

Heulandite can be used in the dispersion of growths and to enhance weight loss. It may also be used in the treatment of disorders of the feet, shortness of breath, and to enable one to re-emerge and recover gracefully after a loss.

Vibrates to the number 9.

HIDDENITE   [Astrological Sign of Scorpio]

Hiddenite is a type of Kunzite [a form of Spodumene] which crystallizes in the form of flattened vertically striated prismatic crystals, and masses that are perfectly cleavable. The colour range includes emerald-green to yellow. For further information concerning the properties of hiddenite, see the KUNZITE section of this book.

In addition, this mineral helps to stimulate the intellect and the loving side of ones nature in order to bring forth the unknown. It prompts the connection with the other worlds and provides for subsequent clarity in the transfer of knowledge.

It can be used to assist one in intellectual or emotional pursuits and can provide insight when diagnosing disorders of the physical body.

Vibrates to the number 6.

HODGKINSONITE   [Astrological Sign of Virgo]

Hodgkinsonite crystallizes in the form of tabular crystals, acute pyramid-type shaped crystals, stout prismatic crystals, and masses. The colour range includes bright pink-to-red/brown.

This mineral helps one to remain "alone in a crowd", if the thought is consciously directed. It also promotes popularity, camaraderie, and honesty. It allows one to recognize the inner bonds with the outer world and to also both acknowledge and comprehend the spiritual connection between the self and the universe.

It assists in eliminating illusion and helps one to understand that the "view from the top" is the same as the "view from the bottom". It promotes sufficient emotional and intellectual advancement such that one may view the inevitably clear way.

Hodgkinsonite can be used to help mend fractures and bone breaks. It can also be used in the treatment of skin lesions and nervous "tics". It is said to improve cellular reconstruction activities.

Vibrates to the number 6.

HOLDENITE   [Astrological Sign of Sagittarius]

Holdenite crystallizes in the form of tabular crystals. The colour range includes clear pink, yellow-red, and deep red. The primary source of holdenite is located in New Jersey, USA.

This mineral can help one to break through during times of plateau delays. It assists one in growing in ones environment and in expanding that environment to include those which one "touches" on the road to progression. It helps one to release negativity and to accept the positive energies of the world. It can also enable one to maintain calm in times of derisive forces. It can destroy the feelings of fear, allowing one to surmount obstacles and to reach the summits of achievement.

It can be used to provide cooperative effort between the loving aspects of the heart, the vitality of the physical self, and the astuteness of the intellect - promoting strength and practicality in emotional situations and decisions.

This mineral can also be used to relieve constrictions in the body, mind and spirit. It can help to improve respiration and to "speed" one to recovery.

Please note that the description above is quite general; this is due to the application of holdenite to the multitude of areas. It is left to the reader to explore this endless realm.

Vibrates to the number 2.

HOLTITE   [Astrological Sign of Aquarius]

Holtite crystallizes in the form of hexagonal-type crystals. The colour range includes brown and orange-to-green.

This mineral can be used to "whisk" one away to "greener pastures", either in body or in mind. If, in mind, once the mind recognizes that the circumstances, in the present, are not "lush pastures", holtite provides support for taking the steps to change the situation - either by leaving, by accepting, or by changing oneself or the situation. If, in body, holtite encourages the adventure and the personal inner growth involved.

It stimulates acceptance of wisdom over intellect and helps to banish confusion. It furthers humanitarian and independent pursuits.

This mineral can be used in disorders involving the hands.

It can also assist in the acceptance of avantgarde healing techniques and metaphysical anomalies. It discourages disorganized growth and assists in restructuring areas of disorder.

Vibrates to the number 8.

HOMILITE   [Astrological Sign of Leo]

Homilite crystallizes in the form of tabular crystals. The colour range includes brown and black.

This mineral can be used to enhance composition qualities and to support proselytizing.

Homilite improves ones conversational and understanding qualities when one is in communication with "inanimate" objects. It provides for a clear transmission pathway during these endeavors. It also provides for centering during activities of writing and speaking.

This mineral also helps one to be constant in ones aim toward an objective, usually, allowing for dispersement of any thoughts concerning the worthiness of the objective. It also enhances love within ones environment and within the self.

It encourages one to take the initiative and to understand and to actively utilize the supreme power available from within the center of ones being.

Homilite provides comfort during dis-ease; the comfort being a "knowing" that all will be well, regardless of the outcome. It also assists in the functions of digestion and elimination, and in the assimilation of nutrients.

Vibrates to the number 1.

HOPEITE   [Astrological Sign of Libra]

Hopeite crystallizes in the form of compact masses, and small prismatic crystals. The colour range includes yellow, white, colourless, and grey.

This mineral is a "stone for the carpet-bagger"; providing for a home in the heart, wherever one may wander and wherever one may wonder.

It provides one with courage to have faith in oneself and enables one to direct the flow of energy toward desired outcomes.

It helps one to methodically itemize difficulties and to retrieve self-reliance from the deep well of obscurity. It allows for a degree of mental and emotional detachment, when necessary, and disallows the magnification of problems.

This mineral can be useful to facilitate the assimilation of zinc, for the treatment of disorders of the skin [elixir for skin is quite helpful], and as an emetic, a purgative, and a diuretic. It can also be used to stimulate the faith necessary to facilitate healing on all levels.

Vibrates to the number 6.

HORNEBLENDE   [Astrological Signs of Libra & Gemini]

Horneblende crystallizes in the form of compact masses and prismatic crystals. The colour range includes yellow, brown, blue, and green. This mineral is one which displays pleochroism - the quality of exhibiting a different colour, depending upon which axis one views. Horneblende usually displays yellow or brown in the X-axis, brown or green in the Y-axis, and dark blue, green, or brown in the Z-axis.

This mineral not only helps one to recognize the aspects of duality, it assists one to synthesize these aspects and to bring them together in an understanding environment. It promotes creativity from the heart and enhances artistic and expressive pursuits.

It has been used as a power stone in ancient ceremonies of the Native American medicine wheel and the African tribal and Australian aboriginal fire wheel. It is a facilitator for speaking with "the others" and for communication with the physical and spiritual animal worlds.

It is a good stone to carry if one is in the circumstances of requesting "another chance"; the outcome will be beneficial to all parties. It allows one to both see and hear with the heart, producing a gracefulness in all interpersonal relationships.

It stimulates the higher mental processes, producing a merging between reason and feeling. It enhances centering in the formulation of plans and assists one in questioning with purpose; it furthers ones talents in precise categorization and in the recording [either mentally or physically] of answers which are given.

It also stimulates vitality with respect to the responsibility at hand, providing for relentless pursuit of the goal until completion.

Use of horneblende during meditation often produces a state of delight and perfect happiness; this state is often carried back to this reality, remaining within the self for a time.

Horneblende helps to insulate one from the abrasiveness of others. It further allows one to "accept" and to release judgmental-ness, bringing to one the tolerance of the un-programmed child.

It can also be used to enhance the assimilation of Vitamins A and D, calcium, magnesium, and iron, and to balance the sodium levels within the body. It has been used in the treatment of disorders of the ears and to stabilize mental disturbances.

Vibrates to the number 3.

HORNSTONE   [See Chert]

HOWLITE   [Astrological Sign of Gemini]

Howlite crystallizes in the form of white nodules, compact masses, and tabular crystals.

This mineral can be used to calm communication, to facilitate awareness, and to encourage emotional expression.

It tends to combine the power of reasoning with observation and patience, providing for discernment, retentive memory and a laudable desire for knowledge, bringing progress marked with triumph. It spurs one toward the ambition to reach ones goals and assists in eliminating hesitation with respect to action.

It dispels criticalness, cold selfishness, and facetious-ness, bringing both strength and innocence to immediate confrontations. It builds an innate decency within ones character, encouraging those attributes which are the building blocks to spirituality.

Howlite can be used to eliminate pain, stress, and rage; hence, it is quite nice to have around. It can help to lessen rudeness and boisterousness, and can provide for a reflection of the offender to the offender. It discourages impertinent behavior and encourages subtlety and tact.

This mineral can be useful for balancing calcium levels in the body, both stimulating increase or decrease dependent upon the area. It can also be used in the treatment of disorders of the teeth, bone structure, and soft tissues.

Vibrates to the number 2.

HUBNERITE   [Astrological Signs of Gemini & Libra]

Hubnerite crystallizes in the formation of tabular and prismatic crystals, blades, lamellar, columns, and grains.

This mineral can be used to dispense vigor to the physical body. It allows for regulation and command of the corporeal processes and expedites appropriate action without imprudent motion.

At the same time it enhances adaptability in ones individuality; promoting the requisite skills for conditional efficiency, while eliminating unsupported claims that any course of action is explicit and unyielding.

It also provides influence with respect to activity, furthering an easy movement in situations and eliminating restriction issues; it helps one to allow a situation to improve naturally.

It can be used to gain information and insight into the antecedent aspects of ones life. Quietly holding the stone and allowing each issue to pass through the mind, one is given visions and, occasionally, actual writings, which provide insight to the resolutions and solutions for the questions.

Hubnerite can be used in the treatment of the disorders associated with abundance of iron. It can also assist in the alleviation of hypoglycemia and in the correction of weakness of the sight. It can be useful in alignment of the vertebrae.

Vibrates to the number 3.

HUMMERITE   [Astrological Sign of Leo]

Hummerite crystallizes in the form of bright orange crusts and tabular crystals.

This mineral can be used to settle or to stimulate the desires and emotions, as necessary, for a healthy emotional system. It assists one in recognizing and attaining the state of dynamic mental and emotional animation.

It also improves creativity, bringing insight to the source of being and providing for a "view to enchant an artist".

Use of hummerite can provide for intense stimulation of the intuition; the mineral is excellent for use by those who are familiar with the avenues of psychic awareness.

Hummerite also allows and encourages one to laugh with pleasure - from the belly - a real laugh.

This mineral can be used to relieve the causes of frigidity and to help one to creatively and peacefully deal with ones sexuality. Holding the mineral promotes a state of silent energy toning to return one to the perfection of health.

Vibrates to the number 4.

HYDRARGILLITE   [See Gibbsite]

HYDROPHILITE   [See Chlorocalcite]

HYDROZINCITE   [Astrological Sign of Gemini]

Hydrozincite crystallizes in the form of compact masses, crusts, stalactites, and flattened, elongated crystals which taper to a sharp point. The colour range includes white, grey, pale pink, yellow, and brown.

This mineral can be used to provide one with insight to the hidden turmoil within oneself, allowing for free expression and for the painless release of the bonding of confusion and strife. It can also help one to allow ones "light to shine", and to take the few moments necessary to "stop" in order to appreciate and enjoy ones world.

It enhances practicality in a "practical nature", bringing the joys of living into the pragmatic realm of self-development.

Hydrozincite crystals can be used, in a fashion similar to the laser wand quartz crystals, in the capacity of opening chakras and clearing and protecting a room or environment.

This mineral can be used in the treatment of brain disorders, both physical and mental. [The configuration of the mass is recommended for this purpose.] It is also useful in helping to balance the liquid in the body, to stimulate the health of the hair, and to assist in the elimination of toxins. It has been used to dispel the fear of water.

Vibrates to the number 4.

HYPERSTHENE   [Astrological Signs of Sagittarius & Libra]
                                          [Also Known as Eulite]

Hypersthene crystallizes in the form of thin plates, masses, and tabular and prismatic crystals. The colour range includes green, brown, and black.

This mineral also exhibits the pleochroic properties; the X-axis displaying the colour brown-red, the Y-axis displaying the colour red-yellow, and the Z-axis displaying the colour green.

It can be used to stimulate contact with the "solution planes" of existence. In the meditative or non-meditative state, answers to problems of all magnitudes seem to "come" very quickly to the user.

In addition, it can help to combat irritability and critical-ness, providing for discriminating judgment. It helps one to "stand-up" for that which is "right" in ones moral structure.

It helps one to maintain business relationships and to further personal relationships.

Facilitation of clairaudience can be enhanced, and discovery of information from the spiritual realm and astral realm is expedited.

It energizes the aspects of self-respect, dispels the negative facets of prideful-ness, and opens the door to the unlimited and desired opportunities at which the energy is directed.

Hypersthene can be used to diminish acidity of the stomach, to decrease pain, to lessen tension in the limbs and shoulders, and to treat fever, spasms, far-sightedness, and over-activity of the pituitary gland. It has been used in the dispersal of growths. It has also been used to ameliorate painful conditions of the Achilles tendon.

Vibrates to the numbers 8 and 9.

**IN YOUR AWAKENING, YOU HAVE BUT TO ACCEPT
THE DAWNING OF YOUR LIFE**

IDOCRASE [Astrological Signs of Sagittarius & Capricorn]
[Also Known as Vesuvianite]

Idocrase crystallizes in the form of granular masses, columnar structures, and short prismatic or pyramid-like crystals. The colour range includes, yellow, red, blue, brown, green, pink, and white.

This mineral can be used to promote patriotism and loyalty to mankind. It represents cooperative effort and is a wonderful stone to present to newlyweds, business associates, and friends and acquaintances.

It also provides for assistance to those endeavoring to invent and discover, assisting in the control of the creative and intuitive aspects of the inner realm.

Idocrase unlocks and stabilizes the mental faculties, helping to clear negative thought patterns from the mental, emotional, and physical bodies. It helps one to recognize that which is important to further ones advancement along the spiritual path, serving to eliminate the feeling of imprisonment, for eternity, of the once living perfect man.

It can be used dispel anger, to banish depression, and to allay fear. It provides for a security with oneself and helps one to fearlessly face danger; it also provides for actualization of the wisdom to discourage dangerous situations.

It brings one closer to the higher realms and provides for "easy access" to ones higher-self. It also facilitates both the observation and comprehension of that which has no substance on this Earth plane. It increases the abilities of clairsentience, assisting one in attentiveness to ones feelings.

This mineral can be used for strengthening the enamel on the teeth, and for strengthening the creative portion of the mental faculties. It can be used in the treatment of the sense of smell, too aid in the assimilation of nutrients from ones intake of food, and to both lessen and ameliorate skin eruptions and ruptures. It has also been used in the treatment of diverticulosis.

Vibrates to the numbers 2 and 3.

ILMENITE [Astrological Sign of Sagittarius]

Ilmenite crystallizes in the form of masses, grains, acute rhombohedral crystals, and thick tabular crystals. The colour is iron-black. This mineral is one of the earliest constituents of magma to crystallize and has been found as a component in moon rock.

It can assist one in matters of utility, providing for guidance in ritualistic activities and bringing forth philosophical expansion.

This mineral can help to dispel both illusion and the ancient "ghosts" of ones life. It can further provide a "knowing" of when that which appears as an illusion is not an illusion. Deceit and misrepresentation cannot hide from Ilmenite.

The crystal form of ilmenite is a "stone for enlightenment". It can, not only, support one on the journey to enlightenment, but it can act as a guide to one on the path, while helping to diminish the obstacles.

Ilmenite can be used in the treatment of all dis-eases. It provides for stimulation of the crown chakra and provides support to the affected areas of the physical, mental, and emotional bodies.

Vibrates to the number 6.

ILVAITE   [Astrological Sign of Cancer]

Ilvaite crystallizes in the form of masses, columnar structures, and thick prismatic crystals with diamond-shaped cross sections and vertical striations. The colour ranges from grey to black.

This mineral can serve to intensify ones patience and to provide information via the higher-self concerning perseverance. It allows for one to understand that success is an edifice built on patience.

It also helps one to appropriate the time necessary to search for the "diamonds" of truth.

It provides for both grounding and centering while enhancing the creative aspects of ones nature, allowing one access to information from the advanced realms.

It helps one to be an epicure of the senses and to apply this distinctive ability to all forms of imaginative originality. It can also be used to align the subtle bodies, enhancing emotional stability and heightening the prospects for gratification and distinction.

Ilvaite can be employed in the treatment of fever [including typhoid fever], diarrhea, hemorrhage, and ulcerations [including the nervous stomach syndrome which precedes the ulcer condition]. It can also be used in the treatment of hepatitis and has been useful as a purgative and vermifuge. It must be noted that ones conscious thoughts of the condition should be made known to the mineral prior to the commencement of the healing.

Vibrates to the master number 33.

INDICOLITE   [See Blue Tourmaline]

IOLITE   [Astrological Signs of Libra, Sagittarius, & Taurus]
        [Also Known as Cordierite]

Iolite crystallizes in the form of masses, grains, and short prismatic crystals. The colour range includes blue, brown, yellow, dark violet, grey, and green. This mineral also exhibits the pleochroic qualities; i.e., X-axis showing clear yellow, Y-axis showing dark violet, blue, or brown, and the Z-axis showing clear blue. In some cases, a metamorphic change has occurred in the iolite and the colours which are seen are shades of grey-green, green-grey, and brown-grey.

Iolite is called the "violet stone". It is one of the major stones for use in the third-eye/crown area during healing, during guided meditations, and during astral travel adventures. Its positioning in this area can determine the nature and the extent of the success of the activity. One must use the intuitive capabilities to determine the correct location for each specific situation. This mineral helps one to change "painlessly", the change being toward spiritual growth and enhanced "illusion".

It produces an electrical charge when in contact with ones auric field and can both strengthen and align this field with the subtle bodies.

It is useful for the stimulation of visions and has also been used in shamanic healing ceremonies to influence the spirits. The iolite ring of the shaman is worn to ensure accuracy within the vision. It is quite powerful "medicine".

It balances the male/female aspects of ones character, bringing harmony to within the self and eliminating dissonance and disruption in relationships. The energy of iolite helps one to release discord from ones life, allowing for progression toward the perfection which may be obtained in this world and the next.

It further enables one to enjoy each moment and to awaken to the inner knowledge which is so patiently awaiting access. It has also been used to simulate a compass, such that one may have knowledge of directions and directional forces.

It performs well when used for the elimination of debts, to enhance precision within ones life, and to facilitate acceptance of responsibility. The energy enables one to understand that the acceptance of responsibility to the self leads to excellence in ones endeavors and in the management of money.

Iolite can help one to attain a constitution which defies physical disorders. It is said to enable one to consume alcohol without exhibiting the effects. It has been used to both protect and to improve degraded conditions of the liver. It can also be used to assist in lessening fatty deposits and to rid the body of toxins. It has been used in the treatment of malaria and other fever-producing disorders.

Vibrates to the number 7.

IRIDOSMINE   [Astrological Signs of Cancer & Leo]
                                                          [Also Known As Osmiridium]

Iridosmine crystallizes in the form of metallic-white irregular flattened grains.

This mineral helps to provide a shaping quality to the subtle bodies and promotes flowering of same. Transferring spiritually from one body to the other is facilitated; this quality provides the user with further information with respect to both the state of the body and the conditions and actions necessary for renewal.

It can be used to activate the potential of an individual, providing for exactness in approach, while enhancing results. It stimulates a magnification of ideas, so that one does not disregard or neglect the slightest detail. Iridosmine can also bring one to the summit of ones intuitive capabilities, allowing for detachment from circumstances and facilitating insight with interpretation.

It can be used in the treatment of gastric disturbances and on areas of the body that could be subjected to poultices. It has been used in the treatment of disorders of the eyes, to provide clarity to sight, and to eliminate fatigued vision. It can also be used in the elimination of parasites from the body.

Vibrates to the numbers 7 and 4.

IRON   [Astrological Signs of Aries, Leo, & Virgo]

Iron crystallizes in the form of grains, and masses. It is sometimes found within meteorites. The colour is grey-to-black.

The natural forms of iron, especially the meteoritic iron, are most effective in manifesting the qualities listed below.

Iron can bring mental and emotional balance, and can bestow new energies to enable one to dismiss traditional issues and to both create and implement those ideals which are new to ones life. It allows one to be tempered by experiences, facilitating "smooth sailing" in ones endeavors.

It has been used to provide contact with the "fairy kingdom" of this world, bringing openness and receptivity to tranquility and abundance.

It has also been used to stimulate contact with other-worldly intelligence, enhancing the connection during the receipt of information, and providing for insight and knowledge concerning the moral structure of the elders.

It confers an invulnerability, and favorably influences the outcome of lawsuits, petitions, and judgments. It augments the qualities of diplomacy.

Iron, used with copper, produces a balancing of the energies of the body and assists one in maintaining the overall well-being of ones body chemistry.

It can be used in the treatment of blood disorders, muscular atrophy, sore throat, gall and kidney stones, and internal bleeding. It can also be used to strengthen the reproductive system and the structures of the nails.

Vibrates to the number 2.

IVORY   [Astrological Signs of Sagittarius & Aries]

This book discusses only the fossilized ivory, the ancient ivory used by the natives of Africa and other countries, and vegetable ivory [e.g., tagua nuts from southern palm trees].

Ivory represents purity and promotes vitality directed towards rightness in purpose and direction. It assists in expelling restlessness, anxiety, moodiness, and derision, while stimulating initiative, dignity, and serenity.

It enhances acumen in areas requiring assessment, bringing forth solutions from ones inner being. It also helps to eliminate obstructive forces in the physical world, providing for a clear pathway for incoming transactions and resources.

It allows for aloofness during the initial meditation process, so that one may easily enter the meditative state. It assists in removing etheric parietal blockages to the meditative entry state.

It can be used in the treatment of bone disorders and in the regeneration activities required to ameliorate these disorders. It can also be quite useful in diminishing problems associated with soreness and stiffness of joints, flexibility of the limbs, circulatory functions, and dis-alignment of the spinal column. Ivory used as a topical elixir is truly soothing to the skin and can be used in the treatment of skin related disorders.

The tagua nuts have been known as "headache stones", allowing for prompt and continual relief of headache pain.

Vibrates to the number 8.

Dreams are part of our heart and soul
Our dreams go to the depths of our thoughts,
Wants, and needs to fulfill our destiny.
In order to fulfill our destiny we must
fulfill our dreams.

[J.R.Davis, 1994]

Jade occurs in the form of jadeite, Transvaal jade, and nephrite. The general qualities of jade are listed here. Further qualities of the respective stones are listed in the JADEITE, TRANSVAAL JADE, and NEPHRITE sections of this book.

Jade is known as a " dream stone" and as a "stone of fidelity", bringing realization to ones potential and devotion to ones purpose. It improves ones remembering of dreams and assists in "dream-solving". It is used to release suppressed emotions via the dream process; for this activity, a piece of jade is placed under the pillow prior to sleep.

It also allows one access to the basic rituals and knowledge used during the Mayan "dreamtime". It furthers the connection with the elders of the Mayan culture, assisting one in obtaining the necessary insights for performing the ceremonial services.

Jade was revered in the Mayan culture as the "Sovereign of Harmony", facilitating peace within the physical, emotional, and intellectual structures, as well as within the materialistic world. It was said to bring accord to the environment, to transmute negativity, and to instill resourcefulness.

It is said to have been one of the stones used in the breastplate of the high priest.

It has been used by the ancient [and some current] primitive tribes as a sacred stone, assisting one in access to the spiritual worlds. It is said to have brought the user a long and fruitful life with a gentle transition from this body to the spiritual world.

The occurrence of jade with the presence of the quartz crystalline structure [see the NEPHRITE section of this book] has been used to expedite meditative travel to the realm of "all knowing".

As the visible world is nourished by the invisible, humanity can be sustained and preserved by the lovely visions of dreamers. One who reveres a beautiful vision or ideal can utilize the energies of jade to assist in realizing those thoughts. Jade helps one to cherish ones desires and facilitates the building of ones dreams in this physical reality. It releases ones limitations such that permission is granted which allows one to actualize aspirations and to attain limitless achievements. It inspires and induces ambition toward the accomplishment of objectives.

It helps to attune one to the needs of others and inspires wisdom during the assessment of problems. It promotes the balancing of ones needs with the requirements of the day, allowing one to recognize and to care for that which is of prime importance to well-being.

It also provides confidence, assisting one in the attainment of self-assuredness, self-reliance, and self-sufficiency.

It can be used in the treatment of disorders of the heart, hips, kidneys, and spleen. It is excellent as an elixir to soothe and smooth the skin, and to stimulate the health of the hair.

Vibrates to the master number 11.

JADEITE   [Astrological Sign of Aries]

Jadeite is a form of jade which crystallizes in the form of grains, masses, and rare small elongated prismatic crystals. The colour range includes translucent emerald green [imperial jade], shades of green [from pale to deep], mauve, lavender, white, brown, red, orange, yellow, grey, black, blue-green to green with white or light green traceries, pastel green with slight bluish cast and interlaced with pure white veins, and white with delicate green veining.

In addition to the properties listed in the JADE section of this book, jadeite exhibits the following qualities.

This mineral was exalted by the Mayan and Aztec cultures as a stone of magic, bringing to fruition, in times of need, the protective forces of the ethers. It represented status and was possessed only by the elite of the realm. It was also carved in the form of deities, representing aspects of protection and favorable fortunes.

It can be used to induce the cohesiveness of groups, allowing for understanding between the members and facilitating cohesiveness in the recognition and actualization of purpose.

Jadeite can also bring forth the abilities to unite and to improve dysfunctional relationships. The emerald green variety [known as Imperial Jade] is recommended for these tasks.

The chloromelanite jadeite [ranging from rich dark hues of green to an intense black] is a stone appropriate for kings and gods. It enhances expressiveness, intelligence, and perception, and helps one to be adept at that which is chosen. It assists one in attaining the royal realm of comfort and elegance, providing for stabilization, via grounding, to the limitless resources of the universe.

Jadeite acts as rather a "stitching" agent and assists both the cellular and skeletal structures to re-bind themselves. It also assists in the removal of pain [e.g., in the sides, hips, legs, etc.] associated with "stitching" and helps stitches to bind and to heal properly.

It can be used in the treatment of disorders of the reproductive organs [primarily male]. It has been used to diminish and to prevent recurrence of cramps and "charlie horses", promoting stabilization of the muscular arrangement and smoothing of the tissues.

Vibrates to the number 9.

JAHNSITE   [Astrological Sign of Taurus]

Jahnsite crystallizes in the form of parallel aggregates and well-developed crystals. The colour range includes brown, purple, yellow, orange, and green.

This mineral can assist one in recognizing and removing the "scars of life" from the memory. It brings forth the remembrance of situations and allows one to release and, subsequently, to eradicate innate anger, grief, and conflict which is associated with the related circumstances.

It allows for progress and change to further a variety of exemplary pursuits.

It provides for charitable action, enhances communication skills, and assists one in understanding and following instructions.

It can assist one to become "un-stuck" in situations and provides a stimulus for enlivening relationships, inducing impromptu variations and improvisations. It contains somewhat of a duality in qualities - helping one to break-away when beneficial, and helping one to stay and to re-arrange ones environment and/or situation when the results would be advantageous to ones development.

Jahnsite is also a "sport stone", helping in the play, promoting flexibility in motion and vitality in action.

It can be used in the treatment of disorders of the hands, heart, throat, and lungs. It can also be used to calm the emotions, to reduce nervousness, to relieve stress and tension in the body, and to diminish speech disorders which have been precipitated by anxiety.

Vibrates to the number 5.

JASPER   [Astrological Sign of Leo - Elemental]

Jasper is a form of opaque, usually patterned, chalcedony and occurs in massive formations. The colour range includes dark red, orange, yellow, tan, brown, green, grey, and blue; it sometimes occurs in the configuration containing stripes or "banding". Properties, additional to those listed in the CHALCEDONY section of this book, are listed below.

This mineral is known as the "supreme nurturer". It acts as a reminder that one is not here, on this physical plane, just for oneself, but is also here to bring joy and substance to others, assisting others to release the bonds of constraint.

It is conducive to awareness and to allowing one to celebrate situations of isolation. It helps one to realize that one is always remembered by others who can, usually, be called upon to provide insight to examples of those who send loving energy toward ones physical manifestation.

Jasper was often worn by shamen to provide protection. It holds an aspect of solar energy and a connection to the solar plexus chakra which also helped shamen in their magical practices. It was considered a sacred stone during the performance of, and adherence to, the "old ways" of the Native American Indians. The jasper which contains the yellow colour was used to assist and protect during times of travel [spiritual or physical]; that which contains the red colour was thought to induce health and re-birth, bringing freshness in ideas and strategies to the holder. The jasper containing the blue colour was used to connect one with the "after" worlds.

It is a stone which accepts intense responsibility in the realm of protection. It protects against negativity and helps one to be grounded to the stabilizing energies of the Earth.

Jasper can be used to align the energy of the chakras and to integrate the attributes of the chakras such that astral journeys can be affected.

It balances the yin-yang energy and balances the physical, emotional, and intellectual bodies with the etheric energies.

It stabilizes the aura, providing for a cleansing effect to smooth dysfunctional energies and to eliminate negativity. It helps one to unite the energy field of the physical with the ethereal in order to balance the form and to direct one toward the goal.

The ancients revered jasper as sacred, protective, and as a facilitator of safe astral travel. [Jasper was placed over the heart and navel chakras prior to astral travel.]

It has also been used during the venture of dowsing.

Jasper has been both worn and used by priests and kings. It is said to have been one of the stones used in the breastplate of the high priest.

Jasper is also is a sustaining stone, a stone representing the elemental "man". It can be quite helpful in times of extended hospitalization and when ones energy is low. On a long fast, it can help to keep ones energy high.

Jasper can be used in the treatment of tissue deterioration of the internal organs, and for disorders of the kidneys, spleen, bladder, liver, and stomach - the energy is more appropriate for deterioration, rather than the actual state of malfunction. Jasper can be used to treat the loss of sense of smell. It has been reported to soothe the nerves.

It can also help with balancing the mineral content and with the regulation of the supplies of iron, sulfur, zinc, and manganese within the body.

Vibrates to the number 6.

In addition to the above properties common to jasper, specific types of jasper possess further qualities.

<u>Arizona Lizard Stone Jasper</u>   [Astrological Sign of Gemini]

Arizona lizard stone jaspoer occurs in the colours ranging from light to dark green. It can be used to promote healing on all levels, to assist in the release of the causes of dis-ease, and to impart hope to situations that may seem desperate.

It has been used to support changes in ones life, to initiate modifications in behavior patterns, and to stimulate action. It is a stone to bring appreciation of heritage and of commonalities, while advancing ones spirit of adventure.

It has been used in the treatment of disorders of the skin, to dispel bloating, to diminish water retention, to alleviate headaches, and to stabelize the emotional balance. It can also be used in the removal of energy blockages which lead to poor circulation.

Vibrates to the number 8.

Bat Cave Jasper   [Astrological Sign of Sagittarius]

Bat cave jasper occurs in the colours ranging from chocolate brown to tan. It can be used to facilitate a very, very deep state of meditation, and to assist one in the attainment of the perfect centering of the self.

It furthers ones appreciation of the joys and delights of living, encouraging one to release stress and to flow with the "gentleness of the summer breeze".

It has been used to stimulate the transition to the astral plane, allowing one to navigate the journey with ease.

It can be used in the enhancement of night vision, in the purification of the body, and to stimulate motor capabilities.

Vibrates to the number 6.

Bruneau Jasper   [Astrological Sign of Gemini]

Bruneau jasper occurs in colour combinations which include the hues of brown, tan, and ivory. The structure exhibits smooth flowing circular or oval patterns, occasionally resembling an eye or an infinite passageway to that which lies beyond this reality.

It allows one to see the "inter-connectedness" between all worlds and, during travel [e.g., astral, past-life ascension], it assists one in maintaining an awareness of the physical world, while at the same time facilitating awareness in the other worlds. It provides for a spiraling toward the infinite space of perception, allowing one to consummate ones goals.

It has been used to enhance practicality in expressiveness, and to assist one to adapt to situations which are new, smoothing the erratic emotional states and helping one to anticipate "the best" in all situations.

It can also be used in the treatment of the eyes, of bacterial infections, of disorders associated with the fatty tissues of the body, and of dis-ease within the reproductive system.

It is an excellent stone for use in assisting one in the development of the body during maturation, and in intuitive preparation of herbal formulas for specific conditions.

Vibrates to the number 7.

Orbicular Jasper   [Astrological Sign of Capricorn]

Orbicular jasper contains the markings of many small circles, and can be used to support pursuits based upon service.

It helps one to accept responsibility and to increase the attribute of patience.

It has been used to facilitate continuity in circular breathing during healing and/or meditative states.

It can also be used to affect nutritional stabilization within the body, to improve the digestive processes and related organs, and to assist in the elimination of toxins leading to the decrease in body odor and dis-ease.

Vibrates to the number 6.

Picture Jasper   [Astrological Sign of Leo]

Picture jasper occurs in colour combinations which include the hues of brown, tan, black, blue, and/or ivory. The structure exhibits a hidden message and/or "picture" from the past. It is a stone of proportion and harmony. It stimulates creative visualization and enables one to understand the basic functioning of "unknown" advanced civilizations. It can be used to further both the development and continuance of business pursuits and to provide for coordination of activities leading to increase.

Biggs-formation picture jasper from the vicinity of Biggs, Oregon, USA, is one of the most beautiful picture jaspers, and also one of the most expensive. It provides scenes from the Earth, and is known as the stone for "GLOBAL AWARENESS". It stimulates the "brotherhood" to work together to save the planet. It emits an energy which promotes the spiritual affinity to achieve perfect accord between humanity and nature; it is one of the "Earth Stones" for the age of redemption and cleansing of the Earth. An unusual form of "Biggs" jasper is known as "Biggs Blue" and has an added property which promotes understanding of the actual advanced technology of the ancient civilizations; it also stimulates the third-eye, and provides insight into the methodology which is available for restoring the planet, renewing the sustaining qualities, and for understanding the prior days of the Earth.

Picture jasper helps to bring hidden thoughts, griefs, fears, and hopes to the surface so that one may face the cause of disorders.

It can be used to stimulate the proper functioning of the immune system, and can be helpful in the treatment of disorders associated with the skin and kidneys.

Picture Jasper vibrates to the number 8; Biggs Blue Picture Jasper vibrates to the number 2; Biggs Brown Picture Jasper vibrates to the number 7.

Red Jasper   [Astrological Sign of Taurus]

Red Jasper occurs in the colour range of red. It has been used to assist one in rectifying unjust circumstances; meditation with the this mineral can provide insight to the method of amelioration. The energy communicates the message that all choice is singularly ones responsibility. It can also assist in providing for rescue in situations of danger.

Red Jasper can facilitate the reiteration of dreams to allow the dreamer to remember the aspects which could be consequential in ones life. It seems to replicate the dream on a video-type mechanism for access during states of meditation.

It can also be used to prevent "set-backs" in disorders. The mineral assists in helping one to learn to progress, and to eliminate the aspects of digression.

Vibrates to the number 6.

Rose-Eye Jasper   [Astrological Sign of Capricorn]

This mineral can be used to assist one in the determination and effectiveness to investigate the untested character.

It helps to provide a protected and secure environment, both physical and mental.

It can also help one to increase the inventive actualization of ones life, providing for rapid rationality, and for common sense allied with the all-knowing universal presence.

Rose-Eye Jasper can be of further assistance in all areas of dispersion, dispersing dissention, dispersing congestion, dispersing crowds, dispersing growths, dispersing overloaded schedules, etc. It appears to be a very supportive, reassuring, and helpful stone.

It can be used in the treatment of pneumonia, for Vitamins A and E assimilation disorders, and hay fever.

Vibrates to the number 8.

Royal Plume Jasper   [Astrological Signs of Leo & Virgo]

Royal plume jasper, coloured a royal purple and exhibiting plumes, can be used in the stimulation of the crown chakra, enhancing ones status and power. It assists in preserving ones dignity and in eliminating contradictions within ones life.

When focused, it can promote the binding-together of energies for direction at a single pre-selected purpose.

It has been used to stabilize the emotions and to treat disorders associated with mental instability and less than adequate memory.

Vibrates to the number 9.

Wonderstone   [Astrological Sign of Aries]

Wonderstone, coloured a soft yellow-tan with waves of light violet, usually, flowing through it, can be used to facilitate and to reinforce the state of tranquility. It can be helpful in eliminating worries, allowing one to recognize that "worry" does not change a situation and that appropriate action can modify results; it also assists one in gaining insight to beneficial action, eliminating distress and depression and increasing ones feeling of well-being. It is an excellent stone for bringing mental clarity to any predicament.

It also stimulates the imagination and furthers faith in, and acceptance, of ones basic impulses and intuitive energies.

It can be used in the amelioration of spasms and convulsions and to remove blockages in the energy path which have led to poor circulation and/or disorientation.

Vibrates to the number 8.

JEREMEJEVITE   [Astrological Sign of Gemini]

Jeremejevite crystallizes in the form of prismatic hexagonal-type crystals. The colour range includes colourless, yellow, and yellow-brown.

This mineral can be used to dispel complexes [superiority, inferiority, etc.], to lessen sorrow, and to stimulate the insight which is necessary and sufficient to enable one to understand the condition which produced the sorrow, so that one can eliminate the condition of regret.

It is excellent in assisting one to progress through changes and to modify the self, or circumstances in which one is involved, in order to progress toward the beneficial development of the qualities which are required to sustain the self.

Jeremejevite can also be used to help one to manifest second-sight in order to provide for the capability of "future-telling". It helps one to understand life and to complete and follow-through with decisions when "at the edge". It allows one to recognize that the resolved course of action is error free.

It can be used to encourage orderly progression in the growth and maturity of the physical body and to eliminate disorganized cellular growth. It has been used in the treatment of disorders associated with the colon. It can also be used to alleviate frost-bite and chills.

Vibrates to the master number 55.

JET   [Astrological Sign of Capricorn]

Jet is a fossilized wood, close in comparison to coal; it, however, is harder than the usual forms of coal. It occurs in the colour black.

Jet can be used to dispel fearful thoughts and can be used to protect the wearer against illness and violence. It also protects one during the pursuit of business and enhances the stability of ones finances.

This mineral aligns the base chakra and stimulates the awakening of the Kundalini. When placed upon the areas of the upper body, it enables the movement of the Kundalini toward the crown.

It is also a calming agent, providing diminishment in depression.

It can be used in the treatment of migraine headaches, epilepsy, glandular and lymphatic swelling, stomach pain, and colds.

Vibrates to the number 8.

JOAQUINITE   [Astrological Signs of Libra, Pisces, & Taurus]

Joaquinite crystallizes in the form of small tabular crystals. The colour ranges from honey-yellow to brown.

This mineral has been known as the "Sweetheart Stone". It stimulates love in relationships and directs the creative self to deter stagnation in same.

It promotes attunement between the partners of affinity, providing for kindness and joy, and bringing both an emotional and an intellectual love to the relationship.

When each person in the relationship carries this mineral, the relationship tends to flourish and is, usually, looked upon as both practical and rational; when unconditional love brings people together, this love is, indeed, eternal.

It also helps to balance the emotional structure, eliminating hostility, and encouraging respect. It can be used to facilitate appreciation of the arts and to stimulate ones creative and mystical nature.

Joaquinite can be used in the treatment of dropsy, gall and kidney stones, gout, rheumatism, an overabundance of uric acid, and for both internal and external infections. It can also be used to ameliorate conditions which manifest fevers and stomach upsets. It can help one to assimilate the correct amounts of calcium and iron and it tends to improves the distribution of same throughout the body.

Vibrates to the number 4.

JULIENITE   [Astrological Sign of Virgo]

Julienite crystallizes in the form of blue needle-like crystals. This mineral is found primarily in Zaire, Africa.

Julienite helps to assist in courage, and disallows intimidation. One can realize, with the assistance of this stone, that "I am myself, and am not required to live-up to the expectations of others". It also allows one to understand where others are "coming from", and enables one to assist, via example, these others in progression.

It enables one to increase ones capacity in work or play; hence, providing additional accessible memory capability, vitality and endurance, communication skills, and time management.

♪ 351 ♫

Julienite can also be used in the treatment of insomnia, gastritis, and disorders associated with the mucus membranes. It has been used in the treatment of disorders of the throat and thyroid gland.

Vibrates to the number 6.

**IF YOU TAKE THE EASY WAY OUT
IT MAY ULTIMATELY BECOME MORE DIFFICULT**

KAINOSITE   [Astrological Sign of Scorpio]

Kainosite crystallizes in the form of prismatic tetragonal-like crystals. The colour ranges from yellow to brown, and from light red to colourless.

This mineral stimulates the connections between all of the energy centers of the body. It easily connects the base chakra to the crown chakra, and allows one the realization that ones physical vitality <u>does</u> support the enlightened state, once attained.

It also allows the intellect to produce grounding conditions, when necessary.

It helps one to say "no" and eliminates the self-limiting concept that one must placate another in order to remain important to that other. It helps one to be truthful with oneself and with others. It also assists one in accessing the practical side of reality, serving to heighten ones employment and social encounters.

It can be used to purge that which impedes progress. It further reveals the many ways in which one may continue toward the enrichment of this reality.

It acts to counter hydrophobia and to balance the liquid aspects of the body. It can provide for cellular renewal and can improve conditions of dehydration.

Vibrates to the number 4.

KAMMERERITE   [Astrological Signs of Virgo & Pisces]

Kammererite is a member of the chlorite group and crystallizes in the form of hexagonal pyramid-type crystals coloured in the range of red to purple. These crystals are both beautiful and lustrous.

In addition to the properties listed in the CHLORITE section of this book, this mineral can be used for the development of the third-eye and for stimulation of the crown chakra toward total spirituality.

It stimulates sensitivity in conjunction with the physical and mental functions, not separately, but as one entity. It takes one through the depths of the fog of ecstasy to unveil the purity of reason.

It provides endurance to spiritual endeavors, activating the chakras and clearing the aura.

It promotes flexibility in ones belief structure, and in the manifestation of that which one "knows". It allows one to proceed from the heart to the inner consciousness in order to determine "truths".

In addition, the utilization of Kammererite in conjunction with Carnelian can facilitate a direct connection between the physical self and the higher-self.

It can be used in the treatment of disorders associated with the male reproductive system and bacterial infections, and in the alleviation of stress related to that which is pending or about to occur. It has also been used to relieve pain and stiffness in the muscular structure and joints of the body.

Vibrates to the master number 55.

KAOLINITE   [Astrological Signs of Pisces & Virgo]

Kaolinite crystallizes in the form of compact masses and hexagonal plates. The colour range includes white and colourless, with tints of yellow, blue, red, grey, or brown. In the "red phantom quartz crystals", discussed in the QUARTZ section of this book, kaolinite is the mineral which initiated the tubular access to permit the growth of the phantom.

During the activities of spiritual evolvement, this mineral helps one over the "high ridges" which could become obstacles in the path. It provides encouragement to continue in the pursuit in which one is engaged, and provides sympathy when one is "down". It further assists one in digesting, processing, and eliminating the problems of life; it seems to transform ragged procession into a smooth flowing toward the infinite state of excellence.

This mineral can also be used to provide strength to the user to rid oneself of unwanted influences from the physical plane and to dispel possession of the body by an outside force. It assists in clairaudient pursuits, bringing forth necessary communication from the spiritual worlds and enhancing transcription activities.

Kaolinite can be used in the treatment to eliminate excess cholesterol, to bring a smoothness and flow to ones skin, and as an anointing elixir when one is in the state of dis-ease. It has been used in the treatment of disorders of the ears, tear ducts, digestion, and intestines.

Vibrates to the number 6.

KASOLITE   [Astrological Sign of Taurus]

Kasolite crystallizes in the formation of minute prismatic crystals. The colour ranges from yellow to brown.

This mineral can help one to become attuned to the Earth and can provide direction to assist one in increasing the ionization of the atmosphere. It can also assist one in communication with the spiritual forces of the Earth and can help one to understand that which is required in order that the Earth may heal itself.

It can produce great inner vitality, helping to sustain one during stressful and/or long-persisting circumstance. It promotes and enhances physical vitality, stimulating the enterprising qualities of ones character.

It can help to regenerate the pancreas, to assist in the regulation of insulin, and to balance the blood sugar. It can strengthen the muscular structure of the legs, arms, back, and abdomen. It has been used in the treatment of blood disorders [e.g., leukemia, etc.] and cellular inadequacies.

This mineral is radioactive. Do <u>not</u> prepare an elixir of this mineral via the normal method. It is best to store this mineral in glass and to utilize the energies which permeate the glass.

Vibrates to the number 2.

KATOPHORITE   [Astrological Signs of Libra & Cancer]

Katophorite crystallizes in the form of prismatic crystals exhibiting a perfect cleavage. The colour ranges from rose-red to brown-black. It also displays pleochroic properties; the X-axis being yellow-brown, the Y-axis being red or green-brown, and the Z-axis being red, green-yellow, red-brown, or green-blue.

The pleochroic attributes, coupled with the properties of this mineral, facilitate seeing all sides of an issue and promotes intellectual decision-making. Katophorite is "a stone for physical awareness and survival", providing for stimulation of awareness by the intellect and for control of perception by the heart/love side of ones personality.

It helps one to sustain courage for defiance and to maintain a calm wariness and respect for danger. It assists in protecting one from immediate physical danger and encourages originality in problem-solving.

This mineral can also bring one to the heights of understanding during healing exercises, such that the memories produced by the auric body are transferred to the physical body to facilitate healing.

It also helps one to traverse changes and to maintain diversity in the physical realm.

Katophorite can be used in the treatment of muscular rigidity, tracheal disorders, mental incoherence, and to alleviated uncontrolled excitability.

Vibrates to the number 3.

KERNITE   [Astrological Sign of Leo]

Kernite crystallizes in the formation of prismatic crystals and masses. The colour ranges from colourless to white. There are sometimes dark brown inclusions in the formation.

This mineral can be used to stimulate the crown chakra, to cleans the chakras and the aura, to access past-lives as well as future lives; it should be noted that the access to the future is also compatible to this life - one will be presented with situations which are very likely to occur during this life on this plane [again, dependent upon the course of progress one chooses during ones lifetime].

It has been used to minimize reticence and to assist one in the procurement of materialistic pursuits related to business. It can also assist one in issues of deduction and can provide the required wisdom and ameliorative energies to promote justice during adjudication of disputes.

It has been used to incite awareness, assisting one to release unconscious assumptions and to promote a re-connection between the conscious self and the mystic which lives within the super-consciousness.

Kernite has been used in to remove toxins from the body, to draw-out infections from inflammations and wounds, to treat disorders related to flexibility, to the thymus, the thyroid, and the stomach, and to ameliorate the symptoms of chemotherapy. It has also been used to alleviate water retention, bloating, and swelling.

Due to the solubility of Kernite, do not prepare an elixir of this mineral via the normal method.

Vibrates to the number 1.

KIDWELLITE   [Astrological Sign of Leo]

Kidwellite crystallizes in the form of masses and in the monoclinic system. The colour ranges from yellow to green.

This mineral can be used to encourage transformation in situations which suppress ones evolution. It can be used to bring one fellowship and to facilitate optimism.

It can also stimulate the mathematical nature, enhancing study of, and performance in, mathematical pursuits.

The energy of Kidwellite can assist in contributing counsel and insight to the resolution of puzzling conditions, encouraging the problem-solving proficiency inherent in the user.

It can align the chakras associated with the heart and love, with the intellect, and with psychic power, in order to produce a synthesis of the qualities and to further promote activities in these realms.

It tends to remind one of contraction of self, of income, etc., providing a gentle restoration of same.

Kidwellite can be used in the treatment of dyslexia, mental confusion, learning disabilities, and instability.

Vibrates to the number 2.

KINOITE   [Astrological Sign of Pisces]

Kinoite crystallizes in the formation of druses, crusts, masses, and miniature crystals. The colour is a transparent medium to deep blue.

This mineral helps one to continue to be in harmony with the physical body and to identify modifications within the body when they ensue.

It can also enhance ones spirituality during the initial stages of growth. It provides a reflection of the self and the inner workings of the body, allowing one to see into the emotional, mental, and physical structures.

It helps one to refrain from delusion and to recognize and to extinguish the self-limiting ideas which have been imparted.

It is an excellent stone for the throat chakra, bringing the energies of communication to the demonstration of psychic abilities; it further instills a beauty and an undisturbed composure to one during the receipt of information during channeling activities.

Kinoite has been used to remove energy blockages while providing a protective energy to the area.

It can be used in the treatment of disorders of the teeth, the throat, the skeletal structure, and the muscular composition. It has also been quite useful in stabilizing the nerves, calming during stressful situations, and increasing ones energy and stamina. It has also been used in general healing and in tissue regeneration.

Vibrates to the number 2.

KOKSHAROVITE   [Astrological Signs of Libra & Gemini]

Koksharovite crystallizes in the form of compact masses and prismatic crystals. The colour range includes white to grey, pale green, and colourless.

This mineral can be used to facilitate contact with those on the physical plane, or elsewhere. Projecting the visualized form of a person into the mineral helps to bring that person near - always in spirit, sometimes in form.

It is a territorial stone and conducts the magnetism of the region of the Earth in which it resides. The energy of this stone is dependent upon the negativity or positivity emitted from the environment from which it was unearthed. Most areas are similar with respect to the amount of energy available; however, the energy accessible in the mining localities bring the strength of renewal and rejuvenation. The locations where this mineral is mined emanate the energies of the vortex structures where the force is abundant, and where this abundance does not rely upon the presence of beings; e.g., one area in the neighborhood of Lake Baikal, Siberia and several areas in the vicinity of the Lapis Lazuli mines in Afghanistan.

Koksharovite can also be used [via gridding] to stabilize chaotic or potentially chaotic areas.

It has been used in the treatment of calcium and magnesium deficiencies, to promote the assimilation of the minerals. It can also be used to assist in stabilizing nervousness, shakiness, and those dis-eases related to these disorders.

Vibrates to the master number 55.

KOLBECKITE [Astrological Signs of Gemini & Libra]

Kolbeckite crystallizes in the form of colourless, yellow, and blue prismatic crystals.

This mineral is lovely for use in community/communal settings to produce camaraderie and team-spirit. It also induces inventiveness and reduces critical speech and actions.

It acts as an orb, an energy field which provides protection and delicate energizing of the crown, throat, and navel chakras.

It also promotes creativity in thought and action.

It can be used in the treatment of colitis, dysentery, urinary tract infections, disorders of the pancreas and gall bladder, and for the repair of structures and the facilitation of movements impaired by hiatal hernia conditions.

Vibrates to the number 3.

KORNERUPINE [Astrological Sign of Scorpio]

Kornerupine crystallizes in the form of aggregates and prismatic crystals. The colour range includes green, pink, yellow, brown, white, colourless, and black.

This mineral promotes understanding of the sacredness of life and the joyousness of death. It allows one to recognize that each moment on this Earth plane and in this body is truly precious; allowing for one to recognize that death brings the end to the deeds we were to accomplish in this body, and providing for a totally clear pathway for ones continued development.

It assists one in seeing beyond the normal illusions of this world, promoting recognition of both the delusion and the actuality. It serves to both stabilize and calm the emotions and to bring refinement to ones character.

Kornerupine can be used to facilitate a change in physical disorders which subsequently brings the body back to the normal healthy state. It can be used in times of crises to stabilize both the environment and those involved. A bit of this mineral in ones environment is quite a survival tool.

Vibrates to the number 2.

In the world of geology, the occurrence of spodumene in the colour pink is known as kunzite; however, there is little distinction made between kunzite and the other forms and colours of spodumene when the mineral is sold. Therefore, for metaphysical purposes, the whole range of colours is addressed in this section.

Kunzite crystallizes in the form of flattened prismatic crystals which are vertically striated, and in massive formations which are perfectly cleavable. The colour range includes colourless, yellow, green, pink, grey, and purple; occasionally the specimen is bi-coloured or tri-coloured and, rarely, rutile inclusions are found.

This mineral activates the heart chakra and aligns the heart chakra with the throat chakra and third-eye. It synthesizes the energies to produce loving thoughts and loving communication. Just holding this stone produces the feeling of a powerful peace, gently penetrating the inner core of ones being. It connects one to the infinite source of love, providing for purification on all levels. It further initiates the internal acknowledgement and external expression of self-love, unconditional love, and romantic love. It is an excellent stone for those who are not totally relaxed when expressing the emotions of the heart space.

Kunzite can be used to remove obstacles from ones path. It further provides indication of the procedural steps required to attain the desired end result and acts as a facilitator in the physical, emotional, and intellectual realms.

It dissolves negativity, automatically raising the vibrations of the area surrounding it; the diameter of the energy field can range from two inches to infinity [if directed properly]. It can be used to dispel possession from outside influences/entities; providing protection on the outer areas of the aura, kunzite produces a shield from unwanted energies.

It assists one in attaining deep meditative states and provides for centering in all situations; it helps one to mentally retire when in the midst of a crowd, to remain calm in the midst of distraction, and to sustain wisdom in the midst of folly. Kunzite also stimulates intuition and creativity during the meditative state. It dispels static un-focused energy and provides for rhythmic centering, inducing precision in all activities. After holding the mineral in a vertical position and aligning the chakras, the energy centers are balanced internally and connected sequentially; a "trip" with kunzite can be quite stimulating.

This mineral promotes maturity in thought and action, while allowing one to maintain the openness of a child. It assists one in understanding and accepting the type of security which does not infringe on ones state of freedom. It helps one to be open, strong, loving, and vibrant, acting as a maintaining force while refreshing the energies of the intellect and emotions. It also stimulates sensitivity and sensuality.

It can be used during radionic analysis; holding a piece of kunzite and placing a piece of kunzite on the witness or using a pendulum of this stone, the energy of the stone interferes with the energy of the user and points to the problem[s] involved.

Use of an elixir, wearing, carrying, or allowing kunzite to rest within ones environment, are all recommended.

Kunzite can be used to both strengthen and reinforce the physical heart muscles. It can be used in the treatment of disorders of the lungs and circulatory functions, and to ameliorate stress-related dis-ease. It has been used to eliminate energy blockages which encourage the onset of dysfunctions within the body. It can also be used to stimulate the secretion of the hormones of well-being.

In addition to the properties discussed above, the very pale yellow kunzite exhibits some additional qualities. This kunzite, aligns the seven major chakras within a twenty-four hour period. It also allows for RNA/DNA structuring and re-building, promotes stability in the calcium/magnesium field, provides blueprint information for cellular development in accordance with the perfect structure, and can be used to deflect radiation and microwaves from ones auric field.

Vibrates to the number 7.

KYANITE   [Astrological Signs of Taurus, Libra, & Aries]

Kyanite crystallizes in the form of twisted fibrous structures, masses, and long-bladed crystals which are either twisted or straight. The colour range includes grey, black, and blue with white, green, yellow and pink.

This is one of the minerals in the mineral kingdom which never needs cleaning or clearing. It will not accumulate or retain negative energy or vibrations. The energy of kyanite is unlimited in application, making it one of the very best attunement stones.

Kyanite aligns all chakras automatically and immediately, with no conscious direction. If directed with the consciousness of the user, it can also open the chakras. Conscious direction of the energy can also align the emotional, intellectual, physical, spiritual, ethereal, astral,..... bodies.

It brings tranquility and a calming effect to the whole being, with particular focus on the throat chakra and the third-eye. It stimulates communication and psychic awareness on all levels. It dispels anger and frustration and helps to facilitate clarity with respect to mental awareness and linear reasoning. It induces one to persevere in activities and situations which would, generally, reduce ones strength; it provides a stimulating energy and supports one in the continuation of projects. It further advances the conscious connection between the higher levels of intuition and heart-felt love, producing compassion in both communication and decision-making. It also assists in dispelling confusion arising from emotional, spiritual, and intellectual issues.

Kyanite Facilitates Meditation! Whenever there is a problem with respect to "getting-into" meditation, the calming, clearing effect of kyanite can be useful because the energy is accessible, gentle, and balanced. It is also quite useful when accessing the astral plane and when connecting with ones guides. It further helps to induce recall of dreams and to promote dream-solving, providing for access to solutions during the dream state.

It provides for balancing of the yin-yang energies, bringing an orderly growth to the intellect, emotions, and physical body. It dispels energy blockages, moving energy from the ethereal plane, in a gentle, yet, forceful way through the physical body.

It can be used during radionic analysis; holding a sample and placing a sample on the witness or using a pendulum of this stone, the energy of the stone interferes with the energy of the user and points to the problem(s) involved.

It should be noted that the black kyanite also provides for grounding during the alignment of the chakras; when the blue kyanite is used in conjunction with the black kyanite, the alignment and the grounding are both spontaneous and self-operating.

In addition, kyanite has occurred with ruby and is discussed in the RUBY section of this book.

It can be used in the treatment of disorders of the muscular and urogenital system, adrenal glands, throat, parathyroid glands, and brain. It is a beneficial stone to place between the heart and navel chakras during the healing activities associated with the "laying-on-of-stones".

Vibrates to the number 4.

**ONE CANNOT ECLIPSE THE GLORY OF LOVE,
ONE CAN BUT BECOME ONE WITH IT**

Labradorite is a type of feldspar which crystallizes in the form of masses, grains, and tabular crystals. The colour range includes white, yellow, and grey. Often, a display of spectral colours, due to the interference of light rays from the plate-like composition, causes labradorite to flame with broad patches of peacock blue, coppery red, or dusky gold labradorescence.

In addition to the properties listed in the FELDSPAR section of this book, this mineral protects ones aura, and helps to keep the aura clear, balanced, protected, and free from energy leaks. It assists in the alignment of the subtle bodies, enhancing the connection between the physical and ethereal realms.

It is said to represent the "temple of the stars", assisting one in sustaining and maintaining, while providing for the understanding of the destiny one has chosen. It brings the light of the other planetary beings to the soul of the user. The labradorescence is a luminescence, derived from extra-terrestrial origin, which is enclosed in the mineral to bring the galactic evolved energies from other worlds to the Earth plane.

The energy of labradorite facilitates the transformation of intuition into intellectual thought such that one can implement the instructions provided. It assists one to traverse changes, attracting strength and perseverance. It has been known as the matriarch of the subconscious mind, providing instructive sessions to the user concerning the implementation of inner messages and the utilization of same in the physical domain. It can help to provide clarity to the inner sight, instilling a passionless peace of imperturbability via the annihilation of disturbing thoughts.

It also symbolizes the moon and helps one to advance, without constraint, through the cycles of progression, heralding the arrival of ascension. It also symbolizes the sun, providing for vitality and for a sense of "self" during transitions, and promoting refinement of action and discernment in direction.

It unites the personal self with the understanding required to both realize and achieve the destiny of this life, relieving insecurity and apprehension, while enhancing faith and reliance in oneself and the absolute purity of the universal harmony.

It assists one in eliminating aspects of familiarity which obscures thought and blurs instinct, helping one with originality and precision, and bringing uniqueness without judgment to ones contemplative patterns.

It helps one to reflect and to facilitate transformations which are beneficial. It also enhances patience and an inner knowing of "the right time".

It allows for recognition that humanity represents the "Being of Light", transcending the limitations of the past and the thoughts of the future, and embracing the infinite possibilities of the moment. It helps one to both "be" and to proceed with the assurance that the light is always there, surrounding and pure.

Labradorite brings the commencement of recognition of ones inherent analytical and rational abilities. It further promotes the synthesis of intellectual thought with the intuitive, mystical, and psychic wisdom.

It assists in inspiring one to introduce the teachings of other worlds to this world of love and light, bringing assimilation and illumination to further the advancement of humanity.

It can be used during radionic analysis; holding a sample and placing a sample on the witness or using a pendulum of this stone, the energy of the stone interferes with the energy of the user and points to the problem[s] involved.

It has been used in the treatment of disorders of the brain, to stimulate mental acuity, and to reduce anxiety and stress. It can assist in digestion, regulation, and metabolism. It has also been used to clarify the eyes.

Vibrates to the numbers 6 and 7.

LAMPROPHYLLITE
[Astrological Sign of Pisces]

Lamprophyllite crystallizes in the form of tabular elongated crystals and needle-like crystalline aggregates. The colour ranges from golden yellow to deep brown.

This mineral stimulates the mental powers, and provides for grounding and stability during physical activities. It assists one during the process of divination, providing insight to prophetic questions.

It promotes the alignment of the subtle bodies and energizes the chakras with the purity of illumination.

Lamprophyllite can also assist in discouraging unkind actions, facilitating both consideration and discretion. It gives rise to ideas which are of utility and are comprised of the loving force of elucidation.

It can be used in the treatment of burns, kidney infections, cholesterol control, stomach and intestinal disorders.

Vibrates to the number 2.

LANTHANITE   [Astrological Sign of Leo]

Lanthanite crystallizes in the form of scales, plate-like layers, and tabular orthorhombic crystals. The colour range includes white, yellow, and pink.

This mineral can be used to provide one with insight to ones character and to initiate changes. It can also be used to help one to both consider and evaluate the genuineness of another, to recognize deception, and to eliminate "indifferent-ness".

It is conducive to supporting tenacity and resolution in decisions, helping one to substitute that which brings both development and joy for that which diminishes ones being.

It is an excellent stone for augmenting the qualities necessary when providing service to humanity.

It can be used in the treatment of gall and kidney stones, and pregnancy disorders, to stimulate hair growth, and to eliminate weakness [in mind or body]. It also assists in emptying and further eliminating boils and skin eruptions.

Vibrates to the number 5.

LAPIS LAZULI   [Astrological Sign of Sagittarius]

Lapis lazuli crystallizes in masses, cubes, and dodecahedral crystals. The colour is a deep blue. Lapis is a combination of minerals, primarily lazurite and calcite; pyrite is also contained in the prized massive Afghanistan lapis, while the Chilean lapis usually contains more visible calcite and minimal, if any, pyrite. The dodecahedral crystals generally come from Afghanistan, and are quite rare.

It is a stone said to have existed since before "time was born", assisting one in gaining admission to the domain of the unknown mysteries of the sacred texts and the esoteric ideas and enhancing the wisdom to understand the information. It further allows one to gain access to, and to explore, the esoteric planetary knowledge.

The afghanistan lapis has been likened to the night sky bedecked with stars. It promotes the connection between the physical plane and the celestial kingdom. It represents the forces of initiation into wisdom and the mystical realm.

Lapis provides for activation and energizing of the throat and brow chakras. The crystalline structure further clears these chakras and provides for unification of all of the chakras for the purpose of maintaining the "perfection" within the person.

Lapis lazuli is a "stone of total awareness", helping to expand awareness and intellectual capacity, and allowing for conscious attunement to the intuitive and psychic aspects of ones nature. It also helps one to remain objective about the subjective, providing for stimulus to the process of reasoning and reinforcing the acceptance of subsequent knowledge.

It enables one to obtain relief from that which has been pressed into the shallow recesses of the mind, providing objectivity, clarity, and mental endurance during release of emotional bondage. It helps for diminishment of the internal smoldering fire which leads to dis-ease. It stimulates the communicative facets of the self, providing for clarity and responsiveness during the release of information.

It assists one in the attunement to the creative source, stimulating the expansion and the realization of consciousness toward the awakening of the perfection of the self. It promotes the insight to a structured plan which can help one to evolve upward toward the light of the total unification with "All That Is".

Lapis can be placed over the third-eye [e.g., a cabochon or crystal] to aid one in developing insight into ones own dreams. It assists in providing a connection with the dream forces which are working to both guide and counsel one during altered states.

It helps to stimulate emotional, mental, and physical purity and clarity, supporting ones courage in activities culminating in the advancement toward universal wisdom.

It can assist one in the organization of ones life and in the routine day-to-day activities in which one is involved.

It is said to have been one of the stones used in the breastplate of the high priest.

Lapis was used by the Hebrews to adorn their ceremonial robes. Legend reports that King Solomon (the greatest stone-wearer of all) was assisted by an angel of the Lord who gave him a special ring which allowed him to control legions of demons which he used to build the temple.

It helps one to overcome depression and enhances the states of serenity and self-acceptance. It is said to bring cheer to the user and to bring success in relationships.

It has been used to further the connected-ness between the male and female attributes of this plane. It assists in balancing the yin-yang energies, focusing on the optimum equilibrium during each situation or circumstance of which one is a participant.

It has also been used as a protective stone, sheltering the wearer/carrier from physical danger and psychic attacks.

Lapis and rutilated topaz have been used together to both shield and build the aura. One method of combining the minerals is via elixir; another method is to use one mineral as an elixir and to carry or wear the other; a third method is to wear both minerals. The reader is encouraged to both explore and discover other techniques which are conducive to personal fulfillment.

Lapis can be used in the treatment of disorders of the throat, bone marrow, thymus, and immune system. It can help to relieve the symptoms of insomnia, vertigo, and dizziness. It can assist in preventing and in rectifying RNA/DNA damage, and has been used to activate the regenerative energies within the body. It can be used to stimulate cellular re-structuring with respect to both hearing loss and the Eustachian tube.

In addition, the crystalline form of lapis can be used to access the energy to sustain health and to restructure cellular, muscular, and skeletal disorders.

Vibrates to the number 3.

LARIMAR STONE   [See Pectolite]

LARSENITE   [Astrological Signs of Scorpio & Taurus]

Larsenite crystallizes in the form of slender prismatic vertically striated crystals and tabular crystals. The colour is white.

This mineral can be used to open and to activate the crown chakra, providing for transparency of issues related to practicality in attainment of spiritual development.

It provides for guidance to illumine the mind that all actions, except those culminating from hostility, unmindful-ness, and meagerness of heart, are acceptable.

It provides for a clarity in understanding situations of stress, and provides a blanket for smothering associated strife.

Larsenite also assists in the amelioration of the anguish associated with hostility, fighting, and wars.

This mineral can be used in the treatment of fevers, trauma, noise fright, and in disorders of the inter-venular structure of the extremities.

Vibrates to the number 4.

LAUBMANNITE   [Astrological Signs of Leo & Virgo]

Laubmannite crystallizes in the form of botryoidal aggregates. The colour ranges from bright yellow to green.

This mineral provides the feeling of praise to the user if praise is lacking in ones life. It also enables one to laugh, for the sake of laughing, and at circumstances in which one has been overwrought and unnecessarily distraught.

Laubmannite assists one in the start of new adventures and in initiating changes; it helps to rid one of those circumstances which have, in the past, prevented growth. It helps one to attain the blessings of the "goods" of this world.

It also enables one to feel pleasurable anticipation instead of anxiety while awaiting or while participating in varying situations; this quality relating to the realization of the elemental nature of all encounters of which one acknowledges and in which one participates.

It can be used to treat disorders of the skin, of the mind, and of the heart. It can be useful in the amelioration of dysfunctional hearing. It can be used to stimulate the acupuncture/acupressure meridians to support weight loss and to reduce the craving associated with smoking.

Vibrates to the number 4.

LAUEITE   [Astrological Sign of Aries]

Laueite crystallizes in the form of wedge-shaped crystals. The colour range includes yellow, orange, and brown.

This mineral assists in victory; it gives one a sense of assurance and courage in ones endeavors while providing for an emotional stability to enhance duration and stamina.

It assists one in recovering from the "low" periods in ones reality and allows one to recognize the lack of both contrast and distinction between "lows" and "highs".

It can also be used to arouse sympathetic action toward others while allowing one to realize that each person is in the situation which is necessary at any one moment. Hence, the sympathy is not for the person, but for the lessons-learned and for the lack of knowledge which that person exhibits.

It is also a supportive stone, one which has been used to facilitate the collection of debts.

Laueite can be used in the treatment of colitis, intestinal disorders, dysentery, and diverticulosis.

Vibrates to the number 1.

LAUMONTITE   [Astrological Sign of Virgo]

Laumontite crystallizes in the form of prisms, columns, and radiating and divergent clusters. The colour range includes white to yellow, grey, and red.

This mineral stimulates gratification, satisfaction, and tranquil optimism in an environment. It clears the environment like a "breath of fresh air" and helps to change "bad" attitudes.

The energy stimulates synchronicity in change, bringing collective initiative toward the application of reformation.

It can also increase ones clairaudient capabilities, providing explicit and direct information and eliminating oblique information.

Laumontite can be used in the treatment of water retention, ruptures, hernia, strains, sprains, acidosis, the cortex of the brain, and hearing problems. It has also been used to increase flexibility in the arms and legs and to assist in the amelioration of arthritis.

Vibrates to the number 4.

LAVENITE   [Astrological Sign of Aries]

Lavenite crystallizes in the form of radial aggregates and prismatic crystals. The colour range includes yellow, brown, and colourless.

This mineral can lead one to abundance in ones life. It produces an attitude of willingness to "do whatever it takes" to reach ones goals; helping to provide insight into what those goals really are.

It opens and energizes the crown chakra, providing a subtle, yet forceful, energy. It also allows for centering and grounding during the meditative state.

It can be used to stimulate the mental capabilities, providing for the state of "transcendental" intellectual development.

It has been used to eliminate negative spiritual beings from ones environment and to decrease noxious odors. It also helps to align the mental body with the higher mind in order to promote the receipt of information concerning self-healing.

Lavenite can also be used in the treatment of skin dis-eases, burns, ulcers, and lesions. Its use as an elixir for these conditions is recommended. It has also been used to supplement the well-being of the pituitary and the adrenal glands.

Vibrates to the number 7.

LAZULITE   [Astrological Signs of Sagittarius & Gemini]

Lazulite crystallizes in the form of masses and acute pyramid-like small crystals. The colour ranges from deep to light blue.

Lazulite is called a "stone of heaven", bringing in the clarity and purity of energy from the omnipresent forces of the universe. This "heavenly" stone is excellent in meditation to take one to the home of euphoria. It promotes calming and enhances sanctity within ones being.

It was used by the ancients as a "worry stone" which provided insight to worries and encouraged the application of intuitive answers.

It allows/promotes one to sense self-worth, and to both recognize and eliminate deficiencies in character and form. It also assists one in attaining balance and perspective in all pursuits.

It can be used to ameliorate sensitivity to the sun, and to treat disorders of the thyroid, pituitary, liver, and lymph glands. It can also be used to increase the mending of broken bones, to enhance the functioning of the immune system, and to relieve dis-ease of the bones and teeth. Lazulite is also a stone to be used to help those with addictive personalities to overcome the traits associated with compulsive behavior patterns.

Vibrates to the number 7.

LAZURITE   [Astrological Signs of Sagittarius & Pisces]

Lazurite crystallizes in the form of masses, cubes, and dodecahedral crystals. The colour range includes blue, green-blue, and violet-blue.

This mineral promotes tranquility and enhances the spiritual quality of the user. It provides for amplification of qualities such as thought transference, intuition, psychic contact with spiritual guides, and problem-solving in the dream state and the state of conscious awareness.

It enables one to conquer superstition and to subdue the generally implacable adversaries of self-discovery, giving one the time, patience, and insight necessary to understand that which "may within man hide".

It allows for the merging of separate "trails", bringing guidance for extension toward the "light".

It can be used in the treatment of food allergies, and disorders of the lungs, and to provide for oxygenation of the blood to facilitate dispersal of toxins. It can also be used to alleviate pain and to provide relief from inflammations and infections.

Vibrates to the number 4.

LEAD   [Astrological Signs of Cancer & Capricorn]

Lead crystallizes in the form of thin plate-like layers, small globular masses, and, rarely, actual crystals. The colour is lead-grey.

This mineral provides for access to ones spiritual guides when questions related to direction and course of action are pending. Lead can also facilitate a "new start".

It assists in the elimination of sedentary aspects and encourages being "on the move", adding strength to the physical and mental bodies.

It is an excellent stone for groups, serving to stimulate advancement and cohesiveness within a group and to increase awareness and understanding of the goals of the group. It further helps to direct elevated energy toward the furtherance of the group, itself.

It is good for pursuits concerning music [i.e., conductor aspirations], sports activities, and for those connected to areas of management and/or business.

Do not prepare an elixir via the normal method.

It assists in the conduction of energy to the flexible portions of the body and in clearing toxins from the cellular structures of the muscular tissue. It can also be used in the treatment of blood poisoning, disorders of the elimination system, and "upset" stomach/digestive systems.

Vibrates to the number 4.

LEAVERITE   [Astrological Sign of All]

Leaverite occurs in many forms, in many colours, and in many localities. A detailed description is difficult to report; however, it is guarantee that the reader, guided by wisdom, will intuitively recognize the stone when permitted the encounter.

The innocence of those in the formative years, and of those participating in the contemporary movement of the new age, has led both children and adults to be attracted to leaverite. I have been carrying leaverite stones with me for years.

These stones are stones of discrimination, providing encouragement for the increase of both knowledge and precision.

They assist in the refinement of taste, the discernment in choice, and the discretion in judgment. They are also helpful in banishing intolerance and prejudicial favoritism.

Leaverite can help one to understand that concepts of superiority and inferiority exist only within ones mind; it can further be useful in the treatment of disorders associated with acceptance of the lesser states.

Vibrates to the number 7.

LECHATELIERITE   [See Glass]

LEGRANDITE   [Astrological Signs of Aries & Gemini]

Legrandite crystallizes in the form of aggregates and prismatic crystals. The colour range includes yellow and colourless.

This mineral can provide insight to the futility of prejudicial views and can help to guide one toward furtherance of the equality of humanity. It allows for the recognition of frailties within ones character and provides support for correction of same. Legrandite assists one to give with pleasure and to receive with humility. It also helps one to recognize personal motive in action.

It was used by the ancient Aztecs in their most powerful ceremonies to ward-off invasions and to bring their enemies to cease and desist in hostilities. It also acts to provide for stimulation of the emotions toward understanding.

Legrandite can be used to treat the disorder of dyskinesia, including spasms, twitches, speech disturbances, etc. It can also be used to clear the sinuses, and to promote the release of endorphins to the body.

Vibrates to the number 5.

LEIFITE   [Astrological Signs of Capricorn & Cancer]

Leifite crystallizes in the form of striated colourless needle-like crystals and hexagonal prismatic crystals.

It can assist to instill courage and leadership qualities when one is involved in a tedious or dangerous situation. It is good to use when one is maintaining clandestine activities; it helps one to realize the "correct" course of action to either protect from, or to relieve oneself of, unpleasant results.

It also helps one to "hang-on" when the time is right <u>and</u> to "let go" when the time is right, providing for the stimulation of inner awareness with respect to the distinction between the variations in the "right" time.

It can assist in lucidity in communication and for acuteness in mental perception. It also furthers ones creative encounters.

Leifite can be used in the treatment of acidosis, in the regulation of the digestive enzymes, and in disorders related to nausea, varicose veins, and circulation. It can also be used to stimulate the meridians associated with the acupressure/acupuncture points.

Vibrates to the number 3.

LEPIDOCROCITE   [Astrological Sign of Sagittarius]

Lepidocrocite crystallizes in the orthorhombic formation and as crusts. The colour ranges from yellow to red to brown. It is also found within clear quartz and amethyst.

This mineral brings grounding with intellectual stimulation, fortifying the structures of enhanced equilibrium between all chakras and auric bodies. It has been used, when within the quartz and amethyst structures, to enhance perception, intuition, and instinct.

It acts to promote realization that ones strength occurs through both spiritual avenues and via love; hence, dissolving aloofness and negativity - within the self and within the environment.

It is related to benefit to the self and to the development of the humanitarian pursuits - the energy is integrated with healing, with storing information, with communicating, with balancing energy, and with teaching. It enables one to both acknowledge and to perceive information which can be used individually and collectively. The use of this mineral as a bridge, between the consciousness and matter, brings practicality to the application of ones insight and powers of manifestation. It is extremely useful in the expansion of knowledge and in retention of same.

In addition, Lepidocrocite with Quartz and/or Amethyst has been used to enhance communication with those of the angelic realm. It serves to advance astral travel and to maintain the connection between the self and the astral body, so that there need be no concern with respect to returning to the physical domain. It also has been used to facilitate the superior actions of others - rather than promoting control of same; it acts to bring energy to situations without any power factors attached. It stimulates awareness with respect to spontaneity, recognition, and focus - further allowing one to understand the path of the energy and to recognize the voluntary increase in energy. It also acts to stimulate and to cleanse all chakras, bringing a purity of energy to the areas where the energy is directed.

It is a stone of the future and will bring knowledge to those attuned to it by clearing mental confusion. It truly awakens the finer, inner self.

It has also been used during Reiki treatments to promote the transfer of energy to the area of need, and during re-birthing to facilitate ease of blockage release.

Use of Lepidocrocite with other crystals acts to facilitate results with greater ease since this mineral enhances the appearance of results.

Wearing/carrying Lepidocrocite has successfully produced hunger suppression; an elixir made of the mineral (the Quartz or Amethyst with Lepidocrocite is recommended] has also produced the same results. It can be used at the physical level to focus healing energy on the systems, glands, meridians, and organs of the body. It has also been used in the treatment of disorders associated with the iris, the liver, and the reproductive organs. It has promoted the shrinkage of tumors and has been used for cell renewal.

Vibrates to the number 8.

LEPIDOLITE   [Astrological Sign of Libra]

Lepidolite crystallizes in the form of masses, scale-like aggregates of short prismatic crystals, plate-like layers, and tabular crystals. The colour range includes pink-to-purple, yellow, grey, colourless, and white.

This mineral activates the throat chakra, the heart chakra, the third-eye, and the intellect. It also opens the crown chakra and allows for the flowering of the inner blue lotus, assisting one to become aware of the subtle vibratory energies both within and without of the self.

It is used for stress reduction and to alleviate despondency.

The energy of lepidolite is refreshing and almost sentimental; it assists in the transformation of the energies of lesser spiritual ideals to the energies of universal light, hope, and acceptance.

It is recognized as a "stone of transition", helping one through situations of variability in this life and assisting in the restructuring and reorganization of old patterns. It further serves to gently induce change and to allow for smooth passage during the change.

Lepidolite can also help one with transitions from one life to another; it facilitates astral travel, assists in birth and re-birthing, and helps one to understand and to cheerfully accept both the departure from the physical realm and the entry to the spiritual dominion.

It can enhance the generation of the life-sustaining negative ions in ones environment, activating the instinct of self-preservation and enhancing the awareness of well-being.

It is an excellent stone for business pursuits, combining the energy of diplomacy with direction and unimpeded communication.

It can induce the attribute of self-love, bringing a child-like love and acceptance to the user, while allowing for the aspect of trust to flourish.

It assists one in openness and honesty, furthering the openness and honesty of those in proximity.

It can be used to locate energy blockages within the body; placing the lepidolite upon the different areas of the body, one can usually feel a slight resonance at the location of the obstruction.

This mineral is also very useful for gridding ones environment; as a calming agent it has been used to grid classrooms, shopping centers, conference rooms, concert halls, etc. It has also been used in gridding disorderly areas of the Earth, helping to bring stability to the structure of the ley lines and tectonic plates.

It also assists in gardening and in agricultural activities, helping to align the energy forces to produce abundance and to eliminate or to rectify dis-ease.

Lepidolite occasionally occurs as a constituent in a six-sided plate-like form of mica. This form, exhibiting the combined colours and energies of the heart and crown chakras, unites the properties of mica [e.g., muscovite, biotite, margarite] with lepidolite to produce limitless uses.

Lepidolite also occurs in a structure containing tourmaline [usually pink or rubellite]. This combination is discussed in the TOURMALINE section of this book.

This mineral can assist in digestion and in the relief of tension and stress related disorders. It can also be used to promote the relaxation of wrinkles [e.g., providing a smoothness to the skin]; an elixir is recommended. It can be used in the treatment of disorders related to tendonitis, leg cramps, "tight" shoulder muscles, and elimination. It can assist in soothing the nervous system, stabilizing the flow of blood, and in calming the heart. It can also be used in activities to restructure the RNA/DNA. In addition, it has been used with Lepidolite and quartz to eliminate candida. It is excellent for use in the mineral form and as an elixir.

Vibrates to the number 8.

LEUCITE   [Astrological Sign of Aries]

Leucite crystallizes in the form of grains, masses, trapezohedral crystals, occasionally as cube-type crystals, and, rarely, in the formation similar to a Celtic cross. The colour range includes white and grey.

Leucite provides a window through which to discover the other bodies. It is an excellent mineral for providing introductory knowledge concerning the connection between ones physical, astral, emotional, intellectual, spiritual, etheric, and other inner and outer bodies.

It can induce the energies of enterprise, helping one to find that which is lost. Note that "that which is lost" not only pertains to physical objects, but also to the awareness which has been lost since ones birth into this world. It stimulates recognition of the gift of remembering which is inherent to humanity.

It can also assist one in understanding the motives of another, allowing one to appreciate the effects of the physical plane upon the spirituality of humanity, and inspiring one toward personal improvement.

This mineral can be used to ameliorate feebleness, and to relieve hypertension, anemia, and over-production of white blood cells in the body. It can also enhance the more efficient utilization of ones carbohydrate intake. It is a stabilizing influence on the body temperature. It can also be used to reduce the pressure created by glaucoma and can assist in the relief of the disorder.

Vibrates to the number 3.

LEUCOPHOENICITE   [Astrological Sign of Libra]

Leucophoenicite crystallizes in the form of masses and elongated, striated crystals. The colour range includes light-pink, pink, purple-red, and the gradations from purple to brown.

This mineral produces a connection with the aspects of physical survival and spirituality, allowing one to recognize the aspects of ones physical reality in relation to ones spiritual development. This is often quite "enlightening" and surprising.

It is said to have been used in the ancient times of Arabia to stimulate both the release of the worldly and the re-birth to immortality. Note that "release of the worldly" is defined as the ability to be at peace with oneself without those worldly attachments, and to be comfortable in the visualization that what you have [your "stuff"] is no longer with you and, in any case, is quite transient.

Leucophoenicite assists in precise analysis of problems and situations. It stimulates a strong and virile intellect and provides for balancing between the loving aspects of ones nature and the rigidity of rationality.

This mineral can be used to ameliorate water retention and swelling of body tissue, to stimulate the heart muscles and the flow of blood, and to reduce fevers. It can help to balance the white/red blood cell production within the body. It can also assist in promoting relief from all forms of phobia and can assist in producing an inner calmness culminating in total relaxation.

Vibrates to the number 7.

LEVYNITE   [Astrological Sign of Aquarius]

Levynite crystallizes in the form of rhombohedral crystals. The colour range includes colourless, white, grey, red, and yellow.

This mineral stimulates the heart chakra and assists in bringing one the quality of compassion toward others.

It helps one in matters of assessment and produces a lightness of mind and a freedom from internal strife.

It is used in the polarization of ones energy fields, to stimulate the alignment of the polarities between the physical body and the etheric body, and to enhance ones physical well-being.

It provides for recognition of the expanding and contracting waves of influences upon the mind, promoting the application of the ideal that mental influences can produce physical action.

Levynite is also an excellent stone for use when one desires to reach ones spiritual guides; it can promote the receipt of information to further ones psychic and "magical" abilities. It provides a bridge between the physical and spiritual worlds.

This mineral can be used for both the treatment and the stimulation of the thymus, to assist in the removal of heavy metals from the body, and to regulate the glucose within the body.

Vibrates to the number 4.

LIBETHENITE   [Astrological Sign of Virgo]

Libethenite crystallizes in the form of crusts, masses, and prismatic crystals. The colour range includes light-to-dark green.

This mineral provides one with freedom from those regulations which have been self-imposed so that one does not feel compelled to "live-up" to the expectations of another.

It facilitates free speech and free action, confined only by the knowledge that to hurt another with malice and forethought is in total opposition to the innate freedom of the universe. It further helps one to decrease mindless speech, and to progress toward the total clarity and inner knowledge which cannot be explained via verbal communication.

Libethenite can also enhance ones status in the worldly environment, bringing possessions closer to attainment and holding that which one has previously attained in balance with ones activities.

It advances ones self-assured-ness, bringing an inspiration to advance; it assists one in appending the beneficial portions of the "old" ways to the "new" journey, helping one to maintain the beneficial course.

It reduces the tendency to procrastinate and induces speed in action.

It enhances perception, allowing for focus on the basis behind plans and situations, while furthering straight-forward appraisals of circumstances of which one is a part.

It is a "stone of progress", stimulating dynamic change, with action, to further ones pursuits.

It is an excellent stone to use when driving; it helps to provide clarity with respect to map-reading and facilitates an intuitive sense of direction.

This mineral can be used to strengthen ones vital force and to increase ones will to live and/or to rid oneself of a debilitation. It can also stimulate ones sexuality, if consciously directed to do so, and can be used in the treatment of incontinence.

Vibrates to the master number 55.

LIEBIGITE   [Astrological Sign of Aries]

Liebigite crystallizes in the form of aggregates, crusts, and short prismatic crystals structured with rounded edges. The colour range includes green, yellow, and yellow-green.

This mineral stimulates the flowing of ones life and provides for a flowering of ones abilities, as well as ones spirituality. It assists in helping one to balance ones daily activities with ones goals.

It also allows for ease in adaptation to, and regulation of, the circumstances and environments which are not usual, bringing freshness and "spirit" to new confrontations and endeavors, and promoting a willingness to find the time to expand ones consciousness.

Liebigite furthers the quest for truth from within the inner reaches of the total consciousness of humanity.

It assists one in the centralization of issues and in building a basis for bonds between service to others and service to the self.

It also promotes both the presentation and receipt of truth. It allows one to recognize the internal mechanisms required for expansion of awareness, culminating in inducement toward pioneering in the areas of service to humanity and the Earth.

This mineral can be used in the treatment of rashes and eruptions, and in disorders associated with the breath. It also can be used to treat menstrual disorders and to decrease those symptoms which "typically" are a part of menopause. It can be used to stimulate the metabolism to bring the body into balance, to enhance the reproductive capabilities, and to increase fertility [when consciously directed].

Vibrates to the number 6.

The limb cast is an ancient tree limb, usually small, in which the wood structure has been replaced with agate; opalized limb casts are discussed in the OPAL section of this book. The qualities listed in the AGATE section of this book are also applicable to the agatized limb cast.

The limb cast helps to provide a flexibility in ones thought structure; this tends to promote an easier access to meditative states and astral travel. This mineral can take one "to the edge", and can then stimulate the intellect, and that "knowing" part within the self, to make the decision "whether to..." or "whether not to..." act in a specific manner. The energy is more like the fruition of a seed, than the seed itself, when it acts in love to produce ones growth. It can help one to understand the eternity.

It represents the living existence of the source of all being, allowing for recognition of the inherent perfection within the soul and for the acknowledgement that each person can access the supreme and loving powers of the universe.

It assists in the development of the potential of the individual, enhancing dignity, definite purpose, and creativity in living. It further provides a stable connected-ness between the physical and spiritual worlds, promoting development of the true and vital self.

It also supplements ones endurance, bringing impetus to thought and action. This structure can assist in the release of inhibitions and in the sweeping-away of reticence.

It can provide for liberation from unshed tears, stimulating the opening of the emotional responses while providing for a nurturing energy to stabilize the emotions.

The agatized limb cast may also be used to encourage success in the maintenance of business or resources. It produces the energy of "firm ground" on which to base resolution to difficulties.

This mineral can be used in the treatment of disorders of the extremities. It assists in providing strength and stamina to the arms and legs, promoting recovery from conditions of atrophy, increasing the flexibility of the body [great for the beginning yogi practitioner], and acting to stimulate and to improve the assimilation of Vitamins A, D, E, and C. It has also been used to ameliorate arthritis, bursitis, and gout.

Vibrates to the number 7.

LIMONITE   [Astrological Sign of Virgo]

Limonite is a generic designation for a variety of oxides of iron. It occurs in the form of masses, stalactites, and botryoidal configurations. The colour range includes brown and yellow.

This mineral can assist one in the alteration of ones life toward stability and comfort. It helps one to remove from the "marsh of existence" and to further gain the "aspirations of the mountain", reaching toward the infinite powers of the mind.

It provides for the strength and virility of youth, enhancing the substance of ones character and providing an "iron hat" for protection against detrimental thoughts, impaired clarity, and psychic attack. It also furthers accuracy in the intuitive processes.

It is one of the minerals which precipitated the formation of the red phantom crystals, discussed in the QUARTZ section of this book.

It can be used in the treatment of disorders of the skeletal system, to ameliorate dehydration, and to assist in the assimilation of iron and calcium. It has also been used to dispel fever and to treat both the liver and the jaundiced conditions produced by disorders of the liver.

Vibrates to the number 7.

LINARITE   [Astrological Signs of Cancer, Pisces, & Scorpio]

Linarite crystallizes in the form of deep blue aggregates and tabular crystals.

This mineral can be used to stimulate the psychic center and to promote astral travel, mainly throughout this plane of existence. It is also used to facilitate contemplation, enjoyment, and telepathy.

Linarite provides a "check" on ones personality to ensure the use of the "thoughts" of the heart prior to the verbalization of intellectual thoughts; hence, it is an excellent energy to access during and prior to situations of confrontations and anger.

It also helps one to say "yes" to life, and "no" to that which impairs freedom. It furthers communication skills and increases the actualization of rational and systematic thought.

It can assist in the alleviation of genetic disorders and in the alignment of the meridians of the body. It can also be used in the treatment of motion sickness, acrophobia, and hydrophobia. It can assist in the rejuvenation of the male reproductive system and can renew sexual capabilities which have been impaired due to glandular dysfunctions.

Vibrates to the number 7.

LINNAEITE   [Astrological Sign of Leo]

Linnaeite crystallizes in the form of octahedral crystals, and granular masses. The colour is grey, sometimes tarnishing to red or violet.

This mineral promotes appreciation of the riches natural to the Earth and allows one to feel a closeness to nature and the natural forces of the universe.

It promotes a connection between the base and crown chakras, bringing vitality with grounding, to the quest for wisdom and spirituality. It helps one to detect and to acknowledge the spiritual aspects of growth in all situations, providing for a painless and beautiful attunement to growth and evolution, via all experiences. It further encourages structure in association, with practicality in the furtherance of ones goals.

It also provides a basis for automatic writing and facilitates the connection to information sources.

It can be used to counterbalance saturated fats in ones diet, and to balance the emissions of the liver, gall bladder, and pancreas. It can assist in the reduction of superficial fat, and can provide for a more thorough change-over of dietary fats into fatty acids and glycerol. It can also be used in the dissolution process for fatty tumors. It can enhance the removal capabilities of the body with respect to toxin elimination. It can also assist in the treatment and diminishment of maligned growths of the cellular structure.

Vibrates to the master number 44.

LITHIOPHILITE   [Astrological Sign of Leo]

Lithiophilite crystallizes in the form of masses and, rarely, crystals of the orthorhombic structure. The colour range includes pale pink to yellow, clove-brown, greenish gray, and blue.

This mineral is one of friendship, bringing a rapport of accord between the self and others. It stimulates popularity, promotes acceptance and approval [unconditional], and inspires prominence.

It is a stone to soothe and smooth the chakras, the energies of the environment, and the mind/emotions. It acts to subdue negativity and to defeat dissention.

The energy extends to others through a fine organization of ethereal threads, reaching all realms concurrently, and acting to bring the auric body to accord with the physical body.

Lithiophilite has been used in the treatment of nervous disorders and to ameliorate schizophrenia, to enhance the assimilation of protein, to stabilize the mind, and to promote the balancing of the metabolic processes.

Vibrates to the number 8.

LODESTONE   [Astrological Signs of Virgo & Gemini]

Lodestone crystallizes in the form of octahedral and rhombdodecahedral crystals, granular masses, dendrites, crusts, and grains; it is also found as a constituent in meteorites. The colour range includes iron black and pale brown.

Lodestone is actually magnetite with an additional property of polarity. [Please note that the configurations of magnetite do not normally possess the polarity attribute.] The additional property is addressed here. The reader may go to the MAGNETITE section of this book for further information.

This additional property of lodestone enables one to both fundamentally recognize and distinguish between the dualities which exist in ones environment. It enhances receptivity and helps one to rejoice in all of the circumstances which enter into ones life. It balances the male/female aspects of ones body, mind, and emotions, and stimulates consciousness for each moment.

It assists in relieving burdens and in bringing to fruition that which is "wanted". It encourages "holding fast" to ones purpose, eliminating confusion of purpose and balancing unexpected occurrences. It also promotes motivation and confidence, eliminating insecurity and dependence.

Lodestone further serves to provide guidance with respect to the most beneficial direction for progression and ultimate ascension, helping one to understand the signs which point toward the easiest lessons and the most advantageous circumstances. It also assists in removing obstacles along the way.

It is said that, in "days of old", the lodestone was used to test fidelity; if unfaithful or un-loyal, ones wife, husband, or partner would "fall out of bed" when touched by the lodestone.

It also acts to balance and to align the meridians of the physical body with the etheric body. It aligns and activates the chakras and aligns the etheric body with the subtle bodies. It also aligns the astral body to the etheric body to stimulate ease in astral travel. Alignment and activation of the subtle bodies is also completed. Please note that the alignment, the chakra activation, and the balancing are not permanent.

It assists in the removal of energy blockages which are present in dis-ease, inducing the free flow of the strength of the body to renew itself.

Vibrates to the number 1.

LOMONOSOVITE   [Astrological Sign of Virgo]

Lomonosovite crystallizes in the form of laminated tabular crystals. The colour range includes dark brown, black, and red-violet.

This mineral can be used to assist in the development of maturity, as well as in the acceptance of maturity; hence, it is a stone for the young and old, and especially for the "young at heart". It provides insight to teach the user that maturity is not what is known as "growing-up", but instead is a state of inner peace which facilitates a subconscious, non-encumbering satisfactory performance of all of the social "requirements".

The energy of this mineral can activate the base chakra, moving upward through the body to the crown, elevating the energies of all of the chakras while providing for grounding to protect one from the interference of static or undirected energy transmissions.

It also acts as a messenger between the intellect and the emotions, bringing messages of peace and redemption to the user.

It further induces the actualization of artistic qualities, allowing for artistry during the fulfillment and realization of ones life.

Lomonosovite can be used for the treatment of spinal disorders, satyriasis, uncontrolled bladder, uncontrolled display of violent emotions, "giddy-ness", selfishness, and to eliminate [quite importantly] aspects of unwarranted selfless-ness.

Vibrates to the number 3.

LUDLAMITE   [Astrological Sign of Scorpio]

Ludlamite crystallizes in the form of small tabular crystals and granular masses. The colour range includes green and colourless.

This mineral can be used to clarify the heart chakra, releasing negativity, destructive tendencies, and insecurity, while cultivating optimistic confidence and love within the self.

It helps one to become "un-stuck" in situations and relationships, furthering the development of the unconscious self toward awakening, and stimulating the opening of one door as another one closes.

It furthers precision and instills loyalty as a mastering force, bringing loyalty to that which is required to further ones advancement.

Ludlamite can be used in the treatment of disorders associated with decay and deterioration. It can assist in stimulating improvement in vision, can aid in dispelling parasites, and can induce an increase in motor abilities. It can also be used to refine the cellular structure of the skin and body, inducing the virtual soothing and smoothing of same.

Vibrates to the number 7.

LURELITE   [See Purple Sage Agate]

**THE OPEN MIND IS ONES BEST ALLY,
BRINGING ONE TO THE PINNACLE OF PERFECTION**

MAGNESIOFERRITE   [Astrological Sign of Aquarius]

Magnesioferrite crystallizes in the form of black metallic octahedral crystals.

This mineral can be used to assist one in "seeing through the clouds", promoting the recognition of the order of that which surrounds, and facilitating the understanding of the meaning implied by those lacking in specificity. It is a grounding stone which also produces an alignment of the meridians of the body and an alignment of the subtle bodies.

It helps to dispel anger and allows one to receive praise with grace. It is quite useful in the realm of business to assist one in securing distinction and contacts. It also helps to place one on a business base which has the potential to reach suitable heights for success.

This mineral produces an energy which is predisposed to discourage chaotic, disruptive, and disorganized growth. It emits an energy which can be used to stabilize and to produce order within the mental, physical, emotional, and spiritual systems. It can be used to initiate order within chaos.

Magnesioferrite can be used in the treatment of convulsions, anemia, osteoporosis, constipation, periodontal dis-ease, and ventricular tachycardia, and to lessen PMS and body odor. It has been used in the treatment of violent and/or highly infective dis-ease, as well as by others who are working with those affected, in order to provide protection from the affectation. It has also been used in the treatment of tumors - at the beginning stages of their growth.

Vibrates to the number 2.

MAGNESITE   [Astrological Sign of Aries]

Magnesite crystallizes in the form of masses, plate-like layers, fibers, grains, and, rarely, as rhombohedral, prismatic, tabular, and scalenohedral crystals. The colour range includes white, grey, yellow, and brown.

This mineral provides for the fruition of unrecognized thoughts and ideas and produces the motivation for one to recognize, analyze, and actualize the underlying stimulus for same.

It can assist in visualization and imagery, and in promoting dynamic, revolutionary ideas.

It relates to the "heart of silence", instilling peace during meditation and furthering the elimination of self-deceit. It brings grounding to the intellect and assists in producing an opening of the crown chakra. It can also be used to stimulate passion and heart-felt love.

Magnesite can be used to enhance the purification of the cells. It can assist in the treatment of convulsions and disorders of the bones and teeth. It has been used to lessen PMS and to control body odor. It can be used to both stimulate and sooth the heart and associated arteries. It can also help to regulate the body temperature to the optimum conditions, and to lessen conditions of fevers and/or chills.

Vibrates to the number 3.

MAGNETITE   [Astrological Signs of Aries, Capricorn, Aquarius, & Virgo]

Magnetite crystallizes in the form of crusts, grains, octahedral and rhombdodecahedral crystals, granular masses, and dendrites. It has also occurred within meteoritic structures. The colour range includes iron black and pale brown. It is strongly magnetic and possesses polarity attributes in the form called Lodestone [see the LODESTONE section of this book].

This mineral temporarily aligns the chakras, the subtle bodies, and the meridians of the physical and etheric bodies. It can be used to dispel grief, fear, anger, and attachment.

It enhances desire for, and facilitates the attainment of, those ideas and "things" which can bring growth to ones spirituality. It also provides the energy conducive to both ease of entry to, and maintenance of, the deep meditative state. One can feel the connection to the universal energy during meditation with magnetite.

Magnetite provides for a connection between the user and the nurturing aspects of the Earth, facilitating grounding and balancing between those bodies. The grounding cord, usually running from the base of the spine to the core of the Earth, is strengthened; hence, all manners of situations are afforded protection, and the environment of a healer during healing situations is provided further protection and stability.

It brings tenacity, durability, and endurance, assisting in the magnification of the answers necessary to remove one from situations which are unwanted. It enables one to project ones mind and to view things from a distance.

Magnetite is a "stone of stability" and can be used to attract love. It has been quite instrumental in activities of manifestation, catching "things" like a net and allowing one to secure that which is desired.

It also assists in balancing the emotions with the intellect, in encouraging the trust of ones intuition, and in producing mental clarity with respect to the determination of the additional minerals which would be beneficial in ones life.

It can be used in the treatment of disorders of the bone structure, hair, skin, blood vessels, and the flesh. It has also been used in the treatment of nose bleed. It can help one to "attract" the healing energies necessary for recovery from disorders.

Vibrates to the number 4.

MALACHITE   [Astrological Signs of Capricorn & Scorpio]

Malachite crystallizes in the form of masses, tufts, rosettes, crusts, botryoidal configurations, compact fibrous layered structures, and, rarely, stalactites and needle-like crystals and prismatic crystals with wedge-shaped terminations. The colour ranges from light to dark green. Some of the formations also exhibit a druse of small malachite crystals on the surface.

It is a "stone of transformation", assisting one in changing situations, and providing for the transfer of sacred information leading to spiritual evolution.

It assists in clearing and activating all chakras and is quite helpful in stimulating the heart and throat chakras. It is an excellent stone for clarifying the emotions and for allowing for both the recognition and the release of negative experiences which one cannot recall; in the re-birthing situation, it provides for ease of disposal of opposing encounters.

It can be used to facilitate insight concerning the cause of any specific condition; e.g., providing insight to the basic disorders within the body, mind, and spirit, and to the conditions associated with interaction with others in this reality.

Malachite is an equalizing and balancing agent; it can create an unobstructed path, leading to a desired goal. It also provides for an indication of the procedural steps required to attain a chosen end-result. It helps one to accept responsibility for ones actions, circumstances, and actuality, bringing understanding and intuitive answers to the forefront prior to response and subsequent action.

It stimulates instinctive and intuitive reasoning, allowing for change which facilitates advancement. It also represents fidelity in love and friendship, loyalty in partnerships, and practicality and responsibility in business transactions.

It has been used as a protective stone by those involved in the field of aviation and is said to dispel symptoms of, and to stimulate awareness of, the inner bases for the condition of vertigo.

The malachite structures exhibiting druse are also especially energetic in facilitating both the rise of spirituality and the enhancement of psychic abilities.

The stalactitic form of malachite also encourages progression toward the spiral of infinite wisdom, while providing strength for the journey.

This mineral can help one to look deep within the self and to acknowledge the reasons supporting an illness, further guiding and supporting one in the release of the emotional causative factors. It is said to protect against radiation and can be used in the treatment of asthma, arthritis, swollen joints, tumors, growths, broken bones, and torn muscles. It can also be used to regulate the RNA/DNA structures, to align and cleanse the cellular structure, to enhance the immune system, and to ease the process of birth.

It is recommended that only the polished form of Malachite be used for the preparation of an elixir via the normal method.

Vibrates to the number 9.

MANGANESE   [Astrological Sign of Scorpio]

Manganese is an ore, usually occurring in masses, and occasionally occurring in crystaline formation. The colour ranges from metallic grey to grey-black to black.

It is a mineral of bonding, bringing others closer and activating the energies of cooperation in group efforts. It furthers a firm impenetrable resolve, such that that which one initiates, one completes. The "rule of the final inch" is depicted aptly through the energies of Manganese - the mineral truly acts to make the "final inch" decrease expediently and with ease.

Manganese also stimulates spontaneity and produces a grounding effect which balances the emotions and the physical body. In addition, it enhances ones positivity and inspires true creativity.

The crystaline formation tends to strengthen all of the qualities listed above and further acts to bring a connection between the conscious self and the angelic realm; the alliance which occurs is one where one is grounded, actively conscious, and intuitively aware.

This mineral can be used to diminish free-radical oxides in both food and in the body. It can provide an increase in the metabolic rate and can produce a homeopathic energy in healing situations. In addition, it acts to stimulate assimilation of the manganese nutrient, bringing relief from headaches, muscular stiffness, and tiredness.

Vibrates to the number 7.

MANGANITE   [Astrological Sign of Virgo]

Manganite crystallizes in the form of striated prismatic crystals, wedge-shaped crystals, radial aggregates, masses, columns, and stalactites. The colour ranges from dark grey to black.

This mineral can help one to dispense with attachment and control, and to recognize that one is responsible for ones actions and not for the actions of another.

It also enables one to desist in relationships which are controlled by another, and to respect oneself sufficiently to "release the grief".

It can be used to provide the physical strength necessary to dispel mental anguish, allowing one to recognize that the reasons for the despair hinge on the lack of self-love and self-respect. It further promotes insight into creative solutions.

It can be used in the treatment of infertility [when consciously directed], and for disorders of the mucous membranes, kidneys, bladder, and blood. It can also be used to strengthen the veins, to alleviate swelling and water retention, and to relieve headaches and the pain associated with dis-ease.

Vibrates to the number 3.

MANGANOSITE   [Astrological Sign of Sagittarius]

Manganosite crystallizes in the form of octahedral crystals. The colour is emerald green, changing to black upon exposure to light.

This mineral can enable one to go to the depths of ones stillness to find the light of ones soul. It is a wonderful mineral for meditative purposes and for centering in the moment.

It improves dream states and enhances "remembering" both during and after the dream.

It can be used to enhance thought transference and to promote the use of conscious feelings and ideas, supplemented by incorporation of unconscious ideas and impulses; this furthers the "knowing" of the method and the conscious production of the results. It helps one to "do it once" and "do it right", providing for insight into righteous causes prior to perseverance.

It provides for independent thought and loving action. It can also be used to facilitate the manifestation of worldly items.

Manganosite is quite useful to one who works with the "laying-on-of-stones"; it provides access to intuitive instruction with respect to the proper placement of minerals for each specific subject and/or dis-ease, and for each problem to be solved or action to be stimulated. It helps one to manipulate the minerals with ease and to provide for the desired situation.

It can be used in the treatment of skin disorders, hair loss, and intestinal disorders. It can help to stabilize mild forms of uncontrollable action and depression. It acts to provide clarity to the eyes and can be used to stimulate the skin.

Vibrates to the number 1.

MARBLE   [Astrological Sign of Cancer]

Marble is a metamorphosed limestone occurring in the form of a coarse to medium-grained rock of re-crystallized dolomite or calcite. The colour range includes white, yellow, red, green, pink, brown, etc. A type of marble, ruin-marble, also exhibits the various shades of yellow-to-brown.

This mineral is used to provide for both clarity and suspension in states of meditation, including tantric activities. It promotes peak states of meditation, and total recall of dreams.

It helps to actuate the "unused" portions of the mind, providing for the strength of self-control, the mastery of thought, and the power of serenity. It further provides guidance in the purification and control of thoughts, assisting one in the actualization of that which is desired.

It can produce a nurturing instinct and can enhance "good common sense" in matters of the home, the heart, and ones sustenance. It further provides for strength of character and is also a "stone to provide protection" - both physical and emotional. It assists in bringing one to balance with respect to both amelioration and improvement of ones physical and worldly circumstances.

It can be used in the treatment of disorders of the bone marrow, and for viral and bacterial infections, sore throat, lower back pain, and to increase flexibility - both physical and mental. It assists one in the aspects of patience and determination during participation in "body fitness" programs.

It has been used extensively in the fields of naturopathy and homeopathy.
Ruin marble exhibits the additional qualities of providing for an intellectual connection with ancient civilizations, furthering ones knowledge concerning reactive social structures and the rare phenomenon of centralization of the goals of ancient cultures.

Vibrates to the number 6.

MARCASITE   [Astrological Sign of Leo]

The chemical composition of marcasite is identical to pyrite; these two minerals are distinguished by their respective crystalline formations. Marcasite occurs in the form of masses, stalactites, fibers, and as tabular and pyramid-like crystals. The colour is bronze-yellow, which may become a deeper yellow upon exposure to light.

The non-crystalline forms of marcasite possess the same properties as pyrite [see the PYRITE section in this book].

The crystalline forms exhibit additional properties which will be discussed here.

Marcasite provides one with the view of oneself from an outside perspective and can produce insight with respect to the methods available for painlessly correcting the qualities which are unwanted; this is occasionally in opposition to the way one consciously appraises the self. It helps one to make these corrections easily, and provides for periodic reminders of any uncorrected and unwanted personal traits. It also shows one how one may appear dull to others and encourages one to "shine".

It further stimulates and illumines the senses and the intellect, softening ones expressiveness and dispelling both the use of rash words and the actions of impatience.

Marcasite represents spiritual development, providing for prosperity by eliminating starvation of the spirit.

It can be used in the treatment of skin disorders, moles, warts, freckles, etc.; placing the stone on the affected area or use of an elixir taken internally or applied topically tends to provide the action.

Vibrates to the number 8.

MARGARITE   [Astrological Sign of Scorpio]

Margarite, a form of mica, crystallizes in the form of plate-like aggregates [the plates in varying directions], masses, and, rarely, in distinct crystals. The colour range includes grey, pink, yellow, green, and red. Further qualities of margarite are discussed in the MICA section of this book.

This mineral stimulates strength to assist one to endure any situation, and acts to bring a pleasant disposition and the ability to laugh.

It also stimulates conversational skills and inhibits shy reclusive behavior tendencies. It works to eliminate feelings of anger and distress.

Margarite provides a subtle energy to the ethereal bodies and provides for soothing and smoothing the meridians of the physical body. It promotes the vitality and the emotional stability to enable one to "spring back" to the state of balance.

This mineral can be used in the treatment of brittleness or softness of nails, to balance the acidity level in the body, and to ameliorate acidosis conditions. It is also excellent as an elixir for the skin and for toning the muscular structure of the body.

Vibrates to the number 2.

MARIALITE   [Astrological Sign of Aquarius]

Marialite crystallizes in the form of masses and prismatic crystals. The colour range includes white, colourless, grey, blue, green, yellow, pink, and brown.

This mineral provides impetus to change - situations of the body, mind, or ones environmental conditions. It can enhance growth in any area consciously chosen, and brings stamina and clarity toward the attainment of a pre-set goal. It allows one to relax unproductive striving, assisting in the attainment of that which relates to agreements made prior to birth into this life.

Marialite also stimulates unconventional, yet loving, thought; facilitating and supporting ones persistent refusal to grant the infringement of negative opinions, desires, and expectations of others. It provides for the precious spirit of independence to be subservient only to the "light" of goodness.

It can be used in the treatment of cataracts, glaucoma, dis-alignment of the iris, dyslexia, and incontinence.

Vibrates to the number 7.

MATLOCKITE   [Astrological Sign of Capricorn]

Matlockite crystallizes in the form of yellow-to-green tabular tetragonal crystals.

This mineral can provide one with a feeling of wonder and curiosity in order to stimulate further development in the chosen area. It can bring one into the controlling situation, while providing the energy to increase the stamina required to exhibit the qualities necessary to remain in control.

It can provide a window through which one can experience intuitive-type astral travel, allowing for the gleaning information without actually requiring the "leaving" of the body.

It "open doors" within the avenues of pursuit, keeping "at bay" that which is not desired; the energy seems to protect one in the areas one determines as requiring protection.

It also furthers forcefulness of character at the moments of ones own choosing.

This mineral can be used to strengthen the teeth and gums, to enhance the enamel coating on the teeth, and to lessen disorders of the stomach which are related to indigestion and hiatal hernia conditions.

Vibrates to the number 1.

MELANITE [Astrological Sign of Scorpio]

Melanite is a variety of Andradite [Garnet] which crystallizes in the formation of grains, masses, plate-like layers, and crystals configured as dodecahedron, trapezohedron, and combinations of the dodecahedral/trapezohedral structures. The colour is either a dull or lustrous black.

The following properties are in addition to those listed in the ANDRADITE and GARNET Section~ of this book.

This mineral can be used for all situations in which there is a deficiency of love [from/to others and from/to the self], the strongest and most ardent energy in the world. It acts to dispel jealousy, envy, distrust, and anger, and releases blockages in the heart and throat chakras.

Melanite further serves to assist one in self-adjusting, such that one may release only those emotions and show others only those facets of the self that one is ready to confront. It helps one to release resentment and animosity and to understand the bases for same, stimulating the learning of the lessons necessary to advance toward ones actualization of the perfect state.

The energy also advances relationships, whether in divorce or in union.

It has been used in the treatment of cancer, strokes, arthritis, and rheumatism. It can also be used to assist ones body to adjust to medication - bringing holistic energies to support the healing of a disorder.

Vibrates to the number 7.

MELIPHANE [Astrological Sign of Gemini]

Meliphane crystallizes in the form of aggregates of plate-like layers, and tabular crystals. The colour is yellow or colourless.

This mineral produces a calming, mellow energy and softens ones harsh attributes. It enhances the appreciation of music, and promotes ones clairaudient abilities. One can, sometimes, even hear, and subsequently communicate, the message of the music of the celestial realm which manifests during meditation with this mineral.

It is an excellent stone for groups, providing for an indivisible entity with diligence and patience to achieve the goal.

It can provide support to other healing stones in producing the relief of a disorder. It can enhance the richness and clarity of ones skin and can be used in the treatment of skin disorders. It can also be used in the treatment of dis-ease related to the mouth and throat.

Vibrates to the number 2.

MESOLITE   [Astrological Signs of Libra & Leo]

Mesolite crystallizes in the form of tufts and groups of radial-type [sometimes needle-like] crystals. The colour is white or colourless.

This mineral opens the network of communication structures to facilitate communication with other worlds, mainly the spiritual world; however, information has been received from ancient civilizations. Mesolite has not yet been utilized as a stone for extra-terrestrial communication.

It provides for intelligent cultivation of relationships and emanates an energy which facilitates the establishment of cohesiveness in relationships and organizations; it furthers the action of the "team spirit".

Mesolite helps one to access the "heart of a problem", assisting one in transforming the heart to love. It further enables one to exhibit control of ones life, assisting in the actualization of the chosen reality.

It can be used to disperse blood clots, to stimulate the arteries to clear their walls, and to enhance circulation. It is also useful in the treatment of bruises and wounds.

Vibrates to the number 8.

MESSELITE   [Astrological Signs of Pisces & Virgo]

Messelite crystallizes in the form of plate-like layers, masses, prismatic crystals, and tabular crystals. The colour range includes white, colourless, grey, green, and brown.

This mineral can stimulate automatic writing and psychokinetic abilities.
It increases the strength of ones essence and can facilitate both the sending and receipt of telepathic messages; it has been used to expedite the receipt of special assignments from the spirit world - these assignments being suited to the recipient and being quite beneficial.

Messelite has also been used as a "merchants stone", bringing orderliness to the activities of business while encouraging beneficial outcomes in business ventures.

It can provide one with both strength and stamina when fasting. It can be used in the treatment of brain disorders, skull fractures or malformations, and for building the cellular structure of the internal cavities.

Vibrates to the number 8.

METEORITE   [Astrological Sign of All]

The composition and colour range of the meteorite is varied. The "irons", chondrites, and achondrites are designated as the three classes of meteorites. The "irons" are comprised, mainly, of iron and nickel; the chondrites are comprised of stone; and, the achondrites [approximately, 1% of the class] are comprised of very rare stony irons consisting of stone fragments and/or beautiful olivine crystals imbedded in a nickel-iron matrix. The material within the achondrites, said to be the result of volcanic activity on Mars and/or the Moon, is believed to predate the formation of the Earth.

The meteorite, rarer than the diamond, originates in outer space, from the heads of comets, the asteroid belt, from Mars, and from the Moon; it is presented to the inhabitants of Earth to use as they may. It is recognized as a gift from another world, containing properties quite specific to each. The qualities common to the meteorites are listed below.

The reader is encouraged to experiment with the varying classes in order to gain the use of those additional tools which have been provided by our other-planetary friends.

The meteorite is held sacred and is esteemed in many cultures. It represents the energy of other worlds and allows for access of this energy by the user. The ancient civilizations of China considered the meteorite to be a sacred stone from the heavens. It has been revered by the Moslems as the sacred stone of Kaaba at Mecca, in Arabia.

The meteorite can be used for balancing and aligning the bodies, within themselves, and to synthesize the alignment between the bodies. It enhances communication on this plane and can provide information, stored within, concerning other-worldly [spacial] aspects relevant to ones needs.

It further symbolizes the aptitude and the strength required for endurance. It enshrines and presents the loving energy of unknown cultures to the residents of the

Earth, allowing for the realization that we are but guests on this planet and assisting in the total actualization of the purpose of our presence.

It emits a trusting energy, helping one to be amenable to exchanges of confidences.

It provides for introspection to the thoughts of enlightened beings and promotes the synthesis of this physical reality with the evolution of the total structure of "All That Is".

It is an excellent stone to be carried by "walk-ins"; providing them with a stabilizing effect with respect to the unfamiliar nuances and divergent behavior patterns which may be residual in their "new environments". It provides for cooperative effort between the "new" being and the "old" beings of the Earth.

It can be used in the treatment of anemia, incoherence, and melancholia. It can be used to assist one in understanding the physical body such that the body becomes one with the spirit and, hence, acts to disallow malfunctioning on the higher levels.

Vibrates to the number 2.

MICA   [Astrological Sign of Aquarius]
                                        [Variety - Muscovite]

The commonest form of mica is Muscovite, and is addressed here. Additional forms of mica are further discussed in the MARGARITE and BIOTITE sections of this book. Muscovite crystallizes in the form of plate-like layers, scales, masses, and tabular crystals. The colour range includes pearly grey, white, yellow, brown, green, red, and violet.

This mineral provides reflective qualities so that one can recognize the flaws of humanity and can remain in a heart space to continue to love this same humanity. It can help one to look at a situation in complete detail, magnifying those aspects of importance. It can also be used to facilitate clarity in visions and mysticism.

It provides for self-reflection, and allows one to recognize that "in each person you see but the reflection of that which you choose to have that person be".

It further allows one to recognize the contrary characteristics of another which are within oneself, and assists one in both acknowledging and eliminating these traits from ones personality.

It enhances ones flexibility in physical, emotional, and intellectual situations. It provides for growth in all areas of pursuit and can be used to diminish anger, tantrums, and nervous energy.

It can be used to grid areas which are prone to earthquakes, acting to relieve the internal stresses of the Earth without producing dysfunctional situations. It also aligns the energy centers of the body and releases energy blockages from stagnant locations.

It can be used when fasting to reduce hunger, to treat both insomnia and the excessive sleeping requirements of mononucleosis, to relieve conditions of dehydration, to bring sparkle to the eyes and sheen to the hair, and to provide energy and purpose.

The category of mica vibrates to the number 8. Muscovite vibrates to both the number 8 and the number 1.

MICROCLINE   [Astrological Sign of Libra]

Microcline crystallizes in the form of masses, grains, twins, and lamellae. The colour range includes white to pale cream-yellow, red, and green.

This mineral is excellent for gridding for polarity balancing, protection, and for releasing that which is unwanted. It also can be used to stimulate clarity in thought and enhances the stabilization of the frequency of brain wave transmissions. It can provide for a connection to the psychic self, awakening the energy of the third-eye and expediting the verbalization of that which is encountered.

It is an excellent stimulant for dreaming, bringing uniform transference from one dream state to the next deeper state.

The energy is comforting, embracing, soothing, and relaxing; it has been quite beneficial during the birthing process and has assisted in relieving stress during pregnancy.

It has been used in the treatment of the eyes and the blood vessels, to assist in ease of childbirth, to release heat from fevers, to ameliorate water retention, and to support cellular reconstruction.

Vibrates to the number 5.

MICROLITE   [Astrological Sign of Aries]

Microlite crystallizes in the form of masses, and octahedral-type crystals. The colour range includes pale yellow, brown, red, and emerald green.

This mineral can be used to enhance speed in physical or mental activities.

It provides for grace with movement and increases ones capacity in concentration and exercise.

It allows one to see the "universe in a mustard seed" and to relate to the inner being of others instead of the outer manifestation. It helps one to expand the consciousness toward both the acceptance and understanding of all which is in ones realm of experience.

It also enables one to both generously give and generously receive.

It can be used in the treatment of artery constriction, candida infections, virulent infections, and premature wrinkles, and to ease the actuality and memory of the discomforts of childbirth.

Vibrates to the number 5.

MILARITE   [Astrological Sign of Virgo]

Milarite crystallizes in the form of hexagonal-type prismatic crystals. The colour range includes pale green, yellow, and colourless.

This mineral enhances the female attributes and balances an over-powerful yang personality. It provides for a wholesome outlook and a compassionate nature.

The energy of milarite "grinds away" at the outer shell of ones character, allowing for the recognition of the inner self and, subsequently, facilitating the conscious recognition of, and impetus to take, the appropriate action in recovering the loving attributes which have been clandestine.

It can provide information, gleaned from looking "at", and not "into" the stone - information which appears as clear and concisely written messages may be recognized by the "eye of the mind" and the inner intuitive systems during this process.

It is recommended for those who are uncomfortable with beginning astral travel and for those who are concerned with manifesting the ability to return to the body; in these cases, milarite eases the apprehension and provides for a firm connection to the "silver cord".

Milarite can also be used in the treatment of disorders of the digestive system, the alimentary canal, and the elimination system.

Vibrates to the number 6.

MILLERITE   [Astrological Sign of Scorpio]

Millerite crystallizes in the form of coatings, braid-like structures, tufts, and very slender crystals [sometimes, in radial groupings]. The colour is a brassy-yellow which tarnishes to an iridescent grey.

This mineral is quite helpful in stimulating both the deep meditative states and the composed states which are required prior to beginning communication with the spiritual worlds. It provides an energy to assist one in the refinement of the techniques and the methods which are conducive to actualizing increased awareness and attunement to the universe.

It helps one to look at the broad range of opportunities with child-like innocence, diminishing those inhibitions which prevent discovery while balancing the mind to obscure inane ambitions.

It stimulates the intellect and helps one to eliminate the negative aspects of the ego.

It smooths abrasiveness and helps to reduce, and to subsequently eliminate, caustic communication.

It tends to expunge guilt from both the conscious and subconscious minds, banishing anxiety and stabilizing and clearing the emotions. It can be used to eliminate inner turmoil, indecision, and the aspects of pandemonium from ones mental, physical, and emotional bodies.

Millerite can be also be used to increase capillary action throughout the body, to increase the elasticity of skin, tissue, and muscles, to eliminate infections in the body, and to relieve pressure in the head and around the brain.

Vibrates to the number 4.

MIMETITE   [Astrological Sign of Capricorn]

Mimetite crystallizes in the form of crusts, granular masses, and needle-like crystals which are sometimes curved. The colour range includes white, yellow, orange, colourless, brown, and brown-red.

This mineral alleviates the proclivity to imitate or copy the mannerisms, demeanor, or life style of another; producing an energy of practical independence.

It can be used to enhance the spirit of adventure and to smooth all aspects of responsibilities to the "tolerable" level. It can bring one to the "spring of wisdom" and can provide for protection while one receives the information therein. It is also a protective stone which facilitates channeling situations and enhances the communicative/receiver modes to provide for clarity and precision.

This mineral can be used to correct conditions of atrophy, immobility, skeletal disorders, and disorders of the throat.

Vibrates to the number 4.

MINERAL STONE   [Astrological Sign of Libra]

Mineral Stone crystallizes in various formations, usually appearing as a conglomerate. The colour range is dependent upon the minerals included.

This mineral brings the qualities of the minerals encompassed to a synthesis of energy and acts to magnify the energy of each mineral, in turn.

In addition, the extension of occurrences to facilitate knowledge with ease is advanced such that approach to each event/condition/experience is with absolute precision and beneficial construction. The concept of approach via strategic techniques is also reflected.

Vibrates to the master number 55.

MITRIDATITE   [Astrological Signs of Pisces & Taurus]

Mitridatite crystallizes in the form of crusts, massive veins, and tabular crystals. The colour is red.

This mineral produces the condition of vitality with love, allowing for the actualization of the positive feelings of love with the strength of truth. It strengthens one commitment to a cause, or to another, and provides for a mixing of the qualities of those involved to produce the desired results. It gives one the courage and initiative to begin relationships on all levels. It also lessens the coarseness of any situation and alleviates misunderstandings. It is useful for recovering ones depth of character, supplementing shallowness and eliminating the vacuous nature.

Mitridatite can be used to further mystic channeling, providing access to the enlightened masters of the spiritual world and opening the door to communication.

It can also be used in the treatment of conditions requiring cellular regeneration, and in the repair of the arteries and valves at the heart locality. It can assist in removing the condition of vertigo.

Vibrates to the number 3.

MIXITE   [Astrological Sign of Libra]

Mixite crystallizes in the form of tufted aggregates, crusts, and needle-like crystals. The colour range includes white and green.

This mineral provides for an open connection between the heart/love center and the crown/enlightenment center. It allows one to produce the bases for an assemblage of the chakras into the configuration of alignment and further promotes the initiation of the rise, or the continuation of the movement of, the Kundalini.

Mixite assists in the both the improvement and the development of the memory, and can be used to stimulate the utilization of unused portions of the brain. It provides the message that the unlimited capabilities of the mind can "sweep-away" confusion and can conquer insuperable difficulties.

It also dispels defiance and enhances cooperation. It is quite useful in guiding one to release prejudice and to accept humanity as one with the self.

It can be used in the treatment of digestive disorders and to enhance the assimilation of the nutrients required to maintain the body in an optimum state.

Do not prepare an elixir of this mineral via the normal method.

Vibrates to the number 8.

MOCHI BALLS ©   [Astrological Sign of Libra, Aquarius, & Aries]
[Also Known As Maqui Marbels]

Iron and Sandstone Concretions from the Southwestern United States, Mochi Balls are said to be named after a tribe of Native Americans who lived in the area of the Moqui Desert and who used them in gaming - the game was similar to the game of "marbles". They are also said to have been used for contact with the extra-terrestrial, for visioning, and for journeying; they were sacred among the shamanic members of the ancient tribes.

They have been used for centuries by the shamanic tribes of the continents. Although newly discovered in the United States, the Mochis have been found on several continents in the ancient archaeological excavations. They are recommended for use by all - bringing knowledge to the user of both the ancient ways and the future ways.

They need no special care - they are lovely to hold and act to protect when placed in ones environment. They adapt to all environments, the energy being like "a good friend". Manifested by nature, enjoyed by mankind, the Mochi Ball brings the synthesis of male/female, duality, and the actualization of singularity, allowing one to recognize and to understand the self, and the independence and liberty of ones nature.

Mochi Balls can be used to align the energy centers, to relieve energy blockages, to stimulate the CHI, to ground and center, and to provide protection. Gridding with two Mochi Balls promotes receptivity to frequencies which are usually inaudible. The journey with the Mochi allows one to live to the fullest while understanding the sanctity of, and performing healing for, the Earth. In addition, they bring feelings to surface such that one recognizes impositions and encroachments upon the self and assists one in activating a "non-selfless-ness".

They have been used in the treatment of physical instability, constrictions and restrictions in the veins, muscles, and arteries, bone loss, RNA/DNA balancing, deficiency of the immune system, and cellular renewal.

Vibrate to the numbers 4 and 6.

MOHAWKITE   [Astrological Sign of Sagittarius]

Mohawkite crystallizes in the form of grains, masses, scales, tabular hexagonal crystals, and short prismatic crystals which taper and exhibit horizontal striations.

This mineral can provide for stability within group structures, and can produce intuitive ideas supplementing ritualistic performance of ceremonies. The energy helps to eliminate stagnation in activities and assists in promoting an openness to improvement possibilities.

It can supplement the energy centering which is required for astral travel, helping to send one "on the way". It can be used to support both the transmittal of messages, and the receipt of information, via the ethereal plane, with respect to the activities of another; it is advised that one gain permission prior to accessing information about another.

This mineral can be used to enhance ones flexibility [both mentally and physically], and to ease the stress related to, the pain associated with, and the actual processes required when one allows the body to submit to operative techniques. It can also help to diminish fatty deposits within the body and to provide a silkiness to the skin [when used topically as an elixir].

Vibrates to the number 6.

MOLDAVITE   [Astrological Sign of All - Scorpio Predominant]
                                              [Also Known as VLTAVA]

Moldavite is a tektite which is found in Czechoslovakia and was formed during meteoritic action which produced a "strew field" of this beautiful green stone. It is one of the rarest varieties of tektite, was formed over 15 million years ago, and is the only known "gem quality" stone of extra-terrestrial origin.

There is a complete book available discussing moldavite. In addition to the qualities listed in the TEKTITE section of this book, the following properties are applicable.

Moldavite is a stone to serve the inhabitants of this planet. It stimulates cooperation between those of extra-terrestrial origins and those who are experiencing life on Earth. It carries one beyond the mirage of life, to a home from which one has been absent, providing the image of eternity and the vision and energy to translate the image into reality.

It holds immense potential, for direct interdimensional accessing of higher dimensional galactic energies, to draw into the Earth plane those thought-patterns and light-vibrations which are optimal to ones preparation for ascension and illumination. It facilitates strong, clear, and direct interdimensional interconnected-ness between ones consciousness and the higher planes of light. It expands the scope and the magnitude of the vibrational spectrums which one can approach, while allowing for a more encompassing passageway to those spectrums of which one already has access; that is, one will "see" more clearly and will "see" with an expansion of vision within the vibrational territory to which one has ventured, and/or one will be provided the inter-connection with the multi-dimensional horizons not yet experienced.

Moldavite works quite well at the third-eye, the throat chakra, and in the area of the crown chakra.

When used in the areas of the hands, it has also stimulated the capability to feel the form of the message and sometimes the form of the communicator from whence the message comes.

It works well with quartz, which adds the factors of amplification, stabilization, and a wide energy range, to the focused and specific access capabilities of moldavite.

It also works extremely well with sugilite, celestite, aquamarine, diamond, lapis, and opal, producing overwhelming combinations of qualities which are quite conducive to healing.

The reader is encouraged to experiment with moldavite and to realize the potential of the stone within ones inner quiet.

Do not cleanse with salt. The stone is softer and more fragile in composition [in comparison with quartz]. [See section discussing cleansing techniques.]

Vibrates to the numbers 2 and 6.

MOLYBDENUM   [Astrological Sign of Scorpio]

Molybdenum is a silver-white to grey high-melting metalloid, usually found in the formation of masses and occasionally with quartz.

This elemental mineral brings constancy, continuity, and reliability to ones life. It acts as a catalyst to maintain that which one has. Molybdenum dispenses an energy of balancing to ones life and has been used to balance the chakras, the bodies, and the mind.

It further fills voids in the aura and stimulates an electric charge to provide equilibrium in all areas of ones life.

An effective utilization of the energy is facilitated by allowing the mineral to remain in ones energy field; this will provide for continuous balancing of ones energy and alignment of ones energy paths. It is not necessary that one be aware of the presence of the mineral in order for the balancing and for the alignment and the support to occur.

It has also enhanced contact between the conscious self and the inner self and between the conscious self and those of other planetary worlds. In the case of the connection between the self and other planetary worlds, it has facilitated the transfer of necessary information to this world such that one may assist others in healing and in actualization.

It produces a voltaic action between the physical realm and the auric bodies to stimulate the movement of electrical charges to strengthen the connection such that when the auric bodies are cleansed, the physical body is stimulated. It further decreases chaotic activity within the body.

Molybdenum with quartz has been used to bring light in the darkness, merging of the auras of two when used by two together, and to promote progression from one understanding to the next. It assists one in acknowledging All That Is, and promotes the knowledge that one is never truly alone.

It is said that Molybdenum was consciously sent to our Earth, landing in a meteorite, and during the process of entry, occasionally adhered to quartz; this melding has processed a union of Earth and the planet from which it came (said to be Kyalpha). It is also said that the synthesis of molybdenum and quartz provided an energy to the Lemurians (during the demise of their land), so that they could travel and establish new colonies elsewhere in this world. Molybdenum on quartz has re-surfaced at this time to help those who wish to establish new lives, assisting in the stabilization of the positive portions of ones being and consecrating the new. It is a metamorphic position enhancer, will stimulate knowledge and illumination, and will serve to remove energy blockages and mental blockages while opening pathways to the future. It is a combination to remove "debris" from ones life and to expedite the transference of light to the darkness.

Molybdenum has been used in the stimulation of the circulatory system, to stabilize the dispersion of oxygen within the body, to treat conditions associated with the immune system, blood disorders, and all organs of the body.

Molybdenum vibrates to the number 7 and Molybdenum/Quartz vibrates to the number 2.

MONAZITE   [Astrological Sign of Aries]

Monazite crystallizes in the form of granular masses, rolled grains, tabular crystals, and prismatic crystals. The crystals are usually large. The colour range includes red, brown, pink, yellow, green, and white.

This mineral can be used to provide comfort during times of sadness, to stimulate the intellect [especially in times of anger] to look beyond a situation and to recognize the cause behind the conflict [hence, to understand and "let it go"], and to enhance ones solitary moments [to increase both ones awareness and appreciation of these moments, and to facilitate the "knowing" of ones inner self].

It can be used as a "shoulder to cry on" in times of sorrow, encouraging one to release the tears, while providing for comfort and calming.

It helps one to be pleasantly captivated by the spirit of practical observation, allowing one to look at otherwise "dull" routines with an excitement that helps all activities to be interesting. It is also said to increase fidelity and loyalty, and to magnify ones sensitivity toward others.

Monazite can be used to relieve intense pain, to combat obesity [when the user is willing to receive the energy of the mineral], and to lessen the burdens of the mind.

Vibrates to the number 4.

MONTICELLITE   [Astrological Sign of Virgo]

Monticellite crystallizes in the form of masses, grains, and prismatic crystals. The colour range includes colourless, grey, and green.

This mineral is the stone of castles and kings. It brings one distinction [when directed], and makes available the riches of the planet. When used in meditation, it conveys the energy to allow one to receive an un-ending stream of inter-connected ideas; it is best to have the assistance of a tape recorder during these exercises. The ideas are from both intuitive prompting and from the kingdoms beyond.

It can take one to the medieval halls of the unconscious self, allowing for recognition while stimulating the pursuit of the synthesis of the power of intelligence teamed with spirituality. It allows one to recognize that the swift and complete understanding of issues and situations is quite natural. It assists in the elimination of archaic bitterness, allowing for awareness of the effects of anger so that one may progress onward from the karmic obligation. It further provides an irresistible lure toward the relentless and deliberate elimination of mental, physical, emotional, and spiritual chaos.

Monticellite has been used by the Native American Indians in ceremonies to assist in the entry to the ancient and sacred grounds of power, and to facilitate communication with the spirit world.

It is said to be quite useful to stimulate learning via self-education and via the use of the senses. It also eliminates feelings of uncertainty and moves one to action.

It can be used in the treatment of afflictions of the head, disorders of the muscular and fatty tissues, and to provide protection from insects.

Vibrates to the number 2.

MOONSTONE   [Astrological Signs of Cancer, Libra, & Scorpio]

Moonstone is found in the orthoclase [adularia] and the albite minerals [both members of the feldspar group]. The properties characterizing moonstone are a chatoyancy, a milky-sheen, or the exhibition of those traits on a portion of the specimen. The following properties are in addition to those listed in the ADULARIA, ALBITE, and FELDSPAR sections of this book.

The energy of moonstone is balancing, introspective, reflective, and lunar. It is capable of helping one with the changing structures of ones life on the physical, emotional, mental, and spiritual levels. The energy relates to "new beginnings", allowing one to realize that these "new beginnings" are, in actuality, the fruition of each "end".

It is a stone for hoping and wishing; it allows one to absorb that which is needed from the universal energies, not necessarily, however, furthering that which is wanted. It helps one to recognize the "ups and downs" and to gracefully acknowledge the changing cycles. It can assist one in sustaining and maintaining, and understanding the destiny one has chosen. It works to bring the galactic evolved energies from other worlds to accessibility.

It is a stone for "feeling", and understanding via intuition and emotional "thoughts", rather than via intellectual reasoning. It brings flashes of insight, banishing the possibility of neglecting ones profit from that which is experienced. It stimulates intuitive recognition and helps one to apply the intuitive knowledge in a practical sense. It also enhances perception and discernment, enabling one to make decisions which painlessly further ones development.

It can be used to alleviate emotional tension and to enhance the positive attributes of creativity and self-expression.

It cleanses negativity from the chakras, enhancing the feminine aspects of ones nature while providing for spiritual nourishment and sustenance, and a loving compassion to further assist one through all changes.

It stimulates confidence and composure and allows one to understand that there is no situation so difficult that it cannot be countered with diplomacy.

Moonstone sustains and supports while promoting growth and supplementing energy. It provides for a connection between the physical, emotion, and intellectual bodies, furthering the advancement and diminishing the obstacles in the path leading to ones progression and actualization as a perfect being; removal of obstacles usually occurs with the release and/or integration of the obstacle. It assists one in the total fulfillment of ones destiny. It also provides for guidance with respect to the most effective procedural steps available to facilitate the attainment of the desired end-result.

Once called the "traveler's stone", it is used for protection against the perils of travel. Moonstone is also a talisman of good fortune. It is said to keep closer that which is dear to one.

It is also said to both arouse tenderness within the self, and to bring happiness to the environment in which it resides.

It can be used during radionic analysis; holding a sample and placing a sample on the witness or using a pendulum of this stone, the energy of the stone interferes with the energy of the user and points to the problem[s] involved.

Moonstone brings calmness coupled with awareness. It helps one to attune to the normal rhythms of the biological forces of ones body such that one can maximize, recognize, and utilize the natural energy cycles of the body. One is not limited, however, by the natural cycles, and can use the energy of the stone to both balance and counterbalance phases of energy depletion as they occur within the body.

The energy of moonstone provides the body with a sustaining force. It can stimulate the properties of rejuvenation and can alleviate many degenerative conditions with respect to the skin, hair, eyes, and the fleshy organs of the body.

♪ 417 ♫

It can also be used to enhance the assimilation of nutrients, to assist in the elimination of toxins, and to treat disorders of the digestive and elimination systems.

It can be used in the treatment of pulmonary consumption, to facilitate and to promote ease in pregnancy and childbirth, to enhance fertility, to ameliorate PMS and change-of-life, to eliminate insomnia [ancient remedy], and to provide remedial action for disorders related to water [e.g., swelling] and insect stings or bites [e.g., allergic reactions to bee stings, anaphylactic shock, malaria, yellow fever, etc.]. It can also be used in the treatment of circulatory disorders.

The energies of moonstone are accessible when worn, carried, or used as an elixir. Topical application to the skin and hair has also been effective in soothing and in stimulating the area.

Vibrates to the number 4.

MORDENITE   [Astrological Signs of Libra & Cancer]

Mordenite crystallizes in the form of fibrous aggregates, masses, and vertically striated prismatic crystals. The colour range includes white, colourless, yellow, and pink.

This mineral can be used to eliminate the trait of sarcasm and to enhance the characteristic of harmony. It furthers the importance of home and friendships, and can be used to bring abundance to ones life.

It has been used to assist in white magic activities and to facilitate the awareness and the mechanisms of the rituals and rites which are associated with these activities.

Mordenite prevails upon the energies of the universe to assist one in eliminating mental distractions and to initiate the pacification of a restless mind.

It provides for a swift release from depression and disillusionment, intercepting chaotic energy and providing for restructuring of same. It promotes detachment from negativity so that one is not blinded by the emotion; hence, furthering the understanding of the symptom[s].

It can be used in the treatment of disorders of the mouth, lungs, and vocal cords.

Vibrates to the number 4.

MORGANITE

Morganite is a type of beryl and crystallizes in the form of masses and prismatic crystals, sometimes vertically striated and sometimes terminated by small pyramid-like faces. The colour ranges from pink to rose.

This mineral is an activator, cleanser, and stimulator for the heart chakra. It helps to bring love into ones life and assists one in maintaining that love as it continues to grow. It also helps one to realize the equality in relationships, between the sexes, and between the races.

It brings the actualization of gain to ones life - gain and supplementation of that which is required to cultivate the spirit and to allow one to consciously align the personality with the ethereal soul.

It also stimulates the transmittal of impersonal wisdom from ones guides and furthers ones accountability for ones personal reality.

It stimulates creativity in issues of self-control, assisting one to act from love, and bringing the beautiful jewel of wisdom to the calmness of the mind.

It opens the door to the vital currents which activate and energize loving thoughts and actions, bringing forth patience and a reverence for life.

Morganite is also a powerful stone, in massive form, for use in ceremonies around the medicine wheel. It provides the experience of the "brotherhood" and facilitates both speaking and listening with ones heart.

It was a stone used to "tell stories" during the early days of civilization; it contains accessible memories relevant to both the history of its use and to the experiences it has seen.

The energy of morganite also provides for access to information concerning the environmental structures of other worlds, helping one to understand and to implement the aspects of love to heal and to maintain the Earth.

This mineral can be used in the treatment of emphysema, tuberculosis, and asthma, and for further oxygenation at the cellular level to enhance rejuvenation of disordered cells. It has also been used to stabilize the heart and to clear the lungs.

Vibrates to the number 3.

MOSANDRITE   [Astrological Sign of Leo]

Mosandrite crystallizes in the form of masses, plate-like layers, and long prismatic crystals which are striated on the faces. The colour range includes yellow, orange, red, green, and brown.

This mineral can stimulate the gift of prophecy and can supplement the skills necessary for divination. It assists in bringing strength to ones convictions, allowing one to gain the flexibility to change opinions based upon "new" insight and/or information.

It can be used to both open and activate the base, navel, solar plexus, and heart chakras, providing for grounding during the process and facilitating concurrent removal of the "muddiness" from both the chakras and the aura.

It can also be used to bring vitality to creativity, love, personal power, intuition, and sexuality.

Mosandrite can help to facilitate freedom [in whichever area one consciously directs the energy], to help one to a "slower pace", and to assist one in the re-direction of the supplemental life force to that which requires the supplement. It is quite useful during healing sessions where the Reiki technique is used.

This mineral can also be used in the treatment of skin rashes, exterior growths, spinal dis-alignment, and constraint in movement.

Vibrates to the number 1.

MOTTRAMITE   [Astrological Sign of Gemini]

Mottramite crystallizes in the formation of prismatic crystals, druses, and globular, reniform, and compact masses. The colour ranges from green to black.

This mineral represents transformation and extensive change throughout all times and is concentrated with resolution to accelerate and to reform the self with ease. The doctrines of motivation and persevering motion are reflected, bringing freedom from oppression and repression.

It has been used to assist in understanding and then practicing the concept of "walk - don't run", helping one to trust the circumstances one is experiencing, and to accept ones position in those situations as a part of the actualization of ones perfection.

Mottramite expedites balance and respite during the attainment of pre-set goals, such that when one attains the goal, one has the energy necessary to enjoy the result. It produces a feeling of well-being and energetic control.

It has been used to provide supplemental energy during competitive sports, great physical stress, and prolonged physical labour.

This mineral has been used in the treatment of the immune system, the adrenal glands, the spleen, insomnia, and lethargy. It also produces an excellent energy for use during convalescence.

Vibrates to the master number 44.

MUIRITE   [Astrological Sign of Aries]

Muirite crystallizes in the form of grains and tetragonal crystals. The colour is orange.

This mineral stimulates creativity and intuition, and enhances sexuality. It increases ones desire and is quite helpful in directing that desire toward creative endeavors.

It provides for intuitive recognition of that which is beneficial and that which is detrimental in ones life, assisting one in the application of this knowledge to decisions and actions.

It can stabilize the emotions and can provide for a feeling that "everything is always okay".

It can assist one in understanding and clarifying "mixed" messages from both the Earth plane and from other worlds. It can induce the actualization of the quality of "second sight", allowing one to be comfortable with the expansion of awareness.

Muirite can be used for cleansing the aura and, hence, removing the unbalanced energy forces which can cause disorder within the physical body, as well as within the emotional and intellectual bodies.

It can be used in the treatment of eye disorders and in the elimination of parasites from the body.

Vibrates to the number 5.

MULLITE   [Astrological Sign of Cancer]

Mullite crystallizes in the form of prismatic crystals. The colour is pale pink.

This mineral stimulates transfer of information from the other worlds concerning the spiritual laws of the universe. It allows for receipt of this information through the heart, with a connection to the intellect, producing synthesis of ancient information which is now being made available to humanity.

This is a "dynamite" stone and requires no special training prior to use. It will be gentle when necessary; as the user is ready for information, it will be provided.

It helps one to recognize all "sides" of an issue, enhancing the contemplative powers and dissipating ineffectual reasoning. It also provides an impetus for one to select the solution and to initiate the resolution in a timely manner.

It further acts to provide encouragement to others to join in the quest for enlightenment.

Mullite can be used to enhance fertility [when consciously directed] and to stimulate personal remembering at the cellular level. It assists one in determining those issues relevant to a disorder or condition, allowing for integration of the issue and, hence, promoting the initiation of the healing processes.

It can provide for purification, cleansing, and elimination of that which is in disorder. It has been used to dispel disorders at the commencement of the symptoms. It can be used for helping with both the structure of the bone and the composition and formation of the cells. It has also been used to assist in the prevention of RNA/DNA damage and can be used in restoration of same.

Vibrates to the number 2.

MUSCOVITE   [Astrological Sign of Leo]

Muscovite crystallizes in the formation of rhombic and hexagonal tabular crystals, folia, aggregated in scaley, stellate, plumose, and globular masses, and compact masses. The colour range includes pink, colourless, grey, brown, green, violet, yellow, and rose-red.

In addition to the properties listed in the MICA Section, this mineral also stimulates the heart chakra and allows the layers of insecurities and uncertainties to disperse.

It can be used to lessen self-doubt, to promote the acts of looking to the past for lessons which truly have been assimilated, and to look to the future with optimism and knowledge that one can advance with success.

The energy of Muscovite brings quick-thinking, succinct and concise expression of ones feelings, and comfort in the exploration of any type of emotional pain which exists within the self. It strengthens the intuitive processes and assists the in the discovery of solutions to problems - personal or those of others.

It activates an awareness of the higher-self, especially when one is struggling with a major life decision.

Muscovite has been used in the treatment of allergies, to balance the pancreatic secretions, to control blood sugar levels, to regulate the kidneys, and to relieve the mind of distress due to dis-ease.

Vibrates to the number 1.

ENJOY THIS MOMENT.......

DO IT NOW!

NADORITE [Astrological Signs of Pisces & Cancer]

Nadorite crystallizes in the form of divergent groups, orthorhombic crystals, and tabular crystals. The colour range includes brown and yellow.

This mineral enables one to grow in the intellectual and spiritual areas of life. It provides for grounding to enhance both study and meditation and can provide insight into the "food for thought". It assists one in reaching the pinnacles of achievement and facilitates the psychological experience of focusing inward such that the realm of the unconscious opens; this further enhances the intuitive assimilation of the total range of thoughts and actions.

Nadorite aligns the physical nervous system with the ethereal nervous system to assist in increasing circulation and to help to arrange the nervous system in the optimum configuration. It also can be used in the treatment of skin disorders, paralysis, numbness, epilepsy, and "nerves".

Do not prepare an elixir of this mineral via the normal method.

Vibrates to the number 5.

NARSARSUKITE [Astrological Sign of Virgo]

Narsarsukite crystallizes in the form of prismatic crystals and tabular crystals. The colour range includes yellow, green, brown, grey, and colourless.

This mineral can be used to enhance the "splitting apart" of the emotional body from the intellectual body such that logical and calm decisions can be reached without static interference.

It can provide one with a sense of self-love in order to alleviate the condition of selfless-ness and to broaden ones horizons. It also provides one the access to a comfortable entry level into the actualization of self-awareness and growth.

It helps one to "drop" the old patterns and actions which have served in the past and which now impede ones progress toward the advancement of the state of perfection; the action of eliminating the outdated thinking helps one to continue toward ascension with openness, clarity, and grace. It further enables one to understand the process of "moving on" and helps one to dispense with everyone and everything which inhibits self-fulfillment.

♪ 427 ♫

Narsarsukite is used in the treatment of addictive behaviors, of afflictions of the blood vessels [not the blood], and to soothe the skin.

Vibrates to the number 3.

NATROLITE   [Astrological Signs of Cancer, Pisces, & Scorpio]

Natrolite crystallizes in the form of fibrous and radial masses, grains, and slender vertically striated crystals. The colour range includes white, yellow, red, colourless, and grey.

This mineral can be used to soften the experience of re-birthing, and to promote contact with the spiritual self at the level just prior to when the spirit entered the body at birth; it can also help to provide contact between the intellect and a channeling entity and between the intellect and a "walk-in" - when the entity is within ones body.

It assists one in the discovery of hidden, yet inherent, resources. It further helps one to extend awareness and centering via attunement to personal, mineralogical, global, and universal energies.

Natrolite can be used to enhance swimming techniques, to overcome the fear of water, and to treat swelling, water retention, localized anemia, and arteriosclerosis.

Vibrates to the number 6.

NATROPHYLLITE   [Astrological Sign of Pisces}

Natrophyllite crystallizes in the form of masses and prismatic crystals. The colour range includes deep yellow, burgundy-yellow, and the shades between.

This mineral can be used to align the intuitive self with the intellectual self in order to provide for increased awareness and for stimulation of fresh ideas. It can be used to facilitate inventiveness and to bring ones inherent ideas to actualization.

It emits an energy of innovation, assisting one in accessing information concerning the correction of internal and external imbalances.

It further helps one to explore the deeper levels of the self and to gain insight into the processes underlying dis-ease and dysfunctional behavior patterns.

This mineral can also be used to thin the blood, to enhance the environment of the unborn, to treat damage to the brain, and to improve flexibility while acting to reduce painful joints.

Vibrates to the number 4.

NEPHELINE   [Astrological Sign of Scorpio]

Nepheline crystallizes in the form of masses, columns, grains, and six-sided and twelve-sided prismatic crystals. The colour range includes white, colourless, grey, green, yellow, red, blue, and brown.

This mineral aligns the first four chakras, combining the qualities of vitality, creativity, personal power, and love.

It can also enhance both illusions and the intellectual recognition of the meaning behind the illusion. It is a stimulating but "soft" stone, which often provides one with a feeling of floating during the state of meditation.

Nepheline teaches one to seek truths and realizations via the meditative state. It further assists one in transforming the lower energies into conscious energies which can be used to invigorate and to rejuvenate the vital functions of the body.

It can also be used to banish sorrow; the sorrow being dismissed via an induced "forgetfulness" [an elixir is often used in this case]. It can be used to calm children [as can a proper diet], to eliminate tantrums, to dispel nightmares, and to reduce tension. It can also be used to control of the levels of high-density and low-density lipo-proteins.

Vibrates to the number 7.

NEPHRITE   [Astrological Sign of Libra]

Nephrite is a form of jade which is comprised of jade and actinolite. It occurs in the formation of masses, botryoidal configurations, and dreikanters [triangular jade nuggets which have been shaped and polished by prevailing winds and native sands].

The colour range includes olive green, green-grey, spinach green, misty green, apple green, light green, brown-green, black, cream, tan, blue-grey, and pink.

It combines the qualities listed in the JADE and ACTINOLITE sections of this book, additionally exhibiting the properties noted below.

This mineral can enable one to balance the male and female energies and to exchange the energies to further provide for balancing between the self and a partner. It provides for integrating the subtle energies of the universe into the body, facilitating the dynamic balancing of opposing energies in both the internal and the external worlds of ones reality.

Nephrite has been used as a talisman of protection, by tribal groups in New Zealand, to provide an invisible barrier against attack and illness.

It was considered to be a sacred mineral during the historical days of China, being used as the material for fashioning sacred implements and articles. It is said to bless that which it touches.

This mineral can be used to stimulate the working mechanisms of the white blood cells to engulf harmful organisms within the blood and to render them harmless. It can provide for stimulation of the adrenal glands, and for assistance in the regulation of metabolism, and acts to ameliorate the reaction of the body to stressful situations. It can also be used in the treatment of colic.

Nephrite also has occurred, rarely, with its massive structure enclosing actinolite crystals, gold, and pyrite. The inclusion of the other minerals produces the combined effects of the two [or more] minerals and the further enhancement of the effects caused by the actual combination.

Nephrite vibrates to the number 5.

Quartz Crystals/Structures within Nephrite

The occurrence of quartz crystals and quartz crystal structures within nephrite is even rarer; the quartz crystal structures have been seen to occur in a state where nephrite replaces the quartz crystal, leaving the outline of the quartz crystal as a pattern within the mass. This combined configuration is one of the "GRAND FORMATIONS", combining the properties, of both the quartz crystal and the structure, totally within the nephrite. The crystals within the nephrite were used in Lemurian healing ceremonies and retain the records of both the knowledge of use and the methods of facilitation leading to results.

This unification of nephrite and quartz will be made available to those who are to work with these advanced energies.

This combination is a catalyst to the acceleration of growth and to the re-awakening and remembering of those with whom one has been closely connected in "previous" lives. It helps one to transcend the third dimension, and to resonate in harmony with the self and with others. It assists one in uniting with the brothers and sisters of this dimension, with those from the realms of the spiritual and astral spaces, and with those from the stars; during these activities, the supreme energies are synthesized to produce the dazzling golden/white radiance of the enlightened state and the shared essence of the heart of the life force.

It further assists one in acknowledging the self as an integral part of the perfection of "All That Is", providing for the empowerment to foster progress toward fulfillment, in love and clarity, of ones final destinies.

The quartz crystals within the nephrite can be likened to arrows of light, assisting one to progress on the path toward the enlightenment of the entire planetary body. The energy of the structure acts as a well-traveled guide, providing mythical arms to encompass all knowledge leading to wisdom. It further marks the end of separation and denial and has been used (being held) to assist one in determining the "where", "when", and "how" one was connected with another in past lives.

It has been used to remove unwanted implants, concurrently healing breaches within the chakra system and filling the voids which remain after the removal of the implant, with the healing light of love.

The quartz/nephrite structure is considered a "stone of the seventh mansion", expediting meditative travel to the realm of "all knowing". It shows one the pathway to higher bliss, providing access to heightened energies which can be used to propel the self into the higher dimensional awareness; this plane of awareness yielding a limitless zone of silence containing greater peace and unity than one has ever known.

The ancient cultures of Indians and tribal natives are said to have used the energies of this structure in shamanic ceremonies to remove the cause of dis-ease.

The quartz/nephrite structure vibrates to the number 9.

NEPTUNITE   [Astrological Sign of Pisces]

Neptunite crystallizes in the form of prismatic crystals exhibiting square cross-sections. The colour is black, exhibiting a red-brown appearance due to internal reflections. It may also, occasionally, demonstrate pleochroistic qualities, the colours ranging from yellow to deep red through the XYZ axes.

This mineral produces a synthesis of personal power and vitality - a dynamic combination for attacking problems, enacting solutions, and attaining the goal. It provides for courage and firmness in "trying" circumstances, and promotes prompt remedial action to situations. It assists one in suspending all judgments of oneself and of others, furthering ones ability to embrace human-ness and to love all.

It is quite helpful in the home to provide stability in structure, to protect against and to help to eliminate infestations, and to provide a sheltered and pleasant environment.

Neptunite can be used to ease the pain of toothache and can help to dispel decay. It can also be used to enhance the quality of the extremities, being good to support body-building activities and to diminish both weakness and atrophy of the muscular structure.

Vibrates to the number 7.

NICCOLITE   [Astrological Sign of Virgo]

Niccolite crystallizes in the form of masses, columns, dendritic structures, and, rarely, crystals. The colour is a metallic copper-red.

This mineral can be used to open and to energize the base, navel, and solar plexus chakras, providing both personal power and creativity to the intellect and promoting intuition in matters of relationships.

It can be used to smooth sexuality, allowing for intellectual and emotional control while facilitating a higher basis for, and more stability and permanence within, sexual relationships.

Niccolite enhances family relationships, providing for an affinity between blood relatives.

It stimulates the actualization of the qualities of tact, refinement, accuracy, and precision. It promotes unselfish motives and actions, and provides for quickness in acts of reconciliation.

It can further higher achievement and accomplishment in sports and in service-oriented activities.

This mineral can also be used to stimulate the appetite, to improve the condition of night-blindness, to assist in the treatment of cataracts and glaucoma, to enhance fertility, and to resolve disorders associated with the reproductive system. It can also be used to treat delicate emotional and physical conditions.

Do not prepare an elixir of this mineral by the normal method.

Vibrates to the number 9.

NISSONITE   [Astrological Sign of Cancer]

Nissonite crystallizes in the form of crusts, tabular crystals, and diamond-shaped crystals. The colour is blue-green.

This mineral can be used to clear and to activate the heart and throat chakras. It enhances ones ability to analyze and to understand the relationship between the parts of a situation or problem and to, subsequently, relate the parts to the entirety.

It further assists one in precise and succinct understanding and verbalization of that which would normally be difficult to comprehend or express.

Nissonite also helps to awaken one to the related-ness of all things, bringing awareness of ones place in the social, intellectual, and physical structures of the Earth. It can help in the elimination of restlessness and emotional imbalances. It can provide an inner peace via the sublimation of pain, worry, and the cares of the external world.

This mineral can also assist in the completion of paperwork, in decision-making, and in the favorable rectification of matters of violations; it also supports ones involvement in the structure of the judicial system and the law.

Nissonite can be used in the treatment of alcoholism, eating disorders, nutritional imbalances, and instability of the pulse. It can also help to stimulate the balance of milk production in nursing mothers.

Vibrates to the number 7.

NORBERGITE   [Astrological Sign of Aquarius]

Norbergite crystallizes, usually, as grains. The colour range includes white, yellow, red, and orange-yellow to brown.

This mineral increases the areas of contact for chakras during the "laying-on-of-stones", hence, allowing for the supplementation of the energies which are normally available. Placement, in this case, would be in suspension in the space above the subject, at the area of the navel; two stones can also be utilized via placing one stone approximately six inches from the crown chakra and the other stone approximately six inches from the feet.

It can be used dispel irritation and uneasiness, helping one to accept and to rejoice in life and to understand that all actions and circumstances are instruments in the fulfillment of ones personal destiny.

Norbergite can be used in the treatment of spinal disorders, numbness, and cellular rejuvenation and re-alignment, and to both protect the enamel of the teeth and discourage pitting.

Vibrates to the number 5.

NORDENSKIOLDINE   [Astrological Signs of Libra, Pisces, & Gemini]

Nordenskioldine crystallizes in the form of thin or thick tabular crystals and in the configuration of lens-like crystals. The colour range includes yellow and colourless.

This mineral stimulates reaching meditative states via the utilization of "gibberish", a technique recognized by Osho, an enlightened eastern Master. It enhances the verbalization of senseless language, allowing for thoughts to disappear and for emptiness to both remain and maintain within the mind.

It can also be used to enable one to "take things at their face value" while providing assistance for intuitive evaluation. This allows for a superficial meaning to be coupled with intuitive thinking, resulting in the recognition of the reality of a situation.

Nordenskioldine helps to dispel the mirage, allowing for passage through the dimensional doorway to ones inner landscape of brilliance; in this beauty, the silence of timely existence can be recognized and understood.

This mineral has been used to lower the histamine levels in the body and to alleviate headaches; it can also be used in the treatment of schizophrenia, liver spots, and osteoporosis.

Vibrates to the number 6.

NORTHUPITE [Astrological Signs of Pisces, Aquarius, & Capricorn]

Northupite crystallizes in the form of octahedral crystals. The colour range includes yellow, white, colourless, and grey-to-brown.

This mineral can stimulate travel [physical plane] and adventures. It can facilitate a connective force between those of the stars and those of this plane, bringing intellectual information which both supplements and relates to that which is already a part of ones intelligence; this stone does not provide for the transmission of random information or information with respect to questions one has not recognized.

Northupite is also used in ceremonies related to the four directional energy forces. In medicine wheel ceremonies, is usually placed at the location of magnetic north. In healing ceremonies, where the directional aspects are utilized and when the intent is to bring in additional forces from the universe, the stone is placed at the head.

It is used to remind one of the existing connection with the "One" of which we are all a part. It further stimulates insight, allowing one to utilize each event which occurs in ones reality, to access, to awaken, and to vitalize ones inner potentials. It assists one in attuning to the resonance of each day, instilling harmony and inner peace within the self.

This mineral can be used in the treatment of narcotic dependency, bacterial infections, colds, instability [physical], and learning disabilities.

Vibrates to the number 2.

NUUMMIT [Astrological Sign of Sagittarius]

Nuummit, the oldest living mineral, was formed over three billion years ago. It crystallizes in the form of laminates. The polished form is black and nearly opaque. The large specimens usually exhibit one colour in the middle and one colour around the middle; however, occasionally, several colours are represented in the configuration of a spectrum. The iridescent spectral colour range includes gold, copper, purple, mauve, silver, green, green-blue, and blue.

This mineral can be used to open, to activate, and to integrate the chakras. It provides for grounding, via the chakras, to both the Earth and the ethereal body. It aligns all of the subtle bodies and both balances and aligns the chakras. It is useful for removal of energy blockages. It is an excellent energy source, exhibiting an electro-magnetic energy field, and providing for the transfer of energy from the etheric body to the physical. It can be used to fill the voids and to remove the "muddy" areas in the auric field; it has also been used to both fill and heal the openings which remain after the removal of undesired implanted thought forms originating in other worlds.

It provides for a circular energy connecting the crown and the base chakras; it further provides for a spiral of energy which provides for the continuity between the chakras of this plane and the purity of the ethereal body.

It has been used to teach one that the bonds and constraints placed upon a person are self-imposed and easily discarded. It helps one to decide, with the heart, that which is really important and to plan for, and to initiate, the release of any binding ideas.

This mineral possesses a defending quality and is an excellent preventive which will shield one from many forms of negative energy. Simply having a piece of nuummit on ones person brings in this protective, shielding aspect of the stone which works on the physical, etheric, and emotional levels.

It can also help to protect against the negative vibrations of pollutants, at the physical level, via the creation of an energy field which it builds within the aura.

It assists one in seeing behind facades, promoting the understanding of that which lies beneath words and actions.

It also stimulates the powers of the intellect, enhancing memory and promoting recall of relevant information when required. It further promotes the synthesis of intellectual thought and intuitive, mystical, and psychic wisdom. It facilitates the transformation of intuition into intellectual thought such that one can implement the instructions provided; it also assists one in the verbalization of those thoughts.

It assists one to traverse changes, attracting strength and perseverance.

It can be used to encourage flashes of intuition and insight. The iridescent quality induces a gentle vitality to ones pursuits in the spiritual realm and assists in the alignment between the spiritual self and the psychic and astral planes. It has also been used by the wise ones of ancient civilizations to invoke visions and to provide insight into the answers required to facilitate healing on all levels.

Nuummit can be used in general healing and in tissue regeneration. It has been used to relieve pain and discomfort associated with headaches and degenerative dis-ease. It can be used to disperse infections, to purify the blood and the kidneys, and to regulate insulin production. It can also be used in the treatment of disorders of the throat, the vision, and the eyes; it has been used to clarify and to strengthen the eyesight and the speech. It is an excellent stone for the stimulation of the triple-burner meridians as defined by acupressure/acupuncture specialists. It can also be used to stimulate circulation, to assist in the recovery from Parkinson's dis-ease, to treat disorders of the central nervous system, to treat disorders of the brain, to stimulate mental acuity, and to reduce anxiety and stress.

Vibrates to the number 3.

BE KIND TO YOURSELF

OBSIDIAN   [Astrological Sign of Sagittarius - Elemental]

Obsidian is lustrous volcanic glass. The colour range and related names are varied.

The intrinsic properties of the numerous forms of obsidian include the reflection of ones flaws and the promotion of a clear picture of the changes which are necessary to eliminate the flaws. The energies of obsidian produce very blunt answers, focusing ones inner vision and, actually, stimulating a picture or vision of the required course of action.

Obsidian is an excellent grounding stone and provides for a connection from the base of the spine to the heart of the Earth. It is an excellent protective stone, stabilizing internal and external energies and gently protecting one from that which could bring physical and/or emotional harm.

It provides a shield against negativity, transforming negative vibrations within an environment. Carrying/wearing obsidian further disperses those unloving thoughts which arise from within the self or are directed toward ones physical form.

It is quite useful in healing, providing both the healer and subject with clarity with respect to both the cause and the amelioration of the dis-ease.

The following types of obsidian are listed to reflect the inclusion of additional properties.

Vibrates to the number 1.

Apache Tear   [Astrological Sign of Aries]

The apache tear, a variety of obsidian, is volcanic glass and is usually found in a vitreous form of black, black/clear, black/smokey/clear, black/mahogany, and, occasionally black/violet or black/green. The shape is somewhat spherical with conchoidal markings. The following properties are in addition to those listed in the OBSIDIAN section of this book.

The apache tear has been traditionally considered to be one of the tears of Native American women, mourning for the warriors driven from a cliff by the cavalry.

It has been used to comfort in times of grief; it, metaphorically, "sheds" the tears for one in times of sorrow, allowing for true understanding of the situation of distress in order to provide insight and acceptance. It allows ones comfort zone to "remain at large".

It provides an energy to stimulate analytical capabilities and precision. It also promotes a forgiving attitude and a release of grievances which have been held against another. The apache tear stimulates spontaneity and facilitates the removal of barriers which are self-limiting.

It is said to expel the venom of snakebite. It can be used to enhance the assimilation of Vitamins C and D, to aid in the elimination of toxins from the body, and to alleviate muscle spasms.

Vibrates to the number 6.

Black, Grey, Brown Obsidian   [Astrological Sign of Sagittarius]

Black, grey, or brown obsidian is, additionally, used for "gazing" and to produce sincerity in action, and insight into future scenes and symptoms.

This obsidian is also used in shamanic ceremonies to aid in the removal of the disorder from the body; one travels with the obsidian to the affected area of the body and visually brings the affectation to the surface, surrounding and transmuting it into white light.

Black obsidian, inducing creativity in all endeavors, vibrates to the number 3; grey obsidian, inducing tact and cooperation in all situations, vibrates to the number 2; and, brown obsidian, stimulating initiative and independent thought and action, vibrates to the number 1.

Blue Obsidian   [Astrological Sign of Aquarius]

Blue Obsidian is also used for stimulation of the throat chakra, to enhance ones communication skills, and to assist one in oration, in articulation, and in the comprehension and pronunciation of new languages.

It has been used in telepathic endeavors to maintain connection with an object. It has also been used to increase knowledge and understanding during the utilization of Tarot Cards, "gazing", and other fortune-telling attendants.

It is an excellent mineral for astral travel, affording purpose and direction during same. It has also been used for protection and for directional knowledge during physical travel.

It can be used in the treatment of disorders of the eyes, to assist in speech therapy, to ameliorate and to alleviate pain, and to bring mental clarity during disorders associated with Alzheimer's dis-ease, schizophrenia, and multiple-personality confusion.

Vibrates to the number 5.

Blue/Green Obsidian   [Astrological Sign of Scorpio]

Blue/Green Obsidian combines the qualities of the Blue Obsidian and the Green Obsidian and further promotes stimulation of the heart and throat chakras concurrently to enable one to speak from the heart and to understand communication with the heart.

It has also been used to assist in energy transfer during Reiki healing, to increase spiritual awareness via the creation of balance between the mind, body, and spirit, and to assist one in gentle communication with others.

In addition, it has been used to assist in the assimilation of Vitamins A and E, to ameliorate skin disorders, and to enhance night-vision.

Vibrates to the number 9.

Electric-Blue Sheen Obsidian   [Astrological Sign of Sagittarius]

Electric-blue sheen obsidian a black obsidian which contains a radiance of electric-blue, ranging from a powder blue [sometimes with a powder pink] to a deep indigo blue. It is an excellent stone for "gazing" and for "journeying". It has also been applied extensively in many of the lay-outs which have been reported within the text of this guidebook.

Used alone, it further assists one in accessing the bases of any difficulties which one is experiencing. It emits an energy conducive to balance the energy fields [personal and those with which one experiences contact] and to assist in the suspension of actions which are ineffectual and/or unavailing.

In "gazing" activities it has been applied to the shamanic and the healing arts, providing for the recognition of the areas within the emotional, physical, and/or intellectual bodies which are creating dysfunctional events/conditions. It further acts to cleanse the mind of contrary and dissenting thoughts of the self and of others, assisting in the promotion of patience and tolerance.

"Electric-blue", configured into spherical formations has served to enhance the activities of "gazing" and "journeying"; the energy transfer, being simultaneously in all directions, has easily facilitated the trance state, and has enhanced all activities associated with psychic communication, astral travel, future-telling, and past-life ascension. It has also promoted a direct access to communication with those of other planetary realms, providing for a direct link to those which whom one *needs* contact.

It is an excellent third-eye stone, stimulating visionary experiences and providing for the activation and energizing of the third-eye chakra. It assists one in traveling deeply within the inner being and in maintaining the depth while integrating the myriad of visual images which are made available. It assists the energy from the third-eye to be transported throughout the body, producing an intuitive understanding of the complete cellular structure.

"Electric-blue" stimulates intuition and enhances awareness. It provides for freedom in accessing pre-determined sites during astral travel and assists one in both lucid dreaming and dream recall. It is an excellent grounding stone [when consciously applied to that purpose]. It has also been applied to the amplification of the auric field, and, via testing with Kirlian photography, has been shown to increase the range and to both intensify and brighten the energies.

It can be used in the application of radionic techniques, enhancing the attunement of the radionics operator and the subject, and enabling the user to more easily recognize the response.

Used as a pendulum, during diagnostic research, the energy of the mineral acts to interfere with the energy of the user and indicates the areas which are involved, as well as, the problems which are implicated [the recognition of the problems is usually expedient].

At this time, spherical configurations have been used primarily in all applications; the smaller pieces of the mineral, when fashioned for the third-eye and additional chakra locations, also work quite well. Jewelry has also been created which includes the "Electric Blue" - wearing the mineral assists one in maintaining a protective field which not only shields one from negativity, but also transforms any negativity to either a positive "thing" or to that which is both meaningless and harmless.

The mineral is of immense benefit in furthering the receptivity of the subject during healing exercises.

It has been used in the treatment of disorders of spinal alignment and to ameliorate the arrangement of impaired vertebrae. It has been used in the treatment of circulatory disorders, to disseminate and disperse growths, to ameliorate toxicity, to enhance and strengthen the structure of the veins, and to allay spasmatic conditions.

It can also be used to improve the eyesight; an elixir, taken internally, is recommended for this application. "Electric-blue" is currently being applied to deficient immune systems and dysfunctional cellular structures. Additional applications are currently in the experimental stages.

Vibrates to the number 7.

Gold Sheen Obsidian   [Astrological Sign of Sagittarius]

Gold sheen obsidian is also used for "gazing" and acts to provide information concerning the "root" of the problem or situation. The energy seems to pierce the outer layers of a problem, allowing for the heart of the problem to become evident.

This mineral also assists in producing a definition of the bases for ones path of action. It is an excellent vehicle for "gazing", usually used by those advanced in the shamanic and healing arts.

Gold sheen obsidian allows one to attain communion with the source of all being. It emits an energy to prompt one to allow beauty to come forth from the inner being as one travels in and through the world of experiences accessed via the sheen.

The energy can further be used to balance the energy fields and to assist one in the elimination of ego conflicts and feelings of futility.

Gold sheen obsidian also reflects that which is needed in ones life; it does not give that which is needed but, instead, provides insight to the avenues available which could bring fruition to those needs.

Vibrates to the number 9.

Green Obsidian   [Astrological Sign of Gemini]

Green obsidian stimulates the heart chakra and provides for cleansing of the area, removing not only extraneous matter and "muddiness", but also gently removing the "hook-up" cords of others. The relief from the removal of these cords can provide for an openness and state of well-being that is likened to euphoria. It also protects the holder from future "hook-ups" and re-directs the cords to an endless vessel filled with white light.

It can be used in the treatment of disorders associated with the heart and gall bladder.

Vibrates to the number 5.

Mahogany Obsidian [Astrological Sign of Libra]

Mahogany obsidian occurs as a combination of the colours red-brown and black.

It can be used to stimulate growth of the physical, emotional, intellectual, and spiritual centers, and to provide strength in times of need. It further provides vitality to ones lifework and/or to the fulfillment of ones aspirations. It can also be used in the elimination of energy blockages and to assist in the relief of tension.

Vibrates to the number 4.

Purple Obsidian [Astrological Sign of Virgo]

Deep purple obsidian, additionally, enhances the growth of the spiritual self and provides for spiritual awareness during participation in the activities which occur on the Earth plane. It is sometimes found as a sheen occurring with the black obsidian. It stimulates clairvoyance and encourages introspection. It provides for a connectedness between the intellect and the intuition, allowing for adequacy in communication of that which is experienced. It opens and activates the crown chakra while providing for grounding via the innate connection to the center of the Earth, thus producing a euphoric energy during the meditative state.

Vibrates to the number 8.

Purple Sheen Obsidian [Astrological Sign of Sagittarius]

Purple sheen obsidian is also used for "gazing" and acts to provide information concerning the "root" of the problem or situation. The energy seems to pierce the outer layers of a problem, allowing for the heart of the problem to become evident.

This mineral also assists in producing a definition of the bases for ones path of action. It is an excellent vehicles for "gazing", usually used by those advanced in the shamanic and healing arts. Purple sheen obsidian assists in bringing one toward the enlightened state and to assist one in seeing beyond the immediate reality. It tends to fill ones mind with clarity and brings the mechanisms of psychic ability to initiation and actualization.

This mineral has been used to stimulate clarity for mental accomplishments and to assist in removal of apprehension and confusion. It has been used in the treatment of Alzheimer dis-ease and to reduce the stress related to daily living.

Vibrates to the number 5.

Rainbow Obsidian   [Astrological Sign of Libra]

Rainbow obsidian bring light and love to ones life, allowing for the recognition of the spiritual side of ones nature. It is also used for "gazing", especially in the areas of love matters, relationships, and total development of ones etheric and physical forms.

It is a "stone of pleasure", bringing gratification and enjoyment to ones life.

Vibrates to the number 2.

Red Obsidian   [Astrological Sign of Leo]

Red obsidian also stimulates physical energy and provides for a balancing of the male/female energies. It further enhances the stability in ones physical attributes and brings validity to ones being. It provides for an endowment of the richness of change, seeking to attract gentleness and to awaken dormant qualities.

It can be used in the treatment of disorders of the blood and spleen.

Vibrates to the master number 55.

Red and Black Obsidian   [Astrological Signs of Leo & Sagittarius]

The combination of the colours red and black in this form of obsidian stirs the flame of the spirit to initiate the rise of the Kundalini.

It also provides for vitality and virility and brings a connected-ness to the "brotherhood" of humanity, eliminating the need to perceive oneself as an individual and/or as an unique unit of consciousness. This further allows for both the expansion of ones identity and the creation of the "life you would love to live".

It can also be used in the treatment of fever and chills.

Vibrates to the number 3.

Red, Black, and Snowflake Obsidian   [Astrological Sign of Sagittarius]

Red, Black, and Snowflake Obsidian combines the qualities of the Red Obsidian, the Black Obsidian, and the Snowflake Obsidian, and further acts to bring automatic grounding during meditation, to open the crown chakra, to stabilize the movement of the Kundalini, and to enhance ones energy fields.

It produces a softness to ones activities and to ones communication to the self and to others.

It has also been used in the treatment of disorders of the skin, the blood, and the ears. It further has been used to ameliorate inflexibility of bones.

Vibrates to the number 1.

Silver Sheen Obsidian   [Astrological Sign of Sagittarius]

Silver sheen obsidian is also used for "gazing" and acts to provide information concerning the "root" of the problem or situation. The energy seems to pierce the outer layers of a problem, allowing for the heart of the problem to become evident.

This mineral also assists in producing a definition of the bases for ones path of action. It is an excellent vehicles for "gazing", usually used by those advanced in the shamanic and healing arts.

Silver sheen obsidian assists in bringing one "the advantage" throughout life. It can also be used as a mirror to the soul, one to stimulate seeing the self as others see you. That which is seen is not always complimentary, but can always be utilized, by the aware individual, to guide one to further refinement and progression of ones personal actualization. It enhances patience and perseverance in the tasks chosen and allows one to understand the underlying reasons for the tasks. Silver sheen obsidian also produces a very strong connection between the physical and astral bodies, assuring that one may always "come home".

Vibrates to the number 2.

Snowflake Obsidian   [Astrological Sign of Virgo]

Snowflake obsidian is a black obsidian with inclusions of a white mineral [phenocryst], whose structure within the obsidian, when polished, resembles a snowflake.

It allows one to recognize the unnecessary patterns which remain in ones life and to re-design ones thought patterns to provide relief from undesired conditions.

It assists one in actualizing the serenity of the isolated state, when isolation is manifested, stimulating the surrender to the totality of the meditative state and further promoting a sensitivity to the most vital powers in the universe - love and beauty.

It is a "stone of purity", bringing both purity and balance to the body, mind, and spirit. It can be used in the treatment of disorders of the veins and the skeletal structure. It can also be used to smooth the skin [an elixir is recommended] and to clear the eyes.

Vibrates to the number 8.

OCHO   [Astrological Sign of All]

The Ocho is very small Geode - it exhibits the properties listed in the GEODE section of this book and demonstrates the additional properties listed below.

It can be used to assist one in victory - during gambling, recreational games, tournaments, and with respect to employment. The energy is conductive to freedom and innocence, bringing the "free spirit" attributes to ones action while providing for impeccability, forthrightness, and trustfulness to ones physical environment and contacts.

It has been used in the treatment of weight disorders, both anorexia and bulimia. It has also been used in the treatment of disorders associated with acceptance of the lesser states, and to assist on to understand that concepts of superiority and inferiority exist only within ones mind.

Vibrates to the number 5.

OCTAHEDRITE   [See Anatase]

OLIGOCLASE   [Astrological Sign of Gemini - Elemental]

Oligoclase is a type of feldspar which crystallizes in the form of masses, veins, and crystals, sometimes clear and glassy. In addition to the properties listed in the FELDSPAR section of this book, the following attributes are applicable.

This mineral emits a sustaining energy, assisting one in maintaining a "hold" on situations or activities of which one is a part.

It assists one in learning to trust, helping one to cease in the definition of personal "territory". It further enhances ones effectiveness in both routine and non-routine activities.

It can be used in the treatment of fractures and disorders of the hands, and to dispel the internal anger which acts to block recovery.

Vibrates to the master number 44.

OKENITE   [Astrological Signs of Sagittarius & Virgo]

Okenite crystallizes in the form of blade-shaped crystals and fibrous interlaced masses resembling snowballs. Some of the very powerful okenite comes from India. The colour is white, sometimes with a hue of yellow or blue. It is the "warm, fuzzy" stone of the new age.

The energy of okenite provides a feeling of "going home".

It assists one in accepting the conscious manifestation of ones higher-self, bringing an end to inhibiting denials, while initiating a beginning to the actualization and manifestation of all aspects of self-forgiveness; hence, it initiates "painless" completion of <u>and</u> total healing via ones karmic cycle.

It acts to purify the chakras and the physical, intellectual, emotional, and spiritual bodies.

It also emits an energy which can both assist in the maintenance of truthfulness and can insulate one from the harshness of truthfulness; it further assists one in assimilating the basis for the perceived harshness, and promotes the correction of faulty patterns. It actually helps one to both gracefully and lovingly acknowledge the mental and verbal "jabs" of others.

This mineral can be used to stimulate the opening of oneself to the experience of channeling and to facilitate the channeling of information relative to ancient sacred writings. An elixir is quite helpful in this activity.

It produces a "halt" to obstacles in ones path, catching and dispersing the obstacles and clearing the way.

It promotes stamina and an open mind in all endeavors.

It provides one with inner approval and allows one to view and to understand the length of ones stay in the physical form, bringing to recognition those karmic debts and learning situations of which one has previously agreed to be a part; hence, producing an understanding of ones current circumstances, as well as those which will manifest due to ones past and future situations - this does not provide actual visions of the situations, but does provide information concerning the subjects which will be covered.

Okenite can also be used to decrease debilities associated with aging, to provide assistance in rectifying former ideas and ways, to help one to dispense with prudery, and to assist one in maintaining both calm and fastidious-ness on an un-compulsive level.

This mineral can be used to stimulate the flow of blood, to treat eruptions [internally and externally], to enhance the mammary glands, and to stimulate circulation in the arms. It has also been used to treat fevers and to alleviate "nervous stomach" disorders. An elixir is especially recommended for application in the cases of eruption.

Vibrates to the number 7.

OLIVINE   [See Peridot]

ONYX   [Astrological Sign of Leo]

Onyx is a type of chalcedony which occurs, usually, in the form of layers of a variety of colours. The predominant colours include black, black and white, red and white, orange-brown/honey and white, etc. It is often carved to produce cameos.

In addition to the properties listed in the CHALCEDONY section of this book, the following qualities are also applicable.

This mineral is an excellent stone for initiating the modes of centering and alignment of the total person with the higher powers. It can be used to banish grief, to enhance self-control, to stimulate the power of wise decision-making, and to encourage happiness and good fortune. It helps one to absorb, from the universe, those energies which are needed.

It can be used to cleanse the intuitive receivers such that one may feel the connection to the whole while continuing to be aware of the many opportunities available for use of intuitive guidance.

It also furthers the quality of sentience of the instincts, helping one to both see and feel the guidance.

Onyx can also help one to see the duality of ones nature and to synthesize the yin and yang into the whole. It can be used to provide glimpses of that which lies "beyond", while providing for activation of the memory with respect to ones "roots" and reality. It further helps one to follow the path alone, promoting the recognition of personal strengths and assisting one in the understanding of the reality of the moment. It helps one to become the master of ones own future.

It is said to have been one of the stones used in the breastplate of the high priest.

It has been used in the treatment of disorders related to bone marrow, to the soft tissue structures, and to the feet.

Vibrates to the number 6.

OPAL   [Elemental Astrological Signs of Cancer, Libra, Pisces & Scorpio]

Opal crystallizes in the form of masses, and, occasionally, stalactites. The colour range and related names are varied. The previous mystery of the cause of colour of opal has been revealed via the electron microscope. When precious opal is viewed through this microscope, it is seen as a uniform stacking and sizing of a great number of tiny spheres. These three dimensionally stacked spheres and the cavities between them, together, act as a diffraction grating which can divide light into the spectral colours, the diameter of the spheres within any grouping determining the resultant colour. Conversely, opal without colour (common opal or potch) contains spheres which are not of orderly size or stacking,

The intrinsic properties of the numerous forms of opal include the amplification of ones traits and characteristics, therefore, providing impetus to overcome the lesser attributes. It helps one to recognize and to feel the creativity which is within the self, providing inspiration and imagination to all situations.

It furthers clean, true, and spontaneous action, enhancing that which one is feeling and allowing for the release of inhibitions.

It can be used to strengthen the memory and to instill faithfulness and loyalty with respect to love, personal affiliations, and business relationships.

It has been used to assist one in becoming "invisible" in circumstances where one does not wish to be noticed. It brings one a quality of "fading-into-the-background" when the energy is so directed.

It is known as a "stone of happy dreams and changes"; the happy dreams arising from the understanding of personal higher potentials coupled with the glad acceptance of ones inherent perfection. The happy changes emanate from those events and situations which allow ones aspirations to surface.

This mineral has been used to awaken both the psychic and the mystical qualities. It helps one to understand the higher powers of intuition and mysticism and to utilize these powers to enhance personal understanding and personal experiences in the realms of the sacred and avantgarde aspects of being.

Opal which exhibits a spectral of colour [commonly called "fire"] contains tiny spheres of silica; it can also be used to encourage flashes of intuition and insight. The ancients believed that the storm god, jealous of the beauty of the rainbow god, broke the rainbow - pieces of the rainbow falling to the Earth to become a part of the opal which exhibits the appearance of the "rainbow-fire". The "fire" represents a glowing inner flame, producing a gentle vitality to stimulate ones pursuits in the spiritual realm, and assisting in the alignment between the spiritual self and the psychic and astral planes.

Opal has been used by the Native American Indian and the Australian aboriginal shamen to invoke visions; it has also been used during the Native American ceremony of the vision quest, and by the Australian aborigines during ceremonial "dreamtime".

It can be used to disperse infections, to purify the blood and the kidneys, and to regulate insulin production. It can also be used in the treatment of disorders of vision and the eyes, to alleviate fevers, and to stimulate circulatory functions. It can be used to clarify and to strengthen the eyesight, to assist in the recovery from Parkinson's dis-ease, and to provide comfort and ease during childbirth.

Vibrates to the number 8.

The following types of opal are listed to reflect the inclusion of additional properties.

Andean Opal   [Astrological Signs of Virgo and Aries]

Andean Opal contains a swirling of pink, black, beige, and sometime, blue colours. It has been used to activate the heart chakra while providing for centering and grounding.

It can be used for spiritual journeying to protect, to assist one in selection, and to bring an availability to the locations one wishes to visit. It has also been used to induce the hypnotic state and to facilitate divination. It further instills a knowledge of "right action" and dispels reaction.

Andean Opal has been used in the treatment of disorders associated with the heart, the lungs, and the thymus. It can also be used to ameliorate water retention, muscular swelling, and spinal dis-alignment.

Vibrates to the number 2.

Black Opal   [Astrological Signs of Scorpio & Sagittarius]

Black opal ranges in colour from black to grey and displays a spectral of colour. One of the most beautiful fiery black opal is found in Lightening Ridge, New South Wales, Australia. The majority of Black Opal is found in the form of seam and small silicious nodules which are generally less than 5 grams in weight. Lightning Ridge black opals are the rarest - their brilliance of colour makes them a true collectable for those seeking beauty and quality.

It is an excellent grounding stone which provides grounding and concurrently stimulates activity.

Black opal can be used for "gazing", providing insights into matters of the past, present, and future, and facilitating prescience and visions from the energy center of the third-eye.

The presence of the "fire", produced by the diffraction of light from the tiny quartz spheroids which are contained within the stone, is a catalyst for the inner knowing, inner seeing, and inner reconciliation of the information.

It can also be used in "reading eyes", providing insight to, and information concerning, the truthfulness and development of the person of concern.

It can be used for disorders related to reproduction, depression, and digestion. It can also be used in the treatment of dysfunctional eyesight.

Vibrates to the number 1.

Black Plume Opal   [Astrological Sign of Pisces]

Black Plume Opal is formed as a seam and in small silicious nodules. It contains tubular/orbicular configurations and plumes.

It is an excellent stone for Sufi Dancing, for stabilization of dizziness, and for the promotion of clairsentient ability. It brings clarity of intent and personal harmony during contemplative states and further assists one in physically seeing the aura.

It has been used to assist one in spiritual counseling, stress management, the furtherance of self-esteem, and in acceptance and non-judgemental action to facilitate grown and self-love.

It has also been used in the treatment of disorders associated with equilibrium, with weight-mastery, with degeneration of cellular structures (stimulating renewal), and with brain dis-ease.

Vibrates to the number 5.

Blue Opal   [Astrological Sign of Taurus]
                                             [Also Known as Girasol]

Blue opal ranges in colour from blue-white to deep blue. There is also a beautiful blue jelly-type opal that has recently been found in Canada.

It can be used to stimulate communication skills and to assist one in voicing thoughts and information which one has not been courageous enough to voice in the past. It provides one with both the freedom and courage to speak freely, and with the wisdom to recognize those with whom this free speech will be accepted.

It further stimulates creativity and ingenuity in "connecting" with another, providing for an inner knowledge of the methods and situations which would be most conducive to the alliance.

The blue jelly-type opal has been used to enhance ones visioning and to activate the third-eye. It seems to provide a clear reflection of that which is of concern and to bring the solutions to the concerns.

It can also be used to balance ones metabolism, to assist in the assimilation of iron, and to treat fatigue and hair loss.

Vibrates to the numbers 3 and 9.

Boulder Opal   [Astrological Sign of Scorpio]

Boulder opal is found in the colour brown, sometimes with "fire" and sometimes without "fire". It occurs within rounded or ellipsoidal-shaped boulders, like nodules or concretions which consist of silicious ironstone. Boulders vary considerably in size, averaging about 30 cm in the largest dimension. These boulders have been formed in the Earth via a slow chemical growth process, usually accompanied by an increase in the iron oxide content. This results in many boulders displaying some form of growth rings, similar to those developed in trees. Through geological time, after their formation, many of these boulders have partially dehydrated, resulting in irregular shrinkage cracks forming within the ironstone. In the rare favorable conditions, silica solutions enter and solidify within these cracks, and in some instances, this material becomes gem opal. The boulders are formed under geologically favorable conditions in stratigraphic sandstone/clay traps and appear erratically within levels, usually in sandstone beds and located just above the clay level. The boulder gem opal occurs with intense colour of reds, blues, greens, purple, and milky.

Many fine pieces of boulder opal do not have a full face of opal, but have bright gem material randomly intermixed with the ironstone. When professionally polished, the blending of the two materials provides an artistically attractive product with each stone having its own distinct individuality.

It provides a connection to the stars, facilitating communication between the Earth plane and the "star people" of this world and other worlds. It provides for a grounding action while enhancing the transfer of information.

It can also clear the "muddy" areas from ones aura, stimulating the healing of those areas which were not clear and assisting one in communication between the conscious and sub-conscious thought systems. This further enhances the properties of healing and initiates the healing state on all levels.

It assists in "sweeping the cobwebs" from ones mind, enhancing mental clarity, emotional security, physical well-being, and spiritual progression toward the perfect state.

Vibrates to the number 4 (without fire) and to the number 6 (with fire).

Boulder Matrix Fire Opal   [Astrological Sign of Virgo]

Boulder Matrix Opal is found in Queensland, Australia, and is configured with an opalized ironstone matrix with random intermixing of gem opal with the brown ironstone. It occurs in the formation of seams, nodules, and stalactites and stalagmites with the cross-section emanating the "electric light flashes" of the opal over the rings of a tree.

This matrix opal frequently displays the highest intensity of striking colour and fire, rarely matched by any other opal form. It is particularly adaptable to incorporation in fine jewelry.

Boulder Matrix Opal is one of purity and intensity. The intensity of the opal portion brings clarity to problematical situations and allows one to remain centered during times of decision-making and stress. It assists in calming the inner soul while facilitating the actualization of the end of dilemmas. The accessing of the bases of any difficulties which one is experiencing is expedited.

It has been found to bring mental and emotional balance, bestowing new energies to enable one to dismiss traditional issues and to both create and implement those ideals which are new to ones life. It allows one to be tempered by experiences, eliminating "stormy weather" in ones ventures, augmenting ones diplomacy, and favorably influencing end results. It is an excellent stone for progress, expansion, and development.

Boulder Matrix Opal assists one in communication between the conscious and sub-conscious thought systems, and has been used in the "Consciousness" configuration of "Gateless-Gate" to assist one in determining that which one **really** desires and in the alleviation of difficulties in ascertaining clarity and comprehensiveness of ones desires, aspirations, ambitions, and dreams. It further expedites the resolution of conflicting desires, aspirations, ambitions, and dreams.

It has also been used to provide a connection to the stars, facilitating communication between the Earth plane and the "star people" of this world and other worlds. It has been used to stimulate contact with other-worldly intelligence, enhancing the connection during the receipt of information, and providing for insight and knowledge concerning structures of creation. It tends to provide a grounding action while enhancing the transfer of information.

It is an excellent stone for clearing and brightening the aura, stimulating the healing of those areas which were unclear and assisting in the maintenance of the status.

It has been used to access ones spiritual guides and ones animal guides. It can be used in medicine-wheel ceremonies to stabilize energy, to bring contact with guides, and to instill permanence to continuity.

The energy is conducive to balancing and to strengthening the electrical connections between the self and others and between the self and the spiritual realm. It also acts to align the meridians of the body with the ethereal plane and with the state of perfection.

It further produces stability in ones life and, if utilized during changing conditions, acts to provide a clear and unobstructed path for advancement.

It has been used in homeopathic and naturopathic remedies to increase healing energy and to provide a directional force. It has also been used in the treatment of disorders associated with aging and fragility. It can be used to treat intestinal blockages, veinular impediments, and brain wave distortions.

Boulder Matrix Opal has also been used in the treatment of circulation disorders, to release blockages and to stimulate the flow of blood.

Vibrates to the number 1.

Cherry Opal   [Astrological Sign of Gemini]

Cherry Opal is a clear "jelly" type opal which occurs in colours ranging from orange-red to pink-red.

It has been used to stimulate, to activate, and to cleanse the base and sacral chakras, to assist one in centering, and to energize ones activities.

It promotes accuracy, effectivity, practicality, and stimulates clairsentience and clairvoyance.

This mineral can be used in the treatment of disorders associated with menopause, to clear headaches, to stimulate the pulse rate, and to alleviate discomfort associated with muscular tension. It has also been used in the treatment of colitis, constipation, prostate discomfort, and spinal disorders.

Vibrates to the number 4.

Common Opal   [Astrological Sign of Libra]
                                                   [Also Known as Potch]

Common opal occurs in the range of colour including white, white-to-green, green, grey, grey-to-black, purple, brown, and colourless. It contains no "fire".

It can increase ones ability to both earn and retain money, and stimulates ones sense of self-worth.

It has been used to balance the male/female energies within the body and to both align and balance the chakras. It produces an attunement with the ethereal realm, stimulating the proper flow of energy to the physical body and facilitating an alignment with the higher-self.

It further enhances working environments and business relationships.

Vibrates to the numbers 8 and 9.

Dendritic Opal   [Astrological Sign of Gemini]

Dendritic opal contains no "fire" and can be any form of opal. It occurs in a variety of colours. The dendritic formation is a branching figure or marking, resembling moss, a fern, or a tree.

It promotes growth, both spiritually and physically, and can be used to enhance ones organizational abilities.

It can facilitate the flow of blood throughout the body and acts to align the nervous system of the etheric body to the nervous system of the physical body. This variety of opal can be used in the treatment of the skeletal structure and in disorders of the veins and arteries.

Vibrates to the number 4.

Fire Opal (General)   [Astrological Signs of Pisces, Sagittarius, Leo,
                                                           Libra, & Cancer]

Fire opal is red to orange in colour, and contains the spectral of colour called "fire".

The energy is conducive to mystery, variety, progress, and change. It assists one in endeavors, to look within the self and to understand the forces for the esoteric, helping one to reflect upon the many facets of ones life and to understand the basis behind the changing tides of ones existence.

It can add a brilliance and clarity to the intuitive and reflective processes and can instill a sense of feeling for the kaleidoscopic mysteries of life.

It assists one in "maintaining" during stressful situations and provides an added energy to ameliorate feelings of "burn-out'. It brings one hope in the future and faith in the self.

It is an excellent stone for stimulation of the triple-burner meridian defined in acupressure/acupuncture techniques. It can also be used to stimulate circulation, to enhance the physical sight, to ameliorate emphysema, and to treat disorders of the central nervous system.

Vibrates to the number 9.

Golden Opal   [Astrological Signs of Leo & Libra]

Golden opal is red to orange in colour and does not contain "fire".

It has been used to assist one in defining and refining those attitudes and "beliefs" which are self-limiting.

It can be used to activate the crown chakra and to provide for the alignment of the chakras with the ethereal plane. It assists in the removal of negativity from the chakras and further stimulates the base, navel, and solar plexus energy centers.

It can be used to remove blockages within both the nervous system and the circulatory system. It can also be used in the dispersal of gallstones, kidney stones, calcium deposits, and other rigid and abnormal complex growths occurring in the body.

The energy is excellent for clearing-away infection and disorder at the onset of the symptom. It can also be used to provide insight to the attitudes which have caused these problems.

Dis-ease has been treated via elixirs and via holding the stone while transfixing the image of the stone to the area of the body which is in disorder.

Vibrates to the number 2.

Green Opal   [Astrological Signs of Sagittarius and Aries]

Green opal has been used to assist one in rational fasting, understanding of healthful dietary habits, and has assisted in cleansing the body internally to promote rejuvenation.

It can also be used to promote a relaxed state similar to meditation, to provide information for problem-solving during dream states and during day-dreaming, and to assist one in maintaining full awareness of surroundings while stimulating comprehension and proper positive action. The energy instills a knowledge that one is always in control of, and may command the outcome of, ones life.

It has been used in the treatment of colds, flus, fevers, and to strengthen the immune system. It can also be used to warm the body during wintry conditions.

Vibrates to the number 3.

Honduran Opal   [Astrological Sign of Sagittarius]

Honduran opal is configured as basalt with flecks of fire throughout the structure.

It exhibits properties of stability and provides for the stimulation of each of the chakras.

It does not cleanse the chakras, but enhances the energy flow to and from the centers.

It can be used in the treatment of brain disorders and to reduce the effects of pain.

Vibrates to the number 4.

Opalized Nature   [Astrological Sign of Leo]

Opalized nature consists of opalized shell, naturewood, limb casts, bog, etc. These formations sometimes exhibit "fire".

Opalized nature, in general, acts to assist one in progression toward ones destiny.

It further provides an impetus to actions which will advance one in the quest for the serenity which is inherent in all life.

Opalized shell possesses the additional property facilitating increased assimilation of Vitamins A, D, and E, calcium, and iodine.

Opalized bog provides properties to connect one to the Earth; allowing one to be part of the activities on the plane, while promoting the recognition of, and the energy to overcome and to conquer, the limitations of the physical form, the mental patterns, and the spiritual constructs.

Opalized limb casts and opalized wood exhibit properties which combine the qualities of opal with the respective qualities shown in the LIMB CAST and/or PETRIFIED WOOD sections of this book.

Vibrates to the number 5.

Pink Opal   [Astrological Signs of Virgo, Libra, & Sagittarius]

Pink opal ranges in colour from pink and white to lavender and cream. It occurs in streaked masses and does not exhibit "fire". It has been known as the "peppermint candy stone".

It is a "stone for renewal", renewing the sacred relationship between the self and "All That Is". It helps to guide one in the journey of life, promoting permanence in the connection between the conscious self and the inner " knowing".

It teaches love and non-violence, providing for nourishment in all aspects of development.

It assists in helping one to release old "patterns", to deepen insights into psychological issues, and to cleanse and to purify the mind and the heart-space.

Pink opal is also a "stone of spiritual awakening", bringing the creative aspects of the universe to the actualization of the holder. It is an excellent stone for activating the mechanisms of inner healing on the emotional, spiritual, intellectual, and physical levels. It assists one in the entry to and the maintenance of the meditative state, furthering conscious connection to those of other planes and existence.

It can be used in the treatment of disorders of the lungs, the spleen, the heart, and the connective tissues. It can be used as an elixir to calm and soothe the mind and body, and to treat diabetes and hypoglycemia. It is excellent for soothing the skin, when applied topically.

Vibrates to the number 6.

Red Opal   [Astrological Signs of Leo & Taurus]

Red Opal has been used to stimulate positive aggression, and to reduce hostility and offensive behavior - one need only to place the mineral within the environment of that which is hostile or offensive and the energy tends to be dissipated.

This mineral has also been used in body balancing, to create a balanced identification with both the left and right sides of the brain, to produce the ideal state of cooperation within the mind; this energy further serves to promote re-programming of the mind with positive thoughts, access to full response and action potential, and to reduce stress. This balancing creates the potential for unlimited actualization and assists one in creation of the positive results.

It has also been used in the treatment of disorders of the lungs, the stomach, and the liver.

Vibrates to the number 8.

White Opal   [Astrological Signs of Virgo & Libra]

White opal is coloured as a milky white mineral containing a spectral of colour.

It can be used to stimulate the crown chakra and to provide deep states of mental clarity. It further helps one to remain calm in the midst of chaos.

It can be used to enhance adeptness in business and to bring inspiration from worldly goods.

Vibrates to the number 8.

Water Opal   [Astrological Sign of Cancer]

Water opal is colourless and clear, exhibiting a spectral of colour suspended within the structure.

It can be used for "gazing" and to stimulate visions from within the realms of eternity.

Water opal helps to clarify and to assist one in understanding that which will continue to exist after the completion of ones "stay" in the physical body. It is an excellent stone for someone contemplating leaving ones body.

It can also be used in the treatment of disorders related to birth, water retention, and stress reduction.

Vibrates to the number 3.

ORPIMENT   [Astrological Sign of Capricorn]

Orpiment crystallizes in the form of small crystals, foliated and columnar masses, and reniform surfaces. The colour is a lemon-yellow of several shades.

This mineral can be used to stimulate the intellect, to cleanse and to activate the solar plexus chakra, and to assist one in reasoning capabilities.

It has been used to bring growth to that which is impaired, assisting in the recognition of that which is conceivable, and promoting action.

The energy can elevate the studious nature, and is excellent for those studying for examinations and for those investigating any course of action; analysis is a key factor of this energy.

It has been used in the treatment of blockage of the canal of the ear, to disperse growths, and to facilitate the removal of unwanted cholesterol.

Due to the softness of Orpiment, the preparation of an elixir via the normal method is not recommended.

Vibrates to the number 2.

ORTHOCLASE   [Astrological Sign of Cancer - Elemental]

Orthoclase is a form of feldspar which crystallizes in the form of masses, plate-like layers, short prismatic crystals, and thin tabular crystals. The colour range includes white, colourless, grey, yellow, pink, and green. The minerals MOONSTONE and ADULARIA are forms of orthoclase and exhibit the distinct properties shown in the appropriate sections in this book, as well as those listed below.

In addition to the properties listed in the FELDSPAR section of this book, the following attributes apply.

This mineral can help one to overcome tragedy, and can provide assistance in the alignment of the chakras, the subtle bodies, and the meridians of the physical body.

It emits an energy of liveliness and pleasantness, stimulating tact, finesse, poise, and refinement.

It is a "stone of cooperative effort", dispelling the aspects of dissension and opposition which occur in ones life. It alleviates fluctuation between states, purposes, and opinions; allowing for insight into each situation.

It is also helpful in providing remedial action for behavioral disorders.

It provides for contact with the ancient builders of Egypt and can be used to initiate insight into the ancient methods and associated wisdom.

The plate-like crystalline form can also be used to stimulate the higher psychic abilities, and to encourage ones faith in the personal intuitive capabilities.

It has been used in the alignment of the spinal structure and the teeth. It can be used in the treatment of tuberculosis and other disorders of the lungs which involve the movement of breath. The plate-like crystals can also be used in the treatment of the eyesight.

Vibrates to the master number 44.

OSUMILITE   [Astrological Sign of Capricorn]

Osumilite crystallizes in the formation of hexagons. The colour range includes black, blue, brown, grey, and pink. It is usually found with a grey porous or metamorphic matrix.

This mineral can be used to stimulate ones personal healing energy and to assist one in sensing the quality and the flow of energy fields. It further serves to help one to release interpersonal problems which have arisen from blockages in conflicts within ones energy fields; subsequently, restoring harmony and balance within the energy realm.

It has been used to assist one in psychic readings, contact with other spiritual realms, and in the manifestation of energy to counteract undesired encounters.

It can be used to smooth ones aura, to cleanse ones environment, and to neutralize negativity.

Osumilite has been used in the treatment of imbalances of testosterone, and to ameliorate diabetes, retinal detachment, and to alleviate the need for kidney dialysis.

Vibrates to the number 6.

OVERITE   [Astrological Sign of Virgo]

Overite crystallizes in the form of plate-like layers and plate-aggregates. The colour ranges from light green to colourless.

This mineral can stimulate independence in ones character and can further the courage to "carry-through".

Overite inspires the placement of love above all else. It brings the entity of love to the body and fills the body with its light; continuing to emit the rays of love, one can transfer this overflow to those in contact zones. It helps one to understand that we share powers and passions with the universe; it is a lovely way to enhance peace on the planet.

It has been used in the treatment of weight problems, anorexia, bulimia, obesity, and infertility in females. It has also been used as an elixir, applied topically, to treat scales and roughness of the skin.

Vibrates to the number 4.

OWYHEEITE[Astrological Sign of Sagittarius]

Owyheeite crystallizes in the form of masses and needle-like crystals. The colour range includes steel-grey to silver-white. It exhibits a metallic luster which tarnishes to yellow.

This mineral stimulates wisdom. It brings the powers of the mind to bear on the development of the soul.

It can also be used to encourage the payment of debts, and, when in the possession of the debtor, can inhibit actions which would culminate in further indebtedness.

This is an excellent stone for dispelling the need of compulsive shopping.

It can assist in bringing oxygen to the blood and in eliminating the "free-radical oxides" which are lurking within ones body. It has been used to provide protection from ozone impurities and from radiation.

Vibrates to the number 7.

PLEASE THYSELF

PACHNOLITE [Astrological Sign of Gemini]

Pachnolite crystallizes in the form of colourless orthorhombic-type crystals.

This mineral can be used to alleviate ones sensitivity to criticism, allowing one to evaluate oneself and to correct the traits which are uncomfortable. It wraps the body in a protective covering, providing for protection from physical harm from the outside world and encouraging one to open to the internal reality.

Pachnolite can be used to "unlock the door" to self-discovery and to assist one in the assimilation of the new ideas which are evidenced. It allows one to progress step-by-step toward a goal, methodically proceeding to achieve the altered state.

It can be used in the treatment of disorders of the fingers, kidneys, lungs, eyes, and ears, and to ameliorate the loss of smell.

Vibrates to the number 4.

PALERMOITE [Astrological Sign of Virgo]

Palermoite crystallizes in the form of white or colourless vertically striated prismatic crystals.

This mineral can provide for a "tuning-in" to those of the pre-historic civilizations of the Earth, mainly with those whom have been pondered historically; it can provide for a fusing of minds, such that the user may immediately relate the experiences of the other. A recording device is quite necessary during these states. The information is presented similarly to a drama, and the information can be used for compilation of an historical novel.

It can stimulate the ability for palmistry and can increase ones ability to utilize the third-eye.

Palermoite can enhance the purity of ones skin and can affect a glowing image, radiant in itself. It purifies the ethereal body and enhances ones youthfulness.

It can also be used in the treatment of allergies, parasitic infections, and inflammation.

Vibrates to the number 6.

PALLADIUM

Palladium is a silver-white metallic element of the platinum group occurring, usually, in the form of irregular grains.

This mineral can be used extensively in healing and in the facilitation of total wellness.

It furthers ones affinity with the outer ethers, providing for a joining of efforts or interests between the self and the infinite energies available. Continual use of palladium provides for a permanent synthesis of energies, bringing an essential oneness to the awareness and the actualization of individual creativity.

The energy contained within palladium has been derived from the distant ancestral form of wisdom; it, therefore, tends to as a catalyst for all "light-based" activities.

It furthers the initiation of, and the continuity in, astral travel and channeling, strengthening the attachment and allowing for consciousness during these activities. It also promotes ease in withdrawal from these states.

It assists one to cease and desist in those activities which are remaining from outdated conditioning, providing impetus to advancement in the transformation of ones life into the vision of the new and conscious humanity. It further assists in providing augmentation to the social skills necessary for both interaction and associations which supplement ones growth.

Palladium represents Athena, the goddess of wisdom, the arts, enterprise, and prudent disputes. It provides the energies to further pursuits in these areas and to inspire triumph.

It was said to have been used as one of the materials comprising a statue which ensured the safety of Troy, providing for protection from dis-ease and assisting in the retrieval of hidden knowledge.

It has also been used to serve as a vehicle for the entry into the realm of ancient knowledge and sacred wisdom, providing for access to, and furthering the "translation" capabilities applicable to, the sacred Buddhist texts.

This mineral has been used to stimulate the electrical energy within the body to maintain the alignment between the physical and ethereal body, and to moderate emotional intensity in all situations.

It can also be used in the treatment of disorders of the lungs, the cerebral cortex, and the circulatory system. It can reduce the violence of dis-ease and can raise the vibratory level of the bodies to resonate with the higher energies of perfection.

Vibrates to the number 8.

PAPAGOITE   [Astrological Sign of Sagittarius]

Papagoite occurs in the form of thin veins, crusts, and as phantom and "snowball" inclusions in quartz crystals. The colour is a lovely clear sky blue.

This mineral emits a gentle and tranquilizing energy, useful for clearing and opening the throat chakra and the third-eye. It assists one in speaking with love and clarity, bringing smoothness to the verbalization of that which is in the mind.

It is a stone for unification, helping in the alignment of the chakras and in the synthesis of the physical, emotional, intellectual, spiritual, astral, and ethereal bodies. It can be used to bring precise and direct communication between the bodies and within all aspects of ones life.

Papagoite provides for an optimistic and broad-minded outlook, supplementing philosophical reasoning capabilities and ingenuity. It further assists one in the actualization of the generosity of giving oneself, totally and without constraint, to others. It can be used to facilitate the release of carefully restrained inhibitions, transforming these limitations to expressions of pleasure.

Used in meditation, it can assist one in the attainment of a state of extreme beauty and delight, providing for an awakening to the "paradise" within the inner reaches of the self. It often induces a state of euphoria when used as an elixir prior to entry into the meditative state.

It is also conducive to removing discordant notes of stress and interference from ones life, bringing one, via an adjustment of ones thought processes, to the understanding of that which is unusual.

Papagoite is also quite useful in strengthening the bonding of relationships; it instills a deep connected-ness between one and the family, the friends, and all of existence.

The combination of papagoite and quartz can also be used in the areas of thought projection and receipt; it assists one in projecting, through space, mental pictures for receipt by minds open to receive them and assists in "cleaning" the mind and erasing thoughts so that one may also receive thought-pictures projected by a distant consciousness. It is quite helpful in astral travel, providing for inner understanding, with respect to the methodology required, while sustaining the state and guiding one toward those areas desired. It also assists one in gaining access to the akashic records, enhancing ones understanding and subsequent communication of that which is written.

The papagoite/quartz formation often brings to one that which is both beneficial and desired, eliminating the restriction of that which is "needed". The use of the papagoite/quartz structure for manifestation is recommended only if one is willing to accept and rejoice in that which is "fancied".

Papagoite can be used in the treatment of disorders of the throat, the brain, the eyes, and the muscular structures. It can assist in relaxing the involuntary muscles of the gastro-intestinal tract and the other smooth muscles of the body. It is helpful in dispelling digestive disorders and pain, providing for a soothing energy [especially effective as an elixir].

Vibrates to the number 9.

PARACELSIAN   [Astrological Signs of Capricorn & Aries]

Paracelsian is a type of feldspar which crystallizes in the form of colourless large well-formed crystals of varied structure.

In addition to the properties listed in the FELDSPAR section of this book, the following attributes apply.

This mineral is helpful in the work of alchemy and, if not physically, can increase ones ability to transmute the lessor areas of ones life into the greater.

It stimulates constructive ideas and further grants one rationality in the attainment of personal goals.

It can be used to both stimulate and cleanse the crown chakra, producing the opening of an unobstructed pathway of energy through which the Kundalini movement is both initiated and encouraged.

It can benefit abilities in the fields of music and the science of physics. It also provides for access to information substantiating quantum physics.

This mineral can be used in the treatment of digestive disorders, to remove toxins from the body, as a cleansing agent for the blood and lungs, and for treatment of skin tumors. It has also been used to increase movement of the limbs and to treat conditions of paralysis.

Vibrates to the number 9.

PARISITE   [Astrological Sign of Scorpio]

Parasite crystallizes in the form of pyramidal and prismatic crystals and as druse. The crystals are horizontally grooved due to an oscillatory combination of faces. The colour range includes tan to brownish-yellow.

This mineral has been used to raise the brain wave frequency, to stimulate increased mental capacity and stamina, and to increase the amount of brain cells which are readily used.

It can also be used to assist one in the strength to voice ones opinion and to recognize and to take action with respect to those who attempt to exploit ones personal good will. The energy serves to stimulate the strength to encounter these negative situations and to rid one of the cause.

Parisite has been used to strength the electro-magnetic connection between the physical energy fields and the perfect ethereal energy fields, bringing well-ness and a calm, but powerful, sense of action.

It has been used in the treatment of carbon monoxide poisoning, to alleviate headaches, to reduce fat content of the cellular structure, and to induce sleep for the alleviation of insomnia.

Vibrates to the number 7.

PASCOITE   [Astrological Sign of Taurus]

Pascoite crystallizes in the form of grains and granular crusts. The colour range includes orange and orange-yellow.

This mineral helps one to "let-go" of previous circumstances and to progress toward the future.

Pascoite presents one with a "ticket" for entry to the realm of choice, providing for an unimpeded path during the journey. It helps one "through the door", but does not facilitate travel on the path, does not clearly mark the different paths, and makes "no guarantees". It is truly an adventure to accept "your ticket" and to "take your chances".

It further acts to increase the abilities of passion, to stimulate the creativity of sexuality, and to benefit ones pursuit of the intuitive knowledge which is accessible to all.

It can be used in the treatment of disorders of the alimentary canal, to mend the areas associated with the knee, and to stimulate motor capabilities.

Vibrates to the number 7.

PEACOCK ROCK [See Bornite]

PEARL [Astrological Signs of Cancer & Gemini]

The pearl is a product of the pearl oyster, both sea water and fresh water. The colour range includes white, black, grey, pinkish-white, yellow-white, bluish-grey, etc.

It signifies faith, charity, and innocence, enhances personal integrity, and helps to provide a focus to ones attention.

It also symbolizes purity and can stimulate that condition in ones body and mind; hence, providing a clear vehicle for the advancing states of wisdom, as well as a clean channel for receipt of spiritual guidance.

The pearl has been known as a "stone of sincerity", bringing truth to situations and loyalty to a "cause".

It has been used to inhibit boisterous behavior and to provide a reflection of the self such that one may see the manner in which one appears to others.

It has been used in the treatment of digestive disorders, and to relieve conditions of biliousness and bloating, to treat the soft organs of the body, and to increase fertility and ease childbirth.

Vibrates to the number 7.

PECOS DIAMOND   [Astrological Sign of Libra]

The pecos diamond is a form of rose-type quartz which is found in the Pecos River Valley, in Texas, USA. The formation occurs in single crystals, usually double terminated or with multiple terminations, and in aggregates or clusters of these crystals. These are not true "rose quartz crystals". The colour ranges from light to deep peach.

This mineral can be used to stimulate the interaction between creativity and intuition. It can also be used to enhance desire [and to subsequently channel it in the direction of personal growth], to stabilize emotions, and to increase sexuality [if consciously directed toward that motive].

It can also be used to cleanse, to energize, and to treat the organs located in the areas of the first, second, and third chakras, while providing for a balance between these chakras and the crown chakra.

This mineral is excellent for use when one is experiencing highly explosive changes; it assists one in the stabilization of the emotions and in the recognition and understanding of that which is needed in order to continue progress.

The pecos diamond is a pleasant stone for the "young-at-heart", bringing a joyful feeling, as well as a feeling of love.

Vibrates to the master number 55.

PECTOLITE   [Astrological Sign of Leo]
                    [Also Known As Larimar Stone]

Pectolite crystallizes in the form of masses, needle-like radial aggregates, and radial groupings. The colour range is from white to grey. The Larimar Stone is a form of pectolite, discovered in the Dominican Republic, which exhibits the colours of blue, red, green, and/or white, sometimes featuring a chatoyancy.

Pectolite can assist one in recognizing the "chains" which have been self-imposed, stimulating one to release the self-constraints in order to facilitate freedom from the bondage of the materialistic world. It assists in precision and forthright-ness in activities, and stimulates the deeper understanding of being in this world.

It further helps one to admit to guilt, when guilty, and emits a love for the user that brings a sense of peace in truthfulness.

It has been used to bring customers to the salesperson, generally a variety quite different than the usual.

It is quite helpful in discouraging pugnacity and overzealous displays.

It has also been used (especially the Larimar Stone) for dimensional work and cellular work. It is an excellent mineral for purging entities from ones environment and from ones corporeal existence.

It can be used to treat the cartilaginous portions of the body, as well as the hair and the feet. In relation to the feet, it can open the acupressure/acupuncture meridians at the feet in order to allow one to recognize which painful spots lead to which areas of the body; this information provides the user with the knowledge of the dis-eases which can be directly affected through healing encounters.

In addition to the properties of pectolite which are listed above, the Larimar Stone is a "stone for Earth healing". It represents peace and clarity, emitting an energy of healing and love. It has been used to stimulate the heart, throat, third-eye, and crown chakras, facilitating inner wisdom and outer manifestation. It helps one to "see" the self from outside of the realm of personal reality, inspiring and encouraging one toward improvement in the actualization of ones realities on the spiritual and physical planes.

It can also be used for gridding, bringing serenity to an environment and providing a message of loving energy to those of other worlds.

Pectolite vibrates to the number 6 and the Larimar Stone vibrates to the master number 55.

PENNINITE
[Astrological Sign of Libra]

Penninite is a member of the chlorite group and crystallizes in the form of compact masses, thick tabular crystals, rhombohedral-type crystals, and six-sided pyramid-type crystals. The colour range includes white, yellow, violet, pink, rose red, grey, and silver-white.

In addition to the properties listed in the CHLORITE section of this book, the following qualities apply.

This mineral can be used to produce flexibility in body and mind. It stimulates the agility of muscles and helps to relieve the pain associated with stretching. It also promotes flexibility in ones belief structure, helping one to realize that which one "knows" from within the self is much stronger than any belief. It allows one to proceed from the heart to the inner consciousness to determine "truths".

It is a good stone for the accountant, the energy provided being conducive to the tracking and control of analyses, investigations, and studies.

It is excellent for those involved in the field of writing, providing for assistance in the development of sequential thought.

It can also be used to provide for a centering of the self which is conducive to the successful use of the pendulum.

Penninite helps one to laugh, from the stomach, which is the location where genuine laughter is released. It gives one the insight that every day is a day for celebration.

It can be used for the treatment of disorders associated with the male reproductive system and with bacterial infections. It has been used in the alleviation of stress related to that which is pending and/or to that which is about to occur.

Vibrates to the number 7.

PERICLASE   [Astrological Sign of Aries]

Periclase crystallizes in the form of colourless-to-white grains, cubes, and octahedral crystals.

This mineral can help one remain "light" in the presence of depressing atmospheres by "taking on" the condition itself. Frequent cleansing, not with liquids, is required, with activation preferably in the sun or in proximity to heat sources.

Periclase can bring one to the state of communication with the faeries of mythology, providing for stimulating insight into paradise and into the karmic conditions with which one must contend prior to reaching paradise. It can also take one beyond the worldly concerns to the concerns of the "brotherhood" of "All That Is".

The octahedral crystalline form can be used to produce an energy which is predisposed to discourage chaotic, disruptive, and disorganized growth. It emits an energy which can be used to stabilize and to produce order within the mental, physical, emotional, and spiritual systems. It can be used to bring order to chaos. It also provides for the purification, the cleansing, and the elimination of that which is in disorder. It can be used to dispel disorders at the commencement of the symptoms. It can also be useful in the treatment of colds, flu, staph and strep infections, infectious cankers, herpes, ulcers, and similar infections.

All forms of periclase can be used in the treatment of weakened ovaries, can assist in the alleviation of fungal infections, and can provide for the grace to overcome any dis-ease. It can also be used to ameliorate acidosis [especially, during fasting], and can help to bring the body into balance with respect to the stabilization of the states of acidity and alkalinity.

Vibrates to the number 7.

PERIDOT   [Astrological Signs of Virgo, Leo, Scorpio, & Sagittarius]
                                        [Also Known as Chrysolite and Olivine]

Peridot crystallize in the form of masses, grains, and prismatic crystals, sometimes flattened. The colour range for precious peridot includes green and yellow-green. Peridot is also known as olivine; the related colours for olivine are dark yellow-green, olive green, and bottle green. Other colours include red, yellow-brown, green-to-brown, and honey yellow [from Ceylon, see the TOURMALINE section of this book].

Peridot emits a warm and friendly energy.

It can be used to magnify the inner aspects of any situation or circumstance. It furthers the understanding of those changes which are occurring in ones life and assists one in the recognition of the detrimental patterns which have been the basis for impairment in attaining that which is necessary for growth.

It can be used to cleanse and to stimulate the heart and solar plexus chakras, bringing openness and acceptance in the intellectual pursuit of matters of love and relationships.

It also helps to regulate cycles in ones life; e.g., physical cycles, mental cycles, emotional cycles, intellectual cycles, and life cycles.

It provides for a shield of protection around the body and should be removed from ones person prior to balancing and the aligning the physical body with the other bodies and prior to cleansing chakras other than those related to its colour; upon completion of balancing, alignment, and chakra cleansing, the wearing or carrying of peridot will prevent outside influences from affecting the aligned, balanced, cleansed structure. Please note that internal disturbances can and, most likely, will eventually affect the optimum condition.

It also helps to heal a "bruised" ego by assisting one in the lessening of anger or jealousy, inspiring happiness within the self and delight in the nature of ones life.

Peridot can be used to bring results to ones search - the seeking and recovery of that which is lost or mislaid in the physical world, as well as the quest for the enlightened state.

It is said to have been one of the stones used in the breastplate of the high priest.

Peridot is an excellent healing stone, acting as a "tonic" to both strengthen and regenerate the body. It can be used in the treatment of disorders of the heart, lungs, spleen, and intestinal tract. It is also used to strengthen the eyesight in conditions of astigmatism and nearsighted-ness. It can be used to provide relief from, and to provide for the healing of, ulcers of the stomach and duodenum. It has been used as a facilitator for the birthing process, stimulating contractions and facilitating the opening of the birth canal.

Vibrates to the numbers 5, 6 and 7.

PEROVSKITE   [Astrological Sign of Virgo]

Perovskite crystallizes in the form of masses, which exhibit small cubes, and cubic crystals with irregularly distributed faces, the faces exhibiting striations parallel to the edges. The colour range includes pale yellow, yellow, yellow-orange, orange, red-brown, and grey-black.

This mineral helps one to bring "things" to conclusion; it discourages procrastination and stimulates one to continue toward the goal. It provides one with tenacity and eliminates mental confusion.

It provides one with an advantage over those who would persecute and harass; this advantage being the knowledge that the connection, between all beings, exists, and that which one "does" to another, he also "does" to himself. It also provides for strength and courage to persevere in these situations.

Perovskite can assist in the treatment of blood disorders which display a deficiency in the maturation of red blood cells. It can also be used in the remediation of spinal disorders which exhibit degenerative lesions in the spinal cord. It has been used to treat inflammation of the tongue and gums, gastric disturbances, and degeneration of the lining of the stomach.

Vibrates to the number 5.

PETALITE Gift from Livia January 2023 [Astrological Sign of Leo]

Petalite crystallizes in the form of the monoclinic system, masses, and cleavable foliates. The colour range includes colourless, white, grey, reddish-white, and greenish-white. The small white to colourless chips of Petalite have been found to be quite powerful with respect to energy release.

It has been known as a "stone of the angels" and has been used to further ones angelic connection, ones connection with the ancient civilizations, and ones alliance with spiritual guides and totem animals. It has been used extensively in medicine wheel ceremonies to provide a safe environment for spiritual contact, to enhance communication, and to bring peace. It has also been carried during vision quests to bring calm, protection, alertness, and prompt success.

It can be used for attunement between those of the physical plane, as well as between one and the spirit world. It is valuable to provide strength and protection during vision quests and astral travel. It is of high spirituality and can bring both valour and protection on the spiritual level, and from the etheric plane. It is also a stone of Earth-grounding; hence, one can remain grounded during spiritual "work". It acts to improve meditation and to further peace of mind.

It was used in ancient times to insure property and to protect against accidents. It has been esteemed, by the Brasilian shamen, as holding both a spiritual and protective property. It has been used in shamanic ceremonies and in the sacred vortices of Bahia. It has also been considered to be both a protective stone and a bestower of goodness.

Petalite can be used to promote the physical sign of auras, and to soothe and to smooth the aura.

It serves to stimulate the throat chakra such that one may speak of that which one sees - clearly, precisely, and succinctly. It further opens the crown chakra, and initiates the movement of the Kundalini.

It can be used to stimulate clairaudience, clairvoyance, clairsentience, and telepathic communication.

♪ 480 ♫

The energy is strong for inducing a "no-mind" meditative state, helping one to return with total relaxation and peace. It further acts to balance the Yin/Yang energies and to provide stability within ones mind, body, and spirit.

It further acts to bring the qualities of an energy vortex to the area in which it is located; hence, carried upon the body, it acts to activate all energy centers and serves to provide a continual source of energy in that location. The same continual source of energy is affected when place within ones environment.

It has been used in the treatment of AIDS, CFS, cancer, tumors, for cellular renewal, and to ameliorate exterior disorders of the eyes. It can also be used to increase flexibility of the muscular and skeletal systems, to cleanse the lungs and the intestines, and to initiate the Triple-Burner fire.

Vibrates to the number 7.

PETOSKEY STONE   [Astrological Sign of Sagittarius]

The petoskey stone is a type of fossilized colony coral which exhibits an "eye" when polished. It is found in Petoskey, Michigan, USA. The colour is a grey-white and the "eye" is white.

The qualities of this stone, in addition to those listed in the CORAL and FOSSIL sections of this book, are listed below.

This stone stimulates the third-eye and the intuitive levels of the inner self. It helps one toward psychic awareness and enhances the awareness of the emotions. It provides for protection of the area of, and around, the head and energizes both the crown chakra and the third-eye.

The petoskey stone discourages infections and infectious dis-ease, eliminates the possibility of mischievous spirits channeling incorrect information, and can bring promotion and actualization to ones creative endeavors.

Vibrates to the number 3.

PETRIFIED WOOD   [Astrological Sign of Leo]

Petrified wood is ancient wood which has been replaced and hardened by another mineral. The two minerals usually involved in the displacement activities are agate

♪ 481 ♫

[chalcedony] and quartz. Petrified bog is ancient wood which has first become a bog prior to petrification.

The "agatized wood" exhibits the properties of agate and chalcedony [see the AGATE and CHALCEDONY sections of this book] in addition to providing access to past-lives via meditation with the stone. "Silicified wood", wood replaced by a form of quartz, exhibits the properties listed below.

It should also be noted that some forms of agatized and silicified wood are also opalized; these woods are discussed in the OPAL section of this book.

Silicified wood can assist in the removal of trifling annoyances by bringing one to the actions required to eliminate the situation. It can also aid in the elimination of worries concerning those things of little importance, bringing with it the motto to "change what you can, and worry not about the rest".

It provides for strength in all areas of ones life and is also a stone for grounding.

It provides access to, and explicit information concerning, past-lives; this action is furthered via meditation with the stone.

Silicified wood can be used in the treatment of atrophied portions of the body, paralysis, and dysfunctional ambulatory capabilities.

It can be used to strengthen the back and to provide alignment to the skeletal structure of the body. It can aid in the treatment of hearing loss and incontinence, and to eliminated odors uncommon to ones environment.

It also provides support to one who is coming through the crisis period of a dis-ease; it provides insight into "why" the suffering has occurred and into the lessons which can be learned and, hence, never repeated.

Petrified wood is also a "stone of transformation", assisting one to advance to ones highest chosen level, to commence ascension to a higher aspect of the self, and to recognize that no action unnecessary - but that all actions bring one to ones ultimate purpose.

An elixir, applied topically, can be used to soothe the skin and to stimulate thickness and luster in the hair.

Vibrates to the master number 77.

PETZITE   [Astrological Sign of Gemini]

Petzite crystallizes in the form of grey or black masses.

This mineral allows one to "slow down", even when ones environment is hectic. It allows one to see all of the details of a situation and to bring those details to the attention of those involved. It brings discretion and cooperation to situations, promoting harmony within the structure of organizations and relationships.

In addition, petzite combines the properties of gold and silver to produce a substantive supplement to the individual qualities and, hence, brings into existence a "dynamite" healing stone. The reader should see the GOLD and the SILVER sections of this book for further attributes of this stone.

It can also be used to lessen the stress of operations when one is hospitalized, and to produce further "knitting" capabilities to the structures which were disturbed. It can be used to treat brittleness of bones and nails, and disorders associated with the large veins of the body.

Vibrates to the number 2.

PHARMOCOSIDERITE   [Astrological Sign of Capricorn]

Pharmocosiderite crystallizes in the formation of tetrahedras, cubes and grains. The colour range includes green, yellow-brown, and honey-yellow. It occasionally occurs with Arthurite to produce a dynamic combination of energies.

This mineral has been used to strengthen and to align all chakras, meridians, and subtle bodies. It actually elevates all chakras and can facilitate attunement between the physical level and the higher planes of existence. It can bring any and all energies to a higher level. It does, however, primarily stimulate the heart and solar plexus chakras, bringing communication skills to intellectual issues, to creativity, and to intuition, while allowing for the application of love in all issues.

It is excellent for spiritual attunement, for healing and cleansing of both the energy centers and the physical body, and for providing protection.

It has been said Pharmacosiderite changes color to warn of impending danger and/or to indicate infidelity in thought or action. It can be used to protect against environmental pollutants as well.

It is valuable for grounding and can help to prevent one from loosing touch with the conscious mind during deep meditations; this facilitates a "no mind" meditative state, but provides the unconscious mind with a "knowing" of the protective mechanism which has been initiated.

It acts to strengthen the entire anatomy, and can be helpful in the amelioration of all dis-eases and disorders. It can aid in the absorption of nutrients, can help to stimulate the regeneration of tissue, and can act to increase circulatory flows to the muscular tissue. It has been used in the treatment for headaches and in the repair of physical damage which has impacted the body. It has also been used to assist one in maintaining stability during ambulatory motions. An elixir has been used to ameliorate skin disorders which were due to stress.

Vibrates to the master number 88.

PHENACITE   [Astrological Sign of Gemini]

Phenacite crystallizes in the form of granular aggregates, radial fibrous spherical structures, rhombohedral [often lens-like] crystals [primarily from Minas Gerais, Zimbabwe, Russia, and Colorado], and prismatic slender wands [primarily from Madagascar]. The colour range includes yellow, pink, brown, yellow-red, pale red, and colourless.

Phenacite is the mineral recently brought to the attention of those active in the metaphysical realm. The dynamic properties have recently been discovered and the stone, although expensive, is quite expansive. It is highly stimulating to the third-eye, allowing the energy of that center to be activated and to be carried throughout the body, producing an awareness of the complete cellular structure.

It facilitates deep meditation, promoting an inner "knowing" with respect to the aspects associated with each of the chakras.

Phenacite can bring the way of love, the way of heavenly being, into ones physical reality. The corresponding energy center for the stone is in the etheric body, above the crown chakra of the physical body. Placement of the stone above the crown chakra can provide a noticeable flowing energy, which covers, connects, and inter-penetrates the total physical body. It is an excellent stone for healing, producing the clear energy patterns of the ethereal to stimulate the healing of the physical; it is also a gathering stone, gathering the energies of other stones used in healing situations and facilitating the effectiveness of the healing; this is a case where "the sum is actually greater than the individual parts".

Application of phenacite to any chakra produces an expedient clearing, cleansing, and activating effect. It can provide purification to the total body structure, energy centers, and energy pathways, while providing for a connection to other planes of existence.

The phenacite from Zimbabwe, Minas Gerais, and from other locations in Brazil, does indeed "contain" a caretaker; although many minerals contain their personal caretakers, the caretaker of a phenacite crystal is quite easily accessed - in fact, the caretaker virtually "knocks at your door" before you even think about the contact. It should be noted that some of the phenacite available from Minas Gerais is stream tumbled - this does not decrease the qualities of the stone, but provides a mellow-ness and "softness" to the energy; if one has not experienced phenacite, it may be suitable to, initially, use the softer energy.

The phenacite from Brazil and Zimbabwe appears to emit somewhat different properties than that from Madagascar. The Brazilian/Zimbabwe phenacite appears to produce a pathway for travel within the dimensions; the travel being on a high awareness level, and the experiences being quite spiritual.

The phenacite from Madagascar appears to provide for a connection with a type of "mother-ship" from another dimension; a ship which has had a long-enduring and extensive contact with the Earth plane, and one from which the user can gain far-reaching and comprehensive information. In addition, the Madagascar mineral is said to be connected to the realm of materialism; producing an advantageous and prompt response to that which one wishes to bring into actuality.

Vibrates to the number 9.

PHENOMENITE   [See Sandstone]

PHILLIPSITE   [Astrological Sign of Cancer]

Phillipsite crystallizes in the form of spherical-type structures, orthorhombic and tetragonal crystals, and twin crystals which have penetrated themselves, sometimes forming the shape of a cross.

This mineral can be used to provide a connection with the higher-self, facilitating improvement in psychic pursuits. It stimulates clairaudience, acuteness of mental awareness, and soundness of judgment.

It also provides for a connection with the protective forces of the universe, and for a connection with the spirituality of our time. It is said to induce and to maintain the state of love.

It enhances the activities of sharing, discourages selfishness, and provides for the regulation of ones life through reason and rationality. When one is in need of some "common sense", this is an excellent source.

Phillipsite stimulates communication skills, allows one adeptness in recognizing feelings via "body language", and produces a benevolent attitude and demeanor.

It can also be used to diminish the "aches and pains" of the body and to act to produce a "hot springs" effect when used in the bath.

Vibrates to the number 9.

PHLOGOPIT

[Astrological Sign of Cancer]

Phlogopit crystallizes in the formation of prismatic crystals, scales and plates. The colour range includes yellow-brown, brown-red, green, white, colourless, and sometimes shows a copper-like reflection. It possesses a pleochroism of brown-red, brown-green, and yellow. It is sometimes asterated due to minute accicular inclusions, rutile, or tourmaline.

This mineral has been used in energy work to bring the energy from the four directions and from Mother Earth and Father Sky. The energy is best utilized by gridding in the configuration of the Star Of David.

The energy expedites revolution and evolution on all levels and imparts a realization of the suitable paths to completion. Flexibility in perception and in the consolidation of past, present, and future actions gains both understanding and appreciation. With the energy of this mineral, the concept of supple adaption to facilitate the integration of all which has transpired, is transpiring, and will transpire, is reflected in ones conscious living.

It has also been used to strengthen channeling activities, to remove spiritual blockages which impede channeling, and to provide for conscious awareness during these activities.

Phlogopit has been used to relieve back pain, to stimulate muscular relaxation, to promote the assimilation of magnesium, iron, and potassium, to assist in the retention of the integrity of the teeth and the bone structure, and to alleviate the symptoms of mononucleosis.

Vibrates to the master number 55.

PHOSPHORITE [Astrological Sign of Virgo]

Phosphorite crystallizes in the form of a fibrous concretionary and partly scaly mineral. The colour range includes green, grey to black, blue, violet, yellow, red, and brown. When occurring with the normal formation of Apatite, the fibers are exhibited in a spider-web fashion after polishing.

In addition to the qualities listed in the Apatite section, phosphorite has been used to stimulate past-life memories in the past-life ascension mode, allowing one to gain information concerning past delightful times and/or traumatic times without actually experiencing the emotional experiences concomitant with same.

It has been used to assist on in ascending the great spiral of knowledge, assist one in gaining knowledge of the self and the environment during the journey. It expedites the journey toward the understanding of the self, bringing wisdom in thought and action.

It has been used to smooth the temperament, to bring a joyful feeling, and to decrease and transmute anger.

Phosphorite has been used in the treatment of skin disorders (eczema, rashes, dryness), and in the strengthening of the hair. It can also be used to assist in the cleansing of arteries and in the removal of toxins from the blood. Use of this mineral has also promoted relief of tendonitis and strengthening of the muscular structure and for enhancing bone development and stability. In addition, it has been used to block the pain sensors of the body.

Vibrates to the number 5.

PICASSO STONE [Astrological Sign of Sagittarius]

The Picasso Stone is a type of marble which is a metamorphosed limestone occurring in the form of a coarse to medium-grained rock of re-crystallized dolomite or calcite. The colour range includes a combination of black, rusty-brown, tan, yellow, and white.

In addition to the properties listed in the MARBLE section of this book, this mineral also can assist one in the development of creative talents, and in the fulfillment of artistic enterprises.

It has been used to assist one in sustaining and maintaining, while providing for the understanding of the destiny one has chosen. It brings the light of the other planetary beings to the soul of the user. The mineral brings the galactic evolved energies from other worlds to the Earth plane.

This energy facilitates the transformation of intuition into intellectual thought such that one can implement the instructions provided. It assists one to traverse changes, attracting strength and perseverance. It has been known as the master of the subconscious mind, providing intuitive sessions to the user concerning the implementation of inner messages and the utilization of same in the physical domain. It can help to provide clarity to the inner sight, instilling a passionless peace of imperturbability via the annihilation of disturbing thoughts.

It acts to stimulate the circulatory system, to reduce anxiety and stress, and to assist in digestion, regulation, and metabolism. It has also been used in the treatment of carpel tunnel syndrome, cellular and organ toxicity, and to promote weight loss.

Vibrates to the number 3.

PICROLITE   [Astrological Sign of Gemini]

Picrolite crystallizes in the formation of columns and fibers which are not easily separable. The colour realm includes the range of dark green to mountain-green, grey, and brown.

This mineral has been used to assist in the maintenance of relationships, bringing conscious realization of the virtues of the other and compartmentalizing obstacles such that each can be addressed independent of the other.

It can calm stressful situations and instill energy when needed. It is excellent for promoting endurance and can augment energy at critical times. It has also been used to assist in protein digestion and in the absorption of foods.

Picrolite has also been used to stimulate the crown chakra and the heart chakra concurrently. It acts to bring the energy of the crown to the heart to assist one in loving actions, forgiveness, and clemency.

It has been used in the treatment of heart disorders, the adrenal glands, the immune system, and the endocrine glands. It can also revitalize and recharge the body with energy after stressful situations.

Vibrates to the number 8.

PIETERSITE   [Astrological Sign of Leo]

Pietersite crystallizes in the form of masses, the structure a result of inclusions in jasper where the inclusions are pseudomorphs after asbestos. The colour is blue/black and the mineral exhibits a chatoyant quality. It was discovered by Sid Pieters, Windhoek, Namibia, and is truly lovely.

This mineral can be used to stimulate the pineal gland and to assist one during meditative states to experience visions and pre-cognitive thoughts. It aligns the energy centers of the body while providing grounding, not to the Earth, but to the etheric body; this rarity in grounding ability has facilitated travel throughout the spheres of existence, culminating in access to the akashic records.

Pietersite has been said to contain the "keys to the kingdom of heaven", dispelling illusion and assisting one in the recognition of the beauty of the soul. It exhibits an energy conducive to the actualization of the loving characteristics of the "brotherhood" of humanity. It brings the potential of the individual to the perfection of the source of all being, stimulating dignified power and loving guidance. It promotes loyalty to the self and to the ultimate experience of life.

It assists one in remaining open to experience, enabling the effect of an illuminated glory when one proceeds to "walk the stage of life".

It further allows one to see beyond the horizon or mirage, helping to support human courage, tenacity, and dauntless effort to both create and maintain beauty.

This mineral can be used to stimulate the pituitary gland to provide the proper regulation of the other endocrine glands and to produce, in the proper quantity, the hormones concerned with growth, sex, metabolism, blood pressure, and body temperature.

This is quite a stone, Sid!

Vibrates to the number 9.

PINAKIOLITE   [Astrological Sign of Scorpio]

Pinakiolite crystallizes in the form of black metallic small rectangular and thin tabular crystals.

It aids one in attaining the solution to mysteries <u>and</u> brings information to the user concerning the unknown - specifically, it can be used as the "detective stone", uncovering information which can be helpful in obtaining solutions.

It is also helpful in games of chance - it provides the energy to stimulate winning.

It can be used in the treatment of frostbite, parasitic infestation, and in the alleviation of hunger. It can help to provide cohesiveness in situations of torn muscular structure or wounds to the skin, and to ameliorate eruptions and coarseness of the skin. It is excellent as an elixir applied to the skin.

Vibrates to the number 4.

PIPESTONE   [See Catlinite]

PITCHSTONE   [Astrological Sign of Aries]

Pitchstone is a type of volcanic glass which is dull and pitch-like in its luster.

This stone can be used to produce clarity in the mental processes and to stimulate and soothe motion and emotion. It can facilitate a "pioneering" spirit and can produce an inquisitiveness into the unknown avenues of the creative forces. It can guide one to the "easy" road in ones endeavors.

It can be used for divining and can produce quick results when used for "cloud-busting". It can also be used to grid ones environment in order to produce an energy field conducive to contact with beings from other worlds.

Pitchstone can stimulate positive interest in those who have lost interest in life; by placement of the stone in ones environment, a change should be evident.

It can be used in the treatment of kidney stones, gall stones, and over-fertility, and to assist in the mending of broken bones and fractures.

Vibrates to the number 3.

PLANCHEITE   [Astrological Sign of Leo]

Plancheite crystallizes in the form of fibrous radial aggregates and large botryoidal masses. It exhibits a pleochroistic colour scheme exhibiting no colour in the X-axis and Y-axis, and a pale to deep blue colour in the Z-axis.

This mineral can be used to stimulate automatic writing and is also useful in design and development activities. It brings to one a clear and energetic positive energy from the planets in this solar system during each respective visit of a planet through the astrological sign. It also helps one in the pursuit of the study of astrology - allowing one access to the "storage files" of the memory in order to bring a state of familiarity and, hence, easily recalled subjective information.

It promotes strength and courage, helps to protect the bodies of the wearer/carrier during experiences with hostile energies, and encourages the tenacity to continue during the stressful situations of life.

Plancheite can also be helpful during intellectual "battles", assisting one in preparedness and stimulating the intellect to both retain and process great quantities of information.

It is said to have been used in ancient times to further ones quest for power and to assist in the rise to fame and fortune.

It can be used to increase the coagulation of the blood, to treat tonsillitis, and to clear the intercellular structures of blockages.

Vibrates to the number 3.

PLATINUM   [Astrological Sign of Leo]

Platinum crystallizes in the form of grains, scales, and, rarely, cubic crystals. The colour is a steel-grey to white.

This mineral can be used to balance the centers and meridians of the physical body, to provide alignment of the physical body to the etheric body, to align the subtle bodies, and to provide the polarity adjustments which are necessary within the physical structure to stabilize the body and to facilitate the maintenance of optimum health. It can also provide permanence to relationships, stimulating self-approval and, hence, facilitating non-judgmental attitudes toward another.

Platinum maintains ones energy level to enhance the accomplishment and completion of goals. It has been used to stimulate the pineal gland and has enhanced ones intuition, psychic abilities, and awareness of other levels of intelligence.

It is the stone of which Archimedes spoke when in search of a centering situation which provided the bases of ability so that one may "move the earth". It also assists one in recognizing, seeing, and feeling the "blossoming" spirit giving forth the light from within the inner reaches of the self.

It can be used to stimulate the health of the eyes, bringing the eyes to an improved condition [the wearing of platinum is recommended to enhance this property]. Platinum also provides a for connection with the cellular structure of the physical body and activates, in the memory of each cell, the recognition of the healthy condition and the processes required to maintain that condition; once the cells understand, they may effectively perform to dispel disorder within their structures.

It also assists in the proper functioning of the digestive tract, and in the better assimilation of nutrients.

Vibrates to the number 7.

POTCH   [See Common Opal]

POWELLITE   [Astrological Sign of Sagittarius]

Powellite crystallizes in the form of crusts, masses, and tetragonal pyramid-like crystals. The colour range includes yellow, grey, brown, blue, and black.

When used in meditation, this mineral can enhance the activity of the crown chakra and can provide for an increase in spiritual clarity. It helps to increase stamina and furthers the ability to attack any task, while producing an energy transfer to facilitate the activities and the completion of the task.

It is a good stone for support during presentations, oratorical displays, and when one is intent on convincing others [in this case, the stone will not interfere with the decisions of others, but will provide strength and mental acuity to the user to facilitate the most logical bases for winning the argument].

Powellite also activates the innate abilities to allow one to overcome physical handicaps and limitations.

It furthers the creative and artistic pursuits, encouraging expressiveness based upon the unity of all within the world. It assists in the advancement of creative spirituality, sustaining one in the recognition of those forces which would be most conducive to progress toward the advancement of humanity.

Powellite can be used to fight the fatty deposits in the body, to provide for increased assimilation of oxygen to the blood, and to ease the processes of puberty [both emotionally and physically]. It is said to be effective in the counteraction of poisoning.

Vibrates to the number 9.

PREHNITE   [Astrological Sign of Libra]

Prehnite crystallizes in the form of compact granular masses, botryoidal, columnar, and globular structures, plate-like layers, stalactites, tabular crystals, and prismatic crystals. The colour range includes pale green, dark green, yellow, and white.

This mineral can be used to facilitate contact with impalpable entities via the visualization process and through meditation. It provides for contact with the entity as determined by the direction of the user; the direction of the user being determined by a conscious decision or an unconscious desire.

It can be used to multiply energy and to enhance ones protective fields. It is quite effective during use as one of the stones in gridding operations; use of prehnite in a grid which is designed to produce calmness, brings a structure of coherence to the environment; use of the stone to complement a grid and to encourage visitation by those of extra-terrestrial origin, provides for a structure of protection and strengthens the invitation.

It is a "stone for dreaming and remembering". It also advances the state of meditation and furthers the avenues available during this unencumbered state.

It enhances ones ability for prophesy, bringing in the aid of the Divine to inspire. It allows the inner "knowing" to prepare, in advance, for situations of which one has no prior conscious knowledge; in these cases, prehnite is considered the stone to assure that the "commandment" to "always be prepared" is followed. The actual predictions which this stone facilitates are usually precise and accurate. Use of prehnite for the activity of prediction should not be taken lightly; the most accurate predictions are made available when the concerns are for ones personal spiritual growth.

It can be used in the treatment of disorders of the kidneys, the bladder, and the connective tissues, and for gout and anemic disorders of the blood.

Vibrates to the number 5.

PROUSTITE   [Astrological Signs of Aquarius & Leo]
                                        [Also Known as Ruby Silver]

Proustite crystallizes in the form of masses, acute rhombohedral crystals, and scalenohedral crystals. The colour is a scarlet red.

This mineral can be used to bring out the feelings and emotions which one has hidden from ones consciousness; it can help to provide a calming stable environment in which to deal with the information.

It is recommended that the proustite be held in the hand during this process. The stone actually takes on the negativity of the situation, in some cases producing alteration of the structure of the surface.

Cleansing of the stone via the visualization of white universal light, and providing for a soft, quiet place in the darkness for it to reside, are both important considerations to ones decision to become an Earth-keeper for proustite.

It furthers the actions related to practicality in ones lifework, bringing the qualities of precision, analytical capabilities, and stability to employment situations. It can also be used to augment ones scientific, and mystical and magical abilities, enhancing personal alignment with the n-dimensional realms of being.

It is excellent for helping one to flow through changes. It provides somewhat of an auxiliary stimulant which says "hey you, let's get on with it".

Proustite can be used to stimulate the activity of the pituitary to raise the blood pressure [when consciously directed to do so], to stimulate the intestinal muscles, and to treat the kidneys and bladder. It can also be used to stimulate the production of estrogen, to ameliorate the symptoms of menopause, to assist in the repositioning of internal organs to the optimum locality, and to treat disorders, and associated symptoms, of the prostate.

Do not prepare an elixir of this mineral via the normal method.

Vibrates to the number 7 and the master number 44.

♪ 494 ♫

PSILOMELANE   [Astrological Sign of Sagittarius]

Psilomelane crystallizes in the form of masses, dendritic coatings, botryoidal structures, and stalactites. It ranges in colour from deep grey to black and, usually, possesses the quality of chatoyancy.

This mineral can help one to re-direct energy and to analyze ones own patterns of emotional thinking and development, based on free associative ideals, revealing to the conscious mind the thoughts and experiences previously unrecognized; hence, stimulating remedial action for emotional disturbances and over-emotional states. It can also be used to correct unwanted, unloving behavior patterns and emotional reactions.

Psilomelane provides for smooth states of meditation and enhances mental travel to other parts of the world [as it is today]. It can be used to facilitate trance states which take the user to the pre-determined destination, and to stimulate a total awareness [in those at that location] to both recognize and understand the nature of the visit.

It has been used for "gazing", providing for insight into that which is occurring in a distant location. Prior to the activation of psilomelane for "gazing", conscious direction of the mind is required - otherwise, one may view situations and activities which are of no relevance or importance to the user.

This mineral can be used in the treatment of pneumonia, to clear the mucus from the lungs, and to provide for the stabilization of the inner walls of the lungs. It can also be used to treat chronic inflammatory conditions of the skin. Psilomelane can assist in the efficient conversion of carbohydrates to energy and in the regulation of the proper flow of insulin to the blood stream.

Vibrates to the number 4.

PUMICE   [Astrological Sign of Capricorn]

Pumice is a form of fine-grained volcanic rock, distinguished by a well-defined cellular structure.

This mineral is a reminder for one not to "sink" into despair when faced with "heavy" problems. It helps to combat abrasive character traits and to alleviate negative attitudes; it takes negativity within itself in any situation, and, hence, should often be cleansed. Pumice also helps to give one insight to negative situations and to adequate responses such that an experience does not require repeating in order to satisfy a karmic burden.

This mineral can be used as an elixir to stimulate regeneration of the skin and to provide for smoothness to the body. It is also a stone to help to keep the heart functioning. It can be used in the treatment of cellular disorders and to reduce abnormal growths.

Vibrates to the number 4.

PUMPELLYITE   [Astrological Sign of Leo]

Pumpellyite crystallizes in the form of minute fibers, tabular crystals, and plates. the colour range includes green and blue-green. In conjunction with Dickite, it brings a lovely combination of healing energies.

This mineral has been used to protect travelers, to ameliorate travel anxiety, and to ease motion sickness. It can be used to stimulate exciting changes, such that the changes bring relief and pleasure and are easily conceived and effected.

This energy has been used to alter ones thought processes such that positive thoughts predominate and one can understand the negative thoughts and dispense with same. It is truly a lovely energy for alteration of ones state of being.

Pumpellyite has also been used to strength beginnings - bringing self-actualization, character adjustment, and clearing of past traumas. It is an excellent stone for energizing the heart chakra, and acts to clear emotional blockages from ones being.

It has been used in the treatment of dis-ease related to anger - i.e., cancer, tumors - and in disorders associated with bone degeneration and muscular spasms. It can also be used to ameliorate anorexia, emphysema, and skin disorders.

Vibrates to the master number 55.

PURPURITE   [Astrological Sign of Virgo]

Purpurite crystallizes in the form of masses. The colour ranges from deep red to purple [occasionally iridescent]. It, sometimes, exhibits pleochroism, producing grey in the X-axis and red, purple, or red-purple in the Y-axis and Z-axis.

This mineral provides strong dispersion capabilities, assisting one to break-out of old patterns and conditions. It allows one the insight to that which would occur if one would retire along the pathway leading to security in the successes already achieved; it also facilitates insight into that which one could accomplish if the choice would be to travel far into "open country" to the unknown and to the "light of the brilliant torch of truth".

It stimulates the crown chakra and increases ones spiritual aspirations. It also provides one with a freedom from the material world and rids one of undue modesty. Purpurite is an "imperial stone", providing access to expedient materialization of that which is chosen. It provides a purity within ones being that both stimulates higher thoughts and facilitates planning and action to help one to continue on the journey toward enlightenment.

It assists one in speaking with both confidence and freedom, providing for protection from interfering energies during the verbalization of ideals and concepts.

Purpurite can be used in the treatment of hemorrhages, bruises, and superficial wounds. It can assist in providing proper transport of the blood from the heart to the lungs. It can be used to control the level of uric acid and to stabilize the pulse rate. It can also assist in the purification of the blood.

Vibrates to the number 9.

PYRITE   [Astrological Sign of Leo]

Pyrite crystallizes in the form of masses, stalactites, grains, globes, striated cubes [the striations at right angles to each other on adjacent faces], and twelve-faced pentagonal dodecahedral crystals. It also occurs as a replacement mineral, supplanting many other mineralogical structure and, hence, occurring in a multitude of configurations. The colour is brass-yellow.

This mineral possesses a defending quality and is an excellent preventive which will shield one from many forms of negative energy. Simply having a piece of pyrite on ones person brings in the protective, shielding aspect of this stone which works on the physical, etheric, and emotional levels. It can help to keep out the negative vibrations of pollutants at the physical level, due to an energy field which it creates within the aura. It is a unique protector and is an excellent stone to keep in ones possession when performing dangerous work; it helps to keep-away all forms of negative vibrations and can work to allay physical danger.

The energy of pyrite can inspire the universal energies to activate the nourishing energies of the body, assisting one in the attainment of the ultimate state of physical perfection. It allows one to recognize the purity of the universe and to understand that each portion of the universe maintains an inherent perfection in order to allow the unfolding of impeccability.

It also encourages and sustains the flawless ideal of health, intellect, and emotional well-being. It symbolizes the warmth and lasting presence of the sun and promotes the recall of beautiful memories of love and friendship.

It also assists one in seeing behind facades, promoting understanding of that which lies beneath words and actions. It can be used to stimulate the powers of the intellect, enhancing memory and providing for recall of relevant information, when required.

It can be used in the treatment of both the structure of the bones and the composition and formation of the cells. It has been used to assist in the prevention of RNA/DNA damage and can be used in repair of same. It can be used in the treatment of bronchitis and disorders of the lungs. It has been used in the treatment of violent and/or highly infective dis-ease, as well as by others who are working with those affected, in order to provide protection from the affectation. It has also been used to lessen fevers and to reduce inflammation.

Vibrates to the number 3.

PYROLUSITE   [Astrological Sign of Leo]

Pyrolusite crystallizes in the formation of columns, granular masses, and reniform coatings. The colour range includes iron-black, dark steel-grey, and blue.

This mineral can be used for transformation and transmutation of ones physical, emotional, and intellectual bodies. It brings an energy for reconstructing ones life and acts to heal any areas of disturbance during the conversion. It is a stone for changing and stabilizing relationships, marriages, mental processes, and emotional and physical imbalances. It allows for the realization that each person shares the powers of the universe, the passions of the planets, and the understanding from the advanced worlds.

It is used for healing and balancing the aura via repelling negative energy. It affects the physical, etheric, and astral bodies.

It assists one in getting to the basic cause of a problem and, hence, provides for access to the reason for a dis-ease, so that one can remove the problem and remedy the situation.

It also dispels unwanted interference from both the physical and spiritual worlds - the mechanism is unclear, but in the physical world, it tends to eliminate circumstances which could facilitate interference; and, in the spiritual worlds, a clear message is sent, asking for no interference.

This mineral has been used in the treatment of bronchitis, to stimulate clarity of the eyes, to regulate metabolism, to strengthen the walls of the blood veins, and to stimulate sexuality [when consciously directed]. An elixir has been used, topically, for the treatment of wounds.

Vibrates to the number 7.

PYROMORPHITE   [Astrological Signs of Sagittarius, Aries, & Leo]

Pyromorphite crystallizes in the form of masses, needle-like crusts, barrels, botryoidal structures, fibers, grains, and hexagonal prisms which taper to a slender point. The colour range includes green, yellow, brown, and orange.

This mineral is a special stone to use in healing situations to enhance the energy of the stones in use. Those minerals placed within the energy field of this stone become further stimulated.

It is a stone for "victory" and it provides for oracular and prophetic abilities in matters of the wit.

It also stimulates personal energy and brings a freshness in attitude and direction.

Pyromorphite can be used to both stimulate and release blockages from the triple-burner acupressure/acupuncture meridians. It can also be used to dispel unwanted micro-organisms from the blood, to aid in the proper assimilation of the B-vitamins, to alleviate chills, and to ameliorate degenerative changes in the gums and connective tissue between the stomach and duodenum.

Do not prepare an elixir of this mineral via the normal method.

Vibrates to the number 7.

Pyrope, a variety of garnet, crystallizes in the form of grains, pebbles, dodecahedral crystals, trapezohedral crystals, and combinations of dodecahedral-trapezohedral crystals. The colour range includes crimson and pink-to-purple. Some pyrope appears to be black due to the depth of the colour.

Properties in addition to those listed in the GARNET section of this book are noted below.

This form of garnet is basically concerned with the protection of the base and crown chakras and in maintaining the rhythms of the subtle bodies in synchrony with the other aspects of consciousness.

It provides for a connection between the grounding force of the base chakra and the opening to the inner wisdom associated with the crown chakra. It is a general stabilizer and does not usually project itself further than the psychic body.

It stimulates warmth and gentleness, assisting one in the unification with the creative forces of the self. It further helps one toward the actualization of experiencing the great spiral reaching from the center of the self to the outer layers of consciousness.

It can be used in the treatment of disorders of the digestive and elimination systems. It has been used to dispel heartburn, to soothe the throat, and to induce vitality in the infirm. It has also been used as an elixir to protect and to soothe the skin.

Vibrates to the number 5.

WHY ARE THERE NO WISE?

Quartz, as silicon dioxide, crystallizes in the form of masses, grains, druses, and prismatic hexagonal crystals. It is also known as rock crystal. Rose quartz, smokey quartz, citrine, and amethyst can be found in the sections of this book designated ROSE QUARTZ, SMOKEY QUARTZ, CITRINE, and AMETHYST.

Quartz has both piezoelectric (pronounced pie-ee-zo) and pyroelectric properties; the polarity of the quartz crystal will change when it is either subjected to pressure or heat, as well as when it is held in the hand - the tip, normally positive and receiving energy, will then change and become negative, thus, emitting energy which will radiate from the tip or from an edge. These properties support the amplification, focusing, storage, transfer, and transformation of energy.

Quartz can be used to dispel static electricity and can provide for conversion and re-direction of the energy toward a beneficial state. It produces a naturally balanced, solid-state energy field, modifying the energy available in accordance with the understanding of the user.

Quartz crystals can be used to amplify both body energy and thoughts. They can assist in the creation of power and can provide for clarity in thinking to enable thoughts to more effectively influence matter.

Quartz is said to bring the energy of the stars into the soul. Traditionally, the natural quartz crystal was said to both harmonize and align human energies - thoughts, consciousness, emotions - with the energies of the universe and to make these greater energies available to humanity. The natural tendency of quartz is for harmony, and it is recognized as a "stone of power".

The quartz crystal is the connection between the physical dimension and the dimensions of the mind. It can be used to communicate with minerals, plants, animals, and intelligent forces outside of the physical dimension. In early times, when all things were thought to be conscious parts of a greater living consciousness, the quartz crystal was believed to synchronize the individual and total consciousness with that of the heavens and the advanced life-forms.

The quartz crystal can be used to facilitate both speaking with, and receiving information from, the spiritual and other-worldly masters, teachers, and healers.

It can also be used to transform thoughts into sound, producing the vibration associated with the thought and affecting the environment with the discharged energy.

The quartz crystal can create altered states of consciousness and can serve as a vehicle for both reaching and utilizing the talents and abilities of the mind. All of the psychic abilities can be stimulated and amplified by the use of this mineral. It further assists one in retaining calmness and clarity in all situations, decreasing the amount of negative affectation which could inhibit emotional stability. It provides for enhanced energy and promotes perseverance and patience, as well as for restful sleep.

Quartz crystals were used in Atlantis and Lemuria for rejuvenation, and in the development of a complete civilization of incredible power and splendor. The mis-use of crystals is said to have induced the destruction of these civilizations; this is a lesson from which to learn - not to experience. If one uses the energy of the quartz crystal, or any other mineral, for purposes other than "for the good of all", the experience of destructive forces within ones life will be invited.

Quartz crystals can be used to clear and to activate the energy centers of the body. It attunes well to the heart chakra and responds very well at the third-eye [or brow] chakra. Placing the crystal at the area of the third-eye, during meditation, seems to enable one to focus more clearly with the mind such that the mind can become empty; this may be attributed to the feeling of "oneness" conveyed during the meditation. It further promotes the reflection and magnification of images and thoughts, so that one may evaluate the inner reaches of the self. Placement of the crystal upon the heart chakra, can help to clear emotional disturbances from ones being; it also further enhances the states of self-acceptance and self-love.

Use of quartz to activate the crown chakra has been quite effective. The spiraling effect of the energy produces a clear pathway for the movement of the Kundalini and for access to the realm of spirituality. If, however, one has not overcome personal "will" and the crown chakra is opened via the quartz crystal, the available energy could produce disruption within the emotional, physical, and spiritual centers. The opening of this chakra provides a pathway for communication from the higher-self; the best results being obtained when the "will" is "willing" and receptive to following the higher guidance.

The quartz crystal provides for purification of the physical, mental, and spiritual bodies. It is also a healer of negativity associated with ones perspectives and judgments; it can be used to focus upon the inner negativity and to stimulate positive thoughts and feelings. It can also direct ones materialistic energies toward the spiritual realm. It can further enhance the flow of, and can direct, ones positive thoughts and feelings toward the "light, love, and harmony of the planet", teaching one to live, laugh, and love with all brothers and sisters.

Quartz induces amplification of the energy field in the location in which it resides. The quartz crystal can produce a force field of healing negative ions while clearing the surrounding atmosphere of positive ions. It also tends to cancel the harmful effects of radiation and radioactivity. Wherever worn or carried, it acts as a physical and mental energizer; it also enhances and protects the aura and provides for amplification of the energy field of the body. Placed pointing toward the crown chakra or beneath the pillow during sleep, it can also bring wisdom and clarity to dreams and can help one to understand the messages and the lessons conveyed during the dream state. If worn close to the neck, it can stimulate the thyroid and parathyroid glands, being also helpful for respiratory problems such as congestion and sore throat. If worn over the heart, it can stimulate the thymus and can increase the efficiency of both the immune system and ones defenses against dis-ease. If worn over the solar plexus, it can provide for the stimulation of total body energies, and can also increase ones emotional fields [this may/may not be so desirable]. If worn on the fingers, it enhances "the midas touch"; if worn on the wrist, it provides stimulation to the meridians which represent survival and protection of the physical and emotional bodies. When worn at the third-eye, it can stimulate mental clarity, facilitating deep meditative states and activating psychic abilities. When worn as earrings, quartz crystals can provide for balancing of the physical body, for alignment with the higher realms, for stabilization and balancing of all chakras, for clearing and activation of the throat chakra and the third-eye, and for synchronicity between the left and right hemispheres of the brain. A single quartz crystal carried on ones person or placed in ones environment will assist in maintaining balance, energy, and protection.

Whether the crystal is worn, carried, or placed in ones environment, the force, the warmth, and the brilliance remain attuned to the energy of the one to whom it is connected.

Experimentation with Kirlian photography shows that the direction in which the point is worn makes very little difference; there is actually an overall increase in the energy field no matter which way the crystal points.

Pointing the crystal "up" has channeled energy into the upper chakras, causing some people to be so stimulated that they felt they were leaving their bodies [tending to make one "spacey"]; using the crystal while positioned in this direction has been quite beneficial for meditation, prayer, study, and taking tests.

Pointing the crystal "down", there has been a slight grounding effect as energy was directed toward the lower body and the Earth, tending to maintain more efficient grounding and assisting one in remaining more "in tune" with the world.

Pointing the crystal horizontally, a small increase has been noted in the energy in front of the body, with large increases on the sides.

Kirlian photography shows that if one holds a crystal in the receiving hand, the etheric fields of the body are, at least, doubled.

"Clear" quartz is used extensively in meditation, spiritual development, and healing. It helps one to recognize the origin of a dis-ease and has been used for this purpose quite extensively by the inhabitants of Atlantis and Lemuria, by the Native American Indians, the African tribal systems, the ancient Egyptian culture, the Mayans and Aztecs, the Australian Aborigines, the Romans, Scots, Celts, Tibetan Buddhists, Brahmans, and many others during the days of the "old ways". It has been used by these cultures in diagnostic healing, in raising the consciousness toward the enlightened state, and in communicating with the spirits and with those from other worlds.

Quartz and quartz crystals have been used for religious purposes since ancient times. Quartz is one of the seven precious substances of Buddhism. It was also said to have been one of the stones used in the breastplate of the high priest. Ancient priests used quartz crystals to render negative energy impotent, to dissolve enchantments and spells, and to destroy all black magic.

Romans used quartz crystals for glandular swelling, to reduce fevers, and to relieve pain.

In the Scottish Highlands, a crystal set in silver and worn about the back was thought to be effective for dis-eases of the kidneys.

In medieval times, the quartz crystal was held against the tongue to assuage fever and diminish thirst.

In addition to the techniques and healing properties discussed in the following HEALING TECHNIQUES section, the quartz crystal can also be used in the treatment of disorders of the circulatory system. It has been used in the treatment of vertigo, to stabilize dizziness, and to promote emotional stability. Holding the crystal to an area of the skin which has been burned, has eliminated pain, blistering, and any trace of the burn. A topical elixir of the quartz crystal has been quite beneficial to skin disorders. An elixir, taken internally, has been used in the elimination of toxins from the body. It can also be used in the treatment of digestive disorders and in the elimination of kidney and bladder infections and dysfunctions.

Vibrates to the number 4.

HEALING TECHNIQUES

The following information provides some examples on healing techniques. Once the reader has tried the techniques, the intuitive portion of the inner mind will provide further techniques for experimentation.

Since most dis-ease which occurs in the physical body is a reflection of disruption/disharmony of the energies in the etheric bodies, healing can more easily occur when harmony is restored within the outer bodies.

Crystals act as both transformers and harmonizers of energy and, hence, act to focus healing energy and healing intent, thereby producing the appropriate energy.

With ones thoughts, one can focus energy precisely where desired; with the additional help of a crystal, one can use this ability to stimulate healing. In many cases, the quartz crystal [or other mineral] enables the higher-self to direct the physical body to both repair and balance itself and, hence, facilitates the integration of the physical form with the "perfect self" of the ethereal.

There are four major accepted brain wave patterns which seem to have connective links to levels of consciousness. The advanced states are useful for healing stimulation and facilitation.

BETA - The BETA brain wave pattern exists on the level of the conscious mind; it is initiated at 14 cycles per second and usually averages about 21 cycles per second.

ALPHA - The ALPHA brain wave pattern exists on the level of the dreaming mind, during the creative state, and with the initiation of minimal extra sensory perception [ESP], cell energy renewal, and the beginning level of suggestibility for the subconscious mind; it ranges from 7 to 14 cycles per second.

THETA - The THETA brain wave pattern activates a deeper state of ESP, is the beginning level for psychokinesis [PK], facilitates painless surgery and dentistry, and initiates powerful levels of suggestibility; it ranges from 4 to 7 cycles per second.

DELTA - The DELTA brain wave pattern is usually recognized during deep sleep; during this time all ESP and PK talents are stimulated and the qualities of total memory and total suggestibility are instilled; it ranges from 1/2 to 4 cycles per second.

should be noted that there is a measurable increase in alpha brain waves after holding a quartz crystal for half an hour. Over a longer period of time, there is an increase in theta and delta brain waves.

The process of healing, when dis-ease is viewed as a discontinuity of energy, becomes simple. When there is an energy blockage in the physical body, the flow of energy to the cells of the affected area is diminished and the related organs, tissues, and structures begin to degenerate; at this time, one usually begins to exhibit the symptoms of dis-ease. When energy returns to the area, rebuilding and renewal of cells can occur and the dis-ease can be eliminated. One method of eliminating both the pain of dis-ease and that which is associated with energy blockages involves holding a crystal in the hand which is located on the same side of the body as the pain, while holding the other hand over the painful area; remain in this position until the pain begins to diminish [usually about thirty minutes]. With this technique, the amplifying ability of the crystal promotes additional direction of energy to the affected area. This technique is not recommended for the treatment of cancer or headaches.

NOTE: Pain killers can interfere with the healing process by coating the nerve endings so that the signals from the cells do not reach the brain. In this case, the brain does not recognize the pain and does not recognize the need to assist. Hence, the brain does not send the energy needed, and the condition of the cells worsens. This is one reason why painful diseases are often debilitating and progressively degenerative [e.g., arthritis, circulatory disorders]. Via the energy of the quartz crystal [or other appropriate mineral], energy can be supplied to the cells such that the cells can now repair themselves; hence, eliminating the cause of the pain because the signal is no longer necessary.

One with a fever can experience a quick restoration of normal temperature by holding a crystal in the hand of preference, at arms length, and pointing the crystal away from the body. The crystal seems to both draw-away and discharge the excess body heat.

The headache remedy is somewhat different. Most pain needs energy to repair, but the headache is thought, in some cases, to be due to too much energy in the head. Energy flows in and out of the head via the crown and brow chakras; when a blockage [usually emotional] occurs, the energy cannot be released and the excess pressure initiates pain. In this case, the excess energy needs to be removed.

One method of removing this excess energy involves placing the quartz crystal in the hand of preference [pointing skyward]; this hand is then allowed to rest on the solar plexus or on the navel chakra. Placing the other hand on the headache pain, this hand can be used to remove the excess energy from the head and to transfer it to the solar plexus or the navel chakra. Upon arrival at the chakra area, the energy would produce a supplemental energy which is applied toward total balancing of the body. This can take approximately thirty minutes to complete. To speed the process, one may close the eyes and picture the headache as a dark cloud of excess energy, visualizing the "removal" hand as a giant vacuum cleaner which is dissipating the cloud. Watch until the cloud is gone and then allow the eyes to open. Upon completion of the technique [and relief of pain], remember to breath deeply for several moments and to thank the universe for thy perfect self.

Example of American-Indian-Method-Of-Healing-With-Crystal
[You As Healer]

1. Breath upon the crystal to remove and "short circuit" any ambient negative forces.

2. Initiate a mental connection, through the third-eye, to the crystal. Then initiate a mental connection, through the third-eye, to the healing spirits working through you.

3. The person requesting the healing places the hand of preference between the hands of the healer, yet not touching these hands. The crystal is in the hand of preference of the healer and is pointing toward the palm of the hand of preference of the subject.

4. The healer rotates the crystal counter-clockwise [in locations of northern latitude] toward the palm of the hand of preference of the subject.

5. The subject is asked to feel the influencing energy from the crystal. When this is acknowledged, the healer rotates the crystal clockwise [in locations of northern latitude]. The subject is asked to determine which position of the crystal conveys the energy which feels more compatible.

   This is an attunement process for adjusting to the specific needs of the subject.

6. At the point which feels most compatible, the crystal is positioned, not touching the hand, but in a position which allows the current from the crystal to be directed mentally into the affected area of the body. The healer continues to allow the energy to channel through him/her [not giving away his/her own energy] until he/she "feels" the energy level change, or until the subject feels it is enough - usually about 20 minutes.

NOTE: You may do this for yourself, pointing the crystal directly to the affected area or sending it through the hand which is not the hand of preference to the desired body location.

PROPERTIES OF QUARTZ CRYSTAL FORMATIONS:

The following formations of quartz possess additional properties which are unique.

The reader will find photographs which are representative of these formations in "Love Is In The Earth - Mineralogical Pictorial".

Activation (Left) Quartz Crystal

The Activation (Left) Quartz Crystal can be recognized by an inclined window located on the left side of the primary face of the crystal.

The primary function which has been realized from this configuration has been the activation and increased performance of the left-brain functions. Used with the Activation (Right) Quartz Crystal, it brings a melding of the left and right brain abilities and a synthesis of same.

By directing the energy of this crystal toward the chakras (from the front side of the body), activation of each chakra is enhanced.

In addition, energy blockages can be removed from the right side of the body via the utilization of this configuration. It can also be used in the treatment of brain disorders which are located on the right side of the brain.

Activation (Right) Quartz Crystal

The Activation (Right) Quartz Crystal can be recognized by an inclined window located on the right side of the primary face of the crystal.

The primary function which has been realized from this configuration has been the activation and increased performance of the right-brain functions. Used with the Activation (Left) Quartz Crystal, it brings a melding of the right and left brain abilities and a synthesis of same.

By directing the energy of this crystal toward the chakras (from the back side of the body), activation of each chakra is enhanced.

In addition, energy blockages can be removed from the left side of the body via the utilization of this configuration. It can also be used in the treatment of brain disorders which are located on the left side of the brain.

Aperture Quartz Crystal

The Aperture Quartz Crystal is configured such that the crystal is cup-shaped, with a hollow "crater" being large enough to contain liquid.

This configuration, filled with water or an elixir, can be used as a "seer stone", to access information from the past, present, and future. It has been used with elixirs to enhance the qualities of same and to provide increased energy to elixirs; the elixir can be consumed from this design.

In addition, this formation can act to establish ineffable logic to ones skills and to promote the increase of ones designs with inventive ingenuity and skill. It actually produces the memory of a "brave new world" such that one perceives that the conception and the development of that world is within the self.

The Aperture Quartz Crystal has been used in the treatment of disorders of the stomach, the liver, the pancreas, the lungs, and to dissolve blockages from the arteries, the intestines, and the colon. It has been effective in the amelioration of bloating and water retention.

Barnacle Quartz Crystal

Barnacle Quartz Crystals are recognized as crystals covered or partially covered with smaller crystals. The larger crystal is the "old soul" and contains the wisdom and trust which attracts the smaller crystals.

This crystal can be used in meditation to provide insights to family and/or community problems. The barnacle quartz crystal is also excellent for those employed by service organizations [e.g., teachers, etc.]; the energy helps to stimulate a group cohesiveness and a willingness to work together. The crystal is a wonderful companion when one is experiencing the loss of a loved one.

It can also be used to increase both physical and intellectual fertility.

Bridge Quartz Crystal

The Bridge Quartz Crystal is recognized by a small crystal which penetrates and is located partially in, and partially out, of a larger crystal.

It facilitates bridging between the inner and outer worlds, between the self and others residing on this planet, and between the self and other worlds. The crystal aids in expressing that which one experiences when one is becoming more familiar with the self. It is quite beneficial when one is working with the aspects of spirituality, and with the advanced metaphysical areas, and attempting to share this knowledge with others. It is also beneficial to public speakers who lecture on topics concerning new ideas and avantgarde concepts.

The bridge quartz crystal is also useful for all types of teaching, promoting communication ties and understanding between teacher and student.

Buddha Quartz Crystal

The Buddha Quartz Crystal is recognized by the existence of an illusion resembling "Buddha-Sitting". The illusion is located by looking through the main face of the crystal, to the back of the crystal, to the position at the top of the back of the crystal. There is a line in this location which resembles a throne, upon which there is a figure similar to the "Buddha-Sitting" position. Danburite has also been found in this configuration.

This configuration has been used to bring the aspects of enlightenment and love toward realization. It intensifies all aspects of the attributes of Quartz, and assists one in the actualization of that which will promote ease in traveling ones chosen path. In addition, it can act as a guide in the physical reality and in astral and spiritual travel. It is a powerful formation, bringing peace to ones life and understanding to ones being.

It has also been used to stimulate meditation [no-mind], and has been used during group meditation to promote same. It holds an omnipotent energy which stimulates the pineal gland, induces the receipt of information from the higher-self, and brings tranquility and harmony to all situations.

In addition, it has been used to contact and to promote the transfer of information from the elders of the ancient civilizations of India, Tibet, and China. It is a stone of Shangrila, and is said to have been used to bring the harmony and accord of this civilization to those who share the energy.

Carved (Natural) Quartz Crystal

The Carved (Natural) Quartz Crystal is recognized by the existence of a carved triangular face - the carving outlines the face and is etched such that the location of the engraved portion is normally white in appearance.

This configuration can assist one in contact with extra-terrestrial information which is beneficial to ones growth and to the growth and increased awareness of our planet. It is a tool for the transfer of information between the self and others who reside on other planes of existence - the ethereal and the astral planes can be accessed without actual out-of-body travel to same.

In addition, this formation has been used to stimulate the recognition of details related to Earth-changes, astrological significance, and weather patterns. It has further been used for dowsing - the carved portion being the "Yes" significator.

Channeling Quartz Crystal

The Channeling Quartz Crystal is recognized by the configuration of a large seven-sided face, located in the center front position of the terminated end of the crystal; a triangular face is located on the opposite [backside] side of the crystal.

The "seven" of the one crystal face represents precision within the intuitive realm of the higher mind and the analytical understanding inherent in the mental and physical bodies. It is symbolic of the student, the professor, the mystic, and the seeker of wisdom.

The three-sided triangle on the opposing side provides for creative and innovative verbalization of inner truths. The "three" represents the both prerogative and the power of speech and the ability to both creatively and joyously express the self.

In this configuration, the "seven" represents the accessibility of innate wisdom and the "three" represents the ability of manifestation and verbal communication. The combination represents initiative and the interdependence between the world of the physical self and the perfection of "All That Is".

The channeling crystal provides for a means of channeling and expressing truth and wisdom from the both the inner realms of perfection and the other worlds. It provides for a conscious connection to the higher wisdom which is available from the higher-self and/or to the wisdom of experience and enlightenment which is available from the "other side".

The channeling crystals can be used to access the wisdom from "within and without". They can be used to bring forth light and love from the most truthful and knowledgeable portions of the self. Sometimes there can be an encounter with other entities from whom one can learn; always check the information, given by the entity, with the personal inner knowing.

Channeling crystals can be used:

- o   for meditation, allowing one to gain both inner clarity and wisdom;
- o   to facilitate specific answers to specific questions;
- o   to gain information in a specific area; and,
- o   with record keepers to access stored information.

One method for using the channeling crystal is to first sit quietly, initiate circular breathing, and call upon protection and guidance, surrounding the self with white light and affirming that the results of the session and the forthcoming information will be for the good of all. A channeler who feels fatigued after a session has had his/her vital energy used by an entity who is less evolved and who could only have participated in the activity if the affirmation of "...for the good of all" and the protection of white light or other mechanisms were not utilized. It is very important to remember that we all have within us the knowledge that we seek.

Now hold the crystal in the receiving hand and allow the mind to quiet; continue the circular breathing and meditate upon the precepts involving love, wisdom, peace, and unity. Identify with the concepts and allow the inner understanding to encompass the total being. Visualize a pure clear blue light beaming into the throat chakra. Visualize an indigo or a deep purple shimmering light at the third-eye. Verbally request the light and wisdom of "All That Is" to accompany, guide, and protect during this activity.

Now, either:

- o   hold the seven-sided face to the third-eye, while continuing the circular breathing, and focus at the third-eye; or,
- o   place the crystal termination between the index and middle fingers of the hand [your choice], with the seven-sided face toward the thumb. Allow the thumb to rest on the seven-sided face, close the eyes, and allow the information to flow to the conscious mind.

The impressions, symbols, images, feelings, or thoughts received should be acknowledged and expressed without doubt or distrust. Do not intellectualize or think about the information.

After the attunement has been refined, one may consciously choose to link the mind to entities who are present, and to receive the transmission of information from one or more, singularly. One is cautioned to maintain personal identity while allowing the entity to express.

Cluster Quartz Crystals

Cluster Quartz Crystals are recognized by the occurrence of crystals in a cluster. They serve to bring the "group" energy of the associated crystal to the surrounding environment, enhancing harmony and peace in groups, in the family, and in other social and/or business environments.

The energy generated is directly proportional to the number of crystals in the cluster.

They have also been used to activate and to cleanse other minerals, to enhance and to increase the energy of other minerals, and to activate the properties of same.

Convoluted Sheet Quartz

Convoluted Sheet Quartz can be recognized by the existence of holes in a milky winding and twisted quartz configuration. The structure occurred during the flow of the quartz over other minerals (usually, tourmaline), and over time, the tourmaline dissolved due to the changes in the condition of the environment. Occasionally there are some pieces of this configuration which contain fragments of the tourmaline.

This formation has been used for chakra cleansing - the chakras are cleansed and each cavity in the quartz acts as a black hole filled with white light, for transmutation of any negativity to positivity. In addition, when removing the ethereal cords which have been sent to ones chakras and attached by others, the formation can be used for the gentle removal of the cords and for sending positive energy to the transmitter of the cords.

The energy of Convoluted Sheet Quartz can be used to assist one in gaining universal energy, to "bloom" in ones environment, and to alleviate clarify interpretations.

Placed at the location of the spine, one can feel the location of the Kundalini, and can initiate the continuity of same. It has been used to delete and to transform blockages in the energy field, such that the Kundalini continues to move due to the awareness of ones centering.

It can instill movement in ones life, to allow for the activity required for progression while providing protection for ones movements.

Carrying this configuration has assisted in the increase of perception of others, such that one can understanding exactly what is being disclosed, more on a spiritual plane; subsequently, the application to the mental and material plane is enhanced; the intent of others and of the self is quite clear when this mineral is used.

Sleeping with this formation in ones environment can facilitate the vividness of dreams and the enhancement of the recall of same - the actual detail becomes lucid and unclouded in the mind; it is similar to recalling a scene that one has just experienced; having sufficient time to record dreams is no longer a problem.

In addition, past-life dreams are prevalent. During meditation with this mineral, one may ask questions and expect to receive clear, concise, and accurate answers.

In addition, this formation has been used to promote astral travel and to assure the maintenance of the ethereal cord which fosters ease of return to the body.

It is useful in multi-directional energy distribution; it appears that the energy, which is directed inward toward the central forces of the mineral, separates and returns at double the intensity. It brings forth a polarizing prismatic energy, which engenders a spectrum of energy to clear and to activate all of the chakras.

Convoluted Sheet Quartz can also be used to remove unwanted implants - both other-worldly and from the physical realm. Again, the cavities act to transform the implants into positive energy.

It has also been used to enhance muscular building and body formation, to ameliorate convulsions and distortions in ones eyes, and in the treatment of disorders of the muscular structure, the teeth, and the bones.

Cross Quartz Crystal

The Cross Quartz Crystal can be recognized by the formation of quartz crystals in the shape of a cruciform shape, and occasionally, by the Celtic cross configuration. It is a tool of the light worker, assisting in the removal of unwanted other-worldly implants. It represents the idea of multiplicity while stabilizing the center of the self, promoting a further uninterrupted connection with the ethereal perfection.

It is a world teacher for all of humanity, facilitating macrocosmic awareness and appreciation of the creative forces of nature. It is an excellent stone when studying the spirituality, and the arts and sciences.

Placing of this formation upon any chakra, has not only cleared and activated that chakra, but has provided a "sweeping" action which cleared the remaining centers.

It produces an excellent energy sources for use at the crown chakra and has also been used at all chakras to provide for the amplification of the energy available.

Curved Quartz Crystal

In the Curved Quartz Crystal curvature is produced during the developmental stages of growth and is rather a rare occurrence. The structure of the curved crystal provides for a continuous [when in ones energy field] alignment of the physical meridians and the nervous system, and the alignment of the physical, emotional, mental, etheric, astral, etc., bodies, singularly and with one another.

The Curved Quartz Crystal emanates a gentle, yet powerful, energy and can be used to cleanse the aura, to promote flexibility in ones attitudes, and to provide strength to ones decisions. It allows one to see the inner workings of any situation and to understand the superficial and the deeper meanings inherent in same. It also allows one to access the interior of the physical body in order to understand existing disorders, providing information with respect to the "fix".

It has been used in the treatment of spinal dis-alignment and in the correction of curvature deformation.

Double Terminated Quartz Crystal

Double Terminated Quartz Crystals are multi-functional; energy moves outward in either direction or in both directions concurrently. They have the capacity to draw or to transmit energy through both ends. "Doubles" are excellent for astral projection and for dreaming - place them under your pillow at night and they can increase and intensify the dream state. They are also excellent for use in meditation.

They can also be used to assist in providing one protection from mental and physical harm. Carrying a double terminated crystal can enable one to maintain ones energy shield.

They symbolize patience and perseverance; this is quite important during healing situations.

In addition, they have been used to move sickness from the body to a location which transforms the disorder from negativity to positive energy [i.e., the location is pre-determined and is, for example, a black hole which is filled with white light].

Elestial Quartz Crystal

The Elestial Quartz Crystal is recognized by natural terminations over the body and face of an etched and/or layered crystal.

It is the "enchanted crystal", bringing with it the concepts of Shiva and the understanding that after transition from one phase of life or from the physical body, the newness will be re-instilled. It provides the user with "a hug from the wind in the willow", allowing for flow in change and actualization.

These crystals can be used to assist one in overcoming emotional burdens, to bring the heart and the intellect into synchronicity, and to help one to look within and to find the love that has always been there. They stimulate the actualization of the conscious self, allowing for percipient recall of astute action, while exhibiting a continuous alignment with the spiritual realm and assisting one in access of same.

The elestial carries the inherent memory of that which was in existence prior to the development of humanity. It can be used to help one to become aware of the immortality of the spiritual being within the self and to enhance ones life on this plane of reality. It further assists one in the comprehension of the processes of life and the levels of death. It serves to provide an entrance to information concerning the past, present, and future of ones personal existence.

The elestial contains the absolute and ultimate essential wisdom and can provide for transfer of this insight to the physical intellect via the higher-self.

By holding an elestial in the hand of preference, after centering and attaining the inner emptying of the mind, one may stroke the etching/layers with the index finger of the other hand. This procedure can be used to bring one into alignment with the wisdom of the universe; it also helps one in translating the information and facilitates an understanding of that which is communicated. The information provided brings forth knowledge with respect to the essential state of the body and the essential state of being in this and other lives. It helps to provide the connection to the insight and realization that one can both love and embrace each worldly and other-worldly experience.

Gazing into the crystal, after centering and emptying of the mind, helps to show one the ways available to enable the "going within" ones being. After gazing, one may close the eyes and access the subconscious self, accepting information to assist one in examination of that which lies behind the reality of the time.

The elestial can be used to both sustain and "maintain" one during changes, helping to prepare one for transformation and allowing for the penetration of the hidden layers of "cause" which support the states of distress and dis-ease. It further assists one in releasing the cause; hence, decreasing or eliminating the effect. It helps one to understand that any control is personal control and that in order to actualize ones full potential, the state of personal action is required.

The elestial can be used to stabilize brain wave frequencies and to ameliorate erratic and/or confused thoughts; it can further assist in producing an expanded state of awareness and an encouraging energy to speed one toward the light. It assists one in summoning vitality in order to produce advancement toward the eternal brilliance of the spiritual self.

The elestial can be used to stimulate the chakras and to bring forth information which has been blocked; it can help to release the blockages and to provide an unobstructed pathway leading toward the retrieval of indispensable information relevant to the state of ones being [past, present, and future].

It assists in enhancing ones awareness of that which needs to be assessed and/or released from the emotional and intellectual bodies. It provides insight into those conditions which hinder the experience, into the validity of ones state of being, and into the concerns relative to the reality which one has chosen to encounter. After centering and relaxation, when the elestial is held, used for meditation, or placed upon the body, it will first provide a view or a message concerning that which needs to be cleared. It will subsequently assist in the removal and dissipation of any confusion and pre-judgmental ideas so that one may maintain a dispassionate, impartial, and composed attitude in order to acknowledge and assimilate the information.

The elestial has been used in medicine wheel ceremonies to reach the ancestral spirits and to provide the channel for the integral knowledge regarding the questions of the participants. It provides for both receipt and dissemination of information, dependent upon the consciousness and loving state of the user.

It assists one in the art of communication and in verbalization of the state of the emotions at the time the state occurs. It assists one in the recognition of the way one actually feels, both emotionally and physically; hence, helping to stimulate the power of personal expression and personal potential.

The energy of the elestial is intensified at the locations of the energy vortices of the Earth and can be of great assistance in the mass cleansing, healing, and re-awakening of the consciousness of the planet.

An example of a procedure which may be used when the elestial is to be a part of healing is as follows. After attuning to the crystal, look within the self and ask whether the elestial should be used at this time. If so, ask the subject of the healing [it could be the self] if there is willingness to "see" the hidden cause behind the distress. Then hold the hand of the subject, allowing the elestial and, if available, a herkimer diamond to rest between the palms of these hands; this furthers the attunement of the elestial to the self and to the subject and, additionally provides for integration between the elestial and the herkimer and the self and the subject.

The elestial can assist in activating and furthering the activities of the third-eye and can stimulate an increase in abilities associated with clairvoyance, clairaudience, and clairsentience.

It can also be used to assist one in access to information relevant to the karmic burdens incurred during past-lives, helping one to both recognize and understand the "easy" lessons which can cancel the karma. It can further be used to access future lives and to understand that which must be accomplished in this life in order to eliminate the need to repeat harsh lessons.

It can be used to facilitate access to shared past or future lives between two or more people. One method of accessing this information is by first initiating circular breathing, while holding hands with the "other" and looking within the self. Next place the elestial between the palms of one set of the hands, while still maintaining the position of holding hands. Now, allow the mind to become open and receptive to the pictures, words, voices, or visions which may appear.

The elestial has also been used in the treatment of epilepsy, schizophrenia, and drug-related burn-out. It can assist in the restoration of emotional and intellectual stability. It can further be used to diminish vertigo and symptoms associated with physical imbalances within the body.

Etched Quartz Crystal

The Etched Quartz Crystal can be recognized by the existence of abrasions located upon the outer areas of the crystal. The abrasions appear to be a type of hieroglyphics.

This formation has been used to facilitate contact and the transfer of information from the ancient Egyptian civilizations and from Lemuria and Atlantis. The transliteration of the symbols bring information relevant to ones life at the time of translation. They were once used in the healing temples of these ancient civilizations and, the markings also contain information of experiences in which they have participated. They also have contained information with respect to the healing methodology which has been proven successful over eons of time and throughout the universe. They have been accessed during the meditative state and have provided information concerning techniques utilized in the ancient civilizations of the Earth and of other locations in the universe.

The Etched Quartz Crystal is usually a personal meditation crystal. Meditation with the crystal is easily accomplished by placing the "hieroglyphics" upon the third-eye. Subsequent to this placement, close the eyes, still and open the mind, initiate circular breathing, relax, and be prepared to receive the information.

If one is meant to experience an Etched Quartz Crystal, the universe will provide. The Etched Quartz Crystal which is made available to one contains the information which will be beneficial to ones personal development and/or will provide information which will assist one in helping another.

Faden Quartz Crystal   [Astrological Sign of Scorpio]

The Quartz Faden [pronounced as "Fah-den"] crystal is one in which the inclusion of one or more white thread-like fibrous formations of quartz occurs. The name "Faden" is derived from the German translation of "thread". If more than one fiber is encompassed, the fibers are separate from each other. The Faden is visible [as a white thread or fiber] within the quartz structure because it is surrounded by either a fluid-filled or gaseous-filled chamber. The fiber is located [usually] at, or in proximity to, the center of the crystal; the geometrical location is perpendicular to the termination of the crystal and may be linear and undeviating or curved/bent. Faden crystals have been found only in the fissures of metamorphic formations; unlike other quartz crystals, they do not form in pegmatite or in cavities of sedimentary rocks.

The Faden crystal is one of *connection*, stimulating and furthering connective forces between the self and that which is chosen as the recipient. Delineation of many methods of unification are given within the description of the preceding arrays.

This crystal facilitates the attunement between the self and another, similar to the action produced by the Herkimer diamond. It assists in producing and maintaining the ethereal connection which one has with another [on any planes, in all dimensions].

It is also a stone for astral travel and for the exploration of the parallel dimensions of ones reality. It strengthens the "silver cord" and produces an energy which both promotes and protects one during flight. [It is also currently being used as a protective crystal for those engaged in air travel.]

In the exploration of parallel dimensions and other planes of existence, it stimulates the opening of the pathway and assists one in remembering the activities which one experiences and/or views as a non-participant. It has been used for past-life ascension, allowing one to maintain a strong-hold on the present reality while observing, without participating in, the events which one accesses; it further provides an understanding of the lessons which were [or could have been] learned, such that one may continue progression beyond the limitations of the lesson.

It is a stone for finding ones complement on the physical plane, serving as a magnetic field to attract ones counterpart and to facilitate an unfathomable energy transfer between the self and the other. The Faden crystal may be programmed to assist in bringing to one that which is desired.

It can be used to promote physical, mental, and emotional stability. It is an excellent stone for centering the self and for gridding disturbed areas of the Earth. It has been used in classrooms [similarly to the utilization of Lepidolite] in order to facilitate a stability within the environment. It has also been used to grid [via photograph and through actual physical placement] areas of the Earth which are prone to unsteadiness.

It provides for a continuous [when in ones energy field] alignment of the physical meridians and the nervous system, and for the alignment of the physical, emotional, mental, etheric, astral, etc., bodies, singularly and with one another.

It can be used to cleanse the aura and to stimulate the opening of the chakras.

The structure which exhibits a curved or bent thread-like fiber emanates a gentle, yet powerful, energy and can be used to promote flexibility in ones attitudes, and to provide strength to ones decisions. It allows one to see the inner workings of any situation and to understand the superficial and the deeper meanings inherent in same. It also allows one to access the interior of the physical body in order to understand existing disorders, providing information with respect to the "fix".

It is a stone of "seeking", assisting one in "ferreting-out" information which is either hidden or unknown. It is an excellent stone for future-telling and telepathic activities. It is also quite conducive to the furtherance of ones meditative state, serving to diminish attentiveness to distractions, and to foster the maintenance of same.

The energy of the Faden crystal serves to stimulate molecular bonding and is, hence, applicable to both superficial and internal healing of cellular loss of integrity and cellular abrasion. It is a stone which facilitates "mending" on all levels, assisting one to trace ones actions/belief systems back to the original cause of a disorder, and subsequently, promoting the restoration of same.

The crystals which exhibit the bent or curved faden can also be used in the treatment of disorders relating to inflexibility; they serve to stimulate ones adroitness and dexterity.

The crystals containing the linear faden can also act to strengthen, and to ameliorate dysfunctional conditions of, the spine.

An elixir constituting the application of the energies of the Faden crystal can be used to further all of the actions listed above.

Vibrates to the number 2 and the master number 88.

Generator Quartz Crystal

The Generator Quartz Crystal is recognized by a configuration of six crystal faces joining together to form the terminated apex. This crystal is "THE" quartz crystal for energy generation.

It is quite useful for energy magnification and for stimulating all portions of the physical, intellectual, emotional, spiritual, and subtle bodies. It has been used to cleanse the chakras, and to supplant any voids and/or any negative energies which are contained, with positive radiant white light.

It is sometimes placed in the center of a group, while the group is involved in healing or spiritual issues, in order to facilitate the connection with the energy between all members. It is quite useful in the healing configuration called the "Star of David", to generate the abundance of energy available.

Excellent results are received when a small generator crystal is used as a pendulum.

The generator crystal has also been used to rectify localized energy disturbances. It acts to dissipate the disturbance and to replace any disorganized energy with a stable, authoritative energy which discourages further disorder.

Natural generators and crystals polished in the configuration of generators have the same properties - they are truly powerful tools for the metaphysician.

Growth Interference Quartz Crystal

Growth Interference Quartz Crystals have been found in Dalnegorsk, Primorie, Russia, and have the appearance of being carved with a trim-saw. They are quartz crystals which have shared their growing expanse with very thin flat calcite crystals of the type that are named "Papierspat (paper-spar) by geologists of Switzerland. The growth interference appears to have occurred during the end of the growth cycle of the long, thin, clear quartz crystals. The calcite crystals were sub-parallel during growth and developed at an angle to the lower prism faces of the quartz crystals;

then they, as "Papierspat" often does, disappeared just prior to crystallization was totally complete. The result is a series of slightly indented lines carving the prismatic faces and sometimes interfering with the growth of the positive rhombohedron.

This configuration of the Quartz crystal has been used to bring access to the astral, ethereal, and higher planes, in order that one may remove barriers and may understand the patience of step-wise progression. It can assist one in proceeding through traumas and through changes with ease - promoting the understanding of the trauma and the bases for change. It further allows the knowledge that the end of each journey, each experience, and each incident is the beginning of a new delight.

It has been used to align the physical body with the subtle bodies, and to bring an electro-magnetic alignment to the energy fields of the body. It can also be used in the removal of energy blockages; when carried or worn upon the body, the chakras are aligned automatically and the Kundalini is activated.

The energy of Growth Interference Quartz Crystal has been applied to facilitate understanding of our emerging culture in order to reveal ones ultimate destiny. It brings information concerning ones increasing vibratory rate with respect to spiritual evolution and demonstrates the method of giving energy to others while constantly allowing for the energy to be replenished by the energy of the universe. The mineral truly facilitates ones connection with the perception and understanding that we are beings of light, with access to an perpetual and continuous source of energy.

This mineral also assists in the removal of doubts. Shakespeare said "Our doubts are traitors and make us lose the good we oft might win by fearing to attempt...." - with the energy of this crystal, ones doubts are recognized and ejected through conscious understanding that one can accomplish anything if one truly has the desire to do so and if one removes self-limitations. This crystal truly places one in the situation of being "completely in command" of ones life.

The energy serves to bring one a universal protective force and acts to stimulate the knowledge of any impending danger. It has been used by children to protect from physical harm during childhood.

It has been used to remove physical blockages within the body, to promote the healing of cuts and abrasions, to mend incisions after surgery, and to provide information concerning the most positive way for rejuvenation and recovery from any disorder.

In addition, the energies of Calcite are combined with Quartz to bring a powerful healing and progressing energy to ones life. Although the Calcite does not normally remain with the crystal, the energy seems to be inculcated and remains to assist one in energy-work.

Horn Of Plenty Quartz Crystal

The Horn Of Plenty Quartz Crystal can be recognized by the formation of a flower-type structure growing around, an encompassing, a quartz crystal. The petals of the flower-type design tend to curve downward to resemble petals.

This formation has been used during the meditative state to produce stellar contact with the highest order of angels, with information imparted which is extremely relevant and of vast importance to the users. Used at the crown chakra, it has aligned the chakras and has bestowed a centering effect. At the heart chakra, it seems to clean the area and to promote protection and love concurrently. It assists one in seeing and in understanding the stages of ones life and acts to provide insight to changes required to promote peace and happiness within ones life.

It can be used to stimulate the energy of the throat and provides an excellent energy to supplement the process of "toning".

It is a "stone of immortality", assisting one to both overcome and to progress toward excellence. It elevates ones sense of self-worth and helps one to understand and to actualize the intrinsic state of perfection which is available.

It can help one to become attuned to the Earth and can provide direction to assist one in increasing the ionization of the atmosphere. It can also assist one in communication with the spiritual forces of the Earth and can help one to understand that which is required in order that the Earth may heal itself.

It has been used to enhance the energy transfer of other minerals to stimulate healing on all levels. It can also be used to stimulate the manifestation of "plenitude" in ones life.

Jacare Quartz Crystal

The Jacare Quartz Crystal is a form of the Elestial Quartz Crystal which can also be used to bring one the qualities of fluency, persuasiveness, and effectiveness in ones aspirations.

It furthers ones assertiveness while eliminating aggression. It is helpful in community work and in the organization structure, assisting one in remembering the "giving" qualities of the Divine.

It also acts to connect one with the source of all being, promoting the acceptance that "everything is, indeed, okay". It is excellent in extracting energy blockages, yielding ease in alignment of the energy centers.

Japan Law Twin Quartz Crystal

The Japan Law Twin Quartz Crystal can be recognized by the configuration of a penetration twin. In addition to the properties listed in the TWIN QUARTZ CRYSTAL section of this book, it has also been used to stimulate the synthesis of the perfection of the subtle bodies to the state of the physical body, bringing an awareness of the disparity and correcting the differences such that perfection is initiated.

It has also been used to dissipate and to transmute deviations, working-out problems on both the physical and subtle levels.

It is an excellent formation for clearing the aura and for aligning the auric body with the physical structure, diminishing the "muddy" areas in both the aura and the physical body. It can act to stabilize the emotions, to dispel anger, and to encourage one to "expect a miracle", to enjoy the refreshing energy of new beginnings, and to understand the reality of excellence.

It is also a "stone of perpetuation", acting to enhance the management of resources within the body. It can be used to regenerate the cellular structure.

Key Quartz Crystal

The Key Quartz Crystal is recognized, usually, by a three-sided or six-sided indented shape located on the crystal. The indent becomes narrower as it goes within the crystal and ends within the crystal, usually in an apex termination.

It is used to unlock the "doors" to healing concepts and to those aspects of the self which tend to be illusive. It further helps one to answer questions like - why can't I...?

It also assists one in accessing that which is hidden in any situation. One can place the crystal on letters, photographs, etc., in order to gain admittance to concealed or obscure messages which are inherent.

It can be used to assist in analytical problem-solving; placing the crystal upon a textbook, which contains the information necessary to arrive at a solution, has stimulated the inner knowledge of the answer.

Laser Wand Quartz Crystal

The Laser Wand Quartz Crystal is recognized as a long slender crystal with small faces comprising the termination. The crystal tapers inversely [i.e., from the base to the termination]. The angles of the sides of the crystal are curved, in many instances, rather than straight. It is said that all "wand" crystals were developed on Earth by other planetary beings; they are said to have developed not by growth, but via thought projection. These crystals have an intimate relationship with both inner and outer space. In addition, there are reversed-laser wands, which have a true taper from the termination to the base - these have recently become available from our Earth and will also be discussed below.

The use of laser wands during meditation facilitates the establishment of a finer communication with the other worlds, the crystalline world, and the inner world of the self. These crystals radiate a lovely energy and have been recognized as a constant source of the brilliant white light. When one holds a laser wand, the energy tends to surround the body, providing for a protective barrier.

The laser wands often have unique etchings and/or markings upon them. They were once used in the healing temples of Lemuria, the markings indicating the records of experiences "they have seen". They contain information with respect to the healing methodology which has been proven successful over eons of time and throughout the universe. They have been accessed during the meditative state and have provided information concerning techniques utilized in Lemuria and on other planets.

The energy of the laser wand crystal is extremely well focused via the small termination. It can be used to clear an area of negativity, to create protective barriers, and to beam healing energy to the self or another. This can be accomplished by holding the laser wand in the hand of preference and directing the energy to flow immediately to the target; when producing protective barriers, allow the energy to flow around the subject or object such that the auric field is not damaged.

Protecting the self with the laser energy field can be accomplished, in a similar manner, by directing the energy to surround the physical body; it can also be accomplished by wearing or carrying the laser wand. In these cases, when consciously desired, one tends to merge with the environment, becoming disregarded and/or un-seen. It facilitates a magical portrayal, allowing one to step into a picture, becoming a painted figure within the composition - a figure that has never, and will never, move.

In advanced healing practices, the laser wands can be used to open the chakras and to perform psychic surgery. The wand assists in "surgically" removing attitudes, feelings, and attachments which may be causing or may potentially cause dis-ease. It should be noted that unless a person is willing to release the thought patterns, concepts, and self-constricting emotional patterns or ties, and to identify with a more positive self-image, the patterns will, most likely, return and the person will be required to learn further lessons. It has also been used to facilitate shamanic healing via the process of removing [by extraction] the unwanted condition from the physical form.

The laser wand has been used in the treatment of disorders involving imperfect form and function. It allows one to recognize the perfection and beauty within the self and to manifest the totality externally.

In addition to the qualities of the non-reversed laser wand the Reversed-Laser Wands have been used to bring forth an arrangement of the divine order of personal life, the sacred order upon, and within, the Earth, and the celestial order of the universe. It further facilitates the concepts of organization and systematic resolutions, and reflects the implementation of same.

When using this configuration for opening the chakras, and when consciously directed, one can open the chakras of the self and of another concurrently. This quality tends to promote a connection between the self and another that is truly conducive to the successful actualization of healing.

It can help one to reach out to others, in the spirit of "brotherhood" and love. It is expressive of warmth and intelligence, promoting both altruistic tendencies and devotion to "right-mindedness". On the other hand, it provides stamina against weariness from adulation.

It can promote inner cellular awareness such that each cell affected by a disorder can singularly, and collectively, recognize the reason for the malfunction and then release the anomaly, facilitating both alignment with the perfect self and the healing state.

Lens Quartz   [See Sheet Quartz]

Manifestation Quartz Crystal

The Manifestation Quartz Crystal is recognized by a small crystal totally enclosed within a larger crystal. These crystals are quite rare.

The use of the manifestation crystal requires the inner knowledge that one is a clear and perfect channel, that a pure white light provides the guiding way, and that the purity of the Divine is within the inner self.

If there is something which one wishes to manifest, the relevant questions are: "Do I really want this?" - "Are there reasons that I may not want this?" If parts of a person do/do not want something, the crystal will not facilitate manifestation because it is receiving mixed messages. One must clear any feelings of ambivalence and inner turmoil prior to using this crystal.

One procedure, which has been quite effective in the use of the manifestation crystal, is as follows:

o   Meditate with the crystal [i.e., clear the mind, initiate circular breathing, and relax];

o   Concentrate on the base chakra, the third-eye, the navel chakra, or the area located two-inches below the navel;

o   Visualize that which is desired and bring it consciously into a clear mental picture; and

o   Feel the emotions associated with the actualization to reality of the visualization.

These crystals can also be used to facilitate artistic creativity, creative thinking, agricultural pursuits, and to increase or decrease [dependent upon the direction of the energy] any aspect of ones life.

Nodule Quartz Crystal

The Nodule Quartz Crystal can be recognized by the configuration of the quartz formation in a nodule with quartz druse overlaying the structure.

This formation has been used to eliminate illusion and to help one to understand that the "view from the top" is the same as the "view from the bottom". It promotes sufficient emotional and intellectual advancement such that one may view the inevitably clear way.

It can be used to fill the voids in ones aura, chakras, and memory. It is an excellent formation to use when one is cleansing the ethereal connections of others from ones chakras - it, without any conscious intent, fills the vacancies remaining after the removal of the cords, with a clear healing energy. It has been used to remove growths and to promote healing on all levels.

Pinnacle Crystal

The Pinnacle Quartz Crystal can be recognized by the growth of the quartz termination to a pinnacle termination.

It has been used to facilitate ascension, providing for a viewing of ones life on this plane [during this lifetime]. It can be used during "re-birthing" sessions to enhance ones understanding of both the blockages which are removed and the reasons for which they existed.

It both opens and activates the crown chakra, and assists one to channel desire toward the "proper" goals, and assisting one to adjust and to be comfortable in all situations.

It further provides for a smooth transition from the beta state to the alpha level, where extra-sensory perception is stimulated.

Pocket Quartz Crystal

The Pocket Quartz Crystal can be recognized by the formation of pockets in a massive quartz structure.

This configuration has been used to assist one in memory stimulation and to increase ones memory capacity. It has also been used to assist one in re-organization of the files maintained by the inner self, such that each file is readily retrievable.

It assists one in rational examination of both ones environment and the issues affecting ones environment. It also promotes a deeper perception of the issue and assists one in looking at the issue intelligently, but with input from the loving side. While allowing one to discard insignificant and irrelevant details, it provides for a clear picture of each issue.

It also directs the state of change to orderliness and calms the attitude, providing for a supplemental physical vitality to the user. It transforms the energy of the crown chakra to energize the base chakra [in contrast with most stones] and actualizes the power of wisdom.

It has been used in diagnosing disorders associated with disorganized cellular patterns. It can be used in the treatment of both the structure of the bone and the composition and formation of the cells. It has been used to assist in the prevention of RNA/DNA damage and can be used in repair of same.

Rainbow Quartz Crystal

The Rainbow Quartz Crystal is recognized by fractures within the crystal. Crystals containing these internal fractures have certain prismatic effects which produce powerful rainbows within the crystal giving additional energy which is lacking in a "crystal clear" specimen.

These rainbow crystals bring rainbows into ones life and are a very special gift from the spirit-keeper of the crystal; they help one to deal with negativity and to maintain the constant awareness that love is within the life one experiences at every moment. They produce the full spectrum of colour, the white light of healing and perfection being dispersed into the individual rays of the rainbow; this dispersion facilitates use of the rainbow crystal on any and all chakras.

<u>Record Keeper Quartz Crystal</u>

The Record Keeper Quartz Crystal is recognized by a raised [or several raised] perfect triangle[s] located on one or more of the crystal faces. It should be noted that the quartz crystal is not the only crystal which is a record keeper; for example, there are a few rare ruby crystals, from the Republic of South Africa and from the Ruby Crystal Mine in India, which also exhibit this property.

The record keeper is a crystal within which wisdom is stored. When one properly attunes to this crystal, the ancient knowledge and profound secrets of the universe can be psychically retrieved. These crystals have been consciously <u>and</u> purposely programmed by the beings who created the energies which have culminated in the actualization of life on this plane, and by their direct descendants [e.g., the Atlanteans and Lemurians].

The purposes of accessing information from the record keeper are:

o   to provide one with information concerning the origin of the human race, the human soul, and all that exists <u>or</u> has existed in ones reality;
o   to facilitate the actualization of each person as a healing agent for humanity and the environment; and
o   to allow one to incorporate higher knowledge, wisdom, peace, and love into this and other planets.

Only those with open minds and pure hearts can access the information via attunement of the consciousness with the inner energies of the crystal.

The information provided by the record keeper enhances ones light, provides for a deeper access to personal wisdom, and promotes a greater peace to be used in this world.

The "three" of the triangle[s] located upon the face[s] of the crystal represents perfect balance achieved when the physical, mental, and emotional aspects of ones being is aligned with the love and purity of the highest spirituality. The triangular shape, of the "doors" which lead to the records, also symbolizes the third-eye, the creation, and the preservation of the state of perfection which serves as a pathway toward the enlightened state.

The information stored within the record keeper could be relevant or non-relevant to physical life on Earth. One must be open and willing to accept all information [even those concepts which one would judge as inconceivable] and must be capable [as we all are] of processing the information and applying it to this physical life.

The record keeper crystal is usually a personal meditation crystal. Meditation with the crystal is easily accomplished by placing a triangle upon the third-eye. Subsequent to this placement, close the eyes, still and open the mind, initiate circular breathing, relax, and be prepared to receive the information.

Another method of accessing information is to activate the triangle by rubbing the thumbnail across the triangle from top to bottom. This provides the opening. Closing-off the source is accomplished by the opposite manipulation.

If one is meant to experience a record keeper, the universe will provide. The record keeper which "comes" to you contains the information which will be beneficial to your personal development and/or will provide information which will assist you in helping another.

Sceptre Quartz Crystal

The Sceptre Quartz Crystal is recognized as a naturally formed crystal which, at the base, is penetrated by a rod; in actuality, the crystal formed around the rod.

These crystals were used in Atlantis and Lemuria in healing ceremonies and were a symbol of the power of the realm; those who carried or wore a sceptre crystal were in the position of "high priest/priestess". The sceptre crystal brings the spirituality of the higher planes into the healing ceremonies and focuses the energy deep within the "heart" of the matter; i.e., the energy is directed to the "heart" of the cell, to the "heart" of the disability, to the "heart" of the subtle bodies, and most importantly, to the "heart" of the energy center of the etheric body, where re-structuring of the physical, mental, or emotional disorders can occur.

It is an excellent configuration for transmission of directional energy.

There are also Reversed Quartz Sceptres which activate the same properties and further serve to return the healing energy to the user. It can also be used to produce a state of mind which is free from impressions. It allows one to see the duality of ones nature, rectifying the negative and building the positive. It can produce deep silence interspersed with visions of the luminous terrain emitted from the crown chakra.

Seer Stone Quartz

The Seer Stone Quartz is river tumbled quartz [sometimes amethyst, smokey, or citrine] which has been polished on one end to permit "gazing" to the inner realms of the stone.

It is used for "gazing" to provide access to the sacred texts of the ancient ones. By directing the mental focus to a period of time and/or appropriate location, one may access varying texts from varying ancient civilizations.

It further stimulates the remembering of that which occurred prior to birth and refreshes ones knowledge concerning the realm of "after" life.

Self-Healed Quartz Crystal

The Self-Healed Quartz Crystal is, usually, recognized by small [usually less in size than the main termination] crystalline structures at the location where the crystal was removed from its matrix or home. The self-healed crystal is one which was separated from a secure base or was damaged during growth, but continued to reach the inherent natural state of perfection by forming smaller terminated faces. These faces together appear like a lace-type design of finished edges.

Another type of self-healed crystal is one which has been broken [exhibiting the break in the horizontal plane or close to the horizontal strata], with the break being healed and the crystal structure being again complete. These crystals have been found in Messina, Republic of South Africa. This crystal is the master crystal in the art of self-healing.

The self-healed crystal, having learned to heal itself, can lend this knowledge to the user and can share the experience of self-healing. One may use the crystal for healing of the self or in "crystal healing" of another person. One method of utilization of this crystal is to place the self-healed crystal in the hands of the subject, or on an area of the body of the subject, in order to send to the subject the knowledge of the art of self-healing.

This crystal takes situations, which appear to be devastating, and helps them to fulfill themselves - utilizing the law of the perfect order of the universe and the creativity of natural completion.

Seven and Eight-Faced Quartz Crystals

Seven and Eight-Faced Quartz Crystals are recognized by the description of the name. These crystals provide conservation of energy, of resources, of .... They stimulate the removal of obstacles in ones path and provide for further installation of energy in all endeavors.

They are said to be of other-worldly origination and to bring the capacity for actualization on all levels. In addition, they are said to bring order to ones life, to impart an energy of manifestation, and to produce a melding of the spiritual and the angelic realms.

Sheet Quartz   [Also Known as Lens Quartz]

Sheet quartz occurs in the formation of flat and, relatively clear, quartz layers.

It has been used as a window to other dimensions, to access information from the astral plane and the akashic records, and to see within the inner self. The action of looking within the self with the sheet quartz has allowed one to recognize disordered states and to mentally rearrange and reorganize the disarray of dis-ease. Sheet quartz has also been used for "gazing" and for sending and receiving messages.

It can stimulate the heart chakra and the third-eye and is an excellent tool for communication between the self and other worlds. It can also be used to stimulate visualization and visionary experiences and to actuate the higher psychic abilities.

It can also be used to stimulate contact with the "solution planes" of existence. In the meditative or non-meditative state, answers to problems of all magnitudes seem to "come" very quickly to the user.

It has been used in the treatment of disorders of, and for pain in, the area of the heart.

Shovel Quartz Crystal

The Shovel Quartz Crystal can be recognized by the shovel formation of the crystal. This configuration can be used to assist one in the approach to solutions and to promote the revelation of same. It further acts to bring information which will assist one in progress towards resolution.

It has been used to assist one in encountering the different aspects of the self and to understand the imagined wonders which exist on the other planes. The energy is also conducive to facilitation of encounters, counteracting ones self-limiting concepts of space and time. It further provides for the elucidation of universal mysteries and for a unity of direction.

This formation also provides encouragement to one to gather knowledge throughout the travels of life. It hinders lasting impressions of undesirable experiences, and encourages lasting impressions of desirable experiences. It does not, however, allow one to forget the lessons learned from any experiences - because of this characteristic, if one is attentive to the inner self, one seldom is placed in circumstances requiring the repeat performance of undesirable lessons.

Singing Quartz Crystal

Singing Quartz Crystals are similar in configuration to the laser wand configuration, albeit usually smaller. They have a clear sweet resonance when gently allowed to touch one another.

They are said to have been developed by thought projection during visitation from other planetary beings who were close to the Earth in space craft. They share a common sound and contain a solution to the obstacles of communication with respect to the sending and receiving of messages between the Earth plane and extra-terrestrial beings.

Singing crystals are said to have also been used to assist space craft from other worlds during navigation and landing processes. Utilization of these crystals in the gridding process produces a superb force field due to the interaction of the "singing energy". The gridding of areas of the Earth with these crystals can assist in stimulating communication and visitation by beings from other physical worlds.

The singing crystal expresses the spectrum of sound and is compatible with the spectrum of light. It creates the very powerful, higher pitched "OM" vibration, bringing about the creative forces. The body can attune to this spectrum and can emanate the energy and reality of the higher-self.

They further help to bring joy to ones life and to encourage one to move to the rhythm of ones own "drum".

In addition, they can be used to open and to release energy blockages, to align the energies of the body, to smooth the aura, and to stimulate clairaudience.

The sending of a clear light frequency through the crystals can assist one in contacting analytical beings of other worlds - both other planetary worlds and other dimensional worlds. They have been used to bring communication from celestial beings.

Singing crystals combine the healing vibrations of Mother Earth with the energy of the stars. They are quite useful in "toning for health" and tend to promote "rearrangement to perfection" of the cellular structures. They have also been used in the treatment of disorders of the ears and to stimulate the correction of hearing deficiencies.

Spade Quartz Crystal

The Spade Quartz Crystal can be recognized by the formation of one or more faces of the crystal being structured in the configuration of a "spade" in a deck of playing cards.

This pattern brings an insight which allows one to see into the "heart" of situations and to determine the benefit, or the detriment, to the continued participation in same; it further acts to promote the inner strength required for continuing or discontinuing the participation.

This is a very good stone for astral travel; it acts as the vehicle, and carries the user through the planes of existence. It provides protection, promoting firmness in perilous positions [i.e., flying], and is the care-taker for the flight. It determines the route and that which should be shown, while other stones for astral travel sometimes allow the energy to be directed toward that which one wishes to see. It is also a protective stone for physical travel, especially by air.

It acts to facilitate all action required to provide one with persistence to maintain "correctness". It provides for a connection with the ethereal energy, with attachment via the intellect; hence, promoting intellectual stimulation on the higher planes. It further assists one to "re-commit to the light", enhancing the connected-ness between the self and all of humanity.

In addition, it has been used in the treatment of disorders related to sight, hearing, and taste.

Spiral Quartz Crystal

The Spiral Quartz Crystal can be recognized by the twisted configuration through the body of the formation. It has been used to bring the universal spiral of energy to the physical body and to assist one in maintaining connection with the physical plane during meditation.

It has been used to activate the movement of the Kundalini, furthering the progression through the energy centers of the body. It tends to remove energy blockages to promote continual movement of energy through the body and to the higher-self such that one can maintain perpetual contact with same.

It provides for an electrical stimulus, facilitated through the subtle bodies, which produces a dielectric charge due to the alignment of the "other" with opposing electrical energy. It is quite interesting to use this stone as a control for ones awareness level with respect to the energy transfer which is actually accepted.

It inspires the energy of love, such that all chakras are activated into a spontaneous flowing movement [similar to a spiral energy extending from the base to the crown chakra], providing for a balance of the male and female energies.

The configuration is also used by many Sufi dancers to provide stabilization. It has also been helpful to mountain climbers, skiers, skaters, and other athletes to promote balance.

It has been used in the treatment of vertigo and to promote stability during recovery from dis-ease or from accidental injury.

Tabby Quartz Crystal

The Tabby Quartz Crystal is recognized as a flat crystal with "notches" on one or both of the flat sides. Rubbing the fingernail in an "downward" motion across the notches [major striations] of the tabby produces an "opening" of the crystal. This opening is similar to opening a file drawer; one can then access the information which the tabby contains. Closure of the "file drawer" is attained by rubbing the fingernail in an "upward" motion across the notches of the crystal.

In addition, this crystal is used to activate other crystals and minerals; one way to accomplish this is to hold the tabby in the "hand of preference" and to rub the tabby across the notches [in a downward motion], while holding the other stone in the other hand.

Trans-Channeling Quartz Crystal

The Transmitter/Channeling Quartz Crystal is recognized by a configuration of three seven-sided faces, each adjacent [on both sides] to a three-sided triangular face.

This structure combines the qualities of the transmitter crystal and the channeling crystal.

It also provides for a continuous connective force between the holder of the crystal and "All That Is".

It is the crystal for creativity and service to humanity through both spiritual and mystical pursuits. It allows access to the records relating to each question or thought and, even without focusing, provides intuitive awareness in all situations.

Transmitter Quartz Crystal

Transmitter Quartz Crystals are recognized by a configuration of two symmetrical seven-sided faces with a perfect triangular face located between them. The "seven" of the two crystal faces represents the ability to activate precise control of the physical senses and desires in order to attain wisdom via strengthening the connection to the higher-self. The three represents creativity in the attainment of unity.

The combination seven-three-seven indicates personal improvement, creativity, and manifestation via the creative forces [3], held in balance and precision by the direct connection to the higher-self coupled with the attributes of both rectitude and analytical capability [7]. The combination of the two seven-sided faces brings the qualities of ease, in change and in progress, together with variety in the experience of higher knowledge. The total combination blends the higher-self with the individual physical and mental consciousness, assisting one in the application of universal knowledge and wisdom in all aspects of ones life; hence, bringing benefits to the realm of service to humanity.

Through the use of these crystals, one can connect to the highest wisdom and can receive specific information to specific circumstances or can receive the universal truth necessary for ones growth to enlightenment.

Thoughts or questions need to be clearly and precisely defined and then projected into the transmitter with an assurance that one is both ready and willing to receive, to understand, and to incorporate the yielded information. The transmitter then "beams" the intellectual resonance "out" to the source of all knowledge. The clarity of the forthcoming information will reflect the clarity and sincerity of the message or question which was sent.

Transmitters can be used:

o   to both connect and align ones mind with the higher-self in order to further ones own spiritual development;

o   to consciously arrange for communication with spiritual guides or master teachers from the other side;

o   to develop ones intuitive faculties and telepathic communication;

o   to act as a "telephone" to send messages to, and to receive messages from, another Earth being [in this case, the transmitter is automatically emptied of the thought form when the transmission has been received by the appropriate person]; and

o   to send thoughts [as energy] toward the well-being of another and the well-being of the planet.

When access to the ethereal plane is more prominent [i.e., sunrise, sunset, periods of the full moon, solstice, and equinox] the most conducive periods, for programming ones transmitter, are available.

Prior to programming the transmitter, one may sit quietly, breathe, and focus on, and align the self with, the numerical attributes discussed above. During this time the crystal would be held in the "receiving" hand.

After the question is clearly defined within the mind, place the triangular face on the area of the third-eye, and mentally project the inquiry or message into the crystal. Then place the crystal in a special place in an upright position, in the sun/moon, and allow it to remain undisturbed for 24 hours. Do not "prop" the crystal with other crystals; energy disturbance, transmission problems, and jumbled messages could occur. An abundance of sunlight/moonlight will facilitate the projective power of the crystal. After 24 hours, sit quietly, still the mind, and be open and receptive. Place the triangular face to the area of the third-eye and receive the information which is being relayed - note the thoughts which enter the mind, for many times this is the mechanism by which you receive.

Even when no question is asked and thoughts of love or healing are sent, messages from the universal center of energy and light are usually returned.

Another method involves similar preparatory steps with the actual transmission occurring during rotation of the crystal within the hands, with the termination of the transmitter end of the crystal pointing toward the sky and leaning, as applicable, in the direction the message is to be sent. As the crystal is rotated, the mind is centered on the programming such that there is adequate focus maintained on the desired results; the message is then released to the ethers, being sent, as appropriate, to the higher-self of the pre-determined recipient.

There are many other methods through which the mechanisms of transmission can be facilitated. The reader is encouraged to experiment and to use that which is most comfortable to the self.

Transformation Quartz Crystal

The Transformation Quartz Crystal can be found in any and all configurations. It is usually not recognized until the beginning of the transformation [i.e., changes in shape, quality, and/or colour].

The crystal is one for progressive change, assisting one in forward movement in all aspects of life. It promotes the understanding that one need not resist existence; it helps one to both relax and trust in the creation of personal reality. It further assists one in listening to the songs of life, eliminating discordance while promulgating that which is of the nature of perfection.

It assists one in surrendering to spirituality, allowing transformation to spontaneously occur, and inspiring the completion of the mundane cycles.

The transformation crystal helps one to replace negative attitudes with positive direction. It further stimulates the ease of movement throughout the vibratory realm of ecstasy.

The crystal, when transformation is via a change in colour, tends to stimulate activity and/or healing in the chakra related to the newly acquired colour. Changes in shape often indicate the creation of a self-healing crystal. Changes in quality may signify the addition or elimination of negativity.

Twin Quartz Crystal

The twin crystal is recognized as a growing-together of two or more individual crystals such that certain portions of each crystal are in parallel alignment and other portions of each crystal are in reverse positions with respect to each other.

It facilitates the building of relationships on all levels, acting to encourage encounters with the soul-mate[s] present during this lifetime. It helps one to create a balance such that the outer manifestation and the inner being are not in opposition and are manifested as movements of the same energy flow.

The crystal promotes the recognition that love gives freedom, bringing the relative synthesis of love and freedom to the level of understanding which is inherent within the spiritual plane.

The twin crystal is also useful for melding the consciousness of groups and for promotion of universal love.

Window Quartz Crystals

The Window Quartz Crystal is recognized by the presence of a large diamond-shaped "window" located in the center front of the crystal, such that the top point of the diamond connects with the line leading directly to the termination, the side points connect with angles forming the opposing faces, and the bottom point connects with a line leading to the base of the crystal.

The four sides of the diamond on the window crystal represent the transmission of information between the various realms of intellectual activity, allowing for both the understanding and the acceptance of the conundrums of this physical reality. The four sides also represent the practical side of ones nature and the impetus to continue with the quest for spirituality in ones lifework. The diamond shape represents the balance between, and the syntheses of, the spiritual and physical realms; it further exemplifies the clarity of the mind, a force which maintains itself as the perfect state, never wavering, always reliable, and sometimes manifested.

These crystals are powerful teachers. They are like open windows through which one can see beyond illusionary identities and into the essence of the self. They may often allow one to become aware of the insecurities which inhibit the expression of the perfect self. The crystals allow for the reflection of ones self-image and the associated perfections or imperfections of the user. They can also be used, with consent, to reflect the state of another. They are quite useful in determining the cause of dis-ease.

Window crystals will come to a person when he/she is willing to honestly look within the self and to accept the truth.

Examples of two techniques for accessing the window crystal, in order to gain insight into pre-specified areas of concern or in order to receive random information from the spirit keeper of the crystal, are as follows:

o   Still the mind, initiate circular breathing, relax, and gaze into the inside of the crystal, via the window. The window will reflect, back to the mind, the impressions, colours, and feelings of the auric body.

o   Close the eyes, clear the mind, and mentally focus on the specific aspect in which there is a desire to find a greater perspective. Project that image into the window, then clear the mind and place the window on the area of the third-eye. Visual scenes will be manifested to you. With these visual scenes, one can more easily look within oneself, within a situation, or within a relationship.

These crystals may also be used to:

o   read the aura of another person by placing the window toward the person and then turning it toward <u>your</u> third-eye; and,
o   assist one in defining the life purpose of the self or another person by facilitating the "seeing" of the interims between lifetimes when decisions were made with respect to which experiences were necessary to fulfill the destiny of that individual;

When working with others [i.e. as above], it is extremely important to clear the mind and center the self so that <u>you</u> do not cloud the issues and answers with personal judgments and beliefs. Clarity of the mind is necessary to ensure total reproduction of the message without any subtle self-held interferences.

Window crystals have also been used to locate "missing persons" and lost items by projecting a clear image of the person or item into the crystal and then accepting the subsequent information.

PROPERTIES OF SPECIALTY QUARTZ:

The following specialty quartz configurations possess additional properties which are unique.

Aqua Aura Quartz

Aqua aura [blue] quartz crystals are clear/cloudy quartz crystals which have been enhanced with pure gold; the molecules of pure gold adhere to the natural electric charge which surrounds the quartz crystal, and are not removed by rubbing or by scraping.

These crystals combine both the properties of quartz and the properties of gold [see the section of this book discussing GOLD, and the general qualities of the QUARTZ section of this book] to produce a very intense energy.

In addition, to the properties of the parts, this crystal form also stimulates the throat chakra and encourages "opening to channel". It has also been used to activate the energy of other minerals for healing.

It has been used extensively to cleanse and to smooth the aura, to activate all chakras, and to release negativity from ones emotional, physical, intellectual, and spiritual bodies.

Citrine/Quartz

The combination of these two minerals brings the synthesis of both and further instills the capacity for a visionary state where the user is permitted to gain the information required and desired.

It allows one to recognize the sacred personal nature and, hence, inspires a curative outcome in the many aspects of ones life. It further assists in reducing futility, noteworthy conceit, and arrogance - bringing supplemental energy to effectiveness and ones path.

The combination of the energies produces a stronger activation for the crown chakra and for the intellect and promotes the understanding of the opening of the crown chakra toward the enlightened state. It is quite beneficial in meditation to further ones "staying power".

Citrine/Smokey Quartz

The combination of these two minerals brings the synthesis of both and further provides a connection with the "star people" of this planet and with those potential "star people" from the other realms. The link can produce physical awareness induced from the other realms, and can help to bring those like-minded others of this plane into ones physical reality.

The energy of citrine tends to maintain clarity of the smokey quartz, such that cleansing is not necessary and such that the combination does not accept negativity. In addition, it has been used to enhance the psychic abilities and can assist in the gentle attunement of third-eye activity, while providing for grounding conditions and removal of obstacles.

Many merchants have used this combination to further business and to increase profits.

The alliance of these minerals sometimes includes the clear quartz composition and further annexes the properties of this mineral.

The faceted form tends to provide the maximum energy potential.

Blue Quartz

Blue Quartz is formed by the inclusion of tiny blue rutile, tourmaline or zoisite inclusions.

It combines the qualities of the included mineral and further serves to activate the throat chakra and to promote the speaking of that which is in ones mind.

It further acts to attune one to the connected-ness of the brothers and sisters of the planet, releasing introversion and fear, while promoting experiences which are fresh and new. It actually assists one in removing the fear of reaching-out to others, and brings stimulation to new relationships.

It produces a comforting resonance, generating a composure during states of disruption and confusion, allowing one to enjoy the actions of being independent and uninhibited.

It assuages fear, helping one to see that the basis of fear is only incomplete knowledge; it assists one in gaining completion of this knowledge. It can be used to encourage consideration and thoughtfulness and is helpful to relationships.

In addition, it has been used in the treatment of disorders of the spleen, the endocrine system, and the blood, and to stabilize the metabolic processes.

Dendritic Quartz

Dendritic quartz contains a branching figure or marking resembling a moss-like or tree form. The dendritic formation is often comprised of manganese and/or chlorite.

It facilitates a closeness with nature and a connection to the Earth Mother.

The combination of the dendrites with the quartz also facilitates "reaching back" to the beginning of the Earth phase and stimulates recall of past-lives relative to this planet.

It can be used to activate the chakras and to sustain the opening of the chakras to facilitate purity in the total connection to the higher consciousness.

It can also be used to treat disorders of the skeletal system, the nervous system, and the small capillaries, and to promote the alignment of the bone structure of the physical body.

Golden Healer

The Golden Healer is a quartz crystal which is partially or totally covered with a transparent golden-yellow mineral (possibly an iron-hydrate). One can see through the golden-yellow material.

This mineral has been used to assist one in attaining and maintaining contact with the spiritual worlds and to incite healing on all levels. It is an excellent stone for use in all healing situations and promotes the recognition of methods and techniques which will further recovery from all disorders.

Green Quartz

Green quartz works quite well with the opening and stabilizing of the heart chakra and promotes an intuitive capability which is coupled with love. It is truly a stone of transformative energies, transmuting negative energy to the positive state without releasing it to the atmosphere. It also acts to inspire creativity, and to attract success, prosperity and abundance.

In addition, it has been used to promote the exchange of both energies and vibratory messages, in order to maintain the integrity of relationships and of the planet.

Green quartz interacts with the endocrine glands to keep the body balanced.

Harlequin Quartz

Harlequin Quartz is quartz containing red dots or red strings of either Hematite or Lepidocrocite. It provides a beautiful "dancing" energy, which, when activated, stimulates the energy flow on all levels.

It can be used to stimulate the base chakra and to provide for a direct pathway between the base chakra and the heart chakra; it can, hence, be used to direct and to intensify devotional proclivities. It activates all of the qualities of the base [first] chakra, the heart chakra, and the crown chakra, and provides physical energy and vitality to the physical body.

It further stimulates the healing qualities of the heart and the associated attributes of loving consciousness.

It can also be used to balance the polarity of ones body with the higher bodies and to open and balance the meridians of the physical body, stimulating the alignment of the physical and ethereal nervous systems.

It has been used to traverse the gap between the physical world and the spiritual world, and can help one to understand transitions.

It can be used in the treatment of disorders related to the blood veins, mental acuity, memory, intravascular coagulation of the blood in the circulatory system, imbalances in the thyroid, and atrophy of the thymus. It has also been used in the treatment of depression, despondency, and to activate the "will" to progress.

Included Quartz

When one is attracted to and uses included quartz, the quartz inclusion will work with the person to provide the further nourishment and qualities required. Usually, the chlorite and hematite included quartz provide the most powerful healing-type of included quartz.

Each inclusion in quartz provides the extra properties of that included mineral to work "hand-in-hand" with the properties of the quartz.

Asbestos-Included Quartz

Asbestos-Included Quartz contains a metamorphosed asbestos which occurs in the colours of green, yellow, and/or orange.

This mineral can be used to automatically align the chakras and to provide grounding concurrently.

It facilitates the changing of states from Alpha, to Beta, to Gamma, and enhances dreaming and recall.

This mineral combines the trinity of the heart, the sacral chakra, and the crown chakra to produce the connection with the optimum self, and to synthesize the optimum self of this plane with the perfection of the ethereal plane. It acts on the premise that each person embraces the perfection of the universe and is capable of the manifestation of all that will benefit everyone; in addition, it bases its action upon the premise and the understanding of the ideal of complete-ness and leads to the rational conclusion with respect to the utilization of this "completeness" in activities of manifestation.

It stimulates communication and psychic awareness on all levels. It dispels estrangement, resentment, and frustration and helps to facilitate intelligibility with respect to mental perception and linear rationality. It induces one to persist in endeavors and in situations which would, generally, diminish ones fortitude; it dispenses an inspiring energy and subsidizes one with energy for the continuance of ventures. It further elevates the conscious connection between the higher levels of instinct and heart-felt altruism, producing compassion in both discussions and in resolutions. It also assists in dispersing confusion emanating from emotional, spiritual, and intellectual issues.

It enhances fairness, yet firmness, and allows one to stand alone when circumstances require. It also assists one in understanding that it is "okay" to ask for, and to accept, help from others; it provides one with the insight to realize that help from another is, in actuality, help from the self.

It has been used in the treatment of disorders of the veins, the skeletal system, the nervous system, and the circulatory system, and to promote coagulation, to ameliorate brittleness of bones, and to dispel chills and complications of inadequate thermal propagation within the body. It has also assisted in the repair of broken bones.

Due to the structural integrity of this configuration, the actual asbestos fibers do not interfere with the preparation of an elixir via the normal method.

Cuprite-Included Quartz

Cuprite-Included Quartz synthesizes the qualities of Cuprite and Quartz and further instills an attribute of nourishing and beneficial energy.

It allows one to recognize the inner bonds with the outer world and to also both acknowledge and comprehend the spiritual connection between the self and the universe.

It assists in eliminating illusion and helps one to understand that all view from one perception are the same. It promotes sufficient emotional and intellectual advancement such that one may view the inevitably clear way.

It has been known as a "stone of luck", bringing opportunity in a serendipity manner and assisting one in the recognition of same.

It has also been used in the treatment of leukemia and for disorders of the kidneys and the bladder.

Carbon-Included Quartz

Carbon-Included Quartz contains carbon; often the quartz crystals containing the carbon are known as "carbon phantoms", but, in many cases, the inclusion is not configured as a phantom. Where the configuration is a phantom, the "Black Phantom Crystal" Section also applies.

This mineral can help to purify ones body and ones surroundings. It can be worn, carried, used as an elixir, or stationed in ones environment.

This mineral stimulates analytical capabilities and precision. It provides for perceptiveness to situations and awakens ones inherent talents and adroitness.

It acts as a composed, yet purifying agent. The energy is mainly attentive to the physical world, but also provides for a connective "thread" between the intellect and spirituality and between physical vitality and meditation.

It provides for grounding and centering during meditation, such that one may eliminate distractions which may impede total reflection.

It has been used to assist in the cleansing of toxins from the intestines and colon, in the treatment of emphysema and the decrease of lung capacity, and to eliminate tumors and growths.

Limonite-Included Quartz

Limonite-Included Quartz synthesizes the properties of Quartz and Limonite and further acts to stimulate the fusion of the energies for the intellect and the crown chakra. It serves to bring intellectual understanding to the concept of the ethereal worlds and motivates channeling activities.

This combination can be used to cleanse negativity from other stones. When directed, it provides for a clearing action while directing any negative energy, which is within the area, toward the light of transmutation.

It has also been used in the treatment of disorders of the endocrine system.

Snowball-Included Quartz

Snowball-Included Quartz is a type of included quartz crystal in which the inclusions are shaped like "snowballs". This configuration also occurs, occasionally, in amethyst, smokey, and citrine crystals. Snowball quartz combines the properties of clear quartz with the properties associated with okenite; although the chemical composition of okenite and the "snowballs" are not the same, the properties are exhibited. In addition, the properties of the mineral comprising the "snowball" inclusion are also applicable.

Lavender Quartz

Lavender Quartz is a type of Rose Quartz which exhibits a lovely lavender colour. In addition to the properties listed in the ROSE QUARTZ section, this mineral has also been used to stimulate the third-eye, to promote clairsentience, clairaudience, and clairvoyance, and to further communication on the physical plane. It has also been used to instill the ability of direct response and instinctual behavior, and promotes the integration of all parts of the personality, contributing to the understanding of the habits and reactions in any given environment with respect to ones instinctive behavior.

It is a very loving stone and is a true asset to ones environment.

It has also been used in the treatment of disorders related to brain-wave frequencies.

Opal Aura

Opal Aura [opalescent] quartz crystals are clear/cloudy quartz crystals which have been enhanced with pure platinum; the molecules of the platinum adhere to the natural electric charge which surrounds the quartz crystal, and are not removed by rubbing or by scraping.

These crystals combine both the properties of quartz and the properties of Platinum [see the section of this book discussing PLATINUM, and the general qualities of the QUARTZ section of this book] to produce a very intense energy.

In addition, to the properties of the parts, this crystal form also cleanses the aura and acts to stimulate and to cleanse all chakras.

Phantom Quartz

The phantom crystal is recognized by a "phantom" crystal within the crystal. The phantom is comprised of a white or colored mineral and may be partial or complete. The phantoms within a crystal provide an indication of the experiences, and the transformations, which the crystal has encountered during its evolution. The phantom crystal has experienced numerous lifetimes, of learning and "being", while continuing in the same physical configuration; the crystal represents the many phases and the many types of life which may be experienced during ones lifetime.

The crystal symbolizes universal awareness. It is one of the Earth stones to be used for redemption and cleansing of the Earth. The energy of the phantom works to bring together the participants of humanity to save the planet. The structure within the crystal exhibits triangular and pyramidal formations coupled, occasionally, with likenesses of mountains and flowers; these formations emanate the energy to save, to renew, and to facilitate the spiritual health of the Earth. The phantom allows the Earth to recall how it was prior to the initiation of destruction; hence, allowing for smoothness in Earth changes during the corrective processes. Both polished and unpolished specimens are excellent energy sources for initiation of the healing; in fact, the beauty of the polished phantom assists in instilling the magnificence of the perfect undisturbed state of the original form.

It is an excellent tool for meditation and for assisting one in connecting with the higher realms of knowledge. It can also be used to access the records of ones progression through past-lives.

One procedure for accessing past-lives is as follows:

o   Sit quietly, initiate circular breathing, relax, and attune to the crystal;
o   Gaze within the phantom portion of the crystal;
o   Close the eyes and allow the after-image [or the image produced] to travel to the inner mind or to the area of the third-eye; and,
o   Allow the mind to travel through the personal memories and to track the history of the soul back to the creation.

Utilization of these stones to facilitate access to past-lives allows one to see these past-lives in a state of ascension, rather than in a state of reality where one is again the participant. The mineral within the quartz, comprising the phantom, can act to facilitate the altered states when the crystal is used in the past-life ascension.

In addition, it provides further energy in healing the emotional and physical situations which may be of consequence to the inner knowledge as it is brought to actualization via the ascension.

The phantom crystal can also be used to assist one in meeting a personal spiritual guide. After surrounding the self in the protection of the purity of the white light, entry to the crystal can be accomplished. One may enter the crystal via "gazing", via holding the crystal to the area of the third-eye, or via the meditative state - walking through the area of the phantom and/or the garden of delight. Finding a place to rest quietly, one may wait until the spiritual guide walks down the path to visit. The wise, compassionate being knows the past, present, and future. You may approach, face-to-face, and meld with the being.

It is quite excellent for use when talking about personal issues with, and when asking questions of, ones spiritual guide. One should await the answers and expect sometimes words, sometimes writing, sometimes pictures; recognition will be by understanding. Convey appreciation to the advisor and make arrangements to meet again. It is quite helpful to evaluate the information upon return from the journey, and to take appropriate action on the information received.

Phantom crystals have also been used in the treatment of hearing disorders and to stimulate clairaudience.

Use the phantom crystal with respect, humility, and patience.

Ajoite-, Hematite-, and Papagoite-Phantom Quartz Crystals are discussed in their respective sections of this book.

Amethyst-Phantom Quartz Crystals also exhibit additional properties. These crystals stimulate recall of ones state just prior to birth; this information can be accessed for each of the beginnings of the life cycle. One can, hence, gain information of the multitude of experiences/lessons which were planned for each life and can further evaluate that which was accomplished and that which remains.

Black-Phantom Quartz Crystals are also very unusual. They provide the energy of the quartz, coupled with the property of grounding; this grounding is via the perfect alignment of the physical energy centers, which occurs with the use of this mineral. Hence, with a black phantom crystal, one does not require an additional stone for grounding.

Chlorite-Phantom Quartz Crystals are also unusual. They combine the energy of the quartz crystal with one of the most powerful healing minerals in the kingdom. They are used to stimulate the state of inspiration and to further actualization.

The chlorite phantom has also been used with amethyst to remove undesirable energy implants; the phantom remembers and helps one to progress back to the time of the implant such that removal is with ease. Chlorite also assists in healing the void which remains after the removal of the implant.

Green-Phantom Quartz Crystals, the green being other than Chlorite (and said to be Caledonite), have also served as excellent healing energies, providing swiftness to recovery. The actual mineral within the quartz synthesizes with the quartz and delivers the properties of both. In addition, these crystals have been used to provide for access to, and transfer of, information from the purity of the angelic realms. It assists in clairaudient endeavors, affording lucid, distinct, and articulate verbalization of the messages received.

It also contains an innate wisdom which is accessible to the user; the data, from within the stone, is useful with respect to ones advancement in the spiritual kingdom, and to the aspects of perfection and the patterns involved in the attainment of that which is desired. In this manner, it can help one to achieve that which would be helpful as the end-product of manifestation, and to recognize the difference between worldly manifestation and a manifestation which would further ones development. It also brings harmony to despair and provides for support and insight in all endeavors.

Orange-Phantom Quartz Crystals can stimulate the vitalization of the entire physical form. It has been used to lessen the degrees of addiction and to both comfort and stabilize the addictive personality. It allows the adjacent energies to transform to positive forces, and brings the focus of the user toward recovery, toward rejuvenation, and toward reclamation of the true self. It has also been used in the treatment of disorders of the spleen.

Orange-Phantom Reversed Quartz Crystals is actually quartz fused with Carnelian, where the Carnelian and the quartz, together, form the outside and the quartz clarity can be seen on the inside; the inspection of the interior quartz is facilitated through polishing the bottom of the crystal. This combination has been used to initiate a chain-reaction of energies within the body, allowing one to sustain oneself for long periods. Endurance, perseverance, and tenacity are enhanced. The initiative to take control of ones life is instilled. In addition, it has assisted in journeying to the interior of the body in order to facilitate diagnosis and to remediate disorders.

Pink-Phantom Quartz Crystals have been used to stimulate the heart chakra and to provide a direct connection between one and another. It can be used to eliminate the feeling of abandonment and restraint, and to assist one in continuing toward ones goals without confinement. It has also been used by healers to activate the receipt of information for restoration of the physical body.

Red-Phantom Quartz Crystals additionally contain the properties of limonite, kaolinite, and hematite. These crystals are rare.

The combination of the properties of quartz with these minerals produces a synthesis, which, in addition to the properties of the four minerals, produces further qualities.

The red phantom is also used to stimulate the first three chakras, to combine the energies in order to produce highly recognizable vitality directed toward creativity, intellectual advancement, and intuitive endeavors.

In addition, the red phantom exhibits qualities similar to dioptase; it provides for stimulation of the intelligence of the cellular structure of the body such that the cells may recognize the reason for malfunction, in conditions of dis-ease; it further provides the vitality and creativity for the correction of the malfunction. This crystal will be made available to those who are ready for the complex powers.

Smokey-Phantom Quartz Crystals retain the additional quality which allows past-life information to be brought forth in an atmosphere of stability; it allows one to return to "time zero" in ones evolution in order to provide information with respect to the connections to the oversoul.

Yellow-Phantom Quartz Crystals additionally contain the properties of limonite and stimulate the intellectual capabilities of the user, bringing clarity of thought to the utilization of the healing energies of the mineral kingdom.

The symbolic presence of the multitude of phantom crystals indicates the multi-faceted lives which we all live. They can reveal the truth of existence to a clear and pure heart and mind.

Raspberry Quartz

Raspberry Quartz is found in the formation of sceptres and standard crystals. It has a raspberry tinge due to the inclusion of Lepidocrocite, Hematite or Goethite, and Amethyst. It combines the qualities of these minerals and, when in the sceptre formation, combines the qualities of the sceptre. It also can be used to synthesize the seven major chakras, bringing attunement to the higher realms and assisting in clearing and activating these chakras. It has been used in the treatment of disorders related to energy flow and systemic dis-ease.

Red Quartz

Red quartz aids in positive action. It produces an abundance of physical energy and vitality, and coupled with the quartz qualities, is a dynamic mineral.

Rutilated Quartz

Rutilated quartz intensifies the power of the quartz crystal. It combines the properties of quartz with the properties listed in the RUTILE and SAGENITE sections of this book. In addition, it affects both the etheric and the astral bodies. It assists one in getting to the root of a problem and, hence, provides access to the reason for a dis-ease or discomfort, so that one can remedy the situation. During astral travel, rutilated quartz provides for insight into the reasons for visiting the locations and viewing the scenes; it stimulates an awareness of the connections between this physical life and the situations viewed.

A type of rutilated quartz, which does not appear to be rutilated, is asterated quartz; asterated quartz exhibits the pattern of a starlike luminous figure on the surface of the stone, during conditions of transmitted light. Asterated quartz occurs in the natural clear/silky/cloudy "white" quartz, as well as in rose quartz, and other varieties of quartz. The additional properties of asterated quartz include the connection to the "star people", the genetic structure and cellular communication configuration being contained within the energy of the stone. This provides for communication with those from other galaxies, as well as other planets in the solar system of the Earth; the asterated quartz which is made available to one is the one containing the transmitter of the "star person" or galactic entity whom one is to contact.

In addition, occasionally, there is curved rutile or curved sagenite within the quartz structure. This configuration brings the qualities of the curved crystal and selenite to meld with the properties of quartz, rutile, and sagenite. It further assists one in flowing with changes and with accepting alterations, adjustments, and insights to further these modifications. The association of the curved rutile or sagenite with quartz is rare.

Strawberry Quartz

Strawberry quartz is a rare strawberry coloured quartz crystal. It usually occurs in portions of a total mass of crystalline structure, but, occasionally, terminations are evident.

This mineral stimulates the energy center of the heart, bringing added energy to the quartz, and filling ones total person with the feeling of love. Use as an elixir is highly recommended.

Strawberry quartz also balances the connections between the physical body and the subtle bodies, and stimulates both the astral body and the psychic system intrinsic in all. It provides for travel to the "center of the universe of life" and fills one with the euphoria of the true loving environment; the connection with the "center of the universe of life" brings one information concerning the creation of planetary forms, the "reasons behind it all", and guidance with respect to enjoying each moment. It further provides the pathway to the source of knowledge which can provide the relevant data concerning the actual reasons one has chosen the reality which is predominant in ones life.

Strawberry quartz was used in Atlantis and Lemuria in healing ceremonies and to stimulate recall of the "beginning"; it was held by the high council, those being the most spiritually developed of the realm.

The stone will be made available to those who are both ready to experience the energy and willing to embrace the information.

Tibetan Quartz Crystals

Tibetan Quartz Crystals have been found in Tibet and have been transported "on the back of a Yak in a sack" to the China border for distribution.

They occur as both double terminated and singly terminated crystals in the clear quartz and smokey quartz compositions.

In addition to the qualities of the composition, the Tibetan Quartz Crystals have been used to promote contact with the ancient cultures of the East, bringing knowledge and information concerning healing and spirituality to the user.

They have also been used to facilitate fasting and abstinence from that which one chooses.

In addition, healing and meditation, have both been enhanced.

Wearing the Tibetan Crystal has induced total centering of the self and has, when accessed, produced an energy conducive to channeling.

The crystal tends to contain a very powerful "OM" vibration, prompting the inventive powers. The body can attune to this resonance and can radiate the energy and verity of the higher-self.

Kirlian photography has shown that, when cleansed, these crystals emanate the total spectrum of colour, and can hence, be applied to all energy medians for stimulation and cleansing - and can be used in the healing of all centers.

Tourmalinated Quartz

Tourmalinated quartz combines the qualities of tourmaline with the qualities of quartz. In addition to the properties listed below, it also exhibits the qualities discussed in the TOURMALINE and SAGENITE sections of this book.

It provides humanity with a tool which produces a "solving atmosphere".

It can be used to assist one in actualizing an innate strength to palliate antipathetic relationships and situations.

It aids in eliminating many "crystallized" patterns which are, or have been, destructive in nature and in ones own life. It also aids in adjusting imbalances throughout the bodies.

QUARTZITE   [Astrological Sign of Capricorn]

Quartzite is a structure of quartz comprised of firmly compacted grains of quartz. It exhibits most of the same properties of quartz; the energy is, however, not directed quite as efficiently. It is an excellent stone for supporting one during the stages of "lesson learning", providing insight to the diminishment of limitations and to those responsibilities which are not necessary. It also furthers ones abilities to maintain cooperation and tact in all situations.

Please note that Quartzite is also known as "Snow Quartz".

Vibrates to the number 2.

TAKE RESPONSIBILITY FOR YOUR HAPPINESS

AND THE CREATION OF YOUR REALITY

RALSTONITE

Ralstonite crystallizes in the form of octahedral crystals. The colour range includes white and colourless.

This mineral assists one in "slowing-down", so that the inner self may become more centered; it, hence, facilitates expediency without uncontrolled speed.

It is a stone to be used for gathering people together to assist in a common goal; used in the group environment, it helps to promote the ability of each member to focus on the same ideal and to provide freshness to the combined vigor and strength. It enhances precision and direction in all activities.

It can be used during any stage of a disorder to facilitate the recovery of strength; it is an excellent stone to use during crisis situations which occur during an illness, in order to provide a "boost" to ones spirits and energy.

Ralstonite can be used to help in the diagnosis of disorders; use of the stone in meditation allows the visualization of both the cause and the consequence to manifest. It can also be used in the treatment of tularemia and during the post-stage manifestations of rabies.

Vibrates to the number 7.

RAMSDELLITE [Astrological Sign of Aries]

Ramsdellite crystallizes in the form of granular masses and black metallic tabular crystals.

This mineral can be used to facilitate super-human strength, to assist one in diversification in fields of endeavor, and to promote, during meditative states and astral projection, a wandering in unregimented directions [producing a variety of scenes, situations, and messages for consideration to the user]. It provides for a dome-like structure over the field of astral travel so that one can relax in the protective barrier, flying freely in a state of perfect bliss.

Ramsdellite can be used in the treatment of cysts and in protection against the over-production of red blood cells. It is also a stone for protection of ones environment against the infiltration of pests.

Vibrates to the number 1.

RASPITE   [Astrological Sign of Capricorn]

Raspite crystallizes in the form of tabular crystals. The colour range includes yellow and brown.

This mineral can provide for a temporary suspension of those events which are distressing. It actually creates a cessation of time, or, in some cases, creates circumstances which allow an interlude to occur, in which the user can reflect and can completely reorganize in order to be better prepared for the forthcoming resolution.

It can be used to discourage dishonesty.

Raspite can assist one in the attainment of the uncommon; in this situation, it works in the realm of manifestation to bring not normal desires to fruition, but to deliver to one that which is not generally abundant.

The mineral can also bring relief to bruises, strains, and sprains. It can also help to bring temporary relief to painful conditions.

Vibrates to the number 7.

RAUENTHALITE   [Astrological Sign of Virgo]

Rauenthalite crystallizes in the triclinic system and is also found in masses. The colour ranges from colourless to white.

This mineral has been used for strengthening concentration and for eliminating the power of distraction. It provides the energy to produce a fully concentrated mind which has immense power and exceptional power through focussing. It brings the mind to a single-pointed-ness, and enhances spontaneity and consecutive thought processes.

It can be used to determine the path of the heart, such that one can control emotional power, alleviate distress, and sooth and comfort the emotional body such that well-ness of the physical body is produced.

This mineral produces a flow of vitality into and through any of the chakras, assisting one in the receipt of the etheric energy when needed. It enhances the fluidity of the nerves to instill the primary life-force.

It has been used to promote rapid recovery from dis-ease, to enhance digestion, and to relieve stress, hypertension, and nervous disorders. It is also been used in the treatment of low blood-sugar and diabetes.

Vibrates to the number 8.

REDDINGITE   [Astrological Sign of Taurus]

Reddingite crystallizes in the form of fibrous masses, grains, and octahedral crystals. The colour range includes pink, yellow, red-brown, and white.

This mineral can be used to assist one in correcting an unjust situation; to "right" a "wrong"; meditation with the crystal can provide insight to the method of amelioration. The energy communicates the message that all choice is "up to you" - it always has been <u>and</u> it always will be. It can also assist in providing for rescue in situations of danger.

Reddingite can facilitate the repetition of dreams to allow the dreamer to remember the details which could impact ones life. It seems to reproduce the dream on a video-type mechanism for access during states of meditation.

It can also be used to prevent "set-backs" in disorders. The mineral assists in helping one to learn to progress, and to eliminate the aspects of digression.

Vibrates to the number 5.

RHODOCHROSITE   [Astrological Signs of Scorpio & Leo]

Rhodochrosite crystallizes in the form of masses, grains, columns, crusts, botryoidal structures, rare rhombohedral crystals, and rare crystals with rounded striated faces. The colour-range includes pale pink to deep red, yellow, tan, orange, and brown. Those crystals in the rose colour range are highly collectable.

This mineral has been called a "stone of love and balance", providing balancing and love on all levels for all bodies. It contains a pulsating electrical energy which emits the strongest power in the universe, the power of love. The energy of rhodochrosite is encompassed by the presence of heavenly energies filled with the golden sphere of light; it assists in creating new worlds for the user - worlds filled with love and dreams.

Using the stone during the meditative state, one may melt into the sphere of golden ecstasy; an encounter with ones twin soul[s] is highly likely, when the energy is so directed.

Rhodochrosite is also an Earth stone for healing of the Earth and for showing love to the Mother of us all. It helps one to serve the planet in her time of need, allowing for one to recognize that the responsibility is actually a joy.

It gently energizes and purifies the base chakra, the sacral chakra, and the heart chakra, restoring balance in these areas. For energizing, it acts with expediency on the physical, astral, and mental planes. For purification, it acts to cleanse and to renew.

It facilitates balancing of the mental process such that the attunement to the higher-self can be attained, and ones awareness and spirituality can be enhanced. It assists in expanding ones conscious awareness of duality and allows for recognition and insight with respect to the method[s] by which the pervasive presence of duality affects ones life. It also assists one in the attainment of the solution to the puzzling concept relating to the contradiction of the duality of nature. It further assists one in accelerating the expansion of ones consciousness, and to both understand and initiate the practice of intensive relaxation, acceptance, and balancing. The crystalline structures are especially beneficial in these areas.

It removes tendencies toward avoidance or denial, and helps one to be willing to both accept and to integrate "new" information while maintaining a clarity of intellect and a moderate ideal of practicality. It assists one in the re-interpretation of traditional values, allowing for the re-emergence and the re-actualization of the validity of living expression in all situations.

Rhodochrosite can also both gently and quickly balance the emotions, providing a stability, or order and structure, to the mind. It assists in balancing the male/female aspects of ones character and physical body, providing for a strong, clear, and tolerant energy. It acts to stimulate the energies of the body, encouraging the maintenance of the optimum state of health.

This mineral has a gentle balancing effect which can maintain the etheric energy at a beneficial level and can help to prevent sickness.

An elixir, taken internally has assisted in the relief of internal infections [e.g., ear, sinus infections, ulcers, inflammations, etc.]. It can also provide a soothing action to external skin disorders; one can place the stone in distilled water [or natural mineral/spring water], energize the mixture in sunlight for several days, and then heat the water and soak a cloth in it for use as a poultice. The energies of the crystalline mineral tend to penetrate the infected areas of the tissues and assist in cleansing the area while removing the dysfunctional negative aspects which are present.

It can also be used in the treatment of various kinds of elimination problems, to strengthen the walls of the intestines, and to promote the production of the proper range of gastric fluids to enhance digestion. It has been used to balance the energies of the heart and to stabilize the heart and pulse rate. It can also be used in the treatment of thyroid imbalances. An elixir is also quite effective in treatment of these disorders.

It is quite useful during the "laying-on-of-stones" for those born under the signs of Virgo, Capricorn, and Taurus.

Vibrates to the number 4.

RHODOLITE   [Astrological Sign of Leo]

Rhodolite, a variety of garnet, crystallizes in the form of masses, granules, plate-like layers, and dodecahedral and trapezohedral crystals [and in combinations of the dodecahedral/trapezohedral crystals]. The colour range includes pale rose, red and purple.

Properties in addition to those listed in the GARNET and PYROPE sections of this book are noted below.

The energy of rhodolite is conducive to application from the base chakra to the crown chakra. It assists in the illumination of intuition and can be used as a stimulant for inspiration in the development of the metaphysical processes which enhance both the meditative and channeling states.

It can initiate the rise of the Kundalini and can support the movement of the energy throughout the chakras.

It helps to provide for excellent protection of the base chakra, and assists in maintaining the rhythms of the subtle bodies in synchronicity with the other aspects of consciousness. It is an excellent stabilizer, stimulating calm assurance throughout the physical, mental, emotional, and ethereal bodies.

This mineral helps to guide one during times of contemplation, balancing peace and solitude with harmony and activity.

It is also known as a "stone of inspiration", bringing the inspiration of love via the heart and the mind.

It can be used in the treatment of disorders of the heart and lungs.

Vibrates to the number 7.

RHODONITE   [Astrological Sign of Taurus]

Rhodonite crystallizes in the form of masses, grains, and tabular crystals, sometimes with rounded edges. The colour range includes pink to rose red, brown-red, green, yellow, and black. It is usually veined by black alteration products [including manganese oxide]. Rhodonite has recently been found in Brasil in the formation of druses and in a lovely gemmy combination with Bustamite.

This mineral can create a clear path to balance the yin-yang energy, synthesizing the qualities of attunement with the spirituality of the universe, and balancing the energies of the Earth plane. It can help one to attain calm assurance in all activities.

Rhodonite has been called a "stone of love" and helps one to achieve his/her greatest potential. It activates and energizes the heart chakra and conveys the resonance of unconditional love to the physical plane.

It is also excellent for stimulation, clearing, and activation of the heart chakra, while providing for grounding of the physical and mental energies at the same time. It can assist one in the attainment of ones "greatest potential", dispelling anxiety and promoting coherence during chaotic encounters.

It further assists one in recognizing and in implementing the actions required to encourage and to further the "brotherhood" of humanity, stimulating the serving aspects of ones nature and encouraging generosity of spirit. It helps one to understand that each individual possesses a relationship to a structure of meaning which can be fulfilled.

It dispels anxiety and promotes coherence, bringing to the user an observant nature and facilitating attention to details and interrelationships.

In addition, the gemmy Brasilian Rhodonite has been found to act in an immediate fashion to activate the pineal gland and to release a dominant and influential energy to stimulate intuitive guidance. It has also been used to facilitate an impenetrable energy which stimulates alignment of chakras and removal of blockages. It is one of the "Grand Formations". In combination with Bustamite, it combines both the properties of Bustamite and Rhodonite and further serves to bring a loving, active, and energetic environment to all actions.

It has been used in the treatment of emphysema. It can also be used in the treatment of inflammation of the joints, light sensitivity, streptococcal throat infections, heart disorders, and arthritis.

Vibrates to the number 9.

RHONITE   [Astrological Sign of Scorpio]

Rhonite crystallizes in prismatic triclinic crystals and in prismatic aggregates. The colour ranges is brown to black.

This mineral tends to increase the available level of oxygen at higher altitudes - the response of increased oxygen in the higher altitudes appears to be due to the increased utilization of the oxygen present, and not actually an increase in the level. When worn upon the body, the altitude change is not noticed with respect to lethargy, breathing impairment, and physical energy levels. Nose bleeds due to altitude change have also been ameliorated.

Carrying Rhonite has also assisted in the increase in strength and stamina when one is in the state of physical exercise.

It has been used to stimulate the vividness of dreams; the recall of dreams are also enhanced - the actual detail appears clearly and the memory is analogous to the remembrance of a scene which has just occurred. With this mineral, there is always sufficient time for the recording of dreams, because the memory does not fade until one records the dream and releases the memory.

It has also been used for gridding environments to produce stability and to provide protection. It can be used to align the physical body with the electro-magnetic energy of the higher realms to create a constant affiliation.

It is a mineral to stimulate transformation and continued change with a constancy of determination to accelerate and to ease the process of the renovation of the self. The theory of motivation and impetus for action are reflected in this energy.

It is said that Rhonite that the stone was part of the mystery of Avalon and that it assists one in gaining the "earthly paradise" both within and without. During meditation, one can experience visuals which involve the scene of Avalon and examples of jewelry which was used during that time period. For example, pendants of Rhonite were created from gold and/or silver in the shape of a diamond and with the Rhonite hanging within the diamond shape; there were four other stones at the corners of the diamond - two amethyst colour, and two turquoise colour); there was also a sacred Celtic inscription mounted at the bottom of the diamond shape as a plate which was also a diamond shape of either gold or silver - the inscription on each of the plates differed from person to person and represented personal protection.

In addition, this mineral has been used to promote deep "no-mind" meditation and to facilitate a "contemplation" meditation through which one may receive information requested.

Rhonite has been used in the treatment of the assimilation of iron, to produce a balance state of acidity/alkalinity within the body, and to relieve congestion. The energy serves to assuage breathing disorders and disorders of the lungs, and acts to stimulate the normal flow of blood.

Vibrates to the master number 44.

RHYOLITE   [Astrological Sign of Sagittarius]

Rhyolite crystallizes in the form of fine-grained felsite, consisting mainly of alkaline feldspars and quartz. The colour ranges includes all colours except for dark grey, dark green, and black. Occasionally the form is fashioned to show a spider webbing, which is quite lovely.

This mineral represents change, variety, and progress. It lights the fire of creativity within the soul, bringing to fruition the quests upon which one has longed to travel. It further assists in providing insight to the subtle energy channels within the body and in promoting insight with respect to the process by which one may raise the energy, breaking through the barriers of the mind, to ultimately reach the profound, transcendental, and joyous state of knowing. It helps one to strengthen both body and mind and to learn how to enjoy the vast potential within the self. It is an excellent stone for promulgating, with humility, the concept and actualization of self-realization.

Rhyolite is also an excellent stone for meditation, bringing forth a systematic methodology, with an emphasis on the search for the highest truth which is inherent in each individual. It can assist one in the advancement of astuteness in all activities, allowing for the understanding that selfless action is as meditation. The energy can assist one to process "things" from the past and to clear the way toward the progression of the future, encouraging focus on each moment in time as it exists in the "now". It is a "stone of resolution", bringing the unresolved to completion.

Rhyolite can be used in the treatment of disorders of the veins, to dispel chills, to eliminate rashes and skin disorders, and to improve the assimilation and action of the B-complex vitamins. It has also been used as an elixir to increase stamina and to improve muscular tone.

Vibrates to the number 4.

RICHTERITE   [Astrological Sign of Sagittarius]

Richterite crystallizes in the form of masses and long prismatic crystals, usually without termination. The colour range includes red, brown, yellow, brown-red, and pale to deep green.

This mineral can be used to "take one flying"; it is excellent for astral travel, and, especially, in accessing the akashic records [particularly with respect to information concerning questions of status and position within the community]. It helps to provide for access to the records relating to the causal factors relevant to status and position. It can, hence, be used to facilitate improvement in ones position. It is also said to enhance love and to stimulate relationships toward further development.

It has been used to reduce the "fight or flight" syndrome and to assist in balancing the reactive state with the active state, furthering the calmness of action and diminishing the distress of reaction.

It can be used in the treatment of deficiency in bone development, and for parasitic infestation, fevers, typhus, disorders of the sight, and imbalances in the thyroid. It can also assist in the treatment of respiratory disorders.

Vibrates to the number 7.

RICKARDITE   [Astrological Sign of Leo]

Rickardite crystallizes in the form of deep purple compact masses.

This mineral is an excellent source for grounding and is an enhancement to spiritual development.

It can clear negativity from ones environment and from ones life. It needs a soft dark place in which to normally reside. When used in healing situations or in the clearing of negativity, some of the brightness of the stone may be diminished; this does not affect the ability of the stone, but allows one to recognize the strength of the condition ameliorated.

It also assists one in the manifestation of that which is desired in the realm of business and materiality. It enhances ones independence of spirit while promoting connected-ness between the self and the universal nature of "All That Is".

Rickardite sometimes occurs with gold and with quartz. If the mineral specimen contains these or other minerals, the properties increase to reflect the new structure and to exhibit the qualities of the other minerals [see the appropriate sections in this book for the additional properties].

It can be used in the treatment of lymphatic tissue, bone marrow, the liver, and the spleen, and in maintaining the optimum condition of the blood cells while eliminating toxins from the body.

Vibrates to the number 8.

RIEBECKITE   [Astrological Sign of Libra]

Riebeckite crystallizes in the form of masses, grains, and long prismatic crystals which exhibit striations parallel to the length of the crystal. The colour usually ranges from dark blue to black; however, in many cases, there is a pleochroistic tendency to exhibit dark blue through the X-axis, blue or green to brown-yellow through the Y-axis, and yellow-green to dark green through the Z-axis.

This mineral can be used to encourage alteration in situations which inhibit ones growth. It can be used to bring one friendship and to facilitate cheerfulness.

It can also stimulate the mathematical nature, enhancing study of, and performance in, mathematical pursuits.

The energy of riebeckite can assist in providing guidance and insight to the solution of puzzling situations, encouraging the problem-solving capabilities inherent in the user.

It can align the chakras associated with intuition, with the intellect, and with psychic power, in order to produce a synthesis of the qualities and to further promote activities in these realms. It tends to remind one of over-extensions of self, of income, etc., providing a gentle chiding to the "offender".

Riebeckite can be used in the treatment of dyslexia, mental confusion, learning disabilities, and instability.

Vibrates to the number 6.

ROSASITE   [Astrological Sign of Virgo]

Rosasite crystallizes in the form of spherical structures, botryoidal crusts, and, sometimes, crusts exhibiting tiny crystals. The colour range includes blue-green, green, and sky blue.

This mineral can be used to calm the emotions and to facilitate the use of mantras. It will stimulate recall of ones "special" mantra; using the stone in meditation, the mantra will be given - sleeping with the stone in the proximity of the head, the mantra will be given - holding the stone or allowing it to remain near, the mantra will be given.

The stone actually helps one to access the memory and to retrieve information [in all situations, concerning all subjects]. It provides a re-affirming energy, supporting, sustaining, and strengthening ones faith in the perfect nature of the universe. It further assists one in recognizing, accepting, and acting on personal insights which originate beyond the realm of normal human consciousness.

Rosasite can be used in the treatment of disorders of any of the internal organs, to renew tissue damage due to the effects of ruptures, and to lessen the affects of measles and chicken-pox [an elixir is applied, topically, in the cases of skin disorders].

Vibrates to the number 7.

ROSCHERITE   [Astrological Sign of Capricorn]

Roscherite crystallizes in the form of plate-like aggregates and tabular crystals. The colour range includes deep green and brown.

This mineral can be used to assist one in the courage and strength to test the untested character. It helps to provide a "safe" secure environment, either physical or mental.

It can also help one to increase the creative actualization of ones life, providing for swift reasoning, and for common sense allied with the all-knowing cosmic power.

Roscherite can be of further assistance in all areas of dispersion, dispersing negativity, dispersing congestion, dispersing crowds, dispersing growths, dispersing overloaded schedules, etc. It appears to be a very supportive and helpful stone.

It can be used in the treatment of pneumonia, for Vitamins A and E assimilation disorders, and hay fever.

Vibrates to the number 3.

ROSE QUARTZ   [Astrological Signs of Taurus & Libra]

Rose quartz is found in masses, druses, granular structures, grains, veins, and quite rarely, as lovely crystal structures. The colour ranges from soft pink to golden-white.

It emits a calming, cooling energy which can work on all of the chakras to gently remove negativity and to reinstate the loving, gentle forces of self-love. It provides the message that there is no need for haste in any situation, bringing calmness and clarity to the emotions and restoring the mind to harmony after chaotic or crisis situations.

Rose quartz is especially helpful at the locations of the heart and the crown chakras. The energy is soft and silky, producing a gentleness from without and from within the user. It has been known as a " stone of gentle love", bringing peacefulness and calm to relationships. It promotes receptivity to the beauty of art, music, and the written word, enlivening imagination, and representing a young, warm love.

It can be used for spiritual attunement to the energy of love.

It provides for balancing of yin-yang energy and can attune each chakra to, and provide each chakra with, the proper frequency of energy vibration.

This mineral is quite effective in the treatment of conditions relating to the emotional body, balancing the love emotions of the upper four chakras - heart, throat, brow, and crown chakras. Rose quartz can act as a rejuvenating agent for both the physical body and the emotions. It is an excellent energy for healing emotional "wounds".

Actual crystals are very rare, and quite small, usually in small clusters. The rose quartz crystals combine the qualities of rose quartz with all of the qualities of the quartz crystal - truly producing a wonderful powerful loving energy. They also instill a permanence to ones loving nature. Placement of the crystal in ones environment, using the energies in an elixir, and wearing and/or carrying the crystal all stimulate the true life force - LOVE.

The Rose Quartz Chevron configuration synthesizes the qualities of the Rose Quartz and the Chevron Amethyst.

The Rose Quartz Elestial configuration combines the qualities of Rose Quartz and the Elestial.

Rose quartz can be used to clear fluids in the cells of the body and to promote the release of impurities. It can be used to enable the opening of the heart center, allowing for the dissolution of stress and tension. It has been used in the treatment of vertigo. It provides for help in the diminishment of disorders of the kidneys and adrenal glands. It can be used [as an elixir] to clear the skin and is said to reduce wrinkles and to provide the wearer/carrier with a soft complexion. Placed upon the heart chakra, it can diminish pain and can stimulate the proper functioning of the heart. Placed upon the area of the thymus, it has decreased coughs and soothed the bronchial and lung areas of the body. It has also been used to diminish burns and to relieve and vanquish blistering due to heat.

Vibrates to the number 7.

ROSELITE   [Astrological Sign of Cancer]

Roselite crystallizes in the form of spherical aggregates, druses, and prismatic crystals. The colour ranges from dark red to pink.

This mineral, sometimes occurring with erytherite, can provide a window through which one can access the entry to the ancient traditions of Egypt, while also providing for guidance in the translation of the hieroglyphics which are displayed within the intuitive thought transfer of the knowledge. The information usually comes to one in the structure of a list, but other transfer structures have been utilized.

Roselite has been used assist one in sharpening communication skills for business and personal relations. It helps one in the understanding of the personal mind and encourages the continuation of personal growth.

It also provides an energy conducive to helping one work directly with the unconscious mind.

It can induce the alpha state during meditation and can be used to facilitate cell energy renewal. It also stimulates ESP.

Roselite can be used to assist in the diagnosis of heart and brain electrical alignment disorders and to aid in determining the axes which require alignment and the stones which would be beneficial in assisting in the restoration of alignment.

Vibrates to the number 4.

ROSENBUSCHITE   [Astrological Sign of Virgo]

Rosenbuschite crystallizes in the form of fibrous masses, needle-like crystals, and prismatic crystals. The colour range includes grey and orange.

This mineral facilitates circular breathing to stimulate states conducive to healing, re-birthing, centering, controlling anger, and meditation. It balances ones sexuality, enhances creativity, and stabilizes emotions. Taken as an elixir, it has produced a state likened to euphoria.

It can help one through times of petty indifferences, problems with the laws of the country, and scandals. It not only provides support, but also assists one in the recognition of information relative to corrective action.

It can be used to promote the recognition of the difference between knowledge and wisdom, leading one systematically toward the realization of ones personal inner truths.

Rosenbuschite can be used in the treatment of fevers, ulcers, conditions of atrophy within the body, as well as the mind, and to provide strength to the vertebrae of the spine. It has also been used to energize flower essences.

Vibrates to the number 5.

RUBELLITE   [See Tourmaline]

RUBY   [Astrological Signs of Leo, Scorpio, Cancer, & Sagittarius]

Ruby is a type of corundum which crystallizes in the form of tabular and rhombohedral prismatic crystals. The colour range includes pink, crimson red, and orange-red. It sometimes exhibits dichroism, displaying crimson red and orange-red in the same stone. It also, occasionally, displays asterism [a starlike luminosity in transmitted light]. Some rubies from Thailand also contain analcime crystals.

This mineral stimulates the heart chakra and assists one in the selection and attainment of ones ultimate values. It further stimulates the loving emotional side toward nurturing, bringing spiritual wisdom, health, knowledge, and wealth.

Ruby is known as a "stone of nobility", gathering and amplifying energy while promoting and stimulating mental concentration. It can improve ones success in controversies and disputes, encouraging gentleness and discouraging violence. It is an excellent shielding stone, protecting on all levels and safeguarding ones consciousness from psychic attack.

In addition, it is said to represent ones rise from martyrdom, the energy bringing support to assist one to recognize that the option exists with respect to whether one needs or does not need to experience anguish, distress, and/or suffering. It further assists one in relinquishing the need to experience the travails.

In ancient cultures, it was also used in the practice of "casting lots", to assist in the determination of resolutions and decisions.

It has been used to induce a stability in ones economic status; it has been said that as long as one retains a bit of ruby, wealth will never depart.

It is also said to have been used to protect the wearer/carrier against unhappiness, distressing dreams, and lightning.

It is said to have been one of the stones used in the breastplate of the high priest.

The energy of the ruby is intense and vivid, bringing lucidity to the dream state and conveying understanding and control of the role and action of the mental state upon the physical realm.

The ruby encourages one to follow bliss. It is said that ruby will light the darkness of ones life, giving birth to a spark of light which progresses throughout the body and spirit, conquering darkness on all levels. The energy can assist one in changing ones world, promoting creativity and expansiveness in awareness and manifestation.

It has been used in the treatment of fever, and heart disorders relating to blood flow through the ventricles. It can be used to decrease the length of time required for chemicals and toxins to exit the body. It can ameliorate the intake of caffeine, acting as a counter-balance to stimulants. It can also help in the optimum formation of children in the embryonic state.

Ruby crystals have recently been available from Merlin's Crystal Mine in India and from Madagascar. They are superior crystals and exhibit additional properties which include further access to the spiritual realms. With the ruby crystal, one may access ancient writings covering the esoteric principles of the religious movements, the structure and attributes of occult knowledge, and information from the akashic records relative to the development of the intuitive, psychic, and astral abilities. The ruby crystals from India are said to be pieces from the spear of Lord Krishna, used during the Vedic ages to vanquish the Lord of Destruction from the Earth. They are now being used to assist in the intense focusing necessary for healing the Earth, for banishing and discouraging the destructive forces, and for the purification of the ethers.

The ruby crystal has been known as the "star of purity" and the "star fire", initiating action and assisting the Earth in receiving the full spectrum of light required for the progression of humanity toward the access of the spiral leading to enlightenment.

The ruby crystal can also assist in purifying and correcting disoriented, trapped energy which leads to atrophy. It helps in the resolution of opposites, promoting the refinement of the will as a love-based force. It further acts to align the bodies - auric and physical - to the full light spectrum, encouraging the optimum state of health and being. It is an excellent stone for re-birthing and for releasing blockages which restrain one from the spiritual path. It acts also to arrest leakages of energy from the chakras and to transmute negative energy to the "golden realm of reasoning". It can also assist one in maintaining a connection with another person, with another area of the world, or with the Earth - allowing for the transmission of loving and gentle energy to the defined location.

The ruby crystal has been used as a rod-like conductor for atmospheric electricity, providing a pathway, to the Earth and to the user, for electrical and magnetic forces. It further assists one in the conscious access of ethereal consciousness, providing a medium through which an understanding and an actualization of the healing process can be manifested.

They are said to have been used in Lemurian ceremonial activities and to maintain the psychic energies of that time period. It has also been used to facilitate access to the teachings of the ancient teachers of India.

It promotes dreaming and stimulates the connection with, and transmission of information from, ones spiritual guides.

Some of these ruby crystals are recognized as record-keepers, containing knowledge from the ancient realms of civilization and awaiting the opportunity to share the knowledge. Astral travel with these crystals has been quite successful.

The employment of Carnelian and Chlorite with Ruby Crystals has been used to eliminate psychic attack and to assist earth-bound spirits to leave an area. Gridding of these three minerals can protect one and ones environment from the return of negative energies.

Vibrates to the number 3.

RUBY IN KYANITE   [Astrological Sign of Gemini]

In addition to the qualities listed in the KYANITE and RUBY sections, this combination tends to produce a melding of the throat chakra, the heart chakra, and the base chakra, allowing for the vocalization and resolution of basic difficulties, issues, and obstacles, in a loving manner.

This mixture not only facilitates immediate alignment of the chakras, but also gathers and amplifies positive energies.

The kyanite portion produces an energy which is beneficial to the ruby, disallowing the accumulation and/or retention of negative energy or vibrations. The kyanite tends to manifest a sweeping energy motion, transforming any negativity which approaches, into a radiant clear and positive energy. The ruby portion produces an energy which is beneficial to the kyanite, providing one with protection and security.

The combination of the minerals assists in astral travel, bringing strength to the connection between the conscious self and the astral body while assisting in the conveyance of understanding and control of ones journeys.

During use as an attunement stone, the combination brings insights to emotional states and initiates the movement of the Kundalini within the users such that the path to movement is traveled by all; the spark of energy is usually felt in the area where the Kundalini is resting and the progression may be both felt and seen with the third-eye.

It provides for an organization of the sacred uniformity of personal life, the blessed order upon, and within, the Earth, and the celestial order of the universe. The concepts of organization and systematic resolutions, and the implementation of same, are facilitated.

Used on the area of the third eye during sleep states, lucid dreaming is enhanced. Carried or worn, the art of manifestation is amplified.

Used in meditation, the state is entered with ease, and the energy becomes quite balanced and accessible. It is also quite useful when accessing the astral plane and when connecting with ones guides. It further helps to induce recall of dreams and to promote dream-solving, providing for access to solutions during the dream state.

It provides for balancing of the yin-yang energies, bringing an orderly growth to the intellect, emotions, and physical body. It dispels energy blockages, moving energy from the ethereal plane, in a gentle, yet, forceful way through the physical body.

It can be used during radionic analysis; holding a sample and placing a sample on the witness or using a pendulum of this stone, the energy of the stone interferes with the energy of the user and points to the problem(s) involved.

It has been used in the treatment of disorders of the muscular system, throat, parathyroid glands. and brain. It has been shown to be a beneficial stone for promotion of de-toxification, for treatment of fever, circulatory constrictions, to stabilize the heart chakra. Placed between the heart and throat chakras during the healing activities associated with the "Laying-on-of-Stones", it has provided for a synthesis between the emotional and vocal.

Vibrates to the master number 66.

RUBY SILVER   [See Proustite]

RUTILE   [Astrological Signs of Gemini & Taurus]

Rutile crystallizes in the form of prismatic crystals, terminated by a bi-pyramid type structure, occasionally in a geniculate configuration [bent, curved, knee-shaped], and as needle-like crystals [especially when penetrating quartz, kunzite, etc.] The colour range includes red, red-brown, black, yellow, gold, blue, violet, and green.

It has been known to represent both the lovely hair of Venus and the "sweet" tipped arrows of love. It has been likened to the appearance of wheat straw and angel hair, especially when found within another crystal [e.g., quartz, topaz, amethyst, etc.]. The ethereal aspects of rutile, when found within another crystalline form, bring strength with love, ease in transition, growth in all avenues of ones development, and calm, reason, and order.

Rutile is used for healing and balancing the aura via repelling negative energy. It affects the physical, etheric, and astral bodies. It assists one in getting to the root of a problem and, hence, provides for access to the reason for a dis-ease, so that one can remedy the situation.

It is a stone for stabilizing relationships, marriages, mental processes, and emotional and physical imbalances. It allows for the realization that each person shares the powers of the universe, the passions of the planets, and the understanding from the advanced worlds.

It also dispels unwanted interference from both the physical and spiritual worlds - the mechanism is unclear, but in the physical world, it tends to eliminate circumstances which could facilitate interference; and, in the spiritual worlds, a clear message is sent, asking for no interference. In the cases of the spiritual worlds, one may relinquish this blockade without relinquishing the blockade in the physical world.

During astral travel, rutile provides for insight into the reasons for visiting the locations and viewing the scenes; it stimulates awareness of the connections between this physical life and the situations which are viewed.

This mineral has been used in the treatment of bronchitis, to stimulate "sparkle" in the eyes, to regulate mothers milk, to strengthen the walls of the blood veins, and to stimulate sexuality [when consciously directed]. An elixir has been used, topically, for the treatment of wounds.

Vibrates to the number 4.

**SOMETIMES THE SAGE
JUST AWAITS THE ANSWER FROM PROVIDENCE**

SAGENITE

Sagenite is a form of quartz or agate which contains inclusions of, or vacant structures which no longer contain needle-like rutile, black tourmaline, goethite, stibnite, asbestos, actinolite, hornblende, or epidote. The QUARTZ section in this book discusses both TOURMALINATED QUARTZ and RUTILATED QUARTZ. This section discusses the properties of all other forms of sagenite.

Sagenite is a "stone for wisdom". It helps one to be judicious in ones experiences and to gain insight into the inner being without being required to repeat onerous situations; i.e., the user is reconciled to one-time learning experiences. It also provides for guidance with respect to the painless way to learn the lessons required in this lifetime.

It is a stone for providing acute mental discernment and enhancement of the practical side of ones nature. It encourages deliberate action via the exquisite art of kindness. It further helps one to acknowledge only beauty and to understand that, that which is non-beautiful exists only in ones limited perception.

The included material [or vacated structure] acts like a net to snare and to remove "muddy" areas in the aura. It is also used in shamanic healing ceremonies to remove the negative spirit which is residing in the area of dis-ease. Carrying sagenite, while smudging, produces a doubly powerful positive energy, encouraging the radiance of the positive white light to shine in all areas of ones environment. It can also be used to cleanse and clear other minerals.

It is a very protective stone and is a good stone for use during pregnancy; the stone can act to stimulate the optimum levels of well-being within the unborn child, while affording protection to the body of the mother.

Vibrates to the number 8.

SAINFELDITE

Sainfeldite crystallizes in the form of pink and colourless rosettes.

This mineral is expressive of abiding content and relays the message that "anything can happen" in the course of ones life.

It is a "stone for adventure", promoting positivity in all aspects of ones environment and life. It provides for protection against negative influences and forms a shield around ones physical body, permeable only to positive influences. Sainfeldite can also be used to augment ones energies in times of need, bringing the activation of both mental and physical capabilities which appear to be beyond the realm of ones capabilities.

It can protect during, and can facilitate, astral travel; providing for grounding via the heart chakra. It also stimulates contact with loved-ones who have ascended to other planes.

It can be used to help re-align cellular structures which have become mutated and to release the dis-eased structure through normal body functions.

Vibrates to the number 5.

SALESITE   [Astrological Sign of Gemini]

Salesite crystallizes in the form of blue-green prismatic crystals.

This mineral can be used to stimulate creativity and intuition concurrently, producing spiritual artistry. With use of this stone, the artist can "vacate the premises" while the creation is being produced, and can use the time to connect to "All That Is", further enhancing the creative state.

This mineral, used in meditation, provides for "concentration" on the highest pinnacle available in the realm of spirituality. It does not transport one automatically to the area, but provides for clarity of the way.

It further allows one to command a clear range of sight, both physical and intuitive.

It has been said to be an excellent stone for any "merchant" profession.

It is quite useful in the activities of the "sweat lodge"; taking the negativity which is relieved from the body and transforming it to useful energy. It tends to alleviate any exhaustion accompanying the ceremony.

Salesite can be used in the treatment of dehydration, as well as in disorders of water retention. It is pleasant in the bath and helps to provide the skin with a fresh, healthy appearance. It can be useful in the assimilation of Vitamins A and C, and in the relief of headaches.

Vibrates to the number 9.

SAMARSKITE   [Astrological Sign of Scorpio]

Samarskite crystallizes in the form of masses, grains, and rectangular prismatic crystals. The colour ranges from brown to velvet black.

This mineral can be used to attain solutions - mental, physical, emotional, etc. It allows one the insight, and the connection with the intuitive self, to assemble the facts and to make the decision. It provides for support, as the detective world says, "to crack the case".

It brings forth the warrior spirit to advance and to be the best at that which one attempts.

It also facilitates pursuits in the fields of astrology, astronomy, and quantum physics.

Occasionally, samarskite appears with a coating; if this coating is not removed, it also promotes an adventuresome spirit and facilitates travel.

Samarskite can be used in the treatment of disorders of the glandular structures of the body. It has been used as an elixir to strengthen the body and to treat digestive disorders. It has also been used in activities related to psychic surgery.

Vibrates to the number 8.

SANDSTONE   [Astrological Sign of Gemini]

Sandstone is a stone of sand. Occasionally, sandstone is found in the petrified form, sometimes in the configuration of small waves, pinnacles, etc. The colour ranges from creamy white to tan to rusty brown.

It is a "stone of creativity" and is conducive to both the building and the strengthening of cohesiveness and solidarity within relationships and/or groups.

It assists one to maintain strength against the distractions of the mind, providing for balancing of ones reality, and facilitating movement and change with ease. It assists in dispelling the mirages of ones reality, providing insight into deceit and encouraging truth. It can help in revealing that which is hidden, and in promoting clarity in thought and sight.

It can also be used to dispel abrasiveness of character and to promote the feeling and understanding of loving acceptance of humanity, while bringing the polished aspects to ones demeanor. It has been used to discourage tirades, temper tantrums, and general grouchiness.

In parts of the world where sand dunes exist, there is an ethereal-like singing which occurs. Sandstone assists one in recognizing the messages of the dunes and in directing ones course of action.

Sandstone can be used in the treatment of wounds and broken bones. It can be used to ameliorate water retention and to assist in the restoration of degenerative eyesight, weak fingernails, and thinning hair.

In addition, there is a Sandstone and Quartz conglomerate, found in India, which is truly a flexible mineral. The colour ranges from pink to peach to tan and it is also known as <u>Phenomenite</u>. It is a lovely and unique mineral. This configuration provides one with adaptability to changing environments and conditions. It furthers ones ability to flow with variations in ones activities, surroundings, and ventures. It is said to have originated from the Earth-changes occurring during the rule of Lord Krishna and to have been used by him to instill stability within the realm. It has also been used in the treatment of dis-alignment of the spinal vertebrae and, as an elixir, to smooth the to re-vitalize the skin.

Sandstone vibrates to the number 3 and Phenomenite vibrates to the number 9.

SAPPHIRE   [Elemental Astrological Signs of Virgo, Libra,
                                                          & Sagittarius]

Sapphire is a type of corundum which crystallizes in the form of tabular prismatic crystals with hexagonal double pyramid structures. The colour range includes blue, white, black, purple [known also as Oriental Amethyst], yellow [known also as Oriental Topaz], and green [known also as Oriental Emerald].

Sapphire also occurs in the form of asterated or "star" sapphire; the "star" results due to the inclusion of small cylindrical cavities within the stone which are parallel to the prism planes.

This mineral can be used to rid one of unwanted thoughts and to bring joy and peace of mind via opening the mind to beauty and intuition. The sapphire brings lightness and joy, with depth of beauty and thought, to the user/wearer.

The sapphire is known as a "stone of prosperity", sustaining the gifts of life, eliminating frustration, and fulfilling the dreams and the desires of the consciousness.

It tends to focus, to emanate, and to radiate energy without ones the conscious initiation.

It is said to have been one of the stones used in the breastplate of the high priest.

The sapphire has been used in the treatment of disorders of the blood, to combat excessive bleeding, and to strengthen the walls of the veins. It has also been used in the treatment of cellular disorders, bringing the energy of cooperation to the cellular level.

The many combinations of the different coloured sapphires are interesting to use in the process of "laying-on-of-stones"; the reader is encouraged to use the intuitive knowledge within the self as a guide to the variety of placements available.

Vibrates to the number 2.

In addition, Sapphire Crystals have recently been available from Madagascar. They are superior crystals and exhibit additional properties which include an approach of ease to the metaphysical realms. With the sapphire crystal, one may access ancient scripts covering the esoteric principles of physical movements in the universal realm and during the life of our civilization upon this Earth.

The Sapphire Crystal vibrates to the number 1.

Additional properties relative to the individual colours of sapphire are shown below.

Blue Sapphire   [Astrological Sign of Gemini]

Blue sapphire assists healing in all parts of the body. It stimulates the throat chakra and assists in communication.

It assists in providing strength to the user and helps one in endeavors of diversification.

Yogo sapphire is a type of blue sapphire which sometimes contains rutile, analcime crystals, calcite, pyrite, biotite, and/or mica; this sapphire also emits the energies associated with the integrated mineral[s].

The structure and attributes of mystical knowledge, and information from the records relative to the development of the civilization, and the intuitive, psychic, and astral selves, are available through this crystal.

These crystals are said to be a one of those minerals implanted upon the Earth by kind and generous ancient Earth-Keepers, in order to assist us learning to live with kindness, to learn with compassion, and to understand with appreciation. They are now being used to assist in the intense energy transfer necessary for healing the Earth, for ameliorating those forces which can be detrimental to the environment, and for the purification of the realm.

The sapphire crystal has been known as the "stone of uniformity", bringing authenticity to ones action and encouraging the progression of humanity toward the fulfillment and well-being which is waiting. ♪

This crystal can also assist in purifying and rectifying disoriented, trapped energy which leads to retrogression in ones life. It helps in the resolution of disparity, promoting the purification of the will to further cohesiveness with unconditional love. It further acts to stimulate the throat chakra, to align the chakras, and to encourage the optimum state of interaction between the self and others. It is an excellent stone for re-birthing and for releasing blockages which restrain one from the spiritual path. It acts also to arrest leakages of energy from the chakras and to transmute negative energy. It can also assist one in maintaining a connection with the Earth and to promote cleansing of the atmospheric energies, and has been used in shamanic ceremonies for that purpose.

It is said to have been used in ancient ceremonial activities and to maintain the psychic energies of that time period. It promotes dreaming and stimulates the connection with, and transmission of information from, that time period.

Some of these sapphire crystals are recognized as record-keepers, containing knowledge from the ancient realms of civilization and awaiting the opportunity to share the knowledge. Astral travel with these crystals has been quite successful.

Vibrates to the number 6.

Black Sapphire   [Astrological Sign of Sagittarius]

Black sapphire provides for protection and centering of both the body and the inherent energy forces. It also provides a grounding force, relieving mental anxiety and dispelling doubtfulness of intuition.

It is an excellent stone to carry when seeking employment and/or maintaining same.

Vibrates to the number 4.

Green Sapphire   [Astrological Signs of Gemini & Leo]

Green sapphire enhances the sight on the physical plane, stimulates loyalty, and encourages the remembering of dreams.

It stimulates the heart chakra and is known as a "stone of fidelity". It provides impetus and means to help improve conditions on the physical plane.

Vibrates to the number 6.

Indigo Sapphire   [Astrological Sign of Sagittarius]

Indigo sapphire provides for alertness and attentiveness, stimulating the center of the third-eye and inspiring creativity in the higher realms of psychic awareness. It assists in eliminating the negative energies from the chakras and from the aura, acting as a reminder that the total responsibility for ones thoughts and feelings lies within the self. It also further facilitates the understanding of ones responsibilities and provides for guidance in acceptance of same.

It is a "stone of encouragement", strengthening ones ambition to continue pursuits and to grow toward the "unreachable" horizon.

This stone is a constant reminder that "the truth shall set you free". It helps one to access information which will strengthen ones resolve and which will further ones growth.

It has been used in the treatment of disorders of the brain and to ameliorate dyslexic conditions in the young.

Vibrates to the number 6.

Parti Sapphire   [Astrological Signs of Gemini, Virgo & Cancer]

The Parti Sapphire, found in Australia, is a combination of several colours of sapphire. The range includes green, blue, yellow, colourless, and yellow.

In addition to the properties of the respective colours, this configuration of sapphire has been used to stimulate all of the chakras of the associated colours and to cleanse and to activate same.

It has been used in Tibetan Pulsing exercises to promote the development of the heart toward innocence and to allow the mind to become unattached to problems. Due to attachments, one can experience only half of ones joy, love, and pleasure, as the mind always functions in polarity. The pattern generated is: right/wrong, yes/no, good/bad, etc. During positive experiences, one clings to the actualization and to the memory, but the function of the mind forces one to automatically experience the negative aspect sooner than would be desired. The heart lives "only in the moment" and provides the rhythmic pulsing, always desiring to unify and to meld with other hearts. The positive energy of the heart neutralizes negative energy through relaxation; pain is transmuted into pleasure, anguish and distress into relief, and tears into exhilaration.

Transformation of disorders has been facilitated with the Parti Sapphire energy; for example, eating disorders have been eliminated via the discharge the tension held in the Vagus Nerve. By relieving this tension with Parti Sapphire, one is able to understand the need for love from outside of the self, and to transform to a new sensitivity and to bring a true love for the self. This mineral also serves to enable one to relate to others with more sympathy and friendship.

Vibrates to the number 3.

A newly named "Watermelon Sapphire" also exhibits the qualities of Parti Sapphire.

Purple Sapphire   [Astrological Sign of Virgo]

Purple sapphire enhances spirituality and diminishes attention to the unnecessary cares and worries of this world. It can be used to stimulate meditation and to awaken the crown chakra. It has been used to clear the path through the chakras such that the movement of the Kundalini is unimpaired.

The advance to spirituality, which is initiated by purple sapphire, brings a condition of peace and oneness to the user. It is known as a "stone of awakening". The recognition of the bonding, of all that exists on the Earth plane with "All That Is", is manifested.

Vibrates to the number 9.

Star Sapphire   [Astrological Signs of Sagittarius & Capricorn]

Star sapphire enhances the centering of ones thoughts. It brings the knowledge of human nature to the user and enhances the ability to understand the intentions of another. It helps to make one cheerful and friendly.

It can also facilitate contact with the advanced beings of planetary worlds other than the Earth plane. It is known as a "stone of wisdom and good luck", helping one to regain the conscious recognition of the perfect order of the universe which exists at birth.

Vibrates to the number 6.

White Sapphire   [Astrological Sign of Libra]

White sapphire provides for focus and directing of attention. It stimulates the crown chakra, revealing the talents of the self and encouraging the pursuit of the lifework.

It is a stone which supports morality, justice, and freedom from greed.

Vibrates to the number 4.

Yellow Sapphire   [Astrological Sign of Leo]

Yellow sapphire is the helper of the Hindu God, Ganeesh; while Ganeesh brings prosperity to the home, the yellow sapphire brings wealth. Many merchants in the Far East wear the yellow sapphire, or keep it on the body. If it is worn, the stone is set such that a portion of the stone, itself, is touching the body.

Yellow sapphire also brings endurance, fulfillment of ambition, and the emanation of a pleasant rapport to the user. It continues to stimulate the intellect, allowing for the emergence of the "big picture" with the focus of the "puddle". It stimulates intensity and vivacity, enhancing wisdom.

It is said to have been used in ancient times to protect the user from poverty and from snakebite.

It can be used in the treatment of disorders of the stomach, the spleen, the gall bladder, and the liver. It has also been used, as an elixir, to eliminate toxins from the body.

Vibrates to the number 4.

SARCOLITE   [Astrological Sign of Aries]

Sarcolite crystallizes in the form of small tetragonal crystals. The colour is a light creamy pink.

This mineral stimulates the furtherance of the study of phrenology and allows one to understand the workings of the brain and the associated and un-associated mental states.

It ameliorates harsh and derisive attitudes and encourages harmony.

It enhances balance and is used to provide stability in meditative whirling activities; the whirling being the spinning of the physical body.

It can be used in the treatment of abrasions, to smooth the skin, to aid in the dissolution of growths and tumors, and to stimulate the meridians of the feet [it has relieved the feelings of sore and tired feet when used in a foot bath].

Vibrates to the number 3.

SARDONYX   [Astrological Sign of Aries]

Sardonyx is a variety of onyx which contains layers or bands of carnelian. It combines the properties of ONYX, CARNELIAN, and CHALCEDONY; see the respective sections in this book. In addition, further properties are listed below.

This mineral can assist in bringing happiness in marriage and "live-in" relationships. It allows one to realize the delightfulness of living. It can be used to attract friends and good fortune, and to encourage self-control. It has been used to diminish hesitation and to provide courage.

It is said to have been one of the stones used in the breastplate of the high priest.

It is known as a "stone of virtue", stimulating and propagating virtuous conduct throughout the many facets of ones life.

It is also useful in gridding the areas of overpopulation in order to decrease crime.

Vibrates to the number 3.

SCAPOLITE   [Astrological Sign of Taurus]

Scapolite crystallizes in the form of masses, columns, and prismatic crystals. The colour range includes pink, white, colourless, green, violet, yellow, grey, blue, and red. The quality of the "cat's eye" chatoyancy is not uncommon in the mineral.

It helps one to delve into the areas deep within the self in order to find solutions to present and past problems.

It further encourages independence and initiative in ones life.

This mineral provides impetus to change - situations of the body, of the mind, or of ones environmental conditions.

It enhances growth in any area consciously chosen, and brings both the stamina and the clarity required for the attainment of the pre-set goal.

Scapolite can be used in the treatment of cataracts, glaucoma, dis-alignment of the iris, dyslexia, and incontinence. It can be used for treatment of bone disorders and constriction of the veins, and to assist one in recovery from physical operations. It can also be used to provide relief from discomforts of the shoulders and areas of the upper chest. It has been used to increase calcium assimilation.

Vibrates to the number 1.

SCAWTITE   [Astrological Sign of Taurus]

Scawtite crystallizes in the form of colourless grains, plate-like layers, and thin tabular crystals [usually in groups].

This mineral is an excellent stone for those who live alone and are, occasionally, uneasy; it helps to dispel anxiety and to provide protection of the premises. It eases critical-ness, and allows one to become more at ease with oneself.

It can be used to overcome the "insufficiencies" in ones life and to promote abundance.

This mineral can be used in the treatment of poor assimilation of nutrients, vitamins, minerals, and information. It helps the mental faculties to perform at an increased rate, and can be used to stimulate metabolism.

It has been used in the treatment of burns and wounds, and, as a topical elixir to diminish permanent markings of the skin. It has also been used in the treatment of fever and "strep" infections.

Vibrates to the number 1.

SCHALENBLENDE   [Astrological Sign of Aquarius & Pisces]

Schalenblende is a closely compact variety of Sphalerite which occurs in concentric layers with reniform surfaces, often with Galena and Marcasite interstratified. The colour ranges from yellow to tan to pale brown.

In addition to the properties listed in the SPHALERITE, GALENA, and MARCASITE sections of this book, this mineral has been used to stimulate peace within localities to where it is directed. It is a "stone of peace", bringing communication and understanding between people who would not normally communicate.

It has also been used to stimulate encounters with those of ones choice.

It has been worn by shamen to provide protection and holds an aspect of solar energy and a connection to the solar plexus chakra which also helped shamen in their magical practices. It was considered a sacred stone during the performance of, and adherence to, the "old ways" of the Celtic civilization; the yellow to tan colour was used to bring the energy to assist and to protect during times of travel [spiritual or physical]; the inclusion of Galena and/or Marcasite was thought to induce health and re-birth, bringing freshness in ideas and strategies to the holder; the full combination is said to assist one in connecting with the "after" worlds.

It is a stone which accepts intense responsibility in the realm of protection. It protects against negativity and helps one to be grounded to the stabilizing energies of the Earth.

It has been used in the treatment of AIDS and to improve deficiency of the immune system.

Vibrates to the number 5.

SCHEELITE   [Astrological Sign of Libra]

Scheelite crystallizes in the form of granular masses, columns, tabular crystals, and octahedral crystals. The colour range includes white, colourless, yellow, red, orange-yellow, green, and purple.

This mineral can be used to dispel haughtiness and to initiate serious, connected thought patterns. It facilitates punctuality and the delivering of a product "on-time".

It provides for insight to the discovery of "a map to the heavens" and allows one to pre-determine the destination prior to, or during, astral travel.

Scheelite also stimulates the female energies and can be used to balance an excess of male tendencies.

It can be used to provide for alignment between the seven chakras and to enhance the recognition and communication of the needs of each chakra. This facilitates ample warning for out-of-balance situations.

In addition, scheelite helps to stabilize the inner self, promoting organization within, and integration of, the personality with the higher-self.

It can be used in the treatment of disorders of the lower back, and can help to dissipate blockages in the nerve structure which supplies blood to the muscles of the thighs, legs, and feet. It can also be used to treat disorders of the male reproductive system.

Vibrates to the number 5.

SCHORL   [See Black Tourmaline]

SCOLECITE   [ASTROLOGICAL SIGN OF CAPRICORN]

Scolecite crystallizes in the form of slender prismatic crystals, masses, fibers, radiated filaments, and nodules. The colour is colourless to white.

This mineral can be used to open the network of information patterns to facilitate communication with other worlds, primarily the spiritual world; however, information has been obtained from ancient civilizations. It is currently being utilized as a stone for extra-terrestrial communication.

It provides for thoughtful cultivation of associations and emanates an energy which expedites the creation of cohesiveness in relationships and organizations; it furthers the action of the "team spirit".

Scolecite assists one in access to the basis of a problem, serving to support the transformation of the heart to love. It further enables one to exhibit control of ones life, promoting the actualization of the preferred reality.

This mineral has been used in the treatment of intestinal disorders, spinal dis-alignment, and to expel parasites from the body. It can also be used for the remediation of disorders related to the eyes, the cortex, and the lungs. It can be used to dissipate blood clots, to stimulate the clearing of arterial walls, and to enhance circulation. It is also useful in the treatment of bruises and wounds.

Vibrates to the number 1.

SEAMANITE [Astrological Sign of Scorpio]

Seamanite crystallizes in the form of pale yellow small needle-like crystals.

This mineral can be used to both initiate and sustain a calm and collected attitude.

Seamanite stimulates desire and provides for a creative direction for that desire. It can bring one back from the depths of depression and can produce the overpowerful attribute of "hope". It can help one to "maintain and gain" during trying times.

This mineral can be used to stimulate the assimilation of iron within the blood, and to help bones to repair themselves [especially, when repair is required due to fractures or breaks]. It also helps to dispel dry skin, and is quite helpful as an elixir applied topically. It can also be used in the treatment of rickets and scurvy.

Do not prepare an elixir of this mineral via the normal method.

Vibrates to the master number 33.

SELENITE [Astrological Sign of Taurus]

Selenite is a form of crystallized gypsum. It is found in the form of colourless to white tabular crystals and needle-like crystals.

This mineral provides for clarity of the mind, expanding ones awareness of the self and of ones surroundings.

It can be used to access past-lives as well as future lives - the future lives being those which are probable at this time, if ones physical life proceeds in the direction in which it is now going. This access is provided by rubbing the crystalline structure with a finger or thumb [not a fingernail]; during this activation process, when the meditative state is attained, the visual images will begin. It should be noted that the access to the future is also compatible to this life - one will be presented with situations which are very likely to occur during this life on this plane [again, dependent upon the course of progress one chooses during ones lifetime].

It has been used to decrease reticence and to assist one in the acquisition of materialistic pursuits related to business. It can also assist one in issues of judgment and can provide the required insight and ameliorative energies to promote justice during adjudication of disputes. It has been used as a sharp sword of awareness, cutting through unconscious assumptions and promoting the re-connection between the conscious self and the mystic which lives within the super-consciousness.

Selenite can be used to provide both flexibility to ones nature and strength to ones decisions. It allows one to see the inner workings of any situation and to understand the superficial and the deeper meanings inherent in same. It also allows one to access the interior of the physical body in order to understand existing disorders, providing information with respect to the "fix".

It has been used to align the spinal column; allowing the selenite to traverse the spinal column from the base of the spine to the back of the head seems to remove energy blockages, while traversing in the opposite direction seems to smooth the flow of energy. It can also promote flexibility within the muscular structure.

It can be used to provide amelioration of disorders associated with poisoning due to the metals in the "fillings" of the teeth. It can also be used to facilitate regeneration of the cellular structure and the protective membrane linings which surround the cells - hence, providing a tool to both prevent and to overcome damage caused by the well known "free radical"; examples of the effects which can be overcome include cancer, tumors, age spots, wrinkles, and light sensitivity. Selenite can also be used to correct disorders and deformities of the skeletal system, and to stabilize epileptic disorders. It has also been used to extend ones life span.

Vibrates to the number 8.

SELLAITE   [Astrological Sign of Virgo]

Sellaite crystallizes in the form of colourless prismatic tetrahedral crystals.

This mineral enhances confidence and assists one in the ability to provide for oneself. It promotes the surrender of ones will to the good of all, allowing one to reflect and to base decisions upon the situations and upon the impact of the situations to all of those involved.

It can assist in providing for an increase in ones manifested ability to learn, discouraging diffidence and encouraging honesty - both within oneself and to others.

It can also be used to provide insight into the experiences which occur, or which one views, during astral travel; it allows for the actualization of the innate logic for analysis of the experiences to the fine detail which is sometimes required in order to produce adequate understanding. This stone is not a facilitator for astral travel, but one to use after the trip has been completed.

Sellaite can be used in the treatment of deteriorating teeth, kidney disorders, and bladder malfunction.

Vibrates to the number 2.

SENARMONITE   [Astrological Signs of Sagittarius & Pisces]

Senarmonite crystallizes in the form of masses, crusts, and octahedral crystals. The colour range includes colourless, white, and grey.

This mineral represents the trinity and allows one to recognize that the connection between all...is one.

It also has a connection with the number six - bringing the help and wisdom of the four directions, Mother Earth, and Father Sky. It is a good stone to use in medicine wheel ceremonies and to have in situations where the sacred pipe speaks - it can provide for a clearing of ones environment and can produce stability in the thought processes.

The vibratory energies, relating to the number seven, bring the synthesis of the four directions, Mother Earth, and Father Sky -the totality of the energies of our planet.

Senarmonite can assist one in "finding" the inner self via the recognition and the willing acceptance of that which is within the loving part of ones nature.

It further promotes rationality in the processes of life, while providing for an opening to a pathway for entry into the sensuality of nature and the creativity of the heart.

It can be used to transmit messages to the spirit worlds, to send love, to ask for guidance, and to stimulate contact. Message transmission within the physical world is also facilitated.

It can be used in the treatment of disorders associated with hearing and, in addition, can stimulate clairaudience.

It can stimulate the senses, can aid in the treatment of disorders of those senses, and can promote the development and furtherance of ESP.

Vibrates to the number 7.

SERANDITE   [Astrological Sign of Virgo]

Serandite is a hydrous silicate of manganese, calcium, and sodium which crystallizes in the formation of elongated crystals and in masses. The colour ranges from rose to red.

This mineral can be used to bring tolerance to dispel jealousy. It serves to allay discontent and frustration and to alleviate envy and vengefulness. It assists one in understanding the reason for mis-understandings and to reduce super-sensitivity.

It has been used to facilitate the definition of goals, providing a balance between the emotional and intellectual bodies such that one can contemplate the higher goals of ones path.

Serandite furthers appreciation by others and instills conscientiousness and total involvement in that which one selects. It acts to promote a living exchange of energies between one and another such that communion is acknowledged and isolation is eliminated. It is an excellent mineral for use during initial contacts with a person or an object.

This mineral has been used to enhance the assimilation of manganese and calcium, and to equilibrate the amount of sodium within the body.

Vibrates to the number 5.

SEREFINA   [See Chlorite]

SERENDIBITE   [Astrological Sign of Libra]

Serendibite crystallizes in the form of granular masses. The colour ranges through the varying shades of blue.

This mineral can be used to induce tranquillity, peacefulness, and calm. It is conducive to activation of the third-eye and to producing undisturbed, clearly expansive visions.

It is known as a "stone of serendipity", helping "things" to occur at the most beneficial time. It also promotes understanding and the peace and power of glad acceptance, helping one to meet all experience with trust and appreciation.

It assists in providing one with the ability to make discoveries, to be in certain locations, etc. - all seemingly, by "accident". It is a stone which helps one to use the intuition and to appreciate the existence of that quality.

It can be used to strengthen the immune system, to ameliorate the effects of tetanus, and to increase the assimilation of Vitamin D and the complete range of minerals, while stabilizing the effects of the sun on the body. It can also be used to lessen the effects of radiation on the body.

Vibrates to the number 2.

SERPENTINE   [Astrological Sign of Gemini]

Serpentine crystallizes in the form of fibers, plate-like layers, masses, and, sometimes as crystals, where the original crystal structure has been replaced by serpentine. The colour range includes green, black-green, brown-red, brown-yellow, and white. It is also sometimes mottled with red, and occasionally exhibits a net-like webbing of magnetite.

When serpentine exhibits the magnetite inclusions, the properties of serpentine are combined with the properties listed in the MAGNETITE section of this book.

Serpentine is useful in the rise of the Kundalini. It stimulates an opening in the pathway through which the Kundalini may travel, and lessens the discomfort which is sometimes associated with this movement.

Placement of the mineral at the crown chakra provides a drawing force conducive to initiating the movement. It can be used to clear the clouded areas of the chakras, and to stimulate the crown. It is also an excellent stone for enhancing the meditative state.

Light green serpentine is said to have been one of the stones used in the breastplate of the high priest.

It can be used in the treatment of diabetes and hypoglycemia, to eliminate parasitic infestations within the body, and to increase the absorption of calcium and magnesium.

Serpentine can render assistance to disorders in all areas of the body, the emotional system, and the mental structure; conscious direction of the energies toward the problem is required.

Vibrates to the number 8.

SHATTUCKITE   [Astrological Signs of Aquarius & Sagittarius]

Shattuckite crystallizes in the form of masses and fibers. It exhibits pleochroism which ranges from light to dark blue. It is a form of plancheite and also exhibits the qualities listed in the PLANCHEITE section of this book.

This mineral both stimulates and combines the energies of the throat chakra and the third-eye, producing clear concise verbalization of psychic visions and of contacts with other worlds.

It can be used in the processes of channeling information from the spirit world, as well as in communication between this physical world and extra-terrestrial worlds. It does not facilitate the contact, but allows for precision in the communication after the contact has been accomplished.

It is also used to provide protection against possession during channeling, allowing for the protection of the physical body against invasion.

Shattuckite can also be used in re-shaping ones reality; this modification providing for further growth in the direction of ones choice.

It can increase ones abilities in automatic writing and can sharpen the higher intuitive powers.

It can be used to increase the coagulation of the blood, to treat tonsillitis, and to clear the intercellular structures of blockages.

It is a lovely "spring tonic" and can be used in the treatment of all minor health complaints and as a general elixir.

Vibrates to the number 2.

SIDERITE   [Astrological Sign of Aquarius]

Siderite crystallizes in the form of masses, botryoidal structures, globes, plate-like layers, tabular crystals, rhombohedral crystals [sometime exhibiting curved faces], and scalenohedral crystals. The colour range includes pale yellow, grey-green, grey-brown, brown-red, grey-red, and nearly colourless.

This mineral provides for the alignment of each body and of all bodies to each body. Use of siderite first facilitates the alignment of the meridians and the chakras of the physical body; from there, the emotional, intellectual, ethereal, astral, etc., bodies align themselves to each other and to the physical body. One can be no more in alignment, than with this mineral.

It emits an energy to strengthen the commitment to ones lifework and to enhance stability in employment.

Siderite is an excellent stone to use in the care of those confined, either to bed, to home, or to an otherwise confining environment. It helps both the one confined and the one responsible for the care to cope in the unnatural-ness of the situation. It also promotes ideas for brightening ones day and for bringing-in the most positivity.

Use of this mineral can help to stimulate the assimilation of calcium, magnesium, and iron; it can be helpful in the treatment of bone deterioration and anemia, and to assist in the proper functioning of the elimination system.

Vibrates to the master number 44.

SHELL   [Astrological Sign of Pisces]

Shell, the homes of the small creatures of the sea, appears in many forms and contains the energies of the god of the sea. The CORAL and COWRIE sections of this book addresses specific types of shell. Additional properties for all shells are discussed below.

These vacated homes have been used to provide boundless growth in all areas of endeavor. They can be used to stimulate intuition, sensitivity, imagination, and adaptability. The structure of the shell can help to enhance clarity in the mental processes and to provide, during periods of decision-making, insight into which option to choose. It further promotes cooperation between the self and others and within the self. It is an excellent source of cohesive energy for groups.

One type of shell, the abalone shell has also been used to enhance smudging activities, bringing the energy of continuity to the environment and instilling a stable atmosphere. It has been revered by the ancient tribes throughout the world as a magical gift from the sea -one which can stimulate fertility of both the mind and body and can protect against un-cooperative attitudes and actions.

The shell can be used in the treatment of hearing disorders, calcium deficiencies, and in dysfunctions of the spinal canal and nervous system. It can assist in the healing of breaks in the skeletal structure and has been useful in enhancing the assimilation of Vitamins A and D. It has also been used to protect the muscular systems of the body from atrophy.

Vibrates to the number 2.

SILLIMANITE   [Astrological Sign of Aries]

Sillimanite crystallizes in the form of masses, aggregates, compact fibrous crystals, and long slender crystals which are, usually, not terminated. The colour range includes colourless, yellow, brown, white, green, grey, and blue.

This mineral can be used to assist in the stimulation of the release of endorphins within the body, producing a state sometimes likened to euphoria, and sometimes associated with the "runner's high". It can further enhance those daily activities which appear mundane, allowing for the realization of the purpose of all things and promoting the recognition of the power and rewards of service.

The energy can go deep within the inner self to stimulate the bodily intuition concerning the intellect, matters of communication, and situations concerning emotions and love. It provides for a foundation from which one may grow, and enhances the flowering of that growth.

It is a "stone for preservation": preservation of the spiritual side when confronted by the allure of the material side; preservation of ones body, ones appearance, ones mental capacity; and preservation of physical structures and objects. It discourages the act of decay in all matters.

It can be used in the treatment of disorders of the lungs and to stimulate breathing. It can help to ameliorate inflammation of the sinuses, and tends to aid in regeneration from atrophy and in preservation of the pituitary gland facilitating mental acuity. It can also be used to help the body to become accustomed to a foreign object placed within it; i.e., it can help, to some extent, to allow the body to accept the donation of an organ or an implant of foreign material which is sometimes used to help a structure to bind together.

Vibrates to the number 6.

SILVER   [Astrological Signs of Cancer & Aquarius]

Silver crystallizes in the form of dendritic wires, scales, plates, masses/nuggets, and, rarely, needle-like crystals. The colour is silver-white which tarnishes to grey or black.

The occurrence of silver within a quartz crystal is not only beautiful, but rare. If one is fortunate enough to become an Earth-keeper for a quartz crystal containing silver, the uses are extensive. The properties of silver and the properties of the quartz crystal are combined to produce "dynamite" results.

Silver brings one "the advantage" throughout life. It can be used to improve ones quality of speech and can bring eloquence to conversations. It tends to bring an air of culture to ones presence and to eliminate abrasive traits while promoting popularity.

It can be used as a mirror to the soul, one to stimulate seeing oneself from outside of the body. This sight is without judgmental attitudes and can provide for a stepping-stone to the furtherance of that which the I Ching [pronounced yee-jing] recognizes as the "superior man". It provides one with patience and perseverance in the tasks chosen and allows one to understand the underlying reasons for the tasks. It assists in increasing perception and helps to regulate the emotional and the intuitive energies.

It provides for a very strong connection between the physical and astral bodies, assuring that one may always "come home" from the astral plane. It tends to strengthen the "silver cord" which connects the astral body to the physical body, providing for diminishment of the unconscious fear of the inability to return.

Silver is used extensively with gem stones because the metal is able to both attract and retain, unto itself, those qualities which are emitted by the stone. The silver provides a steadying influence for the jewel. It is also used during the preparation of elixirs to energize the primary mineral for use in the elixir - occasionally, silver is placed with another mineral during the process of preparation of an elixir of that mineral.

It is known to enhance the powers of the moon and is an excellent mineral for use in energizing other stones during the full and new moons.

It is used to direct the energy of other minerals to the appropriate location: the malleability of silver is conducive to causing energies to bend, and to even become circular, such that the vital energy centers can be concurrently opened, stimulated, cleared, and activated.

It can draw forth negativity from the body while transferring the positive forces of the other mineral; hence, it performs as a balancing agent.

Silver helps to cleanse the body via the pores, and to eliminate toxins at the cellular level. It can be used in the treatment of hepatitis, to increase the assimilation of Vitamins A and E, and to ameliorate disorders associated with unstable vision.

Vibrates to the number 4.

SIMPSONITE   [Astrological Sign of Libra]

Simpsonite crystallizes in the form of crystalline masses and tabular crystals. The colour range includes yellow, brown, and colourless.

This mineral stimulates the crown chakra and the attribute of personal power, while clearing the aura. It provides for freedom from complexity in all matters, and leads one to the inner truth that one creates complexity and can, instead, create simplicity.

It can allow one to both mentally and emotionally "remove" from a situation, while remaining physically present. During the removal, one can access information which will help one to return to the same state of affairs, but with a "more together" frame of mind.

It is conducive to comfort - comfort within ones body, mind, spirit, and environment. It enables one to release "clutter" from the mind and to understand the ease of living on the Earth plane. It further helps one to live ones life according to ones inner sense.

Simpsonite can be used in the treatment of the lymph glands, to enhance resistance to infection, and to relieve fever.

Vibrates to the number 4.

SINHALITE   [Astrological Sign of Virgo]

Sinhalite was originally believed to be a brown variety of peridot. The colour range includes green-brown, brown-green, and golden yellow. It exhibits pleochroism and displays the shades of green-brown and golden yellow.

This mineral is an aid to individuality and is conducive to the promulgation of originality. It encourages one to "walk alone" and to further oneself through innovation. It provides for truth and companionship from within the self, leading one in the direction of love and light.

It is a very loving stone and dispels loneliness, while allowing the user to remain at ease with the inner self.

The golden light emitted through the pleochroism awakens the personal power, while the stone guides one to use this power with heart-felt love.

The stone represents purity and kindness, and can be applied to stimulate well-being on all planes.

Sinhalite can be used to dispel sickness and disorder from the physical body. It is a general healing stone, working on the many facets of the body, mind, and emotions. One can look within the stone and receive the visual images of the truth behind a disorder; this truth stimulates the action which can be taken to alleviate and to remediate the dis-ease.

Vibrates to the number 7.

SKAN   [Astrological Signs of Leo & Aquarius]

Skan crystallizes in the formation masses.

Skan has been used to activate the throat chakra, while providing for grounding; this quality allows one to think prior to speaking, assisting one in the furtherance of consciousness in speech.

This mineral has been used to assist one in clearing the mind, in eliminating misconceptions and judgmental-ness, and in promoting self-worth.

This mineral has been used to increase memory capacity and retention. Holding and/or wearing the stone during learning situations, promotes clarity in assimilation, understanding, and retention of knowledge. It tends to promote the actualization of photographic memory.

It is excellent for use during "Laying-on-of-Stones", to assist in clarity and precision in vocalization of any problems which need to be expressed.

I has been used in the treatment of throat disorders, uncontrolled and/or disoriented n.ental facilities, and for clearing the mind of unwanted thoughts.

Vibrates to the number 9.

SMITHSONITE   [Astrological Signs of Pisces & Virgo]

Smithsonite crystallizes in the form of crusts, grains, masses, stalactites, botryoidal structures, scalenohedral crystals, and rhombohedral crystals with curved faces. The colour range includes white, grey, yellow, green, blue-green, blue, brown, and pink-to-purple. Smithsonite was named for the founder of the Smithsonian Institute.

This mineral provides energies conducive to pleasantness, charm, kindliness, and favorable outcomes. It provides for leadership abilities and tends to build the "bridge over troubled waters", by which one can remedy uncomfortable situations. It further promotes the dynamic celebration of new beginnings.

It can be used to activate each of the chakras, but when held or placed on the body, the strength of the mineral directs the primary energy to enhance physical energy and vitality. Used at the crown, the stone draws the energy of the other chakras into alignment, bringing forth vitality toward enlightenment.

Smithsonite strengthens ones abilities in the psychic realm, providing for increases in the abilities for clairvoyance and clairsentience; it produces confirmation or denial of the messages one receives via these methods.

In addition, it can act as a replacement stone during the "laying-on-of-stones", when a specific stone is not available.

This mineral can be used to ameliorate dysfunction in the immune system, skin eruptions, alcoholism, osteoporosis, sinus disorders, and digestive disorders. It can also help to renew and/or to maintain the elasticity of the walls of the veins.

Vibrates to the number 7.

SMOKEY QUARTZ   [Astrological Signs of Capricorn & Sagittarius]
[Also Known as Carnigorm]

Smokey quartz is a form of quartz, occurring in masses, crystals, etc. The colour range includes light smokey grey to dark smokey grey, and black.

The energy of this mineral is especially applicable to the areas of the solar plexus and the chakras located at the hands and the feet. The rutilated and dark varieties are quite effective in the activities related to the energy frequencies of the physical and etheric bodies. The energy can penetrate and can subsequently transform negative emotions and negative energy patterns; it tends to penetrate and to dissolve energy fields which have been generated from negative thought forms, anger and resentment.

It can be used to gently dissolve negative energies and emotional blockages. It softens negative energy and allows the positive frequencies to enter the realm of affectation. It works to dissolve the resultant formations, effects, disorders, and disease which a problem has created.

It can be used to relieve barriers which may exist between the beta and alpha state of the mind; hence, if one is worried and desires to set aside the thinking mind and to clear the mental channels, smokey quartz can facilitate.

It tends to refine the vibratory energies when one is in the state of meditation, allowing for both the clarity of thought and the elimination of impeding willful-ness. It can be used to initiate a powerful force field which will absorb many forms of negativity, both from within oneself and from outer sources.

This stone does not astound one with its speed; i.e., it is prolonged, yet intense and gentle, in its action; on the higher levels, such as meditation, simply holding the stone will suffice.

It provides for balancing of the yin-yang energy and can be used to facilitate the alignment of the meridians of the physical body with those of the ethereal body. It can also help with mind balance, energy balance, and balancing and attuning the energies required for spiritual development.

Smokey quartz is an excellent grounding stone, enhancing attentiveness to the moment and producing the grounding aspects necessary during the meditative state in order to stimulate higher awareness.

It further acts as a protective stone, providing for an encompassing barrier of energy around the user.

During the activity of "laying-on-of-stones", the placement of smokey quartz pointing away from the feet, the hands, and the base chakra provides for grounding of all bodies to the healing vibration and discourages the "healing crisis" which could occur during activation of the energy centers.

It has also been used in tribal ceremonies to enhance stability and to provide protection from any detrimental forces present in the ethereal realm.

It activates survival instincts and acts to improve ones intuition in matters of responsibilities and in those activities which would be considered to be "challenging".

It promotes personal pride and joy in living.

It has also been used extensively during activities associated with contacting the other worlds, providing for protection and discrimination, and allowing for the link in communication to be strengthened.

Smokey quartz has been used to regulate creativity in business and to encourage astute-ness in purchasing. It is a "stone of cooperation", stimulating the unification of energies directed toward the same goal. It works to diffuse communication deficiencies and to dissolve mental and emotional blockages which limit perception and learning.

The presence of sodium in clear quartz is said to produce smokey quartz; hence, smokey quartz can facilitate the regulation of liquids within the body, and can produce a state of equilibrium within the body with respect to mineral supplementation. It can also be used to dissipate congestion from the physical organs and glands located in the solar plexus area, and to relieve disorders of the hands and feet.

Vibrates to the numbers 2 and 8.

In addition, the combination of Smokey/Clear Quartz (with a very definite line of separation) has produced a melding of the properties of SMOKEY QUARTZ and CLEAR QUARTZ, which are discussed within this book. In addition, it has been used to assist one in matters of discrimination and in delineation of those actions required in ones life to facilitate the furtherance of objectives in any situation. The Smokey acts to ground the energies of the Clear Quartz, promoting ease of energy application. This combination, in the faceted configuration, has an enhanced energy.

There is also a combination of Citrine/Smokey Quartz (sometimes with "clear quartz") with clean definition between the colours, which has been found in Brasil.

This alliance of forces merges the energy of the minerals to produce a dynamic healing stone. The citrine acts to cleanse the energies of the smokey and "clear" quartz, while the smokey quartz provides grounding for all endeavors. The faceted form provides a distinct and bright energy for application to all aspects, combining the singular energies of the minerals to provide an energy greater than the sum.

SOAPSTONE   [See Steatite]

SODALITE   [Astrological Sign of Sagittarius]

Sodalite crystallizes in the form of masses, grains, nodules, and, rarely, dodecahedral crystals and hexagonal prismatic crystals. The colour range includes dark blue, grey, green, yellow, white, light red, lavender blue, and colourless.

This mineral provides for the ability to arrive at logical conclusions via rational mental processes. It helps to eliminate confusion and to both equalize and stimulate ones intellect to be compatible with each situation.

It furthers the aspects and outcomes of unemotional efficiency, providing for direction of purpose with lightness of heart.

It is an excellent stone for use in groups; it provides for fellowship, solidarity, and a commonality of goal and purpose, within the group.

It also facilitates the manifestation of the qualities of companionship and mutual dependence, encouraging self-esteem, self-trust and trust in others.

It can be used to enhance truthfulness in emotions, allowing one to both recognize and verbalize the true feelings.

It can provide one with access to the sacred laws of the universe; calmly presenting the ideas, stimulating thought, and allowing the subtle feelings to permeate the center of ones being. The "knowing" comes without the "work" - how wonderful!

It has been used in the treatment of gland metabolism, and can be used in the treatment of digestive disorders, as a purifying agent for the body, to dispel insomnia, and to ameliorate disorders associated with deficiencies of calcium.

Vibrates to the number 4.

SONOLITE   [Astrological Sign of Sagittarius]

Sonolite crystallizes in the form of fine-grained masses and prismatic crystals. The colour range includes red, orange, brown, and orange-brown.

This mineral can be used to increase the male aspects of the character, providing for strength of character and rectification of highly emotional states.

It can also assist in providing an increase in confidence, especially in the business world.

It is conducive to promoting insight to "fortune-telling" techniques; e.g., the Tarot, the I Ching [pronounced yee-jing], reading the future with mineral lay-outs, and the African tribal method of "throwing the bones".

It also provides an advantage to one when "contending" with personal issues or with others.

Sonolite can be used in the treatment of inferiority, infertility in the male, and disorders of the speech.

Vibrates to the number 1.

SPANGOLITE   [Astrological Sign of Leo]

Spangolite crystallizes in the form of prismatic crystals and tabular hexagonal crystals. The colour ranges from deep green to a lovely emerald green.

This mineral is a "stone for enforcement", providing stimulus to the initiation and completion of projects, while encouraging ones focus. It promotes the actualization of a super-human strength during crises - but a strength filled with love. It can be used in dangerous areas to provide protection.

It encourages patriotism to ones country, love for the "brotherhood" of all, and honesty and truthfulness in relationships. It further assists one in gaining independence from the self or from that which is outside of the self.

It stimulates the heart chakra, opening and energizing the center, while protecting the area from attack. It also stimulates the intuitive survival processes, leading one through the processes required to survive in all situations.

This mineral can be used to stimulate the hands for healing; used as an elixir applied to the hands or placing the stone in the hands for approximately five minutes prior to use, the stone opens the energy centers of the hands to allow the healing energy to flow unimpeded through the hands. It facilitates methods of healing related to the "laying-on-of-hands".

It can be used to provide strength to the spinal column and to strengthen the flesh - not the muscular structure, but the actual fleshy portions of the body. It can also be used in the treatment of cellular disorders and growths.

Vibrates to the number 1.

SPECTROLITE   [See Labradorite]

SPESSARTINE/SPESSARTITE   [Astrological Sign of Aquarius]

Spessartine, a variety of garnet, crystallizes in the form of masses, grains, dodecahedral crystals, trapezohedral crystals, and as a combination of dodecahedral and trapezohedral crystals. The colour range includes orange, orange-red, red, red-brown, brown, and red with a tinge of violet.

Properties in addition to those listed in the GARNET section of this book are noted below.

The energy of spessartine is in the form of a rapid vibration which extends in effectiveness into the subtle bodies, as well as the higher bodies.

When one is attracted to the stone, that attraction is an indication that the consciousness is ready to both absorb and assimilate the higher levels of inner dynamics of growth and structural balance.

It can also be used to initiate the analytical processes of the mind, bringing precise independence in discovery, and facilitating exploration within, the analytical and rational realms.

Spessartine has been used in the treatment of lactose intolerance and to assist in the remediation of deficiencies in calcium metabolism.

Vibrates to the numbers 1 and 7.

Sphaerocobaltite crystallizes in the form of crusts, small spherical masses, botryoidal masses, and, rarely, crystals. The colour is a beautiful lustrous pink-rose-red. The sphaerocobaltite crystals and botryoidal masses which have recently become available are the most beautiful I have seen and are quite rare; these have recently been available from Africa.

This mineral is one of the most loving members of the mineralogical kingdom. A gift of sphaerocobaltite crystals is a gift of love [as is sugilite]. It helps with the formation of friendships, activates and stimulates and clears the heart chakra, and emanates love.

It also encourages positivity, dispels negativity, charges the auric bodies, and facilitates a deep and stable connection/communication with the spirit world.

It can be used to act as a guide to past-lives and to access the ancient wisdom concerning the principles of human-potential, allowing one to create the reality desired.

It acts as an energy vortex center, enhancing all psychic abilities and producing [when directed] experiences which include the direct contact with those of the spirit world, visions, and healings to unusual manifestations.

It further assists one in understanding the cause, effect, and karmic lessons which one has/is experiencing, while stimulating awareness of the methods which can be utilized to transcend undesirable circumstances.

It can assist one in projecting the mind, to allow for visitation to other realms on this plane and in other dimensions. It can be used to enable one to attain an altered state of consciousness and to encourage the higher-self to act as a guide to access the ancient teachings of the universe. At this level of awareness, one can act to reveal the mysteries via automatic writing and/or mystic communication. Placement of a piece of the mineral upon written material which is difficult for one to understand, can increase discernment of the knowledge and perception into the diverse range of information.

Sphaerocobaltite can be used to induce deep relaxation and to generate ideas and solutions. It can facilitate the attainment of awareness and can allow one to open to unconscious impressions. It tends to release images from the unconscious mind and to assist one in achieving the Theta state. It is an excellent stone for meditation.

It has been used to stimulate the balancing of the yin-yang energies and to support the balance of the physical body with the ethereal perfection.

It can be used in the treatment of those conditions which are considered age-related disorders. It helps one to understand that these symptoms are manifested due to issues which, over the course of ones life, have not been adequately realized and released. It can be used to inhibit the degeneration of cellular structures and to balance the RNA/DNA structures to facilitate healthy cellular development and maintenance.

It has also been used as an elixir to enhance the reproduction of enzymes and to promote digestion and vitality within the body.

Vibrates to the number 7.

SPHALERITE   [Astrological Sign of Gemini]
                                                  [Also Known as Blende]

Sphalerite crystallizes in the form of masses, fibers, cubes, tetrahedral crystals, dodecahedral crystals, and sometimes, rounded crystals. The colour range includes yellow, yellow-brown, yellow-black, red, green, and colourless.

This mineral can be used to balance both the male and female aspects of the personality; when masculine properties are in excess, the stone can promote increases in the feminine aspects to provide the balance - when feminine aspects are in excess, the stone can promote increases in the masculine aspects to provide the balance.

Sphalerite promotes the recognition of treachery and deceit. It allows one to immediately recognize the peril of a situation, and to balance the benefits and detriments of that situation prior to concluding or continuing ones part. In these days when there is so much emphasis on psychic information and channeling, this stone can enhance ones intuitive qualities, allowing for the distinction between fraudulent and genuine information. It can also provide for the growth of ones psychic abilities and to encourage one to "be ones own psychic". I would like to stress, again, that each of us has psychic abilities; to remove the blockages in the intellect and to access this quality, one needs to dispel feelings of inferiority.

Rubbing this stone during entry into a meditative and/or trance state seems to allow for actual visual stimulation by a bright white light. This enhances the clarity of the state and aligns one to the astral body. With this alignment, ones inherent psychic qualities are manifested and information becomes readily available. Please note that this is only one method of providing access - there are a multitude more which are, in many cases, totally unique to the user.

During many tribal rituals [African, Australian, American, etc.], the stone was impacted to awaken the energies and an orange spark was evidenced. This sign was taken to mean that the powers of creativity and intuition were also awakened.

Sphalerite can be used to assist one in changes in vocation and can induce the vocation toward the serving aspects of the lifework.

It can also provide for protection from negative forces which may be present when dealing with the public.

This mineral can be used in the treatment of disorders of the eyes, to align the physical nervous system to the ethereal nervous system in order to facilitate the treatment of blood-flow disorders, and to increase the assimilation and to provide balance for the intake of nutrients.

Vibrates to the numbers 5 and 6.

SPHENE   [Astrological Sign of Sagittarius]

Sphene crystallizes in the form of masses, plate-like layers, and flattened wedge-shaped crystals. The colour range includes light shades of all.

This mineral can be used to promote contact with the heavenly bodies within this universe.

It is also a good stone to place in ones garden, in a grid fashion, to stimulate the growth of plants.

It is a calming agent and stimulates the chakras, of the associated colour, with a subtlety, providing a lightness to the physical body.

It can be used as an accessory mineral to promote gentleness in the action of other minerals.

It can also be used in the treatment of muscular strains, sprains, and to soothe the skin. It works well when applied to the skin in the form of an elixir. It can be used to stimulate the immune system, to increase the red blood cells, and to balance the red and white blood cells within the body. Amelioration of fevers and disorders of the muscular structure is common. It can also act to provide protection to the teeth and to induce stability in the teeth during disorders of the gums.

Vibrates to the number 4.

SPINEL   [Elemental Astrological Signs of Sagittarius & Aries]

Spinel crystallizes in the form of rolled pebbles, cubes, and octahedral crystals exhibiting, sometimes, dodecahedral terminations. The colour range includes red [distinguished from ruby by measurement of specific gravity], blue, violet, black, green, yellow, orange, brown, white, and almost colourless.

This mineral can be used to renew energy and to provide encouragement for further attempts at difficult tasks. It can also be used to enhance ones appearance, to increase the positive aspects of ones personality, and to assist in obtaining, maintaining, and accepting victory with humility.

The energy of spinel is the energy of beauty. It is known as a "stone of immortality", bringing freshness to all endeavors and initiating rejuvenation to that which is beginning to degrade.

Additional qualities relative to the varying colours of spinel are listed below. The placement of the appropriate colour of spinel on the corresponding chakra location can assist in the remediation of disorders occurring in that area.

Vibrates to the number 3.

Black Spinel   [Astrological Sign of Taurus]

Black spinel can be used to provide for grounding of ones energy in order to balance the upward movement of the Kundalini. It also promotes insights into problems relative to the physical plane, and facilitates the stamina to "follow through". It emits a protective energy, providing for protection, with grounding to the center of the Earth.

Vibrates to the number 5.

Blue Spinel   [Astrological Sign of Gemini]

Blue spinel can be used to calm sexual desires, to enhance communication, and to stimulate channeling and clairaudience.

It can help to both align and stimulate the throat chakra, providing for verbalization of the Kundalini energy as it moves through the body.

Vibrates to the number 7.

Brown Spinel   [Astrological Sign of Cancer]

Brown spinel can be used to clear the aura and to dispel the "muddiness" of same. It can assist in the activation of the connection between the physical aura and the ethereal bodies.

Vibrates to the number 3.

"Colourless" Spinel   [Astrological Sign of Sagittarius]

Colourless spinel can be used to provide for the synthesis of the energy of the chakras of the physical body and to connect the major and minor chakras to the crown chakra of the ethereal body. This connection enhances visions as well as growth toward enlightenment.

It also furthers endeavors in the areas of mysticism and communication.

Vibrates to the number 7.

Dark Blue Spinel   [Astrological Sign of Sagittarius]

Dark blue spinel can be used to enhance psychic power and higher intuition, aligning the intuitive center with the higher-self, and facilitating astral travel.

It can help to both align and stimulate the third-eye chakra and allows for the knowledge of the movement, position, and blockages in the path of the Kundalini.

Vibrates to the number 5.

Green Spinel   [Astrological Sign of Libra]

Green spinel can be used to stimulate compassion, devotion, kindness, and love.

It can help to both align and stimulate the heart chakra and to protect both the Kundalini and the physical structure during Kundalini movement through the body.

Vibrates to the number 7.

Orange Spinel   [Astrological Sign of Aries]

Orange spinel can be used to stimulate desire toward creativity, to balance the emotions, to enhance the inner intuitive qualities, and to stimulate fertility/dispel frigidity.

It helps to both align and stimulate the navel chakra and is conducive to furthering the course of the Kundalini movement.

Vibrates to the number 9.

Red Spinel   [Astrological Sign of Scorpio]

Red spinel can be used to provide strength, and to stimulate physical vitality.

It helps to both align and stimulate the base chakra and is conducive to the activation of the Kundalini.

Vibrates to the number 3.

Violet Spinel   [Astrological Sign of Virgo]

Violet spinel can be used to encourage spiritual development and to assist one on the path to enlightenment.

It can help to both stimulate and align the crown chakra, providing a cleansing energy conducive to the removal of blockages within the path of the Kundalini.

It assists one in maintaining the astral state and promotes the retention of the information which is made available during travel.

Vibrates to the number 5.

Yellow Spinel   [Astrological Sign of Leo]

Yellow spinel can be used to stimulate personal power and intellect.

It can be used to both align and stimulate the solar plexus chakra and to open the pathway for the movement of the Kundalini through this energy field.

Vibrates to the number 5.

SPODUMENE   [See Kunzite]

STANNITE   [Astrological Sign of Aquarius]

Stannite crystallizes in the form of masses, grains, and tetrahedral-type crystals. The colour ranges from a metallic steel grey to black. It may appear with a tarnish of blue or yellow.

This mineral provides enhancement to ones stature in employment and in community action. It promotes a widening of the pathway leading toward personal power, such that obstructions are removed and the "road is straight". It also facilitates a connection between the physical, mental, and astral bodies; this provides for the transfer of information concerning intellectual aggrandizement and fulfillment of physical needs. In addition, it provides for grounding and alignment to the ethereal body, especially, during trance-channeling and during the provision, from the astral plane, of intellectual information.

Stannite may also be used in the treatment of spasms, dysentery, and bacterial infections, and to straighten and build the portions of the body required for optimum posture, and to increase the sense of smell.

Vibrates to the number 3.

STAUROLITE   [Astrological Sign of Pisces]

Staurolite crystallizes in the form of flat prismatic crystals and short prismatic crystals with cruciform twinning. The colour range includes dark red-brown and yellow-brown.

A pleochroism is exhibited with yellow-red from the X-axis and Y-axis, and hyacinth red from the Z-axis.

This mineral is a talisman of good luck. It is also called the "Fairy Stone" or "Fairy Cross" and was said, historically, to be the crystallized tears of fairies, formed when the fairies were brought the news of the death of Christ. It is used in ceremonies of "white magic" and can facilitate the action of the rituals.

It can also be used to provide a connection to information from the ancients of the Middle East; it is said that the cruciform configuration of this stone was used to heal Richard the Lionhearted of a malarial-type disorder during The Crusades.

Staurolite crystals were worn by Pocahontas, the daughter of Chief Powhaten - it is said that Pocahontas presented Captain John Smith with one of these crystals to protect him from harm.

This mineral can also be used to provide a connection between the physical, astral, and extra-terrestrial planes, assisting in alignment, balancing, and communication between the three.

It can provide for an overpowering relief in situations of stress and can eliminated depression, addictive personality traits, and tendencies toward over-extension of ones time.

It is a good stone to both ameliorate the conditions which are detrimental due to smoking, and to provide incentive, initiative, and support to those who would dispense with the habit. It provides the grounding energy similar to that which the tobacco provides to those who would otherwise "fly away".

It can also be used in the treatment of disorders of the cellular structure, to provide increased assimilation and conversion of carbohydrates, and to alleviate the symptoms and causes of growths. It has been used in the treatment of fevers, malaria, and depression.

Vibrates to the number 5.

STEATITE   [Astrological Sign of Sagittarius]
                                          [Also Known as Soapstone]

Steatite crystallizes in the form of foliates, fibers, thin tabular crystals, and massive formations. It is, actually, a compact form of talc. The colour range includes the shades of green, white, grey, and brown.

This mineral provides for both movement and widening of ones horizons. It can be used to stabilize atmospheric electricity, eliminating interference and amplifying the sending and receiving of messages; the messages being from both this plane and the outer areas.

It assists in fashioning and instilling positive characteristics within the environment in which it is a member. It emits a calming energy, both stimulating one to action and providing for peace at the center of the being. It allows one to release old routines and to create new loving environments.

It also assists one in "changing with the tides", being ever ready for new situations and new challenges. It can be used to assist one in both understanding and applying the rational processes of the intellect, and in remaining open to "new" ways of expressing gratitude.

It can be used in the treatment of fat digestion, to stimulate the liver and gall bladder toward optimal conditions, and as an aid to birth control [an elixir is recommended].

Vibrates to the numbers 7 and 9.

STEPHANITE   [Astrological Sign of Virgo]

Stephanite crystallizes in the form of short prismatic crystals and tabular crystals. The faces of these crystals are, occasionally, obliquely striated. The colour is a metallic black.

This mineral can be used to stimulate the solar plexus and to provide alignment and balancing between the solar plexus of the physical body and ethereal body. It can stimulate and provide access to a constant point of contact between the intellectual, the inner intuitive, and the spiritual planes; this constancy provides for a "recipe" type of access. At the same time, it provides for a grounding through the spinal cord to the center of the Earth, bringing love and stability to the forefront.

It can counteract decrepitude and atrophy. It has been used to provide strength to the bones, and to dispel brittleness [within the body and within the emotional and intellectual centers]. It can be used to stimulate the balance of estrogen and androgen, and to both increase and stabilize muscle tone.

At times, the mineral may appear to become coated with dark material. This extraneous material is a protective device against negativity within the environment and indicates that the stone needs clearing; in many cases, cleaning is accomplished only via ultrasonic equipment. Stephanite enjoys residence, when not in use, in a dark soft environment.

Vibrates to the number 9.

STIBIOTANTALITE   [Astrological Signs of Capricorn & Aquarius]

Stibiotantalite crystallizes in the form of prismatic crystals. The colour range includes brown, yellow-brown, red, and red-yellow.

This mineral can be used to stimulate neural transmissions between the physical and ethereal body, to facilitate the closure of gaps in ones aura, and to assist in the maintenance of the physical life force. It exhibits more affinity with the body, than the head; however, it does assure wholeness in the aura for the complete physical system. Closing the gaps in the aura, the energy also provides for protection from the other worlds and from dis-ease associated with this world.

It provides for a bridge between the grounding energy of the Earth and the aspects of personal power which are manifested via the intuitive self. It allows for "pondering" via intuition. It promotes protection of oneself from emotional situations which could bring disharmony and rejection.

It is helpful in the management of affairs, again allowing the intuitive side to predominate, with satisfactory results.

It can also be used in the garden and around houseplants to stimulate growth.

It can be used in the treatment of coughs, congestion, and hysteria, and to both slow the pulse rate and lower the blood pressure.

Vibrates to the number 5.

STIBNITE   [Astrological Signs of Scorpio & Capricorn]

Stibnite crystallizes in the form of masses, aggregates, columns, blades, radial groups of column-type crystals, needle-like crystals, and prismatic crystals with vertical striations, sometimes exhibiting well-developed faces. The colour is grey, tarnishing to black.

This mineral helps to keep away the intrusive; used in meditation, it facilitates an undistracted entry to the meditative state; used to protect from entities, it enhances the energy field and acts as an impenetrable barrier around the physical body; used to eliminate physical presences, it assists one in the manifestation of the courage to disallow contact.

It is a "stone to stabilize ones economy" and to promote ones ability to satisfy ones needs.

It can be used to eliminate tenacious clinging in relationships, providing for persistence and diligence in relationships, and assisting in attraction - the user defining that which is to be attracted.

It is a totem stone for the wolf; e.g., bringing fidelity in relationships, enhancing astral travel via the speed of the wolf, and stimulating endurance in all matters. It can lead one to the magic of the inner kingdom and can provide access to the all-knowing animal kingdom of the spiritual realm. It also increases understanding between one and the animal and plant kingdoms of this plane.

It can be used in the treatment of disorders of the stomach and esophagus, to dispel possession in the body, and to relieve rigidity and stiffness.

Vibrates to the number 8.

STICHTITE   [Astrological Sign of Virgo]

Stichtite crystallizes in the form of plate-like layers, foliates, and micaceous scales. The colour ranges from lilac to a rose pink.

This mineral is an alteration of serpentine and assists in the movement of the Kundalini into and through the heart chakra. It provides for expansion of awareness in the emotional aspects of ones life and is a good stone for which to allow a special place within ones living quarters. It brings a calming peace to the environment in which it resides, and promotes "thinking with love" prior to "speaking with intellect".

It provides for flexibility and openness in opinions, and for faithfulness in promises. It provides companionship for those who are alone, and stimulates the inner awareness of, and positive behavior modification for, children. It further assists one in being gentle with oneself and with others.

It can be used for the treatment of hernia and ruptures, for regeneration of the skin, and for increasing the expansion and elasticity of skin - quite important during pregnancy and for "springing back" from bouts of water retention or from those extra winter pounds. It has also been used to treat gum dis-ease and to provide for stability of the teeth.

Vibrates to the number 5.

STILBITE   [Astrological Sign of Aries]

Stilbite crystallizes in the form of aggregates, plates, globes, radial structures, thin tabular crystals, and rhombic pyramid-type cruciforms. The colour range includes white, yellow, pink, orange, red, and brown.

This mineral provides for a powerful loving energy in creativity and intuitive endeavors.

It also provides for grounding to this energy while synthesizing the physical manifestation of the creativity with the action of intuitive support.

It can be used to assist one in obtaining the astral state and helps to provide guidance while one is above the world.

It can be used in the treatment of the loss of taste, laryngitis, and brain disorders, and to strengthen ligaments, to enhance the pigmentation of the skin, and to counteract poisoning by providing for enhanced toxin removal capabilities.

Vibrates to the master number 33.

STILLWELLITE   [Astrological Sign of Gemini]

Stillwellite crystallizes in the form of compact masses, and rhombohedral crystals. The colour range includes light blue, brown, and yellow.

This mineral helps one to maintain motionless and stationary, and provides for a tranquil silence during meditation. It is of great assistance to one in attaining the meditative state.

It can provide one with dignity and grace, allowing for the personality to increase in the positive manner to promote open communication channels on the physical plane.

It can provide for a temporary quickening of ones mental capabilities and can promote prepared-ness in any situation.

It can be used in the treatment of disorders of the lungs and the spleen, to enhance breathing, and to promote increases in oxygen intake and assimilation. It also assists in the amelioration of deteriorated night vision.

Vibrates to the number 5.

STRENGITE   [Astrological Sign of Sagittarius]

Strengite crystallizes in the form of crusts, botryoidal structures, spherical aggregates, and, rarely, octahedral crystals. The colour ranges from a pale to a deep violet-red.

This mineral can be used to stimulate the pathways to congruency between the seven [or eight] major physical chakras. It can also be used to activate the hand and feet chakras in order to facilitate the alignment of the meridians within the physical body. It is useful in acupressure/acupuncture techniques to produce an energy flow through, and a dissipation of, the energy blockages.

Strengite can also be used to enhance the power of the "silver cord" connection between the physical and astral bodies, assuring that one may always return "home".

It provides for alteration of the physical, mental, and emotional patterns, encouraging growth toward the highest level. It stimulates meditation during menial tasks and renews consciousness during every moment.

It encourages honour, enhances reliability [even with respect to machinery], and discourages digression and diversion to past lessons.

Strengite can be used to strengthen the tendons, to relieve tendonitis, to alleviate symptoms of shock, to stabilize the metabolism, and to provide vitality during and after operations.

Vibrates to the number 9.

STROMBOLITE   [Astrological Signs of Scorpio & Taurus]

Strombolite, a form of Spurrite, crystallizes in the form of small crystals and granular masses. The colour ranges from grey to pale purple.

This mineral provides a cohesiveness with respect to family ties and closeness within a group. Improvement and refinement in communication is reported; both for inter/intra family structures, work environments, social environments, and other worlds. It can assist one in exhibiting an openness from the heart space, to display real feelings of love and generosity, and to maintain dignity.

In addition, it can be used to stimulate the crown chakra and to provide concurrent grounding. It has been used for thought-transference between the physical realms and the celestial realms and is an excellent stone for meditation.

It acts similarly to an electrical conductor and can be used during healing activities to enhance the energy transfer from a healer, or from other minerals, to the subject of the healing.

It also can be used to align the chakras and to order the connection between the ethereal and physical nervous systems. It is an excellent stone for pendants and for the interior of wands.

Strombolite has been used during the meditative state to produce stellar contact with the highest order of angels, with information imparted which is extremely relevant and of vast importance to the users. Used at the crown chakra, it has aligned the chakras and has bestowed a centering effect. At the base chakra, it seems to clean the area and to promote protection and centering concurrently. It assists one in understanding the stages of ones life and acts to provide insight to changes required to promote peace and happiness within ones life.

This mineral provides for an inner warmth and can stimulate circulation as well as well-being. This attribute applies to both the emotional and physical bodies - the outer world or relationships <u>and</u> the inner world of physical structure. It can be used in the treatment of osteoporosis, bruxism, disorders of the liver, disorders of the eyes, and to lessen leg cramps. It can also be used to improve conditions causing extreme cases of suffering and/or distress.

Vibrates to the number 4.

STRONTIANITE   [Astrological Sign of Aries]

Strontianite crystallizes in the form of acicular and spear-shaped crystals and in fibrous, columnar, and granular configurations. The colour ranges from white to very light green to pale green, grey, yellow, and yellow-brown.

This mineral is a wonderful centering stone and allows one to feel "comfortable" and "at-home" in all environments. It is a useful stone for business-travelers, as well as pleasure-travelers. It allows one to easily adapt to situations and to change as is required; it enables one to realize that these changes are transient and, hence, helps one to be accommodating.

Strontianite helps one to understand responsibility and to increase the capabilities required to sustain ones composure. It provides for the strength to manage the conditions of ones reality, relieving tension and anxiety, and allowing one to recognize that which one can and must change - and that which one must release from ones being.

It further acts to encourage growth in all areas of ones life. It assists by providing the strength of wisdom to all areas of relationships. It can be utilized to help one with decision-making and to initiate diversity in ones life. It is excellent in both stimulating and enhancing communication; it is quite conducive to all aspects of correspondence.

It also assists one in the art of complete listening. It has been used to balance the left brain and right brain, encouraging creativity in the intellect as well as encouraging intelligently directed ingenuity.

It helps to align the network of the nervous system and to provide for free flow of energy. It is also a powerful grounding stone, providing for a clear connection to the powerful basis of love.

It can be use to alleviate introversion, to provide tact to situations, and to instill the art and beauty of cooperation.

It is excellent to use in the ceremonial aspect, promoting a bond between participants while sustaining grounding of the energy centers. It also provides for guidance and assured-ness to activities.

It is useful in helping one to recognize those who have been a part of ones past-lives. The star-like configuration can also facilitate access to a connection with other-planetary beings, allowing for the remembering of other worlds and other times.

As an elixir it is an excellent energizer and protector of house plants; it can also be used in the garden or field situation to help to relieve infestations. It has been used in the home environment to protect against pests.

Strontianite has been used in the treatment of swelling, to ameliorate a highly acid state of the physical body, to promote renewal of red blood-cells, and to remove calcium deposits from the joints. It has also been used to assist in breathing, to clear the veins, and to improve the eyesight. It is an excellent stone for increasing the vitality of those experiencing dis-ease.

Vibrates to the number 2.

SUGILITE   [Astrological Sign of Virgo]
                              [Also Known as Royal Lavulite and Royal Azel]

Sugilite crystallizes in the form of lightly banded masses and, rarely, as tiny crystals and as sugilite inclusions within quartz crystals. The massive formation occasionally contains portions of sugilite known as "gel" - a translucent form of the sugilite. It has also been seen [rarely] in the configuration of a coarse mass where both sugilite and quartz were represented. The colour range includes violet-pink to purple. It is found, mainly, in the Kalahari region of the Republic of South Africa.

This mineral brings about the realization of the connection between the well-being of the body and the well-being of the mind. It has been used in the treatment of all forms of "dis-ease" and attracts healing power. It has surfaced now to bring special healing powers to humanity.

Sugilite is "a love stone for this age", representing the perfection of the spiritual love of "All That Is" and facilitating the manifestation of this energy on the Earth plane.

The energy of sugilite flows from the crown to the base chakra, opening the chakras and providing for a pathway for the movement of the Kundalini. It is quite effective at the heart chakra, stimulating a resonant love which can be felt by others and which is totally "in-tune" with the vibratory energies of the perfect state of the universe.

Sugilite can assist in reminding the user of the reasons for being in the physical body and for living on the Earth plane. It helps one to forgive oneself and others, enhancing ones understanding of the lessons which have been chosen for this visit to the physical realm. It is useful in facilitating memory to answer the question "why am I here?"; it can further help one to determine methods for bringing ones gifts to this world.

It can be used to protect against the harsh realities of this world and to enable one to willingly accept being here and living now. It can help one to believe in oneself, especially if there is an inherent and stable uniqueness which one manifests and which is not universally accepted.

It can also be used to eliminate hostility - it is quite difficult for one to remain hostile toward oneself; in addition, and following the same logic, it can also be used to eliminate anger, abrasiveness, jealousy, prejudice, ..., and all of the negative attributes one could imagine. What an exciting thought!

It is wonderful to wear or carry - it gives one a feeling of being free - "being on top of a mountain with the breeze ruffling your hair"; it infuses the being with inspiration and confidence. The insights are astonishing when meditating with sugilite; one can also hold sugilite and meditate upon the effects which can be expected with further use.

For discouragement or despair, sugilite may be placed at the third-eye and one may breathe-in the comforting energy. It allows for the flow of gentle, loving information from the spiritual world to the mental plane, bringing peace and relaxation to the user.

It furthers ones creative endeavors by providing for cooperation between the physical, mental, emotional, and spiritual bodies while enhancing precision in action.

It is an excellent remedy for headaches; one can hold a piece of sugilite containing the black manganese in order to allow pain to be transferred to the manganese/sugilite stone. It has been used to dispel all types of discomforts and feelings of disorder; one may hold the stone and allow the negative energy of the discomfort to be released into the black manganese of the sugilite.

Vibrates to the numbers 2, 3, and 7.

SULPHUR   [Astrological Sign of Leo]

Sulphur crystallizes in the form of masses, reniform, nodular, and stalactitic configurations, pyramidal and tabular crystals, and granular aggregates. The colour range includes bright yellow, straw/honey-yellow, yellow brown, green, and red/yellow grey.

This mineral is negatively electrified, assisting one in the removal of negative willfulness and in the elimination of distracting intellectual thoughts and emotions which could affect the emotional and intellectual bodies.

It further serves to attract non-caustic attributes and attitudes, providing help during exercises of the mental processes and producing grounding of the reasoning faculties.

It tends to promote an abundance of energy, flashes of inspiration, and a stimulation of the application of devotion toward the realization of the perfection of the self. It can help to gently "melt" the barriers blocking progress.

Sulphur has been used by the South American and Mexican Indians in ceremonial healings. It is said to bring together the synthesis of the four directions, Mother Earth, and Father Sky. It has also been used [in a crushed state, resembling the sacred pollen of the North American Indians] by the ancient nomadic tribes of North America, as an offering to the four cardinal directions so that both darkness would be dissipated and corruption would be cleansed from the Earth.

It has been used as a fumigant and to discourage infestations of insects and negativity within ones environment.

Sulphur has been used in the treatment of disorders related to infections within the body. It can be used in the elimination of fibrous and tissue growths. It has also been used in the bath to alleviate painful joints and to reduce swelling.

Vibrates to the number 7.

SUNSTONE   [Astrological Signs of Libra & Leo]

Sunstone is a form of oligoclase [a type of feldspar] and crystallizes in the form of masses and tabular crystals. The colour range includes grey, green, yellow, brown, orange, pink, peach, and red. Sunstone, usually, shows brilliant reflections due to inclusions [usually goethite or hematite]. For additional information with respect to the further properties of sunstone, see the OLIGOCLASE and FELDSPAR sections of this book. For additional information in the cases of sparkling sunstone, see the GOETHITE or HEMATITE sections of this book.

This mineral can be used to both clear and energize the chakras. It can also provide for a brightening of the chakras, allowing one to exhibit a floral freshness and a feeling of being "squeaky" clean. It assists in gently removing the "hook-ups" which have infiltrated the energy centers, returning them to the source after surrounding them with both love and positive energy.

It can be used to dissipate fearfulness, to alleviate stress, and to increase vitality.

It has been used to encourage independence and originality and to provide "luck" in games.

It has been used by the Canadian Indians, in rituals of the medicine wheel, to show to the spirit guides the connection with the golden white healing light of the sun. In these ceremonies sunstone is placed in the center of the medicine wheel; it has been reported that, during contact with the spirit guides, the stone has emitted a golden glow.

In ancient Greece, it was thought to represent the sun god, bringing life and abundance to those fortunate enough to carry/wear it. It was often used as an ornamental on goblets and plates and was believed to counteract poison and to produce strength.

In ancient India, it was believed to provide protection from the destructive forces of the other realms.

Sunstone is quite helpful with chronic sore throats. It has been used to reduce stomach tension and to relieve ulcers. It can also be used in the treatment of cartilage problems so often suffered by athletes. It was used by ancients for rheumatism [one sits in the sun surrounded by a circle of sunstone]; aching feet and spinal problems were also relieved by physical contact with a large specimen.

Vibrates to the number 1.

SVABITE   [Astrological Sign of Cancer]

Svabite crystallizes in the form of masses and hexagonal prismatic crystals. The colour range includes yellow and colourless.

This mineral can be used to produce an agreeable quality between those in ones environment. It is especially helpful in the work-place, as it also helps to stimulate the intellect while dispelling negativity.

It can assist in providing one with an innate will to attain a set goal; helping one to reach that goal with only minor fluctuations in the path of progress.

It can be used in the treatment of numbness in the body and to enhance joint lubrication via stimulating balance in the synovial fluid.

Do not prepare an elixir of this mineral via the normal method.

Vibrates to the number 6.

**AS YOU DO WHAT IT IS THE HEAVENS REQUIRE,
YOU SHALL RECEIVE PIECES OF YOURSELF**

[ray thompson, 1990]

TAAFFEITE [Astrological Signs of Taurus & Libra]

Taaffeite crystallizes in the form of octahedral crystals, occasionally exhibiting dodecahedral terminations. This mineral was originally thought to be a form of spinel; however, because it displays the quality of double-refraction which is not inherent to spinel, it is defined as a separate mineral. The colour is a pale mauve.

This mineral can be used to produce a state of mind which is free from impressions. It allows one to see the duality of ones nature, rectifying the negative and building the positive. It can produce deep silence interspersed with visions of the luminous terrain emitted from the crown chakra.

It bestows a sense of calmness and a natural ability to attain the meditative state. It furthers initiative and supplements the state of independence.

It also enhances the state of love, producing not only physical love, but also the love of the "brotherhood" of all things.

It can be used to dispel intestinal parasites, to supplement the iron in the blood cells, and to enable the body to both obtain and maintain the optimum balance between acidity and alkalinity.

Vibrates to the number 1.

TANTALITE [Astrological Sign of Libra]

Tantalite crystallizes in the form of short prismatic prisms, rectangular prisms, thin tabular crystals, pyramids, and masses. The colour range includes iron-black, grey, brown, brown-black, and red-brown.

This mineral can be used to deflect, and to protect against, negativity. It acts to preserve one from being victimized by the dissenting energy of another. It has also been used as an energy deflector, being an excellent stone for those with potential for exposure to excessive amounts of radiation. It provides for an increase in ones physical endurance, emotional equilibrium, and intellectual discernment, and can maintain ones "spirits".

It furthers the awakening of benevolence and enhances pragmatism in creativity. As a protective stone against "spells" which are cast by the negative side of another, it has been a special stone to the Nomad Tribes of Russia; not only dispelling the "spell", but energizing the "quarry" and increasing well-being.

It is a stimulus for ideas, bringing inspiration and facilitating fusion between the idea and the action gain actualization of same.

It is also used to mobilize grounding between the first chakra and the center of the Earth, providing for further enhancement of ones well-being on the physical plane, and protecting against those in the spirit world and/or those on the physical plane who are not in the "light" and do not understand the love of the universe.

It acts to stimulate the reflex points associated with the lower back. It can be used in the treatment of additions, arthritis, dyslexia, heart dis-ease, anxiety, and disorientation. It can also provide for both the stimulation and the balancing of the adrenal glands. It has also assisted in the assimilation of potassium.

Vibrates to the number 3.

TANZANITE   [Astrological Signs of Sagittarius, Gemini & Libra]

Tanzanite crystallizes in the form of masses, grains, and striated prismatic crystals. It is a variety of zoisite and exhibits the properties listed below, as well as the properties listed in the ZOISITE section of this book. The colour ranges from colourless to blue or purple.

This mineral stimulates the throat, the third-eye, and the crown chakras. It brings together all aspects of both communication and psychic power, allowing the user to adequately communicate visions.

It can be used to stimulate the crown chakra to produce visions of the higher spiritual realms. The energy acts as a spiraling force, reaching to invite protection and safety during all activities.

It is a "stone of magic", producing the perfect symmetry of personal power and actualization. It brings the "will" to the aid of manifestation, and enhances both the beginning and the end.

Tanzanite was used by the ancient Celtic chiefs to aid in decisions concerning successor-ship. It was used to facilitate the vision which would determine the rights and privileges of those who were being considered for the position.

It also facilitates communication with the spiritual world of the ancient tribal communities which were located throughout the world. It can bring, to the user, the revelations of the gods.

It has been used to assist one in encountering the different aspects of the self and to understand the imagined wonders which exist on the other planes.

The energy is also conducive to facilitation of encounters with other-worldly beings, counteracting ones self-limiting concepts of space and time. It further provides for the elucidation of universal mysteries and for a unity of direction.

Tanzanite can be used in the treatment of skin disorders, mis-alignment of the spinal column, and disorders of the eyes, and to help to bring one from a comatose state.

Vibrates to the number 2.

TARBUTTITE   [Astrological Sign of Cancer]

Tarbuttite crystallizes in the form of crusts and prismatic crystals exhibiting deep striations. The colour range includes white, colourless, yellow, red, green, and brown.

This mineral can be used to slow ones pace and activities and to bring clarity to whether an urgency does, indeed, exist.

It assists in stimulating the intellect and in mellowing it with love and compassion; it can act to further stimulate the physical vitality and to mellow it with clarity. It can be used to help one with both the translation and the understanding of languages unknown; it is also helpful to stimulate automatic writing and ESP.

Tarbuttite can be used in the treatment of zinc deficiencies, to provide for proper development of the bone structure, to eliminate plaque from the veins, as well as the teeth, and to draw-out an infection. It can also be used as an emetic.

Vibrates to the number 2.

TAVORITE   [Astrological Sign of Pisces]

Tavorite crystallizes in the form of granular masses and prismatic crystals. The colour range includes green [sometimes emerald green], and yellow.

This mineral combines the energies of the intellect and the heart; producing a, somewhat, crusading mentality which can be used to convince the world that "love is all that is necessary to maintain the Earth".

It provides for the repetition of an idea which excludes no possibilities; the idea always coming from the mind of love, balanced by the mind of logic. It assists one in attaining the mastery of emotion and surrounds ones being with inspiring natural resources. It further helps one to "please thy self".

It is an excellent stone for communication with animals, both as spiritual totems and as physical life forms.

It can be used to regulate the temperature [especially helpful during menopausal symptoms]. It is also helpful in promoting insight to the cause of symptoms prior to the manifestation of dis-ease; it activates attentiveness to the voice within the self, in order to facilitate transfer of the knowledge.

Vibrates to the number 2.

TEKTITE   [Astrological Signs of Aries & Cancer]

Tektite is a form of meteoritic glass from outer space. Many believe that it is a piece of our moon or a piece of the planet Mars. Moldavite is a tektite and is covered separately in the MOLDAVITE section of this book. The following properties apply to all tektites.

This mineral provides encouragement to one to gather knowledge throughout the travels of life. It hinders lasting impressions of undesirable experiences, and encourages lasting impressions of desirable experiences. It does not, however, allow one to forget the lessons learned from any experiences - because of this characteristic, if one is attentive to the inner self, one seldom is placed in circumstances requiring the repeat performance of undesirable lessons.

It acts to balance the feminine and masculine properties of ones character and to stimulate the natural order of growth, development, and completion.

It has been esteemed in the Orient as a talisman of great power. Polynesian tribal elders believed that tektites would bring wealth and fertility in all endeavors.

It assists in providing one with information concerning the doctrine of final causes or purposes, and allows one to evaluate whether design and purpose are, in actuality, apparent in nature. This insight allows one to see into the heart of situations and to determine the benefit, or the detriment, to the continued participation in same; it further acts to promote the inner strength required for continuing or discontinuing the participation.

Tektite provides for thought transmission within the physical realm and between the physical realm and the location of origination of the stone; since tektites may have been sent from a variety of locations, a variety of tektites may be required to provide communication with all of the initiating sources. Do not be discouraged if messages from one location continue to occur with different tektites; when one is spiritually ready for further information, the tektite of the different locality will be made available. It seems that the beings of the originating locations have a connection with the Earth plane which allows the tektite to provide the "link-up" with those not in the proximity of the tektite. This has caused a bit of consternation - but all unfounded. These beings do not wish to interfere or to become part of the life of this planet; they are quite satisfied to provide information to enhance the development of Earth beings and to further this development by facilitating the connection with the total structure of humanity.

Carrying a tektite acts to strengthen ones energy field and to provide for increased contact during daily activities. Information which is relevant to mundane activities can be transmitted as readily as that which is relevant to spirituality and advancement. One can learn from all transmissions.

Using tektite can also draw one to another, or another to one, due to information provided during transmissions, or due to an attraction which is recognized by others who have the same transmission frequencies aligned in the ethereal body.

Tektite can be used in the treatment of fevers, to reduce transmission of disorders, and to dispel transmitted dis-eases, especially those which have no immediately known origin. It can be helpful in the amelioration of chronic dilation of capillaries and small blood vessels, and can stimulate a balance in circulation.

In addition,there is a Tektite from the Philippines which has been used extensively in healing by psychics and psychic surgeons. This Tektite seems to have an especially concentrated, and distinct energy which sometimes appears in a swirl, enveloping the user/client, and acting to proceed to the area of affliction immediately. It has been used it in a type of psychic surgery; the Tektite is placed upon the area of concern and has served to remove infections and dis-eased cellular structures - that which it extracts does not remain within the stone, but is transmuted without cleansing of the stone. It truly is a stone of light. When using it in meditation, it facilitates a cleaner and easier entry and assists one in attaining the state of "no mind". The spiral of energy which it holds becomes the spiral of the moving Kundalini and the spiral of protection concurrently.

Vibrates to the number 9.

TELLURIUM   [Astrological Signs of Capricorn & Aquarius]

Tellurium crystallizes in the form of masses and prismatic crystals. The colour is a metallic tin-white.

This mineral can be used to promote the actualization of an abundance of physical energy during hostile situations; it provides protection via energy stimulation and encourages the protective mechanisms of the self.

It can balance ones volatility and can stimulate astral travel.

It also provides a softness to ones nature. It acts to purify the emotions and to encourage the discharge of pent-up emotions. It is also a facilitator for communication, bringing softness and subtlety to conversation.

Tellurium can be used in the treatment of pneumonia, as a purgative, and as a cathartic.

Do not prepare an elixir of this mineral via the normal method.

Vibrates to the number 5.

TENORITE   [Astrological Sign of Capricorn]

Tenorite crystallizes in the form of minute black scales with metallic luster and in masses. The colour is black.

This mineral can be used to stimulate healing of the Earth, to ameliorate changes in the Earth, and to provide one with a true grounding connection to the Earth.

It can assist one in the adaptability and variability of ones nature and can bring sublimation to fears and insecurities.

It is useful in the radionics field to intensify the response patterns exhibited during use of the "check-surface".

Tenorite can help to bring together those of like-mind; it is useful in promoting the group effort, interlocking and providing for the unification of the resultant effects.

It is also beneficial to stimulating and to furthering relationships and associations on the physical plane.

It has been used to eliminate free-radical oxides from the body, to promote freeing of endorphins, and to stimulate the spleen. It can also be used to ameliorate hair loss and to assist in the assimilation of zinc.

Vibrates to the number 7.

TENNANTITE   [Astrological Sign of Aquarius]

Tennantite crystallizes in the form of dodecahedral and tetrahedral crystals, masses, and compact structures. The colour ranges from grey to black.

This mineral can be used to convey the feelings and emotions which one has camouflaged from ones consciousness; it can help to provide a calming stable environment in which to deal with the information. The stone actually takes on the negativity of the situation, in some cases producing alteration of the structure of the surface.

It furthers the actions related to realism in ones lifework, bringing the qualities of exactness, analytical rectitude, and stability to employment situations. It can also be used to augment ones scientific, and mystical and magical abilities, enhancing personal alignment with the n-dimensional realms of being.

It is excellent for helping one to flow through changes. It provides somewhat of an auxiliary stimulant which stimulates progression.

Tennantite can be used to prompt the activity of the pituitary to increase the blood pressure [when consciously directed to do so], to stimulate the intestinal muscles, and to treat the kidneys and bladder. It can also be used to stimulate the production of estrogen, to ameliorate the symptoms of menopause, to assist in the assimilation of iron, and to treat disorders, and associated symptoms, of the prostate.

Do not prepare an elixir of this mineral via the normal method.

Vibrates to the number 5.

TEPHROITE   [Astrological Sign of Aries]

Tephroite crystallizes in the form of compact masses and short prismatic crystals. The colour range includes grey, olive-green, creamy-pink, and red-brown.

This mineral can be used to align the energy fields of the physical body with the energy transmission fields of the etheric body. It acts to stabilize the emotional body, bringing energy to love; hence, evolving an energetic love.

This is a very good stone for astral travel; it acts as the vehicle, and carries the user through the planes of existence. It provides protection, promoting firmness in perilous positions [i.e., flying], and is the care-taker for the flight. It determines the route and that which should be shown, while other stones for astral travel sometimes allow the energy to be directed toward that which one wishes to see. It is also a protective stone for physical travel, especially by air.

Tephroite enhances ones position in life, with respect to the material aspects. It helps to strengthen ones faith in ones personal abilities and in the potential actions of others.

It can be used in the treatment of motion sickness, to moderate depression and to alleviate irritability due to stress, to combat fevers and chills, and to discourage less than adequate growth of the skeletal structure.

Vibrates to the number 8.

THALENITE   [Astrological Sign of Scorpio]

Thalenite crystallizes in the form of compact masses, tabular crystals, and prismatic crystals. The colour range includes creamy-pink, brown, and green.

This mineral can be used to mitigate anger and to stabilize ones temper. It can provide relief to internal stress and tends to encourage one to be more flexible in situational confrontations.

It provides for self-restraint in such a way that self-restraint is not required; it actually allows one to see that those situations which would normally call for an unnatural control are, in fact, of less magnitude and less importance than one would lend to them.

This mineral can be used in the treatment of bacterial and fungal infections; the energy is anti-toxic, and can be used to assist one in overcoming conditions related to alcoholism and drug addiction.

It assists in removing the toxins in ones body via the normal elimination system, but at an increased rate, producing sometimes an undesirable outward manifestation of the release [e.g., eruptions] of those materials which would be detrimental if allowed to remain within the body; use of this stone with a stone like dioptase would ameliorate the undesirable effect.

Vibrates to the number 4.

THAUMASITE   [Astrological Sign of Sagittarius]

Thaumasite crystallizes in the form of compact masses, fibers, and needle-like crystals. The colour range includes white, colourless, and yellow, sometimes a beautiful bright yellow in the crystalline form.

This mineral can provide one with insight with respect to the importance of the physical body as a vehicle for the lessons to be learned during this life. It guides one to the inner reaches of the being and encourages respect for the body as a "temple of understanding". It produces an awareness of the damage one consciously does to the physical body and helps one to be more in control of the issues. Similar insight is also made available for the emotional and intellectual bodies.

Thaumasite is concerned with the moment; facilitating all action required to provide one with persistence to maintain "correctness". It provides for a connection with the ethereal energy, with attachment via the intellect; hence, promoting intellectual stimulation on the higher planes. It further assists one to "re-commit to the light", enhancing the connected-ness between the self and all of humanity.

It inspires the furtherance of spiritual awareness, providing for entry to realms of knowledge which are primarily relevant to the issue at-hand; it raises the level of awareness during the experience such that the user can glean the information necessary to successfully act without reaction to present circumstances.

It is a good beginning stone, never allowing progress or intensity to go beyond the capacity of the user.

It also allows one to reach out, without departure from the body, and to gain visions of solutions [again, for present situations]. The activation of the higher intellect, in these cases, produces enhanced mental stimulation toward the rectification of, and subsequent course of action which will be required for, that which one is contemplating.

The energy of thaumasite is conducive to de-programming those ideas and concepts which are self-limiting and constrictive. It allows one to release fear and to dispense with both violence and anger. It assists in defusing communication problems, and in both clearing and rectifying harmful behavior patterns, while reinforcing the ideal that one is blessed with individuality.

This mineral also provides one with awareness, on the emotional and physical levels, of those who do and/or do not have ones "best interests at heart". It provides for an electrical stimulus, facilitated through the subtle bodies, which produces a dielectric charge due to the alignment of the "other" with opposing electrical energy. It is quite interesting to use this stone as a check against ones intuition and to check ones awareness level with respect to the stimulation which is actually received. It further encourages one to act on the impulses which are "born of memory".

Thaumasite can be used in the treatment of disorders of the tendons, in cases where there is a restriction or a less than adequate freedom to the flow [e.g., blood, nerves, digestion, etc.], and in the treatment of bone spurs. The intellectual alignment with the ethereal body can also promote the dissipation of mental disorders and problems related to the pattern of the signals of the brain.

Vibrates to the number 9.

THENARDITE   [Astrological Sign of Aries]

Thenardite crystallizes in the form of crusts, tabular double-pyramid structured crystals, and short prismatic double-pyramid structured crystals. The colour range includes white, brown, and red.

This mineral can be used to stimulate ones energy level and to remove "muddiness" from the aura. It activates the base chakra and provides for clarity, stemming from the base instincts, with respect to ones physical actions.

It helps to dispel irritability and touchiness, and to provide for insight into the to further action required when one believes that the supply of possibilities or resources has been exhausted.

It assists one in releasing the duality of the body and mind, allowing one to understand the ego mechanism and to both recognize and differentiate between the states of desire and need. It further enables one to alter the course of ones life, providing for insight into the new foundation upon which a new life can begin.

Thenardite can be used in the treatment of blood clots, water retention, goiter, spasms, and muscular rigidity. It is also helpful with respect to assisting one in remembering of schedules and times [e.g., for medication, etc.], and has been used in the treatment of Alzheimer's dis-ease.

Do not prepare an elixir of this mineral via the normal method.

Vibrates to the number 5.

THOMSONITE   [Astrological Sign of Gemini]

Thomsonite crystallizes in the form of spherical concretions, columns, radial or plate-like layered aggregates, and needle-like prismatic crystals. The colour range includes white, yellow, pink, red-green, brown, and green.

This mineral provides for an interweaving of the electrical force fields of the physical and the ethereal body, producing a stable connection between the emotional and intellectual bodies, as well. This allows for action with one main body.

It is also a stone for treatment against brashness, treachery, and laziness.

It assists one in eliminating the "fog of mystery" which threatens to defy solution; it promotes the clearing of the mind and the advancement of the swiftness of effort-less ease. It also encourages ones expansion in all areas, promoting both the wit and wisdom to assist one in the alleviation of the blockages in ones life.

Thomsonite can be used in the treatment of high body temperatures, oral fungus, dysfunctional connective tissue, and cysts. It can also act to stimulate the thymus and to increase youthfulness.

Vibrates to the number 3.

THOREAULITE   [Astrological Sign of Sagittarius]

Thoreaulite crystallizes in the form of prismatic crystals. the colour ranges from brown to yellow.

This mineral helps to bring one to the "end" - relationships, environments, homes, employment, life, etc. It does not facilitate the end, but helps to provide stability and joy during these periods of time which could be rather tumultuous. It also promotes insight into the benefit of the end and into that which lies ahead.

Thoreaulite provides for an idealistic visionary state in which writing is "seen"; the writing being in the form of texts which contain testimony on issues of concern. The user is permitted to read the texts to gain the information required. It can also be used to take one to the spirit world of the Kachinas; sometimes allowing one to participate in the religious ceremonies of the other world, and usually allowing one to see the flame of enlightenment "which magically brightens into glittering stars - beautifying the mind while increasing in number and lighting the way toward spiritual development".

This mineral can be used in the treatment of manic depression, brain virus, and violent uncontrolled outbursts. It also acts to alleviate recurrent symptoms [not necessarily affecting the cause].

Vibrates to the number 8.

THULITE   [Astrological Signs of Taurus & Gemini]

Thulite, a variety of zoisite, crystallizes in the form of masses and striated prismatic crystals. The colour range includes grey, white, pink, rose red, yellow, green, and blue. The properties listed in the ZOISITE section of this book apply in addition to those listed below.

This mineral can be used to assist one in dramatic presentations and to promote the entertaining aspect within the self.

It allows one to separate, to examine, and to integrate the duality of ones nature, and to view the integral parts with the combined aspects of logic and love. As the result is often "much to ones chagrin", it also provides for insight with respect to the corrective process.

It allows one to recognize the divine personal nature and, hence, affects a curative outcome in the many aspects of ones life. It further assists in reducing aimlessness, prodigious vanity, and conceit - bringing supplemental energy to eloquence and direction.

It can help in the treatment of calcium deficiencies and intestinal disturbances, and can be beneficial in healing power [when worn beneath a tourniquet] to affect the amelioration of the disorder.

Vibrates to the number 5.

THUNDEREGG   [Astrological Sign of Scorpio]

The thunderegg is a fortification [banded in layers] agate, sometimes also containing opal [usually, pink], and enclosed by a hardened compact matrix; the matrix usually contains silica ash. It is usually found in spherical formations and, internally, exhibits a star-like pattern. It sometimes exhibits an additional flower-like configuration, the most famous being Priday Plume. The properties listed in the AGATE section of this book apply in addition to those listed below. Where the thunderegg contains opal, the properties listed in the OPAL section of this book also apply.

The ancients believed that the thundereggs were a result of the wrath and anger of the gods, being thrown upon the Earth in a fit of rage over that which was occurring in the society below. They also have a connection with the god of thunder [Thor] in Scandinavian mythology, and provide for a link to those ancient thoughts.

The thunderegg can be used to decrease anger and hostility. It can also be used to provide a link with the "star people" of this planet and with those potential "star people" from the other realms. The link can produce physical awareness induced from the other realms, and can help to bring those like-minded others of this plane into ones physical reality. It also acts to instill a community affiliation, promulgating shared knowledge and actions. The energy of the thunderegg can facilitate progress with stability, allowing for "right" thought followed by "right" action. It assists one in listening with intention and in acting with intensity.

The plume thunderegg can, in addition, stimulate ones growth toward the light, allowing for the pathway toward growth to be "lighted by the lamp of inner joy". It facilitates a nurturing quality and assists one to grow in an "ease-ful" manner. The energy is one of joy and peace, and is especially helpful during times of great stress. It helps to stimulate ideas and to give substance and continuity to thought. It is used to manifest the "lovely" into ones life. It also allows one to recognize that, within each person and situation, there is peace and beauty.

Vibrates to the master number 55.

TIGER EYE   [Astrological Sign of Capricorn]

Tiger eye is a quartz replacement of crocidolite [blue asbestos] or of gold asbestos. It differs from cat's eye with respect to the configuration of the fibers; the fibers are twisted or crumpled instead of straight. It exhibits the quality of chatoyancy due to the reflection of light by the fibrous structure. The colour range includes red, brown, gold, cream, black, and blue.

This mineral brings together the vibrations of sand and sunlight, synthesizing the energies of the Sun and the Earth. It combines sharpness and grounding, and is quite practical in its sphere of concern. It resonates to the frequencies of the Earth, encouraging stability with dynamic beauty. The vibration is conducive to peacefulness and stimulates the actions required to advance the encounters with others during the meditative state.

It is helpful for individuals seeking clarity and for those who must deal intelligently with the scattered details which must be brought together into some pattern.

It can be used to enhance the psychic abilities and can assist in the gentle attunement of third-eye activity - this stone being best adapted to "earthy" people.

At the base chakra, it can help to discipline sexual and emotional life, bringing "light" to instances where one must be practical.

It contains a solar energy which helps with those psychic processes which involve the solar plexus chakra - promoting intuitive impressions.

Tiger eye can help one to become practical and of discrete mind, as well as more grounded. It can eliminate the "blues" and can bring brightness and optimism to the user. It also assists in providing insight to those issues which induce internal mental battles, delivering one from the "horns of dilemma" and the conflicts associated with willful pride. It further prompts the admiration for the pure and beautiful, allowing ones life, and ones passion for life, to open and to blossom.

It provides for balancing of the yin-yang energy. It further assists in the integration and balancing of both hemispheres of the brain, bringing awareness to perception.

It can help to prepare the systems of the body for the approach of enthusiasm for flowing with "the river of humanity" toward the "one". It further acts to attune one to the connected-ness of the brothers and sisters of the planet, releasing introversion and fear, while promoting experiences which are fresh and new.

It tends to bring awareness of ones personal needs as well as the needs of others, stimulating understanding with respect to disparity between the pleasure of "wishing" and the act of "having". It has been used to stimulate wealth and to enhance the stability required to maintain wealth.

It produces soothing vibrations, generating a calmness to unsettled turmoil, and allowing one to enjoy the actions of being unfenced and uninhibited.

It has been used in the treatment of disorders of the eye, the throat, the reproductive system, and diverticular constrictions, and to aid in night vision. It can also be used to strengthen the alignment of the spinal column and to facilitate the mending of broken bones.

Vibrates to the number 4.

TIGER IRON   [Astrological Sign of Leo]

Tiger iron is comprised of golden tiger eye, red jasper, and black hematite. It combines the qualities of these three minerals as described in the respective sections of this book.

It can also be used to assist in creative endeavors, prompting the artistic abilities toward wondrous beauty and works, revealing the ultimate in balance and mathematical exactitude.

It helps one to find havens of refuge when danger is perceived.

In addition, is stimulates the physical vitality to "put a tiger in your tank".
It has been used to promote the assimilation the B-complex vitamins and to increase the white/red blood cell count [as directed]. It can also been used to strengthen the muscular structure, and to stimulate the production of steroids.

Vibrates to the number 7.

TIN   [Astrological Signs of Sagittarius, Libra, & Taurus]

Native tin, the natural state, crystallizes in the form of greyish-white rounded grains.

This mineral can be used to clear fogginess from the mental faculties. It stimulates reasoning abilities and alleviates superiority tendencies. It can be used to encourage consideration and thoughtfulness and is helpful to relationships.

It has been successful in drawing-away despondency and in promoting the exhilaration necessary to initiate "new beginnings".

It assuages fear, helping one to see that the basis of fear is only incomplete knowledge; it assists one in gaining completion of this knowledge.

Native tin can be used to relieve the lungs from consumption, to heal sores and ulcers, and to help to rid one of intestinal parasites. It is also of assistance in discouraging insects from remaining in ones environment; being quite helpful with gardens and houseplants.

Vibrates to the number 7.

TINSTONE   [See Cassiterite]

TOPAZ   [Astrological Sign of Sagittarius - Elemental]

Topaz crystallizes in the form of water worn pebbles and prismatic crystals, sometimes vertically striated and sometimes with well-developed terminations. The colour range includes pink, green red, gold, yellow, blue, white, red-yellow, brown, grey, and colourless.

It is known as a "stone of true love and success in all endeavors".

It can promote individuality and creativity, while providing for confidence in trusting ones decisions. It acts to replace negativity with love and joyfulness.

This mineral helps one to understand both the actions occurring in the "big picture" and the interrelationships occurring in the minute detail which comprises the "big picture". It promotes the expression of ideas and instills a trust in the universe such that one may feel comfortable with the potential outcome of a situation without "doing". It assists one in "cutting-through" the curtains of uncertainty and trepidation, precipitating astute reasoning abilities and promoting the release of feelings of annoyance engendered by the loop-hole known as doubt.

It is said to have been one of the stones used in the breastplate of the high priest.

The energy of the topaz acts through the laws of attraction and manifestation. The gentle shades of topaz serve as a catalytic trigger for the manifestation activities, while the vibratory resonance acts with an ethereal magnetic effect.

The ends and facets of a topaz crystal [as well as faceted topaz] provide both positive and negative currents. This is quite different from quartz. These alternating currents are linked via the ethers to the forces of manifestation through which attraction and desire are promulgated. When a request is directed through the topaz to the object or to the thought form which is desired, the topaz acts as a conductor for the message

- sending the message to the ethers via a closed circuit of current which penetrates the energy field related to manifestation. The message is then relayed to the universal mind which, in turn, refines the information and assures that the intent is for the good of all, before sending the transmission directly toward actualization on the physical plane. The energies of topaz transcend both time and space, inducing finely-tuned cooperation and rewards which grow from the idea/ideal which one desires to manifest.

This mineral is the "crystal of potency", quite instrumental in visualization [for healing and/or attracting], in meditation, and in projection. It helps one to absorb that which is needed from the universe, prompting receptivity and willingness to act. It helps one to creatively change ones personal world, enhancing awareness and inducing the states of expansiveness and manifestation.

The topaz crystal is considered quite precious by the African bushmen, being used in ceremonies for healing and for connecting with the spirits who have departed from this plane. It is considered to bring wealth and health to the holder.

Use of the topaz in a silver wand provides an additional conductor to both transmit and activate that upon which there is conscious focus. When the energies projected from the topaz crystal [in the silver wand] are consciously directed into the psychic channels where the health aura can be accessed, the atoms belonging to this area can be modified and altered through ones conscious focus. This usage can aid significantly in the removal of "useless" elements within the aura, making room for expansion and reconstruction to occur. The silver wand responds to mental and emotional intensity; these qualities are fused by the electrical properties of the topaz crystal, bringing forth the laws of attraction and manifestation. The alternating current of the topaz crystal working through the silver wand provides for an additional conductivity factor which amplifies the force field and allows for the maximum utilization of the potential energy.

When the topaz is used in conjunction with amethyst, it both gives and receives energy from the amethyst, facilitating the utilization of the laws of attraction and manifestation for the good of all; the amethyst further provides for the transmutation of undeveloped energies into spiritual vibrations to produce a soothing, clearing, and stabilizing effect. This combination of minerals is quite useful for both white magic and healing.

It can be used to manifest health and to correct disorders within the body. It has been used in the treatment for the loss of sense of taste, and in the healing of wounds and skin eruptions. Use of topaz as an elixir is an excellent method of dispersing the energy throughout the body; it can be taken internally and can be used topically.

When using the elixir, the request is directed through the elixir to the visualized state of that which is desired.

Vibrates to the number 6.

Additional qualities of several specific colours/configurations of topaz are listed below.

Blue Topaz   [Astrological Signs of Sagittarius & Virgo]

This stone can additionally stimulate the throat chakra such that one may consciously, succinctly, and clearly verbalize that which one desires to manifest and/or that which one desires to communicate.

It helps one to be unburdened by arrogance and unconfined by passion, allowing one to see all things as equally important in the overall scheme of life.

It assists one in bringing the body, mind, and spirit into union with the forces of the perfection of the universe.

Vibrates to the number 3.

Golden Topaz   [Astrological Signs of Sagittarius, Leo, & Pisces]

This stone can additionally be used as a path to conscious attunement with the rational principle which rules and governs this universe. If one intends to attune to this "structure", the reasons behind the communication need to be clear and concise.

It acts as a repository stone which stores information, as well as energy, thoughts, and love. If one needs recharged with energy, the golden topaz can be used like a battery.

It is quite useful for activating and stimulating the first three chakras and the crown chakra. It can be used to enhance relaxation, to create lightness of spirit, and to stimulate feelings of peace.

It also acts to initiate faith and to further the quest for the enlightened state.

It can be used to attract people toward one for friendship or business; one needs to be careful that this is not used for selfish purposes. Sometimes, those wearing golden topaz become so busy with the mundane that there is little time for the sacred.

The golden topaz can also be used in the treatment of disorders of the liver, gall bladder, and endocrine glands.

Vibrates to the number 9.

Multi-Coloured Topaz   [Astrological Sign of All]

Multi-Coloured Topaz brings the qualities of the individual colours to synthesis and further assists one in the re-direction of energy and in the analyze of ones own patterns of emotional thinking and development, based on free associative ideals, revealing to the conscious mind the thoughts and experiences previously unrecognized; hence, stimulating remedial action for emotional disturbances and over-emotional states.

It can also be used to correct unwanted, unloving behavior patterns and emotional reactions.

Multi-Coloured Topaz provides for smooth states of meditation and enhances mental travel to other parts of the current world. It can be used to facilitate trance states which take the user to the pre-determined destination, and to stimulate a total awareness [in those at that location] to both recognize and understand the nature of the visit.

This mineral can also be used in the treatment of pneumonia, to clear the mucus from the lungs, and to provide for the stabilization of the inner walls of the lungs. It can also be used to treat chronic inflammatory conditions of the skin. It can assist in the efficient conversion of carbohydrates to energy and in the regulation of the proper flow of insulin to the blood stream.

Vibrates to the number 3.

"Rutilated" Topaz   [Astrological Signs of Sagittarius, Gemini, & Scorpio]

"Rutilated" topaz does not contain rutile, but contains goethite. This form of topaz combines the qualities of the TOPAZ with the qualities of goethite [see GOETHITE section in this book]. It should be noted that goethite inclusions in topaz are rare; but, however rare, the beauty of this configuration is tantamount, bringing the beauty to the field of the user.

The energy is very conducive to the manifestation properties related to the "non-rutilated" topaz, and it acts quite well to facilitate the manifestation of those ideals relative to business, possessions, understanding, appreciation, and healing.

It has been used for "gazing", providing for insight into that which is occurring in a distant location. Prior to the activation of this mineral for "gazing", conscious direction of the mind is required - otherwise, one may view situations and activities which are of no relevance or importance to the user.

It enables one to "light the divine light of imagination", and has been known as a "stone of enchantment", bringing light and love to all facets of ones life.

Vibrates to the number 8.

Sheet Topaz   [Astrological Sign of Leo]

Sheet Topaz occurs in a horizontal flat formation in the colour ranging from clear to white to very pale blue and very pale green.

This mineral combines the properties of TOPAZ with the actualization of knowledge bringing a window to other dimensions. It promotes the access of information from the astral plane and the akashic records, and allows one to see within the inner self. The action of looking within the self with the Sheet Topaz has allowed one to recognize disordered states and to mentally rearrange and reorganize the disarray of dis-ease. It has also been used for "gazing" and for sending and receiving messages.

It can stimulate the heart chakra, the throat chakra, the third-eye, and the crown chakra, and is an excellent tool for communication between the self and other worlds. It can also be used to stimulate visualization and visionary experiences and to actuate the higher psychic abilities.

It can also be used to stimulate contact with the ethereal planes of resolution. In the meditative or non-meditative state, answers to problems of all magnitudes seem to manifest quickly.

It has been used in the treatment of disorders of, and for pain in, the areas of the heart, the throat, and the back of the head. It has also been used to relieve headaches.

Vibrates to the number 9.

TOUCHSTONE   [Astrological Sign of Libra]

Touchstone is a type of chalcedony occurring in the form of a velvet-black siliceous stone.

♪ 652 ♫

The following properties are in addition to those qualities listed CHALCEDONY section of this book.

This mineral can be used to allow one to "see-into" experiences and to examine the depth of the character of another. It helps one to recognize truth as well as deception. The energy of touchstone tends to provide for a balancing between change and progress, enhancing forward movement and tenacity.

It has been known as a "stone of purity and purification". It is an excellent purifier, prompting the release of negativity from the environment in which it rests. It can be used to clear and cleanse the chakras and to allow for the gentle release of hostility and anger.

Activation of touchstone is readily accomplished by rubbing the stone with the hands. When one experiences pain, rubbing touchstone on the affected area can provide for diminishment and the eventual disappearance of the pain.

It has been used as an elixir in the removal of toxins from the body, to soothe the skin, and to relieve aches and pains.

Vibrates to the number 5.

TOURMALINE   [Astrological Sign of Libra - Elemental]

Tourmaline crystallizes in the form of vertically striated prismatic crystals, sometimes slender and sometimes needle-like. The colour range includes deep pink to red to red-violet [rubellite], blue [indicolite], yellow [also known as "Peridot of Ceylon" and as Tsilasite], brown [dravide], green, pink [elbaite], orange, black [aphrizite and schorl], colourless [achroite], bi-coloured, tri-coloured, and colourless.

The energy of tourmaline relates to each of the chakras. It acts to clear, to maintain, and to stimulate each of the energy centers of the body.

It can be used to attract inspiration, to diminish fear by promoting understanding, and to encourage self-confidence. It provides for a balancing of the male/female energies within the body; it further provides for balancing of the mind, of the energy centers, and of the auric body, inducing the alignment of the mental processes <u>and</u> the chakras with the ethereal structure.

The tourmaline and the inherent electrical emanations have been revered throughout the life of the planet. In rituals performed in the ancient eastern Indian culture, the tourmaline was used to provide direction toward that which would bring "good"; it was also recognized as a "teller" stone, providing insight during times of struggle and "telling" who and/or what is causing trouble.

It has been used by shamen among the African, Native American, and Aboriginal tribes. It is thought to bring healing powers to the user and to provide protection from all dangers occurring on the physical plane. The African shamen have used the tourmaline to promote the awakening from the "dream of illusion" and to promote the experience of the self as a part of the universal spirit.

Tourmaline has been used to stimulate balance between the left and right sides of the brain and to enhance cooperative efforts in the areas of creativity and healing. It further helps one to look within the depths of ones being with as much belief in the reality of the inner world as one maintains for the outer world. It helps one to release the concept of being the victim and to maintain fortitude and laughter while retaining consciousness.

Tourmaline wands are quite special with respect to providing complete directional aspects to the qualities present within the structure. The crystals which are wands are terminated and range from two to three [plus] inches in length, with a diameter from 1/4" to 1/2" [plus]. The aspects of the tourmaline are enhanced in the wand configuration and are used to clear the aura, to energize the appropriate chakras, to balance the meridians of the physical body, and to facilitate the optimum balance inherent in the ethereal body. The wand clearly directs the energy to facilitate the actualization of positive patterns and to initiate the fruition of positive affirmations.

In addition to the general qualities of tourmaline, the following information provides descriptions of further properties for selected colours of tourmaline. Please note that the multi-colour tourmaline combines the properties of the respective colours.

Vibrates to the number 2.

Black Tourmaline   [Astrological Sign of Capricorn]
                                            [Also Known as Schorl and Aphrizite]

Black tourmaline can be used to both repel and protect against negativity. It acts to protect one from being victimized by the negative energy of another. It has also been used as an energy deflector, being an excellent stone for those with potential for exposure to excessive amounts of radiation. It provides for an increase in ones physical vitality, emotional stability, and intellectual acuity, and can maintain ones "spirits" even in conditions which appear to emit the messages of "gloom and doom".

It furthers the awakening of altruism and enhances practicality in creativity. As a protective stone against "spells" which are cast by the negative side of another, it is a special stone to Native American Indians; black tourmaline in quartz not only dispels the "spell", but energizes the "victim" and actually increases well-being; black tourmaline used with mica, returns the "spell" to the originating source and allows one to view the sender of the negative energies.

It is also used to activate grounding between the first chakra and the center of the Earth, providing for further enhancement of ones well-being on the physical plane, and protecting against those in the spirit world and/or those on the physical plane who are not in the "light" and do not understand the love of the universe.

It acts to stimulate the reflex points associated with the lower back. It can be used in the treatment of arthritis, dyslexia, heart dis-ease, anxiety, and disorientation. It can also provide for both the stimulation and the balancing of the adrenal glands.

Vibrates to the numbers 3 and 4.

Blue Tourmaline   [Astrological Signs of Libra & Taurus]
                                   [Deep Blue is Also Known as Indicolite]

Blue tourmaline can be used to activate the throat chakra and the third-eye, strengthening the skills associated with communication and psychic awareness. It assists one in relating to others in a loving manner, bringing the true impressions to the surface.

It further helps one to live in harmony with ones environment [e.g., people, places, things]. The energy of blue tourmaline activates the progression toward service, allowing one to recognize the rewards of serving humanity in the areas of expansion of knowledge and in helping all to realize the power of love.

The very deep blue shade of tourmaline, which stimulates the third-eye, facilitates access to the higher levels of intuition. It acts as a vehicle for visions and for contact with the higher realms.

Blue tourmaline can be used in the treatment of disorders of the lungs, throat, larynx, esophagus, thymus, and thyroid. Dark blue tourmaline can also be used in the treatment of disorders associated with the eyes and the brain. Neon blue has been used in diagnostic endeavors and in assisting in the recognition of causal factors.

Vibrates to the number 6 and the master number 55. In addition, the neon blue tourmaline vibrates to the number 9.

Brown Tourmaline   [Astrological Sign of Aries]
                                          [Also Known as Dravide]

Brown tourmaline can be used to clear the aura and to stimulate the auric body to align the energy of the optimum self to the physical body; it does not provide for the alignment, as such, but opens the pathway to facilitate the alignment.

It is a protective stone on the subtle levels, bringing the presence of the Earth to the peace of the higher-self.

It can also be used in the treatment of disorders of the intestinal tract, and to reduce spots on the skin. It has been used to stimulate the growth of plants.

Vibrates to the numbers 2 and 9.

Colourless Tourmaline   [Astrological Sign of Aquarius]
                                          [Also Known as Achroite]

Colourless tourmaline aligns the energy centers and meridians of the physical body to the optimum energy centers and meridians of the ethereal body. It provides for a synthesis of the metaphysical and healing properties of the other colours of tourmaline.

In addition, it can be used to activate the crown chakra, instilling the concept of progress toward service.

It is excellent in healing, combining the forces of all tourmaline properties.

Vibrates to the numbers 6 and 7.

Green Tourmaline   [Astrological Sign of Capricorn]

This mineral can help to teach the user a way of "seeing with the heart" [i.e., opens the heart chakra]. It may be applied in endeavors of visualization and to assist in the attunement of the energy between the third-eye and the heart.

It does possess a masculine energy, but contains the quality of compassion; this facilitates a willful-ness with respect to entering into visions and thoughts.

Green tourmaline holds the essence of the plant kingdom; it provides an energy conducive to healing plants and tends to readily transfer energy from the mineral kingdom to the vegetable dimension of vibrations. It is also quite useful in facilitating the study and practice of herbalism and for increasing the effectiveness of herbs and plants in healing. It shows the world that we are one, trading energies and vibratory messages, in order to maintain the integrity of the planet.

It can transform negative energy to the positive state without releasing it to the atmosphere. It also acts to inspire creativity, and to attract success, prosperity and abundance.

It can be used in the treatment of disorders relating to the eyes. It can also be used to facilitate weight loss and to regenerate the heart, thymus, ductless glands, and the immune system. It has been used as a purgative. The energy of green tourmaline can also assist one in rectifying psychological problems associated with the father and/or other male forces in ones life.

Vibrates to the number 6.

Multi-Coloured Tourmaline   [Astrological Sign of Gemini]

In addition to combining the properties of the respective colours, Multi-Coloured Tourmaline can be used as a "gate" to the inner self and to the higher-self.

Vibrates to the number 8.

Neon Tourmaline   [Astrological Sign of Virgo]

The neon tourmaline further enhances all energies of the colour represented, electrifies transmissions and enhances the properties of the minerals with which it contacts. It enhances the properties given above and has been used as a focal point for long-distance contact and contact with other worlds via meditation and via journeying. It indeed is a powerful stone!

Vibrates to the number 5.

Orange Tourmaline   [Astrological Signs of Leo & Scorpio]

Orange tourmaline is very rare. I have seen a few pieces which have been found in Africa; they usually occur with the yellow and red colours.

The orange tourmaline stimulates the navel chakra and enhances creativity, intuition of the physical plane, and sexuality; it also provides for a leveling of emotions and a furthering of desire - the direction of the desire being facilitated by the intellect.

It can be used in the treatment of disorders related to the reproductive system, to infertility and/or frigidity, and to intestinal disorders.

Vibrates to the number 8.

Pink (Light) Tourmaline   [Astrological Sign of Libra]
                                           [Also Known as Elbaite]

The energy of light pink tourmaline relates to creativity and to conceiving the "new", while allowing one to maintain the connection between the self and "All That Is" and between the self and all which is a part of "All That Is".

It acts to stimulate the crown chakra and the heart chakra, bringing forth the synthesis of love and spirituality, while enhancing the higher aspects of the state of love. It furthers the actualization of love and promotes joy and peace during periods of growth and changes; the changes being guided toward the furtherance of the spirit and the concomitant growth of humanity toward enlightenment.

It allows one to trust in the power of love. It can promote the feelings of joy and enthusiasm for life by releasing destructive tendencies.

It is a stone to assist one in the attainment of peace and understanding, trust and awareness, and love. It is a special stone to give to one you hope will love you.

It has been used to decrease the proclivity for falls and to assist in the release of disorders related to dysfunctional endocrine activities. It acts as a holistic medicament, bringing the body toward unification in order to treat a disorder. It has also been used to treat disorders of the heart, lungs, and skin.

It is excellent as an elixir taken internally and applied topically.

Vibrates to the number 9 and the master number 99.

Rubellite Tourmaline   [Astrological Signs of Sagittarius & Scorpio]
                                  [Also Known as Red/Red-Violet/Deep Pink Tourmaline]

Rubellite tourmaline strengthens the will to understand love and to inspire tactfulness in independence, promoting creativity in the various realms of loving aspirations.

It can be used to stimulate the base chakra and to provide for a direct pathway between the base chakra and the heart chakra; it can, hence, be used to direct and to intensify devotional proclivities.

It activates all of the qualities of the base [first] chakra and provides physical energy and vitality to the physical body.

It further stimulates the healing qualities of the heart and the associated attributes of loving consciousness.

It can be used in the treatment of disorders of the digestive system, the heart, lungs, pancreas, and reproductive system. It has also been used in the repair of the reproductive system and to provide for balance in the structure of the blood vessels and veins.

Vibrates to the numbers 1, 2, 4, and 5.

Rubellite and Lepidolite   [Astrological Signs of Libra & Scorpio]

The formation produced by the combination of rubellite and lepidolite exhibits a powerful and joyous energy which helps to generate happiness <u>and</u> a sensation of physical lightness.

The rubellite stimulates the energy of love, such that all chakras are activated into a spontaneous flowing movement [similar to a spiral energy extending from the base to the crown chakra], providing for a balance of the male and female energies.

The lavender light of lepidolite in this mineral combination erases negative energy patterns from the entire etheric body, expelling static and unhealthy formations while sending healing energies through the meridians, integrating the etheric body with the physical, and balancing both.

There is a purifying aspect to this combination; it deals with emotions and is an overall purifying agent.

It works with all of the energy centers to bring integration and balance; being especially helpful to open the heart and to reconcile yin-yang imbalances in the sub-conscious portion of the being.

Vibrates to the number 5.

Watermelon Tourmaline   [Astrological Signs of Virgo & Gemini]

Watermelon tourmaline is a configuration of tourmaline which exhibits a green or blue rind and a pink or red core. Please note that this is not the same as tourmaline which is bi-coloured, exhibiting both the pink and green or pink and blue colours.

Watermelon tourmaline is the "super activator" of the heart chakra; providing for stimulation, energizing, and connection with the heart chakra of the higher-self. It encourages one to look past the seriousness of an experience or a situation and to recognize both the benefit of, and the humour in, the experience/situation. It helps one to allow oneself the experience of the beauty of nature, while diminishing emotionalism. It also enhances cooperative efforts and inspires tact in all situations.

It has been used in the treatment of nervousness, disorders of the heart and lungs, and in dysfunctions of the emotional system.

Vibrates to the number 2.

Yellow Tourmaline   [Astrological Sign of Leo]
                              [Also Known as Peridot of Ceylon and Tsilasite]

Yellow tourmaline stimulates the solar plexus, enhancing personal power and intellectual pursuits. It also relates to the cycles in ones life, helping one to bring to an opening, or to a closing, that which would benefit ones personal growth.

It stimulates spiritual development by helping one to logically conclude that the pathway is open and inviting. It activates creativity and initiative in business and employment.

It can be used in the treatment of disorders associated with the liver, spleen, kidneys, gall bladder, and stomach.

Vibrates to the numbers 1 and 4, and to the master number 33.

TRANSVAAL JADE   [Astrological Sign of Taurus]

Transvaal jade, a variety of grossular/grossularite, crystallizes in the form of opaque green masses, usually found in veins.

The properties listed below are in addition to those listed in the JADE and the GROSSULAR/GROSSULARITE sections of this book.

This mineral can be used to promote ones organizational qualities and to provide for insight to the solutions to the unresolved current problems and events which contain mystery. It helps one to "find the way through the maze", and provides for guidance with respect to the worthiness of the trip.

It can also be used to unite the separate-ness of groups, organizations, communities, and countries. It works on the level of the heart chakra to enhance the goodness and love within us all and to teach us, again, the "brotherhood" of love.

It can be used in the treatment of disorders of the veins, restrictions in energy flow, problems of the heart [both physical and emotional - which could well be one in the same], dysfunction due to trauma, and irregularities in the area of the throat.

Vibrates to the number 2.

TREMOLITE   [Astrological Signs of Pisces, Scorpio, Libra, & Gemini]

Tremolite crystallizes in the form of masses, fibrous aggregates, short stout crystals, and long bladed crystals. The colour range includes white, grey, colourless, pale green, pink and brown.

This mineral can be used to facilitate contact with those on the physical plane, or elsewhere. Projecting the visualized form of a person into the mineral helps to bring that person near - always in spirit, sometimes in form.

It is a regional stone and conveys the force of the region of the Earth in which it resides. The energy of this stone is dependent upon the negativity or positivity emitted from the environment in which it is located. Most areas are similar with respect to the amount of energy available; the more enlightened and/or spiritual beings there are in an area, the stronger the force.

There are, however, locations upon the Earth [recognized as areas which emanate the energies of the vortex structures] where the force is abundant, and where this abundance does not rely upon the presence of beings; e.g., locations in the proximity of Table Mountain, Cape Town, RSA; Sedona, Arizona, USA; Topo Do Mundo, close to Belo Horizonte, Brasil; Kathmandu, Nepal; Pune, India; South Of England, UK; Browns Mountain, Washington, USA; and many areas in the mountains of Peru.

It can also be used [via gridding] to stabilize and to balance chaotic or potentially chaotic locations.

Tremolite can be used in the treatment of calcium and magnesium deficiencies, to promote the assimilation of the minerals. It can also be used to assist in stabilizing nervousness, shakiness, and those dis-eases related to these disorders.

Vibrates to the number 9.

TREVORITE [Astrological Sign of Pisces]

Trevorite crystallizes in the form of black grains with a green tinge. It is a small stone filled with massive energy.

This mineral can be used to balance the polarity of ones body with the higher bodies and to open and balance the meridians of the physical body, stimulating the alignment of the physical and ethereal nervous systems.

It can also be used to traverse the gap between the physical world and the spiritual world, and can help to prepare one for the transition, promoting ease, love, and calmness during the movement.

It can be used in the treatment of disorders related to mental acuity, memory, intravascular coagulation of the blood in the circulatory system, imbalances in the thyroid, and atrophy of the thymus.

Vibrates to the number 6.

TRILOBITE [Astrological Sign of Capricorn]

The trilobite is a fossilized sea creature which lived in the oceans of this Earth during eons past.

It can promote both leadership and management skills, allowing one to rule lovingly and with patience and fortitude. It assists in the development of patience, strength, and perseverance, allowing one to recognize the desired course and to maintain the pathway which will produce the desired goal. It is an example for humanity that one may be in charge of the world, and still, virtually, be required to "sit in the mud".

It also allows non-leaders to realize that leadership is, indeed, a quality; a quality which produces decisions that are, typically, not agreeable to all, but are in the best interests of all. The trilobite, a mighty soul, allowed the land to be ruled by "man" - when may man gladly give the rule back to the brave trilobite of the expansive oceans?

The trilobite can be used in the treatment of disorders of the eyes, and to correct deficiencies in Vitamins A and D, calcium, and iodine. It can also be used to assist in the amelioration of fading eyesight, brittle bones, skin eruptions, and goiter.

Vibrates to the number 2.

TRIPHYLITE   [Astrological Sign of Libra]

Triphylite usually crystallizes in the form of masses. The colour range includes green, blue-grey, green-grey, pale pink, yellow, and brown.

This mineral is a very soothing stone which can be used to dispel the dismal from ones character or environment. The presence of the stone in an environment acts as a broom "to sweep away the dark" and to "welcome the light".

It is helpful in matters of opposition, promoting guidance to stimulate the intellect in worldly matters. It can provide for "an edge" in gaming activities, stimulating a kind of "quick snap-shot" of the suggested play while encouraging action.

Triphylite can be used in the treatment of feebleness and less than adequate ambulatory conditions, and to provide calming during over-stimulated conditions, to relieve minor aches and pains, and to facilitate the improvement in disorders associated with iron poor blood.

Vibrates to the number 7.

TRIPLIODITE   [Astrological Signs of Aquarius, Libra, & Sagittarius]

Tripliodite crystallizes in the form of fibrous aggregates, crystallized aggregates, and vertically striated prismatic crystals. The colour range includes pink, yellow, and brown-to-green.

This mineral combines the trinity of the mental, physical, and emotional bodies, to produce the connection with the optimum self, and to synthesize the optimum self of this plane with the perfection of the ethereal plane.

It acts on the premise that each person contains, within the self, all that is necessary, in order to manifest anything that is for the good of all; in addition, it bases its action on the premise and the understanding that each person is complete, the human race is complete, the mineral kingdom is complete, the plant kingdom is complete, the animal kingdom is complete, ..., etc.; the logical conclusion leading to the ideal completeness of the "one" and the completeness of the whole. It provides for insight with respect to the utilization of this "completeness" in activities of manifestation. The key idea is that "we are one, they are one, and 1+1=1".

It enhances fairness, yet firmness, and allows one to stand alone when circumstances require. It also assists one in understanding that it is "okay" to ask for, and to accept, help from others; it provides one with the insight to realize that help from another is, in actuality, help from the self.

It can be used in the treatment of the skeletal system, the nervous system, the circulatory system, and the heart. It is antiseptic in action, and can be used to diminish wounds and to dispel toxins.

Vibrates to the number 2.

TRONA   [Astrological Sign of Virgo]

Trona crystallizes in the form of masses, fibers, columns, and elongated flattened crystals. The colour range includes white, grey-white, pale yellow, and brown.
Trona is usually quite fragile, leading to the recommendation for providing a safe, enclosed place in ones environment for its presence. It produces gratification, happiness, and tranquil joyfulness in an environment. It clears the environment like a "breath of fresh air" and helps to change "bad" attitudes.

It can also increase ones clairaudient capabilities.

It can be used in the treatment of ruptures, hernia, strains, sprains, acidosis, and hearing problems.

Vibrates to the number 5.

TSAVORITE   [Astrological Sign of Sagittarius]

Tsavorite, a variety of grossular/grossularite, crystallizes in the form of masses, grains, dodecahedral crystals, trapezohedral crystals, and combinations of dodecahedral and trapezohedral crystals. The colour is emerald green. The properties listed below are in addition to those listed in the GROSSULAR/GROSSULARITE section of this book.

The message and activities of this mineral culminate in the directive "know thyself".

It helps to stimulate the knowledge, within the inner self, that each person is the ruler of his/her own destiny, and that this ruling must be accomplished with love, or the ruler forfeits the position. It helps one to live within this concept and to reflect the eternal love to the outer world.

It also provides for a connection with the higher planes, facilitating contact with the spiritual world, enhancing channeling, and helping to produce visions. The energy of tsavorite helps one to feel the connection via sensitivity, rather than to see via the physical. This stone has been used to facilitate contact with, and to receive information from, both the Egyptian and Greek gods who represent learning, prudence, wisdom, and magic.

Tsavorite can be used to assist one in psychic communications and in pursuits relative to telepathic connections. The crystalline formation and the faceted configuration is extremely powerful for this and all other applications.

It can be used in the treatment of disorders of the senses - hearing, smell, sight, taste, touch, and thought.

Vibrates to the number 3.

TSILASITE   [See Yellow Tourmaline]

TSUMEBITE   [Astrological Sign of Gemini]

Tsumebite crystallizes in the form of crusts, tabular crystals, and six-rayed configurations consisting of three individual crystals. The colour is emerald green.

This mineral can be used to provide equality, familiarity, or intimacy with that which is desired. It stimulates the elimination of problems, when directed properly. It provides for measurement in ones endeavors, providing information concerning each step, no matter how small. It can provide direction in ones life and can bring awareness in action [e.g., thought before speech/action]. It can also be used to bring a synthesis to the well-being of the physical and subtle bodies. It stimulates the action of the heart chakra, bringing love and compassion to a situation.

It activates the inventive side of ones nature, bringing originality to the thought processes and bringing enterprising actions to the physical plane.

Tsumebite can be used in the treatment of elimination and digestive disorders, and in problems of the heart and circulatory system. It can help in providing firmness to the physical.

Vibrates to the master number 33.

TUFA   [Astrological Sign of Taurus]

Tufa is a porous form of calcite, generally formed as a deposit from rivers and springs. The colour ranges from white to grey. It is the building block of the famous Pinnacles of the USA, rising like castles to a height of over 140 feet above the desert floor. The properties listed below are in addition to those listed in the CALCITE section of this book.

This mineral can be used to stimulate artistic pursuits. It acts as a foundation, allowing one to supplement and to build upon the talents previously manifested. It assists in providing flexibility in actions, and helps to dispel judgmental-ness. It is a fine stone to have within ones environment, providing for creative solutions, and amenability in relationships. It also provides for a connection to the creative energy of the higher-self.

It can be used in disorders related to weakness in the body; helping one to take action to correct those weaknesses.

It assists in providing for the assimilation of the minerals necessary for the proper nutrition of the body [excellent as an elixir], and can be used to promote a firm basis from which one can build the strength and vitality of each part of the body. It has also been helpful in the treatment of problems associated with spinal dis-alignment [promoting a connection with the optimum body, facilitating the transfer of corrective action, and assisting in the maintenance of the correct positioning and structuring of the vertebrae].

It can also be used in the treatment of disorders of the canals of the body and to stabilize and ameliorate disorders associated with RNA/DNA imbalances and deficiencies in Vitamins A and C.

Vibrates to the number 3.

TUGTUPITE   [Astrological Sign of Leo]

Tugtupite crystallizes in the form of pink or red compact masses.

This mineral acts to both open and clear the heart chakra.

It helps one to remember and provides support for one to address those events and conditions which have been ignored [either consciously or unconsciously] over the years.

It allows for one to deal with issues which, if left unattended, could at a later time cause dis-ease. It is both a preventive and corrective, also assisting, during periods of dis-ease, to bring the cause to the conscious level of awareness.

Tugtupite stimulates compassion, for others and for the self. It is not a stone for sympathy, but one to facilitate understanding. It also enhances self-expression.

It can be used for gridding an environment in order to produce a continuity of action between those within the area.

It also acts to stimulate the growth of houseplants and to bring a freshness to ones surroundings.

It has been used to stabilize the equilibrium and to relieve motion sickness. It can be used in the treatment of stress, in the prevention of falls, to increase ones agility, to reduce swelling and growths, and to provide for the elimination of emotional disturbances.

Vibrates to the number 4.

TUNNELLITE   [Astrological Sign of Libra]

Tunnellite crystallizes in the monoclinic system in a pearly colourless shade.

This mineral provides a nourishment of energy and love for the operations of mental creation. The energy tends to be accumulated and directed toward the desired objective to facilitate attainment.

It can promote the removal of ethereal "cords" which are sent by others to ones chakras and to assist one in retrieving those "cords" which are personally transmitted. This is accomplished by only carrying this stone and without conscious focus on the removal.

It can also stimulate the Beta state of brain waves and can promote creativity and achievement of ones dreams.

Tunnellite has also been used to increase ones prowess in telekinesis and levitation. It strengthens the "silver cord" during astral travel and assists one in "reading" auras.

It has been used to provide a healthy glow to the skin, to allay wrinkles, and to stimulate elasticity in the skin and muscular system. It can also be used in the treatment of disorders of the arteries, the fluid of the spine, and in the amelioration of cataracts.

Vibrates to the number 3.

TUNGSTENITE   [Astrological Sign of Leo]

Tungstenite crystallizes in the form of grey foliates, scales and masses.

This mineral can be used to connect one to the spiritual plane and to encourage growth in that direction. It provides for the stimulation of the "idea" mechanism within the inner self, and is a good stone for assisting one to recognize, and to act upon, the "new". It can also provide the energy to advance the movement of the Kundalini.

It provides for stamina in pursuits and promotes harmony between the spiritual and intellectual planes. It acts to bring one an orderly, undisturbed state of mind, conducive to introspection and deep thought.

It can be used to assist in the remediation of a coma, and to stabilize mental disorders and problems associated with loss of concentration.

Vibrates to the number 1.

TURGITE   [Astrological Sign of Taurus]

Turgite forms in stalactites, botryoidal masses, and fibers. The colour range includes brown, black, red, and yellow.

It synthesizes the qualities of GOETHITE, HEMATITE, and LIMONITE, as reported within this book and further acts to relieve the feelings and the characteristics of aging.

It has been used to incite intuition and self-knowledge and brings relief to troubled emotional patterns.

It can be used to assist one in seeing the aura, to clear the "muddiness" from layers of the aura, and to stimulate well-ness.

Vibrates to the number 1.

TURQUOISE   [Astrological Signs of Sagittarius, Pisces, & Scorpio]

Turquoise crystallizes in the form of masses, stalactites, veins, crusts, and, rarely, short small, and brilliantly coloured, prismatic crystals [found in Virginia, USA].

Turquoise is another gift from the Earth, bringing the blue of Father Sky to the Earth and melding together the energies of the heavens with the consciousness of Mother Earth.

It strengthens and aligns all chakras, meridians, and subtle bodies. It actually elevates all chakras and can facilitate attunement between the physical level and the higher planes of existence. It can bring any and all energies to a higher level. It does, however, primarily stimulate the throat, heart, and naval chakras, bringing communication skills to emotional issues, to creativity, and to intuition, while allowing for the application of love in all issues.

It is excellent for spiritual attunement, for healing and cleansing of both the energy centers and the physical body, and for providing protection. It has been said that turquoise changes color to warn of impending danger and/or to indicate infidelity in thought or action. It can be used to protect against environmental pollutants as well.

It is valuable for grounding and can help to prevent one from loosing touch with the conscious mind during deep meditations; this facilitates a "no mind" meditative state, but provides the unconscious mind with a "knowing" of the protective mechanism which has been initiated.

It can be used for attunement between those of the physical plane, as well as between one and the spirit world. It is valuable to provide strength and protection during vision quests and astral travel. It is of high spirituality and can bring both valour and protection on the spiritual level, and from the etheric plane. It is also a stone of Earth-grounding; hence, one can remain grounded during spiritual "work". It acts to improve meditation and to further peace of mind.

Turquoise is a healer of the spirit, providing for a soothing energy and bringing peace of mind. It has also been known to guide one through the unknown, protecting while promoting ones independence in action.

It was used in ancient times to insure property and to protect against accidents. It has been esteemed, by the Tibetan shamen, as holding both a spiritual and protective property. It has been used in shamanic ceremonies and in the sacred valley of Shambhala. It has also been considered, by the Native American Indians, to be both a protective stone and a bestower of goodness.

It can be used to balance the male/female aspects of ones character, bringing forth the qualities of mental clarity and spiritual clarity, and providing for the balancing of energies. It also provides for a bit of an increase in ones psychic powers, and can help one to develop ones natural powers. It is said to assist one in communication activities, both written and oral, such that, that which is relayed to others is direct and correct.

It acts to induce wisdom and understanding, and to enhance trust, kindness, and the recognition of beauty. It is said to promote spontaneity in issues of romance and to stimulate the initiation of romantic love.

It has been used extensively in "cloud-busting" [initiating rain]; it has also been used by Native American shamen to initiate rain [the methods of choice included throwing the turquoise into a river or holding it under running water].

Turquoise is also a master healer, emanating a purifying energy which tends to dissipate negativity; it is an excellent anti-negativity stone [where the negativity is not within the self]. It can be used for emotional, mental and physical problems. In ancient times, it was used to heal eye problems [especially cataracts]. It has been used to strengthen work animals. It acts to strengthen the entire anatomy, and can be helpful in the amelioration of all dis-eases and disorders. It can aid in the absorption of nutrients, can help to stimulate the regeneration of tissue, and can act to increase circulatory flows to the muscular tissue. It has been used in the treatment for headaches and in the repair of physical damage which has impacted the body. It has also been used to assist one in maintaining stability during ambulatory motions. An elixir has been used to ameliorate skin disorders which were due to stress.

To facilitate the properties, turquoise may be held for attunement, taken as an elixir, worn, carried, or placed in ones environment.

The turquoise crystals provide a doubling effect of the properties and produce a total polarization of the physical with the subtle bodies.

Vibrates to the number 1.

HAVE NO EXPECTATIONS...

ACCEPT THE BEST

ULEXITE   [Astrological Sign of Gemini]
                                         [Also Known as T-V Rock]

Ulexite crystallizes in the form of silky white fibrous aggregates and rounded masses of fine fibrous crystals.

This mineral can create a clear path to balance the yin-yang energies, bringing the qualities of clarity and clear spirit, and balancing of the subtle bodies.

It helps one to see into a problem in order to actualize a resolution. It helps one to see into others, reading thoughts and evaluating words. It helps one to see within the self, allowing for the attunement to ones spirituality <u>and</u> to the outer dimensions in order to facilitate harmonious polarization.

Ulexite brings solutions to the mind and stimulates an appraising perspective, allowing one to see that which would normally be concealed. It can be used to stimulate the third-eye and to assist in the interpretation of visions.

Using this stone can be rather addictive; awareness to the other facets of life is recommended [i.e., one may be tempted to procrastinate in other areas of ones life so that more time can be utilized in working with ulexite].

It further stimulates the imagination, enhancing creativity in the areas of business and acting to supplement the materials and possessions which one desires.

It can also be used in the treatment of disorders of the eyes, bringing a brightness and sparkle to the iris which tends to emanate from within ones being.

Vibrates to the number 8 and the master number 33.

ULLMANNITE   [Astrological Sign of Aquarius]

Ullmannite crystallizes in the form of masses, and, occasionally, pyritohedral crystals and tetrahedral crystals. The colour ranges from a metallic grey to white.

This mineral can be used to increase the amount of information one can both assimilate and retain in short periods of time. It diminishes laziness, and facilitates aggrandizement.

It is an excellent stimulant for the practical nature and can be used to further ones advancement in areas of employment and hobbies.

It can be used in the treatment of cellular disorders, cancer, and inflammation of tissue. It can also be used to strengthen the arms and the grasping properties of the hands [as well as the mind]. It has been used with the infirm to provide insight to purpose and to assist in the renewal of the will.

Do not use prepare an elixir of this mineral via the normal method.

Vibrates to the number 4.

UNAKITE   [Astrological Sign of Scorpio]

Unakite usually crystallizes in the form of a mottled rock consisting of, mainly, pink feldspar, green epidote, and quartz.

In addition to the properties listed in the FELDSPAR, EPIDOTE, and QUARTZ sections of this book, this mineral can be used to enhance visions on the ethereal plane.

It brings ones consciousness to the present, allowing those "easy" times of unconscious action to dissipate.

It further acts to balance the emotional body, bringing it into alignment with the higher forces of spirituality.

It can facilitate the re-birthing process and can help one to deal with both the information and the events of the past which have instilled blockages within the meridians and energy centers of the body. It provides for a gentle release of those conditions which have been inhibiting ones growth.

It can be used to help one to go "beneath" the physical symptoms of dis-ease and to allow for the determination of the root cause underlying the condition; the cause becoming apparent in the cases of the physical, mental, emotional, and spiritual planes of existence.

Unakite can be used to enhance weight gain such that the weight is added in the areas chosen; i.e., manifestation of where those added pounds should be "stationed". It can be used in the treatment of the reproductive system, and to stimulate healthy pregnancies while facilitating the health of the unborn.

Vibrates to the number 9.

USSINGITE

Ussingite crystallizes in the formation of rolled masses in the triclinic system. The colour ranges from pink to red-violet. This is one of the new minerals which is now available from Russia.

This mineral has been used to provide an aperture through which one may investigate the other bodies. It is an excellent mineral for providing explanatory information concerning the correlation between ones physical, astral, emotional, intellectual, spiritual, etheric, and other inner and outer bodies.

It can encourage the strength of ventures, expediting knowledge of the location of that which is mislaid in the physical world. It further incites the memory of the gift of recall which is intrinsic to humanity.

Ussingite has also been used to stimulate forgiveness and to ameliorate feuds.

It is a macrocosmic mineral, bringing the knowledge of universal truths. It has been used to assist one in the study of the arts and sciences and in the realm of mathematics.

This mineral can be used to ameliorate impotency, to relieve hypertension, anemia, and over-production of white blood cells in the body. It can also enhance the production of T-cells, and can balance the acid/alkaline state of the body. It is a stabilizing influence on the body temperature and has been used to decrease the free radicals in the body.

Vibrates to the number 6.

UVAROVITE   [Astrological Sign of Aquarius]

Uvarovite, a variety of green garnet, crystallizes in the form of masses, grains, dodecahedral crystals, trapezohedral crystals, and combinations of dodecahedral and trapezohedral crystals. The colour is emerald green. In addition to the properties listed in the GARNET section of this book, the following qualities apply.

This mineral helps one to recognize the universal/galactic/endless nature of the soul. Once the thought is recognized, the action can be taken to live with the connected-ness of "All That Is". It furthers precision and acts to transform the energy of intellectual sentiment into the energy of love, such that one may be as love.

It bestows peace, quiet, and solitude - without loneliness. It promotes clarity in the mental processes, stimulates the heart chakra, and provides for enhancement of relationships via the fusion of the souls - one purpose, one mind.

It also encourages patriotism.

Uvarovite can be used in the treatment of acidosis, disorders of the heart and lungs, leukemia, kidney and bladder infections and disorders, and frigidity. It can assist in the removal of toxins from the body [providing a clear route for dismissal].

Vibrates to the number 7.

TIME BECOMES SACRED AS ONE LIVES IT

VALENCIANITE   [Astrological Signs of Virgo & Cancer]

Valencianite is a form of Adularia [orthoclase/feldspar] which is usually found in the form of crystals configured with eight sides, four which are trapezoidal and four which are triangular. It is found only in the silver mines of Valencia, Mexico. The colour range includes white, yellow, red, and colourless.

In addition to the properties listed in the ADULARIA, ORTHOCLASE, and FELDSPAR sections of this book, Valencianite also synthesizes the energies of SILVER.

It can also assist one in facilitating negotiations and has been used to increase sales. It serves to bring energy to situations of arbitration and can inspire settlement. It is excellent for lawsuits and for utilization in court rooms.

It has been used to raise ones conscious awareness, to enhance the life-force, and to stimulate connection with the higher-self.

Valencianite has been used in the treatment of MS and for degeneration of the muscular structure.

Vibrates to the number 7.

VALENTINITE   [Astrological Signs of Gemini & Cancer]

Valentinite crystallizes in the form of white prismatic crystals.

This mineral produces the energy of the sublime. It stimulates both the heart chakra and the crown chakra and provides for a feeling of well-being throughout ones physical body; this well-being facilitates connection to the higher-self and to the astral plane. It has been known to bring a "spring" to ones step.

It helps in communication, bringing the love of the heart to the actualization of the spoken word. It facilitates relationships of physical love, as well as spiritual love. It can bring a loved-one close in heart and mind, and can enhance the telepathic and electrical connections between each two emotional, physical, intellectual, and spiritual bodies.

It enhances the meditative state and assists in the entry to same; it helps one to realize that meditation is not a luxury, and that, in fact, it is frequently quite necessary for the preservation of ones inner peace.

It can also facilitate contact with ones totem in the spirit world; providing for initial contact and the "introductory phase", and furthering additional teamwork.

It can be used to provide for immunity to infectious dis-ease, and can be used in the treatment of frigidity [female], and in the treatment of disorders of the heart, lungs, larynx, esophagus, stomach, and upper intestines.

Vibrates to the number 5.

VANADINITE   [Astrological Sign of Virgo]

Vanadinite crystallizes in the form of globular masses, barrel-shaped crystals, and hollow prismatic crystals. The colour range includes bright ruby red, orange, yellow, brown-yellow, and red-brown.

This mineral can facilitate the mental processes, filling the vacancy between thought and intelligence.

It can also provide for a deep state of meditation, allowing the mind to be entirely "void of course".

Prior to this utilization of the stone, one can consciously decide whether to use the meditative state as a vehicle of emptiness, or as a vehicle to further the psychic process and to provide visions with respect to pre-defined questions.

Vanadinite can promote thrift in spending; either conserving ones energy or ones money. It is a good stone for those who have tendencies to overspend.

It can promote order to ones life, helping one to define the goals and to pursue these goals in an orderly manner.

The hollow prismatic crystals hold an additional property of facilitating a clear center, flowing from the crown, through the core of the body, and to the feet. The clearing and opening of this center provides for pure un-manifested energy to fill the body, stimulating the remainder of the chakras, and providing for a deep peace within the soul. The energy which flows into and through the center of the body provides for the alignment with the optimum self and furthers the transfer of perfection from the optimum self to the level of the cellular structures of the physical body.

Vanadinite can be used in the treatment of exhaustion, breathing disorders, asthma, lung congestion, and dysfunctions of the bladder. It can also facilitate ease with respect to circular breathing - the circular breathing which is conducive to entering meditative states.

Do not prepare an elixir of this mineral via the normal method.

Vibrates to the number 9.

VARISCITE   [Astrological Signs of Scorpio, Taurus, & Gemini]

Variscite crystallizes in the form of nodules, veins, masses, crusts, crystalline aggregates, and octahedral crystals. The colour ranges from pale to emerald green.

This mineral can be used to both connect and align the ethereal nervous system to the physical nervous system. This allows for the flow of messages of "need" from the physical to the ethereal; and for the flow of "energy fulfilling the need" from the ethereal to the physical. It can bring one from the "valley of despair" to a level of calm and peaceful existence.

It can be helpful in dealing with the invalid, to provide for the courage to continue, and to promote the tenacity to deal with, the situation [for both parties].

It stimulates the heart chakra to bring love, with reasoning, to all situations.

It can be used in the treatment of abdominal distention, constricted blood flow, excessive blood flow, impotency [male], and in disorders of the male reproductive system. It can help to regenerate the elasticity in the veins and skin.

Vibrates to the number 7.

VAUXITE   [Astrological Sign of Pisces]

Vauxite crystallizes in the form of radial aggregates and tabular crystals. The colour ranges from sky blue to deep blue, and exhibits pleochroism in the range of almost colourless to blue.

This mineral can promote the settling of disputes without emotional trauma. It eliminates annoying attitudes, and allows one to bring peace to the inner core of being in order to be able to both totally overlook, and to be unaffected by, that which would originally have been considered an annoyance.

It allows one to eliminate being "put upon" by others; bringing the strength of character to allow ones actions to not reflect the expectations of another.

It stimulates the visions of the third-eye and enhances the actions of trance channeling; allowing for awareness of that which is being transmitted, for total memory recall, and for the verbalization of all transactions.

It can be used as an anti-diuretic, to dispel fever, and to aid in the assimilation of the nutrients in vegetables.

Vauxite often occurs with quartz; this combination produces a mineral containing the properties of both the vauxite and the quartz.

Vibrates to the number 3.

VERDITE   [Astrological Sign of Pisces]

Verdite is a serpentine-like mineral, occurring in a deep green colour, sometimes mottled with red, yellow, white, or light green patches.

This mineral can be used to access, and to gain information from, the ancient ones, on both the spirit plane and in "settings" which appear to be identical to the "settings" of a specific time period. It can increase ones fortitude and constancy, thereby promoting ones reliability within the physical plane; it also seems to allow the ancient beings to "know" that the holder of the stone is a stable individual who will use any information for the good of all.

It helps to combat abrasive character traits, providing a polish to even those "steel" characters.

It can also help to stimulate the energy centers of the first four chakras in order to encourage the movement of the Kundalini, marking the progression through the spiritual plane.

Verdite can be used to cleanse the blood, to treat disorders of the heart, to provide anti-poison balances during toxic states, to assist in raising diminished levels of oxygenation within the body, and to counterbalance dizziness. It can also be used to treat genital disorders.

Vibrates to the number 2.

VESUVIANITE   [See Idocrase]

VESZELYITE   [Astrological Signs of Capricorn & Taurus]

Veszelyite crystallizes in the form of granular aggregates and prismatic crystals. The colour ranges from green to blue.

This mineral can be used to clear the mind of matters of triviality. It provides for the balance of both emotions and sexuality, for the stimulation of both intuition and creativity, and for a profitable outlet for desire. It helps one during periods of change and provides a multitude of insights with respect to the available options.

It brings the energy to actualize talent in acting and in participating in the dramatic aspects of situations; providing, in addition, the necessity to laugh at the meaningless aspects of the drama.

It also enhances ones abilities in the pursuit of mathematics, stimulating analytical thinking and inducing the mental state required for problem-solving.

It provides for truthfulness and for conformity to the truth of ones nature. It affords the ability of "correctness" when one is participating in ceremonial activities and when one accesses the spirit world or other physical presences from other worlds.

It promotes fluency in self-expression and in reporting the details of visions, intuitive encounters, and psychic experiences. It further allows one to understand the meanings inherent to these activities.

Veszelyite can be very helpful in the treatment of inveterate dis-ease. It can also be used in the treatment of intestinal absorption problems, viral disorders, and bacterial infections. It can enhance stability in ambulatory disorders, can help to correct posture, and provides energy to the mending of bones.

Vibrates to the number 4.

VIVIANITE   [Astrological Sign of Capricorn]

Vivianite crystallizes in the form of prismatic crystals, stellate groupings, reniform and globular masses, incrustations, and fibers. The colour range includes blue to green and colourless.

The energy of this mineral tends to convey both love and the inspiration for life. It produces a glowing and pulsating beauty to the user.

It has been used in the study of cereology [the analysis of crop markings], bringing information concerning purpose and methods. It can also provide details concerning interrelationships which were awakened during the time of construction.

It is a stone for goal-setting and for attainment of same. It assists one in recognizing that an optimistic goal may always be achieved over the obstacles of reality and the reflections of memory. It further assists one in the specific delineation of intent, bringing right-minded-ness and the knowledge of the clarity of the path.

Vivianite has been used to increase the assimilation of iron, to decrease the presence of free-radicals within the body, to assist in the alignment of the spine, and to treat degeneration of the iris of the eye.

Do not prepare an elixir of this mineral via the normal method.

Vibrates to the number 3.

**THE ULTIMATE WISDOM CANNOT BE EXPRESSED,
IT CAN ONLY BE KNOWN**

[r.r.jackson, 1990]

Wad crystallizes in the form of amorphous and reniform masses and as incrustations and stains. The colour range includes black, blue, and tan to brown.

This mineral has been used to assist one in walking away from people or situations that one finds emotionally upsetting, bringing the knowledge that to remove the self from the situation is not an admission of defeat but a sign of wisdom. It further instills self-confidence and helps to show one that there is truly a difference between selfless-ness and selfish-ness; Wad truly serves to provide permission for one to care about the self. It also assists to provide one with an air that combined liberality with general indifference - especially during situations of stress and tension.

It has also been used to eliminate shyness, modesty, and embarrassment; it tends to show one that perfection has not yet been attained upon the Earth plane and that when one is less than perfect, it is a time to learn and to grow - happily and with humour.

It provides a comforting energy for all occasions and acts to soothe ones emotional bodies.

Wad has been used to assist in the assimilation of manganese and iron. It can also be used in the treatment of cancer, to assist in the decomposition of growths and tumors, and to bring relief from pain. It has shown an antibiotic tendency when applied to bacterial and viral infections.

If the mineral exhibits a softness, do <u>not</u> prepare an elixir of same via the normal method.

Vibrates to the number 1.

WADEITE   [Astrological Sign of Leo]

Wadeite crystallizes in the form of prismatic crystals which exhibit hexagonal cross-sections. The colour range includes light pink, lilac, and colourless.

This mineral can be used to combat irrational thoughts, allowing for the leveling of the mental faculties and the "mellowing" of the level of stress one is experiencing.

It helps to take the "labor" out of progress, lending the experience and foresight to facilitate reaching the goal.

The stimulation of the heart chakra and the connection to the higher mind appears to be a primary contributor to the actions facilitated by this stone.

In times of danger, it provides for a protective barrier around the physical body and "seals-out" the peril. It also provides for an electrical connection to the ethereal body during this period, and transmits the message of possible personal jeopardy; the ethereal body, in turn, acts to send a message to the ethereal body from whence the threat is coming, and the peril is released to the ethers and transformed into the white light of healing.

Wadeite has been said to be useful in levitation.

It can also be used in the treatment of disorders of speech, dysfunctions of the voluntary muscle system, and stomach upsets. It can assist in the process of enhancing fat solubility and removal. It has been used to strengthen the muscular structure.

Vibrates to the number 4.

WAGNERITE   [Astrological Signs of Libra & Virgo]

Wagnerite crystallizes in the form of masses and prismatic crystals. The colour range includes yellow, red, green, and grey-to-brown.

This mineral can stimulate good-naturedness and humour; it assists to incite laughter, the real laughter which is initiated at the naval chakra.

It can facilitate ease of movement and acrobatic and gymnastic endeavors.

It and can also provide for "mini-trips" on the astral plane; this mineral does not facilitate the astral travel, but assists in designing the experience and in providing insight to the realm of short trips which would be available. Please note that in the case of short trips, the benefit is primarily the diversification of situations which one is able to see - all presenting the same relevant information in a variety of ways; this helps the traveler to clearly understand the situation which is being researched.

It can also provide "signals" to the user with respect to matters of love; these signals alert one to sincerity, insincerity, respect, disrespect, etc., and allow one to recognize the duality of nature. It promotes the stimulus to help one to change that duality to a singularity governed by love.

Wagnerite can be used in the treatment of disorders of elimination [body or mind] and water retention. It can also be used to enhance the absorption of minerals by the blood stream. It can be useful in the diagnosis of infections, providing insight to the cause and suggesting the remedy.

Vibrates to the number 3.

WAKEFIELDITE   [Astrological Sign of Gemini]

Wakefieldite crystallizes in the form of yellow masses.

This mineral can stimulate the intellect and can activate the innate power within the self. It provides for patience and awareness in all matters of the physical world. It also allows for the conscious relinquishing of negativity inherent in ones being.

The stone also is protective; it provides one with enhanced intuitive capabilities which are activated during times of danger.

Wakefieldite can be used in the treatment of hormonal imbalance, to stabilize and to regulate the quantities of hormones being released to the body. It can also be used in the amelioration of congestion of the lungs and of conditions producing jaundice. It has been used to alleviate insomnia.

Vibrates to the number 2.

WARDITE   [Astrological Signs of Virgo & Scorpio]

Wardite crystallizes in the form of fibrous aggregates and pyramid-like crystals. The colour range includes pale green, blue, white, and colourless.
This mineral can be used to provide for progress in activities of communication and compassion. The progress, once initiated, is enhanced to proceed at a moderate and comfortable pace.

It is good for pursuits in business and to assist one in the process. It acts to stimulate a positive outcome in situations of bankruptcy.

Wardite also assists in elevating ones self-esteem and enhances the "outgoing" aspects of ones personality; this enhancement produces a genuineness and a natural depth to conversational skills - eliminating the need for the empty attributes of the "jokester".

This mineral can be used in the treatment of the general symptoms of weakness - in body, mind, or spirit. It is a good purification stone, and enhances the purity of liquids. It can be used in garden areas to inhibit the growth of "weeds".

Vibrates to the number 8.

WAVELLITE   [Astrological Sign of Aquarius]

Wavellite crystallizes in the form of radial aggregates, crusts, globe-like shapes with crystalline surfaces, and needle-like crystals. The colour range includes green, white, yellow, brown, black, blue, and colourless.

This mineral assists one in looking "at the whole picture" prior to decision-making. It allows for distraction from the focal point of an issue while promoting attentiveness to all of the out-lying details. It helps one to manage difficult situations and provides information to the inner self such that one can recognize both the direct and the indirect methods of accomplishing a task.

It is especially effective, during the period of the new moon, to increase the intuitive abilities and to activate inner knowledge.

It can also facilitate the flow of energy from the ethereal body to the physical body, producing an increased stability with respect to health and health maintenance within the physical body.

Wavellite can be used in the treatment of flows; energy flows, blood flows, etc.; it can provide assistance in balancing the white blood cell count with the red blood cell count and can facilitate the normalization of that ratio. It can also be used in the treatment of dermatitis.

Vibrates to the number 1.

WEEKSITE   [Astrological Sign of Pisces]

Weeksite crystallizes in the orthorhombic system and is often found as druse and crusts upon host minerals. The colour is yellow.

This mineral has been used to assist one in scheduling activities and has also promoted accuracy during inventory projects. The energy stimulates the memory and brings analytical capabilities to the user.

It has been used to increase mental awareness and to instill the knowledge that, as Somerset Maugham said, "Only a mediocre person is always at his best". With the energy of Weeksite, mediocrity is expelled from ones mentality and brilliance is welcomed.

It further represents meditative analytical thought and intellectual activity and brings stimulation for personal power, ambition, intellect, astral force, desire and emotions based on intellect, and touch.

In addition, it serves to bring strength to the aperture of the solar plexus chakra and the crown chakra, and promotes the opening and/or closure at will.

It has been used in the treatment of disorders of the stomach, liver, gall bladder, sympathetic nervous system [activating involuntary muscles which enhance the mobilization of the physical body], pancreas, and adrenal glands.

Do not prepare an elixir of this mineral via the normal method.

Vibrates to the number 7.

WHERRYITE   [Astrological Sign of Virgo]

Wherryite crystallizes in the form of masses, fibrous aggregates, and needle-like crystals. The colour range includes light green, yellow, and from bright yellow to green.

This mineral is a "caretaker" - placing the user under protective aspects which facilitate the continuity of personal power.

Wherryite does not interfere with ones goals, but stimulates a loving kindness from the inner self which provides a barrier to problems.

It is helpful in the elimination of hostilities, providing for attentiveness to detail and for a quality of watchfulness within the user. It enhances pursuits of logic and reasoning.

It can also be used in the treatment of fatigue, mental instability, and disorders related to fluid retention and swelling.

Vibrates to the number 5.

WHITLOCKITE [Astrological Sign of Leo]

Whitlockite crystallizes in the form of rhombohedral crystals. The colour range includes pink, white, yellow, and grey.

This mineral can be used to help one to "make a last stand" on issues and contentions emanating from the emotional side of ones nature. It provides for intellectual stimulation to allow for the recognition of the information which is required to support a situation. It acts to increase the extent, quantity, quality, and intensity of power - balancing that power with love. It promotes firmness of mind, mellowed by a sympathetic response to the plight of others.

It can be used in the treatment of disorders of the hands, which are related to grasping qualities. It can also provide for assistance in disorders of the mouth [not the teeth], and in the treatment of the other mucus membranes within the body.

Vibrates to the number 9.

WILKEITE [Astrological Sign of Aries]

Wilkeite crystallizes in the form of masses or rounded crystals. The colour range includes pale pink and yellow.

This mineral is often found in blue calcite. In addition to the properties listed below, the qualities associated with the combination of wilkeite and blue calcite also include properties which are listed in the CALCITE section of this book.

This mineral smooths the energy fields of the body and provides for stability in the surrounding force-field. It does not provide a protective barrier, but acts as a tool to both repel and deflect attacks on the psychic level.

It can also be attached to the mid-section of a "cloud-busting" rod to facilitate an increase in the energy field and to further and to enhance the directional aspects of the rod.

Wilkeite can be used in the treatment of obesity, to decrease odors of the body and mouth, to assist in the treatment of disorders of the trachea, and as a general antiseptic.

Vibrates to the number 4.

WILLEMITE [Astrological Sign of Gemini]

Willemite crystallizes in the form of grains, fibrous compact masses, and short hexagonal prismatic crystals. The colour range includes colourless, white, green, red, yellow, brown, and grey.

This mineral provides a "welcoming" aspect to those beginning the journey toward spirituality and psychic development. It provides for a favorable position to "initiates", such that the doors to the other planes of existence are opened and the pathway is free of obstructions. It alleviates intensities and apprehensions which are sometimes experienced during "first time" activities.

Willemite can be used as a mirror to the soul, one to stimulate seeing oneself from outside of the body. This sight is without judgmental attitudes and can provide a stepping-stone to the furtherance of ones growth toward enlightenment. It can provide one with patience and perseverance in the tasks chosen, allowing one to understand the underlying reasons for the tasks.

It can be used in the treatment of dizziness, fungus infections, and hepatitis. It has been used to increase the assimilation of Vitamin A and to ameliorate disorders associated with clear vision of the eyes.

Vibrates to the number 9.

WILLEMSEITE [Astrological Sign of Taurus]

Willemseite crystallizes in monoclinic system in the colour of light green.

This mineral stimulates empathy, regard, group understanding, and a spirituality which is associated with a "oneness" with "All That Is". It provides for an integration between the loving energy of the heart and the analytical energy of the intellect. It promotes the contribution of the energies of love and compassion to all of the chakras.

It represents softness in strength, compassion, empathy, and unconditional love, and brings a soothing, smoothing, healing, exhilarated energy to fulfil anticipation.

It has been used to re-vitalize the heart, thymus, circulatory system, blood, cellular structure, and the involuntary muscles which assist in the restoration of physical energy.

Due to the softness of this mineral, it is recommended that an elixir is <u>not</u> prepared via the normal method.

Vibrates to the number 2.

WILLIAMSITE   [Astrological Signs of Gemini & Sagittarius]

Williamsite crystallizes in the formation of masses, fibers, and foliates. The colour range includes green, red, and yellow.

This mineral can be used to bring a cohesive action between one and the object of ones desires, such that one may easily relinquishment same whenever necessary and/or whenever it has completed its purpose.

It brings an energy of innovation and honesty and serves to instill honor and candor.

In addition, the energy of Williamsite assists one in "discovering" the characteristic within the self which are genuine; it serves to clear the programs of the past and allows one to recognize the domineering techniques which have been used by the self and by others. It assists one in detachment from the regulation of others, but assists one in maintaining control with respect to ones life.

It has been used in telepathic endeavors to both send and to receive messages, assisting one in assuring delivery and acceptance of the information.

Williamsite has been used in the treatment of disorders of the veins and arteries, the pores of the skin (i.e., inflammations and abrasions), lung disorders (including emphysema and irritations precipitating coughs), multiple sclerosis, tissue regeneration, and chronic fatigue.

Do <u>not</u> prepare an elixir of this mineral via the normal method.

Vibrates to the number 6.

WITHERITE   [Astrological Signs of Pisces & Leo]

Witherite crystallizes in the form of masses, columns, and horizontally striated hexagonal-type double pyramid crystals. The colour range includes white, grey, and occasionally, tinges of yellow, green, or brown.

This mineral helps to "whisk-away" ones troubles and to clear the mind of the insignificant.

It conducts one into the meditative state by facilitating the diminishment of mental activity and by inducing a calmness to surround the physical body.

It helps one in repetitive tasks, including exactness in the verbalization of those messages from the spirit world during channeling activities.

It can stimulate clarity of the aura during violent emotional or physical disturbances; hence, providing less impact on the physical structure from the undue stress.

It facilitates ones total involvement in issues of choice and can be used to dispel the "scattered-ness" often encountered in the daily routine.

Witherite can be used for communication with the energy of the stars in Ursa Minor; bringing contact, with a mental transfer of knowledge or with an energy transfer which stimulates both the completion and the understanding of theoretical proofs.

It can be used in the treatment of disorders of the digestive system, providing for a cleansing effect on the unitary whole. It can help to stimulate the thymus, to ameliorate dehydration, and to bring elasticity to the cellular structure of the body. It can also be used to ameliorate conditions of atrophy.

Vibrates to the number 9.

WOHLERITE   [Astrological Sign of Libra]

Wohlerite crystallizes in the form of grains, prismatic crystals, and tabular crystals. The colour range includes yellow and brown.

This mineral can be used to integrate the physical, emotional, intellectual, spiritual, ethereal, astral, ..., bodies to produce grounding of the energy and to further the access to the utilization of that energy at the physical level.

It can further assist in stimulating ones enthusiasm with life and to eliminate frenzy.

It promotes access to the multi-dimensional facets of the personality and assists one in stabilizing the mind sufficiently to facilitate alignment of communication channels between this world and further levels of development.

It can be used in the treatment of circulation disorders, chills, and nervous disorders, and to stimulate the processes of the body to complement the innate healthful-ness of the physical form.

Vibrates to the number 7.

WOLFRAMITE   [Astrological Signs of Libra & Gemini]

Wolframite crystallizes in the form of blades, plate-like layers, columns, tabular crystals, and prismatic crystals. The colour ranges from metallic grey to brownish-black.

This mineral can be used to provide strength for the physical body. It allows for control and regulation of the physical processes and facilitates expedient action without recklessness. At the same time it enhances flexibility in ones character; promoting the necessary skills for situational orderliness, while eliminating unsupported claims that "this way is the only way".

It also provides influence with respect to movement, furthering a "flowing with the situation" and eliminating control issues; it helps one to allow a situation to rectify naturally.

It can be used to gain information and insight into the "why" aspects of ones life. Quietly holding the stone and allowing each "why" issue to pass through the mind, one is given visions and, occasionally, actual writings, which provide the answers required.

Wolframite can be used in the treatment of the disorders associated with deficiencies of iron. It can also assist in the alleviation of hypoglycemia and in the correction of weakness of the sight. It can be useful in alignment of the vertebrae.

Vibrates to the number 5.

WOODHOUSEITE   [Astrological Sign of Taurus]

Woodhouseite crystallizes in the form of cube type crystals with curved striated faces. The colour ranges from white to pink.

This mineral can be used to eliminate the fermentation of anger within the body - hence, eliminating the effects of this emotion on the cellular structure. It brings a calm and peaceful love to the emotions and allows hostility to dissipate, providing for an obliteration, from memory, of the disconsolate and confused emotions <u>and</u> of the ostensible reasons behind the emotions.

It is a mineral for gaming, providing an edge in the material world - the gain proportional to the manifestation of personal power in the realm of receptivity to the intuition.

It enhances the interactive state of the subtle bodies, assisting in both the keen perception and the apt expression of the ensuing ideas which will assist one in personal endeavors.

Woodhouseite can allow one to understand the meaning of the concept that the physical body is the temple of the soul <u>and</u> that in order to learn the lessons and to gain the knowledge for which one journeyed to the Earth plane, the body must be treated with love and respect. It provides for insight into actions which would both facilitate the continuation of an optimum state <u>and</u> would further eliminate the detriments.

It can be used in the treatment of disorders associated with the internal organs and the flow of nerve impulses throughout the body, It has also been used to ameliorate mental discontinuity.

Vibrates to the number 6.

WOODWARDITE   [Astrological Signs of Pisces & Capricorn]

Woodwardite crystallizes in the form of rounded concretion structures. The colour ranges from blue to green.

This mineral can be used to bring creativity to the communication of matters of love and compassion. It stimulates an awareness in the emotions to direct desire toward the highest plane and to allow another the freedom which is conducive to unconditional love.

It promotes reflection into the self, acting to provide the clarity and the intuitive aspects which are necessary to stimulate answers to personal questions.

It also assists one in appearing favorable in matters of selection, bringing to one a "storehouse of supplies" to increase ones self-esteem and attractiveness.

It can be used to provide pain relief, and in the treatment of disorders relative to the internal arrangement of the body. It can also be useful in the treatment of affectations of the lungs and nasal passages.

Vibrates to the number 2.

WULFENITE [Astrological Sign of Sagittarius]

Wulfenite crystallizes in the form of masses, octahedral crystals, prismatic crystals, and square tabular crystals. The colour range includes yellow, golden, orange, green, grey, yellow-grey, brown, white, and colourless.

This mineral promotes the acceptance of the existence of the negative aspects which exist in the world, allowing one to recognize the issues and to not allow "roadblocks" to impede or limit progress toward development. This attribute allows one to recognize the authoritative games of this plane and to continue "in spite of" the potential limitations.

Wulfenite allows one to accomplish the transition, from the physical plane to the psychic and astral planes, with expedience. The time which is usually required to alter ones state is dramatically decreased.

It can be used to promote contact with the spiritual world in the form one manifests; allowing for attunement to those of ancient civilizations, to those of the near distant past, or to those of the futuristic worlds.

It facilitates the knowledge and practice of white magic.

It creates a strong connection between basic structures and higher dimensions, allowing for the channeling of vibrations to the Earth, and for the attunement to higher dimensions. It is quite useful for connecting to higher beings or to the higher-self. It stimulates a bonding between souls who are on the Earth plane and have agreed to meet again during this lifetime.

Wulfenite can be used for preservation and rejuvenation on all levels.

Vibrates to the number 7.

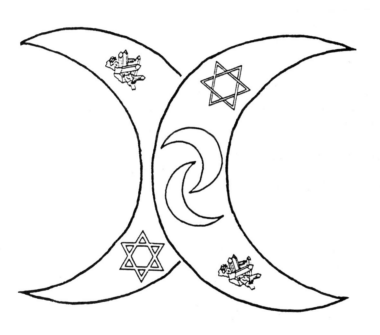

LOVE OPENS THE DOOR TO ECSTASY
LAUGHTER BRINGS JOY
LIFE IS YOURS

XANTHOCONITE   [Astrological Signs of Cancer & Scorpio]

Xanthoconite crystallizes in the form of masses and tabular crystals. The colour range includes yellow, red, and orange.

This mineral helps to increase the cohesiveness of relationships, groups, families, etc., providing for a focus toward any chosen goals.

It provides for stability and rationality in decisions.

It is also used as an auxiliary stone, enhancing the properties of other stones by facilitating a connected-ness between the energy of each.

It can help one to gain true insight into the prospective nature of an unborn child, and to receive knowledge, usually via visions, with respect to the past-life connections between the parents and the unborn child. It can also be similarly utilized to determine the connections between people who are currently on the Earth plane and between those on the Earth plane and those in the spirit world. Meditative access to this information requires specific identification of those involved in the query.

It can also be used to accelerate the healing of cuts, wounds, lacerations, and contusions; it acts to provide for mending on a higher level than the physical plane and to transmit the mended condition to the physical body.

Vibrates to the number 4.

XENOTIME   [Astrological Signs of Virgo & Taurus]

Xenotime crystallizes in the form of rolled grains, rosettes, and prismatic crystals. The colour range includes yellow, orange, red, red-brown, brown, green, and grey.

This mineral can be used to demonstrate that creativity and the laws of creation can produce whatever is desired as long as that which is desired is for the good of all.

It can provide one with the strength to rid one of parasitic attractions in ones life; culminating with the action of removing those from ones environment who feel that "since you have it all together, you **should** take care of us", in one way or another. It also works in the converse direction, allowing one to recognize ones own parasitic or sycophantic characteristics and inducing corrective action to eliminate that obstacle toward growth.

It can be used to facilitate the use of each moment, to dispense with the matters of triviality and to proceed toward ones goals with progress increasing at an exponential rate.

It can also be used to facilitate both the absorption and the metabolism of potassium and phosphorous, to bring the body into balance when there is an excess of alkalinity, to treat the root cause of cancer, and to assist in the elimination of parasites from the system.

Vibrates to the number 6.

XONOTLITE   [Astrological Sign of Leo]

Xonotlite crystallizes in the form of masses, fibers, and needle-like crystals. The colour range includes white, colourless, pink, and grey.

This mineral can be used to produce the stability of the energy of the electromagnetic field which surrounds the physical body. It expedites both the transfer and the receipt of information to/from those with whom one has initiated telepathic communication. With the stabilization of the electromagnetic field, the user can consciously link to another [after gaining permission to do so], for the purposes of development on the psychic and intuitive planes.

It can be used to bring one the inner connection between the physical and ethereal, providing for an "effortless effort" in ones activities. It also promotes the acceptance of realistic expectations.

It can be used in the treatment of tumors, growths, and intestinal disorders. It can also be used to balance the cholesterol levels within the body. Speech impairments have been improved with the conscious focusing of the energies. It can also stimulate the repair of varicose veins and superficial markings which have manifested due to disorders in, and due to the loss of the integrity of, the veins.

Vibrates to the master number 44.

BECOME ONE WITH THE EXISTENCE OF ALL

ZARATITE   [Astrological Signs of Virgo, Taurus, & Aries]
                                [Also Known as Emerald Nickel]

Zaratite crystallizes in the form of emerald green crusts and compact masses.

This mineral can be used to both enhance and fill any breach in the aura, and to protect ones spirit from "capture" by any physical means and/or psychic methods.

It can be used to stimulate visualization and to magnify the most important aspects of the vision, such that the message is not lost in the translation.

It can also be used to gain insight, sometimes from galactic information banks, into the ideals concerning metamorphosis and the alteration of states.

It can stimulate independence in employment and can provide for initiative in the both the pursuit and the attainment of ones personal goals.

It can be used in the treatment of fevers and chills. It can also be used in the diagnosis of disorders.

Vibrates to the numbers 1 and 4.

ZEBRA ROCK   [Astrological Signs of Gemini & Taurus]

Zebra Rock is a mixture of Quartz and Basalt, occurring in a zebra-type pattern. When polished, it occasionally has the appearance of agate.

In addition to the properties listed in the QUARTZ and BASALT sections of this book, this mineral brings one compassion and understanding for others; it serves to assist one in realizing that "If you see an empty house, it does not necessarily indicate that there is no one home". It helps one to look beneath the superficial attributes and to recognize the loving spirit which always abides.

It further teaches that it is not possible to give-away all of ones energy or ones love, but that the eternal source of energy and love is always available and accessible for augmentation.

Zebra Rock serves also to stimulate ones physical energy, even when the biorhythmic charts indicate a subsiding ebb of energy. It is a wonderful energy for athletes, to provide stamina and endurance.

It has been used in the treatment of bone loss, to ameliorate degeneration of the teeth and gums, for dryness of skin, and to assist in the alleviation of muscular spasms, heart palpitations, and vitamin deficiencies.

Vibrates to the number 9.

ZEOLITE   [Astrological Sign of All]

Zeolite is a group name for framework silicates with exchangeable cations; they are well-defined hydrous silicates. The minerals in this book which are in the Zeolite division include Inesite, Xonotlite, Ganophyllite, Pumpellyite, Okenite, Apophyllite, Pectolite, Prehnite, Phillipsite, Chabazite, Natrolite, etc.

It is said that all Zeolites have the capacity to assist in the improvement of the environment and to ethereally absorb toxic products and odors; gridding with Zeolites around waste dumps has been very effective.

Zeolites may also be used to improve agricultural pursuits.

They have been used to dispel bloating, to treat goiter, to eliminate alcohol addictions, and to release toxins from the body.

It is an excellent energy for Reiki, to further ones actions and to stimulate the proper response to the energies applied.

Until recently, Zeolites were said to never occur with Quartz; however, the Earth has produced this combination and lovely specimens are emerging from Pune, India. This combination melds the energy of the specific Zeolite with the energy of Quartz to produce a forceful and dominant energy!

ZINCITE   [Astrological Signs of Libra & Taurus]

Zincite crystallizes in the form of masses, grains, plate-like layers, and hexagonal hemimorphic crystals. The colour range includes deep red and orange-yellow.

This mineral provides for the synthesis of personal power, physical energy, and creativity, producing a stimulation of the electric currents within the body and facilitating the removal or gradual dissipation of energy blockages. It is useful in the radionics field to intensify the response patterns exhibited during use of the "check-surface".

It can help to bring together those of like-mind; it is useful in promoting the group effort, interlocking and providing for the unification of the resultant effects. It is also beneficial to furthering relationships on the physical plane.

Zincite can be used to improve the condition of the hair and the skin. It can also be used for treatment in disorders of the prostate gland. It can provide for purification via catharsis.

Vibrates to the number 5.

There is also a type of semi-natural Zincite which has been named "Polish Zincite"; this formation was produced in a Zinc mine in Poland, nearly 100 years ago, during a mine fire. Although the fire was naturally-occurring and was not due to the action of man, the mineralogical community has not yet accepted this Zincite as natural. This configuration, however, emits the same properties as the "natural" Zincite and further acts to increase the focal emanation of the energy and to enhance same. It has also been used to increase ones conscious connection with the higher realms, to align the subtle bodies with the physical form, to establish a highly-charged electrical connection which brings an electro-magnetic alignment to the physical body (wonderful for healing situations), and to increase mental clarity and perception.

The "Polish Zincite" vibrates to the number 3.

ZIRCON   [Astrological Signs of Virgo, Leo, & Sagittarius]

Zircon crystallizes in the form of grains and short square prismatic crystals, often exhibiting the double pyramid structure. The mineral is also found with curved faces and edges. The colour range includes red, brown, green, yellow, grey, and colourless.

It is known as a "stone of virtue", bringing ones virtuous nature back into the balance with the universal forces.

This mineral promotes unions: physical, mental, emotional, spiritual, etc. It combines the properties of the first, third, and fourth chakras, raising them to a higher level of intensity. It creates a dynamic illumination, via the intuitive self, and allows for the recognition of the "free zones" for travel and exploration.

It also acts to increase ones hardiness and to facilitate continuity in all endeavors.

The zircon symbolizes the central "deity", a force immutable and constant, which is synonymous with the recognition and with the understanding that we are all a part of "All That Is". It is here to remind us of our goals upon the evolutionary spiral and within the human realm.

It also symbolizes innocence, purity, and constancy.

In addition, it can be used to provide assistance in the treatment of disorders of the sciatic nerve and the nerve structures which lead away from the spinal vertebrae. It provides for help in increasing bone stability, in the treatment of vertigo, and in the mending of bones and muscles. It has been used as an antidote for poison.

Vibrates to the number 4.

ZOISITE   [Astrological Sign of Gemini]

Zoisite crystallizes in the form of masses and striated prismatic crystals which are, usually, not terminated. The colour range includes colourless, white, and pink [designated as thulite], colourless to blue or purple [designated as tanzanite], yellow, brown, green, and red.

This mineral can provide for decomposition of negativity and for transmutation of the negative energies to positive force-fields; the positive fields, containing more total energy than the totality of the energy contained in the negativity.

It can be used to dispel laziness and idleness.

It allows for direct connection, via the mental processes, to the celestial latitudes [especially during the astrological cycles of Gemini, Taurus, and Aries]; this can facilitate advancement in all areas of ones life.

It has been used in the treatment of disorders associated with the heart, spleen, pancreas, and lungs.

Zoisite masses occasionally occur with ruby scattered throughout the structure. This combination of stones is also known as anyolite, and is also listed in the ANYOLITE section of this book so that the reader will not overlook the highly energetic properties].

The zoisite and ruby conglomerate is quite magical; in addition to the properties listed above and the properties listed in the RUBY section of this book, the zoisite/ruby combination can create altered states of consciousness and can serve as a vehicle for reaching and utilizing talents and abilities of the mind. All of the psychic abilities can be stimulated and amplified by use of these consolidated energies. In addition, it provides for amplification of the entire energy field of the body. It has also been used by healers in the Asian countries for both diagnostic healing and communicating with the spirits.

The combination of zoisite and ruby increases the awareness of ones individuality while allowing one to maintain connected-ness with humanity. It enhances contact with the etheric bodies and stimulates the crown chakra toward spirituality. It can also create altered states of consciousness and can serve as a vehicle for both reaching and utilizing the talents and abilities of the mind. All of the psychic abilities can be stimulated and amplified via the use of these consolidated energies. In addition, it provides for amplification of the entire energy field of the body. It has also been used by healers in the Asian countries for both diagnostic healing and communicating with the spirits. It acts to improve disorders of the heart and to help one to recover from those disorders associated with diminished physical vitality.

Vibrates to the number 4.

ZUNYITE   [Astrological Sign of Sagittarius]

Zunyite crystallizes in the form of small tetrahedral crystals and twinned octahedral crystals. The colour range includes white and shades of grey to pink.

This mineral can be used in communication with the spirit world, in advancing ones imaginative talents, and in controlling mis-directed energies.

It couples the energies of serendipity with those of the heart, allowing for all aspects of communication to come from the heart.

It is a mineral for the facilitation of the advancement in the arts and for stimulation of the appreciation of the beauty of the naturalness of the all encompassing spirit.

It can also be used in the alleviation of pain, misery, sorrow, and the total range of suffering. It has been used to bring relief from both distress and mental torment, and can stimulate ones sensitivity to the inner causes of all disorders.

Vibrates to the number 3.

THE BEGINNING

INDEX

Earth (cont.) 620, 626, 627, 634, 635, 637, 638, 645, 646, 655, 656, 661, 662, 669, 687, 697, 698, 701, 706

Earth-keeper 53, 54, 101, 298, 305, 494, 602

earthquakes 248, 406

egoless 207, 317

Egypt 36, 39, 464, 571

Egyptian 31, 506, 520, 665

electro-magnetics 108

emetic 318, 325, 635

emotional body 122, 279, 427, 560, 570, 640, 674

emotions 39, 70, 71, 99, 132, 146, 153, 165, 177, 178, 185, 193, 205, 210, 219, 221, 224, 227, 235, 251, 257, 263, 276, 281, 291, 313, 316, 328, 341, 343, 349, 361, 362, 363, 364, 377, 385, 388-390, 395, 396, 402, 408, 421, 475, 481, 494, 503, 519, 526, 529, 562, 569, 570, 572, 576, 601, 604, 606, 608, 616, 627, 638, 639, 657, 659, 683, 691, 697

emphysema 97, 205, 207, 419, 460, 496, 548, 565, 694

employment 81, 184, 189, 199, 256, 260, 293, 294, 355, 449, 494, 575, 586, 600, 617, 639, 643, 660, 673, 705

endocrine 73, 111, 299, 489, 544, 545, 548, 651, 658

endorphins 187, 377, 601, 639

England 76, 661

enlightenment 38, 71, 75, 97, 236, 244, 305, 311, 334, 410, 422, 431, 497, 512, 513, 538, 574, 605, 615, 616, 644, 658, 693

envy 183, 402, 597

enzymes 231, 378, 612

epilepsy 124, 299, 350, 427, 520

epithelial tissues 180

equality 202, 377, 419, 665

equilibrium 113, 214, 246, 280, 316, 371, 378, 413, 455, 607, 633, 667

esophagus 296, 297, 621, 655, 680

ESP 507, 572, 597, 635

estrogen 494, 619, 639

ethereal 37, 69, 72, 74, 75, 79, 83, 84, 102, 108, 109, 119, 120, 128, 140, 164, 177, 188, 194, 205, 206, 209, 211, 218, 222, 235, 246, 251, 271, 289, 291, 296, 297, 302, 316, 345, 363, 364, 367, 388, 400, 412, 419, 427, 435,

ethereal (cont.) 436, 457, 458, 460, 469-471, 473, 484, 507, 513, 515, 516, 521, 524, 529, 536, 539, 545, 546, 548, 563, 574, 576, 584, 600, 606, 607, 612, 613, 615, 617, 619, 620, 624, 637, 641-643, 648, 652, 653, 654, 656, 662, 663, 667, 674, 681, 688, 690, 695, 702

euphoria 310, 374, 445, 471, 554, 572, 601

eustachian tube 371

exhaustion 582, 680

extra-terrestrial 101, 149, 367, 403, 411, 412, 493, 513, 535, 593, 599, 618

eye of the mind 407

eyes 53, 54, 84, 88-90, 92, 93, 96, 103, 105, 113, 116, 117, 128, 129, 133, 156, 182, 189, 196, 198, 201, 203, 224, 225, 236, 255, 258, 279, 280, 284, 293, 300, 336, 346, 368, 398, 406, 417, 437, 442, 449, 453, 454, 469, 472, 481, 492, 499, 509, 514, 516, 518, 521, 532, 541, 550, 577, 594, 613, 624, 635, 655, 657, 662, 673, 693

face 36-38, 163, 168, 179, 301, 333, 348, 434, 456, 510, 512-514, 517, 537-539, 550

fairies 617

faith 241, 244, 265, 325, 349, 367, 459, 465, 474, 569, 640, 650

far-sightedness 330

fasting 404, 406, 460, 555

fat solubility 688

Father Sky 50, 304, 486, 596, 627, 669

fatigue 98, 100, 152, 207, 455, 691, 694

fats 387

fatty deposits 133, 149, 197, 279, 336, 412, 493

fatty tissues 346, 416

fatty tumors 387

fear of water 189, 329, 428

feebleness 381, 663

feet 75, 128, 223, 274, 282, 322, 434, 452, 476, 590, 593, 606, 607, 623, 629, 666, 680

feminine discomforts 232

fertility 35, 94, 131, 147, 171, 206, 209, 214, 226, 235, 303, 305, 384, 418, 422, 433, 474, 490, 511, 601, 616, 636

fevers 157, 160, 165, 166, 169, 194, 197, 198, 227, 241, 244, 351, 372, 382, 394, 406, 451, 453, 461, 498, 506, 567, 572, 613, 618, 637, 640, 705